A Theory of Global Energy Governance

A Theory of Global Energy Governance

FRÉDÉRIC GILLES SOURGENS
James McCulloch Chair in Energy Law,
Tulane University Law School, New Orleans, LA, USA

OXFORD
UNIVERSITY PRESS

OXFORD
UNIVERSITY PRESS

Great Clarendon Street, Oxford, OX2 6DP,
United Kingdom

Oxford University Press is a department of the University of Oxford.
It furthers the University's objective of excellence in research, scholarship,
and education by publishing worldwide. Oxford is a registered trade mark of
Oxford University Press in the UK and in certain other countries.

Published in the United States of America by Oxford University Press
198 Madison Avenue, New York, NY 10016, United States of America.

British Library Cataloguing in Publication Data
Data available

Library of Congress Control Number: 2025935748

ISBN 9780198950295

DOI: 10.1093/9780198950325.001.0001

Printed and bound by
CPI Group (UK) Ltd., Croydon, CR0 4YY

MIX
Paper | Supporting responsible forestry
FSC® C013604
FSC www.fsc.org

The manufacturer's authorised representative in the EU for product safety is
Oxford University Press España S.A., Parque Empresarial San Fernando de Henares,
Avenida de Castilla, 2 – 28830 Madrid (www.oup.es/en or product.safety@oup.com).
OUP España S.A. also acts as importer into Spain of products made by the manufacturer.

Preface

Why do we always seem to play catch up in our energy governance choices? No matter where or when we look, it always appears that policymakers were taken by surprise by events that shaped global energy discourses and that we were ill-prepared to respond to them. This dynamic appears to apply with equal force to the oil shocks of the 1970s as it does to the Russian gas shock in Europe in the 2020s. Climate change responses follow a similar pattern. What is more, some economists have surmised that shocks like the 2008 financial crisis and even the Great Depression were linked to energy governance failures, and particularly failures in managing energy transitions. (In the case of the 2008 financial crisis, oil reached an all-time record price in July of almost $150 per barrel, to drop to slightly above $30 per barrel in December. In the case of the Great Depression, the transition from coal to oil had a major impact on leading industries like the railroads.) Given the current climate transition, I wanted to work out a theoretical approach to energy governance that explains how it works, when it fails, how it shifts, and how it connects domestic energy systems to the global energy system and vice-versa. This book is a step in that project.

This book is not the first book that I have written on the subject. Rather, it is one book of three. The first of these books is *Principles of International Energy Transition Law* (Oxford University Press 2023), which I co-authored with Leonardo Sempertegui. The second is *The Transnational Law of Renewable Energy* (Oxford University Press 2024), which I co-authored with Catherine Banet and Teddy Baldwin. It would be a touch presumptuous to say the three books constitute a 'trilogy'. Still, each book presents variations on a common theme. *Principles* asks how international law governs energy transition problems on a global level and looks to the principles of reasonable use and waste as key lodestars of analysis. *Transnational Law* asks if one can establish a set of transnational legal best practices from how national energy systems have tried to integrate renewable energy projects and how commercial actors in turn have responded to those incentives. This book in a way sits between both—it asks how we can think about the theoretical link between the global and national. I wondered if there were broader lessons we could learn about energy governance in general that could inform the current moment in time. Given that this book has seen the light of day, I think that the answer is 'yes'. I hope at the end of reading the book, you, the reader, will agree with me.

While I am trying to give a theoretical answer, what drove me to this project was 'theory with a purpose'. If we understand better what makes national energy systems tick and how they create feedback loops with the global energy system, we can improve how we respond to the current moment in energy governance. We can have a better compass to guide us through the current climate transition without running into a further major depression and a world war before we enter a new energy paradigm. My theoretical inquiry is very much about imagining a different way forward that can be proactive, pragmatic, and hopefully effective. The main theme that will run throughout is that the best way forward is one of moderation. Rushing headlong into radical solutions makes matters worse, not better. There is a reason for that. Developing what that reason is—and how we might moderate with a purpose to realize specific economic, social, and cultural goals with energy governance is why I set about writing a theory book.

I am not very sanguine that global policymakers are particularly altruistic (the same is true for financiers, innovators, or corporate actors). I therefore do not think that it is worth the effort to write a book that rests on 'we all need to get along better' (something I decidedly will say) without providing a roadmap for how we can get there. That roadmap must be decidedly realist. My realism is that of a humanist's (or, today, civic republican's) *ragione di stato* and its best-known champion Machiavelli. That said, I am just as informed by basic ideas of rational choice, international relations realism, and international legal realism. All of them, after all, share a point of departure with this *ragione di stato*. I therefore very much try to provide a point of view that is consistent with a straightforward appreciation of how power operates in the world. It is almost tautological to say that energy and power are of a kind. To control the first is to have the second. I therefore assume that this motivates global energy competition. The point is that we can tame this mechanism *by using it* if only we know what we are doing. The point is further that we can do so in a way that satisfies the demands of *ragione di stato*—my cooperation will empower me without relative loss of control to any of my rivals—and *virtù* alike. Of course, I do not gain against my rivals, either (which—to *ragione di stato*—is regrettable). Yet, I will take the real improvements in human development outcomes which energy governance provides me to further improve the commonweal and secure the hold of my domestic system on authoritative control mechanisms for effective decision-making. This will do just fine.

Of course, no reader of this book will come away with the impression that I am a fully believing realist. There is all too much talk of the common good and there are all too many references to communitarian sources (whether they be philosophical (Aristotle and Cicero), legal (particularly Roman law), or jurisprudential (John Finnis and Alasdair MacIntyre provide core conceptual tools for many of my key arguments as, to a lesser extent, does Adrian Vermeule). So I confess at the outset that there is a distinct and intentional communitarian character to my argument. To those who disagree with this starting point, I would answer that much of the international legal framework they likely hold dear (international human rights law etc) is entirely suffused with communitarian ideals. I would rejoin further that one can read my argument outside of the communitarian tradition. My arguments are intended to stand on their own merits whether or not one is Aristotelian, Ciceronian, Stoic, Thomist, Republican, or, perish the thought, a Rawlsian liberal. Still, to those who take from the footnotes that I am not convinced by social contracts theories—well read.

It thus may come as an irony that I of course still have to find a link between realism and my own communitarian point of view. Social contracts theorists are likely to shout 'see!' when I land on precommitment devices as perhaps the critical stabilizing tool to take us from realism to global energy community. I think they shout too soon. My point is that we need to build trust to form community. Precommitment is a tool to build trust. Yet, the community we hope to build transcends and precedes these precommitments. Our community is more like a trusting family than a transactional contract: we belong together and come to each other's aid even as we disagree with each other about the most fundamental questions of cooperation. Our choice is to let go of realism once we know that community is possible. I make a case for why—even as purely self-interested actors—we should do so. Yet, here everyone can make up their own mind whether precommitment is all there is. To me the answer is 'no'. Even if one has a different starting point, my hope is that the book makes a sufficiently neutral argument to work either way.

I have to thank many people for their support of the overall project. Most importantly, I have to thank my co-authors on the earlier two Oxford University Press books, Leonardo Sempertegui, Catherine Banet, and Teddy Baldwin. I have to thank them particularly for putting up with my theoretical musings. They have sharpened my thoughts, particularly when they disagreed with me on critical points of my argument. I owe them a huge debt. Obviously, this book does not reflect their own positions. I also have to thank my good friend Diane Desierto for mooting about many of the arguments with me, particularly with regard to the human rights portions of the book. In the same vein, I also have to thank Michael D Nolan for his comments on the early chapters. They helped me sharpen many of the ideas in the book. I also have to thank the current and past members of the advisory board of the Tulane Energy Law & Policy Center with whom I had many occasions to exchange on critical energy law and policy questions: Arif H Ali, Frank E Bayouth, Jason K Bennett, Marcus V Brown, Elizabeth L Craddock, Clairborne P Deming, Jeremy Farr, Stephen M Gill, Jana Grauberger, John C Herbert, Stephanie Chisholm Hildebrandt, Paul L Howes, Lindsey Jaquillard, Alexander Juden, David A Kerstein, Hector Pineda, Christopher F Richardson, Kelly B Rose, Mark Spansel, Gerald M Spedale, David B Strickland, Hugh Tucker, Robert B Tudor III, Richard J Walsh, Neil A Wasserstrom, and Jeffrey A Zlotky. I similarly owe a huge debt of gratitude to the speakers at two Tulane University Future of Energy Fora and in particular to my co-organizers, Pierre Conner III, Daniel Shantz, Eric Smith, and Kerry Stockwell. The spirited interdisciplinary discussions about energy governance issues at these fora were invaluable to my thinking. I am particularly thankful to Secretary Dan R Brouillette, Senator Mary Landrieu, Senator Bill Cassidy, and Deputy Secretary Mark W Menezes in this context. I further owe a unique thank you to James L McCulloch, who endowed the energy law chair I have the privilege to hold; Randel Young, with whom I exchange near daily on energy law and policy; and Randall M Ebner, who other than serving as the chair of the executive committee of the Tulane Energy Law & Policy Center also has been an invaluable interlocutor on energy law and policy. Unsurprisingly, I also owe a huge debt to my colleagues and in particular to Adeno Addis, Evlyn Atkinson, Jörg Fedke, Adam Feibelman, Jim Gordley, Günther Handl, David Katner, Carla Laroche, Vernon Valentine Palmer, Ron Scalise, Jessica Tueller, and Robert Westley for our many wonderful discussions. Tulane University has been a truly outstanding home for this work. I therefore owe a particular debt of gratitude to my University President, Michael A Fitts, my Provost, Robin Forman, my Dean Marcilynn Burke, and my interim dean Sally Brown Richardson who are all in on energy at Tulane.

On a personal note, a big thank you to Father Mark E Thibodeaux, SJ for more or less weekly encouragements to be more discerning. Finally, I owe a huge thanks to my family for putting up with the many late hours. Jeanne, Josephine, and Michael (I listed you alphabetically and thus stay out of trouble?), I could not do it without you!

New Orleans, Louisiana
25 January 2025

Contents

PART I. THEORY

1. The Energy Challenge 3
2. The Bond of Belonging 35
3. World Power Orders 77

PART II. ENDS

4. Development as Human Flourishing 125
5. Cooperation as Belonging 169
6. The Common Energy Good 198

PART III. INSTITUTIONS

7. Finance 223
8. Value Chains 252
9. Rule of Law 277

PART IV. PERSPECTIVES

10. Systems and Choices 305

Select Bibliography 315
Index 341

PART I
THEORY

1

The Energy Challenge

1.1 Introduction

Energy quite literally moves our world.[1] Energy makes economic growth possible. Its absence precipitates decline.[2] Who gets energy, how they get it, and at what price is a matter of a global 'energy system'. This global energy system is the web of all of the relationships and 'value chains' that make the total aggregate global energy flows possible.[3] We can think of this *global* energy system as a quilt of *national* energy systems delivering aggregate national energy flows to domestic consumers at their homes and businesses pursuant to a process administered by state policymakers (eg the US and Texas energy systems).[4] This quilt of national energy systems is knitted together by transnational supply relationships and markets needed to keep each national energy system running (eg liquified natural gas exports from the US and Qatar to Japan).[5]

The global energy system is critical for almost everything we need to live a dignified life.[6] On the most basic level, a dignified life requires food.[7] The global energy system dictates how much, and what, we can eat by controlling the energy that is available for agriculture and transporting agricultural products to end markets.[8] A dignified life also requires shelter.[9] The energy system defines what kind

[1] *See* Vaclav Smil, *Power Densities, A Key to Understanding Energy Sources and Uses* (MIT Press 2016) 162–88.

[2] *See* Peter Sarris, *Justinian: Emperor, Soldier, Saint* (Basic Books 2023) 315–41. Sarris discusses the consequences of a volcanic event that limited the amount of sunlight reaching Earth. The event quite literally destroyed Justinian's empire due to the failed harvest etc caused by the lack of energy.

[3] 'Value chains' link together the producers of raw materials, refinement processes, industrial products, money, and intellectual property. I will discuss the concept in more detail throughout the book.

[4] The US is a federal state. US states have significant authority over energy policy. Wiseman & Osofsky, 'Dynamic Energy Federalism', (2013) 72 Maryland Law Review 773.

[5] 'Japan Natural Gas Security Policy', (18 August 2022) International Energy Agency, https://www.iea.org/articles/japan-natural-gas-security-policy, last accessed 20 January 2025 (showing the percentage of Japanese LNG imports by source); Mills et al, 'Qatar LNG Sales to Key Asian Markets Confronted by US, UAE Rivalry', (21 October 2024) Reuters, https://www.reuters.com/business/energy/qatar-lng-sales-key-asian-markets-confronted-by-us-uae-rivalry-2024-10-21/, last accessed 20 January 2025.

[6] On the concept of dignified life that underlies my discussion, *see* Martha C Nussbaum, *Creating Capabilities: The Human Development Approach* (Harvard University Press 2011) 31–33.

[7] *Ibid* at 33.

[8] Robert Bartlett, *The Making of Europe: Conquest, Colonization, and Cultural Change 950-1350* (Princeton University Press 1993) 143–55 (discussing the 'cerealization' of Europe and its impact on urbanization).

[9] Nussbaum (n 6), at 33.

A Theory of Global Energy Governance. Frédéric Gilles Sourgens, Oxford University Press. © Frédéric Sourgens 2025.
DOI: 10.1093/9780198950325.003.0001

of shelter we can build, and where, by supplying the energy necessary to produce the components for my house and transporting them to me.[10] A dignified life, in addition, involves mobility (be it as part of work or the ability to see others).[11] The energy system determines how, and how far, we can travel by refining fuels I can put in my car or by generating the electricity that powers the train or streetcar we use to get from one place to another.[12] A dignified life, ultimately, is a life that is productive.[13] The energy system defines the very tools we have at our disposal to produce and thus be productive.[14]

Any theory of how global governance should look in the twenty-first century must grapple with energy. If a global governance approach does not satisfactorily deal with energy, it will lead to serious unintended consequences. It will deprive some of basic necessities in order to provide those same necessities to others. That is, it will make distributive choices that are inherently inconsistent with the idea of human dignity.[15] In doing so, it will sow the seeds of significant geopolitical conflict and realpolitik confrontation. This is so for three reasons: the link between energy access and human development outcomes is demonstrable. Further, energy systems are inherently communal, meaning that choice by some stakeholders will necessarily affect others. Finally, climate change exacerbates both the developmental and communal distributive effects of global energy systems, as choices to respond to climate change will of necessity change the current allocation of benefits and burdens from existing energy systems—and are likely to do so to the detriment of those already disadvantaged by existing energy systems, thus compounding a broader energy problem. Worryingly, many of the energy policy choices we make domestically unwittingly sow precisely the seeds of realpolitik confrontation. Global governance today does not adequately grapple with energy.

Firstly, the link between energy and human development is demonstrable. Human development improves with increased energy access until a society reaches the energy consumption levels of Germany and France.[16] At this point, development plateaus. The things that make life 'better' require energy (think

[10] *See* Mark Wilson Jones, *Principles of Roman Architecture* (Yale University Press 2000) 14 (noting the speed of ancient Roman construction).

[11] Nussbaum (n 6), at 33.

[12] Simone Tagliapietra, *Global Energy Fundamentals, Economics, Politics and Technology* (Cambridge University Press 2020) 15.

[13] Nussbaum (n 6), at 33.

[14] Tagliapietra (n 12), at 15.

[15] UN Draft Convention on the Right to Development with commentaries (6 April 2022) UN Doc A/HRC/WG/2/23/2, art 4(2) ('Every human person and all peoples have the right to active, free and meaningful participation in development and in the fair distribution of benefits resulting therefrom.'). A Kantian ideal of human dignity similarly would reject such trade-offs. John Rawls, *A Theory of Justice* (Harvard University Press 1971) 3–4. For an Aristotelian and Stoic-inspired take on dignity that comes to a similar place, *see* Martha C Nussbaum, *The Fragility of Goodness: Luck and Ethics in Greek Tragedy and Philosophy* (Cambridge University Press 2001) xxiii–xxiv.

[16] Vaclav Smil, *Energy and Civilization—A History* (MIT Press 2017) 363; Robert Bryce, *A Question of Power, Electricity and the Wealth of Nations* (Public Affairs 2020) 129–30.

of health care, education, industrial capacity, or computing and artificial intelligence). Critically, much of the world does not have ready access to energy because it has not yet transitioned to energy systems that can provide sufficient energy outputs, relying instead on older, less efficient energy sources.[17] To put this disparity in perspective, in 2020, '3.3 billion people—about 45 percent of all people on the planet—live[d] in places where per capita consumption is less than 1,000 kilowatt-hours per year, or less than the amount used by [an ordinary US] refrigerator'.[18] Even in 2024, the booming economies of India and China continue to lag significantly behind Germany and France in per capita energy access.[19] This distributive consequence of global governance (and global energy governance) is intuitively unstable. Geopolitical confrontation about and around energy therefore is pre-programmed.

Secondly, it is similarly demonstrable that energy is a matter of community. To have access to more energy depends on an ever more complex division of labour. Today's advanced supply chains in leading economies are notoriously complex. For example, until recently, to install new wind power in the EU required Russian coking coal from Siberia to be used in steel production in Ukraine to end up in Italian rolling plants before being fabricated in Germany into the final tower structure to hold up the wind turbine.[20]

The communities that make up energy value chains, of course, were and are subject to manipulation. This manipulation looks to achieve various commercial or political ends. For example, some argue that industrialized nations manipulated commodities value chains to the detriment of producer nations.[21]

Such manipulation is a common tool in global realpolitik.[22] By realpolitik I mean the competition between states for relative advantage—and thus power—in the international state system.[23] Realpolitik uses control over resources and strategic chokepoints to exercise and maintain relative power. Maintaining relative power is a matter of survival: without sufficient relative power, one cannot secure the needed share of scarce resources to safeguard the wellbeing of one's

[17] Smil (n 16), at 363; Bryce (n 16), at 129–30.

[18] Bryce (n. 16), at 127.

[19] *Ibid* at 363.

[20] Margarita Balmaceda, *Russian Energy Chains: The Remaking of Technopolitics from Siberia to Ukraine to the European Union* (Columbia University Press 2021).

[21] Timothy Mitchell, *Carbon Democracy: Political Power in the Age of Oil* (Verso Book 2011) (discussing colonial politics in the early twentieth century).

[22] Finley & Mikulska, 'Wielding the Energy Weapon: Differences Between Oil and Natural Gas', (26 June 2023) Baker Institute Center for Energy Studies Report, https://www.bakerinstitute.org/research/wielding-energy-weapon-differences-between-oil-and-natural-gas#:~:text=Russia%20has%20tried%20to%20use,Russia's%20military%20actions%20in%20Ukraine, last accessed 14 April 2024.

[23] *See* Kenneth N Waltz, *Theory of International Politics* (Random House 1979). The idea, as Waltz notes, goes back to Machiavelli. *Ibid* at 117. Machiavelli's statecraft is subtle. On the influence of Machiavelli on political thought, *see* JGA Pocock, *The Machiavellian Moment, Florentine Political Thought and the Atlantic Republican Tradition* (2nd edn, Princeton University Press 2003); Niccolò Machiavelli, *Tutte le Opere* (Mario Martelli ed, Sansoni Editore 1993).

community.[24] Such realpolitik is inherently dynamic—states counter each other's moves to maintain or reacquire their own respective positions, thus constantly readjusting relative power balances.[25] This dynamic is inherently unstable. It cannot lead to uncontested equilibria but rather lands on equilibria by means of constant contest.

The use of energy in realpolitik is telling. For it to make strategic sense, realpolitik must understand energy as an inherently communal endeavour. A *relative* energy advantage is possible only if we live in a global energy community. Without such a community, there is no point in seeking to manipulate or dominate energy value chains. Each state would have all the necessary resources for its own energy independence on its own territory. This is precisely not the case. Given the importance of energy to national wellbeing, it therefore makes sense to target energy value chains for realpolitik manipulation.

The communal nature of energy also provides the means to answer realpolitik interventions by means of collective counter-actions over time.[26] The previously less powerful participants holding needed raw materials were able to turn this to their advantage in the oil context in the 1970s and completely change the manner in which global energy systems worked in the process.[27] Previously exposed consumers similarly are able to withstand the weaponization of energy access by increasing the market for needed fuels.[28] Over time, the global energy system moves to new constellations—none of which can maintain a balance for long.

An important part of my argument is that realpolitik dynamics find collective solutions to rebalance the global energy system in response to an exercise of energy realpolitik by an adversary. I will argue that this collective response allows us a glimpse of how we can overcome energy realpolitik constraints altogether. We can stabilize global energy governance. This stabilization is premised in the

[24] Waltz (n 23), at 91 ('In a microtheory, whether of international politics or of economics, the motivation of the actors is assumed rather than realistically described. I assume that states seek to ensure their survival. The assumption is a radical simplification for the sake of constructing a theory.') While a simplification, it is certainly consistent with our understanding of why security matters so much. As Thomas Hobbes has burnt into our collective philosophical memory, without it, life is solitary, poor, nasty, brutish, and short. *See* Thomas Hobbes, Hobbes: Leviathan (Richard Tuck ed, Cambridge University Press 1991).

[25] Waltz (n 23), at 102–28. As Waltz points out, states do not strive to maintain a balance of power. They do, however, strive to maintain and, if possible, improve their own relative position in the system. The interaction between such policies brings about a balance of power.

[26] *Ibid* at 126 ('Externally, states work harder to increase their own strength, or they combine with others, if they are falling behind. In a competition for the position of leader, balancing is sensible behavior where the victory of one coalition over another leaves weaker members of the winning coalition at the mercy of the stronger ones. Nobody wants anyone else to win; none of the great powers want one of their number to emerge as leader.').

[27] Harold James, *Seven Crashes: The Economic Crises that Shaped Globalization* (Yale University Press 2023) 168–75.

[28] For an excellent discussion, *see* Ariel Cohen, 'Can Europe Count on US LNG?', Forbes (20 February 2024), https://www.forbes.com/sites/arielcohen/2024/02/20/can-europe-count-on-us-lng/?sh=61a853b6298c, last accessed 14 February 2024.

rule of law and our ability to make and build on credible precommitments. Such precommitment allows us to leverage the logic of realpolitik to escape from its gravitational pull.[29]

The reason that realpolitik can correct manipulation—and the reason that we ultimately can escape a purely realpolitik-driven global energy order—is that states can mobilize a kind of market. This 'market' is a diffuse global economic social organization. States can set incentives that cause private actors to innovate and find others with whom to take risks on the strength of their idea. These incentives provide conditions in which innovation can find finance and build value chains to realize its promise. In responding to realpolitik, states set parameters for innovation.[30] Certainly, such markets can again be nudged by national governments and their respective national energy systems as well as by leading financial and industry actors. But in the end, markets can escape this dynamic by incentivizing innovation. Innovation—cheaper, more secure energy access that can reach broader groups of consumers on closer to real price terms—tends to win out over longer time horizons to rebalance the global energy system away from geopolitical conflict.[31] Innovation transforms the zero-sum realpolitik game of relative power into a positive sum game of collective productivity growth. Innovation allows participants to achieve positive sum gains that are only realizable in their respective (energy) communities.

Inherent in this understanding of the global energy system is that energy can only be harnessed and thus be useful in a global community.[32] That is why energy is susceptible to realpolitik. It is also why realpolitik can respond to these pressures. Managing energy and energy systems is therefore a question of how to keep the community engaged in delivering and improving energy access for an ever-broader group of community stakeholders.

[29] Schelling, 'Strategies of Commitment', *in Strategies of Commitment and Other Essays* (Thomas Schelling ed, Harvard University Press 2006) 1, 6, 8–9. Schelling relies on classical Greek sources to explain commitment in a helpful way for us. He describes Xenophon's choice of fighting with an impassable ravine at his back against advancing Persians as one example of precommitment—there is nothing for it but fighting, fleeing is impossible. He also uses an early Homeric example of the game of chicken—be it in a horse-drawn chariot rather than a car. Both moments put us in front of realpolitik choices. In both, those choices lead us to a potential for collective action that are mutually beneficial precisely because we understand our own self-preservation instincts. These instincts are at the heart of why we act out of realpolitik in the first place.

[30] *See* Joseph A Schumpeter, *The Theory of Economic Development, An Inquiry into Profits, Capital, Credit, Interest, and the Business Cycle* (Redvers Opie trans, Transaction Publishers 1984) 8 (providing a working definition of markets).

[31] Carlota Perez, *Technical Revolutions and Financial Capital, The Dynamics of Bubbles and Golden Ages* (Edward Elgar 2003).

[32] No actor—not even Thomas Edison—could uncouple from the community. Energy innovation, the production of raw materials, the refinement of raw materials, the construction of generating assets, their installation, and their use, all happen within a community even if an end user may in fact use a specific asset 'behind the meter' to gain independence from a larger grid. That very option presupposes the existence of an energy community to facilitate behind-the-meter transactions.

One of the reasons that innovation can rebalance the global energy system as opposed to immediately unsettling it is that energy is 'slow'.[33] Energy projects are highly capital intensive.[34] A new innovation therefore can remove some geopolitical pressure from critical pre-existing energy chokepoints. It cannot replace the old chokepoints with new chokepoints until much later in the 'energy cycle' of diffusion and adoption of the new technology.[35] New technology therefore acts as a kind of reset button and does not immediately add stress of its own on the global energy system. Innovation diversifies. It adds to the energy mix. It does not replace or overturn the energy mix overnight.

Thirdly, climate change is inextricably intertwined with energy systems. Incumbent energy systems rely predominantly on oil for transportation and gas and coal for electricity.[36] These systems burn oil, gas, and coal to power cars, trucks, airplanes, and ships as well as to produce electricity. Burning these fuels emits carbon dioxide (CO_2). At the same time, producing oil, gas, and coal can also release methane (CH_4) into the atmosphere. Carbon dioxide, methane, and other 'greenhouse gases' affect the global climate because they retain more heat (ie solar energy) than do the dominant atmospheric gases, oxygen (O_2), nitrogen (N_2) and argon (Ar). While the total concentration of greenhouse gases like CO_2 seems negligible as percentage of gases in the atmosphere, even these facially small changes in concentration have significant climate consequences: atmospheric CO_2 concentrations increased from pre-industrial levels of 0.028 per cent to 0.042 per cent today.[37] This increase in concentration was responsible for a 1.12°C average increase in temperatures over the same time span measured in 2023.[38]

The average temperature increase linked to incumbent energy systems changes regional and global climates.[39] Climate change has catastrophic consequences for world society. At a level of above 1.5°C of warming, climate change will dangerously increase extreme weather events.[40] It will affect global water (hydrological) cycles.[41] It will affect soil.[42] It will have significant impacts on food supply, disease,

[33] Smil (n 16).
[34] Thijs van de Graaf & Benjamin K Sovacool, *Global Energy Politics* (Polity 2020) 74.
[35] *See* Perez (n 31).
[36] 'Key World Energy Statistics 2021' at 6, (September 2021) International Energy Agency, https://iea.blob.core.windows.net/assets/52f66a88-0b63-4ad2-94a5-29d36e864b82/KeyWorldEnergyStatistics2021.pdf, last accessed 25 March 2024.
[37] Linsey, 'Climate Change: Atmospheric CO_2', (12 May 2023) US National Oceanic Atmospheric Administration, https://www.climate.gov/news-features/understanding-climate/climate-change-atmospheric-carbon-dioxide#:~:text=The%20increase%20between%202021%20and,dioxide%20in%202022%20was%20418.56, last accessed 26 March 2024.
[38] Masters, July 2023: 'Earth's Hottest Month on Record', (14 August 2023) Yale Climate Connections, https://yaleclimateconnections.org/2023/08/july-2023-earths-hottest-month-on-record/, last accessed 25 March 2024.
[39] Hoesung Lee et al, *Climate Change 2023: Synthesis Report. Contribution of Working Groups I, II and III to the Sixth Assessment Report of the Intergovernmental Panel on Climate Change* (Intergovernmental Panel on Climate Change 2023) 9 ('IPCC 2023').
[40] *Ibid* at 14–18.
[41] *Ibid.*
[42] *Ibid.*

eco-systems, and even geography.[43] As it stands, any increase beyond 1.5 °C above pre-industrial levels will cause significant, escalating effects that will themselves be part of broader 'chain reactions' placing eco-systems and the societies which depend upon them under ever increasing stress.[44] To address these new stresses will require 'adaptation' measures—measures that allow societies to cope with the new climate circumstances. This, in turn, will increase energy demand. For example, extreme weather will increase the need for air conditioning.[45] Air conditioning is necessary for school age children to learn.[46] It is also essential to secure the bare survival of the elderly. Having energy therefore is critical to all generations, young and old, as climate change accelerates.

To decrease or 'mitigate' the effects of climate change will require a transition in how energy is produced, delivered, and consumed around the world. Yet, at the same time, this transition collides with greater energy needs to adapt to climate change. It further collides with the needs to increase energy access around the world so as to lift billions out of the human development consequences of living in energy poverty. It finally collides with greater energy needs from the next productivity revolution—large-scale computing and artificial intelligence.[47]

Climate change makes already marginalized people even more vulnerable to hunger, disease, and loss of shelter. The quality of their lives as measured on the human development index is therefore likely to decrease because of climate change. They need more energy and more energy cheaply to avoid this consequence. Changing global energy systems may well work across purposes to this goal. Still, changing global energy systems to protect people in Germany, the Netherlands, or Switzerland against the consequences of climate change cannot do so on the backs of precisely those marginalized people.[48] (Whether one agrees with this as a moral proposition, marginalized peoples can simply continue to use unabated fossil fuels if we do not include them constructively in energy transition decision-making, thus accelerating climate change to the detriment of all.) Not changing global energy systems, on the other hand, will similarly doom the vulnerable first and the more affluent later. Inaction and business as usual, thus, are not an option.

[43] *Ibid.*

[44] *Ibid.*

[45] Matthew E Kahn, *Adapting to Climate Change, Markets and the Management of an Uncertain Future* (Yale University Press 2021) 47.

[46] *Ibid.*

[47] Leffer, 'The AI Boom Could Use a Shocking Amount of Energy', (13 October 2023) Scientific American, https://www.scientificamerican.com/article/the-ai-boom-could-use-a-shocking-amount-of-electricity/, last accessed 13 January 2025.

[48] Germany, the Netherlands, and Switzerland were all involved in significant climate litigation. *See* HR 20 December 2019, NJ 2020, 41 m nt J Spier (De Staat der Nederlanden/Stichting Urgenda); *Neubauer v Germany*, 1 BvR 2656/18 (24 Mar 2021); *Verein KlimaSeniorinnen Schweiz v Switzerland*, European Court of Human Rights, Application No 53600/20, judgment (9 April 2024).

Here, too, we are looking at changing the energy mix and the behaviour of energy technology through innovation. Even so, we cannot replace the dominant energy paradigm at will. It still provides a necessary tool to satisfy significant energy demands that cannot otherwise be met at an acceptable cost point. All we can do is to slowly correct the dominant paradigm where it is economically prudent, to supplement it with carbon neutral generation, and alter its dangerous externalities at the smokestack to meet urgent policy needs. A prudent path is one of moderation and balance.

The different strands of the energy problem I have introduced so far (development, realpolitik, and environmental sustainability) come together in a 'trilemma'.[49] A trilemma describes a kind of choice, in which I want to achieve three things that are partially at odds with each other. I say 'partially' because I can balance them against each other somewhat—still, if I try to maximize two of the three, I am bound to sacrifice the third. One intuitive trilemma is that I would like to get repairs to my car or home done well, cheaply, and fast. The problem is that if I maximize getting the repairs done as cheaply and as fast as possible, the quality is certain to suffer. If I want to get them done well and fast, price will increase markedly. If I want to get them done well and cheap, things will take time. Well, cheap, and fast pull us in different directions so that I have to make a choice of how to balance the three to get most of what I want, even if I cannot have it all.

The relationship between the energy policy goals of inexpensive energy access (to support development), energy security (to maintain or improve my relative geostrategic position), and environmental sustainability (eg to mitigate climate change) move us in different directions. Realpolitik threats are real and must be answered if we want to avoid the lights going out due to geopolitical pressure on energy transactions. Climate change requires us to decrease greenhouse gas emissions from energy. Both energy security and climate change policies intuitively will increase the price of energy. If we want to have cheap energy that is secure and environmentally sustainable, we will have to find a balance between all three. We will have to make choices. These choices are about finding balance. They are not, and cannot be, about rejecting balance in favour of a single goal, no matter how important it seems.

To change the energy system is one of the most fundamental things one can attempt to do because it is difficult and disruptive to rebalance the energy trilemma. The energy system has a logic of its own. This logic is bound up in the energy value chains that tie together distant raw material inputs with technological innovations which, in turn, determine who can flip a switch where to turn on a light or power an assembly line. This logic moves slowly. It finds new, continuously unstable,

[49] For a brief introduction, *see* Tagliapietra (n 12), at 8–10. For a full discussion, *see* Sourgens, 'A Parisian Consensus', (2022) 60 Columbia Journal of Transnational Law 657.

equilibria. It does not allow us to mobilize an energy revolution overnight given the significant size of investments in existing national energy systems.

At the same time, the global energy system also never stands still. We go through energy transitions big and small on a regular basis. Energy innovators and policymakers find a systemic problem that limits our ability to maximize outcomes in our energy trilemma. The systemic problem is like a 'reverse salient'. Although originally a military term, such a reverse salient more generally describes 'an extremely complex situation in which individuals, groups, material forces, historical influences, and other factors have idiosyncratic, causal roles, and in which accidents as well as trends play a part' to hold back the performance of a system.[50] Such a reverse salient can only be overcome by concerted action by innovators and policymakers. It is incredibly difficult and time consuming to find an approach that turns the complexity of a reverse salient into solvable 'critical problems' that we can innovate, engineer, and produce around to 'bring the system back into line—*i.e.*, correct the reverse salient'.[51] Given the tremendous opportunities in resolving a reverse salient, both innovators and policymakers continuously chip away at doing so. They attempt different experiments. It is this steady and slow process that ultimately yields the next big technological breakthrough. This breakthrough, in turn, will need to slowly finds its market. Transition thus is constant even if it proceeds at its own pace following its own inherent logic.

The energy transition challenge we face in the early twenty-first century presses on us from all three sides of the trilemma. Climate change is one obvious reverse salient—if we continue to emit greenhouse gases associated with fossil fuels that are critical to the energy system, there will be catastrophic environmental consequences that threaten the energy system itself.[52] Relatedly, climate change increases energy demand to adapt to a changing environment (eg we need more air conditioning in places that could get by without it before).[53] At the same time, we need to deliver more energy more inexpensively around the world to allow most of world society to participate in an increasingly more energy-intensive 'communication society' looking to harness the power of machine learning and artificial intelligence to boost economic productivity.[54] Finally, as we seek to achieve these outcomes, we are also entering an area of greater geopolitical threats to critical segments of the

[50] Thomas P Hughes, *Networks of Power, Electrification in Western Society 1880-1930* (Johns Hopkins University Press 1983) 79.
[51] *Ibid* at 80.
[52] IPCC 2023 (n 39), at 24.
[53] Kahn (n 45).
[54] *See* Leffer, 'The AI Boom Could Use a Shocking Amount of Electricity', (13 October 2023) Scientific American, https://www.scientificamerican.com/article/the-ai-boom-could-use-a-shocking-amount-of-electricity/, last accessed 4 December 2024; Bristol et al, 'Adopting AI at Speed and Scale: The 4IR Push to Stay Competitive', (21 February 2024) McKinsey & Co, https://www.mckinsey.com/capabilities/operations/our-insights/adopting-ai-at-speed-and-scale-the-4ir-push-to-stay-competitive, last accessed 4 December 2024.

energy value chain.[55] These threats themselves are a reverse salient given the way in which global energy value chains have developed. Any governance agenda that seeks to solve one of them has to solve all of them. This requires a detailed understanding of what energy levers are available to push, which levers create problems, and how we can harness them to formulate the critical problem around which we organize the global response.

My overarching argument in this book is that we must find an appropriate balance to succeed at global energy governance. In responding to climate change, this means that we must look to 'all of the above' answers.[56] Such an approach has the virtue of being realistic—both in the climate change context and in the context of other future energy transitions to follow. Such an approach follows the logic inherent in the functioning of the global energy system. This logic can continue to act as a counterweight to the many growing geopolitical tensions burdening global energy value chains. This logic finally highlights that balanced energy governance can overcome the inherent limitations of realpolitik. The inherent logic of the global energy system dictates that we are all held together by a bond of belonging to the global energy system. I will introduce this bond of belonging more fully in Chapter 2 and then outline its consequences for global energy governance in the remainder of the book.[57] We individually have the power to sever this bond and damage the global energy system. Yet, when we do so, we undercut our own resource base for economic prosperity. To harness energy to maximize its benefits and limit its externalities requires cooperation. Energy is a matter of community. My argument is that the logic for this cooperation is already coded into the global energy system itself. There is a reason energy value chains are long and complex—energy requires vastly different inputs from different places to be generated. Energy cooperation is therefore intelligible in realpolitik terms—it increases relative security if done correctly or undercuts it if not. It also provides a realpolitik path out of impasses—cooperate to dislodge a stakeholder from its systemically dangerous market power. Still, it is not a foregone conclusion that we will follow this logic. At times, policymakers believe they know better. They do so at their own peril.[58]

The point I will make throughout the book is that we ultimately have to choose between three paths. We can act against the logic of the global energy system. This would be to fall into the tragedy of the commons and anticommons. In the context of climate change, this would be highly destructive and potentially irreversible. We

[55] Sourgens, 'Energy Lessons from the Ukraine Crisis', (24 February 2022) EJILTalk!, https://www.ejiltalk.org/energy-lessons-from-the-ukraine-crisis/, last accessed 4 December 2024.

[56] Frédéric G Sourgens & Leonardo Sempertegui, *Principles of International Energy Transition Law* (Oxford University Press 2023) 15–18.

[57] *See* section 2.4.

[58] For a discussion of the dynamics following the first oil shock in this regard, *see* Waltz (n 23), at 151–58.

can follow a rational realpolitik approach by taking what the logic of the energy system allows. Doing so realizes slow, frustrating, and very costly transitions imposing significant, unnecessary losses in particular on vulnerable groups. Finally, we can embrace the logic of the energy system and follow a fully cooperative, prudent, and realistic global energy governance approach premised in our bond of belonging to the global energy system. This book is about how we can realistically follow that last path.

1.2 The Climate Community

Climate change is the dominant driver of today's global energy transition discourse.[59] The most authoritative global scientific body on climate change, the United Nations Intergovernmental Panel on Climate Change ('IPCC'), warned in 2023 that '[t]here is a rapidly closing window of opportunity to secure a liveable and sustainable future for all (*very high confidence*)'.[60] In the words of the 2015 Paris Agreement, acting within this window requires means to obey 'the imperatives of a just transition'.[61] To this end, the 2021 Glasgow Climate Pact urges states to conceive of development strategies 'towards just transitions to net zero emissions by or around mid-century, taking into account different national circumstances'.[62] The 2023 First Global Stocktake reaffirms that 'sustainable and just solutions to the climate crisis must be founded on meaningful and effective social dialogue and participation of all stakeholders'.[63] The focus on 'just' solutions emphasizes the need to expand energy access to provide equitable opportunities to people and peoples living in comparative energy poverty. The global climate regime looks to a balanced, context-sensitive approach to energy governance to address the threat of climate change.

Combatting climate change is about energy governance. We must conceive of ways to structure the raise of the financial resources to act. Cost estimates of energy transition run at approximately US$9.2 trillion *per year* until 2050.[64] To put this number in perspective, global military spending in 2023 is estimated at US$2.2

[59] *See eg* Damilola S Olawuyi et al eds, *Net Zero and Natural Resources Law, Sovereignty, Security, and Solidarity in the Clean Energy Transition* (Oxford University Press 2024).
[60] IPCC 2023 (n 39), at 24.
[61] Paris Agreement, preamble 10.
[62] Glasgow Climate Pact, ¶ 32.
[63] First Global Stocktake, ¶ 9.
[64] 'The Net Zero Transition, What It Would Cost, What It Would Bring' at 5, (January 2022) McKinsey & Co, https://www.mckinsey.com/~/media/mckinsey/business%20functions/sustainability/our%20insights/the%20net%20zero%20transition%20what%20it%20would%20cost%20what%20it%20could%20bring/the-net-zero-transition-what-it-would-cost-and-what-it-could-bring-final.pdf, last accessed 26 March 2024.

trillion.[65] Governance also must support specific energy projects that can use this financing to meet local energy needs in a net carbon neutral manner. Governance finally must create the international interconnections between states, between states and investors, and between investors and energy companies to implement the necessary overhaul of the global energy system to overcome the climate threat.

Any governance approach that insists on meeting climate goals by a complete overhaul of the existing global energy system would be destined to fail. Such an approach was proposed by the International Energy Agency prior to climate negotiations in Glasgow in 2021 at the request of the United Kingdom in its role as president of the conference.[66] The Glasgow Climate Pact rejected this approach in favour of a balanced approach to emission reductions.[67] This rejection was not a matter of complacency. Rather, the speed at which energy value chains form and scale is ultimately inconsistent with such an attempt at radically overhauling the global energy system in a short period of time.[68] Even were it feasible, such a radical reworking of the global energy system would place significant burdens with unpredictable long-term consequences across the energy value chain domestically and across the international system. A balanced approach to energy governance will therefore work within the logic of the energy system. This means we must combine investment in both carbon neutral energy generation and emission reduction technology for existing energy assets by means of carbon capture and increased efficiency measures as well as direct air capture technology to reduce the stock of atmospheric CO_2 concentrations.[69]

Such a balanced approach must begin with domestic energy governance. The Paris Agreement anticipates that domestic energy governance drives progress on global climate mitigation. It leaves the scope and manner of emission reduction to states even as it sets an ambition target at the international level.[70] Consequently, our discussion of global energy governance naturally should begin at the national level.

Though each national approach differs according to context, paradigmatically there are three different dominant paradigms for domestic energy governance: public-utility-based public–private partnerships, dirigisme, and energy market liberalization. As I will argue in this chapter, none of these approaches alone can support the significant expansion of the global energy system while also pushing energy innovation sufficiently to address the current energy challenge.

[65] Taylor, 'Global Military Spending Hits Record $2.2 Trillion Amid Multiple Wars', (13 February 2024) Washington Post, https://www.washingtonpost.com/world/2024/02/13/nato-spending-russia-ukraine-trump/, last accessed 26 March 2024.

[66] Stéphanie Bouckaert et al, *Net Zero by 2050: A Roadmap for the Global Energy Sector* (4th edn, International Energy Agency 2021).

[67] Glasgow Climate Pact, ¶ 36.

[68] Smil (n 16); Sourgens, 'Diligent Zero', (2022) 75 SMU Law Review 417.

[69] McKinsey (n 64), at 10, 60; IPCC 2023 (n 39), at 87.

[70] Paris Agreement, arts 4(1)–(2).

This means that we must think about the starting point of energy governance differently. We will need to find a way coherently to combine the different domestic governance approaches and find a way to combine public–private partnerships, strong state leadership, and markets in a single energy governance paradigm. That will be the task for Chapter 2. There, I will argue that such a conception better captures the inherent logic of energy systems more broadly and thus has relevance beyond the climate change context.

This rethinking will have consequences for global governance. No one state or energy stakeholder alone can bring about the kind of overhaul of the global energy system, which even a balanced governance approach requires.[71] Instead, global energy governance is about the right *interconnection* between the different stakeholders and decisionmakers needed to make the new energy system work.[72] These interconnections need to connect stakeholders in four different dimensions. They must: (i) connect policymakers overseeing national systems better to energy value chain participants operating in their national systems; (ii) tighten the link between national systems; (iii) strengthen the connection between energy value chain participants globally, and (iv) connect each of these dimensions to each other to create a global energy community. These interconnections distribute the responsibility for governance between multiple actors and centres of gravity.[73] As I will argue in Chapter 3, domestic energy governance choices predictably affect global energy governance. To meet the climate challenge therefore requires us to find not just an appropriate domestic regulatory balance or an abstract global energy governance balance. It requires us to understand how national energy systems constitute the global energy system and vice versa to understand where to place our lever to improve global energy governance outcomes.

Climate change demonstrates that these interconnections create a global community, whether we want to be in it or not. Climate change highlights that domestic energy policies have sizeable global impacts. It further highlights that avoiding such impacts depends upon cooperation.[74] Climate change is the most visible evidence of this interconnection and the internal logic that drives it. Still, as I will argue, this logic applies throughout the global energy system beyond climate change. This logic borrows from neighbourly relations in resource communities.[75]

[71] McKinsey (n 64), at 5.

[72] I use 'interconnection' in its ordinary meaning of 'linking together'. 'Interconnection' is also an energy term of art meaning the connection of generating resources to a transmission grid capable of delivering the new energy load to appropriate end markets. This 'interconnection' is one of the important and live policy issues in transmission planning that must be solved to make energy transition work. The challenge we face is not exhausted by this technical interconnection challenge, though that challenge is in many ways symbolic for the larger problem precisely because it requires meaningful coordination and cooperation between different stakeholders.

[73] Elinor Ostrom, *Understanding Institutional Diversity* (Princeton University Press 2009) 255–88.

[74] *See eg* Glasgow Climate Pact, ¶ 60.

[75] *See* Ostrom (n 73).

What my neighbour does deeply impacts me and vice versa.[76] This neighbourliness frame is the thread holding together the international climate regime.[77] Still, it is also applicable in the global energy context. In the energy context, the interconnections between the resource slices we each own in the resource community place us in a kind of 'commons'. This commons logic can help us better understand the interconnections between domestic and global energy governance. It can also help us understand the relationship between different stakeholders in national energy systems and the global energy system.[78] It can point out how to utilize and protect these interconnections to improve energy outcomes on every metric from innovation, to efficiency of value chains, to redundancy in case of unforeseen circumstances beyond what a single actor could have achieved alone.

Building a global governance conception around an energy community treats the global energy system as a shared resource in which all stakeholders have a part and that all stakeholders must maintain and improve together to benefit from it individually. This entails finally that benefits and burdens must be shared such as to hold communities together. Broadly, this means that human development outcomes everywhere must improve and not deteriorate because of energy governance in general or climate change-based energy transition, specifically.[79]

One should not mistake this idea of an energy community as a competition-free space. To the contrary, such communities are fiercely competitive. For instance, one such commons relationship is the relationship between adjacent oil and gas leaseholders in Texas pumping oil from the same reservoir.[80] These leaseholders are obviously in competition with each other to exploit the oil from the shared reservoir. Yet, the reservoir can only optimally be exploited if they work together not to overburden it. This competition is creative in the sense that it is innovative—but it is also inherently destructive of those who fall behind.[81] One can think of this kind of competition as 'co-opetitive'. Competitors can reduce costs by avoiding

[76] *See* Elinor Ostrom, *Governing the Commons, The Evolution of Institutions for Collective Action* (Cambridge University Press 2015) 82–86.

[77] Advisory Opinion on Climate Change, ITLOS Decision No 31 (21 May 2024); *see also* Sourgens, 'Climate Prevention', (2025) 36 Georgetown Environmental Law Review (forthcoming).

[78] For a discussion of the internet as just such a commons, *see* Sourgens, 'Cyber-Nuisance', (2021) 42 University of Pennsylvania Journal of International Law 1005.

[79] Importantly, at some point, more energy access—and more assets—will not improve human development outcomes by much. When looking for an optimal distribution, it is thus not necessarily the case that one cannot make anyone worse off. The question is rather whether a person is made worse off in such a way as to materially affect their human capabilities. A policy that deprives me access to music, for instance, may seem trivial. Yet, it does materially affect human capabilities as they have been developed for instance by Martha Nussbaum. This does not mean that a policy that makes it marginally more expensive for me to go and see my favourite artist at a live concert is going to have a material impact on my human flourishing. True, community and art are both central to flourishing. Yet, it is not typically the case that human flourishing is made materially less attainable because one is not able to see Taylor Swift perform the Eras Tour or Mstislav Rostropovich play the Bach Cello Suites live.

[80] Pierce, 'Carol Rose Comes to the Oil Patch: Modern Property Analysis Applied to Modern Reservoir Problems', (2011) 19 Penn State Environmental Law Review 241.

[81] Philippe Aghion, Céline Antonin & Simon Bunel, *The Power of Creative Destruction, Economic Upheaval and the Wealth of Nations* (Harvard University Press 2021).

duplication of efforts or spreading risk of technological or regulatory uncertainty.[82] Cooperation and shared belonging in a global energy community therefore remains inherently competitive in ways that assist in overcoming the limitations of an existing reverse salient in the energy systems through innovation.[83]

Climate change—and the climate community—reveals something important about energy governance. It evidences the nature of the global energy system as a resource community. It highlights the catastrophic consequences of failures to cooperate in this energy resource community.[84] Yet, it also highlights that the resource community is built on competition as much as it is built on cooperation. Relevantly for our realpolitik analysis, this competition includes regulatory competition. Sharing data and supply chains is beneficial to all resource community participants.[85] Still, regulators can compete with each other for more effective, cheaper, and faster adoptions of winning energy strategies, thus creating realpolitik first-mover advantages in the world economy.[86] Cooperation does not obviate competition. It instead channels competition towards constructive outcomes that ultimately benefit all. The manner in which energy regulation proceeds domestically therefore is critical to the future development of global energy governance. Analysing the dominant paradigms of national energy governance therefore is the logical next step to understanding both climate-based global energy governance and global energy governance more broadly.

1.3 Utilities and Public Law Contracting

The challenge created by today's energy transition is hardly new. Today's energy paradigm, in fact, is itself the result of an energy transition towards industrial, hydrocarbon-fuelled energy systems.[87] There are thus approaches to energy governance that can serve as a potential model for the ongoing energy transition.

[82] Brandenburger & Nalebuff, 'The Rules of Co-opetition', (January/February 2021) Harvard Business Review, available at https://hbr.org/2021/01/the-rules-of-co-opetition, last accessed 26 March 2024. One example is the standardization of supply chains between Apple and Samsung.

[83] *See* Hughes (n 50), at 79–104.

[84] Hardin, 'The Tragedy of the Commons', (1968) 162 Science 1243; Heller, 'The Tragedy of the Anticommons: A Concise Introduction and Lexicon', (2013) 76 Modern Law Review 6; Heller, The Tragedy of the Anticommons: Property in Transition from Marx to Markets, (1998) 111 Harvard Law Review 621.

[85] *See* Anne-Marie Slaughter, *A New World Order* (Princeton University Press 2004). This data sharing is one of the fundamental ideas behind global governance networks. *See* ibid. In the commons governance context, *see* Ostrom (n 73), at 210–15.

[86] On this experimentalist approach to governance in the climate space, *see* Charles F Sabel & David G Victor, *Fixing the Climate, Strategies for an Uncertain World* (Princeton University Press 2022).

[87] Smil (n 16), at 225–384. Peter Cameron notes the nature of the governance approach discussed in this and the next section as a 'paradigm' in Peter Cameron, *Competition in Energy Markets: Law and Regulation in the European Union* (Oxford University Press 2002) 7. I separate this discussion into two paradigms collapsed in Cameron—one based on public law contracts in a utility-based paradigm and one based on nationalization and command or authoritarian control. *See ibid* for Cameron's treatment.

This comparison will only take us so far in the current context: the unique technological, social, and environmental conditions driving today's energy transition are not the same as those that led to the choice of past energy governance systems. Yet, it will provide an important starting point to asking how energy transition might be managed, at all, and what lessons can be adopted from past endeavours.

One compelling theoretical approach to energy governance is a public utility or public law contracting model. This model served as a regulatory starting point around the world and remains the default comparator for any discussion of the development of US electricity governance.[88] The central bargain in a public utility model is that a private investor receives a 'concession'.[89] This concession grants the private investor a territorial monopoly.[90] In exchange for this territorial monopoly, the private investor provides a public service within the territory in question. This public service could consist of building electricity generation and transmission to serve the monopoly territory and distribute electricity within that territory.[91] This public service could also consist of developing oil and gas resources and thus securing revenue from oil and gas to the state.[92]

Because the concession provides a public service at the behest of the state, the concessionaire also benefits from eminent domain powers.[93] To the extent that the concessionaire requires land rights in order to develop a project, it has the ability to compel the transfer of the rights in question. Within reasonable limits, the concessionaire therefore is able optimally to develop the project because the concessionaire has an ultimate power to compel the surrender of all rights needed to complete the project (against payment of compensation which will be added to the investor's cost base and thus recovered from project revenues).

Given the monopolistic position of the concessionaire, the concessionaire typically is subject to price controls. Thus, in the electricity context, electric utilities can only charge reasonable rates set and approved by a public regulator.[94] This

[88] Hughes (n 50); Alexandra B Klass & Hannah J Wiseman, *Energy Law* (Foundation Press 2017).

[89] The same move is applicable in the traditional oil and gas context. *See* Owen Anderson et al, *International Petroleum Law and Transactions* (Rocky Mountain Mineral Law Foundation 2020) 1–91.

[90] Klass & Wiseman (n 88); Largey, 'La place du contrat dans le domaine de l'approvionnement en électricité, en droit suisse', *in La Contractualisation en Droit Public* (Véronique Boillet et al eds, Schulthess 2021) 175, 175–76 (monopoly for distributor who enters into a public law contract with the consumer in Switzerland). In this regulated marketplace, the relationship between generators and the distributor of electricity could be governed by a power purchase agreement, which, in turn, would set a capacity price and electricity price that would guarantee a reasonable return to the investor. There would frequently be an open question as to whether the governing law of the power purchase agreement was the private or public law of the host state.

[91] Klass & Wiseman (n 88); Kim Talus, *EU Energy Law and Policy, A Critical Account* (Oxford University Press 2013) 17; Terence Daintith & Leigh Hancher, *Energy Strategy in Europe: The Legal Framework* (De Gruyter 1986) 88. Notably, different European countries adopted different approaches, with some following a more utility-based approach and others following a more command approach to energy prior to the 1980s. *See* Talus (*supra* this note) at 271.

[92] Anderson et al (n 89), at 51–91.

[93] Klass, 'Takings and Transmission', (2013) 91 North Carolina Law Review 1079.

[94] Klass & Wiseman (n 88).

reasonable return is set by reference to the reasonable costs incurred by the utility or concessionaire. Oil and gas concessions historically were subject to similar price controls. In the early years of oil production in the US, oil producers could only produce a set quota of oil, determined by a regulator such as the Texas Railroad Commission.[95] Similarly, gas prices were heavily regulated so as to allow a reasonable return—but no more than a reasonable return—to the private capital needed to expand energy access.[96] International oil concessions in the Middle East provided the government with a share of oil revenue by reference to a posted price of oil. When Standard Oil of New Jersey changed this posted price unilaterally, oil producing states formed the Organisation of Petroleum Exporting Countries in order to stabilize the price of oil following the precedent set by the Texas Railroad Commission.[97] In other words, *ex ante* price control mechanisms are an inherent feature of the public utility model.

Not only that, but the regulator also maintained regulatory oversight with regard to energy projects to protect their continued social and environmental viability. Regulators stepped in to prevent waste as well as pollution. Regulators similarly were given a significant 'margin of appreciation' or discretion in exercising police powers with regard to regulated industries to protect the public good at large.[98] This margin of appreciation reached all the way down into the law governing the underlying concessionary contracts. Other than in private law contracts, which treat contracting parties as equals with equal default powers, public law contracts in principle grant broader powers to the state to adjust the contract than a private party would have.[99] Even the basic commercial instruments setting up the relationship between the 'utility' (be it an electric utility or the holder of an oil and gas concession) therefore gave an inherent positional advantage to the state, ostensibly to protect the public.[100]

To oversimplify the functional marriage somewhat, in this utility approach, the private sector was responsible for finding the best way to broaden energy access on the basis of the best available technology. It also was tasked with operating the new technology in accordance with industry practice. At the same time, the public sector was charged with policing affordability of energy resources. Similarly, the public sector was charged with protecting the resource base itself against waste by limiting the amount and kind of development of the energy system as a whole.

[95] *See* William R Childs, *The Texas Railroad Commissions: Understanding Regulation in America to the Mid-Twentieth Century* (Texas A&M University Press 2005) 208–15.

[96] *See* Cooper, 'A Note on Deregulation on Natural Gas Prices', (1982) 2 Brookings Paper on Economic Activity 371, 372–73; Daintith & Hancher (n 91), at 84–88.

[97] Daniel Yergin, *The Prize, The Epic Quest for Oil, Money & Power* (Free Press 2012) 496–98.

[98] *See* Arato, 'The Margin of Appreciation in International Investment Law', (2014) 54 Michigan Journal of International Law 545.

[99] Goldman, 'An Introduction to the French Law of Government Procurement Contracts', (1987) 20 George Washington Journal of International Law and Economics 461.

[100] *Ibid* at 462–63.

This approach to energy governance fits a model in which decisions are made by and between multiple actors and centres of gravity.[101] The hydrocarbon energy paradigm relied upon state actors to fulfil a certain function by means of their regulatory power. Still, industry itself was and remains a core player in setting the ground rules for the actual day-to-day operational standards for the energy industry. It is because both regulators and industry work together that investors—lenders and equity holders (shareholders, partners, etc) —in fact place money in the enterprises that make up global energy value chains. The collaboration between state and energy companies creates a case for energy projects and the supply chains on which they depend to become bankable.

This approach also faces important hurdles. In the first place, it is impossible to know what a reasonable return for investment in the energy sector should be in the absence of a marketplace. Yet, such a marketplace could only form with difficulty because energy was seen as a sort of natural monopoly: it does not make sense to build two powerplants to compete over supplying the same town with electricity.[102] Power plants were too expensive and demand was too stable to keep both power plants in business. This means that there was no easy way to introduce competition to test prices. One would have to trust instead that a formula could appropriately assess what return a utility could fairly charge its off-takers.

This natural monopoly applied not just in the context of electricity generation. It applied with even greater force to electricity transmission.[103] It is not economically feasible to build rival electricity transmission infrastructures. There is no demand case for such doubling of efforts. Similarly, the cost and time of permitting and building the transmission system is too high to draw in competitors even if the incumbent provider were to be inefficient.

The same logic initially also applied to the oil and gas sector. Aggressive market-based approaches to oil development led to significant boom and bust cycles that stranded large amounts of oil in the US and made them all but unrecoverable.[104] Stable marketplaces, at the outset, required a significantly greater amount of monopolistic control to maintain. In the global setting, this led to posted price mechanisms to determine the governmental participation in oil production. Yet, because oil was never actually traded, there was no market reference point for this posted price.[105]

Problematically, as important as this paradigm has been in the energy sector, it does not lend itself to efficient investment decisions. Thus, in the electricity

[101] Ostrom (n 73), at 255–88.

[102] *See* Coleman, 'State Energy Cartels', (2021) 42 Cardozo Law Review 2247 (discussing the difference between energy cartels and natural monopoly approaches).

[103] Tomain, 'The Persistence of Natural Monopoly', (2002) 16 Natural Resources & Environment 242, 273–74.

[104] Yergin, (n 97), at 15–17.

[105] van de Graaf & Sovacool (n 34), at 25–27.

sector, there was always a perceived incentive to over-invest: returns were calculated on the basis of investments made.[106] This means that returns would grow with investments. Building out a more expansive and expensive grid therefore was decidedly in the interest of utilities. This had the side effect of creating sufficient excess capacity on the grid to safeguard energy security.[107] It also had the side effect of increasing the overall costs that consumers had to pay for electricity as a whole because there was no competition to limit speculative spending. Again, this risk also exists in the oil and gas space—here, it is known as 'gold plating'—a practice by which a company increases its costs in order to increase the share of oil revenue from a project through cost recovery in more sophisticated oil and gas contracts with the host state.[108]

At the same time, the risk of governmental interference also created disincentives to invest because it increased political risk.[109] This political risk, in turn, increased the return investors expected. This increased return then created an impression of profiteering in regulators, giving rise to a potentially vicious cycle.

The problem of the utility model, in the end, was that it did not return its original promise of efficient development, broad access, and low prices particularly once markets sufficiently matured.[110] Regulators could not in fact secure that prices paid by consumers provided them the most affordable, technologically available energy access. Risk profiles further meant that certain projects would not be undertaken at all because of the needed return to make them prudent to pursue for investors. The attempt at regulatory collaboration by all stakeholders in the energy system therefore was a good start. It was not, however, the kind of success that would provide a basis for governing the current energy transition.

Feed in tariffs to support renewable energy projects provide one recent illustration of why such an approach faces limitations in the current energy transition.[111] Such measures were introduced in order to increase incentives for the diffusion of renewable energy for instance in Europe. The feed in tariffs were set on an ostensible reasonable return basis. Yet, because of the incentives offered, technology improved so fast that there was a perception of windfall advantages for power providers. After the 2008 financial crisis, states significantly curtailed feed in tariffs due to this windfall concern. The feed in tariff model in other words showcases

[106] For a discussion of this concern and some counter-arguments raised at a time of continued, significant state control over energy, *see* Corey, 'The Averch and Johnson Proposition: A Critical Analysis', (1971) 2 The Bell Journal of Economics and Management Science 358, 363. As discussed in section 1.5, market liberalization was driven (successfully in part at last) by this concern.

[107] Todd S Aaagard & Andrew Kleit, *Electricity Capacity Markets* (Cambridge University Press 2022) 39.

[108] Anderson (n 89).

[109] On this concern, *see* Wälde, 'Renegotiating Acquired Rights in the Oil and Gas Industries: Industry and Political Cycles Meet the Rule of Law', (2008) 1 Journal of World Energy Law & Business 55.

[110] Bryce (n 16), at 82–96.

[111] For a full discussion of feed in tariffs, *see* Frederic Sourgens, Catherine Banet, & Teddy Baldwin, *The Transnational Law of Renewable Energy* (Oxford University Press 2024).

that the utility model can both increase political risk and potentially overpay for electricity at the same time.[112]

This risk is a measure of the speed of technological innovation at the current point in time. The utility model is both too successful in setting incentives that actually do technology force and too interventionist to create long-term investment security.

The idea thus had merit as evidenced by the exponential speed of development in the renewable energy sector. It did not set the right kind of interconnections between the different stakeholders to create the kind of energy system that can deliver on increased decarbonization at the same time as expanding energy access at a lower price point. It was a victim of its own success. As a policy approach, it contributed to the drastic reduction in cost of multiple technologies (utility scale wind and solar) that are now capable of contributing to such a result.[113] It just could not fully manage the ascent. It did not share risks, rewards, and responsibilities between the different stakeholders in the energy transition to fully realize and further accelerate the revolutionary potential of what the policy approach had started. That is the cause of a significant number of international disputes involving these support mechanisms.[114]

The approach thus appears on the whole to be too inflexible. It can achieve tremendous advances in diffusing energy technologies by setting what appears to be safe returns.[115] This safety of returns also is uniquely helpful to the support of innovation as safe returns mean that there appear to be 'excess' profits to be made in the field if only one can reduce cost. Yet, this very incentive leads to a vicious cycle. This sort of technology forcing almost by definition sets up the kind of political reaction to change the marketplace *ex post*. Rather than working in the same direction, industry and regulators seem to be pulling in opposite directions when the tipping point of innovation is reached. This is precisely what an energy governance regime for the current energy challenges must be keen to avoid.

1.4 Nationalization and Authoritarian State Energy Planning

Nationalization of relevant energy assets and state energy planning is a common alternative to the utility model outlined in the previous section. Nationalization is part of a command approach. This command approach sees energy as too central

[112] This has led to a slew of international disputes under international investment protection regimes, discussed in more detail in the next section. For a discussion of those disputes, *see* Desierto & Sourgens, 'Investment Law and Decarbonisation', *in Decarbonization and the Energy Industry, Law, Policy and Regulation in Law-Carbon Energy Markets* (Tade Oyewunmi et al eds, Hart Publishing 2020) 157.

[113] *See* Sourgens, Banet, & Baldwin (n 111).

[114] *See* Desierto & Sourgens (n 112).

[115] Klass & Wiseman (n 88).

to the economic and social wellbeing of the state to leave it in private hands. To the extent that strategic energy assets are still in private hands (eg oil and gas production, electricity distribution, electricity transmission, and perhaps electricity generation), these assets are nationalized. This dynamic is certainly well-known in the oil and gas sector.[116] It has also played out in the electricity sector.[117]

The development of national energy resources then is entirely left to the state. Energy planning will look beyond specific regions granted as territorial monopolies in the utility model. Instead, energy planning will be conducted at the national government level. Instead of looking to private actors to make investment decisions on energy sources, the decision is one of national politics. Energy is treated not as a matter of economic return on energy assets but instead as a public good to be generated in line with national geo-strategic, environmental, and economic priorities.

One example of this policy approach is the French reliance on nuclear energy.[118] As of 2022, France has an electricity mix, which relies to 62 per cent on nuclear energy.[119] French nuclear power plants, in turn, are owned by Électricité de France (EDF).[120] EDF, in turn, is owned by the French state (with a small minority stake of private investors).[121] French nuclear policy, known as the Messmer plan, was a matter of state.[122] It was introduced as a response to the oil shocks of the 1970s to provide greater energy security to France and French industry.[123] France therefore shouldered the costs of nuclear power plants without regard to the kind of cost concerns that an investor-owned utility would have brought to bear on fuel mix questions. It adopted the plan as a matter of national (security) policy and followed through. This approach was consistent with a higher level of dirigisme in French economic policy at the time.[124]

[116] Andreas Lowenfeld, *International Economic Law* (2nd edn, Oxford University Press 2008) 465–533.

[117] 'Mexico Power Plant Purchases Touted as 'New Nationalization', (4 April 2023) Associated Press, https://apnews.com/article/mexico-spain-electricity-plants-purchase-ae10392607ee263c2bc87b0fbe2ae9d7, last accessed 3 May 2024.

[118] Many European economies prior to the 1980s relied on a command approach. *See* Talus (n 91), at 271.

[119] 'France: Energy Mix', (2024) International Energy Agency (2024), https://www.iea.org/countries/france/energy-mix, last accessed 3 May 2024.

[120] 'Nuclear Power in France', (25 April 2024) World Nuclear Association, https://world-nuclear.org/information-library/country-profiles/countries-a-f/france, last accessed 3 May 2024.

[121] Francois de Beaupuy, 'EDF Moves Back Into State Hands With a Multitude of Burdens', Bloomberg (8 June 2023), https://www.bloomberg.com/news/articles/2023-06-08/edf-moves-back-into-state-ownership-with-a-multitude-of-burdens?embedded-checkout=true (last accessed 3 May 2024).

[122] James M Jasper, *Nuclear Politics, Energy and the State in the United States, Sweden, and France* (Princeton University Press, 1990) 148–76 (discussing the reasons for and impact of the French Messmer Plan).

[123] *Ibid.*

[124] For a nuanced view of French dirigisme and a policy move away from it in the 1980s and later, *see* Clift, 'French Responses to the Global Economic Crisis' The Political Economy of 'Post-Dirigisme' and New State Activism', *in The Consequences of the Global Financial Crisis: The Rhetoric of Reform and Regulation* (Wyn Grant & Graham Wilson eds, Oxford University Press 2012) 206, 211–13.

Another often-quoted example of such an approach is contemporary Chinese energy policy. Leaving aside whether Chinese energy policy in fact follows a command approach or some hybrid approach combining the different approaches outlined in this section, those praising the Chinese approach similarly are in awe of the decisiveness of Chinese energy planning in the context of the current energy transition.[125] That is, policy can move without having to look to pricing concerns and simply implement a national energy policy even though that policy might appear cost prohibitive. Further, it can force stakeholders to fall in line behind government planning due to the coercive power of the state.

While it does not have to be authoritarian, this state planning approach receives such accolades principally because it is authoritarian or at the very least proto-authoritarian.[126] It can overcome political and economic opposition by means of state power. Things can simply be made to happen for the good of all over the objection even of many.

Tempting though it may appear, this approach similarly cannot achieve the results its champions believe it to promise. The first problem is financial. The reason to look to polycentric governance is that no one actor can shoulder the more than $9 trillion in annual investments needed to see through the current energy transition.[127] This means that a command approach cannot force transition past economic obstacles. It can work on the margins to introduce an expensive technology in one important part of energy systems.[128] It cannot work beyond this. The gravitational force of financial costs is too great.

This gravitational force is on display in the Chinese context hailed by some as the model for global transition. China continues to build a significant fleet of coal-fired power plants to support its continued economic growth.[129] China of course is also building a large fleet of nuclear power plants.[130] Yet, this reliance on nuclear and renewables is not exclusive.[131] Costs, timing, and grid stability do not permit it. An 'authoritarian' approach therefore is unlikely to present a model outside of narrow, limited circumstances.[132]

[125] Peter Drahos, *Survival Governance: Energy and Climate in the Chinese Century* (Oxford University Press 2021).
[126] *Ibid.*
[127] McKinsey (n 64), at 5.
[128] Jasper (n 122), at 148–76.
[129] Lempriere, 'China Responsible for 95% of New Coal Power Construction in 2023, Report Says', CarbonBriefs (11 April 2024), https://www.carbonbrief.org/china-responsible-for-95-of-new-coal-power-construction-in-2023-report-says/#:~:text=China%20accounted%20for%2095%25%20of,the%20global%20coal%20power%20industry, last accessed 3 May 2024.
[130] Wang, 'China's Impressive Rate of Nuclear Construction, What Do Fast Chinese-Led Builds Mean for Nuclear's Future?', Breakthrough Institute (5 March 2024), https://thebreakthrough.org/issues/energy/chinas-impressive-rate-of-nuclear-construction#:~:text=The%20Chinese%20nuclear%20project%20construction,to%20just%20over%207%20years, last accessed 3 May 2024.
[131] *See* Lempriere (n 129).
[132] Drahos (n 125), at 54 (discussing whether China pursues an authoritarian energy policy).

Even then, an authoritarian approach comes at a cost. An authoritarian approach provides less by way of incentive for innovation in the long run. In a centrally planned energy system, stakeholders wishing to exercise decision-making power in the energy sector must rely on connections to the government and government planners.[133] There is thus an incentive to sway government and government planners towards a particular solution by political means. These means become the more powerful, the more entrenched a particular energy player has become due to the political leverage large operations provide.

This dynamic means that innovators have less of an ability to displace incumbent stakeholders on the strength of the technology or process they have devised. Innovators must not only displace existing technology on the strength of their idea. Rather, they also have to work against entrenched stakeholders with an interest to maintain their relative position in decision-making processes.[134] This creates further drag on their ability to establish themselves as a viable alternative to existing approaches.

This problem is particularly great in the context of command economies. Here, the idea of a 'despotic Leviathan' or state with the kind of control powers held by an authoritarian regime precisely underperforms alternatives that more equally balance social against state powers.[135] The reason for this underperformance is partially premised in the incentive for rent-seeking in despotic governance structures.[136] Just as importantly, though, there is a clear link between innovation, creativity, and liberty. Innovation is premised in experimentation—and incentives to experiment premised in an expectation of return for the work invested in an experiment.[137] When there is no such incentive to be creative and further a constraint on creativity due to a personal sense of unfreedom, creativity is unlikely to find expression in useful ways. 'Despotic Leviathans' therefore can command to adopt and improve existing technologies within known parameters. They are unlikely to solve problems in unexpected, paradigm-altering ways. As this is precisely the task at hand in the current transition, purely authoritarian approaches to energy governance are unlikely to yield the desired results.

Even so, it is important to note that a strong state role can have important advantages precisely by overriding market signals particularly for security reasons.[138]

[133] Aghion (n 81), at 87–92 (analysing the impact of lobbying in Western democracies). The analysis is reasonably analogous to central planning given the incentives at play, even if it obviously does not match exactly as electoral competition is less of a concern in this setting.

[134] *Ibid.*

[135] Daron Acemoglu & James A Robinson, *The Narrow Corridor, States, Societies, and the Fate of Liberty* (Penguin 2019) 114.

[136] *See* Aghion (n 81), at 87–92 on the influence of rent-seeking. On rent-seeking and authoritarianism in China, *see* Daniel C Mattingly, *The Art of Political Control in China* (Cambridge University Press 2020).

[137] Acemoglu & Robinson (n 135), at 114.

[138] The same is true in the context of adjacent diversification reasons. Industrial policy requires a significant amount of policy planning. Energy planning thus is of particular importance in states that are

This is a feature that is critical to the development of a functioning governance approach for constructive and cautionary reasons. Constructively, there may come a time when the power of the state to override immediate market concerns may be needed to force technology to move in a direction desired for reasons that are entirely external to energy systems themselves. Climate change today is a partial example of precisely this dynamic. Of course, energy systems themselves are threatened by climate change, meaning that energy system governance must respond to climate change pressures internally to continue flourishing. Yet, there are reasons outside of the preservation of energy systems to be concerned about climate change. Consequently, climate action may well present an additional external impetus to override energy system internal constraints in some instances to force technology to develop in a more climate friendly manner. The development of solar energy is one such example which until reasonably recently was seen as a failure that would not be able to compete on price with incumbent technology.[139] This critique proved incorrect in hindsight.[140] Technology forcing, in that instance, worked.

From a cautionary perspective, national security concerns are likely to override energy decision-making even when market signals would otherwise favour the expansion of energy access in a carbon neutral manner. In this instance, it is not enough for energy governance to develop energy-system internal pathways to foster such outcomes. It must also internalize the national security concerns that could thwart such solutions after the fact. Command dynamics therefore continue to be of particular importance for energy transition governance even as they do not present a viable governance solution in their own right. Still, their long-term risk of stifled innovation suggests that such approaches have shorter shelf lives than one might expect. That is, even assuming an efficient functioning of dirigisme that is not subject to rent seeking, it would plan for fifty years and miss the system-changing innovation to come a year later from view.

1.5 Liberalization and the Creation of Energy Markets

A final dominant approach to energy governance is the liberalization of the energy sector and the creation of energy markets. This approach wishes to eliminate the inefficiencies created by either a utility or a command approach. The vice of

negatively affected by a potential drop in revenue from hydrocarbons. For a discussion of the historical role of such planning in developing economies, *see* Binyamin Appelbaum, *The Economists' Hour, False Prophets, Free Markets, and the Fracture of Society* (Little, Brown & Co 2019).

[139] Cass Sunstein, *Laws of Fear, Beyond the Precautionary Principle* (Cambridge University Press 2005) 171–74.

[140] 'Levelized Cost of Energy+', (June 2024) Lazard, https://www.lazard.com/media/xemfey0k/lazards-lcoeplus-june-2024-_vf.pdf, last accessed 20 January 2025.

both approaches is that they do not allow for competition.[141] Without competition, energy prices paid by the end consumer are invariably higher than they might have been had there been a marketplace. In reverse, price signals will of themselves guarantee a security of energy supply as higher prices will invite more market participants, who will add more supply and thus drop prices.[142] In addition, in a marketplace, innovation can further reduce energy costs by creating real-time incentives to lower production costs so as to achieve a higher profit margin in an existing marketplace. Finally, in a marketplace, end consumers can make choices that can better shape the energy system in light of actual demand.[143] For example, in a competitive retail market, consumers can choose whether to participate in price risk (ie electricity at peak demand times is more expensive than at low demand times. A consumer participating in price risk would thus avoid doing laundry at peak times and may even shut off an air conditioner to save money. A sufficient number of consumers sharing such price risk is likely to affect prices systemwide).

The liberalization of the energy sector leans most heavily into the idea of shared governance of energy systems between a broad variety of public and private actors. Liberalization gives up the planning monopoly of authoritarian energy regimes. It also gives up price regulation and monopoly control from the utility-based approach, relying instead on a market mechanism to shape incentives and behaviour. The state recedes to the background as a regulator of last resort.[144] As this regulator of last resort, the state of course still assures that energy systems perform within adequate environmental parameters. Just as importantly, the state is the guarantor of the competitiveness of the energy marketplace liberalization has brought about. Yet, it no longer has pride of place in planning the grid or regulating prices.

The retreat of the state opens energy governance up for other stakeholders in energy systems.[145] Most notably, energy market participants (such as, importantly, power producers) will take on a far more important role for energy governance as the state retreats. Independent power producers will determine what type of generation will be available on the grid, where it will be located, and how much generating capacity will be added to the grid. Similarly, oil and gas companies determine the extent of new exploration and the speed of new developments. Not only that, oil and gas companies have a significant ability to affect the total volume of oil and gas supply through their production choices. These decisions by leading energy companies in the electricity and oil and gas spaces will themselves impact the incentives for a myriad of other energy value chain participants to deliver needed inputs.

[141] Cameron (n 87), at 8.
[142] Talus (n 91), at 271.
[143] Cameron (n 87), at 8.
[144] For a classic analysis of this phenomenon more broadly, *see* Susan Strange, *The Retreat of the State, The Diffusion of Power in the World Economy* (Cambridge University Press 1996).
[145] *Ibid.*

To provide one example of such market-based impacts across different energy sectors, in 2023–24, electric vehicle sales fell off behind global expectations.[146] The reason appears to have been consumer caution—rather than purchasing fully electric vehicles, many consumers chose hybrid vehicles instead.[147] This had ripple effects in the battery value chain—the demand for lithium dropped.[148] With it lithium became less valuable. This, in turn, puts at risk future lithium projects, those still at comparatively early planning and financing stages as well even as operations at currently ongoing lithium projects.[149] At the same time, less electric vehicles on the road also affects how the electricity grid will behave. On the one hand, overall electricity demand is lower. On the other hand, there will be fewer batteries on the road that could serve as a backstop of last resort for a grid (electric vehicles connected to a charging station can in fact deliver power to the grid as well as charge from the grid, thus providing 'backup power' for grid operators). This, in turn, will set market signals to independent power producers. In yet another area of energy systems, the reduced interest in fully electric vehicles sets a signal for a higher than anticipated demand for oil. This, in turn, leads to greater incentives to develop new oil projects.[150] None of these incentives were exclusively set by governments. They grew out of market decisions made by consumers which, in turn, have impacts in real time on energy systems as a whole.

This is not to say that governments have no ability to set policy. For example, they can offer subsidies and other incentives. They can also announce a policy not to permit the sale of internal combustion engines after a certain point in time. Yet, these policies have only a limited effect on how energy systems as a whole behave. Thus, electric vehicle sales lagged behind expectations in 2023–24 at a time when there were significant incentives available in many jurisdictions to purchase such vehicles and at a time when several jurisdictions had announced phase out dates for internal combustion engines. The market did not move as fast as policymakers had wished.

[146] McLain & Rattner, 'How Electric Vehicles Are Losing Momentum with U.S. Buyers, in Charts', (27 December 2023) Wall Street Journal, https://www.wsj.com/business/autos/electric-vehicle-demand-charts-7d3089c7, last accessed 4 May 2024; Winton, 'Europe To Buy Nearly 9 Million Fewer EVs By 2030 Than Expected: Report', (8 April 2024) Forbes, https://www.forbes.com/sites/neilwinton/2024/04/08/europe-to-buy-nearly-9-million-fewer-evs-by-2030-than-expected-report/?sh=3113e0fa239e, last accessed 4 May 2024.

[147] Ferris, 'Why Hybrid Sales Surge as EV Sales Flatten', (4 April 2024) CNBC, https://www.cnbc.com/2024/04/04/why-hybrid-sales-surge-as-ev-sales-flatten.html, last accessed 4 May 2024.

[148] Simpson, 'Lithium Prices in Free Fall: Implications for Clean Energy Transition in the Private Sector', (1 February 2024) Bradley Intelligence Report, https://www.bradley.com/insights/publications/2024/02/lithium-prices-in-free-fall-implications-for-clean-energy-transition-in-the-private-sector, last accessed 4 May 2024.

[149] Thomas, 'Slow EV Sales Are Proving Problematic for Australia's Lithium Miners', (30 January 2024) Mining Technology, https://www.mining-technology.com/news/slow-ev-sales-are-proving-problematic-for-australias-lithium-miners/, last accessed 4 May 2024.

[150] Penn, 'Oil Companies Expand Offshore Drilling, Pointing to Energy Needs', (3 May 2024) New York Times, https://www.nytimes.com/2024/05/03/business/energy-environment/shell-offshore-oil-gulf-of-mexico.html, last accessed 4 May 2024.

The trade-off for the comparatively smaller impact of policy-making on the overall direction of energy systems is that liberalized energy systems become far more 'sticky' when they have fully adopted a particular problem solution. For example, Texas is the leading wind and solar state in the US despite its facially deeply conservative, pro-hydrocarbon politics.[151] Nonetheless, the market has embraced renewables as the cheapest way to deliver energy to consumers even here. The US under President Trump met the interim goals it had communicated under the Paris Agreement during the Obama administration.[152] It did so despite the fact that President Trump withdrew the US from the Paris Agreement.[153] The diffusion of decision-making power in energy governance meant that energy policies proved ultimately less powerful than the market. The Trump administration did not save the US coal industry.[154] The Obama administration did not kill it. Liberalized markets simply went in a different direction, with coal-fired power plant operators choosing to retire plants and power producers replacing coal with renewables on the grid.

While the idea behind liberalization sounds straightforward, it is in many ways difficult to implement from the perspective of systemwide planning. To provide one example from the electricity sector, the liberalization of electricity markets is intended to bring additional, cheaper generating capacity online to reduce consumer end prices.[155] The problem is that this new generation capacity has to be connected to the grid and then transported through the grid. Notably, the grid was not designed with such competition in mind. Rather, it was built to service regional monopoly territories in the utility context or to support a nationally planned generation strategy. In the context of utilities, regional grids were connected to each other to provide additional redundancy to each other to cushion against an unexpected surge in demand or drop in supply. Yet, in neither case was transmission and interconnection designed to accommodate newcomers. The first step towards liberalization had to be to require the owners of transmission infrastructure to transmit electricity from 'new' independent power producers per the same terms as the electricity produced by the owners of the infrastructure in question.[156]

[151] *See* Gearino, 'One State Generates Much, Much More Renewable Energy Than Any Other—and It's Not California', (9 March 2023) Inside Climate News, https://insideclimatenews.org/news/09032023/inside-clean-energy-texas-renewables/#:~:text=Texas%20has%20produced%20more%20gigawatt,thanks%20largely%20to%20wind%20energy, last accessed 4 May 2024.

[152] Second Nationally Determined Contribution of the United States of America (15 April 2021), https://unfccc.int/sites/default/files/NDC/2022-06/United%20States%20NDC%20April%2021%202021%20Final.pdf, last accessed 4 May 2024.

[153] Secretary Pompeo, 'On the U.S. Withdrawal from the Paris Agreement', (4 November 2019) U.S. State Department, https://2017-2021.state.gov/on-the-u-s-withdrawal-from-the-paris-agreement/, last accessed 4 May 2024.

[154] Lipton, '"The Coal Industry Is Back", Trump Proclaimed. It Wasn't', (18 October 2020) New York Times, https://www.nytimes.com/2020/10/05/us/politics/trump-coal-industry.html, last accessed 4 May 2024.

[155] *See* Talus (n 91), at 16–22.

[156] *See* Kelliher & Farinella, 'The Changing Landscape of Federal Energy Law', (2009) 61 Administrative Law Review 611, 625–26; Talus (n 91), at 70.

In principle, this required that all decision-making with regard to transmission be spun-off from the original owners of the transmission infrastructure to an independent system operator or regional transmission organization to safeguard that transmission was in fact available to all generators connected to a particular grid on equal terms.[157] One of the most successful feats of liberalization was to transition transmission to precisely such structures.

Still, this liberalizing existing transmission is not enough. One of the main contemporary drivers of the success of liberalization is that today's solar arrays and wind turbines can generate electricity at a much lower levelized cost of energy compared to incumbent coal-fired and gas-fired powerplants.[158] Problematically, transmission has been built to accommodate traditional powerplants. These plants could be located reasonably close to where end customers consumed the electricity they generated. This is not the case in the context of renewable energy. Areas with good solar and wind potential can be located at significant distances from population centres, meaning that electricity will have to be transported much longer distances than previously. Similarly, the intermittence of wind and solar energy means that the redundancy needed in the grid to account for drops in energy supply is greater than it previously was because the variability of electricity supply is greater (ie a gas-fired power plant was less likely to go offline due to environmental conditions than a windfarm.) This means that more transmission needs to be built to create precisely such redundancy. The same would be true with regard to utility-scale battery storage—another alternative to creating redundancy in a renewable-energy-heavy grid.

This planning for transmission in the context of a liberalized electricity market is significantly more complicated than it was in the context of a utility-based or 'authoritarian' paradigm. It requires coordination between competitors that is in fact harmful to their respective interests.[159] An owner of a gas-fired power plant is aided if less renewable energy is available in the system given that renewable energy will bring down energy prices. Perhaps ironically, the owner of a renewable energy facility close to a population centre would have a similar incentive to keep out renewable energy generated further away as intermittency of the resource would drive up electricity prices in a way that might allow the close facility to invest in storage and sell to the grid from storage at the times in question. The participants in the system therefore all have interests that appear to be at odds with each other, making planning a grid far more difficult.

Just as importantly, the incentive structure to build redundancy in general into the grid is lower in the context of a liberalized market than it is in any other

[157] Talus (n 91), at 68.
[158] Lazard (n 140).
[159] Kelly & Wiseman, 'No Easy Transmission Fixes', (December 2016) North American Windpower, https://www.akingump.com/a/web/53869/NAW1612_Akingump.pdf, last accessed 4 May 2024.

structure. The point of an electricity market from the point of view of producers is to make money. Making money is a direct result of scarcity: the more demand stretches supply, the higher prices go. This means that, in principle, there is reasonably no incentive for participants in a marketplace to build in redundancies intended to limit the impact of precisely such supply crunches. The exception to this rule is that there is an incentive to build expensive generation that can be flexibly deployed in such instances (ie generation that would not undercut prices in the system at those times, but rather stabilize them at a sufficiently high point to secure significant profit margins to producers). Yet, it is not rational to build such expensive generating capacity on the pricing model available in a marketplace, as the expensive generation in question would remain idle most of the most time, that is, it would not earn enough money to justify the risk of construction. This is the missing money problem in liberalized energy markets: there is a disincentive to invest in enough spare capacity to backstop the grid against failure at expected (yet comparatively infrequent) peak demand times.[160]

Finally, liberalized energy markets are more vulnerable to the kind of geopolitical manipulation discussed above. Markets strive towards efficiency. To the extent that a geopolitical intervention in the market disrupts supplies (or demand) in a key marketplace, there will not be sufficient strategic reserves to make up the shortfall. The unavailability of Russian oil and gas following Russia's invasion of Ukraine is one such example. It created a short-term supply shock after Western governments imposed sanctions on Russia.[161] These sanctions had the ultimate effect of reducing Russian crude oil and gas in their markets. Yet, Russian oil and gas could return to the market at any time. There was no market-based incentive significantly to expand production in other markets to make up for the sanctions induced shortfall. From an energy industry perspective, it was more rational to wait for Russian supply to find the demand that remained available to it than to attempt to cover the shortfall through new production. Sanctions therefore profoundly affected the Western markets in question themselves. And this effect was pronounced because of the liberalized nature of energy markets.

This geostrategic vulnerability of liberalized energy markets must not be underestimated. Energy security is difficult to build into liberalized markets precisely because of the efficiencies it attempts to achieve and the price incentives for investors it wishes to set. Soaring energy prices in Europe pushed the liberalized energy markets in the European Union close to breaking point.[162] Europe arguably

[160] Aagaard & Kleit (n 107), at 14–15.

[161] Alessandri & Gazzini, 'The Impact of Gas Supply Shocks in Europe', (25 July 2023) Center for Economic Policy Research, https://cepr.org/voxeu/columns/impact-gas-supply-shocks-europe, last accessed 4 May 2024.

[162] *See* Tubiana et al, 'Between Crises and Decarbonisation: Realigning EU Climate and Energy Policy for the New 'State of the World'', (July 2022) EUI Florence School of Regulation Policy Brief 2022/42, https://cadmus.eui.eu/bitstream/handle/1814/74737/QM-AX-22-042-EN-N.pdf?sequence=1&isAllowed=y, last accessed 4 May 2024.

began to trend away from the idea of market liberalization before this shock. This trend became more pronounced thereafter in a strategic rethink of market design and the greater role of the state in shaping the energy market.

Liberalization of energy markets has vulnerabilities when it comes to energy security. This is the case in the context of energy system internal stress. Here, the missing money problem is indicative of an internal incentive in liberalized markets to invest less than would be desirable to set an appropriate capacity margin for electricity generation even at peak times.[163] This is also the case in the context of external, geopolitical stress (or indeed any other external stress on value chains).[164] Given the systemic vulnerabilities of liberalization, it, too, is fundamentally flawed as a standalone paradigm to guide the current energy transition.

1.6 Conclusion

Energy governance is critical to human development. Yet, as critical as energy governance is, it appears that existing theories of energy governance have significant blind spots that become particularly salient in moments of transition. As we have seen in this chapter, the dominant theories of energy governance—be they premised on a public contracting model with utilities, on a command or authoritarian models, or on liberalized market models—fail in critical regards. Neither the utility nor the authoritarian model could secure affordable energy access premised in innovation. A liberal market-based approach, on the other hand, proved deeply vulnerable to internal and external energy security challenges to the point of inviting stakeholders to trade for relative advantage from energy insecurity events.

The reason the dominant paradigms of energy governance struggle is that they do not appropriately think about and employ the interconnection between different stakeholders such as to create a shared energy community. To the contrary, the way that the different paradigms link different stakeholders to each other is destructive precisely under the imperatives of the contemporary energy transition. The utility paradigm sets up incentives that create mistrust between regulators and energy stakeholders. Feed in tariffs for renewable energy sources showcased this mechanism—governments wished to draw renewable energy providers in through competitive, cost-plus incentives that would guarantee a reasonable return for renewable energy generation. These incentives worked—they sparked an innovation race that sought to reduce the cost of renewables to generate as much profit as possible from the incentives—profits that exceeded the governmental cost of service analysis. This, in turn, led governments to cry foul and to submit that energy

[163] Aagaard & Kleit (n 107), at 14–15.
[164] Tubiana (n 162).

companies sought windfalls at the expense of the public purse. Policymakers and energy stakeholders were working facially at cross purposes with each other.

Policymakers and energy stakeholders did so because they did not in fact link up to achieve a truly common goal. Their relationship instead was transactional—seeking short-term positional advantages in broader decision-making processes shaping the future global energy systems. Policymakers sought to achieve a relative positional advantage for what they perceived to be critical industries for the new energy order in their respective home jurisdictions. They further sought to limit the cost of carbon neutral generation as much as possible so as not to overburden the public purse. Yet, energy stakeholders sought to maximize profit from the incentives offered. They therefore leaned into global supply chains to reduce costs and innovation leaders to develop technology capable of exhausting available incentive rents as much as at all feasible. In so doing, energy stakeholders did precisely the opposite of what policymakers had hoped for in the manner in which they used incentives. The interconnection between policymakers and energy stakeholders was 'toxic' in the sense that it worked towards parochial and even adversarial ends rather than seeking to understand the interests of the relevant counterparties and working towards a community of interests.

The dynamic was on display in the context of an authoritarian energy model. Here, incentives are just as transactional. Stakeholders seek to maximize government access to gain as much of a positional advantage from government planning as possible. They do not seek to achieve the government's purpose—reducing energy costs through carbon neutral generating technology. Again, the relationship is almost adversarial. It is rent-seeking rather than problem-solving. The interconnection between different participants is off.

What is more, the very idea of an authoritarian energy governance approach is distrustful of non-governmental and foreign governmental stakeholders. Only the national government can set up an energy system that is truly in the national interest. This national interest runs counter to industry interests. They therefore have to be held at arm's length as much as possible. Similarly, national interests of one state clash with those of others. Industrial policy continues to be seen as, in part, a zero-sum game in which energy policy continues to provide an advantage.

Problematically, market liberalization did not cure these ills. It did draw more stakeholders into shaping energy systems. Yet, here, too, incentives did not create positive connections around shared goals for energy system stakeholders. Rather, stakeholders were, and continue to be, at odds with each other and can use their respective position within the energy market to block peers and competitors as much as possible. Further, there is no true incentive to tackle the 'missing money' problem to secure sufficient redundancy in generation to cover peak energy demand. Rather, the 'missing money' problem creates the very incentives to do the opposite—drive up energy prices through managed (though excessive) scarcity (excessive in the sense of scarcity that should not exist under ideal cost-benefit considerations). Finally, geopolitical actors have every incentive to stress vital nodes in energy value chains to achieve a positional advantage. Market systems have difficulty absorbing such shocks, meaning that the global interconnections in an increasingly liberalized energy order in fact also incentivize rivalrous competition rather than innovation coopetition.

It is therefore clear that we need to change the interconnection between stakeholders in energy decision-making processes. What is less clear is what these interconnections should look like and how this reorientation should be accomplished. These are the questions that will occupy us throughout the remainder of this book.

2
The Bond of Belonging

2.1 Introduction

The last chapter showed that the existing dominant theories of energy governance faced limitations because they do not appropriately think about and employ the interconnection between different energy systems stakeholders. To the contrary, the interconnection between different stakeholders can turn almost toxic. Industry stakeholders and government stakeholders appeared to work at cross purposes with each other. When this happens, there does not seem to be an energy governance answer to re-align their efforts within a given governance paradigm.

What I will argue in this chapter is that this misalignment gives rise to distinct energy cycles. The governance approaches we have discussed in Chapter 1 are attempts to bring energy cycles back into balance. Yet, the more pronounced the misalignment, the more violent the energy cycle becomes. This itself can lead to serious governance problems. Managing energy cycles proactively therefore is critical to achieving policy outcomes.

The problems we are seeing clearly in the energy transition context were always in the background even before the current energy transition began in earnest. There was, after all, a reason that states sought to liberalize energy systems: policymakers thought that actual competition would further discourage attempts to gold plate costs to increase profits.[1] Still, the efforts to decarbonize energy systems brought these tensions to the fore more vividly. The efforts to 'technology force' renewable energy systems in particular created an immense stress on existing understandings of liberalized energy markets.[2] This stress got to the point of calling into question the earlier unquestioned commitment in Europe to strong property right protections as one pillar of global energy planning.[3]

[1] *See supra* section 1.6.

[2] *See* Desierto & Sourgens, 'Investment Law and Decarbonisation', *in Decarbonization and the Energy Industry, Law, Policy and Regulation in Law-Carbon Energy Markets* (Tade Oyewunmi et al eds, Hart Publishing 2020) 157; *see also* Kwon, 'Rent and Rent-Seeking in Renewable Energy Support Policies: Feed-in Tariff vs. Renewable Portfolio Standards', (2015) 44 Renewable & Sustainable Energy Review 676. For a study on rent-seeking in the Spanish renewables sector, *see* Espinoza et al, 'The Political Economy of Rent-Seeking: Evidence from Spain's Support Policies for Renewable Energy', (2021) 14 Energies 4197.

[3] 'EU Member States Sign an Agreement for the Termination of Intra-EU Bilateral Investment Treaties', (5 May 2020) European Commission, https://finance.ec.europa.eu/publications/eu-member-states-sign-agreement-termination-intra-eu-bilateral-investment-treaties_en, last accessed 9 June 2024.

A Theory of Global Energy Governance. Frédéric Gilles Sourgens, Oxford University Press. © Frédéric Sourgens 2025.
DOI: 10.1093/9780198950325.003.0002

A better theory of energy governance begins with a better understanding of what is going wrong. We need a better theoretical understanding of energy governance challenges. This means we need a better understanding of the logic of the energy system itself. We saw in the last chapter that energy systems have a logic of their own. We have also seen that this logic is related to the manner in which energy value chains are built and link together. How do these links lead to misalignments? What are the dominant energy paradigms missing about the 'in between' of energy stakeholders that is now coming to the foreground?

The answer I will sketch in this chapter builds on the last: that the energy system has elements of both a 'commons' and an 'anticommons'. Commons describe relationships in which an aspect of an important resource is owned not by a single owner, but jointly by a group of owners.[4] Groundwater, oil, and gas frequently are owned in this way.[5] Different individual owners own a partial right to exploit shared water, oil, and gas reserves. They do not, however, own the whole of a particular water, oil, or gas reservoir. In this context, there is a danger of overuse of the shared resource, or a tragedy of the commons.[6] This overuse in the end leads to the premature exhaustion of the resource base due to overdevelopment.[7]

Anticommons address a similar situation of multiple owners.[8] Yet, anticommons worry about the inverse situation. The multiplicity of multiple different owners can make use of a resource so onerous that the resource will go underused.[9] Roadway tolls imposed on different stretches of a road connecting distant places are one traditional example of a disaster of the anticommons.[10] As each owner of a stretch of road imposes a toll, the cost to travel the whole road increases. At some point, travel will decrease as the cost is not worth the convenience of the road. Yet, there is no reason for any one owner to reduce tolls as only a collective reduction of tolls will increase usage again.[11]

The dominant theories of energy governance run into difficulty because they create the wrong kind of incentives for energy system stakeholders in the shared energy resource space. That space acts as both a commons and anticommons depending upon the circumstances, due to the shared nature of energy resources. This, in turn, can create the wrong interconnections between these stakeholders.

[4] Elinor Ostrom, *Governing the Commons: The Evolution of Institutions for Collective Action* (Cambridge University Press 2015) 182–215.

[5] Carol M Rose, *Property and Persuasion: Essays on the History, Theory, and Rhetoric of Ownership* (Routledge 1994) 165–89; Pierce, 'Carol Rose Comes to the Oil Patch: Modern Property Analysis Applied to Modern Reservoir Problems', (2011) 19 Penn State Environmental Law Review 241, 245–46.

[6] Hardin, 'The Tragedy of the Commons', (1968) 162 Science 1243.

[7] *Ibid.*

[8] Heller, 'The Tragedy of the Anticommons: A Concise Introduction and Lexicon', (2013) 76 Modern Law Review 6; Heller, 'The Tragedy of the Anticommons: Property in Transition from Marx to Markets', (1998) 111 Harvard Law Review 621.

[9] *See* citations in n 8.

[10] Heller 2013 (n 8), at 9–10.

[11] *Ibid* at 13–14.

That is, existing theories assign only a specialized role to most stakeholders. In each of the paradigms, most stakeholders do not have to concern themselves with the success or failure of energy systems as a whole. They only have a more limited, specialized responsibility (eg to operate energy infrastructure according to industry standards on a cost-plus basis).[12] The incentives set by these paradigms focus on exploiting governance approaches to achieve short-term positional advantages within an energy system. This, in turn, undermines any ability by any of these paradigms to deliver efficient and effective solutions in times of systemic change. This is the misalignment that keeps propelling energy cycles forward and provides the incentives for innovation to break deadlocks within energy cycles.

This misalignment is less visible when energy systems function according to traditional pathways to meet a more or less stable demand. In those instances, it is possible to compensate for the risks created by the incentive structure by policing abuse at the margins. When the energy system changes in a fundamental way, the fissures in existing governance approaches simply become more visible. The traditional policing tools do not suffice to bring about the desired state of affairs because the traditional policing tools were not built for the conditions of reasonable uncertainty inherent in any transition.[13] We therefore need to find a different way of balancing the different tools at our disposal against each other to achieve the desired result.

This is not a 'technocratic' task. Balancing these different paradigms is not a matter of technical expertise that can be exercised by a single stakeholder. Instead, it requires all stakeholders to internalize that they share a bond of belonging to the same energy system. They are part of, and provide, inputs towards a larger whole. This larger whole provides them with the very opportunities they would stand to lose through positional, rivalrous action. These opportunities grow when they innovate and compete with each other with the goal of improving that larger whole. This bond of belonging changes each stakeholder's perspective from one that only seeks a positional advantage by maximizing the opportunities a governance approach provides to working towards a different kind of positional advantage—namely a positional advantage they enjoy because they improve energy systems for all participants.

Such a switch in perspective may arise naturally. Owners in resource communities can police themselves to avoid tragedies of the commons and disasters of the anticommons.[14] Yet, it is on the whole unlikely that this will happen in the energy context. It is one thing for owners in a shared water reservoir to agree to a shared use scheme—they are neighbours and physically close to one another. It is another

[12] *See* section 1.4.

[13] For a discussion of one such failure at a critical moment of transition, *see* Duane, 'Regulation's Rationale: Learning from the California Energy Crisis', (2002) 19 Yale Journal on Regulation 471.

[14] For such examples, *see* Ostrom (n 4), at 182–215.

thing to take such a stance in the context of diffuse national and global systems. It is not particularly likely that a person in Los Angeles benefiting from a new transmission line connecting California to the Midwest would ever meet the homeowner through whose proverbial backyard the new line was sited.[15] Benefits and burdens appear more disjointed. This makes spontaneous communal action more difficult.

All this means is that we need to set incentive structures systemically. We cannot set incentive structures to respond to specific problems in an ad hoc manner. We need to set incentives for an entire system to achieve satisfactory outcomes. As national energy systems connect different stakeholders in complex value chains, a failure to think systemically will lead to cascading, unintentional consequences.[16] If one keeps the entire energy system in mind and sets incentives for all participants in the value chains supporting it to participate as desired, one can minimize such unwanted and unintentional consequences.

This task is to come up with a new kind of energy paradigm. The task of this paradigm is to create new interconnections between energy system stakeholders that avoid tragedies of the commons and disasters of the anticommons. To achieve this goal, ends and institutions must instil in stakeholders the necessary trust that others will work to protect a system they value together. Stakeholders must also gain the necessary trust that all stakeholders in principle will fairly share in benefits and burdens of energy transition and energy system expansion and maintenance.

Setting different incentives and developing a new energy paradigm does not mean that we need to come up with a different set of energy governance tools. As we will see, policymakers used these tools successfully to address specific problems. The tools we currently have at our disposal can be used to set a different incentive structure for energy transition if we realign them to deal with our context. The point rather is to use the tools developed by the dominant energy governance paradigms together to create a more stable balance. This joint use needs to be more than a matter of convenience. It must achieve an overall purpose.

Once we have understood the reasons motivating the progress of energy cycles, we can look in more detail at our historical energy experience. I will then introduce the mechanisms of energy cycles by way of concrete examples. I will argue that different governance approaches in fact attempted to realign incentives to support the bond of belonging between energy system stakeholders.

This overall purpose on one level is to balance existing energy paradigms against each other. We have seen that these paradigms each have benefits at different times

[15] Uhlenhuth, 'Power from the Prairie Aims to Link West Coast Sun with Prairie Wind', (24 November 2020) Energy News Network, https://energynews.us/2020/11/24/power-from-the-prairie-aims-to-link-west-coast-sun-with-midwest-wind/, last accessed 9 June 2024.

[16] *See* Betolli, 'Renewable-Energy Development in a Net-Zero World: Disrupted Supply Chains', (17 February 2023) McKinsey & Co, https://www.mckinsey.com/industries/electric-power-and-natural-gas/our-insights/renewable-energy-development-in-a-net-zero-world-disrupted-supply-chains, last accessed 20 January 2025.

in energy life cycles. The question is how we can better utilize the key benefits of each paradigm without suffering its inherent drawbacks. The new paradigm I hope to develop therefore is not a totally different way to think about or organize energy systems. It is instead a kind of background theory of how we should think about orienting the approaches we have available to us to strengthen bonds of belonging to a shared energy system between different stakeholders. The question is one of how to coordinate the actions of these stakeholders with each other according to some overarching logic. This logic is the logic of shared belonging in a slow-moving, highly integrated, and complex energy community.

2.2 The Tragedy of the Energy Commons

The global energy system runs into tragedies of the commons particularly in moments of transition. The classic example of a tragedy of the commons is a communally owned grazing pasture.[17] The pasture provides grazing grounds for multiple farmers. The more cows graze on the pasture, the more stress the farmers place on the pasture. Yet, no farmer is likely to reduce their own use of the pasture unless all farmers reduce their use, in order to share fairly in the foregone profits from grazing. This means that farmers are likely to exhaust the pasture rather than protect it.[18]

This scenario plays out in the context of other resource systems in which it is difficult to exclude other participants from (over-)using a particular shared resource. Water supplies from river basins, groundwater, or irrigation works are one such example.[19] Production from a shared oil and gas reservoir is another example.[20] The protection and maintenance of the internet is a third.[21] In each of these environments, it is possible to overuse the shared resource and under-invest in its maintenance and protection, thus threatening the resource system as a whole.

Climate change plainly looks like a tragedy of the commons.[22] States benefit from economic growth due to energy consumption.[23] This energy consumption is greenhouse gas intensive. There is no incentive to incur the costs of energy transition and its reduction in greenhouse gas emissions unless every state participates. Without such cooperation, catastrophic climate change remains a realistic

[17] Hardin (n 6).
[18] *Ibid.*
[19] Ostrom (n 4); Rose (n 5), at 165–89.
[20] Pierce (n 5), at 245–46.
[21] Shackelford, 'The Law of Cyber Peace', (2017) 18 Chicago Journal of International Law 1, 29–37. For a full discussion, *see* Sourgens, 'Cyber-Nuisance', (2021) 42 University of Pennsylvania Journal of International Law 1005.
[22] Shackelford, 'On Climate Change and Cyber Attacks: Leveraging Polycentric Governance to Mitigate Global Collective Action Problems', (2020) 18 Vanderbilt Journal of Entertainment & Technology Law 653.
[23] *See* section 1.3.

prospect.[24] Without such cooperation, it is therefore better to continue to use existing energy systems to the fullest to get the last remaining benefit of climate systems before the catastrophe. In this tragedy of the commons, we destroy the climate through overuse and not a pasture.

National energy systems similarly are locked in a tragedy of the commons. National energy systems exist because different stakeholders come together to deliver energy to end users in some form of energy marketplace. This marketplace creates incentives through rate and price structures. Rate and price structures encourage collaboration so long as the self-interest and interests of specific stakeholders and the interests of the energy system as a whole coincide as to what outcomes ought to be achieved. Problematically, these interests soon diverge. Energy producers quickly understand how to extract rents from these incentive structures without creating a proportionate benefit to the energy system—they 'arbitrage' the energy governance regime to get higher incentive pay outs more cheaply compared to the investments needed to achieve the same pay out with desired energy systemic benefits. It would take collective action by all stakeholders to resist exploiting such regulatory arbitrage inherent in any energy market design. Yet, once one stakeholder takes advantage, other stakeholders are forced to follow suit even at the risk of undermining the current energy governance regime to protect their respective position within it.[25]

Solving these tragedies is a matter of solving a collective action problem. As Elinor Ostrom has demonstrated in the water context in particular, stakeholders in such a commons can overcome this collective action problem by implementing a 'reasonable use' scheme.[26] Such reasonable use requires each stakeholder to limit its own activities to a level that fairly shares the available benefits and burdens from shared resource use between stakeholders.[27] Such a fair division must allow each participant a reasonable opportunity to use its own respective share in the commons.[28] It also imposes an obligation to make reasonable contributions to collective infrastructure works to distribute and maintain the resource in question.[29] This functions only to the extent that stakeholders in the commons have a sufficient level of trust in the collective compliance with, and realization of, shared values.[30] This level of trust grows when stakeholders observe and gradually correct each other's actions.[31] This observation and gradual correction strengthens

[24] Hoesung Lee et al, *Climate Change 2023: Synthesis Report. Contribution of Working Groups I, II and III to the Sixth Assessment Report of the Intergovernmental Panel on Climate Change* (Intergovernmental Panel on Climate Change 2023) 9 ('IPCC 2023').

[25] For a trenchant critique of liberal energy market designs, *see* Boyd, 'Decommodifying Electricity', (2024) 97 Southern California Law Review 937.

[26] Ostrom (n 4), at 103–42.

[27] *Ibid.*

[28] Schremmer, 'Pore Space Property', (2021) Utah Law Review 1, 4.

[29] *Mfrs.' Gas & Oil Co v Indiana Nat. Gas & Oil Co*, 57 NE 912, 915 (Ind 1900); Kramer & Anderson, 'The Rule of Capture—An Oil and Gas Perspective', (2005) 35 Environmental Law 899, 913–14.

[30] Elinor Ostrom, *Understanding Institutional Diversity* (Princeton University Press 2009) 97–98.

[31] Ostrom (n 4), at 82–87.

the expectation in all stakeholders that they and their neighbours will in fact share in their respective burdens but also receive a fair share out of collective action. This strengthened expectation, in turn, renders the demands of fair burden sharing authoritative (as opposed to a mere theoretical *desideratum*).[32] Neighbourly conduct (and only neighbourly conduct) begets neighbourliness. Neighbourliness, in turn, secures the benefits of a neighbourhood to all neighbours.

Energy systems already function in this way. This is readily visible in the context of oil and gas production. The production for shared reservoirs works only if all stakeholders reasonably use their oil and gas rights.[33] This, in turn, means that they must not create a waste.[34] They must reasonably develop their part of the resource so as to place their neighbour in a position to have a reasonable opportunity to do the same.

The same is also true in other contexts. Unless I travel across continents, I can plug any appliance I buy at the store into any plug and the appliance will work. This experience is so ubiquitous that it seems utterly unremarkable. Yet, until the 1882 English Electric Lighting Act, this was precisely not the norm.[35] What is more, the fact that every household receives alternating current today seems utterly mundane. Yet, it is the result of industry-wide adoption of alternating current over direct current, much to Thomas Edison's chagrin.[36] Similarly, we can fuel up almost any car at almost any gas station and so on. We have standardized energy systems to the point that we can fully benefit from them because multiple stakeholders have acted together reasonably to use different parts of the global energy system.[37] Reasonable use has become second nature to the point of having become almost invisible in many contexts.

Still, it is not always so successful. The problems we have seen in Chapter 1 provide vivid examples of a lack of such collective action. Even in this context, the commons governance root cause of the failure, too, can remain invisible: we mistake the problem of failing to set appropriate monetary incentives only with a failure of collective action more generally.

What frequently eludes us is the inherent logic of the energy system, as such, and its consequences for energy governance. Governing the energy commons is a 'polycentric' affair.[38] No single decisionmaker can dictate how energy stakeholders

[32] Harold Lasswell & Myers S McDougal, *Jurisprudence for a Free Society* (Martinus Nijhoff 1992) 24–26.

[33] Pierce, 'Carol Rose Comes to the Oil Patch: Modern Property Analysis Applied to Modern Reservoir Problems', (2011) 9 Penn State Environmental Law Review 241, 245–46.

[34] Righetti & Schremmer, 'Waste and the Governance of Private and Public Property', (2022) 93 University of Colorado Law Review 609, 633–41.

[35] Thomas Hughes, *Networks of Power, Electricifcation in Western Society 1880-1930* (Johns Hopkins University Press 1983) 94.

[36] *Ibid* at 91.

[37] On the original battle between internal combustion engine and electric cars, *see* Kerry Segrave, *The Electric Car in America, 1890-1922* (McFarland 2019).

[38] On the idea of polycentric governance, *see* Ostrom (n 30), at 255–88.

should work together. For the most part, different stakeholders figure this out by following the logic of the energy system. Of course, different industry stakeholders are subject to different regulations at the municipal, regional, national, and even international level. Yet, even then, there is not a single ultimate decisionmaker to mandate how energy systems should run. To the contrary, it is the interaction between these different industry stakeholders, regulators, and consumers that made the very idea of modern energy systems possible in the first place. Regulators never were innovators, and generally outsourced innovation risk to private capital.[39] Still, innovators could not create markets on their own. On the simplest level, connecting the customers to the first coal fired power plant in the world, Pearl Street Power Station in New York, required Edison to dig up New York streets.[40] This would be impossible without regulator permission.[41] Even the birth of the modern energy system, in other words, was a hybrid arrangement in which private and public decisionmakers each made decisions that ultimately created the modern energy we know today (be it over a slightly more circuitous route). It takes these stakeholders working together towards shared ends to make energy governance work. Yet, this collective action is not 'demonstrative'. Success or failure tend to be silent—and more dangerously—structural. What we can take away is that there is a structural answer to energy governance success. This success leans into how energy systems work and naturally connect stakeholders to each other in the shared energy commons. We can solve the tragedy of the commons. It requires a coordination of polycentric stakeholders rather than the reduction of stakeholders.

Tragedies of the commons can be solved even if, and particularly when, there is no ultimate decisionmaker. This suggests that it is possible to solve the climate commons problem of excessive net greenhouse gas emissions by solving the energy commons problem of securing affordable energy access at a fair price. This requires innovation to decarbonize energy systems. This innovation must not just decarbonize energy systems—it must also reduce net energy costs to solve the underlying energy problem. Importantly, it must then support the diffusion of new technology without exploiting the new regime at the margins. Such innovation is a matter of private capital. Yet, private capital will only invest when there is a public backstop for markets for the new product or process. How the energy system of the future looks like will be determined by the collaboration between all of these stakeholders and not one alone. The history of energy systems, in turn, suggests that this transformation is not only possible but also the natural next step for energy systems to take—even if history also suggests that taking this next step will take a collective effort, and a collective governance effort at that.

[39] Hughes (n 35), at 57–78.
[40] *Ibid* at 58.
[41] *Ibid.*

2.3 The Disaster of the Energy Anticommons

At the same time as running into tragedies of the commons, energy systems are also the potential victims of disasters of the anticommons.[42] The classic example of a disaster of the anticommons is the imposition of tolls by successive 'robber barons' on a single road running through their lands.[43] When the road was under imperial control, there was a single toll. When this central control wanes, robber barons each impose their own tolls. As each imposes a toll, the cost of travel increases. At some point, travellers will abandon the road as it is too expensive and every baron makes less money than they could have in an ideal use scenario.[44] Yet, there is no incentive for robber barons to reduce tolls. This action is unlikely to induce their peers to do the same. To the contrary, they might see such a reduction as a sign to increase their own tolls further to capture the additional value left behind by the price reduction.[45]

The disaster of the anticommons creates underuse. This underuse is disastrous because the incentive structure does not easily lend itself to easy correction.[46] Reasonable use may create the potential for additional harm to a reasonable user rather than additional good. This means that it is on the whole risky for me to agree to reasonable use in this scenario.

We can see the disastrous incentive structures of anticommons in the energy context. Transmission planning in a liberalized energy market is a classic anticommons problem.[47] Comparatively cheap solar and wind energy projects are not always located near end markets.[48] This means that electricity must be transmitted across longer distances.[49] The places through which the electricity is transmitted do not benefit from the electricity being transmitted, as such. Further, if anything, transmission may create economic harm to local players. For example, one US transmission project is slated to cross the state of Utah to connect

[42] Heller 1998 (n 8).
[43] Heller 2013 (n 8), at 10.
[44] *Ibid.*
[45] *Ibid.*
[46] *Ibid* at 22.
[47] Michael Heller, *The Gridlock Economy: How Too Much Ownership Wrecks Markets, Stops Innovation and Costs Lives* (2008) 13–16; Ahdieh, 'The Visible Hand: Coordination Functions of the Regulatory State', (2010) 95 Minnesota Law Review 578, 594. Some describe transmission planning as anticommons adjacent. *See* Wiseman, 'Expanding Regional Renewable Governance', (2011) 35 Harvard Environmental Law Review 477, 511–14. The dynamic Michael Heller analyses fits the transmission problem truly well—and proposes a reason for one of the leading energy transition challenges both domestically, and (as we will see in the next chapter) globally, as well.
[48] O'Donoghue, 'What's Going on with the West's Largest Transmission Line in Decades?', (30 June 2023) Deseret News, https://www.deseret.com/utah/2023/6/30/23773218/transwest-express-transmission-line-renewable-energy-wyoming-wind-western-power-grid/#:~:text=The%20TransWest%20Express%20Project%20will%20connect%20three%20planning%20regions%20in,to%20Nevada%2C%20California%20and%20Arizona, last accessed 26 June 2024.
[49] *Ibid.*

California to Midwestern wind energy.[50] Utah is a coal-producing state.[51] It is also the site for the US only uranium production mill.[52] While Utah is also growing its own renewable industry (mostly by adding solar generation), it thus remains a state that could potentially be harmed economically by cheaper access to wind energy in neighbouring Nevada and Arizona.[53] The transmission project on its face appears to favour a segment of the energy industry (wind) that is not present in Utah and actively competes with the industry that is locally present.

Similarly, incumbent producers in the end markets themselves are not benefited by transmission, as it undercuts their prices. Prices in competitive wholesale markets are set by reference to a clearing price. A systems operator sets this price by calling for bids for the total need to be met through the auction. Typically, the total needed cannot be sourced from a single producer. The systems operator will then accept bids from the cheapest to the more expensive bids until its entire demand put out for bid is met. The systems operator then sets a 'clearing price' by reference to the highest bid it accepted and pays that clearing price to all auction participants.[54] Keeping this clearing price higher, cynically, is in the interests of incumbent producers in the end market.

This means that reasonable use does not of itself solve the incentive problem as it did in the commons situation. Some players are positively better off if transmission resources are underused as opposed to if they are used reasonably. This is not the case in the tragedy of the commons—here all are better off by reasonable use in the long run because they rely on the exploitation of the shared resource.[55] In the anticommons, the problem is that use of the shared resource is precisely problematic for some stakeholders.

Despite this difference in incentive structures in commons and anticommons, the disaster of the anticommons resembles the tragedy of the commons in key respects. Both result from collective action failures. In both cases, reasonable use would lead to a more efficient, and sustainable, use of shared resources. In both cases, unreasonable use patterns arise because there are multiple actors with decisional authority over shares in the resource. In both cases, unreasonable use is in the self-interest of these stakeholders due to the relative immediate loss they will suffer from reasonable use. The theoretical problem we are trying to solve

[50] 'Critical Grid Infrastructure to Connect the West', (2024) TransWest Express, https://www.transwestexpress.net, last accessed 26 June 2024.

[51] 'Utah's Coal Resources', (2024) Utah Office of Energy Development, https://geology.utah.gov/apps/energy-resources/?page=Coal, last accessed 26 June 2024.

[52] 'Utah', (20 June 2024) US Energy Information Administration, https://www.eia.gov/state/analysis.php?sid=UT, last accessed 26 June 2024.

[53] *See ibid* (discussing the growth of solar power in Utah since 2015 but also noting the importance of coal and uranium for the state).

[54] 'Market for Electricity', (2024) PJM Learning Center, https://learn.pjm.com/electricity-basics/market-for-electricity.aspx#:~:text=The%20clearing%20price%20for%20electricity,on%20the%20Markets%20%26%20Operations%20homepage, last accessed 26 June 2024.

[55] *See* Hardin (n 6).

therefore is the same in both cases: setting up an efficient and sustainable use of a resource when decisional authority over, and ownership of, the resource in question is shared between multiple stakeholders.[56]

The tragedy of the commons and the disaster of the anticommons are separate branches of this larger problem of using shared resources. Still, either branch, in principle, responds to a reasonable use logic. 'Tragedies' and 'disasters' are tragedies and disasters precisely because reasonable use is better. Yet, better use was precluded by the fragmentation of decision-making authority. To avoid a tragedy of the commons is to yield to the reasonable demands made by others. This makes each stakeholder better off. Yielding to the reasonable demands others make also solves the disaster of the anticommons. This makes *all* stakeholders better off even if *each* stakeholder may not see an economic, immediate gain. Tragedy and disaster strike because I make myself deaf to those demands. I may make myself deaf to reasonable demands by others for different reasons in each case. Yet, the underlying vice in both is the same: a failure of other regard due to my fellow resource riparians.[57]

This means that pathways to commons governance should in principle be open in an anticommons situation, as well. The question of how to set up such a governance process may be more involved given the underlying incentive structures. Still, this governance process has to be the same kind of process we have already encountered. We are not looking for a different solution at all. We are looking for a different way to deploy the same solution to solve a related problem.

Interestingly, anticommons theorists so far would suggest that the reasonable use solution is not an answer to avoiding anticommons disasters.[58] They rather suggest that we must limit the number of decisionmakers to eradicate the problem at its root.[59] This would suggest that a balanced approach to polycentric energy governance would be doomed to fail.[60] Balanced approaches would still lead to anticommons disasters because of the large number of decisionmakers. A more radical approach therefore would be in order. This means that a command approach is, after all, our only hope to guide energy transition.

This position is too pessimistic. As I will develop in the remainder of the chapter, it is possible to reconcile a reasonable use approach with an incentive structure that is capable of avoiding anticommons disasters. We must share the collective gains from efficient solutions and cannot rely on the fact that they will fairly distribute themselves without external impetus. Theoretical responses that

[56] *See* Heller 1998 (n 8).
[57] Sourgens, 'Polyrelativity', (2025) 52 Pepperdine Law Review (forthcoming).
[58] Heller, 'Common Interest Developments at the Crossroads of Legal Theory', (2005) 37 Urban Lawyer 329, 330–32.
[59] Heller 2013 (n 8), at 19–21.
[60] For the idea of polycentric governance, *see* Ostrom (n 30), at 255–88.

exclude this possibility tend to overreach and land right back in the problems that bedevil command approaches outlined in Chapter 1. They thus correctly diagnose a problem but treat it in a manner that leads to problems of their own. If I am right, these problems can be avoided. We can achieve better outcomes. We just need to see our way to how.

Importantly, we can glimpse that disasters of the anticommons are not quite as disastrous as might at first appear. That is, we can see that the prescription of anticommons theorists may be too far reaching even by looking at the classic example of the anticommons—robber barons.[61] The example is drawn from actual historical practice: the weakening of central power in Germany during the Holy Roman Empire.[62] This weakening of central power enabled 'robber barons' to impose the tolls in question. The tolls in question describe a situation along the German Rhine. This weakening of imperial authority fragmented power in German-speaking realms at a time that France and England were centralizing power. France, therefore, would be the natural centralizing model to follow.[63]

There is an interesting wrinkle to this story. France experienced a decade-long violent revolution in 1789. This revolution was the result of policy failures which deprived 'ordinary' people of basic necessities.[64] Once in motion, the centralized French state was not able to react to the demands of its people for 'both bread and liberty'—setting up the decapitation of the French monarchy in 1793.[65]

Many of the same social conditions that led to the French Revolution were also present in the German-speaking world just east of the Rhine.[66] Yet, the greater geographic proximity between the governed and their lord prevented the same kind of conflagration in Germany. There was no equivalent German revolution to follow the French. Instead, Lords 'settled' affairs with their populations in a way Louis XVI was unable to do. Thus, there was a 'pattern of innumerable minor disturbances in Germany in 1789 and 1790'.[67] Yet,

[61] Heller 2013 (n 8), at 10.

[62] *Ibid* at 9.

[63] As is almost always the case, the story is a good bit more complicated. For one classical discussion of the development of feudal forms of tenure from the Middle Ages through to the early modern period, *see* JGA Pocock, *The Ancient Constitution and the Feudal Law, Study of English Historical Thought in the Seventeenth Century* (Cambridge University Press 1987). The relationship between lord and vassal in the *feudum* and its development was always more complicated than the king/subject duality and existed on an historical continuum. Absolutism was one interpretation of this continuum. To say that it was the dominant understanding of feudal tenure in the thirteenth century seems to go too far.

[64] For a classic account, *see* Theda Skocpol, *States & Social Revolutions, A Comparative Analysis of France, Russia & China* (Cambridge University Press 1979).

[65] *Ibid* at 66.

[66] Of course, not all conditions were the same. France suffered an acute financial crisis due to its support for costly military peradventures. *Ibid* at 64. Some German states were similarly militarily active at this time. Yet, not all were.

[67] Nicholas Boyle, *Goethe, The Poet and the Age, Volume 1: The Poetry of Desire* (Oxford University Press 1991) 650.

> the sovereign power was so widely dispersed through Germany's small territories that order was easily kept locally, grievances could be heard personally, and the organs of national representation and publicity were lacking to give symbolic significance to an individual event or to allow many incidents to cumulate into an identifiable general cause.[68]

The smaller German states were thus to a certain point 'better' for the wellbeing of the governed because they were less centralized.[69] The higher tolls imposed along the roads in the anticommons example did not deprive the populations of the means needed for their human development.

In fact, the German states were capable of working together to secure many benefits for their subjects when economic conditions had changed. Perhaps the most visible sign of this working together was the formation in 1834 of the German *Zollverein*. The *Zollverein* abolished—fittingly for our anticommons example—tolls between its members. In doing so, it created a common German-speaking market even without a single German sovereign (Prussia and Austria both vied for dominance in the German question with the small German solution without Austria prevailing after the German-Austrian war of 1866).[70]

Even prior to the *Zollverein*, German economic and cultural life was not insular, as the anticommons literature's use of the example might suggest. The life of Germany's leading intellectual of the age, Johann Wolfgang Goethe, is testament to this reality. Born in the Free City of Frankfort on the Main, Goethe studied first in Strasbourg and then in Leipzig. He then became a leading government official in Weimar. During this time, he travelled widely in Germany and was in fact the author to create a unified German literary readership. Pre-unification Germany was not a time of decay and contraction. It was a time of burgeoning self-discovery.[71] This self-discovery historically went reasonably far to overcome the disaster of the anticommons through cooperation.

The height of German cooperation was the dream of a liberal united Germany under the banner of the revolution of 1848 (fittingly, the flag of today's Federal Republic of Germany is that of 1848). The 1848 revolution swept through Europe

[68] *Ibid.*

[69] This observation is in a way unsurprising from an Aristotelian perspective. This perspective warned that a state could be too large and too populous for the effective administration of justice. The idea that a smaller state might be better governed due to the greater proximity of governing powers and the governed is not so absurd. Lianos, 'Population and State-State Economy in Plato and Aristotle', (2022) 7 Population and Sustainability 123, 131. It is made the more plausible by the fact that Germany at the time in question was at the tail end of a steady-state economy.

[70] It is true that the *Zollverein* looked a lot like the Germany that was to emerge under Prussian leadership. This is an ahistorical understanding of the nature of the *Verein* at the time. *See* Christopher Clark, *Iron Kingdom, The Rise and Downfall of Prussia, 1600-1947* (Penguin 2007) ('The Customs Union never became an effective tool for the exercise of Prussian political influence over the lesser states.')

[71] Boyle (n 67), at 95–99.

to challenge autocratic rule and demand economic and political liberalization.[72] In Germany, the revolution sought to a create a liberal, united German state. The vision was not to pass then. Still, the failure of 1848 was not a foregone conclusion. True, it ultimately failed precisely because of the *realpolitik* of inter-German rivalry. This rivalry, however, was not the rivalry of the small states. Rather, a united liberal Germany ultimately fell to Prussian unease to lead a united Germany under the ideals of 1848.[73] Even with that failure driven by the eventual intra-German hegemon, the idea that things might have ended up differently is not entirely far-fetched. 'Robber barons' can lay down their powers to act in the joint interest.

This leaves the question of why costs increased for road usage during the time of the robber barons and what had to be done to address it. 1848 suggests important lessons. Prior to the Industrial Revolution, it is not on the whole clear that lower tolls would have materially aided German princes or German societies. These tolls became a problem only with the beginning of the Industrial Revolution reaching Germany—the time that real economic growth became possible. When this happened, initiatives went reasonably far to create a common market through the *Zollverein*.[74] Yet, the political order still tolerated the kind of taxation regimes that hampered the economic growth and innovation potential created by the Industrial Revolution and the new energy systems on which it relied. Liberal protests challenged this economic order. This challenge was politically unsuccessful even as it made ever greater economic strides. The timing of the example thus matters. Anticommons pressures can be resolved through cooperative behaviour when it makes sense to do so. Yet, these pressures may not always suffice to give rise to a liberal or a democratic polity. Economics and politics do not work in lockstep even as they can create parallel impulses for change.

As I will argue in the remainder of the book, energy transitions are moments when cooperation decidedly makes developmental sense.[75] There should in principle be a good reason for different stakeholders to come together around ideas of reasonable use. The consequences of not doing so are different now than they have been in the context of business-as-usual scenarios. It is therefore a question of organizing the incentives to bring about a reasonable use coalition. If the very example that gave rise to the anticommons discussion can teach us anything, it is that

[72] Helena Rosenblatt, *The Lost History of Liberalism, From Ancient Rome to the Twenty-First Century* (Princeton University Press 2018) 131.

[73] *See* Clark (n 70).

[74] Philippe Aghion, Céline Antonin & Simon Bunel, *The Power of Creative Destruction, Economic Upheaval and the Wealth of Nations* (Harvard University Press 2021) 11 (discussing the timing of economic takeoffs as beginning in 1820 in the United Kingdom, then France, and then spreading from there).

[75] As I will discuss in Chapter 4, the meaning of 'development' itself requires further work. There are multiple development paradigms that could guide energy governance. On the level of theory, the bond of belonging functions the same no matter which developmental end we seek to realize. The outcomes, needless to say, look very different.

this is not a futile task and that this task does not require a command approach but can continue to rely on polycentric organization.

2.4 The Bond of Belonging

The core lesson from both the tragedy of the commons and disaster of the anticommons was that each is the result of a failure of due other regard. If I only take into account my own short-term gains and losses relative to the short-term gains and losses of my peers, it is unlikely that I will act in a manner that will protect the resource community as a whole. This, in turn, frequently leads to waste. When this waste reaches extreme proportions, it leads to the collapse of the resource community either due to over- or underuse.

We have seen that energy governance in the face of climate change suffers acutely from this problem. It must respond to climate change and thus decarbonize energy systems. Yet, at the same time, it must increase affordable and reliable energy access. The energy transition—the change in the energy system—that is needed to bring about these results inherently changes the distribution of benefits and burdens derived from energy systems. What is more, the energy transition requires collective action on a dizzying scale. It thus appears to make sense to undertake it only to the extent that a critical mass of stakeholders credibly acts towards achieving the transition. Before that time, the actions towards energy transition of any one stakeholder simply hurt that stakeholder relative to others by reducing their own reliable energy access without positively affecting climate outcomes. At this particular juncture in energy governance, it is therefore indispensable to look for a paradigm that is capable of addressing collective action problems at their root.

Still, the paradigm we need is not one that should function only for transitions or moments of exception.[76] As we have seen in Chapter 1, the dominant energy governance paradigms each suffered from flaws even under ordinary conditions. We also saw that these flaws similarly were the result of collective action problems or at the very least misperceptions by different stakeholders of the goals of the particular governance paradigm. It is therefore similarly true that we need a paradigm that can address and adjust these blind spots. It so happens that these blind spots are particularly pernicious in times of transition. That does not mean that they are not also there in other times, as well.

Analytically, the critical step to overcoming the collective action problem is to posit that there is a bond of belonging between all stakeholders. We are all stakeholders in a common pool resource.[77] In our case, that common pool resource is

[76] Carl Schmitt, *Politische Theologie, Vier Kapitel zur Lehre von der Souveränität* (Duncker & Humblot 1922).

[77] Ostrom (n 4).

the global energy system. Each energy stakeholder (value chain participant, end user, and regulator) belongs to the global energy system. Each stakeholder shares this bond of belonging to the energy system with all other stakeholders.

This analytical step is already inherent in the way we think and talk about the energy system. It is, after all, made up of energy value chains.[78] As we will discuss in more detail in Chapter 8, value chains link together a 'range of different activities and processes that jointly contribute to the transformation of underlying [energy] resources into useable end-products'.[79] Energy value chains typically begin with the production of needed raw materials. These raw materials then are refined and transported. Depending on the value chain, this input is then used for manufacture of components, assembly, and installation. In all cases, an end consumer at some point can purchase the energy output they need.

The very idea of a value chain means that each link in the chain performs a process that only makes sense in light of a whole.[80] A single stakeholder in a value chain cannot exist alone. A gasoline refinery only makes sense if there is petroleum to refine and if there are gas stations to supply, never mind consumers who fill up their cars with gasoline. Value chain participants can exist because they form part of something bigger than themselves.[81]

Sometimes, there are critical stakeholders in a value chain who cannot easily be replaced. There may be actors with significant market power. Such a stakeholder might seek to use its positional advantage within the value chain. If the stakeholder cannot be replaced, the extreme result would be that the value chain breaks. This, in turn, deprives the positional stakeholder of the very advantage they wished to exploit in the first place. The positional advantage of market power is thus relative: it exists only proportionate to the importance of a particular value chain for energy systems at large. Still, even in this extreme example of a value chain participant with market power, our participant with market power can flourish only because it belongs to a shared enterprise. That shared enterprise is what gives it power in the first place. Value chain participants with less market power perforce depend to an even greater extent on their value chain peers. They all share the bond of belonging with every other value chain stakeholder.[82]

The bond of belonging is arguably less visible in the context of facially competing energy value chains. It is certainly true that a refinery needs petroleum to refine and gas stations to supply.[83] Why should a company exclusively dealing in a

[78] On the idea of value chains in general, *see* Michael E Porter, *Competitive Advantage: Creating and Sustaining Superior Performance* (Free Press 2008).

[79] Tordo et al, 'National Oil Companies and Value Creation,' (2011) World Bank Working Paper No 218 at 1.

[80] Porter (n 78).

[81] For the current state of vertical integration in the oil value chain, *see* Christophe McGlade et al, *The Oil and Gas Industry in Net Zero Transitions* (International Energy Agency 2024) 132.

[82] For a realist assessment of this dynamic in the oil context, *see* Kenneth N Waltz, *Theory of International Politics* (Random House 1979) 151–58.

[83] *See* McGlade (n 81), at 132.

competing technology—say electric vehicles—share a bond of belonging with the refinery owner? That is, can we plausibly posit that there is a bond of belonging that ties together these facially rivalrous stakeholders, as well?

Analytically, the answer to this question must be 'yes'. Energy value chains coexist with each other. This coexistence diversifies energy sources. This, in turn, increases the resilience of the energy system as a whole. The energy system can better absorb shocks—the failure of one value chain can be compensated by a stronger reliance on others. The weakening of one value chain therefore is systemically problematic for energy systems viewed as a whole. It weakens energy security.[84] The bond of belonging therefore ties together the different energy value chains for energy security reasons alone.

Pragmatically, the nature of this bond becomes more obvious when we think through what would happen if an energy input suffers an unexpected, but long-term shock. In such a scenario, available energy decreases and the price of the affected value chain increases. This increases the price of energy throughout value chains due to the cross-effects of energy scarcities. This, in turn, would suggest that the most impacted area will see a significant drop in demand due to the destructive effect of increased prices. This demand destruction will have significant ripple effects for adjacent value chains, as well. In our scenario, there will be less car travel. Certainly, persons with the financial wherewithal to buy an electric vehicle would do so. But not everyone is financially able to replace their car. The fewest people are able to do so without changing how they consume goods and services—that is, the money for the new car has to be made up somehow. For example, it is likely that there is less disposable income and thus fewer vacations and thus less car travel. Less car travel means that there will be less of an investment in personal transportation infrastructure, not more. Further, existing infrastructure may well wither (eg rest stops will see lower traffic and therefore may close). This in turn means that it is likely that fewer electric vehicle charging stations will be installed as there are fewer businesses along roadways at which it might otherwise make sense to install them. This in turn impacts the viability of electric vehicles.[85]

In terms of the theoretical lens we have used so far, this second scenario is an anticommons problem. It may appear that self-interest would place the electric vehicles in competition with refineries. Electric vehicle advocates should wish for demand destruction in the gasoline and internal combustion engine segment. Yet, this leads precisely to the danger of underuse that the robber baron scenario showcased.[86] An average family is unlikely to buy an electric vehicle immediately when

[84] *See* Laura Cozzi et al, *World Energy Outlook 2022* (International Energy Agency 2022) 185–87.

[85] This mechanism explains why beggar-my-neighbor policies ultimately worsen rather than improve economic depressions for all actors involved. Martin Daunton, *The Economic Government of the World: 1933-2023* (Farrar, Straus Giroux 2023) 59–88.

[86] Heller 2013 (n 8), at 10.

gasoline becomes more expensive. It may be more interested in doing so.[87] Yet, actual sales are comparatively low.[88] The reason for this is intuitive—many are likely still paying the loan for the car they currently own. Rather, they will simply drive less, thus leading to an underuse of transportation opportunities.[89]

The history of energy systems provides a helpful analogue for this problem—and for its resolution on the basis of a bond of belonging. That analogue is not a transportation example. Instead, it comes from the electricity context: the 'battle of the systems' or 'battle of the currents' in the late nineteenth century. This battle is frequently personified (if also oversimplified) as the battle between Thomas Edison's direct current and Nikola Tesla's alternating current.[90]

Thomas Edison built the first coal-fired power station in the world in order to supply an electric lighting system in New York City. This installation distributed direct current to end users. Edison was thus invested in this technological approach and indeed attempted to market it globally. Direct current, however, had a significant problem: it could not be transmitted over a long distance. If the customer base for electricity was spread out, as was the case in rural areas, this presented a significant technical challenge. Alternating current—the model associated in popular imagination with Nikola Tesla—could overcome this transmission problem.[91] Yet,

[87] Astor, 'As Gas Prices Went Up, So Did the Hunt for Electric Vehicles', (8 April 2022) New York Times, https://www.nytimes.com/2022/04/08/climate/gas-prices-electric-vehicles.html#:~:text=As%20Gas%20Prices%20Went%20Up,Vehicles%20%2D%20The%20New%20York%20Times, last accessed 20 January 2025.

[88] *See* Timur Gül, *Global EV Outlook 2023, Catching Up With Climate Ambitions* (International Energy Agency 2023) 8 (sales share of EVs in the US in 2022 was 8 per cent). By way of comparison, in the second quarter 2024, there were 291.1 million registered vehicles on US roads. Carlier, 'Vehicles in Operation in US Q1 2018-Q2 2024', (5 December 2024) Statistica, https://www.statista.com/statistics/859950/vehicles-in-operation-by-quarter-united-states/, last accessed 20 January 2025. The total estimate of electric cars on the roads in the US is approximately 3.3 million vehicles. Montoya & Ewing, 'How Many Electric Cars Are There in the U.S.?' (17 July 2024) Edmunds, https://www.edmunds.com/electric-car/articles/how-many-electric-cars-in-us.html, last accessed 20 January 2025.

[89] One might suggest that such demand destruction is precisely what is needed from the perspective of strong climate policy. This would not be consistent with the actions of the US (during the Biden administration) and Europe in response to the petroleum supply shock resulting from Russia's invasion of Ukraine and the Western sanctions on Russian oil that followed it. Both the US and Europe at that point sought to obtain additional oil production, for instance, from Saudi Arabia. Demand destruction was not seen as a boon to climate policies favouring electric vehicles but rather as an economic threat to be addressed specifically to avoid demand destruction in the petroleum energy value chain. *See* Sorkin et al, *Biden, Oil and the Middle East*, (14 July 2022) New York Times, https://www.nytimes.com/2022/07/14/business/dealbook/biden-saudi-arabia-oil-middle-east-netflix.html, last accessed 28 June 2024; *see also* Finley, *Is Saudi Arabia Quietly Trying To Help Europe's Oil Consumers?*, (5 May 2022) Forbes, https://www.forbes.com/sites/thebakersinstitute/2022/05/04/is-saudi-arabia-quietly-trying-to-help-europes-oil-consumers/, last accessed 28 June 2024.

[90] This theming is a frequent way to draw attention to the history of energy. For a good example, *see* Jill Jonnes, *Empires of Light, Edison, Tesla, Westinghouse, and the Race to Electrify the World* (Random House 2003).

[91] The battle of the systems could well be described as a battle between single-phase alternating current and direct current. Nikola Tesla was one of the inventors who helped resolve this battle through his work on polyphase alternating current. The juxtaposition therefore is not quite accurate but nevertheless helpful to its evocative nature. *See ibid* at 113 for a discussion of Tesla's work on polyphase alternating current.

the stakeholders in alternating current were at odds with the direct current stakeholders. Both systems battled for dominance in new, suburban markets fit for both technological approaches (direct current and alternating current). Perhaps symbolically for the acrimony of this battle, direct current advocates invented the electric chair (which relied on alternating current) solely as a marketing ploy to warn against the adoption in households of the 'executioner's current'.[92] The acrimony of the battle of the systems in some ways recalls the current rhetorical battles between proponents of renewable energy and electric vehicles, on the one hand, and fossil fuel champions on the other. The rhetoric of direct current, which supports that a rival energy system will kill us, sounds familiar in the 2020s.[93] The battle of the systems therefore provides a good test case for our bond of belonging.

Facially, alternating current ultimately 'won' the battle of the systems. When one plugs into an outlet anywhere in the world, chances are that one receives alternating current.[94] This may suggest that there is no bond of belonging between rival energy value chains after all. Systems battle each other until one completely replaces the other.

That conclusion would decidedly misunderstand both past and present. If one were to read this book electronically on a tablet, phone, or laptop, one is likely to use a device that relies on direct current. Similarly, many of the household appliances we use run on direct current. Direct current therefore was not pushed out of existence.[95] Rather, it was integrated into a larger universal system.

Historically, the battle of the systems was settled when engineers came up with a universal system in the form of a polyphase alternating current. This system permitted the integration of existing direct current investments big and small (lamps and power infrastructure). The expansion of the system would rely on polyphase alternating current infrastructure. But existing infrastructure could be integrated into it too, thus reducing the pain of sunk costs.[96] Importantly for our purposes, the battle of the systems was decided not by some regulatory fiat. It was decided by innovation that permitted all stakeholders to move forward within a single energy system that did not burden potential 'losers' with the cost of having to build power infrastructure twice in a short period of time.

The battle of the systems shows us something important about energy systems. Energy rhetoric sounds 'political'. Carl Schmitt, one of the leading legal theorists of authoritarianism, defines political confrontation as the kind of rivalry that ends

[92] Hughes (n 35), at 108.

[93] Arthur Wyns et al, *The Health Argument for Climate Action, A COP26 Special Report on Climate Change and Health* (World Health Organization 2021) 11 ('The burning of fossil fuels is killing us').

[94] In what is perhaps the ultimate twist, today's ultra-long-distance transmission is best served by high voltage direct current technology. In a universal system, it is possible to innovate around such relative advantages. They are lost in the context of a 'political' fight about energy systems.

[95] For an insightful technical and economic analysis of the battle of the systems, *see* Hughes (n 35), at 32–40, 47–78, 91, 106–08, 113.

[96] *See ibid* at 125–27.

with the complete destruction of one's opponent.[97] That opponent is an 'enemy' rather than an adversary. There is no bond of belonging here. There is simply enmity.

This Schmittian account sounds vaguely like another economic account of adversity: the idea of creative destruction. Joseph Schumpeter developed the idea of creative destruction.[98] Innovation destroys and replaces systems that preceded it. Innovation is highly competitive, meaning that competing innovators may find themselves being pushed completely out of the marketplace. A bond of belonging is hard to see here, as well. Competition is destructive to be creative. Schumpeter thus eerily appears to reprise in economics what Schmitt began in politics.[99]

The reality of energy governance does not follow this rhetoric. As the battle of the systems shows, the relationship between different value chains is certainly adversarial. But it is not a relationship of 'political' enmity. There is fierce competition. Yet, this fierce competition attempts to solve problems across the entire energy system through innovation. It does not seek to shrink or destroy part of the energy system. It integrates technological insight into new and evolving paradigms as it grows and incorporates into a new whole. This is only possible on the basis of a bond of belonging.

This is not to say that energy systems do not reflect the realities of creative destruction described by Schumpeter. To the contrary, the role of innovation and competition in the energy system and energy value chains suggests that creative destruction is indeed a key driver of change in energy systems.[100] Yet, this change is rarely explosive or instantaneous. Even the introduction of paradigm altering innovations like the steam engine or electricity took half a century to alter how

[97] Carl Schmitt, *Der Begriff des Politischen* (Duncker & Humblot 1932).

[98] Joseph A Schumpeter, *Capitalism, Socialism and Democracy* (Harper 1976) 81–86.

[99] On the fascinating relationship between Schumpeter and Schmitt, *see* Cherneski, 'An Unacknowledged Adversary: Carl Schmitt, Joseph Schumpeter, and the Classical Doctrine of Democracy', (2017) 29 Critical Review 447. Cherneski outlines how Schumpeter encountered Schmitt's work from the 1920s and the milieu in which both worked. Importantly, Schumpeter is strongly opposed to Schmitt's political work. It is therefore interesting to see the apparent parallels between Schmitt's political work and Schumpeter's economic ideas. *See* Levinson, 'The Brooding Omnipresence of Carl Schmitt in Contemporary Jurisprudence: Reflections on William Scheuerman's *The End of Law:* Carl Schmitt in the 21st Century,' (2020) 47 Philosophy & Social Criticism 178 (discussing the relationship between these concepts in both authors). While there are obviously points of contact between both ideas, I take them to be almost photo-negative and photo-positive of each other. The creative power of the political in Schmitt is secondary to the act of destruction or annihilation of its enemy. The enemy provides cohesion and direction to a group in a political confrontation. It is in this sense that destruction is creative—to destroy the group has to create and sharpen its own ethos to distinguish friend from foe. In Schumpeter, the inverse is the case. Creation is a matter of innovation that is undertaken for its own sake. Innovation is not directed at an enemy—it is directed at discovery. Once a discovery has been made, innovation destroys what preceded it—though not as thoroughly or as quickly as in Schmitt's political moment. Both men thus find themselves on opposite ends of the same dialectic. As such, they are of course each indispensable for the other and can only be understood in light of this juxtaposition—a juxtaposition that itself is, perhaps ironically, unstable, destructive, and creative. *See* Jacques Derrida, *De la Grammatologie* (Les éditions de minuit 1967); Balkin, 'Deconstructive Practice and Legal Theory', (1987) 96 Yale Law Journal 743.

[100] *See* Carlota Perez, *Technical Revolutions and Financial Capital: The Dynamics of Bubbles and Golden Ages* (Edward Elgar 2003).

energy systems worked and even longer to displace earlier paradigms.[101] The capital cost and sheer complexity of energy systems dictates such a result. This means that creative destruction does not proceed by shock therapy. It proceeds slowly and methodically. In this process, it is certain to 'destroy' the old—and even do so completely. It just does so by subsuming and incorporating the old into the new in much the same way as railway lines of today frequently look back to the tracks laid in the nineteenth century even as today's highspeed trains differ drastically from their steam-powered predecessors.[102]

Positing that there indeed exists a bond of belonging binding together different energy system stakeholders within and across value chains is not enough. We must establish what this bond of belonging requires of these stakeholders. It is this notion of a joint enterprise between stakeholders that provides the backbone for a different way of thinking about energy governance to the manner in which the dominant paradigms discussed in Chapter 1 approach the question. The critical point of this new paradigm is that it does not fundamentally concern the 'who'—who makes decisions, who formally owns what part of energy infrastructure, who finances it etc. Rather, it is concerned with the question of how stakeholders must fulfil their relative roles within an energy governance system. Our commons and anticommons problem was that stakeholders acted without due regard to the goals of other stakeholders. The bond of belonging is concerned with addressing this problem directly by setting out what regard stakeholders owe each other in the first place.

The bond of belonging is a bond of neighbourliness.[103] Belonging is about being in a community while remaining able to pursue one's own ends, and flourishing.[104] Neighbourliness precisely captures this idea. My enjoyment of my home depends

[101] Vaclav Smil, *Energy and Civilisation—A History* (MIT Press 2017) 225–440.

[102] One such example is the 'rechte Rheinstrecke' or Eastern Rhine line. The line was first commissioned in the mid-nineteenth century. The track is of course renovated ceaselessly to support today's highspeed railways. *See* 'Rechte Rheinstrecke wird erneuert', (29 February 2024), Frankfurter Allgemeine Zeitung, https://www.faz.net/aktuell/rhein-main/rechte-rheinstrecke-wird-erneuert-19555370.html, last accessed 16 July 2024. Yet, it is still thought of as the same line. It thus brings to mind the paradox of whether a vessel that once bore Theseus remains 'Theseus's ship' even if every plank has been replaced over the years as a part of routine repairs. The very fact that this paradox might have relevance for energy systems suggests that the pace of change in energy systems is hardly instantaneous.

[103] On the classical idea of neighbourliness in international law, *see* Handl, 'Territorial Sovereignty and the Problem of Transnational Pollution', (1975) 69 American Journal of International Law 50. For a more recent theory of neighbourliness in the climate change context, *see* Dyal-Chand, 'Sharing the Climate', (2022) 122 Columbia Law Review 581.

[104] To be a touch more precise, the bond of belonging owes much to communitarian thought about the relationship of flourishing of (wo)man and the community in which they find themselves. *See here* Alastair McIntyre, *After Virtue* (Duckworth 1987); *see also* Adrian Vermeule, *Common Good Constitutionalism* (John Wiley 2022). Flourishing is only possible in a community because we need each other in order to realize our own good. It is impossible to lead a good life alone. Famously, humans are social beings. Aristotle, *Politics: Book 1, in The Complete Works of Aristotle: The Revised Oxford Translation* (Jonathan Barnes ed, Princeton University Press 1984) 1986. I take this communitarian ideal not in the direction of medieval Aristotelianism as McIntyre does but rather in the direction of civic humanism (a tradition which McIntyre to a point critiqued). For a fuller development, *see* Sourgens, 'Bundles of Freedom', (2024) Rutgers Law Review.

on the conduct of my neighbours and the other way around. If I have long, boisterous get togethers, my neighbours may not be able to sleep. Similarly, none of my neighbours should be able to force me to do in my home precisely what they would like me to do there—it is after all my home and not theirs. The bond of belonging to a joint neighbourhood therefore is not about approximating life in some idyllic pastoral tale. It is rather about assuring that everyone in a neighbourhood acts so as to allow each a fair ability to enjoy their own home.

This bond of belonging has long been recognized in municipal legal systems. In French civil law, for instance, the idea of belonging to a common neighbourhood is a matter of enjoining *troubles de voisange*—or neighbourhood disturbance. I disturb the neighbourhood if I abuse my right of ownership within it. My use of my right may be entirely understandable and indeed there may be nothing wrongful about it. Early risers are not negligent if they mow their lawn at 7 am on a Sunday, nor does their mowing have to be an expression of spite. Still, they are almost certain to act with insufficient regard for the rights of their neighbours to have a lie in on a Sunday morning.[105]

The logic of the civil law follows a Roman law idea. Some of my neighbours' conduct imposes a limitation on my enjoyment of my own land. This limitation in Roman law terms would effectively create a 'servitude'—my land would be 'servient' to my neighbour's use of theirs. It would be 'servient' because my land would be subject to a diminishment of its use. In our example, I now cannot sleep in until 9 am on a Sunday morning without noise disruption. If my neighbour has no right to impose such an inconvenience on my enjoyment of my land, Roman law would give me a right of action to cut short the unwanted servitude and enjoin the underlying conduct—an *actio negatoria*. Again, the point is not that my neighbour does anything wrongful for me to have a right to enjoin her conduct. It is simply that I am limited in my reasonable enjoyment of my 'slice' of my neighbourhood.[106]

In the context of energy governance, this communitarian insight is precisely at the heart of the idea of 'value chains'—no one stakeholder can make energy systems work alone. It takes everyone's joint actions to make value chains work. Importantly, this does not mean that we each must necessarily have the same moral ends or act out of altruism. A Texas oilman is unlikely to follow oilfield practice because he is fond of his neighbour. Rather, he does it because it is in his self-interest as a participant in the oil patch. He gets to make money and compete with his neighbour without risking the collapse of the reservoir. Profit motives—and competition—are decidedly part of this bond of belonging. They just require us to compete cooperatively in a shared enterprise. *See* Branderburger & Nalebuff, 'The Rules of Co-opetition', (January-February 2021) Harvard Business Review, https://hbr.org/2021/01/the-rules-of-co-opetition, last accessed 30 June 2024.

[105] Annie Chalamoud-Trapiers, *Le Droit des Biens* (2nd ed, Breal, 2007) 167; Zile, 'Judicial Control of Land Use in France', (1960) 45 Cornell Law Review 288, 289; *Badoit v André*, Lyon, 18 avril 1856, DP [1856] 2. 199; *Forissier v Chaverot, Req*, 10 juin 1902, DP [1902] 1. 454. For the concept of abuse of right, *see* Herman, 'Classical Social Theories and the Doctrine of "Abuse of Rights"', (1977) 37 Louisiana Law Review 747.

[106] On the *actio negatoria*, *see* Eugene Petit, *Traité Élémentaire du Droit Romain* (Rousseau 1906) ¶ 773. The *actio negatoria* remains influential in many civilian jurisdictions. See, for instance, Podshivalov, 'Models of Actio Negatoria in the Law of Russia and European Countries', (2019) 7 Russian Law Journal 128.

The common law similarly recognizes such a limitation in the law of nuisance. Nuisance provides a property owner with a remedy for the unreasonable infringement of their right to use a particular property. There is nothing wrong with what my neighbour does. Yet, my neighbour's use of their property makes it impossible for me to use my property as I would deem fit. If my neighbour fails to pay due regard to my right to use my property, I can stop my neighbour's conduct in much the same way I can in the Roman law or in civil law—I can ask for an injunction ordering my neighbour to stop the offending conduct.[107]

This leaves an important question—when is use of property in a neighbourhood an abuse of right or unreasonable? There needs to be a standard according to which we can measure whether mowing one's lawn at 7 am on a Sunday is abusive. As both neighbours are likely to disagree on this point, the standard is not immediately obvious. Nor does it suffice to apply the golden rule of 'do onto others'—our early riser may be perfectly content with every neighbour mowing their lawn at 7 am, as well. As we said, the standard was not that the underlying conduct was somehow wrongful, so it is unlikely that we can derive the standard on the basis of some absolute command from ethics or morality. We need a relative standard that nevertheless is objectively ascertainable and opposable to both of our neighbours' respective enjoyment of their land.

We can in fact develop such a standard. In the first place, a neighbourhood is a community. This implies that no neighbour should be allowed to create waste. Such a waste would diminish the neighbourhood or community as a whole.[108] For instance, if my neighbour and I aggressively produce water from a common underground reservoir in such a way as to cause the water reservoir to collapse prematurely, I would have deprived every owner of a part in that common reservoir, a share in potentially recoverable, valuable resources (including, of course, myself).[109] It is only a slight oversimplification to state that such waste is never permissible in a community—unless, of course, acting otherwise would do even greater harm of some other kind (say, everyone needs to pump aggressively to put out a conflagration).[110]

Even this prohibition of waste is relative and not absolute. At first glance, the prohibition of waste sounds like an absolute prohibition that we may never destroy any resource through inefficient land use practices. This is not quite what the rule means. Rather, for the prohibition to apply there must already exist some

[107] *See* Fraley, 'Liability for Unintentional Nuisances: How the Restatement of Torts Almost Negligently Killed the Right to Exclude in Property Law', (2018) 121 West Virginia Law Review 419. For a full comparative law analysis, *see* Sourgens (n 21).

[108] Righetti & Schremmer (n 34), at 633–41; for a different application of the same idea of waste, *see* DuVivier, 'Preventing Wind Waste', (2021) 71 American University Law Review 1, 13. For a comparative approach, *see* Richardson, 'Reframing Ameliorative Waste', (2017) 65 American Journal of Comparative Law 335.

[109] This is one of the starting points for commons governance in Ostrom's work. *See* Ostrom (n 4), at 103–40.

[110] On a correlative-rights understanding in the water law context, *see* Rose (n 5), at 165–96.

communal use of a resource to which 'waste' might apply. Say that there are micro-organisms under my lawn that die when I use a lawnmower. Say further that my use of my lawnmower causes these micro-organisms to die not just under my land, but under the entire neighbourhood. If the micro-organisms in question are not actually used or enjoyed by anybody in the community, it does not matter that my action causes them to disappear. It also does not matter that my use of a scythe instead of a lawnmower might have preserved them. Waste is wasteful only if a threatened resource is valued and valuable. The rule, thus, is radically 'anthropocentric'. It is anchored in human communal enjoyment of resources. It precisely does not care about ecological concerns or value in their own right. These concerns are bracketed out from view. Needless to say, this means that waste is relative. There is no waste as such. Waste instead is inherently social.

At the same time, the prohibition of waste imposes not just obligations on neighbourhood members to refrain from conduct that could hurt the neighbourhood. It also imposes obligations to maintain the neighbourhood.[111] I cannot refuse to participate in reasonable resource use, and carry my portion of its collective costs, if doing so deprives my neighbour of their own ability to use a resource. I must do my part to maintain my neighbour.[112] This may seem like an odd or overbearing requirement. Yet, many neighbourhoods formally or informally impose such obligations on their members in terms of the obligations not to put up certain kinds of fences, build sheds, or allow their house to fall into obvious disrepair. Being in a community therefore means that I must do my part for upkeep. Otherwise, my actions would permit a waste of neighbourhood resources to occur.

Of course, neighbourhoods, communities, and bonds of belonging are not principally about avoiding waste (though this rule is perhaps the most immediately visible consequence of the bond in question). Rather, we own property—and join a community—to make productive use of its resources.[113] The fact that my neighbour may not create a waste does not mean that I receive any benefit from the resource in question. The prohibition of waste is an external guardrail that is intended to protect what I really care about. It is not itself something that I care about in its own right—waste is not about resource preservation as such. The prohibition of waste is intended to protect *me*.

The point therefore is to protect my use rights. This, too, is tricky. What are my use rights? Of course, every selfish person would want to use their own property to the hilt and disregard their neighbours entirely. The problem is that this rule is not generalizable. If everyone used their property to the hilt and disregarded their neighbours, the likely consequence would be the destruction of the

[111] *Mfrs.' Gas & Oil Co*, 57 NE. at 915; Kramer & Anderson, 'The Rule of Capture – An Oil and Gas Perspective', (2005) 35 Lewis & Clark Law Review 899, 913–14.

[112] This, too, is part and parcel of commons governance. *See* Ostrom (n 4), at 82–102.

[113] *See* Honoré, 'Ownership', *in Oxford Essays in Jurisprudence* 113 (Anthony G. Guest ed, Oxford University Press 1961) 113.

neighbourhood. This would be an ultimate waste. Instead, we have to accommodate one another to be secure in our own use rights. This means that I cannot insist on an absolute use right.

What, then, can I generalize? In the first place, I can generalize that I want an opportunity to use my property. Giving everyone an opportunity does not create a waste. Opportunities have to be taken. When they are not, they go away. Opportunities can be limited by the prohibition of waste. Still, this is still not enough. 'Opportunity' is a malleable word. It would be hard to argue that I do not have an opportunity to play for the US soccer men's national team. I hold US citizenship. I have not played for a different national team in the past. I am a man. I therefore could try out for a club soccer team, draw attention to my skill, and eventually be nominated to the squad. Nothing formally excludes me. And yet, as the reader may guess, my 'opportunity' to play for the US soccer men's national team is theoretical only. This cannot be what we mean by 'opportunity'. Instead, what I want is to have a fair opportunity to put what is mine to use.[114] Fair means that it is more than theoretically possible for everyone in the neighbourhood to use the same resource. Everyone must have a means to 'use back' at me so as to achieve their own goals. This will impose an obligation to act—to use labour to bring about a useful change in the land. This labour can be physical—I can till the land for agricultural use. Or it can be mental—I can find an oil company to sign a lease with me to produce the oil beneath my land (assuming I own the mineral rights, of course). Still, if I have this meaningful opportunity, my relative use right is protected. What I do with it is up to me. Others did not, and could not, deprive me of it.

What regard is ultimately 'due' is defined by community expectations.[115] That is—the 'logic' of the resource community itself. In many instances, of course, it is reasonably straightforward to establish waste or an infringement of the fair reciprocal opportunity principle. Overexploitation of oil reserves leads to the premature collapse of the reservoir drive. A veto that my neighbour may never disturb a single molecule in place subject to my mineral rights will trap some of my neighbour's oil.[116] Still, even these two examples tie back to a community expectation—in our case, prudent oilfield practices. The fact that oil becomes unrecoverable is not problematic in the abstract. It is problematic because an energy community has developed around oil resources. It is problematic because it is inconsistent with the logic of the energy system that has grown up around it.

[114] Schremmer (n 28); Schremmer, A Unifying Doctrine of Subsurface Property Rights, (2022) 46 Harvard Environmental Law Review 525.

[115] Lewin, 'Comparative Nusiance', (1989) 50 University of Pittsburg Law Review 1009, 1029; Cribbet, 'Concepts in Transition: The Search for A New Definition of Property', 1986 University of Illinois Law Review 1, 19; Claeys, 'Jefferson Meets Coase: Land-Use Torts, Law and Economics, and Natural Property Rights', (2010) 85 Notre Dame Law Review 1379, 1410.

[116] *Coastal Oil & Gas Corp v Garza Energy Tr*, 268 SW3d 1, 13–17 (Tex 2008).

Whether a particular use is wasteful or abusive depends upon what I can reasonably expect from other community members. Energy communities form value chains around such shared expectations—without these shared expectations, the links of the energy value chains would not join up. These community expectations set the limits for how community members may interact with each other. Abuse of rights and waste therefore do not require some external, objective reference point. Rather, they are anchored in the community which they govern. The bond of belonging in this sense is a bond that looks to the whole of a community to regulate the relationship between individual members and between stakeholder groups.

This means that the bond of belonging is flexible—as stakeholders adapt to new realities and new demands, the community they form changes. With that, value chains change. This, in turn, means that I can no longer proceed on the basis of business as usual. One such example of community expectations changing how stakeholders relate to each other was the resolution of the 'battle of the systems' we discussed above. Energy stakeholders found a means to create a universal polyphase alternating current system. Energy stakeholders further standardized distribution voltages and so on. The battle of systems was resolved through a change in community expectations.[117]

One of the fundamental constants in the energy system is change. Innovation and competition constitute and weaken or even destroy energy value chains over time. At one point, it would have been technologically difficult to transport liquified natural gas from the US to Germany. For one, without hydraulic fracturing technology, the US would have had no gas to export.[118] For another, the liquification and regasification processes are capital intensive, and facilities took time to complete.[119] This means that today, Germany can purchase US gas to replace Russian gas. The value chain linking US gas to German markets has displaced value chains linking Russian gas to German markets. 'Neighbourhoods' are open—newcomers can arrive and change the game.

Innovation is not just a matter of displacing existing producers or distributors of existing energy inputs. It is also about creating entirely new ways of generating energy. Utility scale solar is one such example. Utility scale wind and solar are today the most cost competitive forms of electricity generation we can add to the grid.[120] This has changed energy value chains within the renewable energy paradigm. It has also affected nuclear energy projects and gas projects. This innovation has

[117] Hughes (n 35), at 106, 193.

[118] For a short journalistic account of this change, *see* Rapier, 'How the Shale Boom Turned the World Upside Down,' (21 April 2017) Forbes, https://www.forbes.com/sites/rrapier/2017/04/21/how-the-shale-boom-turned-the-world-upside-down/, last accessed 16 July 2024. For a longer account of the same story, *see* Daniel Yergin, *The New Map: Energy, Climate, and the Clash of Nations* (Random House 2020) 8–12, 28–29.

[119] Yergin (n 117), at 31–39.

[120] 'Levelized Cost of Energy+,' (June 2024) Lazard, https://www.lazard.com/research-insights/levelized-cost-of-energyplus/, last accessed 16 July 2024.

been the defining feature of energy systems as we know them today. The advent of next generation geo-thermal and fusion energy could further disrupt the *status quo*.[121] The fewest of us think of wood and quadrupeds as core energy inputs. That is precisely what the Industrial Revolution—driven by new energy systems—displaced. Energy systems therefore must be open to new uses rather than freezing old ones in amber.

One of the fundamental consequences of this governance approach to energy systems is that maintaining fair opportunities to participate in energy systems may well require financial support. The early story of electrification encountered multiple instances in which the new, and better, electrical lighting technology came just barely too late. Municipalities had invested in gas lighting instead.[122] Stranding these costs was not acceptable and gas interests pushed back against electrification. The battle of the systems provided another example of the same pattern. Investment in a direct current system meant that it was difficult to turn around adopt alternating current. The investment costs were simply too great. The story of the early years of electricity was one of accommodation. Financial support took the form of protectionism of vested interests in the gas context. And it led to a resolution to the battle of the systems that precisely allowed direct current infrastructure to continue to be useful as substations in the new polyphase system.

Financial support did not take the form of outright payments. It instead lurked in the background of energy market designs. Still, these financial support mechanisms were needed in order to diffuse new technology and allow the orderly withdrawal of the old. Energy systems were rarely the province of shock therapy. This meant that past investments in energy assets were effectively carried by new participants who profitably increased their own relative market share. In time, they were certain to increase their market share even further, at times by working together with the erstwhile incumbent competitors by replacing incumbent technology with new, cheaper, and more efficient generation. This could happen only when incumbent assets could be decommissioned or repurposed with acceptable losses for incumbent producers (and acceptability would change if incumbent producers would see a part of the upside of new, cheaper technology). Energy systems therefore historically provided significant financial support by carrying the investment costs previously incurred by incumbent producers.

There is a recent example of this phenomenon: the dramatic reduction of coal-fired power in the US energy mix. For example, energy producers in the US

[121] Blankenship et al, 'Pathways to Commercial Liftoff: Next-Generation Geothermal Power', (March 2024) US Department of Energy, https://liftoff.energy.gov/wp-content/uploads/2024/03/LIFTOFF_DOE_NextGen_Geothermal_v14.pdf, last accessed 18 November 2024; 'The Global Fusion Industry in 2024', (16 July 2024) Fusion Industry Association, https://www.fusionindustryassociation.org/wp-content/uploads/2024/07/2024-annual-global-fusion-industry-report.pdf, last accessed 18 November 2024.

[122] Hughes (n 35), at 65.

retired in excess of 102 gigawatts of coal-fired power generating capacity in the 2010s.[123] As a 2024 US government report explains, 'in 2024, coal retirements will come primarily from older units: the capacity-weighted average age of these retiring units is almost 54 years, about 10 years older than the weighted average of operating coal units'.[124] By comparison, the weighted average age of retiring units in 2015 was fifty-six years and forty-six years in 2018, both of which were peak years for retirements.[125] These plants could be decommissioned and retired in part due to their age and prior productivity. The levelized cost of energy for these 'fully depreciated' (ie paid off) assets remains around US$71 per megawatt-hour.[126] This is well in excess of the favourable end of the levelized cost of energy for wind (US$27–73/MWh), solar (US$29–92/MWh), and combined-cycle gas (US$45–108/MWh).[127] Replacement, in other words, made economic sense for such plants. Plants that were not yet fully depreciated are in a different economic situation. Stranding these assets affirmatively causes losses for the retiring utilities and their lenders. Unless carried, they are far less likely to make the switch unless price environments shift drastically in favour of alternatives (gas, nuclear, renewables).

This support makes sense from a fair opportunity perspective. These producers cannot compete back with new technology due to their past investments. Changing standards with regard to these investments therefore risks exposing them to a loss of a fair opportunity that has not been paid for. This would create a windfall—we benefited before from the presence of these assets through increased energy security as well as favourable energy prices. Decommissioning these assets ahead of scheduled retirement externalizes social costs to the affected producer. If those producers fairly assumed the risk, this may be a fair consequence. To see whether such a risk was fairly assumed, it is instructive to look at pricing and whether it compensated for this risk during the early years of operation.

Given this potential for windfall, it should not be surprising that nuisance law similarly follows a similar logic. There may be circumstances in which new use of a neighbourhood is more socially beneficial. This new use may require cessation of the old use. Yet, in this case, the new users must put the incumbent in a position to 'develop back'. They must pay for relocation. This relocation in the past has been physical. It, in principle, could also be a matter of retiring an asset without

[123] 'More U.S. Coal-Fired Power Plants are Decommissioning as Retirements Continue', (26 July 2019) US Energy Information Administration, https://www.eia.gov/todayinenergy/detail.php?id=40212, last accessed 16 July 2024.

[124] 'Retirements of U.S. electric generating capacity to slow in 2024', (20 February 2024) US Energy Information Administration, https://www.eia.gov/todayinenergy/detail.php?id=61425#:~:text=Coal%20retirements%20are%20scheduled%20to,age%20of%20operating%20coal%20units, last accessed 16 July 2024.

[125] US Energy Information Administration (n 122).

[126] Lazard (n 120).

[127] *Ibid.*

investment loss so as to be in a position to participate in new ventures without the encumbrance of the old.[128]

The idea of the bond of belonging does not just hold together property holders in a neighbourhood. It applies to a far larger group of stakeholders—both in the energy context and outside of it.[129] In the energy context, it holds together fundamentally different stakeholders shaping energy value chains. These stakeholders of course include energy companies and their suppliers—the actors who engineer and distribute innovation in a market place. They also include governmental stakeholders such as national governments, regional governments, and municipalities. Each of the stakeholders make independent and critical decisions for energy systems. Energy governance is 'polycentric' because none of these stakeholders alone can command the entire energy space.[130] Decisional authority is shared.

As decisional authority is shared, its exercise, too, is a matter of competition. Different governmental stakeholders compete with each other nationally and internationally as much as private energy industry stakeholders do.[131] They exercise governmental competence in order to compete with each other. In this exercise of competence, governmental stakeholders (and the private enterprise with whom they engage) are just as much neighbours as any other stakeholder bound by the bond of belonging. The exercise of competence can just as much represent an abuse of right as the use of property. It can just as much create a waste, deprive others of a fair opportunity to use their own competence, or unfairly externalize costs to third parties, thus reaping a windfall. The idea of the bond of belonging constrains these actors just as much as it does private actors as I will argue in the remainder of the book. These actors, too, are subject to the correlative nature of their respective competence over energy systems writ large. The bond of belonging

[128] *Spur Industries, Inc v Del E Webb Development Co*, 494 P2d 700 (Arizona 1972).

[129] In a more general sense, the idea of a bond of belonging is consistent with a communitarian ethics and political philosophy. I hope to develop elsewhere a communitarian theory that situates the idea of the bond of belonging, creativity, and innovation in a contemporary take of the humanist tradition. This humanist tradition may come to the startling insight that we may not have to choose between Nietzsche and Aristotle, Aquinas and Machiavelli, Schmitt and Schumpeter, Heidegger and Ahrens. The fusion of Nietzsche and Aristotle was already well advanced in Schmitt and Heidegger. The idea of *vertù* in civic humanist thinkers is as indebted to an Aristotelian understanding of ethics as Aquinas's—be it from a different direction and with a different point of contact to Aristotle's work. This leaves the question whether we can reconcile the work of Heidegger and Schmitt to a project that is more participatory, less authoritarian, and ultimately more forgiving. One might hope that the deep Catholic roots of Heidegger's and Schmitt's thought would open a path to a more penitent reading of their oeuvre. Their view of the human condition, and of the creative act as the inherently human enterprise, provides one such perilous means of reconciliation. That condition, being human, is as such inherently shared. It ties us to the same moment. This moment should remind us that any of our insights, no matter how searing, are but a fall from grace unless they are directed to the service of man. This leap Heidegger—and hopefully Schmitt, too—might take with us.

[130] Ostrom (n 30), at 255–88.

[131] For a longer discussion of this competition in the US setting, *see* Sourgens, 'States of Resistance', (2019) 14 Duke Journal of Constitutional Law & Public Policy 91. For a discussion in the global setting, Farber, Tsuji & Jing, 'Thinking Globally, Acting Locally: Lessons from the U.S., Japan, and China', (2021) 82 Ohio State Law Journal 953.

therefore is a lens that applies to all of the competence conflicts and to energy governance design writ large. Its lessons are particularly poignant for a balanced idea of energy governance—and thus a reappraisal of the dominant governance paradigms discussed in Chapter 1.[132] The final section of this chapter will explain how.

Before we get to this final section of the chapter, I need to include a placeholder for a discussion a little later in this book. The idea of cooperation according to the bond of belonging is a centrepiece of my argument. I will provide a deeper assessment of the bond of belonging as an end of energy governance as opposed to a means to achieving its goals in Chapter 5.[133] I will explain that the bond of belonging is a virtue of shared, polycentric energy governance. This virtue lies in the agency the bond of belonging empowers. As I will argue, the bond of belonging is a constitutive process of human development.[134] Before we get to that part, I need to place a marker: the fair opportunity principle of reasonable use is already pregnant with the value of agency. It also provides a sense of what agency is about. It is about creating, improving, and protecting shared resources for the benefit of a community of peers. When we arrive at this discussion in Chapter 5, we therefore should be equipped for the direction the discussion will take. It is not about moralizing the bond of belonging. It is about exploring its transformative power for human society, instead.

2.5 Balanced Energy Governance

In Chapter 1, we have seen that the dominant energy governance paradigms all ultimately ran into difficulty.[135] A command approach cannot lean into innovation. A market approach leaves itself seriously exposed to energy security threats. A public contract or utility model ultimately cannot deliver competitive—and thus maximally affordable—energy prices.

We saw that this problem was one of misalignment of incentives. All three models can function exceedingly well. In fact, they tend to achieve their original purpose—and right-side a problem—when they are first introduced. The problem is that as a paradigm matures, and as stakeholders understand how the paradigm works, different stakeholders seek to maximize their own respective advantage. They do so to the detriment of the whole energy system. They do not think systemically. Rather, they think only of pursuing their own fractional and positional advantage within the system as a whole.[136]

[132] For a full explanation of how the bond of belonging applies across the private–public divide, *see* Sourgens, 'Polyrelativity', (2025) 52 Pepperdine Law Review (forthcoming).

[133] *See* section 5.2.

[134] *See* section 4.4.

[135] *See* sections 1.3–1.5.

[136] *See ibid.*

What this experience suggests is that energy systems—like so many other things—function cyclically.[137] These energy cycles are not just a matter of how energy stakeholders become less responsive to systemic needs as governance paradigms become more mature. Rather, it is the underlying nature of energy cycles that is driving the response we have observed in the last chapter. That is, the worsening performance of governance paradigms is a symptom of this larger cyclicity as opposed to its cause.

Some research suggests that the cyclicity of the global energy system is partly responsible for significant economic crashes like the Great Depression and the 2008 financial crisis. Both coincided with an ongoing energy transition (coal to oil in transportation and coal to gas/renewables in electricity and the shale revolution), and each can be linked to energy price pressures. In the context of the Great Depression, the argument is that a switch from coal to oil placed significant strain on the real economy at just the wrong time.[138] The high oil price prior to the 2008 financial crisis similarly was seen as one of its possible causes and further, too, came in the middle of several ongoing energy transitions.[139] An argument has also been made that significant oil price volatility was an overlooked factor in the 1987 Wall Street crash.[140] The correlation is intriguing. For my current purposes, the point is not to take a position on causality (did energy transitions and/or oil shocks cause recessions?). It is, rather, to say that the correlation alone is telling. It supports that the global energy system, and leading national energy systems, follow cyclical patterns.[141] These cyclical patterns, in turn, can have significant consequences in financial markets and the real economy, requiring significant policy intervention.

How, then, do energy cycles work in their own right and what can they teach us about how we ought to deploy the bond of belonging as a governance principle? Carlota Perez's work goes a long way to answer the first part of this question. Perez is a particularly astute observer of energy cycles. A British-Venezuelan national, Perez consulted for the research and development affiliate of Venezuela's national oil company, PDVSA and was actively engaged in the North-South dialogue in the 1970s. The North–South dialogue was in very important ways a dialogue about how to govern global energy systems—and how to share the benefits and burdens of a global economy driven by these energy systems.[142] Perez's work is deeply

[137] *See* Roeben, 'What Drives OPEC Production Policy', (2024) 17 Journal of World Energy Law & Business 19, 29 (discussing the role of production policy in light of investment cycles).

[138] Kennedy, 'Biophysical Economic Interpretation of the Great Depression', (2023) 27 Journal of Industrial Ecology 1197; Kennedy, 'Energy Constraints on Macroeconomic Paradigms', (2024) 226 Ecological Economics 108361.

[139] Hamilton, 'Causes and Consequences of the Oil Shock of 2007-08', (2009) Brookings Papers on Economic Activity 215.

[140] Theramus, 'Was Volatility in the Price of Oil a Cause of the 2008 Financial Crisis', (8 December 2009) The Oil Drum, available at https://www.resilience.org/stories/2009-12-08/was-volatility-price-oil-cause-2008-financial-crisis/, last accessed 25 January 2025.

[141] Kennedy (2023) (n 138); Kennedy (2024) (n 138); Hamilton (n 139).

[142] Giuliano Garavini, *The Rise and Fall of OPEC in the Twentieth Century* (Oxford University Press 2019) 255–65.

Schumpeterian and as such speaks to how innovation and competition affect energy systems and bring about energy cycles. Her leading work, *Technological Revolutions and Financial Capital*, is about technology in general.[143] Yet, her focus is steadfastly on energy (particularly steam, electricity, and oil). This focus on energy as the foundation of technological paradigms is unsurprising given her work on the North–South dialogue—a dialogue that sensitized all of its participants to the reality that economic performance (never mind growth) is inherently tied to the energy systems on which the real economy relies.

Perez notes that energy cycles have two phases—an upswing (the 'installation' phase) and a downswing (the 'deployment' phase). Each phase can be broken in half again. The installation phase begins with an irruption phase. During the irruption phase, excess available capital meets innovation. This innovation is not just any innovation.[144] Rather, it is innovation that addresses 'reverse salients' in energy systems. Such a 'reverse salient' describes a systemic failing 'when a component of the [energy] system does not march along harmoniously with other components' such that 'growth of the entire enterprise is hampered'.[145] To overcome a reverse salient requires systemic thinking—the reverse salient only becomes visible when we understand the systemic implications of problematic component performance. As Thomas Hughes—a leading historian of the birth of the current electricity paradigm—has demonstrated, it is through approaching the problem as systemic (about the system as a whole) that it is possible to isolate the variable that is holding back system-wide performance and then resolve it.[146] It is Hughes's systemic solution to a reverse salient that becomes the innovation, which meets financial capital in Perez's irruption phase.[147] It is not just any innovation—it is critical innovation—an approach that is capable of overcoming a systemic limitation hampering growth in a prior energy paradigm.

What follows the installation phase according to Perez's terminology is a 'frenzy'. During this frenzy, more capital wants to achieve the returns the new technology makes possible—returns that are premised on solving a critical problem, which caused a reverse salient in energy systems. This frenzy leads to a deployment of a significant amount of capital to diffuse the new energy paradigm.[148] Importantly, this frenzy can lead to overinvestment. It typically creates bubbles as more and more capital is attracted to the potential for return made possible by the new technology.[149] Yet, as the term bubble painfully implies, bubbles burst. There is thus a significant risk for participants during the frenzy phase.

[143] Perez (n 100).
[144] *Ibid* at 90–99.
[145] Hughes (n 35), at 79.
[146] *Ibid* at 79–105.
[147] Perez (n 100), at 90–99.
[148] *Ibid* at 99–114.
[149] *Ibid.*

During the upswing phase of energy cycles, one can see how a utility or public contract model would in fact be the best way for energy system stakeholders to organize themselves consistent with the demands of the bond of belonging. The point of a utility model is to limit risk to the public purse. Political organs—municipalities, counties, regions, or states—do not yet know whether a particular innovative solution to a critical problem can realign a reverse salient in energy systems. The idea looks promising, and engineers are generally positive. Yet, there is by definition very little by way of precedent for the new idea working.[150] This means that there is a significant amount of commercial risk. Financial backers of the solution are genuinely willing to shoulder this risk given the significant rewards they anticipate to flow from solving a critical problem. To the extent they are given protection against other entrants who would deploy a similar solution, they are thus willing to shoulder the risk in question.

During this phase, the utility model works uniquely well exactly because technology is relatively young. Investors are concerned with reaping the benefit of solving a reverse salient in energy systems—they thus think systemically, consistent with the bond of belonging.[151] At the same time, investors also have every incentive to price their new entrant competitively in order to displace the existing paradigm and make customers aware of the benefit of the new system.[152] It is thus possible to agree on a public pricing formula that benefits consumers and investors alike. The utility model works precisely because every stakeholder is benefited by benefiting the system as a whole. Being a first mover in adopting a new solution to critical problems is that powerful a motivator.

One of the quintessential examples of success of this utility model is pre-First World War Berlin. Berlin from about 1900 to 1915 had the right mix of private capital (think Emil von Rathenau), industrial expertise (think the Siemens family), and investment banking (think Deutsche Bank) available aggressively to build out Berlin's electricity infrastructure.[153] From 1884 onwards, the public administration of Berlin was a strong partner in developing that infrastructure through a utility model. The city administration was key in establishing 'the kind and extent of services the municipality believed its consumers—whether household, commercial, traction, or industrial—should have'.[154] There thus was oversight and cooperation between industry and the public administration on the design of the grid so as to meet public welfare demands as opposed to maximizing low hanging profit opportunities first. In this context, the utility was charged with assuring technical feasibility and innovating to meet welfare demands. Yet, the shape and performance of

[150] For an analogous problem on the private side, *see* Robert Bryce, *A Question of Power, Electricity and the Wealth of Nations* (Public Affairs 2020) 51–81.
[151] *See* section 1.3.
[152] *See* Hughes (n 35), at 18–47 (discussing the entry into the market of electricity).
[153] *Ibid* at 179–81.
[154] *Ibid* at 184.

electrical systems was a shared enterprise. This shared enterprise also, of course, touched on pricing for electricity. Importantly, this included a differential rate structure that charged different prices for different consumers even at this early in point in time. This differential pricing favoured industrial users and kept private use a luxury. This structure was chosen as it supported the investment by Berlin in a gas infrastructure for lighting.[155] That is, differentiated pricing provided a financial support mechanism to keep existing investments profitable even while the new electric paradigm expanded and took on an ever-increasing market share.

It is not the utility model as such but rather the bond of belonging that brings the energy governance model to its desired end. The public utility model in pre-war Berlin fully reflected how a bond of belonging could create energy systems and energy value chains through systemic cooperation between all energy stakeholders. It was systemic thinking and cooperation in systemic problem solving that made the Berlin experience exemplary. In fact, due to this combination, on 'the eve of World War I, the Berliner Elektricitäts-Werke (BEW) ranked as one of the world's leading electric supply utilities. Engineers and managers looked to it, along with the Commonwealth Edison Company of Chicago, as pacesetters in the establishment of world standards, both technical and commercial, for the electric supply industry'.[156] It is a model that can uniquely distribute risks so as to avoid waste—doubling efforts is unlikely to find customers at this stage, stranding the new idea. Similarly, once the new idea is proven the utility model provides all energy stakeholders with an opportunity to compete and develop back. It does so on the basis of the new community standards set by the changing energy systems—and it does so in a way that is inviting the new entrant into the energy system so as to allow it to build new energy value chains.

Of course, as Perez identifies, there comes a turning point. Frenzies misalign systemic incentives. They invite capital to take advantage of a new opportunity—but this capital may be just too late to benefit fully from the systemic upside of the new technology. This capital is now hunting marginal opportunities. These marginal opportunities begin to be misaligned with the interests of the system as a whole. There will now clearly be losses, and investors will wish to pass these losses on by aggressively utilizing whatever incentive structures are available.[157]

From a governance perspective, we here arrive at an inflection point. The utility model no longer works as well as we might have thought. Partnerships are breaking down. We have to adjust. Carlota Perez labels this point the 'synergy phase'—here we need to deal with the negative consequences of the frenzy. These consequences could be the fall out of bursting bubbles or the passing on of unwarranted costs to the end consumer (unwarranted because no reasonable investor should have

155 *Ibid* at 189.
156 *Ibid* at 182.
157 Perez (n 100), at 99–114.

incurred them in the first place).[158] This synergy phase is the first part of the downswing of energy cycles. It leads to a maturity phase in which the frenzy settles into a new normal running under the new governance paradigm.

This synergy stage can lead one in one of two directions. On the one hand, one could liberalize energy markets and remove the monopoly protection of the utility model. Now, bad investments will simply be allowed to fail. Competition will drive out poor investments through the application of market forces. The territory in question could well be serviced more cheaply by a neighbouring provider etc. Competition would also mean that only those additional investments that are actually likely to yield a return will actually be attempted.[159] We have here the kernels of the neoclassical economic argument for deregulation and market liberalization made famous by economists such as Milton Friedman in the 1970s.[160]

Rather than seeing liberalization through such a neoclassical lens, it is also possible to think of it as matter of the bond of belonging. Incentives in energy systems were misaligned to achieve outcomes that benefit the system as a whole. Liberalization sets new incentives through direct competition driven by pricing.[161] These new incentives cause participants to prioritize systemic needs over chasing distorted incentives from the utility paradigm. A market can flush out bad investments because commercial risk of adopting a new technology is significantly lower than it was before. With risk so lowered, the market is capable of achieving far better prices—and better returns—because the market can flush out the problems—removing excess capacity that needs to fail and installing new capacity on the most economic terms possible.

Viewed through this lens, liberalization is not successful because neoclassical economics is inherently right in all circumstances. Rather, liberalization works because it acts as a counterweight to rebalance energy governance from excesses during the frenzy phase.[162] When we liberalized energy markets, we had both an overcapacity problem and a problem that utilities were not aligning energy systems with price signals in the real economy. Markets set signals to bring stakeholders back to a point of view that is systemically helpful to address both an oversupply and a distorted supply problem. There is thus a reasonably systemic alignment between liberalization at a point of near maturity and the need to limit waste and provide a fair opportunity to all energy system participants to develop out the energy system within the maturing paradigm.

One can understand energy market liberalization in the US and Europe in this way. In the US context, liberalization was a response to both an external shock (the 1970s oil shock following the Arab oil embargo) and an internal misalignment

[158] *Ibid* at 114–37.
[159] Kim Talus, *EU Energy Law and Policy, A Critical Account* (Oxford University Press 2013) 19–65.
[160] Jean-Pierre Favennec, *The Geopolitics of Energy* (Editions Technip 2011) 103–05.
[161] Talus (n 159), at 18.
[162] Perez (n 100), at 99–114.

between rates and price signals. Liberalization was intended to reduce prices and increase energy security.[163] In the European context,

> [c]onsumers—i.e. the people—realized that the monopolies charged them much higher tariffs than were necessary and that the surplus form the higher tariffs—the monopoly rent—was not used for public purposes but, as in the case of all private or public monopolies, was eaten up by the privileged employees and managers of the utilities and by the politicians providing political and legal support for the maintenance of monopolies.[164]

Liberalization thus is necessary to bring stakeholders back to a more systemic approach to the management of energy systems. Competition is not always the cure (competition for the D'Arcy concession in Persia would likely have led to the eventual abandonment of the venture given that on its actual, non-competitive terms it barely scraped by failure) —it is however the cure for the particular moment at which liberalization was attempted.[165]

The goal, end, or purpose, of electricity system liberalization therefore was not dogmatic.[166] It was to solve a particular problem faced by energy systems at a particular point in time. We can understand this problem—like the problem in the irruption phase of energy cycles—in terms of the bond of belonging. Viewed in this way, liberalization of energy markets is not a cure-all to be deployed in any circumstance. Instead, it is a tool in a balanced energy governance kit. This tool can be used to realign systemic incentives to limit waste, provide stakeholders with a fair opportunity to participate in energy systems, and provide the needed financial support to secure the continued functioning of energy systems as a whole.

As a tool, it is most helpful when the frenzy phase has misaligned resources—providing a glut of resources where (or how) they are not needed to benefit from prior incentives at an excessive price.[167] Importantly, liberalization is particularly helpful when there also remains some further build out of energy systems to be

[163] *See* Talus (n 159), at 18.

[164] *Ibid.*

[165] *See* Joskow, 'Lessons Learned From Electricity Market Liberalization', (2008) 29 Energy Journal 9, 10 ('The overriding reform goal has been to create new institutional arrangements for the electricity sector that provide long-term benefits to society and to ensure that an appropriate share of these benefits are conveyed to consumers through prices that reflect the efficient economic cost of supplying electricity and service quality attributes that reflect consumer valuations.'). This reform goal can be achieved by means of liberalization only in a particular context. Typically, this context is present in the synergy and maturity phase of a particular energy system and its supporting value chains. On the D'Arcy concession, *see* Daniel Yergin, *The Prize: The Epic Quest for Oil, Money & Power* (Free Press 1992) 121–36.

[166] I have in mind here the idea of τέλος. Joskow is helpful in writing about an 'overriding goal'. Joskow (n 165), at 10. An overriding goal to my mind here is akin to an Aristotelian end of virtuous living. *See* Julia Annas, *Intelligent Virtue* (Oxford University Press 2011) 75. The link between this end of energy governance and human flourishing will be developed more fully in the coming chapters.

[167] *See* Perez (n 100), at 114–26.

done in order to rebalance the energy system. This additional build out is comparatively risk-free given the maturity of the energy system. Yet, it remains capital intensive. In this setting, a market approach is capable of providing access to capital from private sources against the expectation of long-term profits. It does not burden the public purse. Nor is it able to seek the payment of rents due to efficient market competition.

The build out of the Texas grid demonstrates the advantage. Texas deregulated its power sector at the end of the 1990s. Since this liberalization, energy demand in Texas continues to grow rapidly.[168] This means that there remains a need to expand the grid (both in terms of generating capacity and in terms of transmission capacity). Yet, the commercial risks of expansion are reasonably limited. Texas's liberalization of its energy market in general has lowered prices for consumers while also encouraging a cost-effective and cost-competitive build out of the Texas grid.[169] Achieving the same result by means of central planning would significantly burden the public purse and a utility model did not achieve the desired results. Here, liberalization clearly came into its own as a means to balance the systemic needs of all energy system stakeholders as seen through the lens of the bond of belonging.

Liberalization is not the only response that is possible at the synergy stage. Rather an adjustment could also lead in the opposite direction from liberalization: a governmental stakeholder could adopt a command solution.[170] This command solution resets the misaligned incentives from the frenzy stage differently from liberalization. Rather than letting competition weed out unnecessary infrastructure driving up cost, the state's planning apparatus does so instead.[171] Similarly, the state will take a central planning approach to further grid expansion in order to ascertain that there is a sufficient need to justify expansion to avoid the

[168] On historical additions and retirements to the Texas grid following liberalization, *see* 'New Electric Generating Plants in Texas Since 1995', (October 2013) Texas Public Utility Commission, https://ftp.puc.texas.gov/public/puct-info/industry/maps/elecmaps/gentable.pdf, last accessed 17 July 2024. On demand growth in Texas at the time of this writing, *see* Vargas, 'CEO Board Update', (23 April 2024) Electric Reliability Council of Texas, https://www.ercot.com/files/docs/2024/04/22/5%20CEO%20Update.pdf, last accessed 17 July 2024.

[169] There is no end of controversy surrounding Texas' approach to electricity market design and all sides tend to pick data that supports their respective points. In principle, electricity has become cheaper in Texas. Yet, at the same time, prices are more variable. Trovall, 'Why Have Texas' Elecric Bills Gotten More Expensive and Volatile?, (24 May 2024) Houston Public Media, https://www.houstonpublicmedia.org/articles/news/2024/05/24/488578/why-have-texas-electric-bills-gotten-more-expensive-and-volatile/, last accessed 17 July 2024. The underlying issue is one of market design. Texas did not traditionally rely on a capacity market as part of its electricity market design. For the implications of this choice, *see* Todd S Aagaard & Andrew N Kleit, *Electricity Capacity Markets* (Cambridge University Press 2022) 233–51. Texas has changed its approach since Winter Storm Uri—with somewhat mixed results. *See* Kleit, 'The Texas Electricity Two-Step' (Fall 2023) Regulation, https://www.cato.org/regulation/fall-2023/texas-electricity-two-step, last accessed 17 July 2024.

[170] *See* Peter Drahos, *Survival Governance: Energy and Climate in the Chinese Century* (Oxford University Press 2021).

[171] *See ibid.*

potential for overdevelopment typical at the frenzy stage. The state manages the excess capacity of what is now a proven and mature system with well-developed energy chains through nationalization. As commercial risk has been reduced to close to zero, it is possible for the state to run the energy system as effectively as the earlier investor. Importantly, the state can also write off investments that ought not to have been made and simply operate the beneficial parts of the energy system.

This command solution again intends to align systemic interests with the incentives available for energy governance. Energy is central to economic welfare and economic growth. Once there is a mature system in place, it is therefore possible to view the provision of energy as a public good that can and should be provided by the government at a price point deemed appropriate by policymakers to achieve welfare ends.[172] Here again, there is thus an example of a rebalancing of the energy system that makes sense from a bond of belonging perspective. Private stakeholders are paid out. Public stakeholders can better provide for cheaper energy access.

A good example of this command response completes the story of energy governance in Berlin in the early twentieth century. There had always been political tensions surrounding the utility model. Social democrats had long favoured turning BEW public. This would mean that private partners would no longer be owed a profit from BEW. This revenue flow could now either go to the public coffers to support welfare projects or otherwise be used to support electrification of public welfare priorities. Berlin ultimately took BEW public in 1915. It did so in a reasonably amicable manner by paying the erstwhile utility fair compensation for their stake in BEW. It thus ended the strong collaboration between private and public stakeholders that marked Berlin's energy system in the prewar era.[173]

The reason for this shift was both political and technical. Politically, social democrats had long seen energy access as a public good and bristled at the underlying utility model, particularly once the grid had clearly successfully been established. There was, however, also a technical reason. To satisfy demands for lower rates from the city, BEW needed to grow and take full advantage of advances in technology. It therefore wished to build a plant right at the mouth of the Bitterfeld lignite field. The national government shuttered these plans with the outbreak of the First World War. The lignite deposits were needed for the war effort. There was thus no means for BEW to meet the political moment with technological innovation. War made it impossible.[174]

172 *See ibid.*
173 Hughes (n 35), at 197–200.
174 *Ibid* at 199.

The maturity phase ends the downswing in energy cycles. Importantly, as Perez points out, it is also the point at which a new reverse salient becomes a significant problem for existing energy systems. Maturity takes energy systems as far as they can go—new problems arise due to the full diffusion of the paradigm that stand in the way of even better deployment of energy resources.[175] Capital at this point can make a comparatively limited return in the now mature paradigm (even in a command paradigm, capital of course can still be gainfully employed in energy value chains supporting public energy monopolies). It thus looks for the next innovation to address the reverse salient and start a new irruption phase.[176]

We have seen in Chapter 1 that a command model has difficulty in restarting the energy cycle on its own.[177] The capital incentives to overcome a reverse salient are simply not present in a nationalized energy system. This means that private capital will not fund innovation intended to overcome critical problems.[178] Innovation, in other words, will be slowed. In order to participate in an irruption phase, a command approach will need to find a way to allow private capital back in to develop new, risky, and profitable means to address a reverse salient or develop new energy resources.

This phenomenon is not new. Rather, it is well known in a particular part of the energy world—oil and gas development. Fittingly, in light of Perez's energy cycle model, nationalizations in the oil and gas sector tend to occur when the underlying oil and gas resources could be operated comparatively inexpensively because the heavy lifting of exploration and development had already been completed with private capital.[179] To the extent that oil prices are high—thus leading to a frenzy in oil and gas markets—states are likely to expropriate oil investments in order to limit private participation in what governments perceive as rents generated by the high oil and gas price environment.[180]

When the underlying oil and gas resources near the end of their useful life, jurisdictions that previously nationalized oil and gas resources frequently consider a re-opening of the oil and gas sector to private capital. They need to do so as new

[175] *See* Perez (n 100), at 127–49.

[176] *Ibid.*

[177] *See* section 1.4.

[178] *See* Mommer, 'The New Governance of Venezuelan Oil', (April 1998) Oxford Institute for Energy Studies WPM 23, at 35–36 (discussing the opening to private investment in oil in Venezuela in light of expansion plans).

[179] *See* Jeswald Salacuse, *The Three Laws of International Investment: National, Contractual, and International Frameworks for Foreign Capital* (Oxford University Press 2013) 27 (discussing the idea of obsolescing bargains).

[180] This may not be a correct perception. Oil and gas companies invest for a period of decades. In this timespan, oil and gas prices are likely to go through several price cycles. This means that high price environments must be seen in the context of low points in the cycle to determine whether they lead to rent-seeking. The perception of governments is typically steered by shorter timeframes than a full market cycle or multiple market cycles.

exploration and development—as well as reworking existing oil and gas projects—is capital intensive. It is, further, risky. States typically do not wish to shoulder this risk alone.[181]

Mapping this point in time onto Perez's energy cycle terminology, the reduced recovery from existing projects is a problem that calls for a new irruption phase.[182] This reduced recovery is a critical problem for the state wishing to rely on oil recovery for its long-term fiscal planning. To overcome this problem presents risks and requires capital. This should entail a potential for significant profits to attract the capital that typically is available at irruption phases. In other words, states—even those with a strong command approach to oil and gas reserves—tend to bring private stakeholders in to benefit fully from a new energy upswing. Here, too, balanced pragmatic energy governance displaces dogmatic purity.[183]

Our discussion so far leads to a final and important observation for our discussion in the next chapter. We have seen that energy cycles reach inflection points not only independently due to technological advances or political events in a single country. Rather, energy cycles are intimately tied to global events. Berlin taking BEW public in 1915 was a direct consequence of the outbreak of the First World War. Coal was no longer available to power light, traction, and industry in Berlin. It was needed for the war effort, instead. This deeply affected how energy systems could continue to perform in a utility model. War brought to an end Berlin's standing as the leading example of private–public cooperation to build one of the best energy systems then in existence. It did not have to be so. But geopolitics forced the German and the global energy systems.[184]

Of course, geopolitics in the context of Berlin had little if anything to do with energy systems themselves. The First World War did not break out over an energy dispute.[185] Energy had not yet taken centre stage in geopolitics. It would soon. The decision to switch the British fleet from coal to oil was just one of factors that would see to that. When we look at the 1970s oil shock and its effect on energy systems, we see that energy, geopolitics, and the global economy have come to be fully intertwined.[186] To understand energy cycles therefore requires not just an understanding of how we should govern domestic energy systems and value chains. It requires a global understanding of these value chains and systems. This global perspective of necessity involves the dangers of great power rivalry and geopolitical *realpolitik*. Managing these pressures is critical to managing the global energy

[181] *See* Owen Anderson et al, *International Petroleum Law and Transactions* (Rocky Mountain Mineral Law Foundation 2020).

[182] Perez (n 100), at 70–89.

[183] Venezuela's oil opening and oil nationalizations can be seen through this lens. William Neuman, *Things Are Never So Bad That They Can't Get Worse: Inside the Collapse of Venezuela* (St Martin's Publishing 2022).

[184] Hughes (n 35), at 199–200.

[185] *See* Christopher Clark, *The Sleepwalkers: How Europe Went to War in 1914* (HarperCollins 2013).

[186] *See* Timothy Mitchell, *Carbon Democracy: Political Power in the Age of Oil* (Verso 2011).

commons. We will explore how our theoretical approach measures up to that task in Chapter 3.

2.6 Conclusion

Before we address the global implications of energy governance, we can take stock on the domestic front. We have seen in this chapter that the problem of energy governance is not an ideological problem. It is also not a problem that can be solved with economic dogmatism. Rather, we have seen that what made governance approaches fail—a lack of systemic thinking and a taking advantage of incentives that distort overall energy system performance—can be understood in a different way. The bond that holds all energy stakeholders together in belonging to shared energy value chains and thus shared energy systems begins to fray. We need to fix the incentive structure in order to bring energy governance back into balance.

It is frequently good advice to shy away from simple and extreme prescriptions to solve complex problems. It does not take a detailed study of Aristotle to see the value in moderation and proportionality. The governance frameworks we have examined in the first chapter are no different. They are tools that, taken in moderation, can in fact help provide fruitful outcomes in energy governance. If we think them through to their extreme, however, they simply to fail to do what we ask of them. They oversimplify complex interactions between different stakeholders along separate energy value chains that all interweave with each other to form regional, national, and global energy systems. As we have seen in Chapter 1, following a particular governance approach reflexively will lead to governance failures—failures that moderation could have avoided.

Moderation is not a matter of triangulating midpoints between extremes. Whatever an optimal rate of taxation may be, it is not the mid point between radical libertarians considering all taxation theft and radical communists who consider all private property theft (the mid-point would be an effective tax rate of 50 per cent). To say that one needs moderation is to say that one must act with prudence towards a specific goal. I will discuss this goal in more detail in Chapter 4.[187] Until then, however, the goal is to govern energy systems consistently with their own internal logic.

What this chapter has shown us therefore is a way in which one might be a pragmatic moderate in energy governance—how one might combine different governance approaches to solve a specific problem that arises at a unique moment in time in energy governance. It thus provides a means to test that the performance of energy systems is as well managed as it can be and provides tools to address

[187] *See* section 4.4.

shortcomings. This test so far appears somewhat technical. It is not yet fully linked to the goals we wish to achieve with energy systems. In any exercise of prudence, these goals must be seen as an integral part of governance. We will explore that critical part of energy governance and the bond of belonging in Part II of this book. Before we can get there, however, we must first address the global dimension of energy governance already alluded to at the end of this chapter.

3
World Power Orders

3.1 Introduction

Our focus so far has been on the domestic side of energy governance. We have asked how one state can manage its energy resources in order to support affordable, secure, and sustainable energy systems. This is not the typical focus of a work concerned with *global* energy governance. Rather, the focus of much of that research is on the global interconnection of energy value chains and their susceptibility to energy geopolitics.[1] Or, as Thijs Van de Graaf and Benjamin Sovacool put it, the focus is on mastering 'global energy politics' meaning taming 'the struggle over who gets what, when, and how in energy use from an international perspective'.[2]

It is not that these works do not see the importance of domestic governance and domestic energy use. To the contrary, they depart from the premise (implicit at times and sometimes express) that domestic energy use of course is a root cause of global energy conflict.[3] Yet, what is lost from view is that the domestic governance approaches and their respective incentive structures (and incentive failures) contribute to, and even come to constitute, global energy problems in their own right.

It is this insight that informs why I address the global side of energy governance only after having laid out how governance approaches in the domestic setting interact with, and attempt to balance, domestic energy cycles. Energy historians show how solving global energy problems required one to take a different approach to domestic energy governance.[4] This lesson from energy historians needs

[1] Simone Tagliapietra, *Global Energy Fundamentals, Economics, Politics, and Technology* (Cambridge University Press 2020) 19–26.

[2] Thijs Van de Graaf & Benjamin Sovacool, *Global Energy Politics* (Polity 2020) 2.

[3] *See eg* Van de Graaf & Sovacool (n 2), at 175 ('policy decisions taken to address a short-term issue may have longer-term consequences. It may set a country on a particular path that reinforces itself through mechanisms as lock-in and positive feedback effects.'). The point is left more implicit in Tagliapietra. *See* Tagliapietra (n 1), at 15. In the international legal framing, the matter is inverted altogether. Here the focus is not how domestic energy policies contribute to and interact with global energy governance, but rather assumes that 'the international law of energy would be useful in practice for the design and evaluation of energy policies from a legal standpoint. Depending on their legal form, energy policies may be consistent or inconsistent with different international norms and hence challenged before international courts and tribunals.' Jorge Viñuales, *The International Law of Energy* (Cambridge University Press 2022) 4. Within a positivist international legal frame, this is of course correct as far as it goes. It does not however get at the underlying causalities of energy governance and does not permit international law to provide a roadmap for getting out of the policy quagmires described in the last chapters.

[4] Thomas Hughes, *Networks of Power, Electrification in Western Society 1880-1930* (Johns Hopkins University Press 1983) 199 (discussing the impact of the First World War); Giuliano Garavini, *The Rise*

A Theory of Global Energy Governance. Frédéric Gilles Sourgens, Oxford University Press. © Frédéric Sourgens 2025.
DOI: 10.1093/9780198950325.003.0003

to be brought fully into the frame of how we should understand global energy governance. Global energy governance is not *international* energy governance, nor is it *domestic* energy governance. It is a combination of the two.

I frame the argument in this way to keep us close to an intuitive truth about energy. 'Energy' (or more precisely national energy systems) exist(s) in order to make the lives of the people who use it better.[5] Energy policies fail if they make local constituents poorer.[6] By implication, to think about energy is to think about energy use. Energy use, in turn, is by definition inherently local. Use occurs somewhere. If global energy governance must start somewhere, this 'somewhere' is here.

The problem with this 'somewhere' is that while energy use is inherently local, energy value chains are inherently enmeshed with global forces. Thomas Hughes, one of the leading historians of the transition to electric energy in the early twentieth century observed that '[a]lthough utility managers and engineers could not control contingent events such as wars and depressions, they nevertheless thought through the organization of regional utilities and their related technical characteristic to extend their control over factors outside the electric supply system'.[7] Critically, 'the evolution and style of regional utilities cannot be adequately explained without reference to politics, especially legislation'.[8] As utility managers sought to control contingent global factors, they did so in direct response to the regulatory approach of their respective domestic power systems. Tellingly, the responses by utilities included vertical expansion to control power sources, and to control means of moving and handling power sources from the source to plant, as well as integration with industrial stakeholders to gain security of demand from major consumers. The response to domestic regulation and the attempt to control external contingencies built the very energy value chains that are the focus of the global energy governance problem.[9] They cannot be separated from each other.

This historical assessment still holds true some one-hundred years later in the 2020s. If we need to import much of our oil or gas from abroad, satisfying local energy demand requires us to build and secure global energy value chains. These value chains are vulnerable to geopolitical disruption, forcing a fundamental reorientation of domestic and global policy when such disruption materializes. One

and Fall of OPEC in the Twentieth Century (Oxford University Press 2019) (discussing the response in the US and Europe to the Arab oil embargo); in an adjacent category, much of the work of Daniel Yergin is historical in nature and shows the connections between domestic energy policy and global energy conflict. *See here* Daniel Yergin, *The New Map, Energy, Climate and the Clash of Nations* (Penguin 2020); Daniel Yergin, *The Quest, Energy, Security, and the Remaking of the Modern World* (revised edn Penguin 2012). Yergin's work, while deeply insightful, does not fully theorize the governance implications of his observations but instead lays out a map of geopolitical contestation.

[5] Tagliapietra (n 1), at 19–26.
[6] Robert Bryce, *A Question of Power, Electricity and the Wealth of Nations* (Public Affairs 2020) 166.
[7] Hughes (n 4), at 407.
[8] *Ibid.*
[9] *Ibid* at 407–8.

example is the liberalization of US energy policies in response to the Arab oil embargo.[10] What we frequently lose from view is that the beginnings of liberalization went hand in hand with the North-South Dialogue. This North-South Dialogue sought to ground a new global economic order by stabilizing global energy markets.[11] Another example is the restructuring of European energy markets following Russia's invasion of Ukraine. Before Russian troops crossed the border into Ukraine on 24 February 2022, Germany in particular received a significant share of the natural gas it needed for power generation from the Russian Federation.[12] This changed abruptly after 24 February 2022.[13] What also changed was market design to accommodate the new shocks. Writing about energy governance in 2024, it is therefore absolutely clear that one cannot hold global geopolitics constant when it comes to energy governance. While all energy use is local, energy systems themselves are inherently global. They can be governed as such or not at all.

Even 'energy independence' will not save energy governance from geopolitical considerations. Berlin changed its energy governance paradigm in 1915 after a strong and successful run under the utility model. One key reason was that Berliner Electrizitäts-Werke (BEW) was not able to utilize lignite coal within riding distance of Berlin for electricity generation. The coal was needed for the German effort. The lignite coal in question did not need to be imported. Germany, in fact, had significant coal reserves to hand.[14] The problem is that geopolitics can reprioritize how even domestic energy resources are deployed. Geopolitics therefore introduces uncertainty everywhere. There is nothing we can do to shut it out. We must address it head on to have a workable energy governance paradigm.

This chapter begins this reconceptualization. It begins by linking the domestic energy cycles from Chapter 2 to international energy cycles.[15] Once we have done so, we can see that global energy governance responds to energy commons and anticommons on a global scale. These commons and anticommons give a different twist to our intuitive grasp of the rivalry and mutual dependence in energy

[10] Garavini (n 4), at 267–80.

[11] *Ibid* at 255–326. The North–South dialogue, in turn, sought to bring the transfer of technological advances at the heart of the liberalization efforts—solar energy—into the frame of a successful outcome.

[12] 'How Heavily Does Germany Rely on Russian Energy?', The Economist (4 May 2022), https://www.economist.com/the-economist-explains/2022/05/04/how-heavily-does-germany-rely-on-russian-energy, last accessed 6 August 2024.

[13] *Ibid.* (from February to May 2022, imports shrank from 55 per cent of domestic gas supply to 35 per cent). It is likely that even after direct imports from Russia were halted in the summer of 2022, Germany indirectly imported Russian gas. *See* Humpert, 'Germany Continues to Import Russian Natural Gas Through Belgium and the Netherlands', (27 February 2024) High North News, https://www.highnorthnews.com/en/germany-continues-import-russian-natural-gas-through-belgium-and-netherlands#:~:text=Germany%20stopped%20directly%20importing%20Russian,through%20supplies%20from%20its%20neighbors, last accessed 6 August 2024. These indirect imports are much harder to track. They also are comparatively limited. Still, they demonstrate the limitations on policymakers in making quick adjustments in reforming their domestic energy markets.

[14] Hughes (n 4), at 199.

[15] *See* section 2.5.

systems. This rivalry and mutual dependence can be resolved constructively into a competitive and innovative global energy order by updating the idea of an energy bond of belonging to reflect the global reality of energy systems. It will then place this concept in the context of resurgent energy nationalism and ask whether the idea is not altogether too naïve to be plausible.

3.2 The Link Between Domestic and International Energy Cycles

Domestic energy cycles condition and constitute international energy cycles.[16] Each of the successive phases of the energy cycle (and its governance reaction) sets up the incentives in which particular global value chains can grow and in fact lead to geopolitical vulnerabilities and opportunities. The global response to these vulnerabilities and opportunities again only makes sense in light of the domestic energy governance response to meet local energy needs. The global energy governance paradigm therefore is ultimately fused to the domestic experience and vice versa.

3.2(a) The Irruption Phase

The beginning of a domestic energy cycle is the irruption phase. It sets the baseline for policy and commercial expectations regarding new systemic energy innovations. This phase also provides the impetus for the formation of new energy value chains.[17]

As we noted already, systemic energy innovations occur when entrepreneurs attempt to resolve critical problems for the delivery of energy under the current energy paradigm. For instance, the development of alternating current transmission systems was a direct response to the critical problem for direct current systems to transmit electricity over longer distances.[18] Such innovations typically require significant governance support to get off the ground due to their risk profile. Yet, this risk profile also means that governmental actors are unlikely to take on the technology risk themselves.[19] Instead, the irruption phase typically follows a utility or public contract governance approach. Broadly, this public law contract approach provides security of return to a private venture for energy it actually delivers to

[16] *Ibid.*

[17] *Ibid.* As discussed in Chapter 2, I rely here on the categorization first developed by Carlota Perez. *See* Carlota Perez, *Technological Revolutions and Financial Capital, The Dynamic of Bubbles and Golden Ages* (Edward Elgar 2002) 47–67. As noted in Chapter 2, the categories developed by Perez interact with the cycle in governance approaches we have discussed so far.

[18] Hughes (n 4), at 79–105.

[19] *Ibid* at 60.

off-takers. In return, the private venture carries the risk of completing a project to commercial operation specifications.[20]

In the irruption phase, this governance approach has two consequences. *First*, the energy value chains to develop the new technology tend to be reasonably short. As the technology is not yet at a point of maturity, complex value chains have not had a chance to develop around a new energy solution. Consequently, both to manage risk and limit costs, energy innovation tends to rely on fuel sources in the proximity of power innovations. For example, coal-fired power plants originally were located reasonably close to coal deposits. Energy innovation further tends to rely on the local manufacture of core components, as well. For example, Berlin's BEW relied on components manufactured by Germany's AEG, and Chicago Edison purchased its first turbo-generators from General Electric rather than from the Swiss Bovari & Company where Chicago Edison engineers first observed the technology at scale.[21] Importing such machinery in general tended to be a feature of markets adopting technology later on (as opposed to markets at the innovation frontier).[22] We can observe the same phenomenon during the transition to renewable energy. Here, the manufacture of solar panels and deployment of solar panels first tended to be located in jurisdictions providing significant fiscal support to this new technology (eg the US in the 1970s and 1980s and Germany in the 1990s).[23] During the irruption phase, the physical footprint for the development of the new paradigm tends to be limited.

Somewhat counterintuitively, *second*, while value chains at this phase tend to be local, the intellectual development of technology and technological solutions draws on a global pool of ideas. These ideas are developed, exchanged, and debated globally, for instance in academic discourse and in trade shows. The irruption phase therefore gives rise to a global discourse on energy. Energy solutions are rarely developed in only one country. We can observe this historically in the context of global electrification.[24] We can observe it just as trenchantly today in the field of direct air capture (the technological approach to remove CO_2 from the ambient air).[25] Rather, the exchange of ideas means that there is a rapid diffusion of

[20] This model is not limited to public contracts. Private parties have used similar structures to assign risk in purely commercial transactions involving new energy technologies, as well. *See here* the discussion of the development of electric trains and elevators by Frank Julian Sprague. Bryce (n 6), at 68–81.

[21] Hughes (n 4), at 195, 211.

[22] England imported machinery from Germany and the US in the late nineteenth and early twentieth centuries. *See ibid* at 235. Notably, England was significantly behind Germany and the US in electrification at this time and was not a leader in electricity innovation.

[23] For a discussion of the development of solar value chains, *see* Frederic G Sourgens, Catherine Banet, & Teddy Baldwin, *The Transnational Law of Renewable Energy* (Oxford University Press 2024) 201–06.

[24] Hughes (n 4), at 405.

[25] Kintisch, 'Technologies', in Michael B Gerrard & Tracy Hester eds, *Climate Engineering and the Law, Regulation and Liability for Solar Radiation Management and Carbon Dioxide Removal* (Cambridge University Press 2018) 28, 42–45.

promising technological ideas even though these ideas tend to be implemented by means of short value chains.

With short value chains, the developmental impact of energy systems tends to be local even as there is a global exchange of ideas with regard to the innovative system. This means that the states adopting an innovative solution early see multiple benefits at the same time. They receive the benefit of solving the critical problem holding back earlier expansion of energy systems. This provides further growth potential for the adopting economies due to the increase in energy access. In addition, these jurisdictions also see an expansion in sectors related to the energy industry itself. There is an increase in the development of energy resources (like coal, oil, gas, or quartz/polysilicon). These jurisdictions also tend to develop an industrial base to manufacture needed machinery and components for the new energy paradigm. Both the extractive and the industrial sectors add to the economic benefit of energy access. They are at the beginning of the new energy value chain. The delivery of energy is the result of that value chain. Thus, the benefit of building the value chain at all accrues domestically at this stage of innovation.[26]

This means that there is a virtuous alignment of commercial, financial, and policy expectations at this point. Adoption leads to commercial success that can increase energy markets exponentially. This exponential gain promises exponential financial returns that cannot be achieved in the old energy paradigm.[27] From a policy perspective, this gain is a win-win because it provides greater energy access (which is economically beneficial) while also building value chains domestically. This means that the state at this point is in near full control of integrating energy innovation into its existing energy systems. It can thus guide disruptions and increase economic growth at the same time. At this stage, there is a limited global interlinkage of energy supply chains. Yet, as we will see this illusion of national control disappears almost instantly with the take-off of new energy innovations. Still, the baseline expectation of a true win-win, premised in a sense of innovative energy autarky, has now been set. As we will see in the remainder of this chapter, it can become a dangerous myth for policymakers as they respond to global pressures at later stages in the energy cycle.

There is one notable exception to this pattern that bears mention. Germany is one of the leading jurisdictions for the innovation of automobile transportation. The internal combustion engine as well as the automobile were invented in Germany in the late nineteenth century. International combustion engines rely upon petrol. Petrol, in turn, is a refined oil product. Germany did not have ready access to sufficient oil reserves of its own to meet demand even at the time of the invention of the internal combustion engine let alone at any time thereafter. Instead, Germany first relied on petroleum exported to Germany from the US by Standard

[26] For a discussion, *see* Hughes (n 4), at 18–46, 175–285.
[27] Perez (n 17), at 89–99.

Oil. In the early twentieth century, this created significant strategic problems for Germany as it lacked control over the key part of the automobile value chain—oil. Germany sought to diversify its oil supply away from Standard Oil and towards Romania.[28] Yet, even this diversification was problematic given the geopolitical tensions between Romania and Germany's ally Austria-Hungary with regard to Transylvania at the time.[29] Germany thus found itself precisely in the situation that is not typical in the irruption phase—it had developed a technology that relied on long, fraught, and potentially hostile value chains from the beginning. How could this be? Or more to the point, does this exception discredit the idea that policy decisions at the frenzy stage constitute the very geopolitical problems driving energy policy discourse today?

The perhaps facile answer to the question is that the automobile truly took off as a mass-produced solution to transportation challenges in the US rather than in Germany. The Ford Model T brought the benefits of mass production to the automobile industry.[30] This mass production made it possible for automobiles to have a significant impact on transportation. Ford had the benefit of a booming US oil industry at the time.[31] As a solution to a critical problem in energy systems writ large, there thus was a proximity of fuel, industrial assembly, and end energy use.

This answer provides one part of the picture. Yet, there is another piece to the puzzle. By the time of the invention of the automobile in Germany, there existed a robust petroleum industry that itself had already gone through a frenzy and a bust cycle.[32] The resource itself—petroleum—had already encouraged prospectors to look in truly far-flung places for supplies.[33] At just this time, the petroleum industry, further, was itself beleaguered by the very invention of electric light. (Petroleum in its first boom time was a fuel for lamps rather than for locomotion.[34]) There thus existed a global industry in search of a new market just as the invention of the internal combustion engine came along. There was in fact a geographic diversity in potential oil producing states at the time with Russia as one leading contender and Royal Dutch Shell as another in the 1890s.[35] The innovation thus built on a mature industry with long value chains to do something drastically different with the product (oil) than its original intended use.

What the case of the automobile suggests is that even revolutionary energy innovations, like the internal combustion engine, can at times rely on long value chains. The circumstances are, however, special. A needed commodity for

[28] For a discussion, *see* Munro, 'The Proposed German Petroleum Monopoly', (1945) 4 American Economic Review 315.
[29] Christopher Clark, *The Sleepwalkers: How Europe Went to War in 1914* (Harper 2013).
[30] Bryce (n 6), at 58–59.
[31] *See* Daniel Yergin, *The Prize, The Epic Quest for Oil, Money & Power* (Free Press 1991) 78–95.
[32] *Ibid* at 32–34.
[33] *Ibid* at 65–77.
[34] *Ibid* at 78–80.
[35] *Ibid* at 65–77.

innovation needs to have a pre-existing, mature, global value chain. Further, this value chain must look for new markets due to a lack of growth potential in its traditional marketplace. The material must also be reasonably rare. In that context, fuel sources become no different than other materials. One such reference material could be manganese. Manganese was a critical ingredient in German steelmaking around the same time. It, too, is rare. Germany around the same time as the invention of the automobile imported manganese from Brazil.[36] The German example is thus an outlier. It was an outlier that came of age with the Model T in a context that fits our paradigm. Still, it is a reminder that outliers exist even when they do not represent the norm of energy innovation.

3.2(b) The Frenzy Phase

It is only when a technology has shown its potential decisively to resolve a critical problem that value chains lengthen and the geopolitical implications of energy systems begin to take shape. Importantly, domestic governance choices made during the frenzy phase distinctly nudge the development of global energy chains in distinctive ways. The current energy transition to decarbonize energy systems provides a paradigmatic example of how domestic governance choices set up global challenges policymakers now attempt to address on the international stage.

As a baseline, it is on the whole natural that global value chains would in fact develop once multiple jurisdictions have successfully implemented new, systemic energy solutions to a shared problem following the same approach or idea in broad outline. As we noted in the last section, there was a global pool of solutions that found distinctive domestic implementation relying on initially on domestic value chains. Given the growth in multiple jurisdictions of similar components for a new energy value chain, it is on the whole natural that supply and demand for this new value chain could look to a global marketplace.

This baseline reacts to policy choices made at the domestic level. In Chapter 1, we considered the misalignment of policy incentives and policy goals in the context of the renewable energy roll out in Europe in the early 2000s by means of feed in tariffs.[37] These feed in tariffs were calibrated to decrease annually for new projects to incentivize innovation. The feed in tariffs recognized that solar and wind technology were not price competitive with traditional sources of electricity generation. To support solar and wind projects, feed in tariffs therefore aimed to set tariffs at which power companies could still achieve a reasonable profit for the deployment of renewable energy technology.[38] These subsidies intended to force

[36] Nicholas Mulder, *The Economic Weapon, The Rise of Sanctions as a Tool of Modern War* (Princeton University Press 2022) 29–30.

[37] *See* section 1.4.

[38] For a discussion, *see* Sourgens (n 23), at 153–77.

innovation by providing a revenue target for industry and finance to chase.[39] As we discussed in Chapter 1, this approach was phenomenally successful to the point that solar and wind energy today are the cheapest form of new electricity generation one can deploy (assuming access to favourable sites etc).[40] Yet, as we also discussed Chapter 1, the development of technology in many ways appeared too successful in that it allowed power producers to achieve a higher profit margin on their projects than the governmental support mechanism had anticipated. This, in turn, would mean that sponsors achieved a higher profit margin on projects located on favourable sites. It also made sites that would not otherwise be favourable under normal conditions appear attractive. Technology forcing, in other words, fed a classic bubble that resembled, for instance, railroad expansions along marginal lines in the nineteenth century.[41] Regulatory approaches changed at the end of the frenzy stage to realign incentives and policy objectives, as we discussed in Chapter 2.[42]

These incentive structures had two important global repercussions that are less appreciated. The first concerns how value chains would develop in response to the incentive structures in question. The renewable 'frenzy' was not limited to a single jurisdiction but rather happened in parallel globally.[43] This meant that there now was a global market for components, such as those for solar panels and component parts. This market attracted the attention of export-driven industrializing states like the People's Republic of China.[44] The People's Republic of China built an export-driven solar module industry beginning in its tenth Five Year Plan (2001–2005).[45] This decision led China to import polysilicon from Europe and the US and export finished panels—that is, it led to a lengthening of solar supply chains.[46]

At the frenzy stage, core states adopting energy innovations early are beginning to lose the triple benefit from the irruption stage of holding together most of the energy value chains in their jurisdiction. Longer supply chains tend to distribute energy raw material and manufacturing parts of the value chain more broadly due to the strong price signals of the economic success of a new energy innovation. With

[39] For a price comparison during this technology forcing phase, *see* 'Levelized Cost and Levelized Avoided Cost of New Generation Resources in the Annual Energy Outlook 2014', U.S. Energy Information Administration (April 2014), https://www.eia.gov/outlooks/archive/aeo14/pdf/electricity_generation_2014.pdf, last accessed 29 April 2024.

[40] 'Levelized Cost of Energy+' at 2, Lazard (April 2023), https://www.lazard.com/research-insights/2023-levelized-cost-of-energyplus/, last accessed 29 April 2024.

[41] Perez (n 17), at 24, 82.

[42] *See* section 2.5.

[43] *See* Sourgens (n 23), at 144–98.

[44] China acceded to the World Trade Organization (WTO) in December 2001. For a discussion of the relative changes in the international economic order since then, as well as an assessment of the importance of China's WTO accession, *see* Shaffer, 'Governing the Interface of U.S.-China Trade Relations', (2021) 115 American Journal of International Law 622, 626–29.

[45] *See* Heymi Bahar, *Special Report on Solar PV Global Supply Chains* (International Energy Agency 2022) 105–06.

[46] *Ibid.*

the growth of these supply chains, we see the inception of a global energy order that binds together different jurisdictions. Importantly, the frenzy stage does not set out to build such a global order. Rather, the price signals in early-adopting core jurisdictions create the economic basis for such an order to emerge organically.

Perhaps paradoxically, the frenzy stage does not yet drive the global diffusion of the new energy innovation itself to peripheral markets but rather tends to hold it back. These 'peripheral markets' are further away from the innovation frontier and did not participate in the early adoption of a particular energy innovation. As Perez notes in her study on technological innovation, while there is some outward pressure during the frenzy stage, the true push of a technology to peripheral markets comes much later.[47]

We can observe this trend in the renewable sector. The Chinese experience provides a fascinating natural experiment of this phenomenon. The Chinese experience with renewables is meaningfully split. China was an early adopter of wind technology, experimenting with the technology as early as 1986. Chinese policy supported the formation of joint ventures with leading German providers in 1997. The joint venture structure was intended to provide a path to technology independence and the deployment of 80 per cent local content in the Chinese wind setting.[48] Due to its early investment in technology innovation, China was a global leader in installed wind capacity in 2010, ahead of the US, Germany, and Spain.[49]

China's push into the solar sector, on the other hand, initially was export-driven only. It was only in 2011, a decade after the tenth Five Year Plan, that Chinese policy began a demand creation programme through feed in tariff support within the People's Republic itself.[50] To put this policy choice in further perspective, Chinese adoption of feed in tariff support post-dated Germany's original 1991 *Stromeinspeisungsgesetz* by twenty years.[51] China was a peripheral market with regard to its own adoption of solar energy only and did not catch up with the marketplace for years. The reason for this appears intuitive—there was more money to be made from export than there was from deploying the technology domestically. Capacity therefore had to be directed outwards. As China grew with the wind market from a much earlier point in time, the same is not true in the wind setting—China had domestic need for wind innovations.

[47] Perez (n 17), at 65.

[48] *See* 'China', (2013) IRENA-GWEC: 30 Years of Policies for Wind Energy at 48, available at https://www.irena.org/-/media/Files/IRENA/Agency/Publication/2013/GWEC/GWEC_China.pdf?la=en&hash=E1FC001617FB7AB786A7D831D271853B9404449A, last accessed 12 August 2024

[49] Rachel Gelman et al, '2010 Renewable Energy Data Book' at 55, (2011) US Department of Energy, Office of Energy Efficiency & Renewable Energy, https://www.nrel.gov/docs/fy12osti/51680.pdf, last accessed 12 August 2024.

[50] Bahar (n 45), at 107.

[51] For a discussion of the Stromeinspeisungsgesetz and the policy and political calculations that led to its adoption, *see* Dotterud Leiren & Reimer, 'Germany: From Feed in Tariffs to Greater Competition', in Elin Lerum Boasson, Merethe Dotterud Leiren, & Jørgen Wettestad eds, *Comparative Renewable Policy: Political, Organizational and European Fields* (Routledge 2021) 81, 82.

Just as tellingly, jurisdictions like South Africa had to offer a multiple of the feed in tariffs in developed economies to attract renewable projects. Again, it is not difficult to understand why. The incentive structures in European economies were such as to make even marginal projects financially attractive. These marginal projects still had a lower perceived risk compared to investment in South Africa: South Africa had no meaningful track record with the new technology. To attract capital, South Africa therefore had to offer significantly more by way of incentive despite being in a weaker fiscal position.[52]

The reasonable rate structure underlying the public contract governance model thus drives an unreasonable distribution of technology access at the same time as it drives a global lengthening of value chains. It tends to overcompensate at the beginning of the frenzy stage even in unfavourable applications of new technology in core markets. This overcompensation delays adoption of critical energy technology in peripheral markets. As we will see in the context of the maturity stage of energy cycles, this is a partial explanation why older energy systems such as coal-fired electricity generation continue to grow in peripheral markets even as they are retreating at the innovation core. Needless to say, given the climate consequences of delayed adoption of renewable energy technology, this is not a welcome incentive structure.

3.2(c) The Synergy Phase

The synergy phase corrects many of the excesses from the upswing of the energy cycle. The synergy stage rebalances energy governance.[53] As we have seen in Chapter 2, this rebalancing has its own domestic downsides.[54] Yet, it is in many ways the attempt to realign policy incentives with governance goals.[55] The synergy phase—as the name suggests—is about returning normalcy to the energy cycle after the arrival of a systemic energy innovation to energy systems. At the end of the synergy phase, the new approach to energy governance in principle brings about such a new normal.

Paradoxically, the synergy phase has something of an opposite effect on the global stage. The synergy phase has the potential to be globally disruptive. The changes in governance bringing calm to domestic markets also create the conditions for global energy security threats to emerge. The incentives set during the synergy phase tend to lengthen global energy value chains. They also thin them out at the same time by remaining less competitive participants. The domestic

[52] *See* Sourgens (n 23), at 144–98.
[53] Perez (n 17), at 127–37.
[54] *See* section 2.5.
[55] *See ibid.*

incentive structure during the synergy phase therefore creates the very potential for geopolitical capture that can seed global conflict. The geopolitical tensions dominating the 2020s in fact all are related to—though certainly not exclusively caused by—the synergy stage in energy technologies relevant to the transition.

We have already seen one example of the beginnings of this development in our discussion of the frenzy stage—the lengthening of solar energy value chains. As I discussed in the previous section, the frenzy stage created the incentives to lengthen global supply chains to support the development of solar projects, particularly in North America and in Europe.[56] The synergy phase of the energy cycle had to react to an 'over-heating' of solar investments by changing regulatory approaches to the governance of solar energy.[57] Most markedly, there was a downward pressure on prices.

This downward pressure naturally reverberated through the entire solar value chain. In a globalized economy, downward price pressures send signals to lower prices in the value chain to allow solar project sponsors to continue to maximize their profitability in the new regulatory environment.[58] Global marketplaces reacted to this pressure the way they normally do—they increased the market share of market participants with a comparative advantage in the relevant market segment.

The most marked shift in the context of the solar value chain occurred in the context of the refinement of a material needed to make solar panels, polysilicon.[59] During the irruption and much of the frenzy stage of solar technology, the chief suppliers of polysilicon were Japanese, Korean, German, and American.[60] In 2024, the largest suppliers by far are in the People's Republic of China's Xinjang Autonomous Region.[61] The shift in polysilicon production largely overlapped with the synergy stage of the solar industry in the subsidizing markets (most notably in the EU). The relative advantage Chinese producers gained on the materials side then translated into a comparative advantage on the manufacturing side. This, in turn, further supported the growth of solar panel manufacturing. Thus, the leading manufacturing sites for solar panels migrated to the People's Republic of China, as well.[62]

[56] *See* section 3.2(b)

[57] *See* section 2.5.

[58] *See* Bahar (n 45), at 105 (noting the reverse situation of tariffs increasing the price of solar).

[59] Eriksson & Hack, 'Production of Metallurgical- Grade Silicon in an Electric Arc Furnace', *in SGTE Casebook* (Klaus Hack ed, 2nd edn, Woodhead Publishing 2008) 415–24.

[60] *See* Bahar (n 45), at 108; Pickerel, 'China's Share of World's Polysilicon Production Grows from 30% to 80% in Just One Decade', (27 April 2022) Solar Power World, https://www.solarpowerworldonline.com/2022/04/chinas-share-of-worlds-polysilicon-production-grows-from-30-to-80-in-just-one-decade/, last accessed 8 August 2024.

[61] Bahar (n 45), at 106–07.

[62] *Ibid.* China began its ascent by focusing on solar PV manufacturing as an export market and then built a leading polysilicon capacity to integrate into production. The comparative advantage was the large-scale investment in a systemic production process, which in turn brought down prices. This large-scale investment was subsidy-dependent.

An important relative advantage the People's Republic of China was able to bring to bear at this stage was low energy costs. The refining process to make polysilicon is highly energy intensive.[63] The Xinjiang Autonomous Region in the People's Republic of China has among the lowest energy costs in the country due to abundant access to local coal deposits.[64] Thus, '[a]round 80% of the electricity involved in polysilicon production today is consumed in Chinese provinces at an average electricity price of around USD 75 per megawatt-hour (MWh). This is almost 30% below the global industrial price average.'[65] The People's Republic of China is relying on this competitive advantage of ready coal access to reduce the cost of materials and thus gain an edge in renewable energy supply chains.

The relative advantage gained by China may at first appear ironic: coal-fired power should not provide a relative advantage in the production of needed components for the solar value chain. The fact that it nevertheless does do so runs counter to the narrative that a build out of renewable energy capacity is itself climate friendly.[66]

Still, on closer inspection, it should not strike us as surprising.[67] Cheap energy access is the catalyst for economic growth. It facilitates industrial processes at affordable costs. An industrial stakeholder with comparatively lower energy costs should therefore have a ready competitive advantage in highly energy intensive value chains. Solar energy value chains are energy intensive. The natural advantage gained by the People's Republic of China therefore is simply a result of known economic mechanisms. One may legitimately ask why coal continues to enjoy such an advantage when renewable energy has a levelized cost of energy advantage over coal-fired power.[68] The matter is a question of timing and of scale. In terms of timing, in 2008, the levelized cost of solar energy was at least $131/MWh, compared to $74/MWh for combined cycle gas power and $78/MWh for coal.[69] Current energy advantages of solar therefore have been reasonably recent. Additionally, as one study put it, the production of silicon wafers in 2021 was responsible for greenhouse gas emissions equivalent to 99–213 metric tons of CO_2. The study goes on to estimate that net zero 2050 scenarios could lead to 16.4–58.8

[63] Pickerel (n 60).

[64] Reinsch & Arrieta-Kenna, 'A Dark Spot for the Solar Energy Industry: Forced Labor in Xinjiang', (19 April 2021) Center for Strategic & International Studies, https://www.csis.org/analysis/dark-spot-solar-energy-industry-forced-labor-xinjiang#:~:text=The%20polysilicon%20components%20are%20produced,polysilicon%20factories%20in%20the%20world, last accessed 9 August 2024.

[65] *See* Bahar (n 45), at 11.

[66] *See* 'Solar Explained', (19 January 2024) U.S. Energy Information Administration, https://www.eia.gov/energyexplained/solar/solar-energy-and-the-environment.php, last accessed 20 January 2025.

[67] Hallam, 'A Polysilicon Learning Curve and the Materials Requirements for Broad Electrification with Photovoltaics by 2050', (2022) 6 Solar RLL 220458.

[68] Lazard (n 40).

[69] Levelized Cost of Energy 3.0 (February 2009) Lazard, https://www.solarthermalworld.org/sites/default/files/lazard2009_levelizedcostofenergy.pdf, last accessed 30 September 2024.

gigatons of CO_2 equivalent greenhouse gas emissions.[70] These emissions evidence the large energy consumption of the materials component of the solar value chain. Solar energy or hydropower could significantly reduce the greenhouse gas intensity of wafer production. The problem is—the energy used for wafer production would then not be available to power other things. Energy demand is already growing at a challenging pace. Adding renewable capacity to the grid just for wafer production would place a significant strain on the grid. The same applies for 'behind-the-meter' systems installed by producers on their own property and disconnected from the grid. The relative capital cost to install new capacity does not yet provide a relative energy cost advantage over incumbent power resources in markets with ready access to comparatively cheap coal like the People's Republic of China. It is therefore on the whole uneconomical to deploy cheaper energy for the production of solar wafers in the current environment. (Once it does become economical to make the switch to solar power, Xinjang Autonomous Region again would benefit from a relative advantage as it would be able to produce the cheapest solar panels locally to replace coal. The relative energy advantage gained by the People's Republic of China as a result of the policy measures taken particularly in Europe during the synergy phase are therefore likely to be particularly sticky.)

It is of course tempting to suggest that we should internalize the climate costs caused by CO_2 emissions in the solar value chain to decouple it from coal.[71] The question is—what would have been the effect of such a policy approach on the domestic side of energy regulation during the synergy phase of the energy cycle? The synergy stage precisely meant to stop investments that were not deemed prudent by sending lower price signals—and thus increase the price competitiveness of renewable energy further.[72] Increasing the cost of materials in the solar value chain by means of carbon pricing could well have gotten in the way of realizing the goals of synergy stage domestic energy policies—prices in the renewable sector would not have come down as anticipated. This, in turn, would have threatened the emerging relative advantage of renewables in the energy mix. Every policy choice has consequences. In the energy context, these consequences play out globally and reconstitute value chains that can support stated domestic policy goals. Outsourcing emissions and prolonging the life of coal-fired power until such time as it is profitable to replace coal with renewables in the production process (and thus forgo export revenues) is very much part of this calculus—be it one that is not always front of mind of domestic policymakers.

[70] Hallam et al, 'A Polysilicon Learning Curve and the Materials Requirements for Broad Electrification with Photovoltaics by 2050', (2022) 6 Solar RRL 220458.

[71] Rasool et al, 'Crafting a Robust U.S. Carbon Border Adjustment Mechanism', (8 August 2024) Center for Strategic & International Studies, https://www.csis.org/analysis/crafting-robust-us-carbon-border-adjustment-mechanism, last accessed 20 January 2025.

[72] Perez (n 17), at 114–36.

What we can now see is that at the synergy stage, core states adopting energy innovations early run a significant risk of losing the triple benefit from the irruption stage of holding together most of the energy value chains in their jurisdiction. This stands in marked contrast to the policy creed that 'Green Deals will push early-adopting countries towards developing comparative advantages in advanced green technologies'.[73] Concretely, the expectation behind particularly German incentives had been to support a domestic renewables industry given Germany strength in existing supply chains.[74] This expectation failed precisely at the time of a downward adjustment in the feed in tariffs typically associated with the synergy phase. At the time of this downward pressure on rates in Germany, China made a concerted, industrial policy-driven, effort to enter the marketplace and muscled German competitors out of that marketplace in part because of the differences in energy policy in Germany and China.[75]

The domestic policy environment in many EU member states directly created the incentives that allowed China to rise in the marketplace.[76] There was a profitable export market for jurisdictions like the People's Republic of China to capture due to feed in tariffs. European incentives thus provided a known price signal for Chinese industrial policy.[77] That is, price signals set pursuant to domestic energy policies drive global industrial alignments and policies. Where there is a significant market to capture, producers able to rely on cheaper labour, cheaper energy, and state support can in fact change value chains when price signals attempt to shift production to cheaper producers. Importantly, this is less likely to happen without the swing in price signals set by means of state policy so characteristic of the synergy phase. Without state policy setting early price signals during the irruption and frenzy stages, markets would be too uncertain to attract new entrants. Without adjustments to that state policy during the synergy phase, price signals would not drive project sponsors as quickly to cheaper producers. In that case, incumbent value chain participants would actually have seen the benefit of decreasing energy prices due to the price competitiveness of renewables. They would thus have been able to compete more effectively with Chinese producers.[78] Policy—not

[73] Alessio Terzi, *Growth for Good, Reshaping Capitalism to Save Humanity from Climate Catastrophe* (Harvard University Press 2022) 217.

[74] *See* Bahar (n 45), at 109.

[75] *Ibid.*

[76] *See* Sourgens, Banet, & Baldwin (n 23), at 154–77 (discussing the development of feed in tariff structures).

[77] Bahar (n 45), at 106–07.

[78] This price competitiveness will take longer to materialize in early adopting markets, given that some of the best project sites will be occupied early by first generation technology. There is a downward trend in costs in early adopting jurisdictions. It is just not as pronounced and generalized as it might have been. *See* 'Industry Power Prices in Germany: Extraordinarily High – and Low', (4 December 2019) Clean Energy Wire, https://www.cleanenergywire.org/industrial-power-prices-and-energiewende, last accessed 20 January 2025.

markets—cut short this possibility just as policy—not markets—created the industry in the first place.

These domestic incentives had geostrategic repercussions. Prior to the synergy phase for solar energy in domestic energy markets, no one state had a controlling stake in the value chains supporting solar energy. Due to the synergy stage, the People's Republic of China now holds such a controlling stake.[79] This controlling stake is geopolitically significant.[80] The People's Republic of China has leverage over solar energy supply chains. This, in turn, means that these supply chains are subject to political risk and thus limit the energy security of a domestic policy premised upon a build out of renewables and a phase out of traditional generation like the International Energy Agency's Net Zero 2050 plan.[81] The situation is not an accident. Rather, it is the natural consequence of the interaction between domestic energy governance cycles and economic globalization.

This pattern is not unique. Rather, we can see a similar trend play out in natural gas value chains—be it in response to more complex policy responses to domestic energy needs. To see the mechanism in the gas context, let us build a counterfactual scenario. Assume that Germany invested in liquified natural gas receiving terminals in 2005 instead of proceeding with the Nord Stream 1 gas pipeline project connecting Germany directly to Russian gas exports.[82] What would the incentive structure for the Russian Federation have looked like on 23 February 2022? A German investment in 2005 in liquified natural gas receiving terminals would have led to a more robust market for liquified natural gas exports. This, in turn, should have increased export capacities in gas-rich countries. This in effect means that Germany (and the EU) would have had more ready access to gas supplies to displace Russian pipeline gas. While it is perilous to look for single causes to world conflicts, it is on the whole prudent to ascribe some rationality to policymakers. This rationality would suggest that Russia's invasion of Ukraine would have looked more costly to Russia as Germany would have appeared more likely to be able to decouple from Russian gas quickly. If the decision to invade was a close-run affair, such a shift might have been an important factor in bringing about an alternative policy path in Russia. (The policy path would have been even clearer if the US had significantly larger spare capacity in oil production that could have displaced more Russian crude from global markets.)

[79] Chinese policy was originally export driven and did not aim at supplying a domestic solar PV need. Bahar (n 45), at 106–07.

[80] Elizabeth Press, *Geopolitics of Energy Transition: Critical Minerals* (IRENA 2023).

[81] Laura Cozzi, *Net Zero by 2050, A Roadmap for the Global Energy Sector* (International Energy Agency 2021) 57. As China also has a similarly leveraged position with regard to wind, it is arguably in a position to exercise such geopolitical leverage over both wind and solar value chains.

[82] *See* 'E.On Hatches Plan for Germany's First LNG Import Terminal', (26 October 2005) Energy Intelligence, https://www.energyintel.com/0000017b-a7a9-de4c-a17b-e7eb89700000, last accessed 20 January 2025; Brauers, 'Liquified National Gas Expansion Plans in Germany: The Risk of Gas Lock-in under Energy Transition', (2021) 76 Energy Research & Social Science 102059.

Why did Germany make the decision to enter into the Nord Stream project during Gerhard Schröder's chancellorship and confirm the intention to proceed with the project under Chancellor Merkel as opposed to investing in liquified natural gas terminals? Around this time, some energy stakeholders were investing heavily in liquified natural gas import facilities, highlighting that such a path was not an altogether ludicrous alternative.[83] The answer lies in an energy policy approach typical of the synergy phase of the energy cycle.

The issue in the gas context is slightly more complex than it was in the solar context. Germany at the time in question did not respond to a gas frenzy. Rather, German energy policy responded to a desire to increase support for renewable energy. It also had to contend with expensive subsidies for German coal from North Rhine Westphalia. Finally, the Green Party in particular was intent on a policy of nuclear exit. Together, this policy picture led to both uncompetitively high electricity prices for Germany's export industry and a problem of securing basic demand if nuclear power were indeed removed from the German energy mix. Synergy phase policies typically look to reduce costs by removing costly over-incentives favouring inefficient links in the energy value chain. In 2003, Chancellor Gerhard Schröder's social-democratic government pushed forward structural reforms intended to increase the productivity of the German economy. This set of policies included significant labour market reforms.[84] They also included significant energy market reforms in the mould of making the energy market more efficient in the same way that his government sought to increase the efficiency of the labour market.[85] This policy therefore ended up favouring cheaper gas energy. This cheaper energy meant leaning into and expanding reliance on a partner with a comparative advantage in delivering gas to Germany—Russia.[86] The comparative advantage was that pipeline gas could offer better commercial terms over liquified natural gas at the time.[87] Germany at this time further amplified this strategic advantage through the Nord Stream pipeline

[83] Rapier, 'How the U.S. Became the World's Top LNG Exporter', (5 January 2024) Forbes, https://www.forbes.com/sites/rrapier/2024/01/05/how-the-us-became-the-worlds-top-lng-exporter/, last accessed 17 August 2024.

[84] Möller & Walwei, 'Die Agenda 2010 war ein unerwarteter Erfolg', (14 March 2013) Die Zeit, https://www.zeit.de/wirtschaft/2013-03/agenda2010-reformen-erfolg, last accessed 17 August 2024.

[85] In this context, it was the reduction of subsidies for German coal while maintaining the subsidies for renewables that led to the eventual adoption of a more gas-friendly policy. This policy was driven by the idea—so typical of the synergy phase—that energy policy has to support economic growth by lowering energy costs. *See* 'Schröder will Kohle und Klima schützen', (17 September 2003) Frankfurter Allgemeine Zeitung, https://www.faz.net/aktuell/wirtschaft/energiepolitik-schroeder-will-kohle-und-klima-schuetzen-1112446.html, last accessed 17 August 2024.

[86] On this value chain, *see* Margarita M Balmaceda, *Russian Energy Chains: The Remaking of Technopolitics from Siberia to Ukraine to the European Union* (Columbia University Press 2021).

[87] Anderson, 'Europe's Dependence on Russian Natural Gas: Perspectives and Recommendations for a Long-term Strategy', (September 2008) George C Marshall European Center for Security Studies, https://www.marshallcenter.org/en/publications/occasional-papers/europes-dependence-russian-natural-gas-perspectives-and-recommendations-long-term-strategy-0, last accessed 18 August 2024.

project as this project would further reduce costs to deliver gas to Germany by reducing transport risk.[88]

Had Germany waited in committing to its energy policy, things might have been different. Gas markets were changing in favour of a more elastic international market right around the same time.[89] Germany might also have benefited from the shale gas revolution in the US. With hindsight, this revolution began around 2005.[90] The revolution turned the US from a net importer of natural gas to a net exporter of natural gas. In 2024, the US vies for leadership in global natural gas exports.[91] Reforms to reduce energy prices in 2005 meant tethering Germany to Russian energy exports. It also meant leaving Germany out of the newly developing global gas markets. Synergy energy policies thus again had unintended (if foreseeable) consequences on the geopolitical stage.[92]

The story of German energy policy explored in this section makes it appear that Germany bears outsized responsibility for the rise of Russia and China as geopolitical energy powers. This impression is of course unfair. Occasional exceptions notwithstanding, single jurisdictions acting alone do not and cannot bear such responsibility. Rather, Germany acted in a pattern typical of broader energy transition policy demands that were replicated elsewhere. These policies amplified each other to the point of creating the geopolitical energy instabilities that we face today. The German experience therefore is intended as an example of how domestic energy transition policies and politics lead to geopolitically destabilizing consequences—and have done so particularly in the context of the ongoing energy transition. What is more, it suggests the logic for why they do so: the synergy phase in domestic energy cycles make perfect domestic sense while creating misaligned global incentives. We can therefore do more than simply note that the paradigmatic German energy transition policies of the first twenty years of the twenty-first century were geopolitically imprudent (we will discuss in the next section that they indeed departed from the common sense of realpolitik approaches to global energy systems).[93] We can explain why such policies were and are implemented and why they have such a geopolitically fraught potential.

[88] *See* Karnitschnig, 'Why Merkel Chose Russia over US on Nord Stream 2', (16 July 2021) Politico, https://www.politico.eu/article/vladimir-putin-german-chancellors-nord-stream-russia-energy-angela-merkel/, last accessed 17 August 2024.

[89] Anderson (n 87).

[90] Rapier, 'How the Shale Boom Turned the World Upside Down', (21 April 2017) Forbes, https://www.forbes.com/sites/rrapier/2017/04/21/how-the-shale-boom-turned-the-world-upside-down/, last accessed 30 September 2024 ('From 2005, U.S. natural gas production rose for 10 straight years. The previous production record set in 1973 was obliterated as production grew 50% from 2005 to 2015 to reach 27 Tcf. In the process, the U.S. became the world's largest natural gas producer.'). 'IEA US Shale Upstream Cost Index, 2005-2020', (27 May 2020) International Energy Agency, https://www.iea.org/data-and-statistics/charts/iea-us-shale-upstream-cost-index-2005-2020, last accessed 20 January 2025.

[91] 'The United States Was the World's Largest Liquefied Natural Gas Exporter in 2023', (1 April 2024) US Energy Information Administration, https://www.eia.gov/todayinenergy/detail.php?id=61683, last accessed 17 August 2024.

[92] Anderson (n 87).

[93] *See* section 3.4.

3.2(d) The Maturity Phase

The maturity phase of the energy cycle is the end of the downswing of the energy cycle.[94] It sees to their logical conclusion the efficiency increasing measures encouraged during the synthesis phase. Value chains now can grow to their full complexity due to the certainty of demand and the established players in the field. The maturity phase in general encourages the greatest possible rationalization of global value chains to push the mature paradigm to extract as much by way of profit as remains possible.[95]

Importantly, the per unit profitability of energy value chains diminishes during the maturity phase. There is simply not the same profit available for energy value chain participants as had been the case in the frenzy stage. The relevant processes in application are well-studied. Suppliers can compete globally to bring down costs. This, in turn, means that there is only so much room for profit in this new environment given the potential for competition within energy value chains.

In principle, this has two consequences. The first consequence is that capital is looking to solve the next reverse salient within existing energy systems to gain access to greater profits.[96] That is, capital is looking to support a new irruption phase by supporting innovators who have found a way to conceive of the reverse salient as a critical problem that can be solved by means of a systemic adoption of their invention. The maturity phase by its very incentive structures feeds the next irruption.

But there is a second, arguably less desirable consequence that lasts well into the next frenzy of precisely the kind of technology that is better able to respond to economic and social energy demands. Obsolescent energy technology must look for marketplaces in which to extend profitability for their existing technological paradigm. In core innovating energy economies, there is decreasing room.[97] This pushes technology to pursue peripheral markets more aggressively for adoption.

Here, the incentives of the frenzy and maturity phases create a truly dangerous constellation. During the frenzy stage, incentives are such as to make even marginal opportunities in core markets highly desirable. Further, given the track record for the technology in question in that market, risk is comparatively lower as there is more data available with regard to regulatory and commercial responses to the new technology. This, in turn, means that regulators in peripheral markets will have to compete on price for their most promising projects with marginal projects in core markets. Frequently, this will freeze the technology out of the marketplace. If a jurisdiction cannot generate needed electricity using the best available

[94] Perez (n 17), at 81–90.
[95] *See ibid.*
[96] *See ibid* at 71–90; Hughes (n 4), at 79–105; Perez (n 17), at 49.
[97] *See* Perez (n 17), at 84–85.

technology at a reasonable price, it will have to make a choice about how else to generate electricity. It will not wait half a decade for the technology costs to come down.[98] This means that this jurisdiction has every incentive to lean into the very technologies being displaced by the best available technology in core markets. This leads states to make significant capital investments in projects that are intended to operate for thirty years or more.

Concretely, this meant pushing peripheral jurisdictions towards coal-fired power during the early phase of the renewables and gas frenzies. For instance, China's generation capacity grew 'from 1989, when the total national installed capacity was 100 GW [...] to over 900 GW' in 2011.[99] 82 per cent of total Chinese capacity in 2011 was thermal, that is, mostly coal.[100] From 2000 to 2010, India increased its installed coal capacity by approximately 50 per cent.[101] In the same timeframe, coal consumption in Indonesia (South East Asia's leading economy) tripled.[102] The climate consequences of this push are sizeable as it locks in coal-fired generation for a thirty-year term at least. The trend is not universal in every jurisdiction. Still, viewed globally, 'global coal capacity grew in every year between 2000 and 2019, nearly doubling from 1,066GW to 2,045GW'.[103] Of this, the most dramatic periods of new additions ran from approximately 2005 to 2011.[104]

The question why coal has been 'durable' in the global energy mix can thus partially be answered by the dynamics of maturity of incumbent technologies during the frenzies for their competitors.[105] Part of the reason that newer, less carbon intensive energy technologies do not reach relatively energy poor economies is that frenzies create conditions in which new technologies are too profitable even for marginal projects in economies with abundant energy. These conditions are driven by domestic price-setting decisions following a public contracting logic. Frenzies create an over-abundance of opportunities in some economies and a corresponding dearth in others. Improving global energy and climate outcomes

[98] Bryce (n 6), at 20.

[99] Nan & Moseley, 'The Expansion of China's Generation Capacity' at 1, (July 2011) World Bank PPP Insights, https://ppp.worldbank.org/public-private-partnership/sites/ppp.worldbank.org/files/documents/China_Energy_v1n1_0.pdf, last accessed 12 August 2024.

[100] *Ibid* at 10.

[101] 'Installed Capacity in India, 2000-2020, and Projections up to 2040 in the Stated Policies Scenario', (27 October 2020) International Energy Agency, https://www.iea.org/data-and-statistics/charts/installed-capacity-in-india-2000-2020-and-projections-up-to-2040-in-the-stated-policies-scenario, last accessed 12 August 2024.

[102] 'Republic of Indonesia, The Indonesian Carbon Capture Storage (CCS) Capacity Building Program, CCS for Coal-Fired Power Plants in Indonesia', (June 2015) World Bank, https://documents1.worldbank.org/curated/en/563781468284373788/pdf/FINAL-OK2-Jun-2415Cov-reduced-with-WB-cover.pdf, last accessed 12 August 2024.

[103] 'Mapped: The World's Coal Power Plants', (26 March 2020) Carbon Brief, https://www.carbonbrief.org/mapped-worlds-coal-power-plants/#:~:text=Global%20coal%20capacity%20grew%20in,1%2C066GW%20to%202%2C045GW, last accessed 20 January 2025.

[104] Evans & Pearce, 'Mapped: The World's Coal Power Plants', (26 March 2020) Carbon Brief, https://www.carbonbrief.org/mapped-worlds-coal-power-plants/, last accessed 12 August 2024.

[105] Bryce (n 6), at 170.

therefore requires one to think differently about domestic policy-making and include the global consequences of domestic regulatory decisions in one's calculus. Without such an integration of domestic and international concerns, energy transitions will create significant lock-in effects for older technology.[106]

At the same time, the maturity of a technology pushes prices in core markets to a point that it becomes desirable to achieve comparatively greater profits by entering markets with ostensibly greater risk (greater risk in part due to the lack of existing diffusion of the mature technology). This dynamic becomes the more pronounced when new projects in core markets are displaced by a new, competing projects. This has the doubly problematic consequence of bringing predominantly dated energy technology to peripheral markets and setting price signals in peripheral markets that cause participants to pay a premium for its adoption. The lock-in effect of this combination is predictably strong as phase out not only needs to replace newly built infrastructure. It needs to replace such infrastructure at difficult cost terms. This dynamic explains part of the critique by the Global South of inherent imbalances in the world economy and global energy system.[107]

3.3 Global Energy Commons and Anticommons

We have seen so far that energy cycles link domestic energy policy to global energy decision-making. Each side, domestic and global, affects the other. The relationship between national energy systems is again a commons or shared resource community. It is subject to the same incentive problems as the tragedy of the commons.[108] In addition, we can observe that key realpolitik dynamics between national energy systems follow the underuse logic of the tragedy of the anticommons.[109]

The commons relationship between national energy system is straightforward. Energy systems begin nationally. Yet, each national stakeholder naturally looks to foreign markets as growth opportunities of the future.[110] Similarly, foreign stakeholders hope to benefit from economic incentives set in national energy systems by participating in value chains that benefit from these revenue streams.[111] The jurisdictions are economically connected just like adjacent oil and gas leases in

[106] Of course, in the 2005–2011 timeframe, there was still a need to subsidize renewables. The key point is that the incentives offered by developing states at this time had to be a multiple higher than the subsidies in core early adopting economies even for less advantageous projects.

[107] Perez (n 17). Carlota Perez participated in the North–South Dialogue.

[108] Hardin, 'The Tragedy of the Commons', (1968) 162 Science 1243.

[109] Heller, 'The Tragedy of the Anticommons: A Concise Introduction and Lexicon', (2013) 76 Modern Law Review 6; Heller, 'The Tragedy of the Anticommons: Property in Transition from Marx to Markets', (1998) 111 Harvard Law Review 621.

[110] Stephen G Gross, *Energy and Power, Germany in the Age of Oil, Atoms, and Climate Change* (Oxford University Press 2023) 267–93.

[111] Bahar (n 45), at 106–07.

a reservoir community.[112] To use such shared resources well requires cooperation.[113] Similarly, overuse of strategic advantages by one stakeholder can lead to destructive spirals.[114] This certainly was a fear in response to the oil shocks of the 1970s.[115]

The response to these oil shocks showed that the global energy system is also subject to anticommons dynamics. We associate these dynamics most clearly with realpolitik.[116] As I will discuss in the next section, one of the key fears of realpolitik is to end up in a situation of dependence.[117] Such dependence weakens autonomy. Maintaining relative power in the international system means suppressing processes that can lead to dependence.[118] These processes can be seductive due to the short-term or even longer-term economic benefits they promise—greater economic productivity driven by lower energy prices. Yet, we must resist the temptation of greater productivity if it creates dynamics of relative loss. Like the anticommons, underuse of energy resources is preferable because it does not risk upsetting relative power balances in the international system.[119]

A realpolitik lens similarly would question whether an efficient solution to the commons and anticommons problems is in the national interest of each state. Certainly, if one receives a relative advantage in the international system, it is worthwhile. Yet, some stakeholders will likely need to surrender a current relative advantage to bring this about. Why should they wish to do so?[120]

The currently tempting answer is to look to climate change as the key to overcoming such realpolitik. A realpolitik use of energy resources is more expensive. The price of decarbonization is already significant.[121] Increasing this price due to geopolitical conflicts makes decarbonization increasingly less likely as well as significantly slower (each price increase also increases the interest to be paid on

[112] Pierce, 'Carol Rose Comes to the Oil Patch: Modern Property Analysis Applied to Modern Reservoir Problems', (2011) 19 Penn State Environmental Law Review 241.

[113] Elinor Ostrom, *Governing the Commons, The Evolution of Institutions for Collective Action* (Cambridge University Press 2015).

[114] Hardin (n 108).

[115] Garavini (n 4).

[116] Kenneth N Waltz, *Theory of International Politics* (Random House 1979) 151–58.

[117] *See ibid* at 102–28.

[118] *Ibid.*

[119] *Compare ibid with* Heller 2008 (n 109).

[120] This question was at the heart of the development discourse in the interwar period—a period that remained unabashedly colonialist. It is interesting that ideas of 'development finance' began to sprout at this time at the same time as the period was also perhaps the quintessential example of power fault lines moving foreign policy and international economic policy in equal measure. For a fascinating account of this period—and the development discourse that percolated during it—*see* Jamie Martin, *The Meddlers, Sovereignty, Empire, and the Birth of Global Economic Governance* (Harvard University Press 2022) 99–176.

[121] 'The Net Zero Transition, What It Would Cost, What It Would Bring' at 5, (January 2022) McKinsey & Co, https://www.mckinsey.com/~/media/mckinsey/business%20functions/sustainability/our%20insights/the%20net%20zero%20transition%20what%20it%20would%20cost%20what%20it%20could%20bring/the-net-zero-transition-what-it-would-cost-and-what-it-could-bring-final.pdf, last accessed 26 March 2024.

a project loan; in addition, the price increase reflects increased risk, and as such will also increase the return on capital for the lender—that is, the interest rate.) Everyone suffers from climate change.[122] Consequently, we should act rationally by reducing such costs and thereby maximize our own self-interest.

This answer may look satisfactory at the current moment in time. Still, it hides a larger threat. It is a corollary of this position that solving commons and anticommons problems globally is exceptional. It applies in moments of emergency only.[123] Consequently, the normal operation of energy systems should continue to proceed on the basis of rivalry. The climate logic does not help us solve the problem more generally as it is not necessarily the case that energy systems will cause emergencies like climate change depending on their constellation.

A compelling answer must address both ordinary and extraordinary circumstances. It must be normatively cogent and pragmatically compelling. We ought to cooperate because of an ulterior value we agree is desirable. At the same time, we must ourselves be legitimately better off due to cooperation in such a way that relative losses of power in the international system are less relevant to our decision-making.

Intuitively, commons should precisely lead to such decision processes. The point is not the climate emergency. The point instead is that commons resources are partially shared.[124] Exploitation therefore must be cooperative to protect each share in the resource. In the remainder of the book, I hope to develop such an answer. This answer ultimately looks to how energy systems grow. Energy systems grow by conceiving of a reverse salient holding back the current energy system as a solvable critical engineering problem.[125] Such engineering solutions innovate. Innovation improves as competition increases at the innovation frontier.[126] Cooperation increases the number of competitors at the innovation frontier. This allows us to make qualitative changes to the energy system co-opetitively, which would have been impossible without a critical mass of innovators.[127] The answer is that we will be significantly more productive—jointly and individually—if we work together. Like the 'red queen' made famous by Acemoglu and Robinson, this arrangement will work only if our capacities for innovation grow without upsetting relative power balances, that is, innovation does not create realpolitik dependence.[128] It

[122] Hoesung Lee et al, *Climate Change 2023: Synthesis Report. Contribution of Working Groups I, II and III to the Sixth Assessment Report of the Intergovernmental Panel on Climate Change* (Intergovernmental Panel on Climate Change 2023).

[123] *See ibid*; Paris Agreement, art 4.

[124] Ostrom (n 113).

[125] Hughes (n 4), at 79–104.

[126] *See* Philippe Aghion et al, *The Power of Creative Destruction, Economic Upheaval and the Wealth of Nations* (Harvard University Press 2021).

[127] Brandenburger & Nalebuff, 'The Rules of Co-opetition', (January/February 2021) Harvard Business Review, https://hbr.org/2021/01/the-rules-of-co-opetition, last accessed 26 March 2024.

[128] Daron Acemoglu & James A Robinson, *The Narrow Corridor, States, Societies, and the Fate of Liberty* (Penguin 2019) 33–72.

maintains balance and can self-perpetuate.[129] This balance brings prosperity and the competitive means to increase it in a manner that is limited only by our own collective capacity for invention.

3.4 Rivalry and Mutual Dependence

The fact that energy systems function as a global commons does not mean that there is no rivalry in international energy systems. To the contrary, energy systems have always attracted fierce national rivalries. The nature of the global energy system as a resource community explains why it attracts fierce national rivalries. These rivalries ultimately are the result of the nature of energy systems as a global commons: energy stakeholders are mutually dependent upon each other as they produce energy from deeply interwoven energy value chains. Mutual dependence means that no one stakeholder has a sufficient right to the whole of an energy system to claim outright ownership of all parts needed to deliver energy to its citizens, residents, or customers. Stakeholders compete over, and participate in, a resource community.

If we look at energy systems through this lens, energy rivalries are markers of the tragedy of the commons. Rivalry reflects that some stakeholders use globally shared energy resources unreasonably. The resources in question could be raw materials, intellectual property, the industrial base to refine materials and build energy infrastructure etc. Use is 'unreasonable', as we have defined in prior chapters, if it over- or underuses a shared resource compared to its sustainable, efficient deployment.[130] Rivalry—as a form of unreasonable use—degrades the energy commons. Overuse is actively wasteful of resources. It is affirmatively wasteful. Underuse, on the other hand, is analogous to neglect of the resource—a failure of upkeep—and is permissively wasteful. The fiercer the rivalry, the greater the affirmative or permissive waste.[131] The greater the waste, the less likely it is that the energy commons will recover from such degradation. Rivalry, therefore, can ultimately lead to the destruction of the shared space in which a stakeholder attempts to achieve a meaningful relative advantage. At this tippling point, rivalry becomes self-defeating: rivalry destroys the means by which a rivalrous

[129] On this idea of systems, *see* Niklas Luhmann, *Theory of Society, Volume 1* (Rhodes Barrett trans, Stanford University Press 2012). In Luhmann's terms, the self-perpetuation of the system is its 'autopoiesis'. *Ibid* at 32–33. ('This is what autopoiesis means. The system can constitute operations of its own only further to operations of its own and in anticipation of further operations of the same system.')

[130] *See* section 2.5.

[131] On the development of waste in the common law tradition, *see* Purdy, 'The American Transformation of Waste Doctrine: A Pluralist Interpretation', (2006) 91 Cornell Law Review 653. For a comparative law assessment of waste in the civil and common law, *see* Richardson, 'Reframing Ameliorative Waste', (2017) 65 American Journal of Comparative Law 335.

stakeholder can participate, generate revenue, and have a say in the governance of global energy systems.

Why then is energy rivalry so ubiquitous, given that it is ultimately inefficient, wasteful, and potentially self-defeating? Energy is uniquely important. It is the ultimate economic 'force multiplier': energy allows us to achieve exponentially more than what would have been possible without it. 55 per cent of the world's population lived in urban areas in 2022.[132] Life in urban areas is distinctly energy dependent. Without electricity, New York or any other contemporary population centre could not have grown to its specific width—or its height. Both require energy for transportation. The same is true of most forms of production—whether it is in a factory or whether it is drafting a document and saving it to the cloud.

Given the centrality of energy to national economies, it is intuitive to see why controlling energy would be tempting. If I control the means needed for you to produce energy, I have leverage. If you do not do as I wish, I can deprive you of the means to go about your daily life. Your quality of life will deteriorate severely. Think what would happen to any large city if all refrigeration failed simultaneously and permanently. People would starve, as it would be difficult to resupply such a volume of food for several hundred thousand people (or millions of people) all at once. If the loss of energy goes beyond a city to affect a whole country, the situation is even more dire. Given this reality, you are likely to do as I demand so long as you care only marginally about an issue. It is only if you feel particularly strongly about an issue that you would be willing to suffer the consequences of defying me (assuming that my threat is not a bluff, of course). This is why energy is such a frequent target of realpolitik dynamics.[133]

The classic example of the use of energy resources to achieve foreign policy goals is the so-called 'Arab Oil Embargo'. The embargo began as a more or less spontaneous reaction to US and Western support for Israel during the Yom Kippur War in 1973. The embargoing states were members of the Organization of Arab Petroleum Exporting Countries (OAPEC). The core means of the embargo was a petroleum production cut by OAPEC members, paired with a petroleum export ban. It then evolved into a broader, more organized policy position. This position ultimately was not just about the Israeli-Arab conflict. Rather, it was about a broader readjustment of benefits from trade in oil. Oil trade was dollar denominated. Two years before the Arab Oil Embargo, the US did something to seriously upset the structure of global payments systems—it abandoned the gold standard. This move effectively weakened the dollar. A weaker dollar, in turn, reduced the value of oil

[132] 'Sustainable Development Goal 11', (2024) United Nations Statistics Division, https://unstats.un.org/sdgs/report/2023/goal-11/#:~:text=The%20world's%20population%20reached%208,70%20per%20cent%20by%202050, last accessed 26 August 2024.

[133] *See* Yergin, 'Ensuring Energy Security', (2006) 85 Foreign Affairs 69 (discussing the geopolitical context for energy security concerns).

revenues by oil producing states. The embargo also responded to this broader economic reality.[134]

The embargo imposed a significant economic and psychological toll. It facially did not meet its original military purpose. Even in this context, however, it was part of a broader strategical reset of the conflict. Arab states had outperformed expectations in the early stages of the Yom Kippur War. The Middle East embargo further increased the cost of aid to Israel. The strategic balance in the region therefore shifted. This shift culminated ultimately in the conditions which allowed Israel and Egypt to enter into the Camp David Accords in 1978 and a subsequent peace treaty in 1979.[135]

More importantly, the embargo also coincided with the beginning of a decided shift in the relationship between oil producers and oil consumers. It was one of the factors that spurred on a broader North–South dialogue between the US and Europe on the one hand and developing states in the Global South on the other. States therefore could look to the embargo for the relative advantages energy resources control could bring in the geopolitical arena—even as they would of course also have to recognize the limitations of that power (the North–South dialogue came to an unsuccessful end when Ronald Reagan became US President and Margaret Thatcher became UK prime minister).[136]

More recently, Russia relied on a similar strategy when it invaded Ukraine in February 2022. As noted already, Germany was uniquely vulnerable to a disruption in gas supplies from Russia. Russian strategy thus sought to apply pressure to Germany (and its European partners more broadly) not to support Ukraine due to Germany's (and Europe's) dependence on Russian pipeline gas. Essentially, Russian strategy made an educated guess that Germany (and Europe) did not ultimately wish to pay the economic price of decoupling from Russian gas. The gamble did not come off in the short term. Germany did decouple from Russian gas as part of its response to Russia's invasion.[137] This led to significant increases in German (and European) energy prices, as well as in prices of goods and services, and even led to industrial and economic relocation concerns.[138] Germany did absorb these inflationary pressures in the short-term.[139] Still, Russia did exact a

[134] For slightly different accounts, *see* Garavini (n 4) and Yergin (n 4).

[135] For a contemporary take on the strategic balance, *see* Rabinovich, 'Israel: The Impact of the Peace Treaty', (1980) 78 Current History 5, 11.

[136] Again, *see* Garavini (n 4) and Yergin (n 4).

[137] As noted already, this decoupling was not as complete as has been claimed. Yet, it still represents a monumental and deeply disruptive realignment of supply.

[138] Ward-Glenton, 'German Energy Prices Are so High They're Driving Companies to Relocate, Industry Body Says', (21 June 2023) CNBC, https://www.cnbc.com/2023/06/21/high-german-energy-prices-are-seeing-some-companies-relocate-bdi.html last accessed 26 August 2024.

[139] 'German Inflation Sinks to 1.9% in August', (29 August 2024) Deutsche Welle, https://www.dw.com/en/german-inflation-sinks-to-19-in-august/a-70081684, last accessed 2 September 2024; *see also* 'Economic Forecast for Germany', (15 May 2024) European Commission, https://economy-finance.ec.europa.eu/economic-surveillance-eu-economies/germany/economic-forecast-germany_en, last accessed 2 September 2024.

price.[140] As the long-term economic and political consequences of decoupling remain uncertain, it will take some time to fully understand what that price is.

Further, Russia is also a major oil producer. NATO member states in particular sought to take the lead in limiting Russia's oil revenues to restrict the means available to support Russia's military effort by imposing sanctions targeting the Russian oil sector.[141] Still, the sanctions had the effect of increasing oil prices in the short-term by dislocating oil markets without permanently affecting Russia's ability to supply oil markets after sanctions were lifted.[142] The strategy of containing an energy exporter had significant impact on oil markets, both in states imposing sanctions and in third states. This impact has led states like the US to consider phasing out sanctions against other states running afoul of US foreign policy preferences, such as Venezuela—this led to brinksmanship by the sanctioned states (again, centrally Venezuela) and a reimposition of sanctions.[143] All in all, the sanctions tool did not work as advertised as an effective means to surgically target elites in support of a more pacific, and democratic, world society.[144]

As these examples illustrate, the idea of energy rivalry as a weapon or tool to make relative geopolitical gains has significant currency. There is plenty of state practice to support the worry that such a use of energy value chains is ascendant. Threats to the impairment of the ordinary functioning of energy corridors has been a frequently observed tool in the Russian foreign policy arsenal.[145] It was

[140] *See* 'Economic Forecast for Germany', (15 May 2024) European Commission, https://economy-finance.ec.europa.eu/economic-surveillance-eu-economies/germany/economic-forecast-germany_en, last accessed 2 September 2024 (noting that Germany entered a recession in 2023 followed by a 'sluggish recovery').

[141] 'NATO's Response to Russia's Invasion of Ukraine', (19 July 2024) NATO Report, https://www.nato.int/cps/en/natohq/topics_192648.htm, last accessed 28 August 2024.

[142] On the impact—and its inherent uncertainty—of sanction in the oil sector, *see* Milov, 'Oil, Gas, and War: The Effect of Sanctions on the Russian Energy Industry' at 3, (May 2024) Atlantic Council, https://www.atlanticcouncil.org/wp-content/uploads/2024/05/Oil-gas-and-war-Vladimir-Milov.pdf, last accessed 28 August 2024. Milov notes in particular that 'Russia's state budget, which saw its revenues from oil and gas decline 24 percent in 2023 compared to 2022'. *Ibid.* At the same time, Russian oil revenue in 2024 rose by almost 50 per cent over the previous year. 'Russia Government's Oil Revenue Was Up Almost Up 50% in June', (3 July 2024) Bloomberg, https://www.bloomberg.com/news/articles/2024-07-03/russian-government-s-oil-revenue-was-up-almost-50-in-june?embedded-checkout=true, last accessed 28 August 2024. The impact of oil sanctions therefore has been decidedly mixed and volatile. On the internal policy debates in the Biden White House on a stricter enforcement of the sanctions—and its downside for gasoline prices in an election year—*see* Tanserksley & Rappeport, 'New Plan to Target Russia's Oil Revenue Brings Debate in White House', (7 July 2024) New York Times, https://www.nytimes.com/2024/07/07/us/politics/russia-oil-ukraine-shadow-fleet.html, last accessed 28 August 2024.

[143] 'Experts React. The U.S. Just Reimposed Sanctions on Venezuela. What Does that Mean for Energy Markets and Venezuela's Election?', (18 April 2024) Atlantic Council, https://www.atlanticcouncil.org/blogs/new-atlanticist/experts-react/experts-react-venezuela-sanctions-election/, last accessed 28 July 2024.

[144] For an account of sanctions as just such a tool, *see* Oona Hathaway & Scott J Shapiro, *The Internationalists: How a Radical Plan to Outlaw War Remade the World* (Simon & Schuster 2017).

[145] Kanet & Sussex, 'Introduction: Russia, Eurasia and the New Geopolitics of Energy', *in Russia, Eurasia and the New Geopolitics of Energy, Confrontation and Consolidation* (Matthew Sussex & Roger Kanet eds, Palgrave 2015) 1–5.

also apparently a tool in the Ukrainian arsenal, given the strong suspicions that Ukrainian interests sabotaged the Nord Stream pipelines linking Russian gas to German end markets.[146] It is a tool in the Middle East conflict, with serious threats to energy shipping becoming an increasingly frequent tool of asymmetric warfare.[147] It is a scenario of concern in the South China Sea.[148] Threatening energy infrastructure is a classical tool in geopolitical conflict used by all actors irrespective of their broader strategic alignment. It therefore deservedly takes centre stage.

Still, there is a deeper dimension to geopolitical energy rivalry. This deeper dimension links up with the nature of energy as a global commons. Economies need many of the same resources to fuel their respective energy systems. These resources are reasonably limited. They are also not all domestically available. This means that energy resources must be procured from foreign partners to secure value chains against global disruption.

This is the move that reveals the nature of energy as a global commons—no one state has sovereignty over the whole of the energy system or all critical parts of an energy value chain. Each state is at the mercy of how third states act in a shared energy system. States are in a similar position to each other in the energy system writ large, as oil producers are in a shared reservoir. They can, and frequently do, attempt to gain a relative advantage over each other. Yet, they also ultimately depend on each other not to bring about the collapse of the resource community. Their attempt to gain a relative advantage is itself driven by their keen awareness of the fragile nature of their respective entitlements to a portion of the shared resource. So, it appears smart to 'get while the getting is good'.[149]

The temptation is amplified by the outsized importance of energy for the economy. If I have cheaper, more secure energy access, I have a relative advantage over my competitors in global trade. I can gain just such an advantage by controlling parts of a critical energy value chain. This control is not just a matter of gaining an energy advantage. It now becomes a means to gain a relative advantage for one's economy over the economies of geopolitical adversaries writ large due to the relatively greater energy resource these rivals now need to absorb. Rivalry, therefore,

[146] Dreisbach & Staib, 'Hat Kiew die Nord-Stream-Pipelines gesprengt?', (15 June 2023) Frankfurt Allgemeine Zeitung, https://www.faz.net/aktuell/politik/ausland/ukraine-hat-kiew-die-nord-stream-pipelines-gesprengt-18964913.html, last accessed 28 August 2024; 'Ukraine weist Bericht zu Nord Stream zurück', (15 August 2024) Frankfurt Allgemeine Zeitung, https://www.faz.net/aktuell/politik/ukraine-weist-anschuldigungen-zu-nord-stream-zurueck-19921953.html, last accessed 28 August 2024.

[147] Paris, 'Oil Tanker Attacked by Houthis Is at Risk of Leaking in Red Sea', (28 August 2024) Wall Street Journal, https://www.wsj.com/world/oil-tanker-attacked-by-houthis-is-at-risk-of-leaking-in-red-sea-15672593, last accessed 28 August 2024.

[148] *See* Mandhana, 'In Beijing's Quest for Control of the South China Sea, a New Flashpoint Emerges', (25 August 2024) Wall Street Journal, https://www.wsj.com/world/asia/in-beijings-quest-for-control-of-the-south-china-sea-a-new-flashpoint-emerges-5ac29fc5, last accessed 28 August 2024.

[149] *See* Pierce (n 112); Righetti & Schremmer, 'Waste and the Governance of Private and Public Property', (2022) 93 University of Colorado Law Review 609.

is a matter of gaining control over resources needed simultaneously by multiple states for strategic purposes and thus securing a resource edge to protect one's respective domestic energy ecosystem.

One imperfect example of this dynamic is the campaign to secure sufficient cobalt to support the electrification of transportation. Cobalt is one of the materials needed for batteries used in electric vehicles. It is reasonably scarce. Mining cobalt is also environmentally fraught. Consequently, there are reasonably few cobalt mines in the world. This scarcity leads to resource conflicts. For instance, Chinese and US interests competed for cobalt in the Democratic Republic of Congo. China was able to secure a greater amount of Congolese cobalt, leading to a potential resource gap in the US battery production cycle—and simultaneously to security of supply for Chinese battery producers to the extent that such shortfalls affect the global marketplace. [150]

This deeper dimension of rivalry reflects the global and complex nature of energy value chains. Here, rivalry is a symptom of felt energy insecurity. Cobalt again is a case in point. There was a cobalt supply deficit in 2021—the year of the fiercest geopolitical competition for cobalt.[151] Notably, this supply deficit turned to an oversupply in short order. Alternatives to cobalt became available. Electric vehicle demand also did not fully meet early expectations. Rivalry led to inefficient outcomes. This inefficiency resulted in part form a fear of lacking access to a needed resource in the future that did not trust that global markets would find adequate answers for potential resource shortfalls.[152] The issue was distributive—leading jurisdictions worried about securing their needed share of total supply because of increase in demand by competitors. States translate this insecurity into rivalrous conduct. In the case of cobalt, insecurity gave rise to yet another 'scramble for Africa'.[153] Rivalrous conduct itself creates additional distributive issues which, in

[150] Lipton, Searcey, & Forsythe, 'Race to the Future: What to Know About the Frantic Quest for Cobalt', (7 December 2021) New York Times, https://www.nytimes.com/2021/11/20/world/china-congo-cobalt-explained.html, last accessed 28 August 2024.

[151] *Ibid.*

[152] Viernes, 'Oversupply, Low Prices for Cobalt to Persist in 2024 as Demand Slips', (27 December 2023) S&P Global, https://www.spglobal.com/commodityinsights/en/market-insights/latest-news/metals/122723-oversupply-low-prices-for-cobalt-to-persist-in-2024-as-demand-slips, last accessed 1 September 2024.

[153] Home, 'West Challenges China's Critical Minerals Hold on Africa', (18 February 2024) Reuters, https://www.reuters.com/markets/commodities/west-challenges-chinas-critical-minerals-hold-africa-2024-02-16/, last accessed 2 September 2024 ('But the West is now challenging China's tight grip on the mineral riches lying beneath the soil of the Congo and its neighbour Zambia. This new scramble for Africa comes with a post-colonial twist since both countries have ambitions to be major actors in the critical minerals race.') It is not the first such scramble. The first 'scramble for Africa' refers to the imperialist competition for African resources by European colonial powers seeking to support the Industrial Revolution in the nineteenth century and the colonial order to which it gave rise. Antony Anghie, *Imperialism, Sovereignty and the Making of International Law* (Cambridge University Press 2004) 69. For a granular account of the motivations and manner of French colonialism in Africa, *see* Newbury & Kanya-Forstner, 'French Policy and the Origins of the Scramble for Africa', (1969) 10 Journal for African History 253.

turn, lead to ultimately inefficient outcomes. It in essence creates an overdemand in excess of actual need.[154]

Both types of rivalry—rivalry due to perceived insecurity and rivalry premised in the use of an energy weapon—can only exist because of mutual dependence in energy markets. It can exist because there is a global energy commons. It is a truism that there would be no energy rivalry if every economy was fully energy self-sufficient. Rivalry therefore follows structure—in this case, the structure of global energy resources and the markets on which they are traded.

This structure is premised upon inherent imbalances. These imbalances begin with the fact that energy-intensive economies frequently lack the resources to meet their own energy needs.[155] In turn, energy exporting economies have an overabundance of those resources.[156] This gives leverage to exporters. But leverage is limited, as the exporter cannot itself turn the resource into productive energy use. That is, the importing state also have leverage that is weaker in the short-term but can be more consequential in the long-term: the importing state can diversify away from the exporting state seeking to use leverage. Our exporter now is stuck—find another importer or lose needed revenues. Yet, the alternative importer now has the greater leverage over the exporter. Our energy exporter is in need of a new market. With need comes a discount.

By way of an example of this dynamic, Russian gas certainly continues to find markets after Europe has shifted away from it. Russia is expanding pipeline gas access to China. Yet, the Chinese connection comes at a price.[157] This price is informed by the fact that it would be far more difficult for Russia to diversify its gas supply further to India (never mind the difficulty of diversifying back to Europe).[158] Russia was already in a precarious position once Europe diversified

[154] Such rivalrous conduct as the result of perceived resource insecurity is hardly a new problem. Rather, planners in both the First and Second World War had to wrestle with similar resource issues. In that context, needed raw materials would see price spikes because of insecurity between allied powers—that is, states did not trust that they would be left enough of a needed material for the war by their own allies. In the war context, this distributive problem was solved through centralized planning coordination. *See* Martin (n 120), at 30–44, 204–08. Centralized planning coordination in the context in question, needless to say, also drew on the colonial expertise of the Allies. This coordination ultimately resolved the run on resources and efficiently distributed available supplies. Yet, ultimately, all it needed was sufficient trust to know that one would receive enough of the relevant materials to continue fighting. The centralized planning framework was one means to engender this trust. Thankfully (given its colonial undertones), it is hardly the exclusive tool for doing so.

[155] For a discussion in the oil context, *see* Garavini (n 4).

[156] *Ibid.*

[157] *See* Seddon, Stognei, Foy, & Leahy, 'Russia-China Gas Pipeline Deal Stalls over Beijing Price Demands', (2 June 2024) Financial Times, https://www.ft.com/content/f7a34e3e-bce9-4db9-ac49-a092f382c526, last accessed 1 September 2024.

[158] Corbeau & Mitrova, 'Russia' Gas Export Strategy: Adapting to the New Reality', (21 February 2024) Columbia Center on Global Energy Policy, https://www.energypolicy.columbia.edu/publications/russias-gas-export-strategy-adapting-to-the-new-reality/#:~:text=Russia%20has%20also%20been%20in,and%20India)%20gas%20pipeline%20project, last accessed 1 September 2024. ('Russia has also been in talks for many years about construction of a gas pipeline to India and Pakistan, and Russian minister of energy Nikolay Shulginov said in early 2023 that the country has not ruled out the

away from Russian gas. Once the Chinese pipelines are operational, it is Russia as energy exporter that is in the more precarious position. Taking advantage of a structural imbalance can lead to costly losses due to the mutual dependence of producers and consumers within energy markets.[159]

In addition, there are imbalances in connecting different parts of a single value chain. For a value chain to function, we must link inputs to ever more specialized outputs. The whole chain is not contained in an exporting country. It is thus sensitive to external factors. For example, prior to 2022, most German wind towers relied upon Ukrainian steel produced with Russian coking coal rolled in Italy.[160] If any part of that value chain breaks down, this dislocates the value chain as a whole and no one state controls the entire chain. This imbalance leads to attempts to purchase or otherwise acquire foreign parts of the value chain. Yet, this alone ties the acquiring state more closely to the regulatory control of its neighbours. 'Offensive' rivalry here overlaps with 'defensive' rivalry. I cannot exercise control without also subjecting myself to control, requiring me to do more to limit my own exposure.

These imbalances (and counterbalances) become ever more complex as states diversify their energy mix. Yet, the underlying structure of rivalry remains the same. It is a reflection of insecurity over distribution of shared resources—or more precisely the benefits and burdens of their use. This insecurity maps the commons structure of the relationship between global energy stakeholders. So long as I cannot assure reasonable use by other stakeholders, I must act unreasonably myself to secure the greatest available portion of the shared resource and do as much as possible to block others from doing the same. This conduct is deeply destructive. Yet, due to structural insecurities arising from the commons relationship, it is all I have. This insecurity is at the heart of realpolitik.

This leads to an apparently simple thought. To avoid waste and eliminate the ills of rivalry, all we need to do is to address the underlying structural problems of global energy value chains and global energy systems. A better structure can in fact eliminate rivalry and all the problems it entails. Of course, as simple as the thought may initially appear, it precisely shows how engrained rivalry is in global energy systems and how difficult it will be to address.

In the first place, a structural change might suggest that we get rid of the organization of global energy systems as a commons. The most straight forward way of doing so is to stitch together the entire relevant energy value chains by 'acquisition'. This could be merely economic. Alternatively, it could be military acquisition.

possibility of joining the TAPI (Turkmenistan, Afghanistan, Pakistan, and India) gas pipeline project. The pipeline has struggled to get momentum for decades, however; the economics of these deliveries appear doubtful, and the region it would cross, particularly Afghanistan and Baluchistan, is considered unstable.')

[159] *See* Pye et al, 'The Global Implications of a Russian Gas Pivot to Asia', (2025) 16 Nature Communications 386.

[160] Balmaceda (n 86), at 195–201.

Needless to say, any attempt to 'acquire' a value chain outright is a threat to other stakeholders. Depending on the value chain, this threat can well be existential. Such a structural change therefore can encourage military confrontation. This military confrontation, in turn, is likely to destroy the base of the value chain itself. Ukraine again is an example. The importance of the Donbas region for Russia is linked to energy and particularly the metallurgical link of Siberian coal to Ukrainian steel produced with that coal in Donbas and the use of that steel in wind towers and other end applications.[161] As the destruction of the Azovstal plant in Mariupol highlights, Russia destroyed much of that production capacity to gain military control over it. Structural change by 'acquisition' (first economic then military) did not yield the desired result—at least not in the short-term.[162]

Restructuring value chains less drastically can also be fraught with difficulty. Meaningful change threatens a relative loss of control—or at the very least loss of leverage—for some stakeholders. This, in turn, heightens insecurity for those stakeholders. Such insecurity again feeds rivalry. Rivalry can then upend any attempt at restructuring energy systems. Energy systems are a global commons. That means actors can in fact increase the cost of restructuring for its champions. These champions would likely view such action meant to make restructuring more expensive or arduous as 'interference'. They are likely to react themselves in turn.

This fuels a vicious cycle. Remedying deep structural problems means changing the structure. Structural changes tend to increase relative insecurity and thus erode trust. Any structural change triggers rivalry. This is precisely the problem that structural changes sought to remedy. There is no structural solution for this loop.

How then do global energy commons stabilize? There is an imperfect realpolitik answer to this question. There is also a more effective answer that builds on the lessons learned from realpolitik premised upon an international version of the bond of belonging. I will begin to sketch that more effective answer at the end of the chapter and develop it through the remainder of this book. Before doing so, we need to first understand the realpolitik dynamics to stabilizing global energy imbalances.

Realpolitik picks up the logic of our vicious cycle: if I establish that there is an imbalance in energy value chains and that this imbalance impairs my energy interests, I must act.[163] I must take steps to counterbalance the problem—the instability in value chains that negatively affects my interests. That means I must add to energy value chains somehow to satisfy the long-term security of my energy needs. A build

[161] *Ibid.*

[162] 'Beneath the Rubble: Documenting Devastation and Loss in Mariupol', (8 February 2024) Human Rights Watch, https://www.hrw.org/feature/russia-ukraine-war-mariupol#:~:text=On%20May%2017%2C%20Ukrainian%20forces,a%20place%20of%20shallow%20graves, last accessed 1 September 2024.

[163] *See* Waltz (n 116), at 102–28. The point here is not to re-establish balance but rather to escape my own precarious situation. This has the consequence of creating balance if all stakeholders act rationally and have appropriate means. *See ibid.*

out of core parts of energy value chains requires significant capital investment (eg building new powerplants using a different fuel or expanding hydrocarbons production). Energy infrastructure also takes a significant time to build out (eg pipelines). In light of these limitations, realpolitik counsels that I take steps gradually, if at all possible. Such gradual action spreads costs. Spreading costs means that I can reduce the social cost of my counterbalancing move. At the same time, it also allows us to see how new policies actually affect our national economies. Taking steps to counterbalance strategic problems early and over a longer period of time avoids many of the pitfalls of rushed action.

As noted earlier in this chapter, German energy policy provides an instructive example. Germany sought to exit both nuclear and coal power simultaneously in favour of renewable energy.[164] This position required Germany to rely on cheap Russian pipeline gas to meet its energy needs. Germany did not diversify away from its dependence on Russian natural gas early but instead committed to projects like the Nord Stream pipelines, which further cemented the connection between Russia and Germany. When Russia invaded Ukraine, Germany had to pivot very quickly to make incredibly expensive energy investments. This was not an ideal policy balance. The combination of new energy investments, climate obligations, and support for Ukraine in its war effort put the German budget into a state of upheaval.[165] It undermined many of the long-term energy policy goals Germany pursued by committing to a long-term expansion of gas infrastructure.[166] From a realpolitik perspective, it is an example of the severe costs of what, in hindsight, turned out to be naïve policy choices.

A prudent use of realpolitik in energy policy takes on a dynamic of its own. It counsels that every adjustment by a neighbour in an energy community will spur others to respond. My counterbalancing itself creates potential ripples for my neighbours. That means that my neighbours now must react to me. If I am acting gradually, I typically give my neighbours time to react and add a new layer to their own energy policy. As we react to each other to protect our own interests, we can begin to see a logic in each other's actions. This logic means that I can predict what my neighbour will do. This ability to predict is trust in its most stripped-down form. I may not expect loyalty from my neighbour, but I do expect that self-interest

[164] Gross (n 110), at 267–93.

[165] Graham, 'German Government Averts Crisis with a Budget Agreement for Europe's Largest Economy', (5 July 2024) Associated Press, https://apnews.com/article/germany-budget-agreement-stimulus-coalition-a95dbc1d92c70ee2c10e921b8a5e0762, last accessed 7 September 2024.

[166] Kędzierski, 'At All Costs. Germany Shifts to LNG', (28 April 2023) Center for Eastern Studies, https://www.osw.waw.pl/en/publikacje/osw-commentary/2023-04-28/all-costs-germany-shifts-to-lng, last accessed 7 September 2024 ('Although in autumn 2022 the Bundestag approved the plan to earmark €9.8 billion for this purpose until 2038, the most recent forecasts regarding the initiative's funding indicate that the required sum would be around as much as €10.5 billion'); 'Venture Global LNG Signs 20-Year Contract with German Energy Firm', (22 June 2023) Reuters, https://www.reuters.com/business/energy/venture-global-lng-signs-20-year-contract-with-german-energy-firm-2023-06-22/, last accessed 7 September 2024.

will prompt my neighbour to react to similar external stimuli in the same way it has in the past. I can then internalize that expectation into my own decision-making.

Realpolitik changes the structure of the global energy commons through the responsive actions of self-interested neighbours. There is a logic to how we react to each other. This logic somewhat stabilizes the global energy commons. The dynamic of this equilibrium looks like the realpolitik application of the rule of capture in property law.[167] So long as everyone can act to secure their own needs in a resource community through self-help, we do not need additional governance tools.[168] We just need to gain insight into how we each act in a self-interested manner to avoid misreading intentions and hurtling into tragedy. We need means to signal to our neighbour that defection from a course of action that is in the joint interest of all energy community members will be met with gradual answers.[169] These gradual answers, if seen through to their natural conclusion, would deprive the defecting party of their current (and now short-term) relative advantage in the energy community.[170] This should counsel my neighbour to restraint to meet their own energy interests and relative position in energy value chains. As we see our neighbour restraining from taking action that would imperil the energy community, we can stop from doing so as well. We achieve relative but unstable parity by checking each other's moves.

The realpolitik answer to energy imbalances is to create counterweights early, methodically, and transparently. What brings energy systems into balance is not an attempt at inventing a new structure. It is the dynamic of juggling perpetual imbalance. Realpolitik answers stress with different stress. This allows the system to operate more or less efficiently—and re-perpetuate itself—even as it constantly changes due to the many moves and countermoves we make in response to each other. A realpolitik answer treats energy systems like a vinaigrette dressing. Different, facially incompatible ingredients form a desired whole due to rapid and constant motion into opposite directions. Only rapid and constant motion into opposite directions holds it together. If that motion stops too soon, the vinaigrette begins to fall apart. Realpolitik would tell you that the point of stability is not to find different, more compatible ingredients. It is to find a way to work fundamentally

[167] For the US common law version of this rule, *see Pierson v Post*, 3 Cai R 175 (New York 1805). The rule has since taken on critical importance in oil and gas development in the US. *See* Owen L Anderson et al, *Oil and Gas Law and Taxation* (West Academic 2017) 1–7. The rule itself was expressly drawn from Roman law. James Kent, *Commentaries on American Law Volume 2* (O Halsted 1827) 281–83.

[168] This solution should sound somewhat familiar. It is the efficient solution to the 'prisoner's dilemma' between players with long-term repeat interactions. *See* Robert Axelrod, *The Evolution of Cooperation* (Basic Books 1984) 58–62.

[169] Monitoring and gradual sanctions are also at the heart of successful commons governance, as theorized by Elinor Ostrom. Elinor Ostrom, *Governing the Commons, The Evolution of Institutions for Collective Action* (Cambridge University Press 2015) 94–100.

[170] This is the 'secret' to the success of tit-for-tat strategies in rational choice games, like the prisoner's dilemma. Axelrod (n 168), at 58–59.

inconsistent ingredients into a consistent, dynamic whole.[171] This is the art of answering and keeping the dynamic of the energy system alive.

This fleeting and dynamic balance remains good but not ideal. It looks for constantly changing compromises that have the effect of maintaining relative energy power. It does not look for further energy innovation in its own right. Instead, it innovates only for the sake of relative power. It is thus less than ideal even if it is a liveable arrangement.

3.5 Energy Nationalism as Global Energy Cooperation

The discussion so far raises a question: does energy *nationalism* fit the realpolitik dynamic we have described so far? Energy nationalism is a core attribute of populist politics in the 2010s and 2020s. Energy nationalism is a natural corollary of a 'Homeland First' ethos and economic policy. The goal of energy nationalism is to provide domestic economic opportunity on the basis of nationally available resources. It looks to limit or even expel foreign interests in energy value chains supporting the national energy supply. Further, it would use whatever means necessary to undo any relative advantage of rival energy blocs to achieve as much independence from—and ideally even control over—global energy markets.

If energy nationalism fits in the overall description we have given of energy systems, we might be able to say something more meaningful about energy nationalism than making a value judgement about nationalism as such. Rather, we can then examine energy nationalism as a countermove in global energy commons governance. We can then see energy nationalism not as a form of isolationism or, alternatively, as a kind of jingoism. Energy nationalism instead is itself a mode of engagement with global energy value chains and the global energy systems they support. Such a theoretical appraisal can in fact lead to surprising conclusions.

Even if it is a mode of engagement with global energy value chains, it could of course still be destructive. In fact, it would be normal to assume that energy nationalism must be inherently destructive of anything global. After all, energy nationalism would seem to withdraw from global value chains and from global energy systems in favour of a national system. That is, it would precisely appear to move towards undercutting the commons nature of global energy systems. If this were

[171] Neither the idea, nor the metaphor, are my own. Rather, both come from Heraclitus. Heraclitus noted that stress is definitional. He used two examples—one of which I copied. The first is the idea of a bow—a bow can do the work of a bow only if it can be pulled into two different directions. Alternatively, a barley drink common to the era only held together if it was constantly stirred. As our most popular barley drink does not require constant stirring, Heraclitus' analogy needed an update to speak to us. Thus, the idea of a vinaigrette. Yet, the idea of medium and emulsion trace back to Heraclitus, and are thus nearly as old as philosophy itself. *See* Heraclitus, *Fragments* (Brooks Haxton trans, Viking 2001) 32; Martha Nussbaum, *The Fragility of Goodness: Luck and Ethics in Greek Tragedy and Philosophy* (2nd edn, Cambridge University Press 2001) 81.

the case, energy nationalism would be a policy to be avoided at all costs. It would destroy the global energy commons and as such undercut its own ability to deliver on its promise of energy independence and energy prosperity.

This reaction to energy nationalism misunderstands it. It does not see energy nationalism as a realpolitik move. It instead makes assumptions that leaning into a further globalization is always the better thing for globalized energy governance. As we have seen in the context of our analysis of the interplay between domestic energy policies and the global energy landscape, this is not necessarily the case.[172] To understand if energy nationalism can be constructive therefore we must start at the beginning: what conditions bring on energy nationalism? Once we know the answer to this question we can gain a better sense of whether energy nationalism in fact brings to light and hopes to address a critical problem for the sustainability of global energy value chains.

Think tanks close to the victorious 2024 Trump campaign, like the Heritage Foundation's Project 2025, suggest a nuanced and insightful answer to this question in the US context. The starting point should sound familiar: energy policy must ensure 'abundant, affordable, and reliable energy' access to 'create good-paying [sic] jobs' by 'support[ing] domestic manufacturing', which, in turn, supports national security.[173] Energy nationalism submits that current energy policies must be changed because they increase the cost of energy to consumers through inefficient subsidies. Further, and more importantly, existing energy policies rely on and strengthen energy value chains dominated by foreign adversaries.[174] This means that domestic energy policies strengthen the hand of those foreign adversaries by giving them an outsized influence over needed inputs for domestic energy generation and thus economic productivity. The first goal of energy nationalism is to right-size energy value chains by promoting energy security. This goal, in turn, requires promoting domestic 'energy resources' and using those resources to support geopolitical allies and confront geopolitical adversaries.[175] What is implicit in the policy proposal is that current energy policy has contributed to the formation of global value chains that, in turn, do not 'ensure the existence of markets that will support domestic energy production'.[176] A further implication is that these value chains have indirectly brought about a loss of competitiveness with regard to 'early and advanced science, including materials science, that is related to energy and national security' by offshoring critical materials components of the value chain.[177]

[172] *See* section 3.2.

[173] McNamee, 'Department of Energy and Related Commissions', *in Mandate for Leadership, The Conservative Promise, Project 2025 Presidential Transition Project* (Paul Dans & Steven Groves eds, Heritage Foundation 2023) 363, 363.

[174] *Ibid* at 363–64.

[175] *Ibid* at 364–65.

[176] *Ibid* at 367.

[177] *Ibid.*

If we superimpose this analysis over our own, we can see a natural and surprising overlap. The policy proposal notes the systemic threat of China's position in energy value chains. Though not clearly stated, the very tone of the policy paper makes clear that the value chains viewed with most suspicion are renewable energy value chains.[178] China has indeed been able to secure a market advantage by for instance securing a commanding position in polysilicon production (ie materials).[179] This market advantage has in fact driven previously successful US and Western producers out of the global marketplace.[180] We noted already that this position poses a potential security threat due to the relative position of one power over a needed energy resource.[181] The other concerns raised by the energy nationalist diagnosis similarly are a corollary of this concentration of critical components of renewable value chains in one market. What brings on energy nationalism, in other words, is a serious and sustained imbalance in energy value chains that coincides with a loss of domestic industry to foreign competitors. Energy nationalism therefore presents a picture that is indeed grounded in evidence and flags a threat that clearly requires a realpolitik countermove to maintain a balance in global energy value chains.

Just because a policy position identifies a problem which realpolitik would similarly flag does not mean that the policy prescribes a prudent realpolitik move. Here, some policy positions of Project 2025 are a case in point. Thus, it is certainly critical to 'develop domestic critical mineral sources […] as the vast majority of critical minerals are mined or processed or both in Russia and China'.[182] This policy would broaden the producers of critical minerals and refined products. This, in turn, would add resilience to global value chains. It would thus strive to approximate the competitive advantage of coal in the global energy system—namely the relative redundancy of coal value chains in the global economy. The same is true with regard to policy proposals to 'eliminate political and climate-change inference in […] approvals of liquefied natural gas (LNG) exports'.[183] This proposal too strengthens global value chains—in this case in the natural gas sector—by adding more alternative sources of supply.

At the same time, the policy proposals suggesting eliminating subsidies for renewable energy and carbon capture utilization and storage are counterproductive.[184] Removing such subsidies in principle means a thinning out of competition in global value chains. It leaves core value chains open to capture by economies with cheaper labour costs, competitive energy costs, and laxer environmental

178 *Ibid* at 363.
179 *See* section 3.2.
180 *Ibid.*
181 *Ibid.*
182 McNamee (n 173), at 377.
183 *Ibid* at 369.
184 *Ibid* at 365, 376.

regulations. We have already seen this phenomenon in this chapter—the reduction in renewables subsidies coincided with, and supported, the consolidation of the Chinese position in the polysilicon value chain. A reduction in subsidies in the development of critical technologies is thus a misaligned response to the diagnosed problem.[185] It is likely to increase Chinese dominance in yet further parts of energy value chains, thus further consolidating market power in a single stakeholder, rather than diversifying the mix of stakeholders in critical energy value chains.

Where then does this dislike for subsidies originate? The implication in documents like the Heritage Foundation's Project 2025 is that inefficient subsidies for renewable energy in the US and Europe brought on Chinese dominance in critical solar energy value chains.[186] If domestic subsidies in fact provide the means to fund foreign dominance, realpolitik would counsel avoid subsidies altogether. This analysis is partly correct, as we have seen earlier in this chapter. The subsidy structure in European markets in particular did draw Chinese manufacturing into the renewables market. Yet, it is incorrect in treating China's rise as directly caused by inefficient renewable subsidies. In some ways, the opposite is true. Inefficient subsidies during the renewable frenzy stage kept more polysilicon producers in the marketplace longer. The reduction in European subsidies gave China such a powerful competitive edge for polysilicon production—the lowering of subsidy support after the solar industry had in fact become profitable in principle pushed more production to facially cheaper markets.[187] Had Europe never introduced feed in tariffs for utility-scale solar energy, it is true that China would not have become a leading player in the polysilicon industry. Still, it is not the subsidies that gave China a competitive advantage. It was their rationalization in the synergy phase of the European energy cycle that worked this outcome. The antagonism towards subsidies as such therefore gets the dynamics of energy cycles wrong even as it identifies an accurate, if more complex, correlation between domestic energy subsidies and global market responses. Rationally, a better understanding of global energy market dynamics should thus alter energy nationalist policy prescriptions.

Where does this leave us? Energy nationalism is more nuanced than might at first appear. It is at times a prudent realpolitik move to respond to serious value chain imbalances. That does not mean that it is always a prudent realpolitik move to address such imbalances. The underlying diagnosis may be incorrect (there may not actually be a serious energy value chain imbalance). More likely, the prescriptions to address such imbalances may themselves be counterproductive. Still, there

[185] This misalignment is all the more perplexing when one considers that the policy proposals in question support an all-of-the-above approach to energy governance. *Ibid* at 364. Such an all-of-the-above approach is possible only with carbon capture—without carbon capture, the continued use of fossil fuel electricity generation would be unsustainable from a climate change perspective. Thus, to support an all-of-the-above approach requires technology forcing of carbon removal technology.

[186] *Ibid* at 363–64.

[187] *See* section 3.2.

are times that the prudent thing for global energy commons stakeholders to do is to adopt energy nationalist policies. Sometimes they are necessary to address serious imbalances brought on by a sudden shifts in energy subsidy regimes. One therefore should not dismiss energy nationalist policies as inherently incompatible with global energy commons governance or as existing outside of a global energy commons perspective.

This leads to a surprising corollary: energy nationalism can be a constructive form of global energy *cooperation*. Energy nationalism can diagnose a critical problem that threatens the proper functioning of global energy value chains. This threat is itself a reverse salient—it prevents energy systems from achieving the full realization of their energy potential due to the geopolitical risk they pose.[188] There is a common thread to the energy nationalist critical problem: without intervention, one, or more likely many, jurisdictions will no longer be able to guarantee for themselves a fair opportunity to compete in the global economy due to a structural disadvantage in how global energy value chains are constituted.[189] (For example, a geopolitical actor—acting alone or in concert—might have to be checked because that actor can credibly deprive its neighbours in the energy commons of critical energy resources.) In diagnosing the critical problem, energy nationalism sets out the criteria for a successful problem solution—the ability to compete back on a more or less level playing field once the new policies have had a chance to take effect.[190] This ability to compete back could take two forms—build out alternative value chains to compete with existing energy value chains and thus mitigate the geopolitical risk of that value chain. Alternatively, it could in theory look to degrade the value chain through sabotage or military force. It is notable that no energy policy playbook of even the most hardened energy nationalist looks to this destructive option.

Energy nationalism, as we have encountered it, is about broadening energy value chains. This creates redundancies. Such redundancies are helpful for the resilience of global energy systems as a whole. These redundancies occur because economies vigorously defend the role of national champions in global value chains. Such energy nationalism may look like it distorts equal access in international trade in the short-term. It has been adjudicated to be inconsistent with the international economic law free-trade regime (though this jurisprudence is itself questionable as I will discuss later on).[191] Yet, it does not necessarily undermine the competitiveness of the energy value chains writ large. To the contrary, it can increase competitiveness by presenting credible alternatives to stakeholders holding a market position that is itself capable of distorting competitive markets.

188 Hughes (n 4), at 79.

189 For the fair opportunity doctrine in a correlative rights context, *see* Schremmer, 'Pore Space Property', (2021) Utah Law Review 1; *see also* section 2.4.

190 Schremmer (n 189).

191 *See* Sourgens (n 23), at 112–16.

If we look at energy nationalism through this lens, there are many champions of this point of view in energy history. They obviously include President Donald Trump. These champions also include leaders like General Charles De Gaulle and his insistence on French exceptionalism.[192] There is a throughline between this insistence and French nuclear policy.[193] This policy has greatly strengthened the diversity of the global nuclear sector. These champions also include leaders like Juan Pablo Pérez Alfonzo—one of the architects in the formation of Organization of Petroleum Exporting Countries (OPEC). The emergence of OPEC broadened the scope of decisionmakers in global oil markets even as it tried to bring these decisionmakers into a coalition of the likeminded.[194] They also should include Kwame Nkrumah and his insistence on an African economic resurgence built on electricity-driven industrialization. In each case, energy nationalism was part of a broader order-building project.[195] It was not a retrenchment from the world, but rather a means to engage with it. It was not always successful. This is hardly surprising. Any order building move rooted in a realpolitik reaction to structural imbalances in global energy value chains is as likely to succeed as it is to create upheaval. What remains surprising is that energy nationalism is a faithful expression of the 'rule of capture' brought to the international stage. Of course, each stakeholder will diligently and ruthlessly act to further its own self-interest. Yet, in doing so, it must acknowledge the role of its neighbours in jointly building an order in which such self-interested action becomes possible. When my neighbour is pushed to the point of being deprived of a fair opportunity to participate in the energy commons, all should welcome a resort to energy nationalism given the destructive alternative they might also have to hand: the attempt to destroy shared energy resources as a way to cover their retreat.

3.6 A Global Bond of Belonging

As we have seen in this chapter, there is a direct throughline between domestic energy policy and global energy governance challenges. Domestic policies create the conditions in which global energy value chains form. They further provide the incentives for those value chains to develop during the synergy and maturity phase

[192] Warner, 'Gaullist Foreign Policy', (1965) 21 The World Today 112; Hajiyeva, 'Gaullism as a Legacy of Charles De Gaulle', (6 July 2017) Modern Diplomacy, https://moderndiplomacy.eu/2017/07/06/gaullism-as-a-legacy-of-charles-de-gaulle/, last accessed 13 September 2024. For a contemporary take on the cooperative nature of Gaullism, *see* Soustelle, 'France and Europe, A Gaullist View', (1952) 30 Foreign Affairs 545.

[193] Hannah Holtzman, *Through a Nuclear Lens, France, Japan, and Cienema from Hiroshima to Fukushima* (State University of New York Press 2024) 38–39 (discussing the origins of the Messmer plan).

[194] Garavini (n 4).

[195] *See* Adom Getachew, *Worldmaking After Empire: The Rise and Fall of Self-Determination* (Princeton University Press 2019) 147–48.

of the energy cycle. This, in turn, causes domestic policies to change to respond to changing global repercussions of past policy choices. The bond of belonging that we theorized as constituting these domestic energy policies is, by necessity, global in nature. Domestic energy policy cannot be severed from global energy policy and vice versa. Each is an integral part of the other.

This consequence is reasonably straightforward to understand on the domestic side of energy policy-making. I theorized that what provides a conceptual frame for domestic policy-making is the bond of belonging holding different energy stakeholders together. The different substantive energy policy approaches (the public contract/public utility model; the market liberalization model; and the command model) experienced a breakdown in efficacy when different stakeholders acted without the relevant other regard for each other in light of how they themselves responded to incentives. This, in turn, leads to policy changes to realign the reaction of different stakeholders to incentives so as to support the development of energy systems to deliver cheaper, more secure, and sustainable energy outcomes for their respective societies.

This bond of belonging must incorporate the effects of the global nature of energy value chains on domestic energy systems to be effective. If the bond of belonging does not incorporate this particular feedback, it will stop being a helpful guide for energy policy-making altogether. The domestic response to global disruptions of energy systems would no longer realign the reaction of different stakeholders to incentives intended to strengthen domestic energy systems against these 'exogenous', and apparently foreign, shocks. Domestic policy-making does in fact respond to strengthen domestic energy systems. The bond of belonging therefore connects domestic regulators to all global energy value chain stakeholders.

This, however, is not enough. As we have seen, there are realpolitik consequences of how global energy value chains constitute themselves. If stakeholders in global value chains are to be held together by a global bond of belonging, we must account for this realpolitik reaction to global value chains. These value chains are now not seen as purely a means to secure energy needs. They have become tools in the conduct of foreign affairs. The question therefore is whether the bond of belonging in fact also applies at this global level in light of the foreign affairs implications of energy systems. Do sovereign stakeholders also act consistently with a global bond of belonging when they implement their foreign-facing energy policies?

The last two sections have shown that prudent realpolitik responses to geopolitical threats to global energy value chains are in fact anchored in a mode of energy cooperation. Energy foreign policy seeks to limit the influence of any one actor or group of actors over global energy value chains. It can do so by limiting the influence of a particular stakeholder in a value chain. This can mean providing support for domestic competitors to that stakeholder. It can also mean diversifying the energy mix away from the value chain in question. The first response immediately benefits all other like-situated stakeholders by increasing competition in the respective value chain. The second response does not immediately benefit all such stakeholders.

The relationship between these responses and global energy security becomes clearer in a counterfactual. Say Poland would have diversified away from Russian gas imports prior to 2021 by importing a larger share of gas from Qatar and the US than it did.[196] This would have strengthened Poland's energy system vis-à-vis a potential dependence on Russian gas imports in 2021. It would not have immediately helped Poland's neighbour Germany unless Germany took a similar approach. It would have some residual impact, as Poland would have the ability to transmit electricity to Germany. Still, this impact would be comparatively small as Poland may not have much by way of spare capacity to share. Alternatively, assume that Poland would have displaced Russian gas by significantly increasing domestic production.[197] In this scenario, there would be more non-Russian gas available in the region. This would more immediately help Germany by making available a local gas alternative to Russia. To fully understand the difference, we need to consider context. If Poland had imported more LNG from the US, this should in principle have stimulated growth in US production to meet a growing export market. This means that the same increase in global, non-Russian production would have been achieved in both scenarios. The difference is the location of that production. In the context of gas, the location of production matters: gas is more easily moved by pipeline than LNG.[198] If there is more regional gas available, this changes the calculus as displacing Russian gas production is now comparatively cheaper. This means that Russian realpolitik leverage decreases not just with regard to one customer nation (Poland) but several customer nations (Poland, Germany, and other Central European states).

What can we learn from this scenario? The realpolitik response to threats to domestic energy security brought on by geopolitical considerations is imperfect. As energy value chains are communal, any state's action to shore up its own energy security will have a residual positive impact on the energy community at large. Still, this impact can be far from optimal or efficient. What is more, in the context of our example, it is not readily apparent that the greater global benefits of one solution will outweigh domestic political concerns speaking against it. This point does not need a counterfactual example. We in fact have seen this dynamic play

[196] Maj, 'Energy Without Russia—The Consequences of the Ukraine War and EU Sanctions on the Energy Sector in Europe' at 4, (2023) Friedrich-Ebert-Stiftung Country Report Poland, https://library.fes.de/pdf-files/bueros/budapest/20475.pdf, last accessed 16 September 2024 ('Poland's gas import dependence (net imports relative to consumption) in 2021 was 78%. The Russian share of Polish net imports was 74%, while the share of imports from Russia in domestic consumption was 56%. Qatar (13%) and the United States (9%) were also significant gas suppliers.').

[197] Andruleit et al, 'Reserves, Resources and Availability of Energy Resources' at 37–38, (December 2013) German Federal Institute for Geosciences and Natural Resources (BGR), https://www.bgr.bund.de/EN/Themen/Energie/Downloads/energiestudie_2013_en.pdf;jsessionid=17D704B1546E57D7441A22581077EE5B.internet012?__blob=publicationFile&v=2, last accessed 16 September 2024.

[198] *See* Van de Graaf & Sovacool (n 2), at 34–41.

out in real time in the same context of Russian energy leverage. Germany could have significantly reduced Russian leverage by reversing its choice to exit nuclear electricity generation. In this scenario, Germany would have required fewer LNG imports to meet energy demand. Yet, Germany held steadfastly to its withdrawal from nuclear energy even after Russian gas became unavailable.[199] Domestic environmental policy here trumped European energy security. Energy cooperation even within as consolidated a bloc as the European Union therefore has significant limitations: domestic politics still outweighed communal security concerns.[200] Domestic politics, in other words, tend to trump policies that would achieve the best overall global outcome. The rational choice of realpolitik is not altruistic. It secures national goals, not global goals.

We can observe the same dynamic in the context of the export of obsolescing energy technology to 'peripheral' states during the maturity phase of the energy cycle. This export of energy technology helps the exporting economy (and energy stakeholders within that economy). Its positive impact on the importing economy is more complicated. It locks the importing economy into a less competitive form of energy generation and consumption compared to the innovation frontier in 'core' economies. This is on the whole not efficient or altruistic. This mechanism allocates new energy technology not to where it could most helpfully be deployed from an energy perspective. (Marginal projects in core economies are frequently preferable to the most promising projects in peripheral economies due to the appreciation of risk by technology innovators.)

In the context of the current, climate-driven energy transition, this has obvious drawbacks. It explains partly why coal-fired generation remains competitive in 'peripheral' energy markets. Coal stakeholders have every interest in pushing coal-fired generation to those economies. At the same time, there are strong profits to be earned from advanced gas and renewable generation in 'core' energy markets. There is thus less support for those projects in peripheral jurisdictions. Still, as peripheral jurisdictions are likely to engage in more energy intensive production processes due to the combined effect of economic globalization and lower labour costs in the jurisdictions in question, buying behaviour in 'core' jurisdictions is likely to increase global greenhouse gas emissions. Lower labour costs mean that goods are more affordable. If goods are more affordable, consumers with greater purchasing power in 'core' economies are more likely to buy them (eg increase demand). This, in turn, increases demand for energy in the producing country. This demand is likely to be partially met by coal. This, in turn, is likely to increase overall global greenhouse gas emissions. We have thus entered a dangerous circle

[199] 'German Politicians Split as Last Nuclear Plants Close', (16 April 2023) Deutsche Welle, https://www.dw.com/en/german-politicians-split-as-last-nuclear-plants-close/a-65332978, last accessed 20 January 2025.

[200] *See ibid.*

simply by virtue of the manner in which energy cooperation functions in a world guided by an uncorrected operation of global energy cycles.

This does not mean that matters have to remain this way. The logic that supports realpolitik cooperation in foreign affairs would suggest that it is possible to lean more fully into a truly global bond of belonging. This truly global bond of belonging would seek to incorporate an exponentially increasing proportion of economies to the economic global core by means of innovation and productivity. Still, the logic of how such a system would work requires greater exploration. We would need to establish both the ends of such cooperation and the means of its implementation. The remainder of this book provides such a case.

3.7 Conclusion

The first part of this book concerned the theory of international energy governance. We have seen in this context that we traditionally think about energy governance in terms of three dominant paradigms—a command paradigm, a liberalized market paradigm, and a public contracting or utility paradigm. These paradigms all met their limits in dealing with energy challenges. They misaligned incentives between stakeholders to achieve energy systems outcomes. We therefore took a deeper look at what actually was going on in energy systems when these misalignments happened. That led us to see that energy systems respond to commons and anticommons dynamics. For energy systems to function, energy value chain stakeholders must make reasonable use of their respective contributions to those value chains for the value chains and the energy system to thrive. Energy value chains form a bond of belonging between energy system stakeholders. When that bond is honoured by all stakeholders, energy systems strive. Misalignments of incentives, by contrast, lead stakeholders to act in their own short-term self-interest without regard to the bond of belonging. It is these types of situations that lead to tragedies of the commons and disasters of the anticommons. To avoid such tragedies and disasters requires purposeful collective action. This collective action, in turn, requires governance—and regulatory—intervention.

The key to understanding energy governance therefore was not to focus on the traditional energy governance paradigms as such. It was to focus on how and why they were deployed in the first place. When we focused on this question, we saw that domestic energy governance paradigms were not actually employed in the abstract. They were intended to balance incentives to strengthen the bond of belonging between different energy stakeholders. We further saw that different phases of the energy cycle naturally required different regulatory responses to address potential misalignments. We therefore could better understand, predict, and critique governance interventions in energy systems.

In this chapter, we have now brought to the fore what was already reasonably clear from the beginning: these governance interventions themselves have international repercussions. They do not constitute a quilt of domestic energy systems and value chains. Once we enter the later stages of energy frenzies and the early stages of synergy, they constitute global value chains. These global value chains, in turn, determine how domestic energy systems can perform by making available the inputs needed for them to function. We therefore saw that a new global dimension of energy governance opened up simply from how energy systems were constituted to deliver energy outcomes to facially local energy users.

This chapter has shown two things in particular. The first is that domestic energy policies have unintended global consequences. They create incentives for global value chains to form. These global value chains, in turn, do not act in the national best interest of any state. Rather, they take on the logic of a global marketplace of its own. This, in turn, significantly impacts the domestic trajectory energy systems can take.

The second impact is that these global marketplaces themselves create geopolitical risks and opportunities. Energy is central to the functioning of the real economy. Energy vulnerabilities therefore are particularly significant. They create important targets of opportunity for geopolitical stakeholders.

In this chapter, we saw how it is that we can address these global energy problems from a realpolitik perspective. We must solve global and domestic energy policy problems together. This means responding to geopolitical imbalances in global value chains early and gradually to strengthen a global bond of belonging in internationally constituted energy systems. We saw that this is by no means an ideal governance approach: it continues to lead to significant waste in that it underperforms how a bond of belonging would organize global energy marketplaces without such geopolitical distortion. Yet, it performed better than the alternatives. The tragedy of the global energy commons and disasters of the global energy anticommons could be forestalled if not entirely avoided.

This conclusion proves particularly problematic in the context of the current, climate-driven energy transition. Both the costs and the urgency of energy transition requires us to think more fully about how we might achieve better, less wasteful outcomes. The remainder of this book will do precisely that. The point therefore must be to find a different, more cooperative way to harness the internal dynamic of global energy systems. As we will see in the remaining chapters, such an approach will lead to more growth in global energy systems. This, in turn, will support greater opportunities in global real economies and societies. We all benefit when we take the logic of realpolitik and channel it differently. How we might go about doing so is the work of Parts II and III of this book.

PART II
ENDS

4
Development as Human Flourishing

4.1 Introduction

In Part I, we outlined a theoretical approach to global energy governance premised in a global bond of belonging. This global bond of belonging tied together the links of energy value chains to national energy systems. These national energy systems, in turn, form part of one overarching global energy system, writ large. We saw that this bond of belonging works reasonably well to bring coherence to domestic energy governance approaches. The problem was that at the global level, realpolitik concerns intervened. These realpolitik interventions delivered less than optimal outcomes for global energy systems. While even these realpolitik concerns were ultimately driven by a global energy bond of belonging, the tether loosened. From an energy system internal point of view, we could therefore conclude that there will be waste—and that energy resources were, are, and will be unreasonably used—if we look at them through the logic of the global energy system.

Needless to say, once we have identified such waste, it is important to at least propose a way in which it can be remedied. The idea that waste is bad is as fundamental as it is intuitive. Waste is an outcome that is antithetical to the exercise of prudent judgement. It deprives everyone of something good—something good that might have been employed to the betterment of people, states, and peoples. The same is true in the energy setting.

Energy governance theory provides us with a helpful starting point for how we should reimagine the energy system to reduce such waste. It provides us with a point of view internal to the functioning of the energy system. This internal point of view shows us that there is a breakdown in how domestic and global energy value chains interlink with each other. They do not govern the shared energy resource community consistently with the ideas of neighbourliness and reasonable use. We are not achieving optimal outcomes, because realpolitik gets in the way. Realpolitik here is still preferable to pure rivalry. Yet even rational realpolitik is seriously limited. It is therefore natural that energy stakeholders should push for an adjustment to global energy governance to achieve less wasteful outcomes as well as energy system growth. Given that global and domestic energy governance are linked, any such change will have domestic consequences as well.

As we face the problem of waste in energy governance, we now need to refine our understanding of the bond of belonging developed in Chapter 2. In Chapter 2, I submitted that the bond of belonging is the tether that holds together all energy

A Theory of Global Energy Governance. Frédéric Gilles Sourgens, Oxford University Press. © Frédéric Sourgens 2025.
DOI: 10.1093/9780198950325.003.0004

stakeholders in a resource community of the global energy system.[1] Each of these stakeholders could function only because of the actions of other stakeholders. They are thus meaningfully bound together in energy value chains that begin with the extraction of raw material and end with the actual use of energy by an end consumer. In light of the waste introduced by the international realpolitik dimension of energy value policy on energy value chains, we now must both defend and mobilize the bond of belonging to reimagine why and how we can overcome these limitations and truly realize the benefits of the bond of belonging for the global energy system.

In terms of defending the global bond of belonging, I must provide a cogent account of how it is better to avoid waste according to some energy external metric. I have to address that waste might well serve ends outside of the energy relationships of our bond of belonging that are more desirable than an efficient functioning of global energy value chains themselves.

In Part I, we have already encountered this end: development. There is a developmental reason for improving energy systems. Energy is uniquely important for all manner of economic and social outcomes. It provides the means to achieve tasks beyond the ability of one human acting alone on the basis of their sheer muscle strength. It may sound tautological. Still, energy empowers. This empowerment allows us to produce more, and live differently than before we had the energy in question. Energy is a driver of development. Development is intuitively a good thing we should want.[2] If the bond of belonging between energy value chain participants provides us with greater developmental gains, we should indeed strengthen it. I argue in this chapter that it does. This means that the realpolitik response to geostrategic threats to energy security discussed in Chapter 3 then is truly suboptimal. We must find a way to cabin defections from the normative logic of the bond of belonging by means of a mechanism that improves net developmental outcomes over the realpolitik alternative. We need a different understanding of cooperation, which I will develop in Chapter 5.

Still, this begs the question what we mean by 'development'. Development can measure fundamentally different things. Depending on the end of the change, tying energy systems to 'development' can lead to radically different outcomes. Consequently, I must be more precise in defining what development can and ought to mean for the purposes of overcoming the realpolitik challenge to global energy governance.

This chapter therefore explores two rival views of development. The first of these conceptions is the economics-first view of development. Problematically, a purely economic view creates the very incentives described in Chapter 3—it is a constituent of the vulnerabilities of global energy value chains to geostrategic

[1] *See* Chapter 2, section 2.4.
[2] On this link, *see* Vaclav Smil, *Energy and Civilization: A History* (MIT Press 2018).

manipulation. A purely economic view further does not of itself guarantee a distributive counterweight to override the use of a realpolitik lens to govern global energy value chains. This means that an economics-only view of development leaves us at an impasse. An economic paradigm of development cannot answer the realpolitik challenge, or at least not do so fully.

When we look to what we mean by development we therefore should think of an alternative. That alternative is the second idea of development. It is a human good-centred view of development. This view of development is codified in core global human rights instruments such as the International Covenant on Civil and Political Rights (ICCPR), the International Covenant on Economic, Social, and Cultural Rights (ICESCR), and their regional counterparts. Human development as the fulfilment of human rights therefore can help us overcome the impasse that economic development alone could not master.

The human good is not measured economically. Rather, it is measured by the capabilities we each have to grow towards a good life. Of course, many of these capabilities will require money. Shelter, food, health, and education to name a few are not free. Money, in turn, is more abundant with economic growth. Still, these capabilities value more than money. They value human agency. Money is a means to supporting human agency, not an end in its own right.

This idea of human development can in principle overcome the impasse, which economic development could not overcome. The bond of belonging in energy systems ultimately serves human development. This human development, in turn, progressively realizes human rights. This progressive realization of human rights is already an obligation of states under international human rights law. As we will see, this achievement of human rights ends also constitutes global value chains and domestic energy systems in a drastically different way than an economically focused energy governance paradigm. This difference in fact responds to the realpolitik challenge, as I will discuss in more detail in Chapter 5.

4.2 Two Rival Concepts of Development

In this chapter, I will discuss two rival concepts of development: economic development and human development. Both are tremendously popular in their own right. When we think about development in lay terms, it is likely that we do so through an economic lens. Newspapers report ceaselessly on employment data, inflation, and growth (or decline) in gross domestic product (GDP).[3] Human development, on the other hand, is typically the measure we use when we question

[3] For one such recent story, *see* Casselman, 'U.S. Economy Grew at 3.3% Rate in Latest Quarter', (25 January 2024) New York Times, https://www.nytimes.com/2024/01/25/business/economy/economy-q4-gdp.html, last accessed 29 October 2024.

whether a classical understanding of economics really has all the answers. This measure has become a benchmark of UN efforts to measure and support 'sustainable development' around the world.[4]

As we look at these two yardsticks of development, it should be clear that they are not the only conceivable measures of development. For instance, one could measure development ecologically and track the growth or decline of biodiversity.[5] For that matter, one could analyse whether populations are becoming more or less religious not just by tracking attendance at religious events but also by analysing whether their behaviour broadly tracks the precepts of the relevant religions etc.[6] When I choose to contrast these two concepts of development (economic development and human development) I therefore owe an explanation. The first explanation for this choice is that both of these conceptions are about humans in society rather than about some other relationship (eg relationships with nature or relationships with God). The reason we use energy, intuitively is precisely to change what humans, acting together, can accomplish for humankind. Energy does not have ecological or religious meaning even as it does have effects on nature and may affect how we can interact in religious service (online congregations function because of the energy infrastructure in place that allow us to come together online in the first place).[7] The lens therefore fits our energy frame better than many alternatives.

I have also chosen the economic and human development lenses because they are comparatively 'thin'.[8] They do not require us to agree on a complex moral system for the lens to make sense. (For instance, a theological or religious development lens would make most sense if one agreed that a particular religion is in fact true. Yet, one could not easily persuade non-believers that such a development matrix has any meaning for them as non-believers. It is, after all, folly to try to

[4] 'Human Development Index', (2024) United Nations Development Programme, https://hdr.undp.org/data-center/human-development-index#/indicies/HDI, last accessed 29 October 2024 ('UNDP').

[5] 'Biodiversity', (2024) United Nations System of Environmental Economic Accounting, https://seea.un.org/content/biodiversity, last accessed 29 October 2024.

[6] 'Key Findings From the Global Religious Futures Project', (21 December 2022) Pew Research, https://www.pewresearch.org/religion/2022/12/21/key-findings-from-the-global-religious-futures-project/, last accessed 29 October 2024.

[7] *See eg* 'Vatican Media Live', (2024) The Holy See, https://www.comunicazione.va/en/servizi/live.html, last accessed 29 October 2024.

[8] I pick up here on the work done by John Rawls in 'Political Liberalism'. *See* John Rawls, *Political Liberalism* (Columbia University Press 1993). I fundamentally disagree with Rawls in many respects. As the remainder of this chapter will show, my own thinking is indebted to communitarianism and civic republicanism and not the liberalism championed by Rawls. Nevertheless, the point that we should have a means of understanding justice that is accessible to us no matter our particular moral and ethical point of view is certainly correct. For us to have the ability to have a discourse with each other, we must assume that there is some way for us to communicate about the topic at hand without having to agree with each other at the outset already. That is why I adopt this thinner understanding here—if energy governance is about anything, it must be about something we can all agree on even if we do not share a common faith, moral outlook, language, or culture.

persuade faith.[9]) The point of both of these development lenses is that they allow broad moral agency. They are not about measuring development according to a predetermined set of moral benchmarks. They instead measure what is available for human beings to use so as to act according to the benchmark of their choice. When we read reporting in newspapers about GDP, inflation, and employment data, we think about what we ourselves and other people can likely do or not do (buy groceries, a house, or go on a vacation). Economic choice of what to do with economic resources (eg money) is up to us. The same is true in the context of human development. Human development measures what people could do should they choose to do so. It is a measure of the agency available to them.[10] It does not prescribe how people should act but rather measures how far they might act in accordance with their own moral agency.

Adopting such thin theories of development helps us answer the 'why' question. If asked why we should eliminate waste in energy systems, we can now communicate with as broad a range of people as possible. Further, we can tell them that eliminating such waste gives our interlocutors additional options—positive development increases a conception of human agency. If a person responds that they'd rather not use that additional room for human agency, this is a choice they can make within the framework we have built. This means we do not constrain them conceptually to agree with our framework *ex ante*. At the same time, if our interlocutor would wish to constrain our room for action against our will, we would have a basis to reject such an argument on the basis of the framework we have chosen.[11] Our agency remains our own. This means that these thin theories of development are uniquely well-positioned to explain how we should address and improve the distributive outcomes we have noted in the previous chapters. We should all agree in principle that development according to one of these thin metrics is indeed a desirable goal and therefore should show us that any argument about 'national interest' that lessens them is simply misguided. Action in the 'national interest' in the context of global energy value chains makes sense as a stable choice in rational choice games like the prisoner's dilemma (we can make sure no one takes advantage of us).[12] We know, however, that it a meaningfully suboptimal choice in that cooperation would have yielded a more desirable result.[13] The question then becomes how we should cooperate not if we should cooperate.

[9] A person who accepts the prudence of a belief in God because of Pascal's wager is unlikely to gain the benefits of that wager simply, because they never truly believed in the first place.

[10] *See* Martha C Nussbaum, *Creating Capabilities, The Human Development Approach* (Harvard University Press 2011).

[11] The idea is one of liberty as non-domination. *See* Philip Pettit, *A Theory of Freedom and Government* (Oxford University Press 1997).

[12] *See* Robert Axelrod, *The Evolution of Cooperation* (Basic Books 1984) 58–62.

[13] *Ibid.*

This switch is momentous. If we can get to it, we can meaningfully defend that the waste we have identified must indeed be avoided because it is not in anyone's best interest. We must find the how to overcome it. That is precisely the work I hope to do in this chapter.

This leaves the question of how we should understand the relationship between both understandings of development. I start by saying that these concepts are rivals. This idea of rivalry must be explained. The point is not that these two concepts of development cannot and do not overlap in meaningful ways. As we will see below, they absolutely do and must. I cannot talk of human development without talking about the economy. I similarly cannot talk about the economy without talking about the people (consumers, workers, etc) in it.

The point is rather that both lenses cannot be ultimately correct at the same time. At some point, I need to make a choice between the two. If I care about human development, I am willing to make sacrifices in economic growth. If I care about economic development, the inverse is true. Both theories are related in that I will, in each case, have an explanation of why my policy choice can secure economic and human development in the long run.[14] But I cannot avoid having to make the short-term choice between both. In this short-term choice, both theories are 'rivalrous' in the sense that one must displace the other to be a meaningful guide for action.

This matters for our discussion. Most immediately, it matters for the bond of belonging. The bond of belonging holds together energy value chains. When we say that, we need to understand what the bond of belonging is for. It will work differently if it is concerned with economic growth or human growth. Energy value chains constituted for and held together by simply economic growth will form differently from energy value chains constituted for and held together by human growth. It will distribute benefits and burdens differently and consider different things 'externalities'. The point of this chapter therefore must not only be that we need to prevent waste and unreasonable use in energy systems due to our understanding of development. We must also define what we mean by 'unreasonable' or 'wasteful'. Reasonable against which yardstick? This is the work of the rest of the chapter.

[14] To put my cards on the table even at this point, I personally doubt that this 'long run' in the economic context is a realistic time horizon for the reasons that will become apparent. Economic development can and does create structural inequities that economics alone will simply not address in any time horizon worth waiting for. The inverse, critically, is not true. A human development lens will lead to greater economic growth in a foreseeable—if multi-generational—timeframe. It does so because it brings in more people to push economic growth compared to a purely economic growth model. The distinction will become apparent as we discuss the concepts in greater detail below.

4.3 Economic Development

Economic development is the currently prevalent lens of 'development' in our everyday lives. This is intuitive. When we consider the change that societies have made, it is natural to look at their standard of living. In the 1930s, there was a shortage of calories in Central Europe—the question was how to feed people. As Timothy Snyder recounts in gruelling detail, the cruelties visited upon Poland and Ukraine in the twentieth century had much to do with this caloric imperative: both the Soviet Union and National Socialist Germany looked to the region as their respective breadbasket to secure sufficient food for a hungry population.[15] When we look at the Russian Federation and Germany in the 2020s, no matter what else is the case, there has been a marked change. Russia's invasion of Ukraine was not about food as Germany's invasion of Soviet Ukraine had been a little more than eighty years earlier. Standards of living are significantly improved today in many places around the world. They are significantly improved due to economic growth, due to innovation, due to our ability to overcome existential problems through access to a global marketplace.

The idea that economic development is central to our ability to provide for the good of people around the world is not far-fetched. Look at pictures of Dubai in the 1960s and compare it to pictures of Dubai today.[16] The difference is staggering. The same is true in Seoul, Taipei, Ulaanbaatar, Lagos, or Santiago.[17] Looking at these pictures, one would assume that people living in those cities today have a far better quality of life than they did then. If one looks at pictures of the early 1950s, the same story would hold true for Berlin, Bonn, or for London (England stopped rationing food as late as the 1950s).[18] Economic lift off has empowered people. Equating social miracles with economic miracles therefore is a natural thing to do given our recent track record.

If we look at 'development' economically, our measure of 'development' is material. We look at wealth. This wealth can be expressed in different terms. Yet, the most well-known way is the idea of gross domestic product, or GDP. GDP 'measures the monetary value of final goods and services—that is, those that are bought by the final user—produced in a given period of time (say a quarter or a year)'.[19]

[15] *See* Timothy Snyder, *Bloodlands: Europe Between Hitler and Stalin* (Basic Books 2010).

[16] Jacobs, Dramatic Photos Show How Radically Dubai Has Changed in 50 Years, (14 December 2018) Business Insider, https://www.businessinsider.com/dramatic-photos-show-how-radically-dubai-has-changed-in-50-years-2018-12, last accessed 29 October 2024.

[17] *See* 'South Korea Looked Just Like North Korea 50 Years Ago', (26 July 2021) Business Insider Asia, https://www.businessinsider.in/stock-market/south-korea-looked-just-like-north-korea-50-years-ago-photos/slidelist/21199867.cms, last accessed 29 October 2024. The experience in other cities is just as startling.

[18] 'British Rationing Ends Next Summer', (6 November 1952) New York Times, https://timesmachine.nytimes.com/timesmachine/1953/11/06/84070351.html?pageNumber=11, last accessed 29 October 2024.

[19] Callen, 'Gross Domestic Product: An Economy's All', (2020) International Monetary Fund, https://www.imf.org/en/Publications/fandd/issues/Series/Back-to-Basics/gross-domestic-prod

GDP 'counts all of the output generated within the borders of a country'.[20] The greater the monetary value of final goods and services, presumably the greater the wealth of a particular country.

'Development' tracks change. Economic development tracks economic change. That means that in GDP terms, economic development refers principally to the change in GDP in a particular economy. Positive development is a growth of real GDP (that is GDP adapted to inflation).[21] A shrinking economy would see a regression of real GDP. Development would in the first place be defined in terms of measurable economic growth.

4.3(a) Economic Growth

The be-all-end-all of public discussion of the economy is economic growth as measured in terms of growth in GDP. If there is economic growth in terms of real GDP, the idea is that an economy is thriving. If real GDP is shrinking, the inverse is true. Economic growth becomes a goal for economic policy.

One of the assumptions of economic growth is that it is ultimately good for all members of society. If there is no economic growth, there are less resources available to address social needs. This reduction in resources means that fights about resource allocation in a polity are fights over the distribution of assets in zero-sum games. There is no way to make everybody better off. To make someone better off, I instead have to make somebody else worse off. Such fights over distribution are unlikely to end well. Those who lose in the allocation of resources will likely fight to gain it back. Social arrangements changing distributive outcomes therefore are unlikely to be stable—in the near term at least (if they ever are).

To the extent that there is economic growth, this reality changes. I can make everybody better off without making anyone worse off. There is more to go around. As there is more to go around, in principle any distribution of the excess does not make anyone worse off. It rather distributes net gains. Of course, there will still be fierce debates as to who should have a larger share of these net gains. Still, this fight is nowhere near as fierce as a fight over a zero-sum game. In any event, the argument is that distributing the gains broadly is likely to enhance further growth by injecting more money to be spent by a larger group of consumers. This means that there is an incentive for the holders of capital to distribute an optimal share of gains to sustain growth and thus increase their

uct-GDP#:~:text=GDP%20is%20composed%20of%20goods,the%20residents%20of%20a%20country, last accessed 6 October 2024.

[20] *Ibid.*
[21] *Ibid.*

own absolute share even if they may give up part of their relative share of GDP year-to-year.[22]

A focus on economic growth therefore is a proxy for the material wellbeing of an economy and thus a society. The more material wealth a society has, the more of that material wealth it can share within that society. This sharing means that living standards improve. As living standards improve, people directly benefit from economic growth.

Importantly, economic growth does not seem to make value judgements. It does not distinguish between bibles and guns, Shakespeare and Fabio romance novels, or Bach and Kid Rock. It is as good for the economy to spend any given amount of money on Kid Rock concert tickets as it is to go and see Rostropovich play the Bach Cello Suites. We therefore do not need to make any judgements about the human good. We can leave it to people to decide what is good for them, instead. This means that economic growth looks like an inherently neutral measure. I can convince any person that growth is good simply because it means that they will have more available to do what they themselves want to do. Who in their right mind would disagree with more?

4.3(b) Development as Eradication of Poverty

It is obviously not *quite* so simple. The assumption that an increase in GDP will help everybody in society does not account for distributive outcomes within a society. All of the increase in GDP could well be distributed to less than all members of society. This would leave the poor without a means to escape from poverty simply by means of economic growth. Development in economic terms has to account for this wrinkle.

There is a straightforward economic measure to deal with this problem. 'Development' need not only refer not only to GDP growth. It can also mean that GDP growth needs to be deployed to reduce poverty.[23] If there is growth in GDP, and there is also a reduction in poverty, those least well off are able to participate in the fruits of growth. This means that growth fuels equitable access to the new resources. Those least well off in a society are better with growth than without it.[24]

This leaves a lingering question—why should we focus on the eradication of poverty in the first place? Much research has been conducted to show a correlation between poverty reduction and economic growth.[25] Still, there is no economic

[22] For a discussion of this line of argument, *see* Alessio Terzi, *Growth for Good: Reshaping Capitalism to Save Humanity from Climate Catastrophe* (Harvard University Press 2022).

[23] Subedi, 'Declaration on the Right to Development', (2021) United Nations Audiovisual Library of International Law, https://legal.un.org/avl/pdf/ha/drd/drd_e.pdf, last accessed 6 October 2024.

[24] John Rawls, *A Theory of Justice* (Oxford University Press 1971).

[25] Adams, 'Economic Growth, Inequality, and Poverty, Findings from a New Dataset', (February 2003) World Bank Group, https://openknowledge.worldbank.org/server/api/core/bitstreams/

necessity for this link. To put the point in reverse, it is not necessarily true that poverty reduction is going to be helpful to economic growth. The opposite may well be true. Economies grow with greater consumer spending on goods and services. Productivity growth is a key metric in GDP growth.[26] The largest increase in consumer spending due to poverty reduction is likely going to be food and basic necessities. By contrast, 'mining, information, finance and insurance, and wholesale trade all enjoy above-average productivity and have grown most rapidly since 2005'.[27] If one wanted to distribute resources to benefit future economic growth, it stands to reason that more households with an interest in mining, information, finance, and insurance should receive distributive benefits from economic growth ahead of poor people. This distribution would provide additional consumer growth in high productivity industries and thus leverage growth in those industries over others. The idea that poverty reduction is going to help GDP growth *in the short to mid-term* therefore seems suspect—it may be true in some circumstances. Still, the link seems intuitively attenuated. To put it bluntly, if poverty alleviation had the economic potential for disproportionate growth, why are there food deserts, health deserts, and other avoidance strategies by industry of precisely those potential customers?[28]

The addition of poverty reduction to the concept of economic development is a fairness measure.[29] It introduces an external yardstick into economic decision-making. Economic development alone does not give us desired outcomes because it is distributively blind. This means that we need to add to an economic development lens to account for this weakness.

This in its own right suggests that there is a fundamental problem with an economic development lens. An economic development lens runs into fundamental fairness concerns. The idea of development as it has come to the fore in the context of international human rights law at a minimum insists on poverty reduction.[30] Yet, this insistence is ultimately external to an economic perspective. There is nothing within an economic lens that makes this insistence a rational guide for policy-making. To the contrary, depending upon the circumstances, it may even

fe3b85f2-bcc5-56bd-ba40-fdb450626f38/content, last accessed 6 October 2024; Adams et al, 'Macroeconomic Policy and Poverty Reduction', (August 2001) International Monetary Fund, https://www.imf.org/external/pubs/ft/exrp/macropol/eng/, last accessed 6 October 2024.

[26] *See* Atkins et al, 'Rekindling US Productivity for a New Era', (16 February 2023) McKinsey Global Institute, https://www.mckinsey.com/mgi/our-research/rekindling-us-productivity-for-a-new-era, last accessed 6 October 2024.

[27] *Ibid.*

[28] *See* Leslie, 'Food Deserts, Racism, and Antitrust Law', (2022) 110 California Law Review 1717, 1721–22.

[29] Hadiprayitno, 'Poverty', *Realizing the Right to Development* (Office of the High Commissioner on Human Rights 2013) 137, 137–38.

[30] Navanethem Pillay, *Human Rights, Health, and Poverty Reduction Strategies* (World Health Organization 2008).

be harmful. The economic lens therefore cannot get away from the idea of a more substantive engagement of the human good.[31]

The economic perspective cannot in fact rely on the winning move of the last section. There, we suggested that economic growth was good for everybody because it provided everybody with more means to achieve their own personal goals. We now need to amend this proposition. It is certainly true that it is economically desirable to have economic growth so as to diversify gains from existing economic growth to fuel future growth. The problem is that this mechanism can leave significant groups out in the cold. If one were a member of this group, it is on the whole unlikely that one would agree that one's own life had gotten better because of economic growth.[32]

To the contrary, members of this group may actually be affirmatively averse to economic growth. Economic growth typically goes along with greater resource use (whether that greater use is raw materials for goods or energy for services). This greater resource use typically involves environmental burdens. Economic rationality would suggest that these burdens fall on places with the lowest property values. Those of course are the very places that are already home to the poor.[33] Economic development therefore may in fact impoverish the poor further in terms of things they are likely to care about more than money: life expectancy.[34]

The idea of economic growth therefore provides a powerful driver for social mobilization. The problem is that it does not of itself distribute the potential for social mobilization fairly. To the contrary, left to its own devices, it is likely to distribute this potential outright *unfairly* (at least from the point of view of those it leaves behind).[35] We need a corrective outside of economics to reflect a better understanding of development. If this is the case, poverty eradication cannot itself be the be-all-end-all of development. The point is not an economic measure. The point is an ethical matter that poverty imperils human dignity. The measure of our policy success then cannot be poverty—an economic measure—but instead must look to an ethical measure that can harness and ethically correct economics.

[31] This is economist Amartya Sen's key point. For a compelling articulation, *see* Amartya Sen, *Development as Freedom* (Knopf 1999); Amartya Sen, *The Idea of Justice* (Belknap Press 2009).

[32] This point undergirds the appeal of candidates like Donald Trump. Badger et al, 'They Used to Be Ahead in the American Economy. Now They've Fallen Behind', (26 October 2024) New York Times, https://www.nytimes.com/interactive/2024/10/26/upshot/census-relative-income.html, last accessed 29 October 2024. For a theoretical explanation of the same phenomenon, *see* Francis Fukuyama, *Identity: The Demand for Dignity and the Politics of Resentment* (Profile Books 2018).

[33] Bratspies, '"Underburdened" Communities', (2022) 110 California Law Review 1933.

[34] *See ibid* at 1988 (discussing this experience in the COVID-19 context).

[35] For an interesting account of the underlying unfairness as a motivator for Donald Trump's first presidential campaign from a left-leaning point of view, *see* Hochschild, 'I Spent 5 Years With Some of Trump's Biggest Fans. Here's What They Won't Tell You', (October 2016) Mother Jones, https://www.motherjones.com/politics/2016/08/trump-white-blue-collar-supporters/, last accessed 29 October 2024.

4.3(c) The Economic View of Energy Governance

Despite these inherent flaws in an economic understanding of development, it remains uniquely 'sticky' for energy governance. It is almost a reflex to think of 'waste' in the bond of belonging in terms of economic waste. Waste and unreasonable use introduce an inefficiency into how global energy value chains hang together and, in turn, affect domestic energy value chains and energy systems. When we think of this waste, we tend to assume that this waste is *economic* waste.[36]

In terms of an economic model of development, 'waste' and 'unreasonable use' in energy systems means that resources are not optimally used to support maximum economic growth. If we apply this perspective to energy systems internally, the economic growth we wish to support is somewhat narrower than growth in the real economy. The goal is maximum growth of the energy system itself. This means that strengthening the bond of belonging and reducing waste has a more defined goal: we must develop and deploy energy value chains to maximize the relative advantage of each energy value chain stakeholder to increase productivity within each energy value chain. Further, we must expand energy access in a way that supports the deployment of the energy value chains inputs exhibiting the greatest increases in productivity with further demand growth, to fully realize the productivity gains in energy value chains.

This approach translates productivity gains in energy value chains into increased energy access (and lower prices) for the real economy. Cheaper, more abundant energy access in principle should lead to productivity growth in the real economy in the short-term.[37] In the longer-term, productivity gains through lower prices would depend on the use of energy savings by firms. To the extent that those funds are reinvested into the company to update technology and further increase efficiencies, these productivity gains should increase over time. If savings are paid out as dividends, however, productivity increases would plateau quickly and might even lag behind productivity in a higher price environment (that higher price environment causes firms to invest to increase efficiency, thus boosting productivity).[38] An energy system internal lens therefore would have to assume that firms will make such reinvestments as part of their case for broader growth in the real economy due to improvements in productivity.

Alternatively, one can take an external vantage point to energy systems and energy value chains. The goal now is to deploy energy value chains to maximize

[36] For a discussion of the idea of 'economic waste' in a private law context, *see* Farnsworth, 'Legal Remedies for Breach of Contract', (1970) 70 Columbia Law Review 1145, 1171–75.

[37] *See* André et al, 'Rising Energy Prices and Productivity: Short-Run Pain, Long-Term Gain?', (23 May 2023) Organisation for Economic Co-operation and Development Economics Working Paper No 1755, https://one.oecd.org/document/ECO/WKP(2023)8/en/pdf#:~:text=The%20estimates%20suggest%20that%20a,gains%20in%20the%20medium%20term, last accessed 7 October 2024 (discussing the short-term negative impact of energy price spikes on productivity).

[38] *Ibid.*

productivity in the real economy (as opposed to maximizing productivity in energy value chains themselves). In this scenario, 'waste' and 'unreasonable use' would refer to a loss in growth in the real economy. The bond of belonging therefore now has a slightly different goal: we must develop and deploy energy value chains to maximize the relative advantage of stakeholders in the real economy to maximize productivity gains in the real economy. This means that we must expand energy access and reduce prices where this strategy will increase productivity in the real economy and force deployment of capital towards investments in energy efficiency measures and better production processes where productivity gains could best be achieved in that way (ie we would have to anticipate whether earning gains from energy savings would be reinvested or whether one should force investment through higher price signals instead).

Finally, there is a third approach. This third approach would look to poverty reduction as a goal of energy deployment. Here, waste and unreasonable use of energy resources would be the relative poverty increase one use would cause over another energy pathway. The bond of belonging here would be about limiting global poverty through efficient energy deployment.

As it stands, the economic approach to energy governance tends to mean the first and not the other two options. Conceptually, the task of energy governance is to make available excess resources through increased productivity in energy systems. What to do with these excesses is a policy question that is ultimately unrelated to *energy* governance. Energy governance makes available tools and resources. In an economic view, energy governance does not impose value-based outcomes on society. Economic views tend to look to Kaldor-Hicks efficiency to deal with distributive questions involving the optimal use of resources. Kaldor-Hicks efficiency is a measure that helps to explain how to think about distributive outcomes, in which no party could be made better off without making another worse off. Distributive outcomes are Pareto superior if we can make someone better off without making someone else worse off. Problematically, in real life we tend to make someone worse off. Kaldor-Hicks efficiency answers that a distribution is in fact more efficient to the extent that it leads to surplus resources in excess of the loss imposed on a person who has been made worse off by a distributive change. The loser could be compensated with room to spare. The point is, though, that a party who is made worse off does not actually have to be compensated for a state to be Kaldor-Hicks efficient.[39]

We can follow this logic in an economic development understanding of a bond-of-belonging-driven energy governance approach. The bond of belonging treats waste and unreasonable use as purely internal to energy systems. It thus looks at

[39] For a discussion of the relationship between Pareto optimality and Kaldor-Hicks efficiency, *see* Posner, 'The Ethical and Political Basis of the Efficiency Norm in Common Law Adjudication', (1980) 8 Hofstra Law Review 487, 488–98.

productivity gains that could have been achieved in the real economy (as opposed to the actual investment decisions of firms). Economic waste is avoided, and energy use is reasonable, if there is a surplus in productivity and thus growth that could be translated in the long-term to the real economy. The choice of what to do with the surplus is not an energy question. It is a broader policy question about how fiscal incentives should be set to encourage investment or how government money should be spent to limit poverty. These are not concerns that are inherently energy governance concerns in an economic model.

Where does this leave us? Somewhat unsurprisingly, an economic view of development would tell us that realpolitik is inefficient and should simply be done away with wholesale. That is, what the economic model of development would tell us is that we need to lean more firmly into a Friedmanesque neoliberal idea of economic globalization.[40] Any action to the contrary is simply inefficient, wasteful, unreasonable, and therefore to be avoided. At the same time, a purely economic vision focused on growth also feeds realpolitik rivalry. As I have discussed in this section, relative economic growth matters to attract more investment. This, in turn, means that a focus of energy governance on global economic growth will counsel increasing a state's relative energy access and relative energy affordability. Instead of overcoming the realpolitik problem, an economic-growth-based global energy policy ends up unwittingly reinforcing it.

This answer also leaves us at an impasse. Globalization constituted the very value chains that are now susceptible to geostrategic manipulation.[41] It also created conditions in which the benefits and burdens from energy value chains are distributed so as to invite realpolitik as well as populist responses.

The main problem on both the realpolitik and the populist front is that an economic understanding of development has the practical effect of concentrating energy value chains. As we have seen in Chapter 3, energy systems tend to concentrate value chains in when regulators directly take issue with the price signals set during the frenzy stage of the energy cycle.[42] Price signals are significantly reduced. This, in turn, leads to the rationalization of energy value chains. The effect of this rationalization is that a smaller set of actors and industrial hubs will have a greater share of the value chain under their control. Efficiency thus leads to consolidation across value chains. This consolidation will distribute different parts of the value chain in different places around the globe—yet it will limit the number of actors who provide key inputs into the value chain. Value chains, in other words, become both more hierarchical (in terms of leading to apex actors within the value chain) and more geographically diffuse (in terms of the operations of those apex actors).

[40] For an appraisal of this form of neoliberalism in action, *see* Sebastian Edwards, *The Chile Project: The Story of the Chicago Boys and the Downfall of Neoliberalism* (Princeton University Press 2023).

[41] *See* section 3.2.

[42] *See ibid.*

This is not the answer we were looking for. It does not get us out of the realpolitik deadlock. The realpolitik deadlock grasps that actual distributions matter even though they do not matter to Kaldor-Hicks efficiency concerns (these care about theoretical distributions).[43] In the realpolitik context, they matter as between states. They confer power. This power in theory (though again the theory sounds in Kaldor-Hicks) should benefit the citizens and subjects of those states. To say that there is Kaldor-Hicks efficiency without making a state whole simply does not work. It does not capture something inherent about fairness: I must put you in a position to compete back at me if I make you distributionally worse off or you are not going to agree to the change in distribution.

The same plays out on the domestic front. Here, too, actual distributions matter. It is not enough to say to a citizen in Mississippi, where growth was 0.5 per cent, that the US economy has grown by 3.0 per cent over roughly the same time.[44] Greater economic growth is not evenly distributed. This means that realpolitik, populism, and energy protectionism can and do in fact serve to support a domestically fairer distribution of the benefits and burdens of economic growth compared to its globalist cousin. Economic development therefore may get us part of the way out of the impasse in that it tells us that a more efficient configuration of energy value chains will provide us with more means to address social goals. Still, it tells us nothing about how we should distribute those means and what goals we should achieve. It consequently cannot overcome the realpolitik challenge in its own right.

These problems are further compounded in the context of the policy assessment of the environmental impact of the energy system and energy value chains. An economic perspective begins by assessing the costs of such an environmental impact.[45] These costs are not straightforwardly negative from an economic growth perspective. They may in fact lead to economic productivity in their own right (environmental remediation, medical treatment, and drug development all are economically productive).[46] Environmental costs are only problematic to the extent that they are not offset by additional economic growth. If growth offsets environmental costs, the world with environmental burdens is still more Kaldor-Hicks efficient than a world without such costs. In such a Kaldor-Hicks efficient outcome, there would be no economic need to respond to environmental burdens, at all.

[43] Posner (n 39).

[44] 'Revisions Show US Economy Grew Faster, 2021–23, Boosting Real Incomes', (26 September 2024) The White House, https://www.whitehouse.gov/cea/written-materials/2024/09/26/revisions-show-us-economy-grew-faster-2021-23-boosting-real-incomes/, last accessed 7 October 2024; Miller, 'Mississippi Economic Outlook', (Spring 2023) Mississippi State Economist, http://www.mississippi.edu/URC/downloads/outlook/0423mseo.pdf, last accessed 7 October 2024.

[45] *See* William D Nordhaus, *The Spirit of Green, The Economics of Collision and Contagions in a Crowded World* (Princeton University Press 2021).

[46] For an interesting journalistic account, *see* David Pilling, *The Growth Delusion: Wealth, Poverty, and the Well-Being of Nations* (Penguin 2018).

An economic growth assessment of climate change follows a similar logic even as it has to deal with different datapoints. Unmitigated climate change is likely to 'reduce world real GDP per capita by more than 7 percent by 2100'.[47] Adaptation to climate change is likely to limit the long-term growth effects of unmitigated climate change.[48] Nevertheless, adaptation 'is highly unlikely to offset them entirely'.[49] An economic-development-based assessment of climate change therefore would assess the comparative efficiency of adaptation and mitigation measures. It would counsel to combine the most efficient adaptation and mitigation measures in light of this assessment to deliver the greatest possible economic output as judged by cost. Depending on the discount factor used to assess future loss of growth, this economic analysis may further find that future losses are not worth significant present investments.[50] These investments would not yield a sufficient return on investment, and will therefore be inefficient. Consequently, an economic development perspective may well suggest taking comparatively fewer measures to adapt to climate change—using available resources to invest in sectors outside of the energy sector may simply be better long-term from an economic growth perspective than adapting to climate change. While growth will stagnate in light of climate change, it will stagnate less if capital is rigorously invested in the highest growth potential as opposed to giving climate change mitigation or adaptation an ordinary preference over other approaches. Given the very real consequences of climate change for a significant number of people, communities, and states, this answer should strike one as ethically counterintuitive.[51]

4.4 Human Development

There is an alternative to an economic account of development. That account is focused on human development. This understanding of development undergirds critical, near universally subscribed human rights conventions. It therefore provides a theoretically cogent and legally salient understanding of development.

[47] Kahn et al, 'Long-Term Macroeconomic Effects of Climate Change: A Country-Country Analysis', (October 2019) IMF Working Paper, https://www.imf.org/-/media/Files/Publications/WP/2019/wpiea2019215-print-pdf.ashx, last accessed 11 November 2024.

[48] Matthew E Kahn, *Adapting to Climate Change: Markets and the Management of an Uncertain Future* (Yale University Press 2021).

[49] Kahn et al (n 47), at 9.

[50] *See* Weisbach & Sunstein, 'Climate Change and Discounting the Future: A Guide for the Perplexed', (2009) 27 Yale Law and Policy Review 433.

[51] Encyclical Letter 'Laudatio Si' of the Holy Father Francis on Care for our Common Home (24 May 2015) ¶¶ 20–26; Encyclical Letter 'Fratelli Tutti' of the Holy Father Francis on Fraternity and Social Friendship (3 October 2020) ¶ 91.

Human development asks fundamentally different questions from economics—even though both are related to each other.[52] The idea of human development begins from the premise that humans are social beings.[53] The statement that humans are social beings inherently means that we have a bond of belonging to each other. That bond holds us together in community. The bond of belonging in the energy context is part of a broader bond of belonging as further human development. In this broader context, we first ask: what does the social bond of belonging strive to achieve?

The point of a social bond of belonging is to aim for some good. This good must be the good of the community it holds together. That is, those who are held together by a bond of belonging must strive for the common good.[54] This common good includes a significant material component. A community that has more resources is likely to be able to look after the common good more effectively than a community that lacks those resources. But resources are not sought in their own right. They are tools for a purpose. That purpose is to strengthen life within the community.

The obvious next question is whether we ought to have a social bond of belonging in the first place. What is in it for me? The answer to this question is two-fold. *First*, the point of the common good of a community is to allow each member of that community to flourish.[55] That is, each member of that community must be able to live a good life. When a community provides its members with the opportunities to live a good life, the bond tying the community together strengthens because members of the community thrive in their community. *Secondly*, one can only ever thrive in community. What I need to flourish can only come from participating in a community or in a society. It is impossible to live a good life truly alone. That is why we bonded together in the first place. We need kinship, friendship, and care to live a fulfilled life.[56] We need each other. This need for each other begins with, and is rooted in, the family and familial love and radiates from there to more abstract concepts of love of country, fraternity, and human fellowship.[57]

[52] For a critical assessment of how human development must be seen at the heart of economic governance, *see* Desierto, 'The Human Right to Development as a New Foundation for International Economic Law', (2023) 31 Tulane Journal of International and Comparative Law 57.

[53] Aristotle, 'Nicomachean Ethics', *in The Complete Works of Aristotle, The Revised Oxford Translation* (Jonathan Barnes ed, W D Ross & J O Urmson trans, Princeton University Press 1984) 1729.

[54] Pettit (n 11), at 121–24; Adrian Vermeule, *Common Good Constitutionalism* (Polity 2022) 56; Cicero, 'De Legibus' I.42 in *Cicero, The Republic & The Laws* (Niall Rudd trans, Oxford University Press 1998) 112.

[55] Nussbaum (n 10), at 125–31; Alasdair MacIntyre, *After Virtue* (2nd edn, University of Notre Dame Press 1984) 189.

[56] Cicero, 'De Oficiis' I.xvii.47-xvii *in Cicero Volume XXI: On Duties* (Walter Miller trans, Harvard University Press 1913) 51–61.

[57] *See ibid.* For discussion, *see also* O'Connell & Day, 'Natural Law as Source of Extrapositive Norms', *in Oxford Handbook of the Sources of International Law* (Jean d'Aspremont & Samantha Besson eds, Oxford University Press 2018) 562.

The common good of social beings then is to provide the means for each member of the community to live a good life. Energy governance—and its bond of belonging—is just one piece in this broader enterprise. Development here then is about human development as measured by the ability to live a good life and a good life in society. Development is not measured by a single resource. It is measured against the realization of basic human capabilities through the use of resources.

4.4(a) The Good Life and Human Capabilities

When we talk about living a good life one may have visions of being well-fed on a tropical beach without a care in the world.[58] It turns out that this picture does not in fact capture a good *life* even as it captures an enjoyable moment in one's life. While it might be nice to fantasize about a life that is one endless, all-inclusive beach vacation, ethics would tell us that it is not in fact a fantasy one should pursue. This fantasy is about idleness. And such idleness taken to an extreme is in fact the opposite of living a good life.

A good life, instead, is about human flourishing.[59] Human flourishing is about agency—works—undertaken in the pursuit of realizing discerning judgement. Agency is creative. It makes something. Making something is meaningful (full of meaning).[60] 'Meaning' here reflects an understanding of being in the world as acting through the world.[61] This understanding can come only by practising care for the world. Without such care, we cannot reflect how we come to be in the world, how the world comes to be with us, and how we act in it. Without care, we thus relinquish agency because we lose the ability to contribute meaningfully to the world.[62] In other words, we lose our ability to live a good life.

What ties together the ability to live a good life is care.[63] The bond of belonging is one version of care. It should therefore be reasonably intuitive that we cannot develop care alone. Care, and flourishing more generally, is the result of one's deployment of human capabilities. These capabilities, in turn, are available to us socially. Our community has to aid us in developing the capabilities in question through the bond of belonging to the community.

[58] One of the protagonists in the Disney movie *Tangled* sings that his dream is to be 'on an island that I own, tanned and rested and alone, surrounded by enormous piles of money'. *Tangled* (2010). We may sympathize with this feeling. Still, this is not what a good life looks like even if we may think that it does.

[59] Nussbaum (n 10), at 125–31; MacIntyre (n 55), at 189.

[60] *See* Aristotle, Nicomachean Ethics 1106b35-1107a26, *in* Barnes (n 53), at 1748; MacIntyre (n 55), at 220–22.

[61] Martin Heidegger, *Sein und Zeit* (Max Niemeyer Verlag 1993).

[62] *Ibid.*

[63] Martha C Nussbaum. *The Fragility of Goodness: Luck and Ethics in Greek Tragedy and Philosophy* (revised edn, Cambridge University Press 2001) 353–55.

Martha Nussbaum has developed a catalogue of ten human capabilities that tracks our definition of the human good. These central capabilities are (1) life; (2) health; (3) bodily integrity; (4) an educated ability to use senses, imagination, and thought; (5) care for others; (6) educated, discerning judgement; (7) belonging; (8) environmental stewardship; (9) play; and (10) political and material agency.[64] These capabilities each sound intuitively desirable. Still, it is the use of these capabilities together that allows us to flourish. Just having capabilities available to us is not enough. We need to actively participate.

Each of these capabilities form part of a broader practice. This practice is at the heart of the social bond of belonging. A practice here means a "coherent and complex form of socially established cooperative human activity through which goods internal to that form of activity are realized in the course of trying to achieve those standards of excellence which are appropriate to, and partially definitive of, that form of activity, with the result that human powers to achieve excellence, and human conceptions of the ends and goods involved, are systemically extended".[65]

Life—'not dying prematurely, or before one's life is so reduced as to be not worth living' requires us to protect each other.[66] For example, life requires us to act together to rescue one another from natural disasters. Protecting each other to secure conditions for a life 'worth living' aims at an excellence of human dignity in society. Health similarly requires cooperative activity—we need to feed and shelter each other, we need to participate in inoculation drives to protect each other from fatal illness, etc. Bodily integrity requires not just protection against harm but affirmatively working to allow us to move freely from place to place—we must build an infrastructure together that allows each of us to enjoy bodily integrity. Education and judgement obviously are a result of social practices and so on. We learn to use human capabilities from each other, we protect them for each other, and we practice them with each other to achieve ends that together make for a good life, flourishing, through action in our socicty.

To say that human capabilities function in a social practice and that this practice is at the heart of the social bond of belonging means that the bond of belonging is indeed a necessary condition for the realization of human capabilities. The bond of belonging explains how we can cooperate by reference to values that are internal to the practice.[67] It sets the parameters for neighbourliness and care. It gives me my space within the social enterprise. Human capabilities therefore are about social belonging and about how that belonging empowers me to flourish in turn.

Each of these capabilities require material means. The capability of health tends to require health care, which in turn costs money etc. In pursuing the common

[64] Nussbaum (n 10), at 18–20.
[65] MacIntyre (n 55), at 187.
[66] Nussbaum (n 10), at 18–20.
[67] MacIntyre (n 55), at 187.

good for society through the realization of these capabilities we must make available the material preconditions for their realization to each other to the maximum of available resources. This does not mean that we need to collectivize economic organization—to the contrary, such a structure would limit available resources in the long-term by limiting innovation and the potential for growth that is so central to any distributive discussion. Still, we need to share the benefits of growth such as to make available the means to support human development. In other words, Kaldor-Hicks efficiency is decidedly not enough.[68] Purely relative gains must be reinvested to maintain human capabilities. Growth further must also be fairly shared, for example by means of ordinary fiscal mechanisms.[69] This fiscal means must then be deployed by society towards the common good, that is, the progressive realization of human capabilities as flourishing in society.[70] This progressive realization of human capabilities—and their use towards human flourishing—is human development.

Human development should be similarly as enticing as the economic model of development. I do not prescribe how people are to live a good life. A good life by definition requires each person to determine that good life for themselves through human agency. Human development simply requires that we make available the means and opportunity so that everyone is able to live a good life. It is difficult to disagree with such a prescription. Why should we not act so as to make it possible for as many people as possible to live a good life?

One might ask whether someone else's ability to live a good life takes away from mine. As policies distribute access to resources, one may feel that they are themselves part of a zero-sum game.[71] This impression departs from a mistaken

[68] *See* Sen (n 31), at 116–20.

[69] *Ibid.*

[70] Nussbaum (n 10), at 18–20; Vermeule (n 54), at 59. A reference to both Nussbaum and Vermeule might at first blush appear odd given that one would associate each author with fundamentally different political points of view. On this critical point, both agree as both draw on fundamentally Aristotelian source materials (together with Stoic and civic republican source materials) for their respective positions. Vermeule notes that 'human flourishing, including the flourishing of individuals, is itself essentially, not merely contingently, dependent upon the flourishing of the political communities (including ruling authorities) within which humans are always born, found, and embedded'. Vermeule (n 54), at 59. Nussbaum takes up the same point in Aristotle but pushes to extend the relevant community within which such flourishing occurs. Nussbaum (n 10), at 129-32. Both thus tie human flourishing to being in society in a non-trivial way. That is, society is not just the provider of material means for human flourishing. Human flourishing rather can only ever take place in society because a good life is itself inherently social.

[71] As I will explain in Chapter 6, the common good is inherently non-rivalrous. Yet, policy choices can at times appear to be rivalrous at the margins by adopting one path to progressively realizing the common good over another. These distributive outcomes should be short lived as progressive realization of the common good continues. Further, the realization of the common good appears rivalrous only in the sense of 'megalothymia' of making a different group that used to be worse off than mine better off as opposed to making my group absolutely worse off. As Francis Fukuyama points out, however, in a society that does not pursue a common good premised in a shared identity, this policy choice will be taken as partisan conduct. *See* Fukuyama (n 32).

premise.[72] Excellence—human flourishing—is a social exercise.[73] We teach each other to live well and to deploy our human capabilities together towards excellence. That is why artists and novelists create such fantastic works of art in close proximity to one another: they improve each other's work simply by observing each other's exploits and engaging with each other to improve themselves. If my neighbours flourish, I am more likely to flourish myself because human capabilities are a social practice. Human capabilities and human flourishing are not rivalrous. They are mutually supporting.[74] The bond of belonging holds together this mutual support and realizes human capabilities in society.

4.4(b) Human-Rights-Based Belonging as Realization of Human Capabilities

Human development is grounded in an ethical point of view. As we have seen in the last section, it is about providing us with the means to live good lives. It is about supporting rather than restraining agency. This understanding of development does not have the distributive problems we encountered in the economic context. The social practice of the bond of belonging non-rivalrously realizes human development by extending deeper human capabilities to more people. We now have a yardstick by which to measure distributive concerns through the bond of belonging. This distributive concern requires us first to use resources so that we place others in a position to be able to 'compete back' at us within society and use their own agency.[75] If our course of conduct aimed at improving material conditions for ourselves also harms others, we must share harms and benefits proportionately. Proportionately here means that we should encourage growth (and thus greater resources) while also limiting the negative impact on vulnerable communities.

The lens of the bond of belonging as human development has left the purely ethical sphere. The United Nations Development Programme uses human development to track development.[76] It is at the heart of UN sustainable development

[72] Its premise of 'megalothymia' insists on social hierarchy and as such admits the social nature of flourishing. *Ibid.* It refuses to extend the idea of a common good to all groups in society by insisting on hierarchical ordering. It resembles the Spartan state and its relationship to the helots. This relationship highlights the cost of megalothymia—institutionalized civil war that itself severely limits policy choices. Donald Kagan, *The Outbreak of the Peloponnesian War* (Cornell University Press 1969) 10–27.

[73] *See* MacIntyre (n 55), at 202.

[74] Vermeule (n 54), at 59.

[75] This pattern was at the heart of Athenian farming. This practice, in turn, laid the foundation for Athenian democracy and the philosophical underpinnings of the common good in conservative philosophers such as Aristotle (conservative in their own social context, as opposed to necessarily conservative in ours). *See* Victor Davis Hanson, *The Other Greeks, The Family Farm and the Agrarian Roots of Western Civilization* (Free Press 1995) 127–78.

[76] UNDP (n 4).

goals.[77] It is thus not a theoretical construct only. It is a measure of development that is already actively guiding global policy-making.

This human development lens is also at the heart of broadly subscribed, constitutive global human rights instruments.[78] Several of the human capabilities we outlined in the previous section are at the heart of the most traditional understanding of human rights, namely civil and political rights. The International Covenant on Civil and Political Rights (ICCPR), drafted in the mid-1950s and concluded in 1966, is a crucial framework convention emblematic for 'first-generation' human rights. It includes the following critical protections for human capabilities—turning them from capabilities to international human rights enforceable against the state in their own right:

- *The Right to Life (Capability 1).* Article 6(1) of the ICCPR codifies that '[e]very human being has the right to life'. It goes on to say that this 'right shall be protected by law' and that '[n]o one shall be arbitrarily deprived of his life'. Article 6(1) of ICCPR protects the first human capability needed for human flourishing—life—by requiring states to take active steps to protect life.[79] To belong means that my political community respects and protects my right to exist.
- *The Right to Bodily Integrity (Capability 3).* ICCPR Articles 8, 9, 11, and 17 protect bodily integrity. Article 9 protects bodily integrity against the state. It provides that '[e]veryone has the right to liberty and security of person'.[80] It goes on to prohibit arbitrary arrest or detention and entitle persons arrested or detained a right to the due process of law. Article 8 compels states to take action to protect our bodily integrity as against other members of our community by requiring states to take care to prevent slavery, servitude, or forced labour.[81] Article 11 adds that states must not allow their justice system to be used as a means to imprison anyone 'merely on the ground of inability to fulfil a contractual obligation'.[82] Article 17 meanwhile requires states to protect the privacy of those under their jurisdiction.[83] To belong means that my political community respects my liberty, protects my security of person, and does not intrude upon my seclusion and privacy.

[77] 'Transforming Our World: The 2030 Agenda for Sustainable Development', (25 September 2015) United Nations General Assembly Resolution 70/1.

[78] *See* Diane A Desierto, *Public Policy in International Economic Law, The ICESCR in Trade, Finance, and Investment* (Oxford University Press 2015) 127.

[79] International Convention on Civil and Political Rights (1966) (ICCPR), art 6(1); *see also* European Convention on Human Rights (1950) (ECHR), art 2; American Convention on Human Rights (1969) (AmCHR), art 4; African Charter on Human and Peoples' Rights (1981) (ACHPR), art 4; Asian Human Rights Charter (1998) (AHRC), ¶ 3.2.

[80] ICCPR, art 9; ECHR, art 5(1); AmCHR, art 7(1); ACHPR, art 4; AHCR, ¶ 4.3.

[81] ICCPR art 8; ECHR, art 4; AmCHR, art 6(1); ACHPR, art 5; AHCR, ¶ 2.4.

[82] ICCPR, art 11; ECHR, art 1; AmCHR, art 7(7).

[83] ICCPR, art 17; ECHR, art 8; AmCHR, art 11(2).

- *The Right to Freedom of Thought (Capability 4).* ICCPR Article 18 provides for 'freedom of thought, conscience, and religion'.[84] This, together with the privacy protections codified in Article 17, restrict the state from interfering with my ability to form thoughts and opinion. Article 19 goes on to protect the right to hold opinions.[85] This means that I am not only allowed to have thoughts and opinions—I am also allowed to share them by means of the freedom of expression. To belong means that my political community does not restrain my ability to think and believe for myself and share my thoughts and beliefs with others in a public forum.
- *The Right to Care for Others (Capability 5).* ICCPR Article 23 follows the approach outlined in the last section that the 'family is the natural and fundamental group unit of society and is entitled to protection by society and the State'.[86] It thus provides the basic unit of care in the family and affords it protection by the state.[87] It goes on to guarantee the right to marry and found a family.[88] ICCPR extends this basic unit of society to other endeavours by recognizing the right of assembly and association in Article 22 discussed below.[89] To belong means that my political community respects and protects my belonging to my family and does not interfere with the family.
- *The Right to Belonging (Capability 7).* One of the most important components of the right to belonging is that one must have 'the social bases of self-respect and nonhumiliation; being able to be treated as a dignified person whose worth is equal to that of others'.[90] This right to belong is undergirded in the ICCPR by the prohibition of discrimination in its Article 26.[91] Article 26 codifies a right to 'equal protection of the law' and requires that 'the law shall prohibit any discrimination and guarantee to all persons equal and effective protection against discrimination on any ground such as race, colour, sex, language, religion, political or other opinion, national or social origin, property, birth or other status'.[92] ICCPR Article 23 further affirmatively protects the right to belong to a family.[93] Article 22 protects the right to belong to groups outside the family.[94] Article 18 expressly recognizes the freedom of religion. To belong means that my political community protects me as an equal and allows me to form social attachments outside of the political community.

[84] ICCPR, art 18; ECHR, art 9; AmCHR, art 12; ACHPR, art 8; AHRC, ¶ 6.3.
[85] ICCPR, art 19; ECHR, art 10; AmCHR, art 13(3); ACHPR, art 9; AHRC, ¶ 7.2.
[86] ICCPR art 23; ECHR, arts 8 & 12; AmCHR, art 17; ACHPR, art 18.
[87] AmCHR, art 17; ACHPR, art 18.
[88] ICCPR, art 23; ECHR, art 12; AmCHR, art 17(2).
[89] ICCPR, art 22.
[90] Nussbaum (n 10), at 19.
[91] ICCPR, art 26.
[92] *Ibid*; ECHR, art 14; AmCHR, arts 1(1) and 24; ACHPR, art 3; AHRC, ¶ 5.2.
[93] ICCPR, art 23; ECHR, art 12; AmCHR, art 17(2).
[94] ICCPR, art 22; ECHR, art 11; AmCHR, art 16; ACHPR, art 10; AHRC, ¶ 15.2(f).

- *The Right to Political and Material Agency (Capability 10).* ICCPR Article 22 codifies that '[e]veryone shall have the right to freedom of association with others, including the right to form and join trade unions'.[95] Article 25 goes no to protect the right to 'take part in the conduct of public affairs'.[96] Together, these two rights require the state to allow political agency. To belong means that my political community does not impair my political agency.

These rights are mostly negative. They require the state to refrain from acting.[97] To the extent that the state must act, it is required to put in place the mechanisms of administration of justice that will allow people to vindicate their own rights.[98] These rights do not require the state to *make policy* or do so in a particular way. In fact, it is only a slight exaggeration to state that most of these rights could be safeguarded simply by pushing the presence of the state to a libertarian vanishing point.[99] The political community so far forms with a minimal state charged mostly with the establishment of a system of justice and little else. The rights codified in the ICCPR consequently do not go far enough to address the distributive problems arising in policy-making. In many ways, this conception of rights, when thought through to its logical conclusion, denies that these distributive problems are problems for the political community in the first place.[100]

Denying the existence of distributive problems in the energy context is reasonably self-defeating. We have seen that state action is frequently critical in launching and managing energy value chains as well as the national energy system. We have also seen that this state action has significant impacts on global energy value chains. We therefore must grapple with distributive problems to stabilize global energy value chains in light of geostrategic threats to these very value chains. What is more, we must do so in a manner that is more efficient than realpolitik adjustments as this realpolitik response to geostrategic threats proved significantly wasteful.

The answer to how we should conceive of the distributive problem in a human rights frame comes from positive human rights. These distributive problems are addressed in treaties like the ICESCR, concluded like the ICCPR in 1966. The ICESCR creates positive human rights that require the state to create material

[95] ICCPR, art 22; ECHR, art 11; AmCHR, art 16; ACHPR, art 10; AHRC, ¶ 15.2(f).

[96] ICCPR, art 25; AmCHR, art 23; ACHPR, art 13; AHRC, ¶ 5.2.

[97] Philip Alston & Ryan Goodman, *International Human Rights* (Oxford University Press 2013) 527–28.

[98] *See* AmCHR, art 7(6).

[99] *See* Robert Nozick, *Anarchy, State, and Utopia* (Basic Books 1974). Even if the exaggeration is slight, it remains an exaggeration. Thus, the question of the right to life in the context of environmental protection would suggest that absolute binaries are dangerous things. *See* The Environment and Human Rights (State Obligations in Relation to the Environment in the Context of the Protection and Guarantee of the Rights to Life and to Personal Integrity – Interpretation and Scope of Articles 4(1) and 5(1) of the American Convention on Human Rights), Advisory Opinion OC-23/18, Inter-Am Ct HR, (ser A) No 23 (15 November 2017).

[100] Nozick (n 99).

circumstances for human flourishing. The core principle that runs through the ICESCR, codified in its Article 2(1), requires that

> Each State Party to the present Covenant undertakes to take steps, individually and through international assistance and co-operation, especially economic and technical, to the maximum of its available resources, with a view to achieving progressively the full realization of the rights recognized in the present Covenant by all appropriate means, including particularly the adoption of legislative measures.[101]

The key switch in the ICESCR is that it does not just require compliance with rights (as was the case with ICCPR). Rather, it also requires the realization of rights.[102] This realization of rights means that states must not just respect human rights in the sense of not interfering with rights by means of state action. States must also take positive steps to protect and fulfil human rights. Protection requires states to take steps to prevent others from violating individual or group rights. Fulfilment, in addition, demands that states make and institute policies that put people, groups, and peoples in a position of enjoying their rights.[103] Fulfilment in particular requires states to take affirmative steps through policy-making to nurture the human capacities of persons within their jurisdiction.

ICESCR affirmatively seeks the realization (or fulfilment) of rights that coincide with the human capabilities we have outlined in this chapter already. The ICESCR makes clear that the realization of human capabilities are inherently interconnected. This means that the realization of rights with regard to one capability requires the realization of all rights supporting other capabilities. This is why the fulfilment of rights requires policy judgement to assure the progressive realization of all rights (as opposed to any mechanical attempt to rank rights *ex ante*).[104]

- *The Right to Life (Capability 1).* The ICESCR does not expressly codify the idea of a right to life. Still, the right to life permeates the whole of the Convention. To understand how it does, consider how the Human Rights Committee explains the right to life in its General Comment No 36 of 3 September 2019, discussing the right to life codified in ICCPR Article 6(1).[105] That comment notes that 'Environmental degradation, climate change and unsustainable development constitute some of the most pressing and serious threats to the ability of present and future generations to enjoy the right to life'.[106] The right

[101] ICESCR, art 2(1); AmCHR, art 26.
[102] ICESCR, art 2(1).
[103] Alston & Goodman (n 97), at 182.
[104] ICESCR, art 2(1).
[105] Human Rights Committee, General Comment No 36 (Right to Life) (3 September 2019).
[106] *Ibid* at ¶ 62.

to life therefore is broader than just bare subsistence. As noted by the Asian Human Rights Charter: '[t]he right to life is not confined to mere physical or animal existence but includes the right to every limb or faculty through which life is enjoyed. It signifies the right to live with basic human dignity, the right to livelihood, the right to a habitat or home, the right to education and the right to a clean and healthy environment for without these there can be no real and effective exercise or enjoyment of the right to life.'[107] Acting to limit threats to the right to life requires more than state restraint or protection. It requires the state to deploy resources through policy-making. This deployment of resources through policy-making aims at the protection of human dignity and not just bare life.[108] That is precisely what all the rights codified in ICESCR viewed together hope to achieve. As the Committee on Economic, Social, and Cultural Rights noted in the context of its General Comment No 12 on the Right to Adequate Food of 14 May 1999, the rights in ICESCR and ICCPR when viewed together are intended to uphold 'the inherent dignity of the human person'.[109] The realization of the conditions needed to uphold the inherent dignity of the human person is what ICESCR aims to achieve. That is why the right to life—though not expressly mentioned in the Convention—is so central to its design. To belong means that my political community, and I as a member of that community, must realize the conditions in which I and my fellow community members can live a dignified life.

- *The Right to Health (Capability 2)*. ICESCR Article 12 codifies a right 'the enjoyment of the highest attainable standard of physical and mental health'.[110] In addition, ICESCR Article 9 codifies a right to social insurance.[111] This right to social insurance is an important backstop to the right to health given that health and the need to draw on social insurance frequently coincide. There is thus a means for persons to support their own health in times of crises. The fulfilment of this right also includes '[t]he creation of conditions which would assure to all medical service and medical attention in the event of sickness'.[112] The right to housing, discussed in the context of the right to bodily integrity, similarly are relevant to the right to health. As with the rights related to other core human capabilities, General Comment No 14 of the Committee on Economic, Social, and Cultural Rights of 12 May 2000 highlights that health is 'indispensable for the exercise of other human rights'.[113] It further notes

[107] AHRC, ¶ 3.2.
[108] *Ibid.*
[109] Committee on Economic, Social, and Cultural Rights, General Comment No 12 (Right to Adequate Food) (14 May 1999), ¶ 4.
[110] ICESCR, art 12; ACHPR, art 16; AHRC, ¶ 7.1.
[111] ICESCR, art 9.
[112] ICESCR, art 12(d).
[113] Committee on Economic, Social, and Cultural Rights, General Comment No 14 (Right to Health) (12 May 2000), ¶ 1.

that the 'right to health is closely related to and dependent upon the realization of other human rights, as contained in the International Bill of Rights, including the rights to food, housing, work, education, human dignity, life, non-discrimination, equality, the prohibition against torture, privacy, access to information, and the freedoms of association, assembly and movement'.[114] Importantly, General Comment No 14 highlights that the realization of the highest attainable standard of health depends a state's 'available resources'.[115] To belong means that my political community, and I as a member of that community, care for the wellbeing of community members by creating and supporting institutions charged with maintaining my health and the health of my fellow community members.

- *The Right to Bodily Integrity (Capability 3).* ICESCR Article 11 centrally recognizes the 'the right of everyone to an adequate standard of living for himself and his family, including adequate food, clothing and housing, and to the continuous improvement of living conditions'.[116] Article 11 adds in particular that there is a right to be free from hunger, highlighting the link between health and the conditions at issue in the provision.[117] This protection is central to the right to health as it provides the material conditions for a healthy life. General Comment No 4 of the Committee on Economic, Social and Cultural Rights, submitted on 13 December 2014, expressly address the right to adequate housing.[118] General Comment No 12 of 12 May 1999 highlights the importance of the right to adequate food, noting in particular that 'the right to adequate food is indivisibly linked to the inherent dignity of the human person and is indispensable for the fulfilment of other human rights'.[119] To belong means that my political community, and I as a member of that community, establish the institutions that foster my access, and the access of all community members, to the basic material means needed to live a good life.
- *The Right to Freedom of Thought (Capability 4).* ICESCR Article 15(3) adds to the demands for respect of freedom of conscience and the private sphere. It requires states 'to respect the freedom indispensable for scientific research and creative activity'.[120] This respect stands in the context of an obligation codified in ICESCR Article 15(2) to 'achieve the full realization of this right shall include those necessary for the conservation, the development and the

[114] *Ibid* at ¶ 3.
[115] *Ibid* at ¶ 9.
[116] ICESCR, art 11; AHRC, ¶ 7.1.
[117] ICESCR, art 11.
[118] Committee on Economic, Social and Cultural Rights, General Comment No 4 (Right to Adequate Housing) (13 December 2014).
[119] Committee on Economic, Social and Cultural Rights, General Comment No 12 (Right to Adequate Food) (12 May 1999), ¶ 4.
[120] ICESCR, art 15(3); AmCHR, art 26.

diffusion of science and culture'.[121] Without this diffusion, the right to freedom of thought would be meaningfully limited. To belong means that my political community, and I as a member of that community, act as stewards of cultural and scientific growth by supporting cultural and scientific institutions.

- *The Right to Care for Others (Capability 5).* Like ICCPR Article 23, ICESCR Article 10 recognizes the significance of the family as the 'natural and fundamental group unit of society, particularly for its establishment and while it is responsible for the care and education of dependent children'.[122] It now requires the state to accord the 'widest possible protection and assistance' to the family.[123] To belong means that my political community, and I as a member of that community, support the unique place of the family in political community.
- *The Right to Educated, Discerning Judgment (Capability 6).* ICESCR Article 13 recognizes 'the right of everyone to education'.[124] It provides further that the goal of education is 'the full development of the human personality and the sense of its dignity, and shall strengthen the respect for human rights and fundamental freedoms'.[125].Article 14 requires states promptly to make available free primary education after ICESCR enters into effect with regard to them.[126] Article 15(1)(c) continues to recognize a right to 'benefit from the protection of the moral and material interests resulting from any scientific, literary or artistic production of which he is the author'.[127] General Comment No 13 of 8 December 1999 highlights the importance of the realization of this right for the realization of all rights protected by ICESCR, noting that '[a]s an empowerment right, education is the primary vehicle by which economically and socially marginalized adults and children can lift themselves out of poverty and obtain the means to participate fully in their communities'.[128] To belong means that my political community, and I as a member of that community, establish and participate in institutions that foster learning and grant access to a basic education.
- *The Right to Belonging (Capability 7).* ICESCR Article 15(1)(a) recognizes the right to 'take part in cultural life'.[129] Cultural life sets the parameters in which belonging can itself development. Cultural life presents the context in which, and the opportunity for, meaningful attachments to form to broader groups that experience, and related to, the world like me in a significant way

[121] ICESCR, art 15(2); ACHPR, art 17(2).
[122] ICESCR, art 10; ICCPR, art 23; ECHR, arts 8 and 12; AmCHR, art 17; ACHPR, art 18.
[123] ICESCR, art 10.
[124] ICESCR, art 13; ECHR, art 2; ACHPR, art 17(1); AHRC, ¶ 3.2.
[125] ICESCR, art 13.
[126] *Ibid* at art 14.
[127] *Ibid* at art 15(1)(c).
[128] Committee on Economic, Social and Cultural Rights, General Comment No 13 (Right to Education) (8 December 1999), ¶ 1.
[129] ICESCR, art 15(1)(a).

(religious belonging, artistic and literary belonging, scientific belonging etc). To belong means that my political community, and I as a member of that community, support and defend cultural institutions.

- *The Right to Environmental Stewardship (Capability 8).* ICESCR Article 12 recognizes as part of the right to health that steps to realize the right to health include 'the improvement of all aspects of environmental and industrial hygiene'.[130] General Comment No. 14 further specifies that this right includes 'the requirement to ensure an adequate supply of safe and potable water and basic sanitation; the prevention and reduction of the population's exposure to harmful substances such as radiation and harmful chemicals or other detrimental environmental conditions that directly or indirectly impact upon human health'.[131] To belong means that my political community, and I as a member of that community, act as environmental stewards to protect the environment of the community for the community.
- *The Right to Play (Capability 9).* The right to play is not included expressly in the ICESCR. As General Comment No 21 of 20 November 2009 clarifies, it is included in the right to cultural life codified in Article 15.[132] General Comment No. 21 explains that 'culture, for the purpose of implementing article 15 (1) (a), encompasses, inter alia, ways of life, language, oral and written literature, music and song, non-verbal communication, religion or belief systems, rites and ceremonies, sport and games, methods of production or technology, natural and man-made environments, food, clothing and shelter and the arts, customs and traditions through which individuals, groups of individuals and communities express their humanity and the meaning they give to their existence, and build their world view representing their encounter with the external forces affecting their lives'.[133] General Comment No 21 explains part of the reason play is important— '[c]ulture shapes and mirrors the values of well being and the economic, social and political life of individuals, groups of individual and communities'.[134] In play, we can relate to culture in a uniquely joyful way.[135] Play further provides us with a store of shared experiences from play in which to establish and test cultural meaning in play and through play in a broader cultural context.[136] To belong means that my political community, and I as a member of that community, will support my enjoyment of leisure in society and that of my fellow members in community.

[130] ICESCR, art 12.
[131] General Comment No 14 (n 113), at ¶ 15.
[132] General Comment No 21 (Right of Everyone to Take Part in Cultural Life) (20 November 2009).
[133] *Ibid* at ¶ 13.
[134] *Ibid.*
[135] Nussbaum (n 10), at 19.
[136] Ludwig Wittgenstein, 'Philosophische Untersuchungen', *in Werkausgabe* (Suhrkamp Verlag 1984) 255.

- *The Right to Political and Material Agency (Capability 10).* ICESCR Article 6 recognizes the right to work, including 'the right of everyone to the opportunity to gain his living by work which he freely chooses or accepts'. The realization of this right requires states to provide training and guidance and make policies 'to achieve steady economic, social and cultural development and full and productive employment under conditions safeguarding fundamental political and economic freedoms to the individual'. Here, the economic perspective outlined in the first part of the chapter becomes a tool to achieving material agency needed for human flourishing. To belong means that my political community, and I as a member of that community, will make decisions to all members of the community to flourish in its economy by means of their own labour and intellectual pursuits.

This frame has been further strengthened in the UN Convention on the Right to Development. This Convention sets out that 'the human person and peoples are the central subjects of development and must be the active participants and beneficiaries of the right to development'.[137] It explains that 'development, as described in the present Convention, is essential for the improvement of living standards and the welfare of human persons and peoples and contributes to the enjoyment of all human rights'.[138] The Convention then codifies that the right to development entitles every human person and people 'to participate in, contribute to and enjoy civil, cultural, economic, political and social development that is indivisible from and interdependent and interrelated with all other human rights and fundamental freedoms'.[139]

The Convention on the Right to Development further squarely places the distributive question with which we began at the core of the right to development in Article 4(2). Article 4(2) is a kind of pivot for the right to development. It begins with the guarantee that '[e]very human person and all peoples have the right to active, free and meaningful participation in development'.[140] This formulation recalls the idea of human development as a means for human flourishing through free agency—making something meaningful through discerning judgement by participating in care for the world.

This plainly is not enough. There is necessarily a distributive component to development. We must make available the resources for every human person and all peoples to participate actively, freely, and meaningfully in development. Article

[137] Convention on the Right to Development, art 3(a), https://www.ohchr.org/sites/default/files/2022-04/A_HRC_WG_2_23_2_AEV.pdf, last accessed 1 November 2024.

[138] *Ibid* at art 3(d).

[139] *Ibid* at art 4(1). For a discussion of the central importance of art 4 to the Convention, *see* Desierto (n 52), at 68–70.

[140] Convention on the Right to Development (n 137) art 4(2).

4(2) also addresses this distributive aspect. It codifies that every person and all peoples have a right to 'the fair distribution of benefits resulting therefrom'.[141]

How are we to understand this distributive idea of fairness? Plausibly, given the link of the right to development to human development and the link of human development to human flourishing, we should look at this fairness concern through the lens of the practice underlying the social bond of belonging. This practice required us to deviate from the economic understanding of Kaldor-Hicks efficiency.[142] It is not enough that excess growth could compensate people who are losing out due to policy changes. We must in fact make everyone progressively better off in terms of their capabilities for human development. That means that we may not burden persons and peoples to provide a benefit to third parties. We must share benefits and burdens alike. How do we share fairly? In a social practice, we share fairly if we distribute the load of burdens so as to allow for the greatest exercise of human excellence.[143] We cannot trade flourishing of one for the flourishing of another—rather, we must aim to realize human flourishing for all persons and peoples progressively.

This last point may seem strange to our economically minded ears. Policies always create material trade-offs and we fight about improving or at least protecting our own relative share. Human development rejects this lens as self-defeatingly hedonistic and outright slothful. Human development is precisely non-rivalrous because human flourishing of any one person requires the support and flourishing of many others. It is premised in a social practice that is strengthened with each new participant. One might call this point of view moralistically naïve—'that is not how the real world works'. After all, if it did, why would we still fight over our respective relative shares?

And yet, one of the fundamental truths at the heart of the economic perspective is that competition is good. It drives innovation. Innovation big and small creates efficiencies. These efficiencies cause us to have to use less for one task, leaving us with more to invest elsewhere. This fuels growth. This growth done right is frequently exponential at the point of major breakthroughs. This exponential growth, in turn, supports a significant increase in standards of living.[144]

If we analyse this economic truth discerningly, we discover a virtuous social practice that follows the same principles of excellence as human development. Economic activity is quintessentially social activity. Needless to say, we do not compete alone. A monopolist would precisely not compete or innovate but simply collect the rents inherent in their monopolist position. The same is true of other

[141] *Ibid.*
[142] Posner (n 39).
[143] *See* Vermeule (n 54), at 59; John Finnis, *Natural Law and Natural Rights* (Oxford University Press 1980) 169.
[144] Philippe Aghion, Céline Antonin, & Simon Bunel, *The Power of Creative Destruction, Economic Upheaval and the Wealth of Nations* (Harvard University Press 2021).

market actors who disproportionately benefit from markets dependent upon political favour.[145] We compete as a social practice. Not only that, the more competitors there are, the more robust the practice and the greater its collective rewards. We improve at this form of economic practice because we push the innovation frontier further.[146] We learn from each other. Draw on a pool of global ideas that help each of us invent and thus compete better (as we have seen in the energy context already).[147] The better we become at this form of competition, the more we have both in real terms and in terms of our standards of living. If we focus on growth, we precisely should not focus on protecting relative shares of a fixed pie. We must focus on growing the pie. And this growth focus only works as a social practice.

If we want to focus on even just economic growth, we still need each other. How do we need each other? We need as many people to be as educated as possible to push the innovation frontier and thus push me at the innovation frontier. This education, in turn, depends on other human capabilities—I do not learn well if I have to live with food insecurity or lack shelter or health. But this means that we need as many people as possible to flourish. With as many people at the fullest realization of their human flourishing as possible we maximize cultural capital (scientific, literary, artistic, and religious creative insight). This is what ultimately pushes the bounds of innovation as far as is at all feasible. This benefits me more materially than any other course of conduct could, everything else being equal. Even as *homo economicus*, the artificial economic human, we maximize our self-interest (ie exhibit the virtue of excellence of this mode of being) only if we are virtuous together.

4.4(c) Development as Human Empowerment

Development along the lines of human capabilities and human flourishing is ultimately about empowerment. Empowerment in the human rights context can be used narrowly. Then, it refers to human rights efforts to increase control over their lives by disadvantaged groups and communities.[148] This definition is helpful due to its focus on communities carrying a facially disproportionate burden. Still, it also at first blush appears too narrow. The problem is that empowerment appears to be only for a subset of people as opposed to a universal idea.

[145] *Ibid*; *see also* Daron Acemoglu & James A Robinson, *The Narrow Corridor: States, Societies and the Fate of Liberty* (Penguin 2019) 133.

[146] Aghion (n 144) at 61.

[147] Thomas Hughes, *Networks of Power, Electrification in Western Society 1880-1930* (Johns Hopkins University Press 1983).

[148] Di Giovanni & Bercovich, 'Legal Empowerment in Informal Settlements: Lessons on Using the Law to Overcome Urban Exclusion and Poverty in the Global South', (2021) 54 NYU Journal of International Law & Politics 93.

There is a broader sense of empowerment. Empowerment is about increasing the scope for, and efficacy of, agency.[149] By extension, empowerment in the human rights context increases human agency. Empowerment does so for everyone. That is, empowerment is not tied to a particular group or a particular location.

Instead, empowerment increases human agency wherever and whenever persons, groups, or peoples find themselves without the needed resources or support to live a flourishing life. At some point, agency is no longer curtailed by external constrains or a lack of support. At some point, we can fend for ourselves. Of course, a billionaire can fail to live a flourishing human life.[150] In that context, the problem is not one of empowerment but rather one of using one's agency towards human flourishing. By implication, this means that empowerment at some point stops being a meaningful metric. At some point, human flourishing is up to us and to use of human capabilities as opposed to us lacking human capabilities. Still, the point is that empowerment is generalizable to everyone as opposed to being limited to the empowerment of certain predetermined groups.

The human development lens shows that the narrow and the broad understanding of empowerment still get at the same thing. Empowerment offers a counterpoint to the *status quo ante*.[151] There is someone who needs to be empowered. If someone needs to be empowered, the *status quo ante* imposes external limitations on human capabilities. It deprives some people, groups, or peoples of capabilities which support human flourishing. Those whom it deprives of the means for human flourishing, the *status quo ante* leaves 'disaffected'.[152] I take disaffected somewhat literally—to be disaffected means that society strains the bond of belonging.[153] I despair of the care of my community for my wellbeing. In turn, this means that I no longer feel belonging to that community. I thus no longer care to support my community. Losing this bond of belonging leads to a vicious cycle. I can only strive for human flourishing in community. If I abandon my community, I abandon any hope of virtue (and flourishing). Yet, when too many people lose their virtue, they undermine their society's capacity for virtue as a whole. The vicious mechanism (in the sense of a mechanism that leads away from flourishing) becomes self-reinforcing. Empowerment therefore is about redeeming society for the disaffected and vice-versa. I can only empower someone who lacks agency in a meaningful way. And I need to empower them to bring them back to virtue. Their

[149] *See* Antony Anghie, *Imperialism, Sovereignty and the Making of International Law* (Cambridge University Press 2004) 105.

[150] Cockrell, 'I'm a Therapist to the Super-Rich: They Are as Miserable as Succession Makes Out', (22 November 2021) The Guardian, https://www.theguardian.com/commentisfree/2021/nov/22/therapist-super-rich-succession-billionaires, last accessed 17 October 2024.

[151] Anghie (n 149), at 318.

[152] For the juxtaposition of disaffection as lack of equal recognition (isothymia) or of a desire to be recognized as inherently superior (megalothymia), *see* Fukuyama (n 32).

[153] In this sense, Fukuyama's understanding of thumos or spiritedness comes reasonably close to my understanding. One feels cutoff from the spiritedness of one's community and thus is disaffected due to the lack of regard of one's community. *See ibid.*

ability to be virtuous redeems my own capacity for virtue in turn. As human flourishing is mutually dependent, we must empower each other together or fail apart.

Empowerment means to strengthen the bond of belonging. It means to create conditions in which human flourishing—agency—is possible due to the mutual support community members provide each other. This agency strengthens agency of others in turn. We break the vicious cycle of rivalrous action and move to act in common.[154] This action in common provides a means for us to grow—grow because we can increase the means we have available to support a dignified life. This growth, in turn, leads to a more stable society—a society that is able to react by means of the efforts of its members to new challenges and master them.

This idea of development looks to deploy resources to achieve more than just economic outcomes. It deploys resources to achieve human outcomes. These human outcomes are not just material. They are material and ethical. It is not enough to eradicate poverty. Many persons who have escaped poverty still cannot meaningfully flourish. It is possible to have escaped poverty and yet not have completed a secondary education curriculum—let alone have attended university. It is even possible to be comparatively materially well-off and still lack access to education, culture, freedom of thought, etc. This lack of access can be due to an outright attack by the state on the culture of a particular community by subjecting the community to 're-education' and otherwise limiting its members' ability to develop a more advanced understanding of their own (or truly any) culture. One can think here of the Canadian residential school system or similar Australian school systems.[155] Other contemporary examples abound.[156] Still, the state can also fail to realize rights related to core capabilities without outright failing to respect human rights. It can simply not provide schooling sufficient to allow the survival of a dying language (and with it, a dying culture).[157] This, too, may strand persons or peoples in a developmental desert. The same is true in less extreme circumstances. There are spheres of human activity that people cannot touch even though they are not poor. They can live decent enough lives. Still, the full realization of human flourishing has been denied to them by the circumstances in which they found themselves.[158]

[154] Vermeule (n 54), at 59.

[155] 'What We Have Learned, Principles of Truth and Reconciliation', (2015) Truth and Reconciliation Commission of Canada, available at https://ehprnh2mwo3.exactdn.com/wp-content/uploads/2021/01/Principles_English_Web.pdf, last accessed 1 November 2024; Smith, 'Indigenous Peoples and Boarding Schools, A Comparative Study', (26 January 2009) United Nations Permanent Forum on Indigenous Issues, UN Document Number E/C.19/CRP.1, https://www.un.org/esa/socdev/unpfii/documents/IPS_Boarding_Schools.pdf last accessed 1 November 2024.

[156] *See* Sean R Roberts, *The War no the Uyghurs* (Princeton University Press 2020).

[157] *See* George Steiner, *After Babel: Aspects of Language and Translation* (2nd edn, Oxford University Press 1992).

[158] MacIntyre notes that Aristotle would similarly look to varying degrees of material preconditions for human flourishing. MacIntyre (n 55), at 187–89. One can thus live a life that is good enough—decent—without actually being able to realize the human good of flourishing fully. Still, we need more than favourable material conditions. We need favourable ethical conditions as well as material

A human development perspective sees that empowering is itself a social task. We must empower all. That means, it wishes to do more than remove the harshest of privations on human agency (poverty). It does not aim at a minimum standard of living. It aims at the opposite end: excellence. This excellence, in turn, helps to achieve precisely the kind of human and economic growth outcomes we hope for—we bring in every mind capable of pushing the innovation frontier. This innovation frontier is not just scientific or economic. It is ethical: we are looking progressively to increase the number of people who live good human lives because they support our own efforts at doing the same through economic, social, and cultural exchange.

4.5 Human Empowerment as Energy Governance Goal

A human development lens meaningfully navigates us past the impasse of treating development in purely economic terms. It does so both in terms of its 'why' (its goal) and in terms of its 'how'. It thus adds to our understanding of the energy bond of belonging by providing a better understanding of what the common shared energy resource is and what it serves. The rest of the book will flesh out in more detail how such a goal would be achieved in detail. Yet, there are important differences to a purely economically centred approach that are helpful to orient the discussion to follow.

4.5(a) The Human Empowerment Energy System

The goal of the energy bond of belonging is not blind growth. We do not aim to install capacity where that capacity leads to the greatest absolute capacity gain. We also do not aim to install capacity where that capacity leads to the greatest possible global economic growth. Instead, the goal is to increase human capabilities in such a manner as to progressively empower persons, peoples, and communities.[159]

A human development lens leads to a differently constituted energy system compared to the economic development lens. The priority for energy policy is to support human capabilities and to fulfil human rights. It is not to grow the economy for its own sake (with all the distributive problems this entails). Human capabilities are energy-intensive. For instance, the right to education requires air conditioning in areas suffering from significant heatwaves.[160] Similarly, basic electricity

conditions. Ethical conditions here refer to both the availability of human capabilities and their actual use.

[159] *See* ICESCR, art 2(1).
[160] Kahn (n 48), at 7.

access to power small refrigeration units and the ability to charge a mobile phone supports human capabilities, particularly of women, to leave the home around the world.[161] To have the opportunity to participate in an innovation economy further requires communication access (which again requires energy).[162] Energy policies supporting such outcomes would realize multiple human rights at the same time. Obviously, different policy pathways will prioritize differently. Yet, the goal is always progressively to realize multiple rights and capabilities and to support the growth of energy systems over time. Having the means for such policies is likely to require economic growth to support the additional expenditure to realize the projects in question. Yet, economic growth is instrumental.

An energy system that aims to achieve these goals is likely to look meaningfully different from one built around maximizing economic growth. It likely will aim to deliver electricity by means of smaller, distributed generation and transmission.[163] The cost of providing energy access on a 'traditional' grid-based scale is frequently too high to warrant providing energy access in particularly energy poor regions.[164] These energy poor regions, on the other hand, are the most disaffected and have a significant need for energy access. They are also areas with significant untapped intellectual resources that are currently shut out of the innovation economy. Bringing more people into a modern energy world means that we are likely to increase our innovation potential going forward by adding more minds to solving the innovation challenges of our day.[165] These minds, in turn, are likely to help create economic opportunities close to home, thus broadening the economic distribution of economic innovation rents over time.

Achieving such a 'smaller' energy policy will differ according to circumstances.[166] In the context of communities looking to electrify for the first time, rural

[161] For an account of the impact of such electrification in India particularly for women, *see* Robert Bryce, *A Question of Power, Electricity and the Wealth of Nations* (Public Affairs 2020) 111–23.

[162] Johnson & Persico, 'Broadband Internet Access, Economic Growth, and Wellbeing', (May 2024) National Bureau of Economic Research Working Paper 32517, https://www.nber.org/system/files/working_papers/w32517/w32517.pdf, last accessed 6 November 2024.

[163] *See* Zhao, 'Cost–Benefit Analysis of Distributed Energy Systems Considering the Monetization of Indirect Benefits', (2024) 16 Sustainability 820; *See* Tonrey, 'Distributed Energy Resources: How Utilities Have Stared Death in the Face and Emerged Victorious', (7 July 2023) Kleinman Center for Energy Policy, https://kleinmanenergy.upenn.edu/commentary/blog/distributed-energy-resources-how-utilities-have-stared-death-in-the-face-and-emerged-victorious/, last accessed 3 November 2024.

[164] Abhijit Banerjee & Ester Duflo, *Good Economics for Hard Times* (Public Affairs 2019).

[165] Bryce (n 161) provides such an account of women in particular going to local universities in India because they are no longer needed in the home given the advances in electrification.

[166] This 'smaller' energy policy may at first blush sound like the 'soft' path to energy transition outlined in Amory Lovins classic *Energy Strategy: The Road Not Taken?* Lovins, 'Energy Strategy: The Road Not Taken?', (October 1976) 55 Foreign Affairs 65. Lovins proposes a softer path to energy governance that relies on easier (renewable) energy technology that can be used in a distributive generation network close to the point of energy use together with energy efficiency measures to reduce energy usage. He contrasts this path with a hard path of technologically challenging, centralized forms of energy generation, most notably nuclear energy. The 'smaller' energy footprint for which I argue here very much takes Lovins' point that such an approach to energy is significantly more democratic. I reject, however, that it entails a choice of technology. Read in the extreme, Lovins' point is deeply sceptical of energy innovation and its ability to provide technologically advanced energy access. I do not

or municipal cooperatives provide a means to align resources around a shared goal of electrification of the relevant community. Such cooperatives are self-regulating, not for profit entities, in which the customers of the cooperative are also its voting members.[167] Here, the bond of belonging immediately ties together new electricity users as the decisionmakers in generating and distributing electricity. It further connects those users with the (likely) external financing to make it possible. One example of such an effort is the Pedernales Electric Cooperative in the Texas Hill Country.[168] It was formed after the breakup of the holding companies in the US power market during the new deal, in response to the vigorous lobbying by then Congressman Lyndon B Johnson.[169]

On a bigger scale, the deregulation of the electricity markets had a similar effect in the early 2000s. For example, the 2002 deregulation of the Texas electricity market similarly purposefully aimed to displace large, incumbent utility-based generation with smaller, more nimble generation, leaning expressly into wind power as a means to serve Texas's energy needs.[170] Today, Texas is the leading US state for both wind and solar power and has a strong mix of different energy sources.[171] Increasingly fewer power companies have the ability to exercise market power in the Texas electricity market. This, in turn, means that users benefit from comparatively lower, competitive prices for their electricity due to the relatively 'flat' structure of the Texas electricity market.[172]

share that scepticism. Rather, technologies like small modular reactors or next generation geothermal energy may well be able to help institute a 'small grid' energy policy focused on human development while also leaning into complex, engineering and operationally complex, innovation-based 'hard' energy systems.

[167] Klass & Chan, 'Cooperative Clean Energy', (2021) 100 North Carolina Law Review 1.

[168] Bryce (n 161), at 96–110.

[169] *Ibid*; *see also* Hughes (n 147), at 392–401.

[170] Seely, 'Texas Power Grid Update', (2024) 63 South Texas Law Review 429, 432.

[171] '2023 State of the Market Report for the ERCOT Electricity Markets' at A-35-A38, (May 2024) Potomac Economics, https://www.potomaceconomics.com/wp-content/uploads/2024/05/2023-State-of-the-Market-Report_Final.pdf, last accessed 4 November 2024.

[172] *Ibid* at 87–88. The Texas experiment is in many ways imperfect. For example, residential customers in the deregulated market segment, pay, on average, more than residential customers receiving their electricity from exempted cooperatives. The main savings instead accrue for business customers. One of the key problems is that residential customers lack the means to understand, and then adjust to, different pricing offers. *See* Gold, 'The Year the Texas Legislature Changed the Energy Game Forever', (November 2023) Texas Monthly, https://www.texasmonthly.com/news-politics/the-year-the-texas-legislature-changed-the-energy-game-forever/, last accessed 6 November 2024. This deficit may be overcome with better technology to assist in guiding home energy usage in light of the current price environment. In addition, the Texas market came under severe criticism following winter storm Uri in February 2021. 'The February 2021 Cold Weather Outages in Texas and the South Central United States', (16 November 2021) US Federal Electricity Regulatory Commission, https://www.ferc.gov/media/february-2021-cold-weather-outages-texas-and-south-central-united-states-ferc-nerc-and, last accessed 4 November 2024. The issue ultimately was not one of market design but rather one of winterization. FERC 2021, at 17. The storm affected both incumbent coal generation and new gas-fired and renewable generation, highlighting that the underlying issue was not purely one of market design. Storrow, 'How Coal Failed Texas in the Deep Freeze', (18 March 2021) E&E News, https://www.eenews.net/articles/how-coal-failed-in-the-texas-deep-freeze/, last accessed 6 November 2024.

The point is not that human development is only consistent with the full liberalization of energy markets. As discussed in Chapter 1, this liberalization itself runs into limitations. Further, as discussed in Chapter 2, liberalization is part of a broader set of policy tools at the disposal of energy policy-making guided by the bond of belonging to realign the incentives for all energy system stakeholders. It is not the exclusive tool.

The point is instead that a human development lens will move away from concentration and towards increasing the number of stakeholders with meaningful agency in the energy system (more energy companies, different governmental stakeholders, and a broader set of communities). Increasing agency is at the heart of the human development lens. Agency, in turn, is a matter of more direct community action. This is particularly the case when community action secures needed core resources like water or food—and indeed energy—for community members to flourish.[173] Such an approach balances the growing capacity of competition-based innovation against a greater capacity for governance by the state to harness it towards a shared common good.[174]

A human development lens introduces human agency into the operationalization of energy governance.[175] Energy is important to support greater agency. This does not of itself mean that we need to increase agency *over* energy governance to improve human development agency outcomes. The need for greater agency instead is a matter of the underlying choices energy policy ultimately supports. Means are limited. Consequently, we must choose how an energy system supports the progressive realization of human rights and capabilities. This choice of how we constitute the energy system therefore is itself value laden. It is not a matter of

[173] Elinor Ostrom, *Governing the Commons, The Evolution of Institutions for Collective Action* (Cambridge University Press 2015) 58–141.

[174] *See* Acemoglu & Robinson (n 145). The resulting energy system looks ordoliberal, in the sense of trusting in a strong state to balance economic opportunities for a broad set of independent actors who in turn counterbalance a strong state (as opposed to supporting consolidation in the name of greater efficiency). On ordoliberalism in general, *see* Thomas Biebricher ed, *The Oxford Handbook of Ordoliberalism* (Oxford University Press 2022). On the relationship between Ordoliberalism and Carl Schmitt's thought on the essential importance of a strong state, *see* Cristi, 'Carl Schmitt: Decisionism', *in The Oxford Handbook of Ordoliberalism* (Thomas Biebricher ed, Oxford University Press 2022) 243–60. Whether the argument I advance is ordoliberal ultimately is a question of emphasis. The reason that there is overlap is the fundamental importance of competition both here and in the ordoliberal tradition. *See* Ergen & Kohl, 'Rival Views of Economic Competition', (2022) 20 Socio-Economic Review 937. I tend to view the matter as one of balance between state and the economy in much the same way as Acemoglu and Robinson. Competition is a matter of finding socio-economic equilibria supporting stable economic growth by means of innovation. This balance is similarly critical in the historical example of the apex of the Greek polis. *See* Hanson (n 75). It is similarly critical to the civic humanist tradition. Quentin Skinner, *The Foundations of Modern Political Thought, Volume One: The Renaissance* (Cambridge University Press 1978). The idea of ordoliberalism weaves together many of the same strands.

[175] In technical terms, there is agency in a reflexive paradigm—it is both the goal of the operation of the paradigm and a means according to which it operates. *See* Gralf-Peter Calliess & Peer Zumbansen, *Rough Consensus and Running Code: A Theory of Transnational Private Law* (Hart Publishing 2010). For additional discussion, *see* Frédéric G Sourgens, *Good Faith in Transnational Law: A Pluralist Account* (Brill Nijhoff 2022).

technocratic expertise. It is a matter of discerning moral judgement. The broader the set of stakeholders in energy decision-making, the more we empower those who are affected by energy design choices both directly and indirectly. We empower those affected by energy design directly to the extent that we give them an active means to means to participate in decision-making about how the energy system is constituted. We empower those affected by energy design indirectly to the extent that we give them a means to influence active decisionmakers through consumer choices or community engagement.

Energy cooperatives present a conceptual ideal—all affected community members are direct decisionmakers.[176] Yet, this ideal is conceptual only. Cooperatives are an unworkable governance paradigm when the size of the affected community grows so large as to deprive community members of an effective means to voice their views and participate in shaping collective decisions. Consequently, the pragmatic approach is instead to increase the scope for agency by broadening energy value chain participants at the end of the value chain (distributors, generators, regulators, etc). This broadening makes the energy system more responsive to the demands of a larger cross section of affected persons by providing them greater means to engage with, and contest, energy decision-making. Given the significant impact of those decisions on human development, this increased agency is itself a human development imperative.

This human development imperative also stabilizes energy choices at the local, national, regional, and ultimately global level. The ultimate choices we make are not about the expert management of an abstract system. These choices are subject to the kind of realpolitik manipulation we discussed in Chapter 3. Realpolitik treats energy decision-making as an abstract, technical calculation as to which geostrategic chess piece to imperil, which to protect, and which to use to project power. It is not a concrete choice to achieve specific results for the improvement of the lives of particular people. Nor is it a choice made by these affected people themselves.

The more we 'own' our energy choices, the more carefully we will understand what these choices entail. We exercise prudent judgement. The word prudence implies a certain degree of caution. This implication is borne out by moral psychology—we are instinctively and inherently risk averse when we put our minds to exercising judgement.[177] All things considered, it is thus less likely that we will make decisions that increase the threat to our own energy access and more likely that we will act to manage risk. Such decision-making in its own right is a critical counterweight to the real and volatile geostrategic incentives for value chain distortion discussed in Chapter 3. Still, they are not enough. The human development lens will also need to consider how value chains are constituted.

[176] Klass & Chan (n 167); *see also* Klass & Wilton, 'Local Power', (2022) 75 Vanderbilt Law Review 93.
[177] Roger Fisher, William Ury, & Bruce Patton, *Getting to Yes, Negotiating Agreement Without Giving in* (2nd edn, Houghton Mifflin Company 1991) 22–23.

The focus on agency also provides an important distinction between the economic and human development with regard to environmental and climate change concerns. The human development lens assigns significant decision-making authority to those affected by energy generation. In the cooperative setting, this decision-making authority is formally delegated to members of the cooperative, that is, its customers.[178] In a market setting, consumer choice fulfils a similar function in directing which generation choices will be accepted by end consumers and which rejected. In both instances, end users of energy have greater agency in making energy as well as environmental choices.

This kind of agency obviously is not enough to secure human development. It does not provide a backstop against the imposition of unacceptable burdens on any one particularly affected group. Human development requires the progressive realization of human rights and capabilities.[179] Progressive realization implies a presumption against backsliding in the realization of human capabilities due to policy choices or governance outcomes.[180] Backsliding by imposing a climate or environmental burden on a community would not only fail to realize the rights of the affected community. It would also fail to *respect* and *protect* the human rights of those community members, that is, it further impairs their then-existing human capabilities due to the new environmental burden.[181] To impose any such burden directly or indirectly through the permitting of new energy infrastructure requires the state to put the affected community in at least as good a position (in terms of their human capabilities) as it was before.

This does not impose a veto on new energy development. Rather, the point is the overall realization of human capabilities as a whole as opposed to maintenance of the *status quo ante* with regard to any one capability. Still, to make energy choices that impose climate and environmental burdens requires states to implement active adaptation to the new conditions.[182] It requires further that the distributive choices are consistent with a fair apportionment of benefits and burdens. It finally also requires that these decisions about how to adapt and how to mitigate be consistent with the overall idea of agency. It thus requires a particular means of cooperation. I will discuss this in further detail in the next chapter.

[178] Klass & Chan (n 167).

[179] ICESCR, art 2(1).

[180] Ben Saul et al, *The International Covenant on Economic, Social and Cultural Rights: Commentary, Cases, and Materials* (Oxford University Press 2014) 145.

[181] Christian Tomuschat, *Human Rights: Between Idealism and Realism* (3rd edn, Oxford University Press 2014) 142.

[182] Communities may well be benefited and burdened by new developments. In that case, benefits and burdens may well be weighed up against each other. Still, such weighing can only occur to the extent that it does not diminish the agency of the affected community. The human capability analysis is thus not only driven by material means but by human development.

4.5(b) Human Development-Based Energy Value Chains

The human development lens brings a similar change in focus to bear on energy value chains. A human development deconcentrates energy value chains, as well. The concentration of value chains is problematic from a human development perspective because of its environmental impact. Such concentration means that the environmental burdens associated with any one part of the energy value chain are disproportionately borne in one place. If the segment of the value chain in question involves particularly toxic processes, this concentration can lead to the de facto creation of 'sacrifice zones', in which 'vulnerable and marginalized groups bear a disproportionate burden of the health, human rights and environmental consequences of exposure to pollution and hazardous substances'.[183] A key risk in creating such 'sacrifice zones' stems from the cumulative impact of different facilities on a particular community.[184] A human development approach aims to avoid the creation of such 'sacrifice zones' to the extent that is possible.

To avoid concentration of environmental impacts means to broaden energy value chains. We need to diversify the places in which environmentally burdensome activities occur. Rather than expanding extractive industry where it is already ongoing, we need to shift extraction to more locations. Similarly, rather than adding refining capacity in a place that already has a significant refinery presence, we should add refineries in places that are not currently home to refining capacity.

This same strategy will also share benefits. It will increase the number of key stakeholders who can participate in energy value chains. This, in turn, increases agency within energy value chains. This increased agency improves economic outcomes by driving employment. This growth potential is now realized in more places thus distributing the economic benefits from energy value chains.

Just as importantly, the human development lens insists that we must increase the number and diversity of intellectual contributors to energy value chains. Innovation is a core economic growth driver.[185] It is also a core cultural driver. The human development lens counsels that we encourage policies that support such growth. At a minimum, this means that local support measures for a nascent domestic energy industry are a welcome development. These measures do not distort international trade. To the contrary, they support international trade by increasing the number of actors who can compete at the innovation frontier over the long-term. In addition, as I will discuss in the next section, cooperation also demands a robust engagement in technology transfer that allows areas suffering

[183] Boyd (Special Rapporteur on Human Rights and the Environment), 'The Right to a Clean, Healthy, and Sustainable Environment', (12 January 2022) UN Doc A/HRC/49/53.

[184] Guillot, 'Environmental Justice in Pollution Hotspots and Sections 7 & 15 of the Charter: The Case of the Aamjiwnaang Community in Chemical Valley', (2023) 53 Environmental Law 273, 281–90 (discussing one such example in the Canadian First Nations' context).

[185] Aghion (n 144), at 55–74.

from energy poverty—and the related human development impairment—to stand on their own feet.[186]

There is thus a contrast between a human-development-driven energy policy and an economically driven energy policy. In broad outline, an economic growth approach concentrates benefits and burdens to increase the efficiency of the overall energy system and to meet the greatest possible short-term growth potential. A human-development approach aims for the progressive realization of human capabilities. This approach is premised in extending agency within and over energy. Such an approach deconcentrates energy as far as feasible to increase agency to as many stakeholders as possible. It provides greater ownership to more stakeholders. This, in turn, strengthens the authority of energy value chains and energy system governance by providing a greater reason to participate and grow them.

4.6 Human Empowerment as the Logic of the Energy System

The internal logic of the global energy system follows a human development rather than an economic development approach. The energy bond of belonging is not about achieving single metric outcomes. Rather, it is a means to balance the energy trilemma.[187] It does so by determining what is reasonable. Its reasonableness assessment is informed, in turn, by community practice.[188] Community practice can be—and frequently is—economically inefficient.[189] We therefore cannot make economic growth the sole measure of the bond of belonging. Economic growth is important. It still does not alone determine policy or even commercial outcomes.[190]

The reference to community standards by the bond of belonging is about human empowerment and decision-making through 'organic', neighbourly deliberation.[191] The bond of belonging is about putting us in a position from which we can exercise our own agency and 'compete back' against our neighbours through our labour and ingenuity.[192] It gives us power. Similarly, community standards arise by collective deliberation. This deliberation is not the result of debate in parliament or civic assembly. It arises organically from the repeat interaction between community members. It is the result of their gradual alignment of conduct and land and resource use.[193]

[186] Global oil and gas operations here provide a helpful example of how to require such local content and technology transfer to host states. Owen Anderson et al, *International Petroleum Law and Transactions* (Foundation for Natural Resources and Energy Law 2020).

[187] *See* section 1.1.

[188] *See* section 2.4.

[189] Frédéric G Sourgens, *Good Faith in Transnational Law—A Pluralist Account* (Brill Nijhoff 2022) 73–134.

[190] *See ibid* at 135–249.

[191] *See* section 2.4.

[192] *Ibid*; Hanson (n 75), at 127–78.

[193] Sourgens, 'Bundles of Freedom', (2024) 76 Rutgers Law Review 393.

The deliberation and empowerment of the bond of belonging is reflected in the human development approach. This approach is precisely about empowerment.[194] The human development approach provides the 'why' for us to find each other in community and exploit resources jointly. It is to realize our own personal capacities as constituent part of that community. The energy bond of belonging is such a human development bond of belonging, as it applies to national energy systems and the global energy system.

We can confirm as much when we re-appraise balanced domestic energy governance.[195] The goal of balanced governance is to set incentives for national energy systems to grow in a socially desirable way. The reason national energy systems set incentives is that energy markets neither design themselves nor deliver the outcomes we desire from them on their own. To achieve desirable outcomes requires balance.[196] This balance, in turn, requires a goal. The goal of energy governance—quite literally—is the progressive, long-term empowerment of its respective community. That is also the goal of the human development approach.

4.7 Conclusion

The energy system serves human development. When we ask how we can conceive of a better way to govern global energy value chains and domestic energy systems than reliance on realpolitik, the answer must be human development, as well. We saw in the last chapter that realpolitik introduced significant inefficiencies into global energy value chains and global energy markets. These realpolitik distortions themselves became possible because of, and responded to, the incentives set by domestic energy policies. Realpolitik therefore created real impairments for the realization of energy outcomes domestically as well as globally.

If we look through a human development lens, we now have the beginnings of an answer to the realpolitik conundrum. Greater human development is a desirable reason to limit realpolitik. It is a reason that does not redistribute a limited set of global resources in a rivalrous fashion. Instead, it provides a way to escape the rivalry trap of realpolitik. It fashions a means of realizing growth that benefits all participants. This, in turn, sets a potential incentive for participation by realpolitik actors in a different kind of global energy system.

Perhaps as importantly, a human development lens increases agency. There are more decisionmakers in the energy system. There are more decisionmakers in energy value chains. This increase in stakeholders is a direct consequence of the deconcentration of the energy system.

[194] *See* section 4.4(c).
[195] *See* section 2.5.
[196] *Ibid.*

This increase in agency is itself a counterweight to realpolitik. Realpolitik was a matter of deploying and responding to the deployment of geostrategic market power. Such market power goes hand in hand with concentration. If there are few actors in key bottlenecks of the energy system, states controlling one or more of those actors can exercise market power. A deconcentration strategy addresses this problem by distributing energy value chains more broadly around the world. It further addresses this problem by increasing the number of decisionmakers in the energy system writ large. This deconcentration is directly responsive to the realpolitik concern expressed in the last chapter. It aims to achieve the same task. The difference is that it does so with a different value in mind. That value is the realization of human agency through energy.

This increase in human agency is itself an antidote to realpolitik. Realpolitik, as the name indicates, is a matter of politics. Politics, in turn, depends on the ability to make decisions palatable to core decisionmakers in a polity (whether these decisionmakers are the democratic citizenry, an oligarchic aristocracy, or a kind of politburo). The greater the number of stakeholders in energy decision-making and the broader the number of energy value chain participants, the more difficult it becomes to manipulate energy decision-making for non-energy related ends. There are more stakeholders with a deeper interest in the efficient functioning of energy value chains to support human development. Overcoming more stakeholders is on the whole more difficult than overcoming fewer stakeholders. Overcoming more stakeholders who agree on a fundamental value proposition is even more difficult to achieve.

We have seen that this different energy system—one that is driven by human development rather than economic development—is itself likely to be far more resilient. It is likely to distribute benefits and burdens more broadly. It seeks to limit concentration and broaden participation. This, in turn, means that more stakeholders have a stake in energy governance. This greater number provides a stronger base from which energy systems can grow materially, economically, and intellectually. This policy approach, finally, is not a matter of desire or conjecture. It is the direct result of core human rights obligations constitutive of the global human rights system. The approach therefore is what the law on the books already requires. It does not alter the current law-based international order. To the contrary, it confirms and strengthens it.

Needless to say, this approach requires cooperation to achieve. Chapter 5 outlines how we should think about cooperation in this setting. The final chapter of this part, Chapter 6, then outlines a conception of the common good of such energy governance.

5

Cooperation as Belonging

5.1 Introduction

The idea of a bond of belonging holding together global energy governance is central to this book. We are neighbours in a shared energy system. To benefit from the energy system, we must make reasonable use of the energy resources we share in common. We must not waste these resources. Instead, we must align our own use with the standards of our respective energy value chain communities. We are bound together because we achieve energy outcomes together. Negatively, this means that we can severely impair each other's ability to benefit from the energy resources we share in common to the point of destroying these resources through wasteful use. (This is the plot of the tragedy of the commons and disaster of the anticommons we discussed in Chapter 2.[1]) Still, we also saw that we can secure better energy outcomes for ourselves by working together.

The bond of belonging demands cooperation. This cooperation is an essential precondition for securing our energy future. It is just as critical to maintaining our energy present. Without cooperation, energy value chains cease to function. When energy value chains cease to function, scarcities abound. These scarcities, in turn, can lead to an unravelling of value chains in their entirety and a serious impairment of the energy system as a whole.

Energy governance writ large is not about which traditional energy paradigm is right. It makes little sense to argue whether market liberalization, nationalization of energy resources, or private public partnerships to build new energy infrastructure are preferable in the abstract. Instead, each approach is a better means to align incentives to strengthen the bond of belonging to the energy system in specific concrete circumstances. An understanding of energy governance through the lens of the bond of belonging views each approach as providing a set of tools for balanced energy governance. This understanding eschews any economic or philosophical purism. It simply looks optimally to align the cooperative synergies different energy stakeholders could harness together.[2] The bond of belonging explains why and how we cycle through different, facially inconsistent energy governance paradigms to achieve a common end.

[1] *See* sections 2.3–2.4.
[2] *See* section 2.5.

A Theory of Global Energy Governance. Frédéric Gilles Sourgens, Oxford University Press. © Frédéric Sourgens 2025.
DOI: 10.1093/9780198950325.003.0005

The global nature of energy value chains threw up significant obstacles to organizing national energy systems around a national bond of belonging. Energy value chains grow globally. We have seen that they do so sometime during the frenzy phase of the energy cycle when a new energy approach has proved its viability.[3] The global nature of value chain growth accelerates as an energy technology grows during the synergy and maturity phases of energy development.[4] Domestic incentives act as an additional catalyst for the global realignment and reorganization of energy value chains.[5] These global realignments of energy value chains created a distinct geostrategic energy security problem. Global energy value chains are susceptible to geostrategic manipulation to support non-energy goals. This potential for geostrategic manipulation in fact changes how national energy governance proceeds to secure domestic energy access against such manipulation. I argued that the global nature of energy value chains invited a realpolitik balancing of energy affordability against energy security.[6] This balancing meant in practice that any overconcentration of energy value chains within the sphere of authority of a particular power rationally would be answered by finding new sources of supply to deconcentrate value chains and by finding other energy source to balance energy value chains against each other.

Realpolitik is problematic. It is wasteful. It distorts the global energy system to protect the national energy system against manipulation. Realpolitik actively appears to constrain cooperation. This has very real costs. We can perhaps best understand this cost when we look to the role of coal in the German and Chinese energy mix in 2024.[7] In both instances, coal plays a significant part because coal is not subject to geostrategic manipulation in German and Chinese markets.[8] Yet, in both cases, coal is not in fact the feedstock that either Germany or China wish to rely upon, given coal's greenhouse gas intensity and relative cost. Realpolitik, in other words, entrenches energy systems and does not allow for ready transition even when transition would be the rational thing to do. This is problematic in the context of climate change.[9] Still, it is problematic in any setting given that energy policies have very real distributional consequences in the 'real' economy.

To get at the problem, we therefore need to re-evaluate the bond of belonging. In this chapter, I will provide a fuller view of what cooperation pursuant to the bond

[3] *Ibid.* For further discussion, see Carlota Perez, *Technological Revolutions and Financial Capital* (Edward Elgar 2002).

[4] *See* section 2.5.

[5] *See* sections 3.2(b)–(c).

[6] *See* section 3.4.

[7] *See ibid.*

[8] 'China: Coal', (2023) International Energy Agency, https://www.iea.org/countries/china/coal, last accessed 21 January 2025; 'Germany: Coal', (2024) International Energy Agency, https://www.iea.org/countries/germany/coal, last accessed 21 January 2025.

[9] Jakob, 'The Future of Coal in a Carbon-Constrained Climate', (2020) 10 Nature Climate Change 704.

of belonging means. What emerges is a perhaps surprising understanding of cooperation as belonging. In the first place, cooperation as belonging is not a means to achieve a particular end. It is an end in its own right. We typically think of cooperation as a tool to achieve a specific concrete outcome. In the context of energy governance, the ultimate outcome we hope to accomplish is the progressive realization of human development. This human development is itself a matter of the progressive realization of human agency. Human agency, in turn, is possible because of our being embedded in society. It is inherently cooperative. Cooperation as belonging therefore posits that energy governance is about this form of social agency. Belonging is an end in its own right that is ultimately more important than any specific concrete energy outcome (say, the construction of a linked distributed generation network to address energy poverty in Ghana). The point is that in making decisions together about energy developments, we progressively realize the means for our own future agency. This is impossible to achieve without belonging.

This belonging takes on a distinct colour. Belonging is about a particular kind of agency. I noted in Chapter 2 that the bond of belonging was about reasonable use and the avoidance of waste.[10] More to the point, when I argued what constituted reasonable use and waste, I looked to community standards.[11] These community standards informed us of what the strictures were within which everyone had a reasonable opportunity to use their own rights to innovate and compete back.[12] The use of this reasonable opportunity improved community resources through the agency of their respective stakeholders. What we can add now is that this belonging is not the belonging to a strictly economic community. It is not about maximizing economic outcomes in their own right. Belonging is about human capabilities. It is about flourishing in community.

I will end the chapter by reappraising the realpolitik response to global energy governance. I will argue that some of that realpolitik governance response is in fact about strengthening belonging. It aims at the right thing—the same kind of structure of the global energy system as the human development perspective I developed in Chapter 4.[13] Both approaches fundamentally aim at deconcentrating energy value chains. Both further look to establish an energy mix to protect against shocks in any particular value chain. Both therefore hope to achieve outcomes that provide a more resilient energy system. Done right, both hope to achieve this greater stability through a fair distribution of benefits and burdens. This fair distribution places every stakeholder in a position that allows better human development outcomes for each by leveraging comparative advantage while avoiding the

[10] *See* section 2.4.
[11] *Ibid.*
[12] *Ibid.*
[13] *See* section 4.4.

dangers of overconcentration of that comparative advantage. Everything here, too, is a matter of moderation.

Still, I argue that the bond of belonging also provides for two important additions to the realpolitik approach. *Firstly*, beggar my neighbour energy policies fail. They fail to help neighbours—this being their design. They also fail those who deploy them. The realpolitik response to beggar my neighbour policies is well-trodden, effective, and ultimately proves to make everyone worse off.[14] An understanding of belonging adds that such policies undermine agency precisely because they destroy the very social fabric that is necessary for agency to come in its own. *Secondly*, belonging allows us to direct realpolitik towards the common good. Realpolitik is a form of state intervention to guide energy markets. States can aim their interventions to achieve stronger energy outcomes by lifting more participants—including national stakeholders—to the innovation frontier of different, complementary energy value chains. When realpolitik interventions do so, they obviously support national energy needs. They also expand energy choices for all states and thus provide greater room for agency by supporting innovation.

Cooperation as belonging, in short, is a means to increase agency over the global energy system. It deconcentrates decision-making. It strategically deploys state interventions to improve cooperative strategies premised in innovation and to dissuade rivalrous strategies premised in zero-sum thinking. Cooperation as belonging is an end in its own right. It is an essential condition for energy agency. It is an end because it is a constituent facet of human flourishing. Belonging's understanding of agency is inextricably linked to a third part of the trio of the ends of energy governance—the common good. These three parts—human development, belonging, and, finally, the common good—each reflect a different aspect of what energy governance sets out to achieve. We will discuss this common good and its relation to the other parts of the trio in Chapter 6.

5.2 Cooperation as Belonging

Cooperation is frequently seen as a means. We have a personal goal in mind (sell 1,000 packets of cookies to raise money for a school excursion). I might try to meet this goal single-handedly. Still, it is questionable that one person could reasonably meet the goal alone. One therefore joins together with people who have a similar goal (fellow parents and students who would like to provide, or take advantage of, the educational opportunity the excursion promises). Cooperation as a means is the most efficient path to achieving an end. Yet, cooperation is a way or manner of achieving a goal. It is not a goal in its own right.

[14] Rational choice theory proves that this strategy of defection to earn an advantage for oneself is disastrous. Robert Axelrod, *The Evolution of Cooperation* (Basic Books 1984) 58–59.

Cooperation as belonging posits that cooperation means something different entirely. Cooperation is not a means to an end. Cooperation as belonging *is* an end. I do not belong in order to do something else. I *aim* to belong.[15] I do not belong to aim at something else. I do not belong because I wish to flourish. Rather, belonging is a necessary part of flourishing that is an end of our action in its own right. Citizens exercises civic virtue because they belong to the commonwealth.[16] They do not exercise civic virtue to receive personal, non-civic advantages in return for their civic engagement. Cooperation as belonging posits that flourishing demands active membership in a community as one facet of the human good.

This switch in perspective appears radical to the 'liberal' mind.[17] From this 'liberal' vantage point, cooperation is simply a means for individuals to secure their own ends. Each seeks their own advantage. We see each other (or each other's labour) as expedient means to achieve our own ultimate goals. I treat others fairly because otherwise, I might suffer injury myself if I agree to different rules of engagement. Still, cooperation remains a means to stave off that injury—and ultimately nothing else.[18] More precisely, whatever it is, it is not an end in its own right.[19]

Belonging inverts this relationship. It holds fast to the idea that belonging is itself a necessary constitutive part of human excellence. It is this perspective that brings home the horror of banishment for the Greek, Roman, and Renaissance mind.[20] Being cut off from one's polity was an ethical tragedy precisely because it undercut a central component for truly flourishing action. Belonging is valuable because it gives meaning to our actions.[21]

The bond of belonging in Chapter 2 already ceased on the nature of energy value chain to show the intuitive role of belonging for energy governance.[22] Here, too, the idea of cooperation as an end makes sense. The end of an oil producer

[15] Francis Fukuyama, *Identity: The Demand for Dignity and the Politics of Resentment* (Profile Books 2018).

[16] Skinner, 'Two Concepts of Citizenship', (1993) 55 Tijdschrift voor Filosofie 403; Quentin Skinner, *Visions of Politics* (Cambridge University Press 2012) 165–85.

[17] I use 'liberal' in the sense of the modern political thought that sees the state as a means for me to secure my own liberty while keeping the state at arm's length to avoid oppression by the state. Quentin Skinner, *Liberty Before Liberalism* (Cambridge University Press 1998) 17–18. I contrast liberal thinking with republican thinking. Republican thinking conceives of liberty as available only through the exercise of civic virtue in the commonwealth.

[18] This is the motivation behind the stalwart of liberal thinking—the original position in John Rawls's theory of justice. The veil of ignorance works because I do not know my own eventual position in society. This means that justice is a means to choose a society in which the potential injury I suffer by banding with others is as minimal as might be achieved. What justice does not do is to make me choose civic virtue. I just choose my own advantage in the context of a particularly constructed rational choice hypothesis. John Rawls, *A Theory of Justice* (Oxford University Press 1971).

[19] *See* here the treatment of fraternity in Rawls, which he tellingly demotes to 'a lesser place in democratic theory'. *See ibid* at 90–91.

[20] *See* representatively Publius Ovidius Naso, *Tritia. Ex Ponto* (AL Wheeler trans, Harvard University Press 1924); Dante, 'Paradiso, Canto XXI', *in Dante Alighieri, La Divina Commedia Vol. 6* (Gaetano Ferraro 1830) 163.

[21] Alasdair MacIntyre, *After Virtue* (2nd edn, University of Notre Dame Press 1984) 151.

[22] *See* section 2.4.

is to participate in the oil value chain. Without that value chain, developing an oilwell would make no sense. The end of production is participation in a value chain and in an energy system. Certainly, this value chain allows oilmen to earn a living and even strike it rich. Still, there is a deeper ethos of being an oilman than simply earning a living. There is a sense of belonging to a meaningful activity that supports broader and important national and global aims. One takes pride in, and fulfilment from, one's work because of one's belonging to this larger enterprise.[23]

As the oil context makes unmistakably clear, belonging is still competitive. Oilmen were and are fiercely competitive with each other. This competition turns to innovation as a guide to success. A prominent example of this innovative, competitive spirit is the role of independent oil and gas producers in the US shale revolution. Independent oil and gas producers found a way to produce from sites in the US that had long been thought to be unprofitable due to their challenging geology. When oil prices hit record highs in the late 2000s, these independent oil and gas producers leaned on and perfected hydraulic fracturing and horizontal drilling techniques. Each were not new in their own right. Yet, the manner of their deployment revolutionized the oil and gas industry in the US in the span of a decade, turning the US from an oil and gas importer into an oil and gas exporter. They achieved this aim due to the competitive and innovative spirit of US oil and gas independents.[24]

The energy industry showcases how the idea of competition and belonging go together. The ability to take a personal risk is a matter of broader industry context. In this context, innovation stands on the shoulders of others. We learn from each other and improve on each other's work. It is not possible to do this work alone. Again, the shale revolution uniquely showcases this. This revolution was not championed by vertically integrated oil and gas supermajors. Rather, independent producers spearheaded this revolution. They did so by relying on a vibrant ecosystem of oil field services contractors. These contractors, together with the independents, were able to compete and innovate together. Belonging, innovation, and competition are part of the same larger energy story.[25]

[23] On this historical connection, *see* Dochuk, 'Blessed by Oil, Cursed with Crude: God and Black Gold in the American Southwest', (2012) 99 Journal of American History 51. The idea of oil as God's bounty, which Dochuk discusses in the context of Rockefeller, continues to echo in the twenty-first century—President Aliyev of Azerbiajan referred to oil as the gift of God when opening the 29th Conference of the Parties under the UNFCCC. Gelles, 'The Unmistakable Backdrop of COP29', (12 November 2024) New York Times, https://messaging-custom-newsletters.nytimes.com/dynamic/render?uri=nyt%3A%2F%2Fnewsletter%2F551102f3-9524-56ff-9ee2-12933766f221, last accessed 18 November 2024.

[24] For a commons governance approach to shale development, *see* Ilia Murtazashvili & Ennio Piano, *The Political Economy of Fracking, Private Property, Polycentricity, and the Shale Revolution* (Routledge 2018).

[25] For an article exploring how independents benefited from deconcentration in US gas markets, *see* Golden & Wiseman, 'The Fracking Revolution: Shale Gas as a Case Study in Innovation Policy', (2015) 64 Emory Law Journal 955, 964–89.

The shale example also reveals a deeper mechanism of belonging. We belong, innovate, and compete because different stakeholders in a value chain are uniquely positioned to take on different necessary risks of innovation. These different stakeholders are partners with whom to innovate. Specialization makes sense because there are other specialists. Each can shoulder more risk because it can mitigate this risk through specialization and innovation. This risk assignment draws in more capital from more producers. This capital is invested to improve upon drilling techniques by contractors etc. Belonging ties stakeholders closer together in an energy value chain and propels this value chain forward. Innovation by a broad group of independent, deconcentrated actors completely changed the energy landscape without much by way of hierarchical command or direction. Instead, belonging to a 'polycentric' community of stakeholders, each doing their job, created exceptional energy outcomes through innovation. This innovation makes previously marginal opportunities productive. The logic of this belonging—as we noted already in Chapter 2—is a matter of commons governance. I will therefore begin our discussion of cooperation as belonging there.

5.2(a) Cooperation in Commons Governance

The bond of belong requires cooperation.[26] The energy system is a shared resource community in which decision-making is inherently shared.[27] What, though, do we mean by cooperation? We intuitively think of cooperation as a means to achieve a particular end.[28] Still, this intuitive understanding is imprecise in consequential ways.[29] If cooperation is purely a means, we look at it as a tool that can and should be deployed only to the extent that it is efficient to bring about the end we are really after. In the context of realpolitik, this end is securing domestic power and domestic economic growth. In a more traditional economic analysis, cooperation is a

[26] *See* section 2.4; Elinor Ostrom, *Understanding Institutional Diversity* (Princeton University Press 2009) 255–88.

[27] Elinor Ostrom, *Governing the Commons: The Evolution of Institutions for Collective Action* (Cambridge University Press 2015).

[28] For example, Elinor Ostrom posits (correctly) that commons governance is a means to cope with problems. Ostrom (n 27), at 54.

[29] As Ostrom also points out, the means of solving commons problems creates nestled constitutive and operational processes of decision. *Ibid* at 52. Constitutive processes of decision are about more than simply solving a problem. They set up a community that itself becomes constitutive of 'meaning' in that community. *See* W Michael Reisman, *The Quest for World Order and Human Dignity in the Twenty-First Century: Constitutive Process and Individual Commitment* (Brill Nijhoff 2012) 112–33. It shapes fundamental expectations about who gets to make what decision how and how we relate to each other. *See* Reisman, at 81–82. This, in turn, deeply influences our view of self as we find our own place in the community and experience self-worth and dignity through being in the community. Fukuyama (n 15).

means to support economic growth—making more money—in its own right.[30] In a realpolitik or economic-growth minded world, cooperation is decidedly not an end. It is a tool we deploy if it suits our goals.

To fully understand this difference, it is important to see how both approaches part ways. In both contexts (cooperation as a realpolitik or economic means and cooperation as an end), we still begin in a similar starting place. Cooperation is a practice. It is something we habitually do together according to complex socially authoritative rules in order to achieve an outcome.[31] In the realpolitik context, we aim to achieve national power. In the economic context, we aim to achieve economic growth. In both, the goal (power and growth) is external to the practice. It makes sense to say that I will cooperate only if it grows the economy or makes my home state more powerful.

If we treat cooperation as an end, this changes. A practice aims at realizing a goal that is inherently internal to it. Chess is a classic example of such a practice—we play chess because we value the game of chess in its own right. We do not play chess to gain an advantage outside of chess.[32] There is an 'excellence'—ἀρετή or virtue—of chess. That excellence is an active love of chess by becoming an ever-better chess player.

Inquiring about cooperation as an end *as such* is slightly more complicated. It asks a 'meta' question. All practices are already by definition inherently cooperative—they are things we habitually do *together*.[33] The question of cooperation as a practice therefore applies the idea of practice to practice itself—it enquires about the practice of practising rather than the practice of playing chess. In this context, we have to answer the question: 'What is the inherent internal virtue of practise in its own right?' We can answer this question by reformulating it so that looks like a simple algebraic equation. Consider the statement 'I will stop cooperating with you if not cooperating with you makes me more *x*'. We need to find the value of *x* at which the statement is absurd. That value of *x* is the internal excellence of cooperating as such. Now substitute 'belonging' for *x*. The statement now says: 'I will stop cooperating with you if not cooperating with you makes me belong with you more' (adjusting slightly for grammar). This statement is absurd because it involves a self-contradiction. Not cooperating naturally walls us off from the very community to which we wish to belong. Such conduct is ultimately self-destructive

[30] This loosely tracks the logic of Ricardo's comparative advantage in global trade. For a concise introduction to the idea, *see* Abhijit V Banerjee & Esther Duflo, *Good Economics for Hard Times* (Public Affairs 2019) 53.

[31] MacIntyre (n 21), at 187. I here use authoritative in a descriptive sense as 'participation in decision in accordance with community perspectives about who is to make what decisions, by what criteria, and by what procedures'. Harold D Lasswell & Myres S McDougal, *Jurisprudence for a Free Society: Studies in Law, Science and Policy* (New Haven Press 1992) 26.

[32] MacIntyre (n 21), at 188.

[33] *Ibid* at 187.

for all involved.[34] We can therefore conclude that belonging is the inherent good of cooperation.

We can get at the same point differently. What if I asked—'what is the point of togetherness?' Togetherness simply turns the phrase 'things we habitually do together' (a practice) into a more accessible noun. Togetherness is a different way of describing cooperation. Asking about the point of togetherness gets at the same idea. We can therefore doublecheck—does it make sense to say that belonging is the point of togetherness? We simply get behind the everyday turn of phrase 'we belong together'. Belonging gathers the together of multiple people into a 'we'. It makes intuitive sense to say that togetherness is about belonging. That is how we use the ideas of belonging, togetherness, and cooperation in everyday speech.

We can now put the different pieces together to advance the point. Belonging is a virtue. We have seen that belonging is itself critical to human development. We have a capacity for belonging. International human rights law respects, protects, and fulfils this capacity.[35] What we have seen now is that belonging is not just a human capacity. It is the critical capacity to come together to realize the others. We cannot flourish alone. We can only flourish by cooperating.[36] This means that we must belong to cooperate at all. It also means that we must in a real sense make others belong with us if we wish to cooperate with them.

Given the argument so far, we can take an additional step. Belonging is the cardinal *civic* virtue. Civic virtue is the virtue of acting in a commonwealth.[37] Civic virtue asks us to act and to treat each other so that we can all take part in a community that provides for the welfare of its members. The founding myth of civic virtue is that the commonwealth—the Roman '*res publica*'—is an extension of family through an ever-growing alliance of clans or tribes.[38] This myth continued to be reflected in the public law of the Roman republic. Voting occurred by tribe, to which Roman citizens were assigned, in a '*comitia tributa*'—a 'tribal assembly'.[39] Roman public law principles at the heart of the civic republican tradition confirm this understanding that we form a commonwealth because we belong together. To practise 'civic virtue' in light of this background is to practise belonging.

[34] The example is drawn from Sophocles's *Antigone*. The Theban cycle had a lasting impact on Aristotle's own ethical thinking. I find it helpful because 'walled off' still speaks to us metaphorically today. The punishment Antigone endured for her defiance of Creon in burying her brother Polynices was to be walled off in a cave to die. *See* George Steiner, *Antigones: How the Antigone Legend Has Endured in Western Literature, Art, and Thought* (Yale University Press 1996).

[35] *See* section 4.4(b).

[36] *See* Martha Nussbaum, *The Fragility of Goodness, Luck and Ethics in Greek Tragedy and Philosophy* (updated edn, Cambridge University Press 2001) 81.

[37] Skinner 1993 (n 16); Skinner 2012 (n 16).

[38] Cicero, *De Oficiis* I.xvii.47-xvii *in Cicero Volume XXI: On Duties* (Walter Miller trans, Harvard University Press 1913) 51–61.

[39] On the role of the assembly in Roman public law under the monarchy, republic, and principate, *see* Theodor Mommsen, *Römisches Staatsrecht, Dritter Band* (Verlag von S Hirzel 1887) 300–28.

This idea of the '*commonwealth*' begins quite naturally with the idea that the '*wealth*' of the community is '*common*' in the sense that it is employed towards a mutual benefit. The familial analogy is instructive again—the civil law to this day employs a Roman standard of care of acting as a '*bonus paterfamilias*'—a good head of family.[40] This good head of family is a 'diligent guardian of the rights and interests of his [...] ward'.[41] Such a guardian naturally must dispose of wealth and resources for the mutual benefit of his ward. This means in practice that any commonwealth must make available such meaningful, mutual opportunities to those whose allegiance it expects. Civic virtue is to act as if we were family, securing this meaningful mutual opportunity for all who belong to the commonwealth.[42] At a minimum, it requires me to abstain from acting in a way that threatens the commonwealth and the sustainable exploitation of its resources.[43] To belong is to care. To care means to look out for the interest of my kinsman. Civic virtue extends this care to the entire civic community.[44] Though it sounds old-fashioned, civic virtue is love of country. Love of country is fundamentally a love of its people. This love means securing to everyone a fair opportunity to partake in the common wealth of the commonwealth.

To belong in this sense means to trust. Cooperation requires members of the commonwealth and stakeholders in a commons to make investments. These investments take me away from my own pursuits (both hoplite military service at Athens and the building of irrigation works in the Philippines take farmers from their fields).[45] The benefits of cooperation take time and are less visible (ie I see only the present day benefit from cooperation and cannot easily see the value of continuous inter-generational efforts).[46] This trust requires that each member has a sense of agency in deliberation and implementation of joint decisions.[47] This trust requires supervision—we must verify that we limit free riders and that all who belong in fact cooperate.[48] We build such trust when we each hold each other to account by observing that we in fact all act with civic virtue. We do not rely on some external supervisor but rather spur each other on to more effective participation. Hoplite warfare did not have 'officers' to keep order. Instead, the greatest incentive to do well in battle and keep one's nerve was that each hoplite was flanked by his neighbours—and knew he was.[49] Similarly, when we observe infractions, the

[40] James Gordley et al, *An Introduction to the Comparative Study of Private Law* (2nd edn, Cambridge University Press 2021) 460.
[41] Aaron X Fellmeth & Maurice Horwitz, *Guide to Latin in International Law* (Oxford University Press 2009).
[42] Ostrom (n 26), at 263.
[43] *Ibid* at 279.
[44] Cicero (n 38).
[45] Victor Davis Hanson, *The Other Greeks: The Family Farm and the Agrarian Roots of the West* (Free Press 1995) 221–89; Ostrom (n 27), at 82–87.
[46] Ostrom (n 27), at 82–87.
[47] *Ibid.*
[48] Ostrom (n 26), at 97–98.
[49] Hanson (n 45), at 221–89.

point is not to punish. It is to re-instil civic virtue. The key is not to punish repeat offenders we catch harshly. It is to prevent repeat offences through early care.[50]

This cooperation is a practice of belonging. It is a mutual enterprise to see to our joint and mutual benefit. It is premised in a deep care for each other. This care gives rise to trust. This trust builds up through shared exercises of shared decision-making to undertake and achieve tasks none of us would have been able to achieve on our own. We see that our agency is enmeshed in joint action. Our goal is to strengthen this agency and joint action through ever stronger habits of shared social action around institutions we shape for the achievement of shared goals and mutual benefit. This belonging is the proper foundation not just of exploitation of natural resources but of all economic resources. This economy is simply a composite of the collective households of the commonwealth—it is derived from the idea of the οἶκος or household estate. Economic growth is the growth of the collection of οἶκoi. It is a matter of belonging.

Such civic virtue—belonging—is not collectivism. We cooperate in a commons because we belong to the commons. Because we belong to the commons, we have to act for the good of the commons. Acting for the good of the commons means that we have to give each other a fair opportunity to benefit from the commons. This precisely means that I may act for my own ends, as well. To benefit from the commons, I must act to exercise my right to a fair opportunity. Belonging to a commons means that I can exercise my own agency more fully. I can do so, because I am no longer at risk of being hurt in the enjoyment of my rights by my neighbour. This only works if we protect each other in the commons reciprocally: in order to exercise my own agency, I must empower my neighbour and vice versa.[51] The virtue of belonging is non-rivalrous. Belonging is empowering. When we each act to empower the other, we have more agency than we would have had without our respective actions. There is more over which I have a fair opportunity to compete. This means that I am better off because I collaborated. I have been put in a far better position to live a flourishing human life. That flourishing remains 'mine' because I have to take my opportunity. I must labour to reduce opportunity to reality. I therefore very much earn my keep. No one built my enterprise for me. I did.

Controversial though it may sound, to have something in such a commonwealth is the fruit of one's own virtue. It is merited.[52] It is the result of agency duly exercised. We just cannot exercise agency, or be virtuous, outside of community. The opportunity to act is constituted by my community. Yet, my actions still are my own. Farmers relying on common irrigation have an opportunity to farm due to the communal irrigation work.[53] Still, the harvest they collect depends on their

[50] Ostrom (n 27).
[51] *Ibid.*
[52] Hanson (n 45), at 99.
[53] Ostrom (n 27).

own use of irrigation and their own effort. The community does not grow the farmer's crops. The farmer does. And the farmer's effort fundamentally matters to the result of the harvest.[54]

My agency must not impair my neighbour's use right. It must leave my neighbours with a fair opportunity to use their agency to compete with me. Together, we must respect, protect, and grow the commons from which we each benefit. 'Mine' in other words is interwoven with the 'mine' of my fellows. This weave does make an 'ours'. This 'ours' strengthens each of our 'mine' by giving it stronger support. Still, the system as whole is built on each of us *acting*. Collaboration is not a command we obey any more than chess playing is a command we obey. It is something we actively do for our own good.

5.2(b) The Human Development Commons

Human rights law tracks the understanding of cooperation in the commons. Human rights instruments reflect our belonging to the community of humankind.[55] This community of humankind, in turn, is a commons. It is not governed by a single world government. It is also not subject to lawlessness. Rather, it is governed by states. These states each have sovereignty over a particular territory.[56] Yet, the actions of each state with regard to its own territory affect the rights of other states over their own. Further, states affect the ability of non-state actors to act on and across their territories.[57] Non-state actors, in turn, also practically affect what states can achieve.[58] The community of humankind is the largest polycentrically governed commons. This governance can function if and only if it is held together by cooperation as belonging. The human rights obligation to cooperate fashions precisely such a legal relationship of belonging between states, people, and peoples that is itself dispositive of energy governance.

The International Covenant on Civil and Political Rights (ICCPR) incorporates a commons-based idea of cooperation. ICCPR Article 1(2) states that '[a]ll peoples may, for their own ends, freely dispose of their natural wealth and resources without prejudice to any obligations arising out of international economic co-operation, based upon the principle of mutual benefit, and international law'.[59] Cooperation here makes two appearances. The first is negative—the ICCPR applies 'without prejudice to any obligation arising out of international economic

[54] Hanson (n 45), at 405–34.

[55] Universal Declaration of Human Rights (1948), art 1.

[56] Declaration on Principles of International Law concerning Friendly Relations and Co-operation among States in Accordance with the Charter of the United Nations, (24 October 1970) UN General Assembly Resolution 2625 (XXV).

[57] *See ibid.*

[58] UN Guiding Principles on Business and Human Rights (2011).

[59] ICCPR, art 1(2). The same article appears at ICESCR, art 1(2).

cooperation'.[60] The second, however, is positive. The free disposal by peoples of their natural wealth and resources proceeds 'based upon the principle of mutual benefit'.[61] To unpack this provision, natural wealth and resources are held by peoples for the mutual benefit of all peoples. The logic of Article 1(2) ICCPR does not collectivize natural wealth and resources by including a reference to 'mutual benefit'.[62] Rather, the ICCPR sets up a commons relationship: each people forms part of a global resource community. Each people is the primary locus of the right to free disposition of resources.[63] Still, this right is limited by the principle of neighbourliness—it can only be exercised when it does not impair the rights of every other people to do the same.[64] The mutuality in ICCPR is one of belonging to a global resources commons.[65] Each people must protect the common resource base as a whole. Each people must further secure for each other a fair opportunity to dispose of natural resources.[66] This principle of mutual benefit reflects the same obligation to cooperate we have seen in the other critical human rights instruments.

The International Covenant on Economic, Social, and Cultural Rights (ICESCR) axiomatically codifies the obligation of states to cooperate. Its Article 2(1) requires the progressive, full realization of all economic, social, and cultural rights. This obligation applies to each state individually. It is also a collective obligation that must be fulfilled 'through international assistance and co-operation, especially economic and technical'.[67] Article 2(1) obligates states to act 'to the maximum of its available resources'.[68] This applies in the first place to the state's obligation to fulfil the rights in question on its own territory and for its own citizens. It

[60] ICCPR, art 1(2).
[61] *Ibid.*
[62] Spector, 'Two Conceptions of Justice and the Dystopia of Global Justice', (2015) 52 San Diego Law Review 1077, 1114.
[63] This squares both the American and Soviet positions at the time of drafting of the provision in question. On these positions, *see* Domke, 'American Protection Against Foreign Expropriation in the Light of the Suez Canal Crisis, (1957) 105 University of Pennsylvania Law Review 1033, 1035. For the relationship of the provision to permanent sovereignty over natural resources, *see* Cambou & Smis, 'Permanent Sovereignty over Natural Resources from A Human Rights Perspective: Natural Resources Exploitation and Indigenous Peoples' Rights in the Arctic', (2013) 22 Michigan State International Law Review 347, 357–61; Gathii, 'Food Sovereignty for Poor Countries in the Global Trading System', (2011) 57 Loyola Law Review 509, 535–36; Mtambierweki, 'Biotechnology and International Law Within the North-South Context', (2001) 14 Transnational Lawyer 103, 109.
[64] For a contrary interpretation, *see* Williams, 'Can International Legal Principles Play a Positive Role in Resolving Central and East European Transboundary Environmental Disputes', (1995) 7 Georgetown International Environmental Law Review 421, 441. This reading brackets out the principle of mutual benefit in its entirety.
[65] On the link between mutual benefit and commons, *see* Righetti & Schremmer, 'Waste and the Governance of Private and Public Property', (2022) 93 University of Colorado Law Review 609, 664; Rose, 'Privatization—The Road to Democracy', (2006) 50 Saint Louis Law Journal 691, 719–20.
[66] For the link between ICCPR art 1(2) and the nascent right to development, *see* Sohn, 'The New International Law: Protection of the Rights of Individuals Rather than States', (1982) 32 American University Law Review 1.
[67] ICESCR, art 2(1).
[68] *Ibid.*

also applies to the obligation to provide international assistance and cooperation. As the Committee on Economic, Social, and Cultural Rights noted in its General Comment No 3, 'the phrase "to the maximum of its available resources" was intended by the drafters of the Covenant to refer to both the resources existing within a State and those available from the international community through international cooperation and assistance'.[69] The importance of cooperation is reflected in many of the specific provisions of the ICESCR, such as Articles 11 (adequate standard of living) and 15 (cultural life and enjoyment of the benefits of scientific progress), as well as Articles 22 (role of the committee) and 23 (international action to achieve the rights recognized in the Convention).[70]

The UN Convention on the Right to Development similarly places a premium on cooperation. Like ICESCR Article 2(1), it requires, with regard to the obligation to fulfil the right to development, that '[e]ach State Party shall take measures, individually and through international assistance and cooperation, with a view to progressively enhancing the right to development [...]'.[71] Cooperation is thus critical to the progressive realization of rights in both contexts.

The Development Convention also places the idea of cooperation as we have developed it above at the heart of the obligation to respect and protect human rights. With regard to the obligation to respect the right to development, the Convention requires states to 'refrain from conduct, whether expressed through law, policy or practice, that [...] impairs the ability of another State or an international organization to comply with that State's or international organization's obligation with regard to the right to development'.[72] This prohibition is analogous to the prohibition to interfere with the efforts of a neighbour to use their share in common pool resources. Each state has to respect the efforts undertaken by their peers.

The Convention extends the same logic to the obligation to protect the right to development. This obligation requires states 'to adopt and enforce all necessary, appropriate and reasonable measures [...] to ensure that human or legal persons, peoples, groups, or any other State or agents that the State is in a position to regulate do not nullify or impair the enjoyment and exercise of the right to development within or outside their territories [...]' so long as regulating or enforcing such measures is within the scope of a state's legislative or enforcement jurisdiction.[73] The Convention emphasizes the overarching nature of the duty to cooperate in several other places.[74]

[69] Committee for Economic, Social, and Cultural Rights, General Comment No 3 (The Nature of States Parties Obligations) (14 December 1990), ¶ 13.
[70] *Ibid*; ICESCR, arts 11, 15, 22, 23.
[71] UN Convention on the Right to Development, art 12(1).
[72] *Ibid* at art 10(b).
[73] *Ibid* art 11.
[74] *See Ibid* at arts 8(2), 13, 18(b),

The duty to cooperate ultimately reflects the idea of civic virtue I introduced above. The idea of civic virtue asks us to act and to treat each other so that we can all take part in a community that provides for the welfare of all of its members. The Development Convention codifies this idea of civic virtue at the heart of the duty to cooperate. It sets out that:

> States have primary responsibility [...] for the creation of international conditions favourable to the realization of the right to development for all, and shall take deliberate, concrete and targeted steps, individually and jointly, including through cooperation within international organizations and engagement with civil society.[75]

The community of states are in a relationship of civic virtue with each other. The goal of this civic virtue is belonging. This belonging is expressed in the care for each other.

This care must establish the requisite international conditions such that each state can provide for the welfare of its peoples, people, and relevant groups. This means that we must put each other in a meaningful position to have a fair opportunity to compete with each other in the global commons. This obligation, in turn, requires us to 'mobilize appropriate technical, technological, financial, infrastructural and other necessary resources to enable State Parties, particularly in developing and least developed countries, to fulfil their obligations under the present Convention'.[76]

The Development Convention makes a similar point in slightly different terms. The duty to cooperate in the Convention is anchored in the idea of solidarity.[77] The Convention defines solidarity by reference to 'unity' and 'union of interests, purposes and actions'.[78] Unity or union entails belonging 'among individuals, peoples, States and international organizations'.[79] This unity or union causes the individuals, peoples, States and international organizations it binds together 'to sacrifice, or at least to limit, [their] individual interests for the overarching interest of the international community' and in turn sees to it that 'the benefits of [such] cooperation accrue to every member of the international community'.[80] What civic virtue captures better than the idea of solidarity is the relationship between stakeholders and community.

[75] UN Convention on the Right to Development, art 13(2).
[76] *Ibid* at art 13(2)(e).
[77] *Ibid* at arts 3(i), 13(2).
[78] *Ibid* at art 3(i).
[79] *Ibid.*
[80] Rüdiger Wolfrum, *Solidarity and Community Interest: Driving Forces for Interpretation and Development of International Law* (Brill Nijhoff 2021) 90.

Solidarity does not perfectly capture this idea. Civic virtue is a better fit. Here, the solidarity discourse lands on an idea of 'self-centred solidarity' due to the benefits each stakeholder receives through solidarity.[81] It then seeks to balance this self-centred aspect of solidarity against a healthy egalitarianism. This egalitarianism, in turn, 'strives for the abolition or at last the amelioration of substantial inequalities among States'.[82]

Self-centred solidarity begins with 'me' and asks why I would want to exhibit solidarity.[83] This lens ultimately treats solidarity as a means and not an end.[84] It looks to achieving a goal that is external to the practice of cooperation as solidarity to ground its usefulness. This external goal is anchored in both enlightened self-interest,[85] and a duty-based sense of justice sounding in the social contract tradition.[86]

Cooperation as belonging inverts that relationship. It treats belonging as an end rather than a means. The consequence of this switch is that the demands of union are more immediate. I no longer look for an external referent or reason for cooperation (self-centred or altruistic). In the context of civic virtue, the question 'what do I get out of it' would misunderstand the concept. I do not act with civic virtue to achieve an external reward. I act as a good citizen. Still, my motivations are not altruistic. A chess player is not altruistic by offering a match to a fellow traveller.[87] The same is true in the context of civic virtue. The demands of cooperation as belonging become part of my own decision-making process. I display civic virtue because I practise citizenship. I practise citizenship because I belong to the republic. The exhortation to act for the good of my community is ingrained in my role. I further know that the consequence of rejecting the role of citizenship is calamitous—it deprives me of belonging, and as such undermines my very ability for human flourishing. Still, I do not act with civic virtue to avoid that consequence. I do it for its own sake just like I act as a son, husband, and father for its own sake.

[81] *Ibid.*

[82] *Ibid* at 93–94.

[83] The same is true in the context of altruistic solidarity. I have to be altruistic to display it.

[84] *See* n 86. The *obligatio in solidum* is a means to securing the payment of a debt. It is not an end in itself.

[85] Hestermeyer, 'Reality or Aspiration? Solidarity in Environmental and World Trade Law', *in Coexistence, Cooperation and Solidarity: Liber Amicorum Rüdiger Wolfrum* (Holger Hestermeyer et al eds, Martinus Nijhoff 2012) 45–63.

[86] Wolfrum (n 80), at 91. Wolfrum draws on Gentili, Grotius, and Pufendorf as source material for the idea of solidarity. *Ibid* at 42. His work here draws on authors who, on balance, take the natural law tradition in a contractarian direction. The contractarian link is also apparent in Hestermeyer's excellent derivation of the origins of solidarity in the *obligatio in solidum* in Roman law. *Obligatio in solidum* is an obligation owed between several debtors and several creditors. It thus presupposes a debtor–creditor relationship at the outset. *See* Roscoe Pound, *Readings in Roman Law* (Jacob North & Co 1906) 186. This is not the anticipation of civic virtue in the same Roman source material, which founds civic virtue not on contract but expanded civic kinship.

[87] MacIntyre (n 21), at 188.

The idea of cooperation as belonging strengthens the idea of cooperation found in international human rights treaties. Cooperation is necessary because agency is possible only to the extent we cooperate. This is the flipside of the idea of man as a social animal.[88] As social animals, our agency is constituted by our community. Acting with civic virtue means that I will cooperate for the betterment of my commonwealth. This betterment of my commonwealth, in turn, looks to empower the agency of my community, which then empowers me by expanding my capabilities for human flourishing. Treating cooperation as belonging as an end is the beginning of a virtuous cycle. Human development is community development. Understanding this relationship means that strengthening one will strengthen the other.[89]

Thinking of cooperation through the lens of civic virtue helps us to answer another question that is at the heart of the solidarity question. Why sacrifice? The solidarity discourse is premised in the idea that cooperation requires stakeholders to make a sacrifice in fulfilling their own interests in order to further the common interest.[90] Cooperation as solidarity therefore *appears* inherently rivalrous—I get less so that someone else gets more. Still, I ought to sacrifice because my sacrifice is good for the community as a whole.[91] Even this communal gain, however, may not always make up for the size of the immediate sacrifice.[92] The more altruistic the demands for self-sacrifice sound, that is, the more speculative the gain and the more tangible the immediate loss, the less likely a state is to heed them.

This is at the heart of the realpolitik problem. Why should I act for the good of others when doing so potentially weakens me? Realpolitik counsels that I should never sacrifice for others. I may make a short-term investment for long-term gains (for instance by building nuclear power plants or LNG terminals). Still, even such investments must make long-term, self-centred sense. Anyone acting on an entreaty to invest more without security of sufficient return is simply paying a gullibility tax. A champion of realpolitik would admit that justice and equality sound like nice enough goals. But they are basically appeals to charity. Such charity is best dispensed from a position of strength and abundance. A state therefore should not do anything that weakens its relative strength in the international system as that

[88] Aristotle, 'Politics', *in The Complete Works of Aristotle, The Revised Oxford Translation* (Jonathan Barnes ed, WD Ross & JO Urmson trans, Princeton University Press 1984) 1986.

[89] This see-sawing relationship is in effect at different levels. The red queen effect made famous by Acemoglu and Robinson is another version of the same phenomenon. The red queen effect describes the idea of competition between society and the state—a stronger society causes the state to strengthen which, in turn, causes society to strengthen. Acemoglu and Robinson cast this as a result of competition between social and political power along a narrow corridor. *See* Daron Acemoglu & James A Robinson, *The Narrow Corridor, States, Societies, and the Fate of Liberty* (Penguin 2019). We can now see what holds stakeholders on this narrow corridor—civic virtue.

[90] Wolfrum (n 80), at 91.

[91] *See ibid.*

[92] Here, we would get into the territory of the potential applicability of Kaldor-Hicks efficiency to the idea of solidarity.

would weaken its very ability to be charitable. In other words, realpolitik can easily invert the idea of solidarity to suggest that its goals are best met when the powerful gently extend a civilizing hand to the less fortunate.[93] To do so, they must of course maintain their perch. Any suggestion to the contrary would simply undermine the good that can realistically be achieved, given current economic and geostrategic realities.[94]

The answer to realpolitik must recast the question. There simply is no 'sacrifice'.[95] I cannot be better off by refusing to cooperate, as the solidarity lens implicitly appears to suggest. One of the interesting features of virtue is that it is precisely non-rivalrous. My exercise of virtue does not lessen the opportunity for anyone else to be virtuous. Someone else's exercise of virtue similarly should not make me worse off. Consequently, it is inapposite to think of cooperation as requiring a sacrifice.[96]

This is not to say that one may not achieve an undue material benefit by failing to cooperate. The point is just that such conduct is the beginning of a vicious cycle that is ultimately in no one's interest. Defection—refusal to make the 'sacrifice' in question—is itself cause for realpolitik alarm in others. Trust is eroding. Eroding trust requires a response to counter the new threat and improve our own energy security. Such policies undermine predictability and certainty in international affairs. This lack of certainty, in turn, will bring more realpolitik responses to the table. One thus enters a vicious cycle of mutually escalating realpolitik responses which serve no one.

As we confront realpolitik, the question is rather whether national resource use is reasonable and thus cooperative, or unreasonable and thus illicit. In the words of the ICCPR, reasonable use is 'based upon the principle of mutual benefit'.[97] Mutual benefit, in turn, means that, at a minimum I may not myself impair third-state policy efforts aimed at human development.[98] I must also restrain those within my legislative and enforcement jurisdiction from doing so.[99] It also means that I must invest to protect and maintain the resource community: I must put others in a position to have a reasonable opportunity to compete back and benefit from resources themselves.[100] This means that I have to support other

[93] For an interesting historical critique of this view of international law, *see* Martti Koskenniemi, *The Gentle Civilizer of Nations, The Rise and Fall of International Law 1870-1960* (Cambridge University Press 2004).

[94] *See* Martin Daunton, *The Economic Government of the World 1933-2023* (Farrar, Straus and Giroux 2023) 369 (discussing the US trade negotiation position at the beginning of the Kennedy round).

[95] Wolfrum (n 80), at 91.

[96] This claim is universal in nature. *See* Nussbaum, 'Non-Relative Virtues: An Aristotelian Account', *in The Quality of Life* (Martha Nussbaum & Amartya Sen eds, Oxford University Press 1993) 242, 265.

[97] ICCPR, art 1(2).

[98] UN Convention on the Right to Development, art 10(b).

[99] *Ibid* at art 11.

[100] *Ibid* at art 4(1).

stakeholders to put them in a position responsibly to use their respective natural wealth and resources. This use of resources must be for both their own good (ie realization of economic, social, and cultural rights),[101] and for our mutual global benefit in turn.[102] The typical means states use to support the means of third states to use their natural wealth and resources is through supporting foreign investment and global trade. In this scenario, both home and host state have respective obligations to secure the sustainability of this new economic activity by adopting appropriate fiscal regimes that limit risk, secure a sufficient return to attract capital, and provide appropriate means for development to the host state from the venture.[103]

One consequence of the civic virtue lens is that it treats cooperation as forward looking only. Cooperation seeks to improve development outcomes by protecting and maintaining the commons. It is not intended to compensate for past wrongdoing. One example of such cooperation is the provision of Marshall Plan aid to Germany after the Second World War. German war guilt precisely did not enter the picture. Securing the continued viability of European economies after the destruction of the war did.[104] Solidarity, on the other hand, is in principle consistent with a corrective justice lens. It would look to address inequalities as social wrongs.[105]

Civic virtue here may be self-sustaining in a way that solidarity may not be. It strengthens the trust needed to improve future cooperation. It has rewards for all involved. Addressing past wrongs, on the other hand, can have the consequence of leaving all more aggrieved—those who make recompense for having been called to order and those who have been recompensed for having received what is typically an inadequate remedy for the wrong suffered. Realpolitik here is correct that reparations are most sustainably given from a position of mutual strength to increase trust that we have indeed turned a page from past horrors. Otherwise, notions of guilt for past wrongs are typically at odds with attempts to restart cooperation.

The idea of cooperation as belonging in human rights law dovetails with reasonable use. I must use my own resources reasonably. This does not mean that I sacrifice or give up my ability to use my own resources unreasonably. Rather, it means that my exercise of rights in a shared resource space is precisely limited by the community in which I act. If I want to make use of my own resources, at all, I must respect these limitations.

101 ICESCR, art 2(1).
102 ICCPR, art 1(2).
103 UN Convention on the Right to Development, art 4(2).
104 Daunton (n 94), at 250–51.
105 *See* Wolfrum (n 80).

5.2(c) Energy Belonging: Agency, Cooperation, and Competition

Energy governance is a strong candidate for applying this idea of belonging. Different components of an energy value chain work in much the same way as adjacent rights to produce resources from a shared reservoir. In an energy value chain, I thrive because others 'ahead' and 'behind me' in the value chain thrive. I do not thrive alone. In an energy value chain, I also thrive because I compete with others in my own segment of the value chain—competition causes me to innovate. This innovation improves my outputs in an appreciable way for those who come after. This, in turn, strengthens the viability of my energy value chain as a whole because my value chain now can deliver energy more cheaply, more sustainably, or more reliably. My place in the value chain—my belonging to the value chain—constitutes my actions in the value chain.

The point for me to join the value chain is to participate in the value chain. That means that the 'end' of the value chain for a value chain stakeholder is belonging to the value chain, pure and simple. Consequently, belonging from an energy perspective is not a means. I act for the purpose of transforming an input into an output that, in turn, becomes someone else's input. This transformation is premised in cooperation because I neither generate my own input nor further transform my output into end use of energy. Energy value chain participants are consummate 'middlemen'. To these middlemen, transforming an input into an output is not a means. It is the very essence of their being in the middle to begin with.

The idea of acting in a value chain drives home that energy agency is bound up with the idea of energy belonging. Energy agency is possible because of a larger web of global and overlapping policy, market, and techno-commercial decisions by a broad set of independent actors. Each energy stakeholder can make effective decisions because of, and against the background of, this larger web.[106] It is impossible to have any agency in the energy context without this larger frame.

The same is fundamentally true of public stakeholders in the global energy system. As we have seen in Chapter 3, it is not possible to have an exclusively national energy system premised in complete national energy autarchy.[107] National energy policies have global spill-over effects. They help to constitute global value chains. These global value chains, in turn, support the realization of domestic energy priorities and prompt adjustments in domestic energy policies.[108] Belonging therefore shapes not just energy value chains. Belonging is at the heart of global energy governance more broadly speaking. Global energy value chains demonstrate this logic concretely. Still, the policy responses to global energy value chains

[106] *See* Wilhelm Röpke, *A Humane Economy, The Social Framework of the Free Market* (Elizabeth Henderson trans, 3rd edn, Intercollegiate Studies Institute 1998) 236.

[107] *See* section 3.2.

[108] *See ibid.*

are just as embedded in a global energy system as the value chains themselves are. Realpolitik is an attempt at establishing greater national energy agency through confrontation with the global energy system.[109] Still, given the practical impossibility of national energy autarchy, this realpolitik was premised in an instrumental view of cooperation—it counterbalanced the energy policies of third parties with energy alliances that, for the moment, increased national control over energy access. In a sense, the global energy system behaves like quicksand: even as policy-makers seek to exercise greater control over their respective parts of the global energy system, they become only more embedded in the global processes from which they wish to escape. Realpolitik wastes a lot of energy (literally and figuratively) because of the inherently inefficient nature of global governance.

This chapter has shown that there is an alternative—treat cooperation and belonging as an end in its own right. Doing so gives rise to an alternative paradigm for structuring energy value chains and the policy responses to harness them appropriately. We now no longer fight against the quicksand. We are instead escaping its pull by distributing the 'weight' of energy decision-making across a wider group of stakeholders who work together to escape the downward pull of wasteful realpolitik decision-making.

The overarching policy principle guiding such a cooperative paradigm is the idea of 'mutual benefit' codified in Article 1(2) ICCPR.[110] In the energy context, it means that we must deploy our respective energy resources for mutual benefit. These energy resources in the first place include the inputs needed to constitute functioning energy value chains. Most intuitively, these resources begin with 'natural resources' in the sense of primary materials like oil, gas, quartz, copper, rare earths, water, etc. As noted in Article 1(2) ICCPR, these resources also include capital resources (ie 'wealth').[111] They further involve each of the processes employed at each link of the energy value chain to transform consecutive inputs into consecutive outputs. These resources are obviously intellectual (ie intellectual property) and techno-industrial (ie refineries and assembly lines).[112] They similarly include markets in which these inputs and outputs can be traded to connect value chain links to each other.

The disposal and use of energy resources for mutual benefit means that every people must mutually benefit from the use of these energy resources. At a minimum, this means that peoples must not be cut off from energy access. Peoples cut off from energy access are deprived of a crucial precondition for belonging to the global energy system. They are left out. Such a disposal and use of energy resources

[109] *See* section 3.4.
[110] ICCPR, art 1(2).
[111] *Ibid.*
[112] *See* Gathii, 'Beyond China's Human Rights Exceptionalism in Africa: Leveraging Science, Technology and Engineering for Long-Term Growth', (2013) 51 Columbia Journal of Transnational Law 664, 687.

is precisely not for the mutual benefit of all peoples. Global policy informed by the idea of cooperation as belonging therefore must be deployed to address this failure. It is not possible to cooperate to realize human rights outcomes without bringing energy access to energy poor people, peoples, and societies.[113] The idea of cooperation as belonging now can provide a more granular understanding of this imperative. It is a matter of constituting a sense of a truly inclusive energy *community*. It is thus not a matter of handing out 'aid' to the less fortunate. It is a matter of creating a qualitatively stronger community capable of sharing in the benefits and burdens of the global energy system.

Similarly, a use of energy resources must be for the mutual benefit of all peoples who are already actively part of the global energy system. In principle, advances in energy technology are indeed mutually beneficial. These advances improve energy value chain outcomes by bringing down the price of energy inputs and by reducing the externalities of producing value chain outputs. Technology-forcing advances through policy means (ie by providing incentives and regulating externalities at the smokestack) are, in principle, mutually beneficial—they achieve desirable outcomes for the respective policymakers instituting a technology-forcing policy and benefit the global energy system by broadening sustainable energy access.[114] This is not to say that any energy policy is consistent with mutual benefit. Beggar-my-neighbour policies are decidedly not. Similarly, policies that concentrate benefits and burdens do not cohere with the idea of mutuality of benefit—they deprive some of a fair opportunity to compete back and participate in energy value chains and in the energy system by imposing additional barriers to entry on those stakeholders (environmental burdens and simply the prohibitive capital cost of participating, as well as broader social costs).[115]

The ultimate design of the global energy system under a paradigm of cooperation as belonging is open and 'flat' rather than hierarchical and diffuse. Cooperation as belonging is organized around the idea of mutual benefit. Mutual benefit is best realized by broadening energy access through broadening value chains themselves. Such mutual benefit extends the necessary benefits of belonging for stakeholders to feel a sense of belonging.[116] It also increases the stakeholders with active participation in energy decision-making. This broadened structure of decision-making itself strengthens belonging by providing more opportunities for deliberation and decision by a larger group of stakeholders in more varied roles.[117]

Such decision-making is 'thicker'. Stakeholders make more policy, commercial, and environmental decisions with regard to the energy system. They do not just rubber stamp the decisions of others, they are themselves intimately involved in

[113] *See* Vaclav Smil, *Energy and Civilization—A History* (MIT Press 2017) 363.
[114] The diffusion of solar and wind energy is one such example.
[115] *See* Röpke (n 106), at 236.
[116] *See* Ostrom (n 26), at 263.
[117] *Ibid.*

a much larger set of energy decisions on a commercial and on a policy level. It creates a common vocabulary for cooperation by exposing a greater number of stakeholders to greater detail about the problems we have to overcome. (It is one thing to say that 'someone should decarbonize the electricity grid'. It is another to make active decisions about energy investments that must earn a sufficient return to support companies and economic sectors.) This common vocabulary allows us to deliberate across relevant social sectors. This deliberation reorients value chains internally through innovation and externally through policy support to achieve our shared aims. This deliberation focuses on solving the critical problem posed by reverse salients within the energy system that prevent it from achieving energy outcomes optimally.[118] Belonging and agency mutually strengthen each other.

This idea of mutual benefit also translates to the interactions between energy value chains making up the energy system. Here, the stakeholders are value chain participants. Acting for the mutual benefit of all value chain stakeholders means to support a broad energy mix. A broad energy mix accommodates the largest number of existing energy value chain stakeholders. It thus provides for the greatest possible competition to improve the energy system in terms of providing cheaper, more secure, and more environmentally sustainable energy outcomes.

In the context of the value chain, mutual benefit means that we are building a universal energy system. This universal energy system does not destroy any one major value chain. The universal system emerged as a solution to the battle of the systems between direct and alternating current (AC/DC). The universal system made sure that as much of the existing value chain and existing capital investments could be worked into the energy system as it developed. It did not strand investment and value chains. It repurposed them as the system continued to evolve.[119] The same lesson is likely to hold in the context of the decarbonization of energy systems in the twenty-first century. The point is not to displace any one input to the global energy system, even as champions for some systems suggest precisely that.[120] Instead, the point is to build a universal system that can incorporate all value chains while reducing greenhouse gas emissions. Mutual benefit in the value chain context means that competition occurs within a universal system rather than within a system that predetermines who may participate in the first place.

This universal setting allows for innovation to take hold. Innovation here is mutually supportive rather than rivalrous. One object lesson of this mutually supportive innovation is the benefits provided to non-fossil fuel chains by advances in horizontal drilling and hydraulic fracturing. Firstly, hydraulically fractured wells

[118] Thomas Hughes, *Networks of Power, Electrification in Western Society 1880-1930* (Johns Hopkins University Press 1983) 79.
[119] *Ibid* at 125–27.
[120] Laura Cozzi, *Net Zero by 2050, A Roadmap for the Global Energy Sector* (International Energy Agency 2021).

are likely to become a source of lithium from produced water.[121] Water from these wells is rich in lithium. As it is produced as a byproduct of oil and gas development, it is a reasonably cost-effective means to produce lithium.[122] It also does not impose additional environmental burdens from extraction. It therefore perfectly complements a battery value chain that is in facial competition with oil and gas. Still, innovation in one value chain benefits another. Similarly, drilling expertise permits us to develop next generation geothermal generation. This geothermal generation taps into geological heat. Drilling advances allow us to run a water/steam loop through geothermal formations to power a turbine. The loop is closed, meaning that we simply recirculate the water to generate electricity.[123] This is possible precisely because we have become better at drilling for oil and gas. Innovation in renewables thus can be the byproduct of oil and gas innovation. It is likely that future energy technologies like fusion energy will add similar synergies between energy systems.[124] This is not to say that innovation will not displace parts of the energy system over time. Energy technology cycles always do.[125] Yet, when they do, they tend to draw on what was there before. Innovation is destructive at a pace that permits adaptation and synergy. It is mutually beneficial to value chain stakeholders in general because it allows them each to make a home in the value chain on the basis of competitive innovation.

5.3 Energy Belonging and Energy Realpolitik

This leaves us to explore the relationship between energy belonging and energy realpolitik. As I have shown in the chapter so far, energy belonging and energy realpolitik are alternative ways to conceive of the relationship between global energy policymakers. Still, is it possible to transform energy realpolitik into energy belonging and vice versa? If so, what are the relevant mechanisms and consequences for global energy governance?

The discussion so far suggests that energy belonging and energy realpolitik share a critical 'fixed point'. That fixed point is trust. In the absence of trust, realpolitik becomes the only rational paradigm for interaction with other energy stakeholders.[126] Energy value chain participants now must organize around

[121] Mackey et al, 'Estimates of Lithium Mass Yields from Produced Water Sources from the Devonian-aged Marcellus Shale', (2024) 14 Scientific Reports 8813.

[122] *See ibid.*

[123] Blankenship et al, 'Pathways to Commercial Liftoff: Next-Generation Geothermal Power', (March 2024) US Department of Energy, https://liftoff.energy.gov/wp-content/uploads/2024/03/LIFTOFF_DOE_NextGen_Geothermal_v14.pdf, last accessed 18 November 2024.

[124] 'The Global Fusion Industry in 2024', (16 July 2024) Fusion Industry Association, https://www.fusionindustryassociation.org/wp-content/uploads/2024/07/2024-annual-global-fusion-industry-report.pdf, last accessed 18 November 2024

[125] Perez (n 3).

[126] Axelrod (n 14), at 58–59.

mutually distrustful policy stakeholders. Realpolitik continues a kind of global cooperation—still, this cooperation is a means rather than an end in its own right. Cooperation is a means to securing and bolstering energy agency. Realpolitik defects from cooperation as soon as defection in fact secures or bolsters national energy agency better than cooperation.

Given the absence of trust, national policymakers (and rival value chain participants) are constantly gathering intelligence on each other. They do so in order to react quickly to any move that might threaten energy agency. This quick reaction is critical to safeguarding that a counteraction will in fact have enough time to be effective—slow action may allow a rival a significant leverage at a critical point. Realpolitik is optimally deployed when it does not permit such critical moments to come about due to proper counter-planning. At the same time, quick action must be gradual so as to avoid jumping from the frying pan into the fire. Gradual action allows one to navigate the thin line between rival threats to one's energy agency by not placing too much weight on any one part of one's energy strategy. Realpolitik engages in each of these steps to secure the independence of the realpolitik stakeholder—it will therefore err on the side of seeing a threat and responding to it.[127]

One core tool for realpolitik to prevent any one state, stakeholder, or group of states or stakeholders from threating energy agency is to deconcentrate energy value chains. The concentration of critical parts of energy value chains can give market power to strategically placed stakeholders. Market power, in turn, means that the strategically placed stakeholder can achieve rents from its fellow stakeholders—it can use its market power to receive more than the fair value because it has become a central participant in a value chain. The strategically placed stakeholder can use this market power to achieve financial or policy benefits, meaning that it is a significant threat to energy agency. The deconcentration of value chains reduces the risk of the exercise of market power by increasing the number of suppliers who could step in should a stakeholder attempt to manipulate the market to its own advantage.

As realpolitik counterbalances the potential for the exercise of power through energy resources, it does not tip over the realpolitik board. It moves gradually. This gradual movement allows global energy value chains to adjust to the new unstable equilibrium. This equilibrium reflects a transparent status quo that allows a certain amount of planning security for all stakeholders. Still, this status quo is never quite stable. Any innovation, any new policy initiative, any new critical market entrant in an important energy value chain threatens the equilibrium or balance of energy power. This instability is at the heart of the tendency of energy realpolitik to waste. There is simply no ability to act with sufficient foresight in energy value chains.

[127] Kenneth N Waltz, *Theory of International Politics* (Random House 1979) 102–28.

The situation is obviously quite different if there is a strong basis of trust. In this scenario, energy belonging can become an alternative paradigm for energy governance to realpolitik. Here, the engagement with other stakeholders focuses on mutual benefit premised in shared decision-making. In an environment of trust, I am no longer fearful about the security of my energy agency. I can now exercise my energy agency with a view to long-term cooperative development, disposal, and use of global energy resources with a view to maintaining a reasonable opportunity for all energy stakeholder to have a fair opportunity to develop, dispose, and use their own share of these resources.

A mechanism of neighbourly supervision and gradual response to defections is also constitutive of this organization of the global energy system. This mechanism is of course at the heart of realpolitik—it is the critical early warning system to protect one's energy agency. In a commons governance paradigm premised in belonging, trust is constantly nourished in much the same way that suspicion was constantly nourished in realpolitik. Belonging is premised around communal action. In theoretical terms, this communal action is constituted by a collective and mutual exercise of civic virtue. In more prosaic terms, we watch our neighbour sweating next to us whether we dig an irrigation trench or stand side by side in the face of danger. In the context of the energy system, we each gradually act on the signals we send to each other through collective decisions. The more we confirm a course of action through our individual energy decisions (investments, innovations, and regulatory actions), the more committed we become to the course of action. Our respective conduct becomes mutually reinforcing out of a sense of belonging.

Finally, belonging also follows realpolitik in preferring a broader base of actively participating stakeholders in the energy system. It does so for a different reason—it expands the group of active decisionmakers maintaining the energy system. This strengthens the authority of energy decision-making because decisions are carried by a broader cross-section of energy stakeholders. This, in turn, increases the trust of these stakeholders in each other in light of the broad-based consensus around collective decision-making.

The mechanisms of realpolitik and belonging share many processes in common that make a transition from one to the other distinctly possible. They each look to action by a broad number of stakeholders. These stakeholders constantly monitor each other's actions in both settings. They further look to deconcentrate value chains and thus strengthen the agency of each stakeholder in a diffuse global energy system.

What then is missing from the realpolitik paradigm to turn it towards the idea of belonging? The critical process that is missing is a richer collective deliberative process to make decisions together with a view of securing a common good. Without a common good, it is not possible to leverage existing decision processes towards the idea of belonging. This idea of a common energy good is what I will discuss in the next chapter.

Still, even without this missing element, we can already see that the preconditions to move from realpolitik to belonging (and sadly vice versa) are already built into the respective processes of decision in each. It is easier to see how belonging might turn to realpolitik. If our neighbourly supervision finds that I am working harder than my neighbours and that no amount of exhortation encourages them to do more, it is increasingly likely that I will similarly slack in my effort. Action towards a common good can wither as we see others abandon it.[128]

The idea of a reverse salient uses precisely this image. A reverse salient is a military metaphor. In its original context, it refers to the collective lagging behind by part of a military force that impedes the ability of the whole to achieve its goals. This reverse salient is typically the result of a kind of 'contagion' within that force—there is a lack of common belief and this lack of common belief leads slowly to an approach of each for himself. Reverse salients are so dangerous because they risk unravelling the whole. When they unravel the whole, the only place to go is realpolitik—saving my own skin before anything else.[129] Still, the same mechanism can work in the opposite direction, as well.

As we constantly observe each other, we can in fact build a stronger trust in each other's actions through greater understanding of our respective motivations. All we need to do is network more with each other. This networking will lead us to a better understanding of what we each are trying to do and why we are taking our respective actions.[130] This understanding, in turn, can lead to more meaningfully cooperative efforts (it turns out that I can assist my neighbour without much cost and actually make us both better off even in a realpolitik world). Though it may sound quaint, watching each other improve our respective lots is motivating.

The initial trick for turning realpolitik to belonging is thus to increase the density of energy decision-making networks. The good news is that this is already ongoing at almost every level of energy decision-making. One of the most visible such efforts is the annual Conference of the Parties under the United Nations Convention on Climate Change and the Paris Agreement concluded pursuant to it (known simply as 'COP'). The COP is a networking event for policymakers and energy industry stakeholders to exchange ideas about the decarbonization of the global energy system.[131] It meets annually, and has access to an increasing amount

[128] *See* Ostrom (n 27).

[129] Hughes (n 118), at 79–104.

[130] Anne-Marie Slaughter, *A New World Order* (Princeton University Press 2004); Levit, 'A Bottom-Up Approach to international Lawmaking: The Tale of Three Trade Finance Instruments', (2005) 30 Yale Journal of International Law 125; Koh 'Triptych's End: A Better Framework to Evaluate 21st Century International Lawmaking', (2017) 126 Yale Law Journal Forum 338; Harold Hongju Koh, *The Trump Administration and International Law* (Oxford University Press 2018); Osofsky & Levit, 'The Scale of Networks?: Local Climate Change Coalitions', (2008) 8 Chicago Journal of International Law 409; Welton & Eisen, 'Clean Energy Justice: Charting an Emerging Agenda', (2019) 43 Harvard Environmental Law Review 307.

[131] Daniel Bodansky, Jutta Brunée, & Lavanya Rajamani, *International Climate Change Law* (Oxford University Press 2017) 142–43.

of relevant data that can guide networked decision-making from self-interest to our common interest. There are many other similar governmental fora. Similarly, there are many similar industry fora that provide a similar networking opportunity for energy value chain participants. Realpolitik, even in the early twenty-first century, is not a cold dog-eat-dog world. It is a far more networked world that can in fact work towards the ideal of belonging far more readily than one might have assumed.

5.4 Conclusion

Cooperation is critical for the global energy system to function. Energy value chains inherently depend on cooperation between value chain participants. Similarly, energy policymakers depend on third parties and third states to achieve their own policy goals due to the nature in which global energy resources are shared around the world. As I noted in Chapter 3, this distribution of energy resources creates a mutual global dependence which makes cooperation inevitable.[132]

In this chapter, I have argued that the human development lens we deployed in the last chapter requires us to look at cooperation as an end rather than a means. The realpolitik answer to energy governance looks to cooperation as a means to secure relative advantages within the global energy system. These relative advantages are a safeguard for domestic energy agency. Yet, this understanding of cooperation as a means fundamentally misses that cooperation cannot function optimally when it is deployed as such a means. At a minimum, hardnosed realpolitik itself leads to a greater default level of suspicion. This suspicion in its own right increases transaction costs at most every step of every energy value chain. This means that we cannot optimally realize human development because too many of our resources are 'trapped' in the costs of realpolitik policy-making.

I have shown that there is an alternative to realpolitik. This alternative treats cooperation as an end rather than as a means. Treating cooperation as an end looks to cooperation as belonging. The bond of belonging holding together energy value chains is an end of energy governance in its own right. The bond of belonging ties us together in a community. This community is established around the idea of mutual benefit and shared decision-making. I have argued that the idea of cooperation as belonging pivots from cooperation as a realpolitik means by introducing greater trust in shared decision-making. I have argued that we can build towards such greater trust through increased networking of decision-making. This, in turn, means that we can use the mechanics of realpolitik to achieve more than just our own end of increasing our own energy agency. We can support and increase the energy agency of all stakeholders. This, in turn, can help us to overcome the inherent

[132] *See* section 3.4.

waste of realpolitik decision-making by creating stronger incentives for reasonable use of energy resources.

Before I set out to discuss the idea of our common energy good, I need to make a final and pragmatic observation. In this chapter, I have juxtaposed the idea of cooperation as the end of belonging and cooperation as a realpolitik means. Theoretically, these ideas are incommensurate and mutually contradictory. I either treat cooperation as an end or as a means. Treating them as both fails to appreciate that each builds on ultimately inconsistent theoretical starting points.

Practically, this juxtaposition is overdrawn. Cooperation as a means and cooperation as an end in reality exist on a continuum. We rarely if ever treat cooperation as an end and an end only. We of course create myths around this ideal. Few of us ever fully live up to it. Still, it would be distinctly uncharitable to say that we always treat cooperation as a means for selfish ends. Frequently, we truly do act out of a sense of belonging—we do not hold the door, help someone carrying their groceries, or yell to stop a pedestrian crossing the street from being hit by a car because we expect anything tangible in return. The same goes in the energy setting. Energy cooperation lives on a continuum. Sometimes, we are closer to an understanding of belonging. Sometimes, we find ourselves closer to a pure realpolitik driven engagement.

The fact that energy cooperation exists on a continuum is ultimately a good thing. It is means that we can always rebuild. We never fully lose our ability to belong even when cooperation turns distrustful. We can always turn the same processes of decision in a different direction towards a shared value. Cooperation as belonging therefore is a goal that ultimately will rarely if ever be fully realized and yet is also never completely abandoned. It is realized more or less effectively. The remainder of this book will identify how we can realize it more fully. In the next chapter, I will outline why we might wish to do so by sketching the common energy good such a conception would help to support.

6
The Common Energy Good

6.1 Introduction

Part II sets out to answer—how do we improve on a global energy order ruled by realpolitik? This required us to have a metric of this 'improvement'. I argued that the appropriate metric was human development (as opposed to economic development). The point of improving a global energy order as against one that was ruled exclusively by realpolitik is to further human development. Needless to say, this end can only be achieved through cooperation. Still, the quality of this cooperation remained an open question. A realpolitik perspective is transactional—it treats cooperation as a means to selfish ends. The question therefore was—is there an alternative to this view of cooperation as a means? I answered that indeed there is—true cooperation ultimately is not about me. It constitutes an 'us' to which each of us belongs. This belonging is an end in its own right.

The mechanics of belonging should have given us some hope in two important respects. Firstly, belonging is premised in a relationship of trust. This trust permits us to achieve significantly more jointly than would have been possible in a realpolitik world. We avoid a significant level of waste due to the greater trust inherent in relationships of belonging. The idea of cooperation as belonging therefore is meaningfully supportive of the overall goal of improving on realpolitik governance of energy systems. Secondly, the mechanics of cooperation as belonging could in fact exist on a continuum of realpolitik. We need not turn swords to ploughshares to achieve our aim (at least, not immediately). We can build on the logic of existing realpolitik cooperation to achieve this improvement of constituting the global energy system as a community to which we can truly belong.

This chapter now picks up the thread. In Chapter 5, I said that belonging constitutes a process of decision that secures a common good of decisionmakers. If I know what this common good is, it is possible to nudge existing decision processes towards this common good. In doing so, I can create a sense of belonging and constitute a community where I previously found a random assemblage of 'rogues and knaves' out for their own good. I can transform lone actors into a fellowship.

In this chapter, I ask three questions to attempt this feat. I begin with a baseline question: what is the goal of energy cooperation in a realpolitik frame? Energy realpolitik, of course, is about energy agency. Realpolitik seeks to secure energy agency for the stakeholder adopting it as a toolkit by maintaining or increasing

A Theory of Global Energy Governance. Frédéric Gilles Sourgens, Oxford University Press. © Frédéric Sourgens 2025.
DOI: 10.1093/9780198950325.003.0006

relative power over key parts of energy value chains constituting the global energy order. Realpolitik uses cooperation as a means to secure my own in a zero-sum game.[1] Cooperation aims at the opposite of a common good. Realpolitik is a paragon of knavery—unreliable, unscrupulous, and ultimately selfish.

This sets up the next question. What common good does energy belonging realize? This common good is something that is a product of deeper cooperation—it is fully realized only to the extent that the cooperation is pursued as an end. It cannot be gamed but must be earned. This common good is the procurement of core public goods needed for the proper functioning of the energy system as a whole. These public goods are the equivalent of the three limbs of the energy trilemma. The quest for energy access finds the common good of energy abundance. The quest for energy security finds the common good of energy peace. The quest for energy sustainability finds the common good of circular energy stewardship.

The final question is in many ways the critical question of Part II. I argued at the end of Chapter 5 that cooperation as belonging and realpolitik cooperation exist on a continuum. Neither is absolute and neither is ever absolutely banished or exorcised. With the public goods constituting the common energy good in mind, how can we nudge along energy governance towards energy belonging? I suggested the networking of energy agency as a key missing ingredient of governance in a purely realpolitik world. We can now answer what networks we need and how they should be constituted to realize the common good of the energy system.

6.2 Realpolitik Energy Power

The starting point of analysis is the default position of well-executed energy realpolitik. What good does energy realpolitik realize? The question is important for two reasons. The first is to get our bearings about what we are up against in seeking to improve global energy governance. The second is that if we are to hope to replace energy realpolitik as the mode of global energy governance, we must, to a point, be able to achieve its ultimate end by different means. It does us no good to insist on the desirability of utopias. If we wish to move towards them, we must find a path that can satisfy the hardnosed and the cynic that at the very least, they have not lost more than a little time in attempting to journey down our path.

Energy realpolitik is about energy agency.[2] Stakeholders engaging in energy realpolitik hope to carve out for themselves a space in which they can have authority over their own energy choices.[3] These choices are critical because of the

[1] *See* Kenneth N Waltz, *Theory of International Politics* (Random House 1979).
[2] *See* Yergin, 'Ensuring Energy Security', (2006) 85 Foreign Affairs 69.
[3] Waltz (n 1), at 118.

significance of energy for economic productivity. To have energy agency is to have economic agency.[4] This economic agency, in turn, supports social agency through increased communication opportunities and more opportunities to combine together for our respective social ends. Economic and social agency finally undergird cultural richness. Energy agency therefore is about realizing for oneself the realization of critical economic, social, and cultural capabilities necessary to lay claim to supporting the welfare of one's respective subjects, citizens, and stakeholders.

The path of realpolitik to securing energy agency is to look to build energy power. I use energy power here akin to military power. In the military context, one can think about military power as a state's level of ability to use violence to secure national security goals.[5] Energy power has both a defensive and an offensive component. Defensively, is the level of energy capacity sufficiently great to withstand the use of energy as an offensive tool of policy-making?[6] Can one overcome a shutdown in access from a particular supplier? Offensively, does one have the ability to overcome the defensive tools of other stakeholders to achieve a material security success? Energy power together refers to the level of ability of the stakeholder to use its energy resources to secure economic and national security ends.[7]

As I have argued in the context of Chapter 3 already, realpolitik is typically a zero-sum game.[8] It looks to power over others and the power of others over us.[9] This means that one will always be on the lookout to improve one's defensive energy power to escape the dangers of an 'energy attack' by a rival stakeholder. Due to this focus of a well-played realpolitik game, offensive energy power should be fleeting. It should lead stakeholders who are vulnerable to offensive energy power to work together to counter the threat of this offensive power. This, in turn, will diminish the impact of offensive power. In a truly well-executed realpolitik policy, offensive power should emerge only for truly brief moments in time. A new energy innovation may in fact concentrate energy resources despite the best efforts of energy rivals to prevent such a state of affairs (the US held a strategically relevant relative oil advantage through the 1960s).[10] Yet, even then, the concentration should be limited, as other rivals catch up to the innovation frontier or adopt alternative means of achieving similar energy outcomes.

Cooperation as a means is a critical tool to reach dynamic global equilibria of relative energy power. By working together, stakeholders can counteract, limit, and

[4] *See* Martin Daunton, *The Economic Government of the World 1933-2023* (Farrar Straus & Giroux 2023) 567–70.

[5] *See* Fletcher, 'Strict Subordination: The Origins of Civil Control of Military Power in State Constitutions', (2023) 14 Harvard National Security Journal 254, 267–68.

[6] *See* Waltz (n 1), at 127.

[7] *See ibid* at 106.

[8] *See* section 3.4.

[9] *See* Waltz (n 1), at 102–28.

[10] *See* 'Oil Dependence and U.S. Foreign Policy 1850-2023', (2023) Council on Foreign Relations, https://www.cfr.org/timeline/oil-dependence-and-us-foreign-policy, last accessed 30 November 2024.

balance the power of other rival stakeholders. This would not be possible working alone. Stakeholders ultimately need each other to create such an equilibrium.[11]

This kind of cooperation gives rise to a vanishingly thin idea of a common good. We can break down the logic of this kind of energy cooperation. In principle, stakeholders act together because 'each, in order to attain his *own* objective, can agree to assist the other to attain *his* objective, but the condition of such assistance is that it shall be reciprocal'.[12] Realpolitik adds the element that each stakeholder seeks to observe the activities of others towards the reciprocal end and adjusts its activities in light of the conduct of its peer to react quickly to any sign of defection. Energy stakeholder A acts together with energy stakeholder B to block the growing power of energy stakeholder X. A and B work on the basis of reciprocity—A and B need each other's reciprocal assistance to counterbalance X; A is vulnerable to a defection by B to X or even to a third party, C, (thus dealing a serious blow to A's defensive energy power) and vice versa. (Say X is an exporter of pipeline gas with potential market power. A and B coordinate their action to cause L to build a liquified natural gas export facility to decouple from X. A is able to drive down the price of L's gas causing C to buy a greater volume of gas than B could have, thus increasing the yield from the facility for L. L terminates its relationship with B and enters into an arrangement with C instead, leaving A more vulnerable to X than before.[13]) A and B should build in guarantees of reciprocity—still, the nature of their coordination makes this comparatively difficult. A and B are not in privity *with each other* (in our example, they would be in privity with L).[14] This means that the guarantee of reciprocity is purely premised in the ability of each stakeholder to apply counter-pressure to prevent defection. The common good here is purely transactional. A and B each need each other to attain their own individual good and care nothing about the good of the other.

These equilibria are unstable. Combination with C might serve A (and L) better than the coordination with B. A (and, more importantly, L) would consider their respective defections 'efficient' for their own purposes.[15] Similarly, energy innovation may throw entire networks of cooperation into disarray (the macroeconomic vulnerability of offshore wind projects to commodities prices leaves the door open for other technologies like small modular nuclear reactors, next generation geothermal, or fusion energy to displace a significant proportion of its

[11] *See* section 3.4.

[12] John Finnis, *Natural Law and Natural Rights* (Oxford University Press 1979) 139.

[13] The scenario is a seriously oversimplified hypothetical premised in the idea that Germany would have entered the Qatari LNG significantly earlier than it did in 2022, thus changing the terms on which Asian importers could purchase LNG from Qatar. On Germany's late entry, *see* 'Qatar Signs Gas Export Deal with Germany', (29 November 2022) Deutsche Welle, https://www.dw.com/en/qatar-signs-gas-export-deal-with-germany/a-63923323, last accessed 30 November 2024.

[14] On the nature of this triangular relationship point, *see* Finnis (n 12) at 139–40.

[15] *See* Posner & Sykes, 'Efficient Breach of International Law: Optimal Remedies, "Legalized Noncompliance", and Related Issues', (2011) 110 Michigan Law Review 243.

'default' growth potential).[16] This unstable nature of equilibria highlights how thin the common good in a purely transactional relationship is. In this context, 'the co-ordination of action is not valued by any of the parties as a component or aspect of his objective'.[17]

A realpolitik energy world is situated on the thinnest, transactional end of the common good scale. Everyone is vulnerable to defection at all times because no one sees an inherent value in cooperation. This vulnerability itself must be accounted for in defensive energy power calculations, thus increasing the potential for waste in a realpolitik of this paradigm in direct correlation to the systemic risk of defection. This systemic risk of defection reflects the thin nature of the common good shared by energy stakeholders.

6.3 The Common Energy Good

The idea of energy belonging builds out a far more robust idea of the common good. It moves away from a purely transactional understanding of the common good to securing a good for the community through the community. This understanding stabilizes the instability of transactional arrangements. This stability comes at a cost—it creates a vulnerability to exploitation by free riders and realpolitik actors.[18] It therefore requires a constantly reinforcing trust premised in the conspicuous exercise (and observation of) 'virtuous' conduct for the betterment of the community.

Like the realpolitik paradigm, energy belonging is also about energy agency. Energy belonging wishes to secure the greatest possible energy agency by maximizing reasonable use and minimizing waste. To that end, unlike energy realpolitik, energy belonging begins from the starting point that energy action is always embedded in an energy community consisting of a broad variety of different global actors. Energy agency can only be harnessed when we deploy our efforts towards shared goals.

The fact that we are part of an inherently shared energy enterprise means that the common good is appreciably thicker than it is in the context of a realpolitik understanding of energy governance. The common good now is part of a relationship of care. The most intuitive such relationship of care is friendship. A relationship of care between friends means that '(i) A acts ... for B's well-being, for the

[16] On these macro-economic pressures on offshore wind, *see* 'Offshore Wind: Strategies for Uncertain Times', (12 July 2024) McKinsey & Co, https://www.mckinsey.com/industries/electric-power-and-natural-gas/our-insights/offshore-wind-strategies-for-uncertain-times, last accessed 30 November 2024.

[17] Finnis (n 12) at 140.

[18] Elinor Ostrom, *Governing the Commons, The Evolution of Institutions for Collective Action* (Cambridge University Press 2015) 45.

sake of B, while (ii) B acts for […] A's well-being for the sake of A, (iii) each of them knows of the other's activity and […] knowledge, and (iv) each of them co-ordinates […] his activity with the activity […] of the other so that there is a […] community […] and reciprocity not only of knowledge but also of activity'.[19]

A relationship of belonging differs from friendship by mediating the relationship between individual members of the community through the community, as opposed to linking friend immediately to friend. Thus, a relationship of care between fellow members of a community of belonging means that (i) each member acts for the wellbeing of the community, for the sake of the community, while (ii) the community provides for the welfare of each member for the sake of each member, and while (iii) each member knows of the activities of other members to this common and reciprocal end, and (iv) each of them coordinate their respective activities to secure a reciprocal good that is only possible in community. The common good in this relationship is the good that can only be achieved, if at all, through the collective efforts of the community for the welfare of each of its members.

This posits that there are energy goods that can only be achieved through co-operation. To some extent, one can think of these as public goods. Such public goods are goods that are best achieved through pooling of resources. National defence is a public good because it would make little sense for each to secure their own defence. The cost of effective private armies is simply too high. The same might be said about large infrastructure. Such public goods benefit everyone, their enjoyment by anyone does not diminish its value to others, and does not vary according to our preferences.[20]

Still, while the common good is also a public good, common goods are qualitatively different from many public goods. The common good is inherent in community. It is unachievable but for community. This is not true for all public goods. To return to the example of defence, it makes sense to speak of a private defence force in excess of the public military even if such a force is expensive to retain (in fact, such forces are reasonably ubiquitous and effective). (A similar phenomenon was on display in the context of the 2025 Los Angeles wildfires. Residents of threatened neighbourhoods tried to hire private fire fighters to protect their own homes privately.[21])

What does not make sense is to speak of a private *peace*. Peace is not the same as the ability to respond to, or deter, an (unprovoked) foreign attack.[22] Peace is a condition or state of mutual trust. We do not anticipate attack because we each

[19] Finnis (n 12), at 140.

[20] John Rawls, *A Theory of Justice* (Oxford University Press 1971) 266.

[21] Arango & Kamin, "'Will Pay Any Amount': Private Firefighters Are in Demand in L.A.", (12 January 2025) New York Times, https://www.nytimes.com/2025/01/12/us/private-firefighters-la-wildfires.html, last accessed 21 January 2025.

[22] *See ibid.*

contribute to peace and see each other contributing to peace. I can only have this peace, and the security peace offers, in community. In a sense it might make sense to speak of peace as a public good because, like national defence, it is non-excludable and non-rivalrous. Yet, it differs from other public goods in that peace cannot be ransomed even though a cessation of hostilities can be. A cessation of hostilities is a public good. Peace is more than a public good.[23] It requires active, constant vigilance to keep. Each member of the community at peace 'belongs to' this peace. Each member must safeguard the peace for the benefit of the community. And the community safeguards it for each member. Each member must do so even when there is no appreciable risk of hostilities. This vigilance perpetuates the sense of security, and the incumbent ability to plan peace entails.

As I will argue in the remainder of this chapter, energy belonging gives rise to a common good of this kind. It is a common good that is instrumental to the solution of the energy trilemma with which I began this book.[24] That trilemma pulled us in different directions when facing a reverse salient in the energy system.[25] Our answer aims to realize energy affordability, energy security, and environmental sustainability. Still, we can only maximize two of the three. In doing so, we would undermine the third. We therefore need a means to balance all three limbs of the trilemma against each other optimally to realize outcomes consistent with each of the three limbs to the maximum extent possible. We cannot achieve this goal transactionally. We must create a community of mutual benefit.[26]

This community will always be imperfect. The common good does not require perfection. It can be partially achieved. Most teams function well enough even if each team member does not always pitch in a maximal effort. We can pick up the slack for each other. We also can work together while still somewhat mistrustful of each other. We just have to trust each other enough to take the next step. Tolkien's re-imagining of myths is replete with near enemies learning to trust each other over time to the point of friendship.[27] The scale Tolkien conjures is a near enough representation of reality. We can trust and work together even when we are not yet at a stage of full friendship or full belonging. One should therefore not take my argument to suggest that we must realize the energy common good perfectly or not at all. Rather, my point is that if we do not realize it *im*perfectly, we have no hope of solving the energy trilemma.

[23] O'Connell, 'The Arc Towards Justice and Peace', *in Arcs of Global Justice: Essays in Honor of William A. Schabas* (Margaret M de Guzman & Diane Amann eds, Oxford University Press 2018) 467, 468, 481–82 (arguing that peace is a human right due to its inherent connection to human flourishing.)

[24] *See* section 1.1.

[25] *Ibid.*

[26] *See* section 5.2.

[27] I think here in particular of the relationship between Gimli and Legolas. John R R Tolkien, *The Lord of the Rings* (HarperCollins 2021).

6.3(a) Energy Peace and the Universal System

Naturally enough, the starting point for the common energy good is the idea of peace. One of the key dynamics that have occupied a good part of this book is the geostrategic exposure of energy value chains, and consequently, of the global energy system.[28] One meaning of 'energy security' is precisely to counteract these kinds of threats.[29] This 'energy security' is a public good.[30] A national grid is susceptible to geostrategic pressure *as a whole*. Measures to harden energy security therefore benefit the entire grid, including all of its customers.

Tantalizingly, there is something beyond this kind of energy security premised in mutual deterrence and ability to counterbalance geostrategic manipulation. There is the possibility of 'energy peace'. This idea of 'energy peace' differs from energy security by reducing the uncertainty associated with the constant realpolitik adaptation to external threats to one's own energy agency. Such 'energy peace' is not without parallel. Economic globalization in the long nineteenth century largely followed such a pattern—here, even though there was significant tension and occasional warfare between Great Powers, global commerce was largely exempted from it. The gold standard epitomized the Great Power approach to coordination. There were few if any international institutions. Yet, standards were set to permit global exchange through constant neighbourly supervision.[31] One consequence was that needed raw materials for industrial activity would tend to flow unimpeded around the world, giving significant planning security to the Great Powers in managing their own economic policies. Parts of the economic order were simply exempted from geostrategic tensions for the perceived benefit of all Great Powers.[32] Tellingly, the metaphor chosen by participants in this order was one of a 'Family of Nations' ordered around an ideal of shared 'civilization'.[33]

The idea of 'energy peace' reimagines a similar order around energy belonging. It drastically increases who may belong compared to its distant nineteenth-century

[28] *See* section 1.1.

[29] Yergin, 'Energy Security', (March/April 2006) Foreign Affairs, https://www.foreignaffairs.com/world/ensuring-energy-security, last accessed 2 December 2024.

[30] Leal-Arcas, 'Sustainability, Common Concern, and Public Goods', (2017) 49 George Washington International Law Review 801, 805.

[31] On the moral underpinnings and functioning of the gold standard, *see* Martin Daunton, *Wealth and Welfare, An Economic and Social History of Britain 1851-1951* (Oxford University Press 2007) 274–97.

[32] *See* Nicholas Mulder, *The Economic Weapon: The Rise of Sanctions as a Tool of Modern War* (Yale University Press 2022).

[33] This idea of civilization was also at the heart of the colonial order. It demarcated insiders from outsiders. This idea of civilization was cruelly exclusionary and exploitative. *See* Adom Getachew, *Worldmaking After Empire: The Rise and Fall of Self-Determination* (Princeton University Press 2019). Interestingly, it did exercise a true gravitational pull of community between its members even as it was falling apart for economic reasons after the First World War (most importantly, the cost of the war on many of the (former) Great Powers. On the fascinating 'twilight' of this era in international economic history, *see* Jamie Martin, *The Meddlers: Sovereignty, Empire and the Birth of Global Economic Governance* (Harvard University Press 2022)).

cousin. 'Energy peace' is a creature of human rights rather than the gold or 'civilization' standard. Still, it does continue the original familial metaphor—it succeeds the Family of Nations with a community of free peoples.[34] This community is premised in an idea of belonging. Instead of coordinating this belonging through a gold standard, it is premised in an idea of universal peace.[35] This universal peace, in turn, supports human development as human agency by creating the collective decision processes needed to allow human agency to flourish, at all.[36]

'Energy peace' is part of this broader project. It centres on collective *energy* agency. Energy agency in conditions of energy peace functions in ways that are vaguely reminiscent of the gold standard. Both are premised in coordination around a marketplace or forum. Such a forum is a space in which to buy and sell value chain inputs and outputs transnationally and the environment in which to grow the global pool of ideas for energy innovation.[37] In both instances, it is also a *deliberative* space shared between government and business actors on the management of the world economy. The gold standard sought to mechanize this deliberation by permitting capital flows to determine more or less immediately which policies and business ideas would attract the means for further development and which would have to be rethought to stem capital flight.[38] Still, the point of mechanization was to sustain the possibility of a global (financial) economy.[39]

The energy forum 'demechanizes' this decision function. It is a place for joint energy deliberation about how best to develop the global interlinkages within energy value chains. This deliberation occurs in the interaction between policy incentives set by states and the value chains that develop in response, as well as in the regulatory dialogues between global energy regulators.[40] Still, the goal remains the same: how best to grow and maintain the global (energy) system.

Energy peace—just like energy security—is a public good. Its benefit, like energy security, accrue to everyone. As I will argue below, it allows us both to create conditions for energy abundance and to become better environmental stewards. Yet, every member must also maintain this global forum for it to remain efficacious. It thus shares in the free rider problems of non-rivalrous and indivisible goods.

[34] United Nations Charter, preamble ¶ 1; ICESCR, art 1.

[35] United Nations Charter, art 1(2).

[36] *See* section 4.2.

[37] Thomas Hughes, *Networks of Power, Electricifcation in Western Society 1880-1930* (Johns Hopkins University Press 1983).

[38] On the problems of this mechanization in the modern economy, *see* Martin Daunton, *The Economic Government of the World: 1933-2023* (Farrar, Straus & Giroux 2023) 19–25, 45–48, 77.

[39] Earlier financial orders backed by lending premised in exploiting currency arbitrage as a way to avoid usury laws ended up in dire straits because too much money was travelling in the same direction, thus creating unsustainable financial balance of payments issues. For a fascinating account of finance in this age, *see* Tim Parks, *Medici Money: Banking, Metaphysics, and Art in Fifteenth-Century Florence* (Atlas Books 2005).

[40] *See* Anne-Marie Slaughter, *A New World Order* (Princeton University Press 2004). This data sharing is one of the fundamental ideas behind global governance networks.

One should not mistake energy peace with a *laissez faire* global marketplace without any barriers for trade or national support for energy policy priorities. Historically, commitments to free trade in energy value chain inputs and outputs did not require states to abdicate all energy dirigisme. This understanding of global *laissez faire* requirements in international trade law are instead a more recent development.[41] It is further utterly wrongfooted, as it fails to account for the historical role of state support in the development of energy value chains in postulating rules that would prohibit newcomers from adopting similar strategies to catch up to their peers.[42] To the point of our discussion, this version of *laissez faire* trade law is beholden to the wrong idea of 'development'. It is driven by the idea of economic efficiency.[43] This economic efficiency naturally concentrates segments of the energy value chain in order to benefit fully from economies of scale and relative advantage.

If trade law is driven by the imperative of the progressive realization of human development, as opposed to economic development, the picture changes.[44] This idea of human development is inextricably entangled with policy judgements. These policy judgements require more than the establishment of an efficient marketplace. They must see, for example, to the realization for 'everyone to an adequate standard of living for himself and his family, including adequate food, clothing, housing, and to the continuous improvement of living conditions'.[45] Energy is a core ingredient for policymakers to realize this right. An efficient energy market can help to bring it about—it can leverage economic stakeholders into creating the conditions needed for the progressive realization of this right. Yet, economic stakeholders must not substitute improvements in efficiency in the energy market for the ultimate goal of improvement of living conditions. Rather, there must be deliberation about how to deploy the full resources of world society for mutual benefit to achieve this end—realization of human rights—collectively.

This vision may sound like collectivist global planning. It is far from it. Mature energy value chains already mirror much of this idea. Oil, for example, is produced around the world despite stark differences in costs for the exploration, development, and exploitation of oil reserves.[46] Further, project documents allow policy stakeholders to take a more or less active role in economic decision-making about exploration, development, and exploitation of oil resources from private

[41] Anna-Alexandra Marhold, *Energy in International Trade Law, Concepts, Regulations and Changing Markets* (Cambridge University Press 2021). This is not to argue that energy was completely excluded from international trade law. It is just to say that international trade law did not adopt a hostility to state intervention in energy markets until reasonably recently.

[42] For a discussion, *see* Frédéric G Sourgens & Leonardo Sempertegui, *Principles of International Energy Transition Law* (Oxford University Press 2023) 312–16.

[43] *See* section 4.3.

[44] *See* section 4.4.

[45] ICESCR, art 11(1).

[46] Ayed S Al-Qahtani, *World Oil Outlook 2045* (Organization of Petroleum Exporting Countries 2023) 137–64.

ownership all the way to full state ownership. In much of the world, national oil companies work with international oil companies to develop and exploit oil reserves. When they do so, national oil companies frequently include local content requirements to support the domestic oil sector. National oil companies further take on significant managerial roles alongside international oil companies to advance to the innovation frontier in oil development themselves. In every context, the development of oil reserves is intuitively linked to the idea of improving standards of living. This development of oil reserves is deeply cooperative—'deeply' because it involves a large cross section of actors. These actors have to act with a true sense of mutual regard successfully to develop projects. This mutual regard extends beyond the fence line to local affected communities: international oil companies are well served to build up trust to have a social license to operate. This social license is directly linked to the empowerment of local communities.[47] In principle, energy governance therefore can create a forum for shared decision-making across different kinds of actors. This forum is far more sophisticated than a *laissez faire* marketplace because it aims to increase more than just one value. And yet, it is not a collectivist development of energy reserves premised in state central planning.

So far, I have focused on the idea of energy peace as a counterpoint to geostrategic disturbance. Still, it is just as central in the domestic setting. In the domestic setting, the threat to energy peace comes not from 'external' geopolitical actors. Instead, it comes from the confrontation between and against specific energy value chains. The paradigmatic example of this style of confrontation was the battle of the systems (between alternating and direct current systems) discussed in detail in Chapter 2.[48] Such 'battles of the system' are facially inconsistent with the idea of energy peace—they seek to banish a particular set of actors from the domestic energy system. Such attempts at 'banishment' are inconsistent with the idea of belonging. They thus threaten the energy peace on the domestic scale in much the same way that geopolitical threats do on the global scale.

The solution to this confrontation was not to aim for an either/or but rather to construct a universal system. The universal system protects existing investments by repurposing them to serving a different function in a broader system. Each technology is fitted with its alternatives to fashion a new system that can accommodate all, or at least nearly all, stakeholders.[49]

An energy transition that follows a human development approach, cooperation as belonging, and a thick common good must follow in the footsteps of such a universal system, in aspiration at least. Energy transition is a response to a reverse salient in the global and/or domestic energy system.[50] Belonging requires that each

[47] For more detail, *see* Owen Anderson et al, *International Petroleum Law and Transactions* (Rocky Mountain Mineral Law Foundation 2022).
[48] *See* section 2.4.
[49] Thomas Hughes, (n 37), at 125–27.
[50] *See* section 1.1.

stakeholder acts for the wellbeing of the energy community for its own sake while protecting the welfare of each stakeholder belonging to the community.[51] This means that addressing the reverse salient should, as far as is possible, not exclude stakeholders from the community. To do so would sever the bond of belonging and pit stakeholders against the community. This, in turn, would destroy the possibility of achieving a common good inherent in that community—at least for the time being. A universal system bridges this problem by re-arranging the position of each stakeholder in the new whole.[52] It thus can leverage every stakeholder in finding a new solution by means of innovation and cooperation towards implementing a solution to the critical problem holding back the energy system.

The universal system is the domestic flipside of geopolitical energy peace. It permits stakeholders to come together to find a new place for themselves in the energy community in light of energy transition. It provides a means for each to invest in their community to bring about a solution to a critical problem for the community. This effort requires energy peace to combine or connect the strengths of each stakeholder to shield against the weaknesses of another (such as combining gas-fired generation together with solar generation to address the intermittence of solar electricity). Energy decision-making strengthens collective energy agency.

This leaves the question of the relationship between energy peace and fervent opposition to a particular form of energy generation. The German nuclear exit is a case in point.[53] One answer is that the German nuclear exit was the result of political path dependencies and that a more informed debate about nuclear power would likely have led to a different result. Still, this is perhaps too cheap an answer. It is theoretically possible that a society would reject a particular technology due to its inherent risks or due to its reasonably certain costs and externalities. Germany might well fit this mould, too—the Green party long prepared the groundwork for a decision against nuclear technology on economic and environmental grounds.[54] The arguments against nuclear energy were, and are, that it is too dangerous to operate, that spent nuclear fuel storage is similarly an unacceptable environmental externality, and that nuclear power plants by the very size of their nameplate capacity overly concentrate generation in the hands of few utilities owning a few plants. How should a community wishing to maintain the benefits of energy peace deal with contestation from civil society advocates?

On the one hand, it must be possible for energy peace to allow for such discussions. Otherwise, it would deprive critical stakeholders in energy decision-making of a voice and of agency. This would drive these stakeholders out of the community. On the other hand, the arguments against a particular stakeholder as belonging in

[51] Finnis (n 12), at 140.
[52] Hughes (n 37), at 125–27.
[53] *See* Stephen G Gross, *Energy and Power, Germany in the Age of Oil, Atoms, and Climate Change* (Oxford University Press 2023).
[54] *Ibid.*

the energy system as such runs into the same problem in reverse—the Green Party did in fact wish to exclude nuclear energy stakeholders from the German energy mix.[55] A universal system would provide a technical solution—it would develop technology to limit the environmental externalities of spent fuel storage,[56] increase safety measures in plant design and operation,[57] and work on decreasing the reactor size to deconcentrate generate.[58]

This still does not quite go far enough. The objection of the German Green Party was not technological; it was ethical. The universal system therefore has to provide a means to resolve the ethical question, as well as the technical question to implement the ethical solution. The universal system measures these contestations with one yardstick. There is a problem with the ethical argument against nuclear power if it is inconsistently deployed. If *only* the nuclear sector comes under attack for an overconcentration of generation and *only* the nuclear sector comes under attack for serious risks of environmental degradation, the ethical argument is wrongfooted. It seeks to exclude a stakeholder on the basis of who they are as opposed to their conduct. This is fundamentally inconsistent with the demands of belonging and non-discrimination.[59] The ethical objection therefore needs to provide parameters for a technological solution. These parameters will be the result of ethical contestation within the energy forum. So long as these parameters cannot be met, the ethical objection against a particular conduct by stakeholders is actionable without running afoul of energy peace. Still, the moment parameters can be met, the objection should cease. The point is that the debate is one about conduct as opposed to a technology as such. Energy peace as the universal governance system must accommodate the former. To be stable, it must prohibit the latter. All energy stakeholders are part of the energy community. No matter how firm one's ethical commitments, one cannot exclude a set of actors as such without vitally threatening energy peace.

6.3(b) Energy Abundance

Energy peace has two important corollaries for the solution of the energy trilemma. Energy peace takes significant pressure off energy security. It provides an

[55] *Ibid.*

[56] *See* Y R Alvarez et al, *Status and Trends in Spent Fuel and Radioactive Waste Management* (International Atomic Energy Agency 2022) 24.

[57] *See* 'Safety of Nuclear Reactors', (23 August 2024) World Nuclear Association, https://world-nuclear.org/information-library/safety-and-security/safety-of-plants/safety-of-nuclear-power-reactors, last accessed 5 December 2024.

[58] *See* Ingersol, 'Small Modular Reactors (SMRs) for Producing Nuclear Energy: International Developments', *in Handbook on Small Modular Reactors* (2nd edn, Daniel T Ingersoll & Mario D. Carelli eds, Elsevier 2021) 29–49.

[59] *See* Rudolf Dolzer & Christoph Schreuer, *Principles of International Investment Law* (2nd edn, Oxford University Press 2012).

alternative means to provide energy security compared to the realpolitik solution. This alternative means frees up capital and resources to realize the other two goals of the energy trilemma (energy affordability and energy sustainability).[60]

The idea of energy abundance as a consequence of energy peace in the first place is a consequence of this greater amount of resources. If it is not necessary to invest as heavily in energy security, there are more opportunities to invest in energy affordability. Even if the general investment in energy resources remains stable, it stands to reason that some of the surplus saved from energy security would be invested in energy affordability.[61]

The idea of energy abundance also follows from the idea of energy peace as a universal system.[62] A universal system does not have to displace existing energy assets to duplicate efforts already undertaken by existing assets. It further can rely on economies of scale achieved by mature energy technologies to deliver more energy at a greater speed. The idea of a universal system therefore makes available more and cheaper energy resources with which to meet growing demand.

Energy abundance is more than a corollary of energy peace. It is also a common good in its own right by changing the manner in which communal decisions about energy deployment are made. If energy decision-making is purely economic, there are marginal energy projects that will not readily find investors. They are capable in principle of making a return on investment. Yet, the return on capital does not justify the risk of investing in the venture in the first place. This risk is particularly pronounced in young energy markets. These young energy markets do not have a significant track record of returns by investors. This uncertainty translates into risk perception. This risk perception, in turn, increases the needed return to justify an investment.[63]

Belonging changes this equation. Decision-making about energy is not driven purely by traditional economic considerations. Rather, decision-making looks to the deployment of global energy resources and capital for mutual benefit.[64] This mutual benefit, in turn, is measured in terms of human development outcomes.[65] Decision-making about the deployment of global energy resources must return human development outcomes to all relevant stakeholders (ie peoples).[66] The organization of energy decision-making around an energy community of belonging therefore takes a different view of the desirability of energy investments, particularly in opportunities at the margin of profitability.

[60] *See* section 1.1.
[61] For a discussion of the factors increasing the costs of energy security, *see* section 2.4.
[62] *See* Hughes (n 37), at 125–27 (discussing the idea of the universal system).
[63] For a discussion of this phenomenon, *see* Frédéric G Sourgens, Catherine Banet, & Teddy Baldwin, *The Transnational Law of Renewable Energy* (Oxford University Press 2024).
[64] *See* ICCPR, art 1(2).
[65] *See* section 3.4.
[66] *See* ICCPR, art 1(2).

The mechanics of community-based energy investment decision-making is already on display in Africa. State-sponsored stakeholders from the Persian Gulf (Saudi Arabia and the United Arab Emirates in particular) have made significant investments in increasing renewable energy generation in Africa. These investments exceed those by other stakeholders.[67] The logic for these investments ultimately must be a greater level of trust by investors in the stability of the investment opportunity. This trust allows them to structure energy transactions to reduce risk to an acceptable level to make the investment in the first place. There is thus a greater abundance of energy resources deployed in conditions of trust compared to that under normal economic risk assessments.

The difference is significant because of what it can jump start. The more energy resources are deployed in the markets in question, the more of a track record there will be for the performance of energy investments in the new markets in question. This additional track record—to the extent that trust was well-placed by the original investors—will provide proof of concept that profitable operations in the market are possible. This, in turn, means that uncertainty decreases. With decreases in uncertainty, risk similarly decreases and more capital is available to invest in additional projects. At this stage, energy demand growth will likely mean that there is also a growth in human development outcomes and at least a moderate take-off in economic opportunities within the country. This take-off will fuel more energy growth by increasing energy opportunities.

Energy abundance is a matter of self-reinforcing mechanisms. In a universal system, energy scarcity is unlikely to be a limiting factor for global energy growth. The key limiting factor is the energy marketplace itself. Does it make economic sense to invest in generation in new markets? If this limiting factor is addressed, conditions are ripe for energy abundance as there will then be a response by global value chains to deliver more inputs, growing these value chains in turn. This growth in principle will provide the means for additional investment in the energy sector, either as reinvestments or as external investments to participate in a growth industry.

The bond of belonging therefore has the inherent good of increasing the abundance of energy and energy resources. There is more to go around to meet growing demand. The bond of belonging in this sense fuels a virtuous cycle of energy growth. This manner of growth is only possible in the context of increased trust. This increased trust, in turn, is a matter of a strengthened bond of belonging.

6.3(c) Energy Stewardship

The idea of energy peace also reaches into the sustainability of energy systems. I use 'sustainability' broadly in this context. Narrowly, the energy system is sustainable

[67] Sourgens, Banet, & Baldwin (n 63).

if it can continue to rely on existing value chains for the foreseeable future.[68] An earlier wood-based energy order was unsustainable because it consumed more wood than it could regrow.[69] The energy system is not sustainable more broadly if it causes significant dislocations in the human environment that cannot easily be counterbalanced with available technological means.[70] This sustainability measure is broader, as acid rain or air pollution did not imperil the function of the energy system as such even as they significantly impacted human capabilities.

The current climate crisis threatens the sustainability of the energy system in both the narrow and the broader sense. In the broader sense, climate change has the potential to have catastrophic impacts on human life around the world.[71] It affects most every natural system needed for human flourishing. In the narrower sense, climate change will also impact energy usage. In the short-term, energy needs will increase to adapt to climate change. To the extent that climate change reaches catastrophic proportions, energy use is likely to collapse as economic activity becomes impossible in an increasing number of places and as natural disasters and pandemics become increasingly more likely.[72]

Energy peace is responsive to both senses of sustainability. On the one hand, energy peace requires action by energy stakeholders for the preservation of the energy system itself. These actions require stakeholders to protect and preserve the energy community. On the other hand, energy peace demands that the energy community in fact support the welfare of all energy stakeholders.[73] Significant environmental degradation that undermines human capabilities cannot be reconciled with this imperative. Consequently, stakeholders must adjust the energy system to mitigate and adapt to the new conditions to protect human capabilities.

In both cases, belonging produces stewardship.[74] Stakeholders have a stewardship obligation with regard to the system to which they belong as a whole. They must protect and maintain the system. As the system must support the wellbeing of stakeholders in return, this stewardship obligation reflects back onto the environment. We must act as stewards of the environment to secure its continued availability to support human development.[75]

This understanding of stewardship is internal to the practice of energy belonging. Energy peace is impossible without stewardship. Without stewardship,

[68] *See* Heffron & McCauley, 'Achieving Sustainable Supply Chains through Energy Justice', (2014) 123 Applied Energy 435. Heffron and McCauley look in particular to locally sourced, carbon neutral supply chains in this context.

[69] Vaclav Smil, *Energy and Civilization—A History* (MIT Press 2017).

[70] Gro Harlem Brundtland, *World Commission on Environment and Development, Our Common Future* (UNDP 1987).

[71] Hoesung Lee et al, *Climate Change 2023: Synthesis Report. Contribution of Working Groups I, II and III to the Sixth Assessment Report of the Intergovernmental Panel on Climate Change* (Intergovernmental Panel on Climate Change 2023) ('IPCC 2023').

[72] *See ibid.*

[73] *See* UN Development Convention, art 3(b).

[74] *Ibid* at art 13(1)(a).

[75] *See ibid.*

the energy system incurs and imposes losses that undermine the functioning of the system itself. Stewardship, therefore, logically does not impose an obligation external to energy systems on energy stakeholders in this way. To understand the difference, consider the slogan 'don't mess with Texas'. The slogan was part of a campaign to stop public littering on Texas roads.[76] There is no inherent relationship between driving on a road and littering. The obligation not to litter therefore is external to the activity. In an ordinary understanding of energy consumption, we think of climate change or exhaustion of resources as an 'externality'—that is, something that is external to the practice of energy consumption, as well. It is this externalization of the environmental relationship that creates the conditions for a tragedy of the commons. We take as much as is possible, understanding that the resource from which we take is likely to collapse. In fact, the very anticipation of collapse only accelerates and heightens our use of the resource. In the context of energy belonging, this changes. Because we belong to a resource community, our practice of belonging to the resource community is to take care of the resource. It internalizes the exhaustion of the resource we use into our use patterns. It does so by leaning into innovation to address and mitigate the dangers to the resource community.[77] This taking care is stewardship.

Stewardship is not the same as ecologism. The point is not the protection of the ecology for its own sake. Stewardship is to make a resource useful while preventing harm from its use.[78] By definition, use 'uses up' the resource. The point is to use it up responsibly. This means that one may in fact use a resource even when it does harm so long as one also acts to undo the harm in question. Still, the idea is to reduce and limit the intensity of use to the extent feasible to protect and maintain shared energy resources.

Stewardship is closely related to the idea of circularity. A circular economy 'shar[es], leas[es], reuse[s], repair[es], refurbish[es] and recycl[es]' resources 'in an (almost) closed loop' in order 'to retain the highest utility and value of products, components and materials at all times'.[79] A circular energy economy attempts maximally to reuse, refurbish, and recycle as many energy 'inputs' in energy value chains as is possible. Practically, this typically means to reuse, refurbish, and recycle the resulting waste products of energy production. One of the best examples of this circularity is the recycling of spent nuclear fuel. This recycling limits the amount of fissible material that needs to be stored. It also limits the amount of

[76] 'Don't Mess With Texas – Origin Story', (2024) Don't Mess With Texas, https://www.dontmesswithtexas.org/about-us/, last accessed 5 December 2024.

[77] *See* Williams et al, 'A Guide to the Circular Carbon Economy (CCE)' King Abdullah Petroleum Studies and Research Center (August 2020).

[78] *See* The Human Right to a Clean, Healthy and Sustainable Environment, GA Res 76/3000 (28 July 2022) UN Doc A/76/L 75 (2022).

[79] 'Closing the Loop, New Circular Economy Package', (January 2016) European Parliament, https://www.europarl.europa.eu/RegData/etudes/BRIE/2016/573899/EPRS_BRI%282016%29573899_EN.pdf, last accessed 5 December 2024.

fissible raw material that needs to be produced. It therefore uses existing materials in as closed a loop as possible.[80] 'Circular carbon' is another example of this approach. 'Circular carbon' captures CO_2 from the combustion of fossil fuels. The captured CO_2 is then made useful in other processes like the production of oil and gas.[81] Alternatively, it can be used as a feedstock for other industrial processes.[82] It could even be used as feedstock synthetically to create natural gas (even though this process is not cost effective given the abundance of natural gas reserves).[83] Other such circular solutions include 'cross-vector' integration of energy systems to use residual outputs of energy generation or industrial processes for additional useful purposes (such as heating of homes).[84] Stewardship counsels to develop circular solutions for energy value chains to the extent feasible. It therefore counsels to develop and support carbon capture, utilization, and storage as well as direct air capture of CO_2 as a critical means to combat climate change.[85] It does not however *require* such circular solutions when it is possible to address the inherent harms to human development by other means more efficiently (ie with a greater realization of human development outcomes).

The next generation of energy technologies likely to make it to market address the reverse salient of the relative lack of circularity in existing energy technologies from the outset. The two most important technologies are next-generation geothermal and fusion energy. Next-generation geothermal is fully circular. It uses advanced drilling to access geothermal energy (heat from the Earth's core) to heat water to power a steam turbine to then reuse the water in the same loop again once it has cooled down.[86] Fusion similarly is reasonably circular (if not quite as literally circular as geothermal energy). A fusion reaction generates energy by 'fus[ing] two hydrogen isotopes into helium'.[87] The helium is not then split to provide more hydrogen to restart the fusion reaction.[88] Rather, helium itself is a comparatively

[80] Alvarez (n. 56).

[81] Duda et al, 'Carbon Dioxide Enhanced Oil Recovery, Untapped Domestic Energy Supply and Long Term Carbon Storage', (March 2010) US Department of Energy National Energy Technology Laboratory, https://www.netl.doe.gov/sites/default/files/netl-file/co2_eor_primer.pdf, last accessed 6 December 2024.

[82] Muthuraj & Mekonnen, 'Recent Progress in Carbon Dioxide (CO_2) as Feedstock for Sustainable Materials Development: Co-polymers and Polymer Blends', (2018) 145 Polymer 348.

[83] Bane, 'Making Methane from CO_2: Carbon Capture Grows More Affordable', (2 September 2021) US Department of Energy Pacific Northwest National Laboratory, https://www.pnnl.gov/news-media/making-methane-co2-carbon-capture-grows-more-affordable, last accessed 6 December 2024.

[84] van Nuffel et al, 'Sector Coupling: How Can It Be Enhanced in the EU to Foster Grid Stability and Decarbonise?' at 7, (November 2018) Policy Department for Economic, Scientific and Quality of Life Policies European Parliament, https://www.europarl.europa.eu/RegData/etudes/STUD/2018/626091/IPOL_STU(2018)626091_EN.pdf, last accessed 6 December 2024.

[85] IPCC 2023 (n 71).

[86] *See* Li et al, 'Life Cycle Sustainability Assessment and Circularity of Geothermal Power Plants', (2023) 35 Sustainable Production and Consumption 141.

[87] Sadik-Zada, 'Back to the Future: Revisiting Perspectives on Nuclear Fusion and Juxtaposition to Existing Energy Sources', (2024) 290 Energy 129150.

[88] *Ibid.*

valuable byproduct of the reaction.[89] This byproduct further is produced only in limited quantities given the energy density of the fusion reaction.[90]

Renewable energy similarly can employ a circular approach in its end-of-life planning. (solar, wind, batteries). Modelling suggests that the components of solar photovoltaic plants can usefully be recycled thereby reducing the burden on landfills and requiring fewer new resources to replace decommissioned solar plants.[91] Similar efforts are ongoing in the wind context.[92] Battery technologies further are also currently expanding their recycling capabilities.[93]

Frequently, circular or near-circular approaches to energy and resource use will not be practical. Further, in many instances, circular or near-circular approaches may become prevalent at a time that emissions and waste from energy technologies will already have contributed to significant degradation of the human environment. In this context, stewardship requires the collective implementation of adaptation measures for those negatively affected by current technology.[94] The energy community otherwise would concentrate burdens in a manner that is inconsistent with the idea of mutual benefit. Neighbourliness therefore requires that each energy community stakeholder contribute to the forward-looking adaptation of living conditions for affected groups to this new scenario.[95]

In the climate change context, adaptation measures are likely to include solar radiation management.[96] Solar radiation management technology limits the amount of solar energy to enter the atmosphere. This, in turn, reduces the global climate balance. Solar radiation management is likely a necessary measure, given the increase in global average temperatures measured in the 2020s. Solar radiation management itself can have significant negative impacts on the human environment. The deployment of this technology is similarly subject to the obligation of

[89] For a quick primer on the value of helium, *see* Brumfiel, 'The World Is Running Out of Helium. Here's Why It Matters', (8 November 2019) National Public Radio, https://www.npr.org/2019/11/01/775554343/the-world-is-constantly-running-out-of-helium-heres-why-it-matters, last accessed 5 December 2024.

[90] For a quick primer on the quantities involved, *see* 'Fusion in Brief', (2024) UK Atomic Energy Authority Culham Centre for Fusion Energy, https://ccfe.ukaea.uk/fusion-energy/fusion-in-brief/, last accessed 5 December 2024.

[91] Dreves, 'Working Out the Details of a Circular Solar Economy', (22 April 2024) US Department of Energy National Renewable Energy Laboratory, https://www.nrel.gov/news/program/2022/working-out-the-details-of-a-circular-solar-economy.html, last accessed 6 December 2024.

[92] Smithson-Paul et al, 'Decommissioning Case Study, Circular Economy in the Wind Sector—Summary', (29 April 2024) Catapult, https://tethys.pnnl.gov/sites/default/files/publications/Smithson-Paul_et_al_2024.pdf, last accessed 6 December 2024.

[93] Peplow, 'Lithium-ion Battery Recycling Goes Large', (19 November 2023) Chemical & Engineering News, https://cen.acs.org/environment/recycling/Lithium-ion-battery-recycling-goes/101/i38, last accessed 6 December 2024.

[94] First Global Stocktake (11 December 2023), ¶¶ 51–94.

[95] For a full discussion, *see* Sourgens, 'Climate Prevention', (2025) 36 Georgetown Environmental Law Review (forthcoming).

[96] On solar radiation management, *see* IPCC 2023 (n 71), at 72–73.

consultation fully to engage stakeholder agency and adaptation measures for those who are nevertheless negatively affected by its deployment.[97]

6.4 The Common Good Energy Network

Few communities are perfect communities. If the common good is to be something practical as opposed to utopian, it must be possible to realize it gradually and to varying degrees. It cannot be an all or nothing proposition. Otherwise the discussion in this part of the book would be pointless. It may well be true that energy governance ought to aim to improve human development, cooperation ought to be a matter of belonging, and that we ought to enjoy energy peace, abundance, and stewardship. We would nevertheless do none of those things as we very clearly live in the realpolitik world I outlined in Part I.

Common goods can in fact be partially realized. Most of us have had the experience of participating in a group activity with a group of relative strangers. For example, we may have played sports, done theatre, or performed a choral piece with people whom we did not know well. In the beginning, it was likely an awkward affair. Over time, our collaboration became more than the sum of its parts: my teammates worked hard to make up for a ball I lost and the effort led to a gratifying score, my opposite actor played along with the way I said a line, my choir hit a complex harmony just right. Yet, none of us were part of a perfect sports team, acting troop, or choir. There is no such thing. Still, we all have experienced partially achieving a common good. In all likelihood, our experience was that we wanted to do more of that (both achieve it more often and achieve it more fully).

How then do we turn individual performers into a team and how do we realize more of a common good? The question matters for our purposes. Part I concluded that realpolitik could provide many answers to energy governance. Still, it left much to be desired because it left a significant part of the potential upside of collaborative governance on the table. In Part II, I identified what that upside is. What we do not get in a purely realpolitik world is the common good of an energy community. This common good of an energy community, in turn, is critical to solving our energy trilemma. Without it, we can realize less with regard to each goal. Still, in light of the current policy challenges (climate change, energy poverty, increased energy demand in significant economic sectors, etc), the energy system needs to do more to meet the basic demands we make of it. It is likely impossible to address the critical problem of the energy system today without *growth*.[98] Part II outlined

[97] For a full discussion, *see* Sourgens, 'The Dark Sun Network', (2023) 94 University of Colorado Law Review 681.

[98] *See* Alessio Terzi, *Growth for Good: Reshaping Capitalism to Save Humanity from Climate Catastrophe* (Harvard University Press 2022).

that this growth must be human development growth premised in cooperation as belonging. The problem is getting there.

I will provide a blueprint of how we reorient the critical institutions needed to realize the common good of the energy system in Part III. Still, before I get there, Part II provides the theoretical answer for how we have to proceed in Part III. As I started out in this chapter, the common good is an inherent 'by-product' of a certain kind of relationship of belonging. To recall, in this relationship, (i) each member acts for the wellbeing of the community, for the sake of the community, while (ii) the community provides for the welfare of each member for the sake of each member, and while (iii) each member knows of the activities of other members to this common and reciprocal end, and (iv) each of them coordinating their respective activities to secure a reciprocal good that is only possible in community. By contrast, in a transactional realpolitik relationship, stakeholders act together (i) each for their own respective wellbeing without regard for the wellbeing of their peers, because (ii) each can better secure its respective own wellbeing by working together on condition of reciprocity, but (iii) each stakeholder observes the activities of the other to secure a reciprocal effort and (iv) taken counter-measures the moment either observes a defection.

The critical part in either context is what each stakeholder observed the other doing. Realpolitik and belonging both are premised in a mutual observation to secure the benefit of cooperation and prevent defection. The first step therefore must be to tighten the relationship between the relevant stakeholders to make conduct more transparent. The greater the transparency in the relationship, the greater the risk of detection of defection—and thus the graduated sanction that would limit the potential benefit of defection.[99] Transparency lowers this risk, thus protecting realpolitik cooperation.

The second step is to change the nature of reciprocity. In the context of a transactional realpolitik engagement, reciprocity is a reciprocity of performance. It is not a reciprocity of ends. (In fact, we may well want radically different things from each other—I may want natural gas and my counterparty may wish to have money to diversify their economy away from natural gas exports). We therefore need to observe each other working towards shared ends in the energy specific context. (Even in the context of the gas sale transaction, we are both part of the same value chain and must act to maintain and protect the value chain together to each get our respective end from the value chain. Notice that now we have a reciprocal interest in the same community—the gas value chain). Any interaction that increases our respective observations that we are working reciprocally towards a shared end begins to transform our cooperation from a transactional cooperation to one of belonging.

[99] *See* Ostrom (n 18), at 76.

At this point, both relationships exist side by side. As our reciprocal observation allows us to have a better understanding of the relationship at issue, the relationship will move more firmly one side to the other. As it does so, it will allow for greater trust and thus for the greater realization of a common good (or its impairment). The common good of any particular community is a direct result of a stabilizing of the overall edifice of total stakeholder relationships into relationships of firmer reciprocal belonging to a shared community.

Under the right conditions, realpolitik can therefore lead to the realization of the common good. It is, in fact, one of the few ways in which one can safely traverse the gulf between transactional relationships and relationships of belonging. Realpolitik limits incentives for advantage taking and free riding from a community. It therefore provides an important backstop for community building in its own right. As defection and free riding decreases, trust in a communal enterprise should increase. It does so without risk of a 'long con' given the continued observation even in reciprocal observations of belonging.

6.5 Conclusion

The common energy good is critical for our ability solve the energy trilemma. The common energy good creates conditions of energy peace. These conditions of energy peace significantly reduce geopolitical risks on the international stage. Further, energy peace also works towards a universal system in which all energy value chains can continue to have a place. This significantly limits the risk of sunk costs and further increases the number of stakeholders available to overcome the critical problem facing the global energy system of providing more energy to support global productivity growth while reducing the global environmental impact of the energy system.

The common energy good also creates the conditions for energy abundance. Energy abundance is in part a consequence of energy peace. There are more resources available within the energy system to develop additional energy sources that can be strategically deployed to reduce conditions of energy poverty. These resources are no longer needed to invest in sizeable realpolitik safeguards. Still, energy abundance is more than a consequence of energy peace. It is a means to decrease uncertainty inherent in a transactional understanding of the global energy system. This decreased uncertainty can itself support additional opportunities for virtuous cycles in energy investment that reduce energy poverty while strengthening the energy system as a whole.

The common energy good finally creates the conditions for energy stewardship. Energy stewardship looks to secure the mutual benefit of the energy system for all stakeholders. This means reducing the environmental burden the energy system imposes on society and providing for adaptation measures where an environmental burden cannot feasibly be avoided. Energy stewardship in principle aims for a circular energy economy. Such a circular economy can only feasibly be created over time as more capital is available to support further innovation in a particular energy paradigm. Still, energy belonging will yield circular solutions for energy problems as a matter of its own internal operations more frequently than other governance paradigms.

Finally, I have argued that the common good is not a matter of utopian fantasies. It is attainable by structuring realpolitik relationships around reciprocally shared interests. The more such networks can be tightened, the more relationships of belonging (and the common good they entail) can take hold. This in turn assists in realizing increasingly greater shares of the common energy goods of energy peace, energy abundance, and energy stewardship.

PART III
INSTITUTIONS

7
Finance

7.1 Introduction

In Part I, I laid out the theoretical framework for global energy governance. This framework showed that energy governance sought to set appropriate incentives for energy development. I argued that these incentive structures required constant re-adjustment to counterbalance a misalignment of incentives in different parts of the energy cycle. Problematically, I showed that these governance responses created their own repercussions—what started out as purely domestic interventions in the domestic energy system became global phenomena and brought on a realpolitik order that impaired the original domestic regulatory design to deliver affordable, secure, and sustainable energy to consumers.

In Part II, I argued that we need to understand the ends of energy governance if we want to realign these international imbalances in global energy governance. I argued that global energy governance must seek to realize the greatest possible human development outcomes.[1] I argued further that such governance requires deep and broad cooperation between energy stakeholders. This cooperation was premised in the idea of a shared belonging to the global energy system.[2] Such co-operation, I argued, leads to the realization of a critical set of common energy goods—energy peace, energy abundance, and energy stewardship. These common goods go a long way to solving the global energy trilemma that started us on our journey in Part I.[3]

My argument throughout was that there are three different ways that energy decision processes can function. The first is conduct that ends up in the tragedy of the commons or anticommons—a self-centred and unreasonable use of energy resources that ultimately threatens the global energy system as a whole. The second of these follows a realpolitik logic. This realpolitik logic cooperates with others to achieve purely domestic energy goals. It is suspicious of defection and therefore constantly monitors the conduct of other stakeholders to intervene and correct any attempt at exerting realpolitik pressure on energy systems. This logic limits our room for action to respond to the current energy transition challenge. At the same time, another decision process follows the logic of belonging. This logic

1 *See* section 4.4.
2 *See* section 5.2.
3 *See* section 6.3.

A Theory of Global Energy Governance. Frédéric Gilles Sourgens, Oxford University Press. © Frédéric Sourgens 2025.
DOI: 10.1093/9780198950325.003.0007

of belonging cooperates with others to support a shared energy community. This logic, too, monitors the conduct of others to model cooperation for the common good. As stakeholders cooperate towards shared ends, they can in fact enjoy an increase in energy peace, abundance, and stewardship due to the positive feedback generated by this deeper form of cooperation.

In this part, I will argue that we need to rethink the role of critical parts of the institutions supporting the global energy system in order to reap the benefits from this deeper form of cooperation. I will outline how we can orient realpolitik decision-making towards progressively weaving a bond of energy belonging between energy stakeholders.

The first logical problem we have is finding a way to pay for the costs to upgrade the global energy system to meet the critical problem of climate change and energy scarcity at the same time. Analysts in the early 2020s estimate that the cost of this upgrade will run to US$9.2 trillion per year.[4] I will approach this problem by asking first what kind of energy transitions there are to get at how each type of transition is financed in turn. I will argue that there are three kinds of energy transitions—innovation-based transitions in which innovation itself drives transition, regulation-based transitions in which regulation has to solve a 'missing money' problem to provide public energy goods which innovation based growth cannot yet provide, and coordination-based transitions in which regulation has to provide a sufficient return for existing innovations to be usefully employed in national energy systems. Climate mitigation and climate adaptation fall between the last two kinds of transitions. They therefore require significantly greater regulatory initiative compared to innovation-led transitions. Traditional market-based finance is not going to support climate mitigation as there is no market into which to sell mitigation outcomes. Further, climate adaptation in developing economies faces a similar market problem.

I will argue throughout this chapter that the finance gap can in fact be closed. I will outline how we can do so even in light of strong realpolitik headwinds. I will outline, in light of the work of the last chapter, that we can turn realpolitik processes towards one that progressively realizes the common energy good inherent in a bond of belonging approach. I will submit that it will take all stakeholders—regulators, innovators, energy companies, investors, and international development finance institutions—to pull off this feat.

The core institutions that finance energy transitions begin with national regulatory energy markets. These markets coordinate the conduct by regulators, energy innovators and energy industry, as well as investors to provide public energy goods not available in the current configuration of the national energy system. When

[4] 'The Net Zero Transition, What It Would Cost, What It Would Bring', (January 2022) McKinsey & Co, https://www.mckinsey.com/capabilities/sustainability/our-insights/the-net-zero-transition-what-it-would-cost-what-it-could-bring, last accessed 26 March 2024.

these national regulatory markets secure global public energy goods, they need to be coordinated globally to be tenable from a realpolitik perspective. This requires a different kind of institution—it requires institutional verification mechanisms for the realization of reciprocal international commitments. The Paris Agreement currently makes available such a verification mechanism. Finally, such efforts also require global development finance institutions to facilitate the flow of finance to prove the concept in developing markets. Without such proof of concept funding, global public energy goods, and the global common energy good, lack a critical catalyst to be adequately realized. In this chapter, I outline what processes constitute and operate these institutions and how they can be oriented towards forging a bond of energy belonging as well as the realization of the common energy good.

7.2 The 'Missing Money' Problem

Electricity market liberalization traditionally leads to a 'missing money' problem.[5] In both a utility model and in a command model, the total needed generating capacity to meet anticipated annual peak loads can be set as a matter of policy. In a command model, the state or state-owned entity will then contract to build sufficient capacity to meet the policy goal. The state can then either recover the cost by charging for electricity, through general revenues (eg taxes) or both. In a utility model, the utility will receive approval to build out its generation base in line with the capacity target in light of regulatory decision-making process. The utility will charge the investments in the relevant generation as part of its cost base in electricity tariffs.

In a liberalized electricity wholesale market, things work differently. The market price is supposed to signal that it is lucrative to invest in new generation. The market price is set on the basis of a clearing price for electricity. This clearing price is the marginal price for electricity purchased by the system operator in a specific auction (ie the price of the most expensive electricity it needs to purchase to meet its auction target).[6] This market price signal will be successful in attracting investors if and when investors anticipate that they can earn a sufficient return on a new investment under normal market conditions at the average prevalent clearing price (ie they have a good basis to estimate that they will clear the market for a sufficient portion of their name plate capacity at a sufficiently high price to provide a return on their investment in the generating asset.) The 'missing money'

[5] Joskow, 'Capacity Payments in Imperfect Electricity Markets', (2008) 16 Utility Policy 159. For a summary of the missing money discourse thereafter, *see* Hogan, 'Follow the Missing Money: Ensuring Reliability at Least Cost to Consumers in Transition to a Low-Carbon Power System', (2017) 30 Electricity Journal 55. For a longer discussion, *see* Todd S Aagaard & Andrew N Kleit, *Electricity Capacity Markets* (Cambridge University Press 2022).

[6] *See* Aagaard & Kleit (n 5).

problem materializes because it concerns the capacity needed to meet annual peak loads that occur reasonably infrequently. This means that an investor investing in building out that last generation will have to earn a sufficient return to justify investing in a vanishingly small number of hours of actual peak demand.[7] The greater the difference between ordinary load and peak load and the less frequently peak demand occurs, the less likely it is that an investment in that last generation to meet demand will in fact generate a sufficient and sufficiently certain return to justify investing.

The 'missing money' problem suggests a deeper problem than mapping out electricity demand curves. Liberalized electricity markets run into a problem when it comes to meeting systemic needs that are ultimately non-excludable and non-rivalrous (ie public goods). The 'missing money' problem is about grid reliability and grid resilience.[8] Both reliability and resilience are public goods.[9] They benefit every customer. Short of instituting a draconian competitive retail market, I cannot target specific customers to exclude because they do not pay for electricity at its scarcity value at such peak times.[10] Further, the greater grid resilience is not 'used up' by any one customer more than another. Consequently, the peak estimate does not put customers in competition with each other.[11] (Notably, even a competitive retail market may well discourage installation of additional capacity as scarcity pricing in fact helps all generators in the marketplace. For comparatively rare peak events, it may not be worthwhile to invest in more generation even at such prices.)

The 'missing money' problem therefore is not limited to its traditional context (the context of insufficient generating capacity on the grid to meet estimated peak demand). It is a problem that affects market design every time that we are looking to invest in something that looks like a public good. By their very nature, these

[7] Joskow (n 5).

[8] *Ibid.*

[9] Klass et al, 'The Key to Electric Grid Reliability: Modernizing Governance', (Mar. 2024) University of Pennsylvania Kleinman Center for Energy Policy, https://kleinmanenergy.upenn.edu/wp-content/uploads/2024/03/KCEP-Paper-15-Key-to-Electric-Grid-Reliability.pdf, last accessed 7 December 2024.

[10] Proposed solutions to the missing money problem suggest different coupling mechanisms between wholesale and retail pricing. *See eg* Hogan (n 5); Woo, 'A Wholesale Electricity Market Design sans Missing Money and Price Manipulation', (2019) 134 Energy Policy 110988.

[11] One proposal to address the missing money problem is to require end users to enter into a demand subscription service that sets the firm service level. Woo (n 10). By way of analogy, one could think of this approach like data streams in a smart phone plan—one has full services up to the amount subscribed and assumes the risk of slow or interrupted service thereafter. This does not change the non-rivalrous nature of grid resilience but rather seeks to charge it *ex ante*. It also does not make grid resilience excludable even as it tries to create an excludable order of blackout preferences. The two, however, are different concepts. Every customer still benefits the same from a grid that does not suffer catastrophic failures even if some customers pay to extend their connection to the grid longer than others during peak scarcity times. The customer paying more does not pay more for increased resilience. Rather, the customer is paying for an additional amount of power delivered through a grid that must be sufficiently resilient to allow the purchase in the first place.

public goods cannot be charged to specific customers to improve their *individual* use. Consequently, investment in meeting demand for such public goods cannot easily be financed through a normal marketplace. There is no easy market return for the investment.

Regulators in liberalized electricity markets have attempted to address the 'missing money' problem in its traditional context by creating 'capacity markets'. In these capacity markets, regulators hold auctions in which generators sell capacity to generate electricity on demand to meet potential peak demand (as opposed to selling electricity). Capacity markets pay for capacity whether it is called upon or not, and therefore provide a separate price signal to encourage investment.[12] Still, these auctions themselves can set reasonably inefficient signals, for instance by placing *ex ante* price caps on auctions to protect the public purse (and ultimately the ratepayers who will have to pay for the cost of the capacity market in their respective tariff base). Due in part to the price-capping mechanisms, capacity mechanisms therefore have come under criticism as insufficient to overcome the 'missing money' problem.[13]

Whether one uses capacity markets or a different mechanism, the 'missing money' problem ultimately can only be solved through regulatory intervention. Regulators create mechanisms by means of which they buy—or force consumers to buy—public goods. As these public goods are non-excludable and non-rivalrous, consumers cannot opt out of these mechanisms. This feature protects against the risk of free-riding.[14] Consequently, they must live with a price increase created by virtue of the regulatory purchase mechanism.[15] Individual actors in a competitive market cannot themselves bring about such a result. They face a tragedy of the anticommons-like situation in which the competitive market creates incentives to under-invest in order to be able to offer more competitive (ie cheaper) energy prices. As every generator competes to do so, they under-invest in meeting the demand of the grid community.[16] To solve the 'missing money' problem and other problems like it, therefore, takes the market *as a whole* to secure such public goods. In the context of the missing money problem, national regulators are the natural institutional actors to bring about this coordination.

Here, it makes sense to pick up the idea of balanced governance from Chapter 2. In Chapter 2, I argued that the bond of belonging requires a form of

[12] Joskow (n 5).
[13] *See* Aagaard & Kleit (n 5).
[14] Vince et al, 'What Is Happening and Where in the World of RTOs and ISOs?', (2006) 27 Energy Law Journal 65, 96.
[15] In a truly liberalized capacity market, these price increases should hit every customer evenly on a per kilowatt-hour basis (they then would pay for their fair share of the increase in resilience). This would be a regressive pricing model, as it would create a greater hardship for electricity customers with comparatively less disposable income. It is therefore tempting to restructure market design to account for this unfairness. Needless to say, by the time one has does that, one has created a reasonably distorted 'market' for public goods.
[16] *See* Joskow (n 5).

balanced governance that combines different governance approaches (public utility, market liberalization, and dirigisme) to secure cheap, reliable, and sustainable energy for energy consumers.[17] I noted in particular that this balanced governance favoured a public utility model during the installation phase of a new energy innovation.[18] This innovation entered the marketplace in order to solve a critical problem within the energy system. The innovation was able to think systemically to engineer a better approach to remove a reverse salient that held back the performance of the energy system as a whole.[19] The failure of a national energy system to deliver public goods is a reverse salient within the system. It limits the national energy system's ability to grow or even to deliver needed service under conditions of stress. Importantly for our governance discussion, as of yet this problem has not been solved through new innovation. For instance, there is no technology that can scale energy output at will without increasing investment costs. Here, market design needs to step in to address the reverse salient and create conditions for innovation to meet the reverse salient with improvements in system performance. This market design need is best met in the same way as it was in the installation phase of a new energy innovation—through public–private partnership to secure the specific public good through public contracting. Regulatory intervention and grid coordination through systems operators attempt to achieve precisely this outcome. They therefore realign incentives for energy system stakeholders according to the bond of belonging to the energy system as whole to deliver needed public goods through better coordination between all stakeholders.

From a financing perspective, this means that such investments are only possible because of regulatory intervention and the creation of a regulatory market. Financing is available against the expected return from a regulatory pricing mechanism. It is not available from an unregulated market. It is therefore pragmatically difficult to conceive of a purely market-based solution for the provision of core public energy goods. This suggests that financing common energy goods (which are a particular kind of public good) exclusively by means of market mechanisms will run into similar difficulties. We therefore need different mechanisms, and additional institutions, to finance common energy goods.

7.3 'Missing Money' and Three Energy Transitions

The discussion of the 'missing money' problem links up with how we can finance energy transitions. To explain this link, I need to distinguish between three different types of energy transitions. In the first type, an innovation 'outpaces' a

[17] *See* section 2.5.
[18] *See* section 2.3.
[19] *Ibid.*

reverse salient and can improve the system before it imperils the provision of a public energy good. This is an *innovation transition*.[20] In the second type, a reverse salient 'outpaces' innovation and imperils the ability of the energy system to provide a public energy good. This is a *'missing money' transition*.[21] In the third type, there is an innovation that can overcome a reverse salient in principle but there is no ready consumer for it—here the transition is systemically financed. When market design does not favour coordination, this type of energy transition can also lead to a 'missing money' problem. This is a *coordination transition*.[22]

7.3(a) Innovation Transitions

Energy transitions are frequently innovation driven. As we have seen in Chapter 2, the normal way in which energy transitions unfold is that a new, systemic innovation allows the energy system decisively to overcome a reverse salient by recasting the reverse salient as a critical problem that can be solved by means of innovation.[23] These innovations can find a market because the new technology improves the ability of each individual customer to whom the innovation is marketed to use energy. For instance, in the context of alternating current, a countryside household can be connected to the electricity grid, thus allowing the household to participate in the benefits of electrification.[24]

Still, the new technology is at the installation phase. This phase is costly because it requires a lot of infrastructure investment. For innovation to find a market at the installation phase, and to finance the capital cost for the needed energy assets, it makes most sense to go through a public utility model to share commercial and regulatory risks.[25] The electrification of Chicago or Berlin in the early twentieth century are key examples of this dynamic.[26] The reason financing innovation through a public–private partnership model in the installation phase makes sense is that it guarantees both a customer base (through monopoly protection) and price certainty (set by the regulator on a cost-plus basis).

Still, the public–private partnership is innovation led. The regulator does not need to force technology to deliver a particular public good. Further, the technology and the means of diffusion of technology is principally in entrepreneurial hands. The regulator principally assists in installation to prevent external

[20] *See* section 7.3(a).

[21] *See* section 7.3(b).

[22] *See* section 7.3(c).

[23] *See* sections 2.4–2.5.

[24] *See* Thomas Hughes, *Networks of Power, Electrification in Western Society 1880-1930* (Johns Hopkins University Press 1983) 106–39.

[25] *See* section 2.5.

[26] *See* Hughes (n 24).

factors stifling innovation and to ensure the delivery of public energy goods in the process. The regulator does so by protecting the price of the new innovation on a cost-sensitive basis and by protecting the customer base through grant of a monopoly.[27]

Because of the timing of innovation, policymakers never quite perceive a 'missing money' problem. The problem still lurks in the background. Innovators identified both a reverse salient holding back the energy system and formulated this reverse salient into a critical problem capable of an engineering solution.[28] When innovators find a solution to this critical problem in time, their innovation is capable of drawing money into fixing the reverse salient because there is a ready marketplace for the new innovation that can grow the energy system.[29] The new innovation expands the marketplace to new (private) paying customers and provides a public energy good *at the same time*. Still, the very fact that engineers identified a reverse salient to be resolved lets us know that a 'missing money' problem was just around the corner. The energy system failed to function so as to provide energy goods. As a reverse salient can only be resolved systemically, the energy goods in question almost by definition are public goods. Systemic solutions inure to the benefit of all system participants rather than just new entrants. The 'missing money' problem in innovation transitions would have materialized fully if we did not innovate quickly enough to draw more customers into the energy system to defray systemic costs (or at the very least innovate so that existing customers would like to pay more for energy services). If we are too slow to innovate in this fashion, market-based financing will not be available to pay for the needed upgrades to provide public energy goods without regulatory intervention.

7.3(b) 'Missing Money' Transitions

The second kind of energy transition happens when innovators 'miss their moment'. In this scenario, the reverse salient of the energy system has in fact overtaken innovation. Policymakers now see that the reverse salient is in fact holding back desired policy outcomes: the energy system cannot deliver necessary public goods for the energy system to function properly.

In the 'missing money' transition, policymakers rather than innovators define what constitutes the critical problem to be resolved. The energy system does not

[27] The change from such a cost measure to a measure that looks to prudence of investment as an important factor is a good indicator that we have progressed further from the installation phase. For an interesting contemporaneous study of precisely this development in the electricity industry, *see* Rose, 'The Hope Case and Public Utility Valuation in the States', (1954) 54 Columbia Law Review 188.

[28] *See ibid* at 79–105.

[29] *See* Carlota Perez, *Technological Revolutions and Financial Capital, The Dynamics of Bubbles and Golden Ages* (Edward Elgar 2003) 47–59.

deliver public energy goods well enough. Regulators therefore set the desired level of realization of the public energy good through policy-making.[30]

In this situation, market design has to step in and 'hold the line' until innovation can again take on its traditional role to grow the energy system and provide the public good organically as a natural byproduct of innovation. Policies do not deliver energy or energy goods. The national energy system does. This means that regulators have to work with stakeholders operating the energy system—ie the energy market. 'Missing money' transitions, therefore, also work best in a public–private partnership model.

The 'missing money' problem provided one somewhat mundane such example.[31] Here, regulators create regulatory incentives to draw private stakeholders into investing capital to deliver the assets and services needed to provide a public good. Another example of a similar dynamic is the support of renewable energy projects through technology forcing by means of aggressive feed-in tariffs alongside the liberalization of the energy market more broadly.[32]

Facially, the mechanism to address the second type of transition is the same as the first. We look to some kind of public–private partnership that sets policy goals outside a marketplace and then provides regulatory price incentives for private capital to finance those goals. Still, the underlying mechanism is different. In the second type of transition, public–private partnerships are regulation led. The regulator defines the critical problem. We therefore need a regulator to create the market. Financing is wholly dependent upon the regulator defining the public energy good to be realized and making credible financial commitments through which to realize it.

If the regulator does not make credible financial commitments for industry to realize the public energy good, the policy will be an 'unfunded mandate'.[33] It will force the provision of a good without making money available for its realization. Such unfunded mandates are unlikely to deliver goods, all things considered, as they cannot be financed by accessing new revenue streams. They can only be financed against existing revenue streams. This would make investment in the energy sector on the whole less attractive and thus lead to an overall deterioration of the national energy system by encouraging under-investment.

[30] The mechanics are precisely not competitive, meaning that there is a potential for over-investment to meet the missing money problem as targets are set by policymakers rather than by market force. This is a critique raised for instance in Aagaard & Kleit, 'Too Much Is Never Enough: Constructing Energy Capacity Market Demand', (2022) 43 Energy Law Journal 79. This is one of the side effects of conceiving of the critical problem through a policy rather than a market/innovation lens. In many ways, it is a feature rather than a problem as it leaves significant room for engineers to address the same reverse salient through a market-based approach.

[31] *See* section 7.2.

[32] Frédéric G Sourgens, Teddy Baldwin, & Catherine Banet, *The Transnational Law of Renewable Energy* (Oxford University Press 2024) 144–79.

[33] For the definition of unfunded mandate, *see* Rapawy, 'Federal Mandate Procedures', (1999) 36 Harvard Journal on Legislation 571, 571–72.

7.3(c) Coordination Transitions

The third kind of energy transition is stuck between the first two. In the third scenario, an innovation capable of overcoming a reverse salient exists. The problem is that it cannot just be marketed to end customers directly. End consumers do not draw immediate, clearly cognizable benefits from this innovation.

One key example of this kind of transition is the implementation of the universal system.[34] It integrated direct current and alternate current parts of the electricity system into a universal system. The universal system improved the energy system as a whole. Yet, its new benefits were difficult to market to individual customers as such. The implementation of these innovations in a sense had to be 'self-financed' by the energy system—first, for instance, through industry consolidation, and then charged on to consumers. (That is, energy companies needed to coordinate and finance the switch to the universal system before charging it on to consumers through rate increases.)[35]

This scenario, too, looks like a 'missing money' problem. There is a financing gap that has to be overcome to set the energy system to rights. Here, a private–public partnership again is needed to get past the hurdle. What is different from the traditional 'missing money' problem is that an innovation exists that can solve the critical problem holding back the energy system. It is simply not economical for companies to invest in its installation even through consolidation if it cannot count on the regulator approving price increases for it to recoup its investment. Here, both regulators and industry are in equipoise, with *both* leading part of the time. Industry provides much of the technical solution. It just needs the regulator to set both the price signals, and, potentially, the regulatory mandate to implement it. Otherwise, innovation, brilliant though it is, will simply never find its market.

One technology in this position in 2025 is direct air capture.[36] Direct air capture technology exists.[37] It is useful in addressing greenhouse gas stocks in the atmosphere.[38] Still, there is no ready customer to buy CO_2. The price of the technology will therefore remain too high to be deployed at the necessary scale.[39] To bring this technology to bear requires coordination between innovators with a stake in the technology and regulators with a stake in its deployment at scale.

Another transition that is stuck in this position is the electrification of particularly energy-poor jurisdictions. Here, technology to deliver electricity readily

[34] *See* Hughes (n 24), at 79–105.
[35] *See* Hughes (n 24).
[36] *See* section 7.4(a) for further discussion.
[37] Hoesung Lee et al, *Climate Change 2023: Synthesis Report. Contribution of Working Groups I, II and III to the Sixth Assessment Report of the Intergovernmental Panel on Climate Change* (Intergovernmental Panel on Climate Change 2023) 87 ('IPCC 2023').
[38] *Ibid.*
[39] *Ibid.*

exists. It just does not exist at a deployable price.[40] Here, again, there is a need to coordinate a global public response to address energy poverty.[41]

7.3(d) Transition Institutions

All three types of energy transition require similar institutions. As each relies ultimately on a public–private partnership, all types of energy transition require a robust national energy policy-making regime. This regime, in turn, must be able to regulate to set specific price signals capable of supporting the financing of public energy goods. Regulators therefore need to be energy literate. Otherwise, regulators cannot formulate the failure of the national energy system to deliver public energy goods into a critical policy problem. A critical policy problem is one that can in fact be resolved—in the sense of providing the requisite public energy goods—through regulatory intervention. To conceive of the reverse salient of the national energy system in this manner therefore requires significant energy expertise and particular policy-making expertise to design an appropriate intervention capable of delivering public goods. Without such regulatory capacity, energy transitions cannot be accomplished.

At the same time, energy transitions also require energy innovators, energy industry stakeholders, and equity and debt investors. Without energy innovators, only the second energy transition type is conceivable as energy policy needs will, by definition, outpace innovation. Even in the second transition type, energy policy can only function if innovators ultimately respond to the policy signals to match the critical policy problem with a critical engineering problem as policy does not deliver energy, energy companies do. Energy industry stakeholders are thus similarly necessary to navigate transitions successfully. They are the stakeholders with the knowhow to install innovations and thus resolve the critical problem successfully.

Energy industry stakeholders, in turn, need investors to fund installation. This investment can include equity investment. More importantly, it also includes debt investment (eg loans). Without such investments, private industry stakeholders are limited to a relatively limited capital to manage installation. This would slow the pace of transition significantly and thus prolong the reverse salient's salience. These investors will make their investment decisions in terms of ordinary market diligence—they will look to the return of investment they stand to make, the risk of their investment, and the certainty of the regulatory environment.

Finally, there needs to be a robust global cooperation to support optimal outcomes. Regulators should coordinate information about their respective

[40] Abhijit Banerjee & Ester Duflo, *Good Economics for Hard Times* (Public Affairs 2019) 188.
[41] Sourgens, Banet, & Baldwin (n 32), at 336.

approaches.[42] Further, international investment and technical assistance is needed to overcome resource and expertise problems to manage each kind of transition. There thus must also be an international regulatory network to address this need.

All four types of actors need a space in which they can make their decisions. They need a marketplace or forum. In most instances, the regulatory environment (rule and ratemaking processes etc) provides a significant part of this forum. This regulatory environment is backed by ordinary capital markets to provide investments and energy value chains to provide energy inputs. I will discuss the role of energy value chains in Chapter 8.

7.4 Between Transitions—Financing Climate Policy

A reason that we have difficulty financing the currently ongoing energy transitions is that what we call 'the energy transition' today in fact runs across all three types of energy transitions I outlined in the last section. Each type of transition is financed differently and requires regulators to act differently to support financing. This means that we cannot rely on a single financing approach to bring 'the energy transition' about. Rather, to be successful we need to blend our financing models to push forward each transition in its own right. A bond-of-belonging based approach can and will in fact support such a model, as it is itself premised not in a dogmatic attachment to any one economic theory of energy governance but rather is driven by a pragmatic focus on achieving energy system outcomes in light of specific market conditions.

The current 'energy transition' is even more complex. The three types of energy transition I introduced above involved actors in a single national market. The money from the 'missing money' problem was missing *domestically* and domestic regulation and domestic public–private partnerships could in principle supply it. This is not the case in the current energy transition. The current transition implicates not just national energy systems. Rather, it is a problem that affects the *global* energy system, as such.[43] We therefore cannot resolve the second and third kind of transitions through purely national regulatory leadership. We need to coordinate different national responses globally.

Such global coordination has serious realpolitik repercussions. Each geostrategic actor will have to weigh the implications of coordination on the balance of power between them. Realpolitik therefore limits transition, as we have already seen in Chapter 3.[44]

[42] *See* Sourgens, 'The Dark Sun Network', (2023) 94 Colorado Law Review 681.
[43] *See* Frédéric G Sourgens & Leonardo Sempertegui, *Principles of International Energy Transition Law* (Oxford University Press 2023).
[44] *See* section 3.4.

We can now say more than we could in Chapter 3. We can identify that realpolitik functionally replicates the 'missing money' problem at the international, geostrategic level. On the domestic level, the 'missing money' problem is a problem of misalignment of incentives between policymakers and industry stakeholders. Policymakers wish to secure public goods, while industry stakeholders look to remain competitive in a given market structure and secure their own economic good. The 'missing money' problem arises when market structures do not allow industry stakeholders to secure returns on investment to provide the public good in question. There is no economic upside for firms to realize the public energy good in question. We therefore need regulatory intervention.[45]

Realpolitik misaligns incentives in a similar way but does so not between regulators and industry stakeholders but between different national policymakers. Each policymaker seeks to secure its own national public energy good. In focusing on a national public energy good in a global discourse, policymakers now focus on individual good, not public good as measured in the context of the global community.[46] They therefore become like industry stakeholders in a key respect—they do not see meeting a shared public good as an end worth pursuing in its own right. National policymakers acting on the international stage and industry stakeholders instead look to maximize their own individual good (in the case of the national policymaker, this good is the national public energy good; in the case of the industry stakeholder, it is shareholder value).[47]

Realpolitik replaces the industry's concern with economic returns with a concern for relative geostrategic power. A realpolitik deployment of resources makes no sense if it does not provide me with a clear, short-term competitive advantage.[48] Yet, the attainment of public goods precisely does not create competitive advantages—they are by definition non-excludable and non-rivalrous.[49] Realpolitik therefore risks getting stuck in a 'missing power' problem alongside the 'missing money' problem.

Critically, we cannot solve the 'missing power' problem like we solved the 'missing money' problem. We solved the 'missing money' problem by introducing regulators. These regulators have policy-making authority over industry stakeholders.[50] There is no similar global regulator of last resort with authority over states' exercise of realpolitik. Each state exercising realpolitik judgement is sovereign and does not recognize a superior regulator with jurisdiction over its energy policy.[51] We therefore need to find an institutional answer that can escape

[45] *See* section 7.2.
[46] *See* Kenneth N Waltz, *Theory of International Politics* (Random House 1979) 106.
[47] *Ibid.*
[48] *See* sections 3.4–3.5.
[49] *See* section 6.2.
[50] *See* Joskow (n 5).
[51] Declaration on Principles of International Law concerning Friendly Relations and Co-operation among States in Accordance with the Charter of the United Nations, (24 October 1970) UN General Assembly Resolution 2625 (XXV)

realpolitik. To find a way to finance the current kind of energy transition—one that implicates global public energy goods that are geostrategically sensitive—requires action that coordinates regulatory responses somewhere on the spectrum of the bond of belonging. This is easier said than done.

7.4(a) Climate Mitigation

Climate mitigation is a public good. It is also part of the common energy good of energy stewardship.[52] Climate *mitigation* reduces the impact of climate change on everyone by reducing the flow or stock of greenhouse gases in the atmosphere. I cannot exclude anyone from the benefit of climate change mitigation. One person also cannot use climate mitigation more than someone else.

Climate mitigation means investment in technologies that reduce net greenhouse emissions from existing energy assets, as well as investing in new energy assets that do not increase net greenhouse emissions going forward.[53] Some of these technologies impose a new cost item (eg carbon capture and storage).[54] Other technologies may not be available at scale (eg renewable generation with battery backup, next generation geothermal, or fusion energy) and may increase the cost of energy systems during this installation period.[55] From an energy perspective, we face a 'missing money' problem: there is no energy technology that can improve energy outcomes and achieve the public energy good of climate change mitigation at this point in time. Several innovations may well be close. Yet, savings from these innovations are not yet sufficient to warrant a transition like the transition from steam to electricity on their energy merit alone. To meet the public energy good of mitigation therefore requires regulatory intervention to define the reverse salient of climate change as a critical energy policy problem.[56]

There is also no ready market for climate mitigation alone. Voluntary carbon markets have received a tepid response.[57] They do not set sufficient price signals to secure financing for any kind of mitigation technology.[58] At the same time,

[52] *See* section 6.3(c).

[53] IPCC 2023 (n 37), at 86.

[54] *Ibid.*

[55] *Ibid.*

[56] *See* section 7.3(b).

[57] Dawes, 'What's Plaguing Voluntary Carbon Markets?', (2 February 2024) Center for Strategic & International Studies, https://www.csis.org/analysis/whats-plaguing-voluntary-carbon-markets, last accessed 9 December 2024.

[58] *Compare* Choudhury, 'Commodities 2024: Price Slump in 2023 Clouds Outlook for Voluntary Carbon Markets', (5 January 2024) S&P Global, https://www.spglobal.com/commodity-insights/en/news-research/latest-news/energy-transition/010524-price-slump-in-2023-clouds-outlook-for-voluntary-carbon-market, last accessed 9 December 2024 (noting 2023 closing price of carbon offsets at US$0.74/mt$CO_{2e}$) *with* 'Carbon Capture and Storage in the United States', (December 2023) Congressional Budget Office, https://www.cbo.gov/system/files/2023-12/59345-carbon-capture-storage.pdf, last accessed 9 December 2024 ('CBO') ('An indicative range of estimates is from about

technology is available to reduce both flows and stocks of CO_2 emissions. The technology just cannot be sold to end consumers because CO_2 only has a value as a public good (ie the value of not accelerating climate change). The deployment of carbon removal technology therefore also faces a coordination transition problem.[59]

To complicate matters, climate mitigation is a global problem rather than a national problem. It further implicates realpolitik metrics. For example, climate policies overlay economic policies that together have led to a significant loss of manufacturing, and the related industrial base, from both the US and the EU to the People's Republic of China.[60] Part of this migration of manufacturing is energy price sensitive.[61] Realpolitik therefore in general would counsel against further undercutting US and EU industrial performance by means of energy regulations to respond to the 'missing money' problem. It leads to a relative loss of industrial power to a rival. This realpolitik concern is alarmingly acute in light of the classic purview of realpolitik—defence policy. Western powers may already not have a sufficient industrial base to increase to war time production in a Great Power confrontation.[62] In the mid-2020s, the realpolitik concern of preparing for a direct military Great Power conflict have left the wargaming stage and actively entered policy-making.[63] There is thus also a 'missing power' problem: addressing the 'missing money' problem through domestic regulatory action is potentially diametrically opposed to the national security interests of key geopolitical blocks.

\$15 to \$120 per metric ton of CO_2 captured, with additional costs for transporting and storing the CO_2' for CCUS and \$135 to \$345 per metric ton of CO_2 for direct air capture.)

[59] *See* section 7.3(c).

[60] *See* Doshi, 'As Europe Deindustrializes, Can Economic Suicide Be Avoided?' (10 May 2024) Forbes, https://www.forbes.com/sites/tilakdoshi/2024/05/09/as-europe-deindustrializes-can-economic-suicide-be-avoided/, last accessed 9 December 2024; Borgonovi et al, 'The Effect of the EU Fit for 55 Packages on Labour Markets and the Demand for Skill', (28 July 2023) OECD Social, Employment and Migration Working Papers No 297, https://www.oecd.org/en/publications/the-effects-of-the-eu-fit-for-55-package-on-labour-markets-and-the-demand-for-skills_6c16baac-en.html, last accessed 9 December 2024 ('Employment in the Fit for 55 scenario is projected to decrease by 3% for blue collar and farm workers (2% in the Baseline) and increase by 4-5% for other occupations (5-6% in the Baseline). The most demanded skills following the implementation of Fit for 55 will be those related to inter-personal communication and the use of digital technologies, whereas the demand for skills related to the use of traditional tools and technologies is projected to decline.'); Lipke et al, 'Trust and Trade-offs: How to Manage Europe's Green Technology Dependence on China', (29 May 2024) European Council on Foreign Relations, https://ecfr.eu/publication/trust-and-trade-offs-how-to-manage-europes-green-technology-dependence-on-china/, last accessed 9 December 2024.

[61] Doshi (n 60).

[62] Harper, 'Vital Signs 2020: Industrial Base Could Struggle to Surge Production in Wartime', (24 January 2020) National Defense Magazine, https://www.nationaldefensemagazine.org/articles/2020/1/24/industrial-base-could-struggle-to-surge-production-in-wartime, last accessed 9 December 2024; Jones, 'The U.S. Defense Industrial Base Is Not Prepared for a Possible Conflict with China', (2024) Center for Strategic & International Studies, https://features.csis.org/preparing-the-US-industrial-base-to-deter-conflict-with-China/, last accessed 9 December 2024.

[63] 'China Wants Ability to Invade Taiwan by 2027, U.S. Admiral Says', (24 April 2024) Nikkei Asia, https://asia.nikkei.com/Editor-s-Picks/Interview/China-wants-ability-to-invade-Taiwan-by-2027-U.S.-admiral-says, last accessed 9 December 2024.

States therefore simply do not have the relative power 'reserve' to engage in policies that benefit the global public good but undercut their own relative geostrategic position.

The particular intersection of innovation, domestic policy, and geopolitics at which the climate transition finds world society is inauspicious from a finance perspective. Innovation cannot currently solve the climate mitigation problem by means of engineering alone. Domestic policy could treat the problem as a 'missing money' problem or a coordination problem and create a regulatory marketplace to finance climate mitigation technology. Still, doing so creates direct military advantages for geostrategic rivals whom leading defence policy stakeholders view on an escalatory military footing with each other. An attempt to use regulatory means to solve the 'missing money' problem, and increase energy prices, looks geostrategically naive. The geostrategic uncertainty therefore creates significant difficulties for financing the steep costs of climate mitigation.[64]

In this constellation, it is cold comfort that the bond of belonging can overcome precisely such deadlocks in theory. The bond of belonging requires a level of trust that key geostrategic stakeholders do not currently have towards each other.[65] The fact that a solution would be possible under different geostrategic conditions therefore is not helpful. Instead, we must find a way to institutions that could bring about an alignment of incentives to fix the 'missing money' and the 'missing power' problem in the face of global tensions unprecedented since the early 1960s.

Still, even in this context, financing climate mitigation is not hopeless. Rather, the structural similarities in how realpolitik and the bond of belonging function provides a potential pathway. One of the critical similarities between realpolitik and the bond of belonging was the verification of the efforts of one's neighbour.[66] As I argued in Chapter 6, this mechanism permits cooperation along realpolitik lines while also building a bond of belonging. The verification mechanism in that context must serve two goals—attaining an individual goal through cooperation and achieving a good for the sake of the community.[67]

If verification can be secured, cooperation is helpful from a realpolitik perspective because it mitigates national economic losses attributable to climate change.[68]

[64] 'The Net Zero Transition, What It Would Cost, What It Would Bring', McKinsey & Co (January 2022), https://www.mckinsey.com/capabilities/sustainability/our-insights/the-net-zero-transition-what-it-would-cost-what-it-could-bring, last accessed 26 March 2024.

[65] *See* Elinor Ostrom, *Governing the Commons: The Evolution of Institutions for Collective Action* (Cambridge University Press 2015) 82–87.

[66] *See* section 6.3.

[67] *See* section 6.4.

[68] Mikaelsson et al, 'Executive Summary', in European Climate Risk Assessment, (2024) European Environmental Agency EEA Report 01/2024 at 11 ('Hundreds of thousands of people would die from heatwaves, and economic losses from coastal floods alone could exceed EUR 1 trillion per year.'); 'Climate Change Impacts Are Increasing for Americans', (14 November 2023) National Oceanic and Atmospheric Administration, https://www.noaa.gov/news-release/climate-change-impacts-are-increasing-for-americans, last accessed 10 December 2024 ('NOAA') ('The impacts of extreme climate

At the lower end of carbon capture costs, removing all US CO_2 emissions from electric power and transportation for 2023 would cost US$35.85 billion.[69] At the lower end of direct air capture costs, removing all US CO_2 from transportation would cost US$250.56 billion.[70] Current estimates of US economic losses due to climate change are US$150 billion annually.[71] China similarly has significant climate exposure.[72] As most of these losses can only be avoided to the extent that *all* emitters reduce emissions, there is a case to be made for realpolitik cooperation. The main question in this realpolitik equation is what reciprocal reductions are efficient to avoid a geostrategically and economically optimal amount of losses. Each will likely deploy different solutions that favour domestic industry and thus protect the domestic industrial base. Both are also likely to shield industry from energy cost increases. Such cooperation therefore must be flexible to yield realistic results.[73]

This realpolitik cooperation also supports an entirely different goal—the common energy good of environmental stewardship.[74] This good is ultimately more ambitious. It looks to realize the maximum feasible amount of environmental stewardship as opposed to the realpolitik optimal amount of emission reductions. Still, the goal—reducing climate change—is ultimately a global goal. As geostrategic stakeholders make progress towards that common goal, the conditions for a bond of belonging approach to climate mitigation improve drastically. One can therefore advance financing climate mitigation even under the currently challenging conditions, assuming that verification mechanisms can in fact be sufficiently designed.

There is an analogue for this approach at the height of geostrategic tensions. This mechanism supported one of the most notable realpolitik successes of the Cold War era—nuclear disarmament achieved through treaties like the Intermediate-Range Nuclear Forces (INF) Treaty.[75] The premise of this success was the Russian proverb made famous by President Reagan: 'trust, but verify'.[76] This mechanism

events are costing the nation an estimated $150 billion each year. With every increment of global warming, costly damages are expected to accelerate.')

[69] *See* 'U.S. Energy-Related Carbon Dioxide Emissions, 2023', (25 April 2024) US Energy Information Administration, https://www.eia.gov/environment/emissions/carbon/, last accessed 10 December 2024 (US emitting 963 million mt CO_2 in industrial sector and 1,427 mt CO_2 in electric power sector); CBO (n 58) (CCUS cost of $15 to $120 per metric ton of CO_2 captured, with additional costs for transporting and storing the CO_2' for CCUS and $135 to $345 per metric ton of CO_2 for direct air capture.)

[70] *See* sources in n 69.

[71] *See* NOAA (n 68).

[72] *See* David Sandalow et al, *Guide to Chinese Climate Policy 2022* (Oxford Institute for Energy Studies 2022) 26–28 (noting a trillion-dollar exposure).

[73] This flexibility is built in to the Paris Agreement. *See* Paris Agreement, art 4(2).

[74] *See* section 6.3(c).

[75] Leich, 'Arms Control and Disarmament', (1988) 82 American Journal of International Law 341.

[76] Abbott, '"Trust but Verify": The Production of Information in Arms Control Treaties and Other International Agreements', (1993) 26 Cornell International Law Journal 1, 36–37; President Reagan, 'Farewell Address to the American People', (12 January 1989) New York Times, https://www.nytimes.

allowed the US and the Soviet Union to cut their respective nuclear arsenals. The idea of acting out of both concern for a global public good (reducing the risk of nuclear war borne from a nuclear arms race) and in a realpolitik manner is therefore not absurd even when discussions are about the central-most topics of national security.

Financing climate mitigation is more demanding than nuclear disarmament. Nuclear weapon states have it in their sole power to stock and organize their nuclear forces. State agreement is not sufficient to decarbonize global energy systems. Rather, states must act with private stakeholders in the energy industry and in the investment community to innovate, finance, and install the needed energy technology to meet decarbonization goals. This means that states must combine their geostrategic efforts with their domestic regulatory efforts to be successful. On the domestic level, this will require regulatory action to absorb the cost of existing technology like carbon capture, utilization, and storage or direct air capture as well as renewable energy. Still, this regulatory action needs to be tied to a global enforcement mechanism that can verify and enforce reciprocal decarbonization commitments or unilateral but mutually beneficial unreciprocated decarbonization outcomes. Unilateral carbon border adjustments tied to the non-fulfilment of such commitments are one such tool for economies with significant markets like the US. The revenue generated from such carbon border adjustments could then be employed to pay for further upgrades to carbon removal capabilities in the imposing state.[77] This would mean that the enforcement mechanism would not itself affect the relative balance of power between the states in question. Rather, it would use enforcement to achieve the originally shared goal of decarbonization. Institutionally, this means adding a global enforcement mechanism to the domestic mechanisms discussed in the last section to give sufficient credence in state commitments to decarbonize the energy sector to attract private capital.

The architecture of the Paris Agreement has aimed to provide the infrastructure for such a decarbonization verification process. It requires each state to submit an emissions inventory,[78] as well as 'information necessary to track progress made in achieving its nationally determined contribution' (NDCs).[79] The NDCs, in turn, represent a state's stated emission reduction goal, towards which the state 'shall pursue domestic mitigation measures'.[80] Since the Conference of the Parties negotiations at Katowicze (and later Glasgow), Paris Agreement parties agreed to a

com/1989/01/12/news/transcript-of-reagan-s-farewell-address-to-american-people.html, last accessed 9 December 2024.

[77] For a climate proposal along similar lines, *see* Siegel, 'Senate Republicans Introduce Climate Bill—Aimed at China', (2 November 2024) Politico, https://www.politico.com/news/2023/11/02/senate-gop-climate-bill-china-00124909, last accessed 9 December 2024.

[78] Paris Agreement, art 13(7)(a); *see also ibid* at art 4.13.

[79] *Ibid* at art 13(7)(b).

[80] *Ibid* at art 4(2).

Paris Rulebook to give definition to how to account for emissions and emission reductions in the stocktake process, as well as to guide an expert review process for reports.[81] This reporting structure provides a robust verification mechanism that, combined with other outside verification efforts by non-governmental organizations and others, can provide a reasonably good picture of decarbonization efforts. The Paris Agreement reporting mechanism therefore plays a critical part in a realpolitik, and transactional, form of cooperation by providing a common basis to verify both ambition and performance. In doing so, it provides a critical building stone for the bridge from transactional realpolitik to energy cooperation premised in a global bond of belonging. With this reporting mechanism in place, it is possible to solve both the 'missing money' and the 'missing power' problem. Consequently, a path is available to create global regulatory markets for climate mitigation in the energy sector. Given that this marketplace does not rely on good will but makes transactional, realpolitik sense, it can provide the right kind of credibility to bring investors forward to invest in mitigation technologies. This investment, in turn, will permit innovators and entrepreneurs to conceive of and solve the critical problem of energy-based climate mitigation from the engineering and not just the policy side.

The US will leave the Paris Agreement for the second time following its withdrawal from the treaty in 2025.[82] This withdrawal states that '[o]ver the decades, with the help of sensible policies that do not encumber private-sector activity, the United States has simultaneously grown its economy, raised worker wages, increased energy production, reduced air and water pollution, and reduced greenhouse gas emissions'.[83] The withdrawal therefore is not a rejection of the goal to 'reduce[] greenhouse gas emissions'.[84] It rather concerns the means to do so, including the rejection of current climate finance mechanisms benefiting third states.[85]

Bilateral climate efforts with the US and any other non member states of the Paris Agreement will continue to be able to draw on the verification mechanisms created under the Paris Agreement. The key verification process concerns reporting. The reporting metric adopted pursuant to the Paris Agreement remains available for bilateral communications about climate mitigation efforts and outcomes. Bilateral communications can further adapt and improve the reporting metrics to better fit specific circumstances of exchanging states. The US can

[81] *See* Rajamani & Bodansky, 'The Paris Rulebook: Balancing International Prescriptiveness with National Discretion', (2019) 68 International & Comparative Law Quarterly 1023; Paris Agreement, art 14.

[82] Executive Order 'Putting America First in International Environmental Agreements', (20 January 2025) The White House, https://www.whitehouse.gov/presidential-actions/2025/01/putting-america-first-in-international-environmental-agreements/, last accessed 21 January 2025.

[83] *Ibid* at ¶ 1.

[84] *Ibid.*

[85] *See ibid* at ¶¶ 1, 3(e).

continue to draw on information submitted by Paris Agreement member states as part of the verification process pursuant to the Paris Agreement. Should the US wish to rely on policy mechanisms like the carbon border adjustment bill sponsored by Senator Cassidy of Louisiana, the US would require a metric against which to measure foreign emissions against US emissions.[86] In such a scenario, the US would also have a record of greenhouse gas emissions.

The architecture of the Paris Agreement further allows this market to trade on the idea of relative advantage by setting up a global mitigation market.[87] There is a potential comparative advantage to reducing emissions in newly industrializing economies with a higher emission profile—as noted already, carbon capture at large source points is cheaper than direct air capture of CO_2.[88] Similarly, one of the biggest improvements in climate outcomes comes from switching from coal-fired power to gas and renewables, as the US power journey has demonstrated.[89] There is thus low-hanging fruit in cooperating to reduce emissions in industrializing economies at the same time as decarbonizing the easiest sectors in post-industrial economies. The Paris Agreement sets up a structure for just such exchanges, thus creating the potential for a global regulatory market.[90] To take advantage of this market, national regulators must incorporate this market design possibility in their regulatory market design.

This mechanism, too, can be replicated bilaterally. The policy purpose of the US withdrawal from the Paris Agreement makes it somewhat unlikely that the US would in fact use such an opportunity.[91]

Even with a global market mechanism, and with the security to reduce emissions in large economies, there is a sizeable climate mitigation gap. The 'rest of the world' requires both more energy than it currently consumes and must decarbonize its existing energy assets to achieve global climate mitigation efforts. Without such efforts, states will continue to rely on inexpensive available power resources to meet rudimentary needs. In practice, this means turning to coal for electricity and for heating.[92] Development finance in principle is capable of addressing both the decarbonization and the electrification needs in the 'Global South'. This development finance is not a 'hand out'. Rather, even from a realpolitik perspective, it is an inexpensive investment in achieving climate outcomes without

[86] *See* Siegel (n 77).

[87] Paris Agreement, art 6; Daniel Bodansky, Jutta Brunnée, & Lavanya Rajamani, *International Climate Change Law* (Oxford University Press 2017) 179–92, 237–38.

[88] CBO (n 58).

[89] *See* Second US Nationally Determined Contribution under the Paris Agreement (April 2021), at 2.

[90] Paris Agreement, art 6.

[91] Executive Order (n 82), at ¶¶ 1, 3(e).

[92] Hummer et al, 'Just 15 Countries Account for 98% of New Coal-Power Developments', (3 September 2024) Carbon Brief, https://www.carbonbrief.org/guest-post-just-15-countries-account-for-98-of-new-coal-power-development/, last accessed 11 December 2024 ('Despite the concentration of coal-plant development in fewer countries and projections that global coal demand could be peaking, new coal-fired power station proposals continue to outpace cancellations.').

benefiting a geostrategic rival directly. It is thus an efficacious component to close the emission gap (and thus avoid national losses) without incurring significant geostrategically destabilizing consequences.

The current global climate regime provides a starting point to coordinate global energy transition policies. It does so even in the face of geostrategic competition. Energy finance can serve an important alliance building function akin to development finance during the Cold War.[93] The People's Republic of China is already proceeding along this route.[94] The key to any such efforts ultimately is the verification mechanism that emissions are indeed reduced. The current regime continues to make available such tools for members and non-members of the Paris Agreement alike.

7.4(b) Climate Adaptation and Energy Expansion

Financing global climate adaptation (including an increase in energy capacity to power adaptation) is, if anything, more challenging than financing climate mitigation. In many jurisdictions, global climate adaptation runs into a different version of the 'missing money' problem and 'missing power' problem. Yet, even in this context, there is a realpolitik rationale for collective adaptation action. Just as in the mitigation finance context, this realpolitik rationale can ultimately support global action consistent with the bond of belonging, the pursuit of human development, and the common energy goods of energy peace, energy abundance, and energy stewardship.

Financing climate adaptation differs in important respects from financing climate mitigation. Climate adaptation consists of local investments to improve the climate resilience of a particular community.[95] Climate mitigation, on the other hand, requires global cooperation to be effective, at all. In comparatively richer jurisdictions, climate adaptation is readily financeable. There is a marketplace for individual adaptation measures. For instance, extreme temperature events will increase in severity and frequency in the European Union.[96] To protect against extreme heat, private persons and businesses will need to invest in air conditioners.[97] Given the improvement in their respective quality of life and productivity, private

[93] Martin Daunton, *The Economic Government of the World 1933-2023* (Farrar, Straus and Giroux 2023) 367–426.
[94] *See* Liu, 'China Is Providing Billions in Climate Finance to Developing Countries', (7 November 2024) World Resources Institute, https://www.wri.org/insights/china-climate-finance-developing-countries, 21 January 2025.
[95] *See* Paris Agreement, art 2(1)(b).
[96] Mikaelsson (n 68), at 11.
[97] Matthew E Kahn, *Adapting to Climate Change: Markets and the Management of an Uncertain Future* (Yale University Press 2021).

persons and individuals are likely to purchase air conditioning solutions.[98] This will bring both industry and finance to support European adaptation efforts by making more air conditioning available for purchase. The increase in air conditioning will also increase electricity demand.[99] This increase will be reasonably predictable. It will require an expansion of the grid. Yet, again, there is a basic market case for this expansion and industry and finance are readily available to support it. This leaves true local public adaptation goods like levee systems. In sufficiently affluent communities, these levee systems can be built through regular appropriations or property taxes on communities protected by the levee. In economies like the US, the EU, or Singapore, there are no particular conceptual impediments to financing adaptation measures—even as these measures are no doubt expensive.[100]

The problem is radically different in less affluent communities. In less affluent communities, purchasing power to buy air conditioners is more limited. Given the productivity impact of air conditioning, the limited adoption of air conditioners will have significant repercussions for relative opportunities in those societies.[101] The same is true of other private adaptation measures. The same thread weaves through all other areas of adaptation (upgrading the grid to power with new adaptation measures and public works to protect communities). Industry and finance are less likely to support an adaptation market in the communities in question because there is too little demand even as there is disproportionate need.

This, again, is a 'missing money' problem. There currently exists no innovation that could meet the demand for public energy goods through market expansion. In this case, the reason is one of price. Still, it is not true that the economies in question will never be able to self-sustain adaptation measures on a market basis. Economic growth can and does change this equation. Abu Dhabi, Seoul, and Taipei each highlight that different pathways to economic growth (extractives, heavy industry, and chip manufacturing) can drastically change the case for market-based adaptation measures in the 2020s compared to the economic situation in the 1950s.[102] 'Developing economies' can and do develop. When they do, they can self-sustain climate adaptation. The problem is that inaction on climate

[98] Barry & Winfield, 'As Summer Breezes Fade, Sweltering Europeans Give Air Conditioning a Skeptical Embrace', (2 August 2023) Associated Press, https://apnews.com/article/air-conditioning-ac-extreme-heat-europe-3f1b8ad9275297da02ae137a72b77a8d, last accessed 11 December 2024.

[99] Jamet, 'Air Conditioning Is "Exacerbating the Climate Crisis" But How Many Europeans Use It?', (18 June 2024) Euronews, https://www.euronews.com/green/2024/06/18/air-conditioning-use-has-more-than-doubled-in-europe-since-1990, last accessed 11 December 2024.

[100] Lee et al, 'How the Tiny Island City-State of Singapore Fights Rising Sea Levels', (10 October 2023) Time Magazine, https://time.com/6322111/singapore-fights-rising-sea-levels-climate-change/, last accessed 11 December 2024.

[101] *See* Kahn (n 97).

[102] *See* Binyamin Appelbaum, *The Economists' Hour: False Prophets, Free Markets, and the Fracture of Society* (Little, Brown 2019) (discussing the economic growth pathway in different developing economies around the world).

adaptation today threatens permanently to deprive the societies in question of a path to both economic and human development.[103] The 'energy hill' the societies must climb is too step to get to development. They need a finance catalyst to lower the energy hill and make development self-sustaining. Yet, they cannot provide this catalyst themselves.

Facially, solving this 'missing money' problem is more treacherous than solving the 'missing money' problem in the climate mitigation context. Climate adaptation finance for the economies in question must come from the outside. It needs to be public money given that there is no clear market case for more adaptation in the economies in question. There facially is no reciprocal climate benefit for the sending state from adaptation measures in the receiving state. Given the fiscal situation in the mid-2020s in the US, the EU, and beyond, it is therefore facially difficult to make a transactional case for climate adaptation finance for the receiving states in question.[104]

Somewhat surprisingly, the current geostrategic situation is helpful in providing such a case. Many of the states requiring climate adaptation assistance are strategically located.[105] Further, current geostrategic tensions have crystalized around a web of potential conflicts between Great Powers. The most important area of such tension is between the US and the People's Republic of China. This is not the only relevant area. Russia and the European Union, Iran and Israel, India and its neighbours all have significant geostrategic conflict potential.

This conflict potential entails a need for realpolitik alliance building. The People's Republic of China is already engaged in such alliance building by providing adaptation assistance to low lying islands in the Pacific in exchange for militarily valuable access (access that can be used to station military assets that can interdict passage by hostile fleets).[106] Other powers lag behind the People's Republic of China in this respect. Realpolitik therefore would suggest it prudent to increase similar activities in geostrategically important areas.

The same realpolitik logic applies to alliance building more generally. It is not possible to predict with certainty which economies will become the next South

[103] *See* Diffenbaugh & Burke, 'Global Warming Has Increased Global Economic Inequality', (2019) 116 Proceedings of the National Academy of Sciences of the United States of America 9808-9813.

[104] Rappeport, 'U.S. National Debt Tops $35 Trillion for First Time', (29 July 2024) New York Times, https://www.nytimes.com/2024/07/29/us/politics/national-debt-35-trillion.html, last accessed 11 December 2024; Alderman, 'Investors Punish France Over Budget Turmoil', (2 December 2024) New York Times, https://www.nytimes.com/2024/12/02/business/frances-credit-rating.html#:~:text=France%20is%20in%20worse%20fiscal,the%20country's%20gross%20domestic%20product, last accessed 11 December 2024; Sing, 'China's Risky Answer to Wall of Debt Is More Debt', (18 June 204) Reuters, https://www.reuters.com/breakingviews/chinas-risky-answer-wall-debt-is-more-debt-2024-06-17/, last accessed 11 December 2024.

[105] For one example, *see* Fujii-Takamoto, 'Strategic Competition in the Pacific: A Case for Kiribati', (7 December 2022) Journal of Indo-Pacific Affairs, https://www.airuniversity.af.edu/JIPA/Display/Article/3237885/strategic-competition-in-the-pacific-a-case-for-kiribati/, last accessed 11 December 2024.

[106] *See ibid*; *see also* Rush Doshi, *The Long Game: China's Grand Strategy to Displace American Order* (Oxford University Press 2021).

Korea and which will fail in that regard. Any one alliance viewed on its own therefore may be of limited realpolitik value. Forward-looking alliance building with *baskets of economies* changes the dynamics. It increases the likelihood of success and also deprives one's rival of a potentially increased base for the projection of geostrategic power. Such a realpolitik strategy would suggest that one invest comparatively smaller amounts more widely. This in turn will provide opportunities for developing economies to receive assistance from multiple geostrategic competitors.

This realpolitik logic mirrors somewhat the logic of development lending during the Cold War. Lending adapted to geostrategic realities from a reasonably transactional 'bankers' approach at the height of US post-war power to an approach that was premised in alliance building in light of the shifting scenarios in the Cold War.[107] Realpolitik therefore provided opportunities for development finance outside of the strict requirements of project bankability.[108]

Instructively, thinking at the International Bank for Reconstruction and Development highlighted these rival approaches to development funding in its early years. One of the early approaches to development finance discussed at the time was to 'start[] from micro-foundations of social agents who responded to local difficulties according to local conditions, rather than programmatic aid which might benefit some social groups and others with the risk of domestic political conflict'.[109] In the adaptation context, this approach could be deployed in a manner not dissimilar to proof-of-concept funding in the innovation context. Proof-of-concept funding provides the bridge between an idea and venture capital support for an innovation.[110] A micro-foundations approach to adaptation development finance and adaptation energy finance would focus on small footprints first. This small footprint would be within the scope of proof-of-concept funding. It would also tie development funding to 'micro-agency'—agency at the smallest feasible community level—thus embedding the response best in local conditions and giving it the best chance of success. If successful, it could then be scaled in light of better, and hopefully soon 'bankable', economic modelling—modelling that would bring funding in on a self-sustaining basis.

The realpolitik lens to adaptation finance, like its climate mitigation sibling, builds a bridge between a purely transactional form of cooperation towards one that is premised in a shared common good. The idea of alliance building already suggests as much. It conjures the idea of a 'union' that is deeper than convenience. Alliance hints at a mutual organization around a shared understanding of a common good. Adaptation finance will be successful in broadening the realization

[107] Daunton (n 93), at 307–13.
[108] *Ibid* at 395–96.
[109] *Ibid* at 314 (discussing Albert Hirschman's approach to development finance in the early 1950s).
[110] *See* Andrea Alunni, *Innovation Finance and Technology Transfer: Funding Proof of Concept* (Routledge 2019).

of human development outcomes when it observes what forms of finance are successful, how they might be further improved, and what tools are available to make them more widely accessible. As adaptation policy improves, it is likely to grow the adaptation marketplace and make adaptation more self-sustaining in the long-term in more places. As more adaptation means more energy in more places, this strengthens the global energy system by broadening the global energy stakeholder community. The institutions to bring about this result largely exist today. The next and final section of this chapter will briefly address the role of transnational development finance institutions as a particularly salient institutions to help coordinate the policy processes I have discussed so far in this chapter.

7.5 The Role of Development Finance Institutions

Global energy transition finance must rely on more than 'ordinary' investments. 'Missing money' transitions and coordination transitions in particular rely upon regulatory bridge markets. These bridge markets allow for the development and deployment of energy resources to provide public energy goods when the market on its own is not yet in a position to deliver these goods through growth alone. Standing up such regulatory markets will require development finance support to the extent that the market cannot easily absorb the additional costs through rate increases. This will frequently be the case in economies with comparatively lower rates of energy consumption. These economies by definition do not yet have a sufficient consumer and infrastructure base to support higher rates of electrification without external impetus. In these markets, even the basic supply of energy to a broader population base becomes a 'missing money' problem because the cost of expanding the national energy service to more consumers is too high relative to the disposable income in the community that is to be connected to the grid.[111] In these markets, development finance would be an obvious means to accelerate the installation of energy infrastructure needed to realize energy-driven economic and human development outcomes by reducing costs of capital and by supporting the installation of energy solutions with a footprint fit for the local environment. Development finance is also a key facilitator of global climate mitigation and climate adaptation efforts.[112]

This raises the question of which institutions should provide the development finance in question.[113] Realpolitik and the bond-of-belonging lenses provide

[111] Abhijit V Banerhee & Esther Duflo, *Good Economics for Hard Times* (Public Affairs 2019) 187.
[112] *See* section 7.3.
[113] For a fuller technical discussion of classical development finance, climate finance under the Paris Agreement, export–import finance, and their relationship to traditional project finance, *see* Sourgens, Banet, & Baldwin, (n 32), at 234–56.

conceptually different answers. In practice, however, realpolitik can again build a bridge to a bond-of-belonging-based finance approach.

A realpolitik lens counsels for a state to make available foreign energy transition finance when doing so achieves national security goals. In the climate mitigation context, the chief goal is to avoid domestic economic losses caused by climate change escalation.[114] In the climate adaptation context, the chief goal is to build and grow alliances.[115] In both contexts, a subsidiary goal is to support the national economic of the lending country. This means that finance would in the first place seek to support exports of the lending state.

The natural realpolitik model for such development finance is export finance. Export finance can take the form of direct export loans. These loans are typically for part of the financing cost of the overall export contract.[116] They are thus part of a broader package of commercial loans. These loans typically include political risk insurance and/or loan guarantees.[117] Export finance is available to sell and install domestically manufactured products to foreign jurisdictions. Realpolitik ideally would tie both climate mitigation finance and climate adaptation finance to such export facilities to maximize geostrategic advantages.

The bond of belonging, on the other hand, looks to energy transition finance as a means progressively to realize human development by achieving the common energy goods of energy peace, energy abundance, and energy stewardship. The bond of belonging seeks to empower agency. It would therefore look to embed as much of the climate mitigation and climate adaptation project in a *local* process providing *local* value. In principle, it would therefore be at the opposite end of the spectrum of national export finance and would benefit from a regional development bank model to provide financing independently of realpolitik constraints.

In reality, international financial institutions and export lending are not as monolithic as these ideals would suggest. International development lenders, for one, are themselves part of a broader geostrategic outlook, with some tethered to existing geostrategic alliances. Some international development banks have close ties to the US[118] Others have close ties to the People's Republic of China.[119] Others

[114] *See* section 7.3(a).
[115] *See* section 7.3(b).
[116] *See* Fact Sheet, 'Supporting Renewable Energy and Environmental Export', U.S. Export- Import Bank (2024), https://www.exim.gov/about/special-initiatives/ctep/fact-sheets/supporting-renewable-energy-environmental-exports#:~:text=Since%201992%2C%20EXIM%20has%20had,for%2018%2Dyear%20repayment%20terms, last accessed 11 February 2024.
[117] 'Medium and Long-Term Loan Guarantee', (2024) Export-Import Bank of the United States, https://www.exim.gov/solutions/loan-guarantee, last accessed 11 December 2024; Nolan et al, 'Political Risk Insurance and Guarantees from Public Providers', *in* Transnational Law of Public Contracts (Mathias Audit & Stephan Schill eds, Bruylant 2016) 737–71.
[118] *See* Daunton (n 93).
[119] *See* Doshi (n 106).

try to navigate in between and wish to serve regional geostrategic interests.[120] Global institutions therefore exist on a spectrum. Similarly, national lending support is frequently less beholden to national interests than one might assume. That is, the eligibility criteria for export lending reflect the realities of a globalized world economy.[121]

Most importantly, development finance and export finance facilities can be stacked together to increase the capital available for a particular project.[122] This means that different actors—frequently with different geostrategic constituencies—support the deployment of energy infrastructure through development lending. These different actors may each have entered into the transactions for their own geostrategic reasons. Still, they each have an interest in the success of the underlying project and in expanding energy deployment around the world. Structurally, facially competing geostrategic actors thus come together to work for shared goals of the success of energy projects that support human development goals. The more interwoven these transactions become, the closer lending will come to a bond-of-belonging ideal.

Development finance institutions are important institutionally to advance energy transition finance. They house expertise about how to select, finance, and support energy projects. They are a critical network of stakeholders capable of underpinning solutions for global 'missing money' problems like the climate energy transition. They can instrumentalize the finance solutions discussed in the previous section. They are therefore a critical institutional player in the organization of energy transitions.

Their structure further provides an additional important bridging function. Development finance is right at the interface between realpolitik and human development. Development finance institutions translate the demands of human development into realpolitik-intelligible policy options to spend money abroad that could also have been invested domestically. Given the gravitational pull towards the domestic, the close connection between development finance institutions and leading centres of global power are precisely helpful to continue the support for globally needed initiatives that are in the global common interest to pursue. The perceived flaws of these institutions—their ties to realpolitik interests of capital

[120] *See* 'Distribution of Voting Power', (31 March 2024) African Development Bank, https://www.afdb.org/en/documents/afdb-statement-voting-powers-31-march-2024, last accessed 11 December 2024.

[121] *See* Runde 'The U.S. Exim Bank in an Age of Great Power Competition', (18 June 2024) Center for Strategic & International Studies, https://www.csis.org/analysis/us-exim-bank-age-great-power-competition, last accessed 11 December 2024.

[122] Li, 'Scaling Up Climate Finance for Emerging Markets and Developing Economies', (27 February 2023) International Monetary Fund, https://www.imf.org/en/News/Articles/2023/02/28/sp022823-scaling-up-climate-finance-for-emerging-markets-and-developing-economies, last accessed 11 December 2024.

exporting states—therefore very much become an asset to secure the greatest possible support for financing critical energy transition energy projects.

7.6 Conclusion

Financing energy transitions is central to meeting not just the moment of the climate transition but to global society's continued ability to progressively realize human development goals. This financing problem is particularly acute in two types of energy transitions—'missing money' transitions and coordination transitions. In both types of transition, there is no energy innovation that can meet the social demand for public energy goods by means of traditional markets in the respective national energy system (or in the global energy system, writ large). Without regulatory intervention, traditional equity or debt financing to develop and deploy the needed energy resources to meet social demand for public energy goods similarly will be scarce in such circumstances. There is no reasonably certain return on investment for such transitions. Without such a return, financing them is all but impossible by traditional means.

I have argued in this chapter that national regulators can and do work to provide the needed stability to finance such transitions by creating regulatory markets. These regulatory markets provide certainty of returns if they solve a critical energy policy problem. The regulator defines this critical energy problem through the regulatory market structure—and the outcome the regulator wishes to purchase from energy stakeholders. I have argued that public–private contracting and its cost-plus remuneration method is the ideal form of energy governance: the regulator (as opposed to innovators) are seeking to install a new energy solution. As discussed in Chapter 2, the installation phase of the energy cycle is particularly well-suited to promote the installation of new energy solutions. When regulators set up a such a credible regulatory market on a cost-plus basis, traditional forms of finance again become available to meet the demand for public energy goods as investors can calculate and count on a reasonable return on their investment.

In the context of the climate transition, this financing approach encountered another wrinkle: regulatory energy markets have geostrategic effects particularly when we are trying to address the provision of global public energy goods like climate change mitigation. In this context, national regulatory markets increase the price of energy. This energy price increase is only tenable from a realpolitik perspective if it is borne proportionately by relevant geopolitical actors. I have outlined that a realpolitik response to this problem can, over time, lead to a bond-of-belonging solution to the geostrategic stalemate by providing verification mechanisms that allow states to coordinate their domestic national regulatory markets and trust the respective reciprocal performance by their peers. The Paris Agreement provides a sufficiently credible verification mechanism to achieve this goal. It is therefore possible in principle to finance a global climate mitigation market by relying on domestic regulatory commitments.

This regulatory market hits a further wrinkle when it comes to climate adaptation. Here, there is no facial reciprocal interest of supporting foreign adaptation measures. Yet, many developing states in particular lack the financial capacity to make credible regulatory commitments sufficient to attract climate adaptation investments. I argued that this particular problem again can be solved through a realpolitik lens of alliance building in light of currently rising geostrategic tensions.

Financing in both contexts—climate mitigation and climate adaptation—could usefully rely on international development finance. Drawing on the history of development finance, I have argued that development finance approaches indeed are available to support the climate transition. My emphasis again was on the realpolitik motivations for development finance. My point was that the structure of international development finance supports an overall transition from a purely realpolitik lens to one that will strengthen the bond of belonging over time.

Financing energy transitions is necessary to realize optimal solutions to the energy trilemma with which I started the book. If we cannot pay for our policy solutions to the trilemma, they will be solutions on paper only. To make them real, we must link regulators, innovators, and industry stakeholders, as well as investors in a process of shared global decision-making to secure that national energy systems, as well as the global energy system, do not just facilitate the production of valuable private goods but also progressively realize the common energy good. As I have shown in this section, each stakeholder has a different role to play in this process. Setting up this process is complicated and complex given the respectively different motives of each participant. Still, it is the complementary nature of their respective roles that makes this process work. Ultimately, financing even transitions with costs as steep as the climate transition is possible because the different expertise each brings to bear. But success is not a foregone conclusion. It requires the expert, prudent, and discerning exercise of judgement by all stakeholders to be realized. Such judgement leads to a particular configuration of global energy chains. I will turn to that configuration in Chapter 8.

8
Value Chains

8.1 Introduction

Value chains are at the heart of the global energy system. It takes a huge number of different inputs to make a lightbulb come on when I flip the switch in my office or turn my engine on when I start my car. In the first place, to turn on my lightbulb, I need electricity. This electricity comes to me through transmission lines after it is fed into the grid by various generators. These generators use different paradigms to make electricity that each requires different raw materials and a different plant to work (gas, coal, uranium, solar cells, etc). To procure all the pieces each plant needs to deliver energy is a complex task. Not only that, I actually need a lightbulb that works with the electricity that is delivered to my house. Otherwise electricity would be useless. The same is true in the transportation context—I need petroleum refined into gasoline that is delivered to a gas station near me—and I need a car that can run on the grade of gasoline delivered to that gas station.

To make energy available for my use requires energy value chains. The idea of a value chain is that it is unlikely that one company alone will be able to provide each input, make each transformation, and deliver each component needed to make a whole national energy system work (never mind the global energy system). Even at the time of truly integrated global oil companies controlling oil from the well to the pump, these oil companies did not also sell people their cars.[1] It generally takes multiple companies to deliver energy in a useful way to end consumers. This is generally a good thing: there is room for specialization at each 'link' of the value chain (whether it is doing seismic studies to site an oil well or geothermal plant or drilling the well or delivering oil or electricity etc.). This specialization, in turn, allows for deeper innovation at each link as different providers of the relevant input in question compete for business from the next downstream buyer in the value chain. This innovation and competition repeats at each link in the chain. It therefore advances the energy system as a whole.

As each of these steps is both risky and lucrative, it is a perfect place for the deployment of private capital. Energy companies—and energy investors—are the main players within these value chains. Each uses their respective advantage

[1] Thijs van de Graaf & Benjamin K Sovacool, *Global Energy Politics* (Polity Press 2020) 59 (discussing the extent of virtual integration in oil until the 1970s).

A Theory of Global Energy Governance. Frédéric Gilles Sourgens, Oxford University Press. © Frédéric Sourgens 2025.
DOI: 10.1093/9780198950325.003.0008

to improve the functioning of a particular link in the value chain. This, in turn, achieves a return on in investment that draws in more expertise and more capital.

The energy finance piece I discussed in Chapter 7 provides the capital for the techno-commercial solutions to each problem or link along the energy value chain—how can I get more efficient at generating an energy service or material needed by downstream energy clients? The more efficient I become at each link, the cheaper energy can become. The cheaper energy can become, the greater my potential return on investment to deliver this innovation to the marketplace. Capital therefore is not deployed in the abstract. Rather, it is deployed within a specific context that allows us to pay for desired outcomes (say, a cheaper solar panel or a horizontally drilled oil well) and make use of those outcomes (say, power an air conditioner in a Houston office building in the summer or profitably extract oil from the Permian basin).[2] Finance alone is not enough to deliver energy. I need the 'stuff' to translate an idea backed by money into physical outputs. Energy value chains provide that 'stuff'.

We have seen in Chapter 3 how these value chains 'grow up'. We have seen that they tend to begin locally. We source and grow the inputs for new energy ideas close to where we hope to market the idea first. As an idea takes off, we can then diversify out inputs. As the technology is adopted in more and more places, we naturally create marketplaces for different kinds of inputs that are needed everywhere. These inputs can look and act like intuitive 'inputs' (fuel). These inputs also include more sophisticated machinery (say turbines) and companies that are able to construct plants and install turbines in them.[3]

As technologies mature, it is therefore natural that there would be some consolidation in energy value chains.[4] Some companies are simply better at engineering, procuring, and constructing power plants than others. They are able to take on more risk at lower prices because they have found ways to 'innovate' (innovation here is not so much coming up with better turbines than it is coming up with a better purchase structure for components and services—the innovation here is legal and commercial rather than technical). This means that stragglers will simply go out of business. Consolidation then intensifies as there are distinct economies of scale. These economies of scale allow me drop my price further if I have a certain volume of work. This makes it even harder for stragglers to compete with me thus

[2] *See* Goodman, 'America's Oil Country Increasingly Runs on Renewables', (18 September 2024) New York Times, https://www.nytimes.com/2024/09/18/us/texas-grid-renewables-battery-storage-solar.html, last accessed 7 January 2025.

[3] *See* section 3.2.

[4] For one recent appraisal of the potential for consolidation in the U.S. solar sector, *see* Baker, 'U.S. Renewables M&A: A Cautious Road to Recovery?', (4 November 2024) White & Case, https://mergers.whitecase.com/highlights/us-renewables-ma-a-cautious-road-to-recovery#, last accessed 22 January 2025. Comments from in-house counsel at solar companies in January 2025 at public events suggest that consolidation will be significantly more pronounced than the law firm analysis suggests.

hastening their demise in the marketplace. None of this is particularly specific to the energy industry. One is likely to see similar trends in almost any segment of the economy.

What does set energy value chains apart somewhat is that they are incredibly capital intensive.[5] The 9 trillion a year figure to finance energy transition is symptomatic of this large cost of building up energy value chains.[6] This high cost has an additional lock-in effect—once we have built systems around some actors who have consolidated a significant share of the market, it is really costly to move away from them. The infrastructure is built around them. And this infrastructure is expensive to replicate.

This means that 'path dependence' is particularly great in the energy sector. Path dependence means that once I have chosen a particular path, and invested in it, my own prior investments require me to continue down this path even if what I am doing is no longer the most efficient way of doing business. The QWERTY keyboard configuration is an example of such path dependence. It is not the most efficient keyboard set up. Yet, because enough people have learned to type on it, it would be more expensive to replace it with a more efficient keyboard simply because we would have to retrain a significant number of people.[7] Making choices about how we constitute energy value chains are therefore likely to stay with us for the foreseeable future. Consolidate 'wrong' and you will pay for it.

In this chapter, I will begin by looking back to Chapter 3 and the key geostrategic risk that such a constellation of value chains can bring. I will contrast it with the risk from too much national policy counter-steering: too much realpolitik protectionism in and of energy value chains leads to a kind of energy 'stagflation'. (What I mean here is that energy costs go up even as there is less by way of energy growth: I pay more for less and suffer the natural consequences of this in the real economy through loss in economic growth and rising unemployment.) The point therefore must be to set up a balanced value chain, in which a broadly diversified set of actors remains highly competitive and innovative while adding resilience to the energy system by preventing overconcentration. While this sounds too good to be true, I will outline that oil and gas in particular has provided an instructive analogue. The question is how to bring about such reconstitution of global energy value chains. I will here again draw on the hard lessons learned from the development of global oil and gas projects to sketch a path forward.

[5] Van de Graaf & Sovacool (n 1), at 74 ('energy is the world's most capital-intensive sector').

[6] 'The Net Zero Transition, What It Would Cost, What It Would Bring' at 5, McKinsey & Co. (January 2022), https://www.mckinsey.com/~/media/mckinsey/business%20functions/sustainability/our%20insights/the%20net%20zero%20transition%20what%20it%20would%20cost%20what%20it%20could%20bring/the-net-zero-transition-what-it-would-cost-and-what-it-could-bring-final.pdf, last accessed 26 March 2024.

[7] Hathaway, 'Path Dependence in the Law: The Course and Pattern of Legal Change in a Common Law System', (2001) 86 Iowa Law Review 601.

8.2 Between Energy Dependence and Energy 'Stagflation'

The key problem value chain consolidation poses from a geopolitical perspective is dependence. Sourcing a critical material, refined product, or component from a single supplier creates vulnerabilities. As we have seen in Chapter 3, this vulnerability can be a double-edged sword.[8] The single supplier only has power so long as it is indeed essential to the functioning of the value chain in question. Using its dominant position for geostrategic ends leads to an inevitable long-term loss of power. States and economies will look for ways to restructure away from dependence on the single source. History suggests that they will be successful in the medium term. At that point, however, the use of a dominant position tends to cause economic and geopolitical problems of their own making.[9]

We have also seen that realpolitik counsels for early action to prevent such concentration of market power from emerging in the first place. In the context of Chapter 3, we focused on geostrategic competition and conflict; the same lesson holds in the purely domestic context as well. A domestic actor can also hold a national energy system hostage if that actor has too much market power. Screening for and preventing such market power is therefore also critical for the proper functioning of national energy systems.[10]

Quite naturally, as we have already noted in Chapter 3, realpolitik is inefficient, at the very least initially.[11] There is a market reason for consolidation. That market reason for consolidation is that certain inputs can simply be sourced more cheaply by consolidating to a single set of suppliers.[12] These suppliers frequently have a comparative advantage with regard to the input in question. The input can be produced more cheaply in a particular place due to geology, energy prices, labour costs, etc. If I insist on diversifying away from the source in question, I naturally pay more than I ought to have done under efficient market conditions. There is thus a cost to realpolitik. This cost can be significant.

Energy realpolitik can create conditions that are even worse than simply increasing prices at the margins for certain inputs. Energy realpolitik can set incentives that lead to energy 'stagflation' and structurally harm its economy. The word 'stagflation' was coined to describe economic conditions in the 1970s. Inflation in the 1970s was stubbornly high. At the same time, there was also high unemployment and meagre economic growth. The economy was stagnating.[13]

[8] *See* section 3.4.

[9] *See* Giuliano Garavini, *The Rise and Fall of OPEC in the Twentieth Century* (Oxford University Press 2019) 301–60.

[10] *See* section 3.4.

[11] *Ibid.*

[12] For a discussion of the historical development of consolidation and competition in the global economy, *see* Chandler, 'The Evolution of Modern Global Competition', *in Competition in Global Industries* (Michael Porter ed, Harvard University Press 1986) 405–48.

[13] One surmised cause of stagflation is government intervention (ie economic realpolitik). *See* Helliwell, 'Comparative Macroeconomics of Stagflation', (1988) 26 Journal of Economic Literature

There is no easy policy way out of 'stagflation' as policy approaches to address one end of the problem (stagnation or inflation) will likely make matters worse for the other problem (for instance, one could lower interest rates or spend more government money in public works projects to address stagnation—yet this would worsen inflation. Increasing interest rates will bring inflation under control but worsen stagnation.)

Energy 'stagnation' is a scenario in which realpolitik keeps inefficient business alive that ought to have been allowed to fail. Supporting such businesses increases costs. Worse still, it incentivizes inefficiency. There is no benefit to innovation. Rather, one simply receives one's secure return without taking any risk. This means that taking on risk is irrational. Yet, this means that productivity is likely to decrease further even as prices continue to increase in reliance on support from realpolitik policymakers.[14] I pay more for less. As energy prices have an impact on the real economy, this energy 'stagflation' will have an impact on the real economy. It is a trigger for stagflation in the real economy, as well. (In fact, rising energy prices were a key driver of stagflation in the 1970s.[15])

Energy stagflation creates a structural problem for energy value chains. Value chains now build around purposefully inefficient incentives. These incentives do not lead to innovation and increased productivity. They lead to complacency and decreased productivity.[16] As expensive infrastructure is built to facilitate such value chains, it becomes increasingly more expensive to break with this constitution of energy value chains.[17] What is more, it will increase the real cost for a significant number of domestic stakeholders who rely on the politically distorted market structure for their livelihoods. This, in turn, makes it difficult to move away from such inefficient incentive structures due to the political fallouts such a course correction would entail. The best way to avoid such energy stagflation would therefore seem to be to recognize its beginnings and never venture down its path in the first place.

Constituting global energy value chains seems to be stuck between two extremes. On the one hand, complete *laissez faire* tends to lead to the consolidation and concentration of energy value chains. This consolidation is deeply concerning from a realpolitik perspective. On the other hand, realpolitik intervention creates

1. The same idea is consistent with the ideas of lobbying as a means to secure a (non-competitive) increase in market share. *See* Daron Acemoglu & James A Robinson, *The Narrow Corridor: States, Societies and the Fate of Liberty* (Penguin 2019); Philippe Aghion et al, *The Power of Creative Destruction: Economic Upheaval and the Wealth of Nations* (Harvard University Press 2021).

[14] Aghion (n 13), at 87–93; Acemoglu & Robinson, (n 13), at 97–125.

[15] The cause for rising energy prices was not support for inefficient energy production methods. Instead, it was a shock in monetary policy when the US abandoned the gold standard to address domestic economic inefficiencies and yet global oil prices were paid in US dollars.

[16] Aghion (n 13), at 87–93.

[17] David Singh Grewal, *Network Power, The Social Dynamics of Globalization* (Yale University Press 2008) 64–65.

the risk of energy stagflation by perennially supporting inefficient firms. This creates path dependencies that are economically and politically sticky. They are difficult to correct once put in place.

This means that setting up energy value chains to realize the benefits from financing energy transitions is problematic. Even solving the finance problems I discussed in the last chapter requires us to build energy value chains that can translate capital into molecules and electrons. Yet this translation sputters because it leads back to the realpolitik problems we had hoped to escape. We therefore need to solve the realpolitik problem once more to set up a global energy system that can in fact deliver on the promise of progressive realization of development.

8.3 The Balanced Value Chain

To find a pathway to get to a realpolitik-tenable constitution of global value chains that does not fall into either the trap of dependence or stagflation necessarily needs to look for inspiration. What would an ideal constitution of value chains look like, never mind whether it is achievable as a matter of realpolitik. How would we constitute global energy value chains under a bond-of-belonging paradigm? Once we have the idea in mind, we can then see if we can employ the same mechanism of translating between realpolitik and the bond of belonging.

As I discussed in Chapters 2 and 5, value chains interact with each other *vertically*.[18] For example, a polysilicon refiner sells polysilicon to a solar cell producer who then sells cells on to the next participant in the value chain and so on.[19] These relationships are partly adversarial—all things being equal, buyers will want a lower price and sellers a higher price. Yet, they are also cooperative. Viewed from 30,000 feet, each link in the value chain needs all other links to function properly to return a predictable profit. Viewed up close, suppliers and their immediate buyers can and frequently do form long-term relationships with each other. These relationships reduce risk through stronger mutual understanding and improve the efficiency of that connection in the value chain.[20] Obviously, these relationships are not permanent—a sufficient price difference may well cause the buyer to look somewhere else. Still, there is a sense of belonging within value chains. This sense of belonging means that each participant must leave enough value to make participation worthwhile for every other participant. It means that when we interact closely for a long period of time and can monitor our respective conduct, we can improve outcomes for everyone in the value chain by limiting risk. It finally means

[18] *See* sections 2.4 and 5.2(c).

[19] *See* Frédéric G Sourgens, Teddy Baldwin, & Catherine Banet, *The Transnational Law of Renewable Energy* (Oxford University Press 2024) 201–06.

[20] For a discussion, *see* Frédéric G Sourgens, *Good Faith in Transnational Law: A Pluralist Account* (Brill Nijhoff 2022).

that when it comes to obligations to maintain and protect the value chain as a whole, the cost of this upkeep is generally borne proportionately by all value chain participants (proportionately in the sense that each value chain participant must continue to have a reason to participate in the value chain).

As I have also discussed already in Chapter 2, value chain participants interact with each other *horizontally*.[21] They are part of a resource commons. This relationship is competitive—each supplier in theory fights for the same buyers, even if only to increase their respective market share. At the same time, this relationship, too, is cooperative. Participants are constrained by the limits of the marketplace to connect with their buyers (eg oil is a commodity with a stronger global marketplace than gas, which tends to be more difficult to transport across oceans than oil, thus affecting how oil and gas can be traded).[22] Improving marketplaces in principle helps all stakeholders compete for market share. Improving the marketplace means that we must cooperate—suppliers must leave each other a fair opportunity to compete for buyers and buyers must leave each other a fair opportunity to compete for supply. This marketplace, too, functions better if it is transparent—that is, when we can observe each other transact in it. It, too, must be maintained, with upkeep falling proportionately on all participants. This same relationship exists between value chains—that is, facially competing value chains require a universal system to function optimally.[23]

In all three types of relationships—the vertical and horizontal relationships in a single value chain and the horizontal relationships between value chains—the bond of belonging counsels for an optimal 'mix' of participants. For value chains to function vertically, there must be a good level of specialization within the value chain. A complex or expensive process can become cheaper if an actor specializes in that particular part of the value chain. They understand the process better, can find ways to innovate, and then assume more risk at a lower price, helping the value chain as a whole. There is thus a benefit of more specialized actors in a value chain to reduce the risk to the overall value chain by finding appropriate shoulders for each appreciable segment. This does not mean that vertical integration is not also desirable—vertical integration reduces inefficiencies between links and provides greater certainty of demand and supply in a single firm. Rather, there must be a balance between both to spur competition and innovation to move the value chain forward and increase the productivity of the whole. The same is true horizontally. The more competition there is between suppliers, the better. This again does not mean that there should not be some market consolidation—this too creates efficiencies. Rather, it means that one must find a good balance. Finally, the

[21] *See* section 2.4.

[22] Simone Tagliapietra, *Global Energy Fundamentals: Economics, Politics and Technology* (2020) 20–49; 41–46, 69–79.

[23] *See* Thomas P Hughes, *Networks of Power: Electrification in Western Society, 1880-1930* (Johns Hopkins University Press 1983) 106–39.

same is true of the energy mix as a whole—the greater the redundancies created by different energy value chains, the more secure our overall national energy system. Again, one can exaggerate here too. Yet, on the whole, a broader mix is preferable all things considered to a narrower mix because it provides more opportunities—more pathways—for continued innovation and growth.

This last point highlights the ethical dimension of the bond of belonging. The more pathways there are for innovation, the more people within the energy system have meaningful energy agency. They can make choices. These choices are not 'passive' ('which kind of energy do I want to consume?'). These choices are active ('how to innovate to make the national energy system realize greater development outcomes?') The broadest feasible value chain is the value chain that has the greatest potentiality for energy agency because it offers the greatest amount of opportunity for the greatest number of people.[24] This, in turn, helps the value chain as a whole—the greater the number of actors at the technological frontier, the fiercer the competition. The fiercer the competition, the more innovative a value chain must become.[25] This competition does not necessarily make us smarter. Rather, it forces us to take a chance on more ideas, first by thinking them through more thoroughly and then by seeing if we can prove the concept and whether the idea actually works well beyond the paper.

This means we can now determine when we have reached the broadest feasible value chain. It is the value chain with the greatest number of actors at the technological frontier. The technological frontier describes a situation in which 'productivity is close to the maximum level of productivity in the sector'.[26] The key implication of this frontier is that '[f]irms close to the technological frontier innovate in order to escape competition, whereas firms that are far from the technological frontier will be discouraged by competition'.[27] If we can boost this number further through financial, commercial, or policy action, a broader value chain configuration remains feasible. If financial, commercial, or policy action simply encourages actors who are far removed from the technological frontier to survive, we are not improving the value chain through broader access but are instead weakening it.

The bond of belonging posits that the broadest feasible constellation of value chains is a necessary but not a sufficient condition for the cooperative realization of human development.[28] This cooperative realization of human development can be achieved only by means of a fair distribution of energy benefits and energy burdens.[29] Broad value chains deconcentrate benefits. They rather share benefits

[24] *See* Wilhelm Röpke, *A Humane Economy, The Social Framework of the Free Market* (Elizabeth Henderson trans, 3rd edn, Intercollegiate Studies Institute 1998) 236.
[25] *See* Aghion (n 13).
[26] *Ibid* at 58.
[27] *Ibid* at 59.
[28] *See* sections 4.4–4.5.
[29] UN Convention on the Right to Development, art 4(2).

from energy value chains among the greatest number of actors feasible, that is, the greatest number of actors to maximize innovation potential for the value chain as a whole through competition within the value chain. Broad value chains also deconcentrate burdens. Horizontal value chain competitors will naturally look for different relative geographic advantages to compete in the energy marketplace. Energy infrastructure therefore does not lock-in path dependencies that concentrate burdens in any one community.

This alone still does not demonstrate that this constellation of value chains is necessary to achieve fair distributive outcomes. Instead, I need to define 'fair' in the context of the bond of belonging.[30] How do I distribute the opportunity to live a good life? In the first place, my distribution has to be consistent with a progressive realization of this opportunity for everyone.[31] That is, it must be the greatest achievable current realization of human capabilities which also has pathways to spare to progressively bring opportunities for a good life to everyone still left out. Living a good life, as I established in Chapter 4, is about agency.[32] Consequently, a fair distribution has to progressively realize agency. In our current context, it must progressively realize *energy agency* so as to secure that the global energy system reflects the active choices of the greatest number of stakeholders rather than an external imposition of what is supposedly best. Such an imposition is inimical to the idea of agency (including, naturally, energy agency).[33] It is also inimical to agency more broadly given the centrality of energy to the realization of human development capabilities. The correct constellation therefore must be the currently greatest possible realization of energy agency that also leaves pathways for those who currently lack an aspect of agency to gain it. The broadest feasible constellation of energy value chains achieves precisely this. It gives the greatest current number of actors energy agency by providing them with the capability to compete as energy innovators. This innovation can itself be a piece to strengthen energy value chains so as to broaden value chains in turn.

This constellation is still not sufficient. Agency still needs to be applied. This application could in principle concentrate benefits and burdens—just in a broader group than before.[34] It thus takes financial, commercial, and civic engagement to realize the fair distributions of energy benefits and burdens. Value chains do not guarantee this on their own. They only provide the space in which such

[30] *See* section 4.4(a) for a fuller discussion.

[31] ICESCR, art 2(1).

[32] *See* section 4.4(a).

[33] Agency is closely related to liberty as non-domination. *See* Philip Pettit, *A Theory of Freedom and Government* (Oxford University Press 1997); Sourgens, 'Bundles of Freedom', (2024) 76 Rutgers University Law Review 393.

[34] Sparta immediately before the Peloponnesian war had a broader distribution of benefits and burdens, defined as agency, than other societies at the same time. This, however, would have been of little comfort to the helots held in active bondage by Sparta to the point of informing foreign and military policy. Donald Kagan, *The Outbreak of the Peloponnesian War* (Cornell University Press 1969) 10–27.

deliberations can occur and do not suffice to guide those deliberations towards the realization of universal human development.

One may ask 'why broad value chains as opposed to simply political agency'? In the first place, as the discussion has shown throughout the book, states have an extraordinary influence on how energy value chains are constituted at each phase of the energy cycle. States and civic engagement therefore are constitutive actors of energy value chains even if they do not have to transact within them. Still, energy governance is not a matter for governments alone. Capital, technology, innovation, materials, etc are all needed to make energy work. Their governance is not just a matter of states. It is also a matter of how persons with capital, technology, innovation, materials, etc interact with each other and with the state. To realize energy agency, we must therefore look to all these actors.

The bond of belonging is 'polycentric'.[35] It looks to the exercise of energy agency by a host of different actors concurrently to achieve a common goal. Here, the goal in the broadest sense is global energy governance. The actors participating in this governance are our energy value chain participants. The governance process is constituted by the relationship between innovation, regulation, and finance. In the ordinary course—that is, when energy governance is innovation-led—this process begins with the installation of a new energy technology at the irruption phase and continues on through the energy cycle.[36] In this process, innovators, energy companies, their suppliers, investors, and regulators align incentives for each participant to achieve the goals of the national and global energy systems. I have outlined the domestic logic of this process in Chapter 2 and then have explained its globalized interactions and feedback loop in Chapter 3.[37] To address these feedback loops, I sketched the ends of the global energy system (human development, cooperation as belonging, and the common energy goods of energy peace, energy abundance, and energy stewardship) in Chapter 6. The interaction between these stakeholders in setting and responding to market and regulatory incentives constitutes the framework in which value chains can operate. The value chains that form within this framework then 'operationalize' this energy system—they run the day-to-day transactions that are sensible within this framework on ordinary and prevalent commercial terms.

The bond of belonging constitutes value chains differently than other lenses might. In the first place, it creates room for significant operational redundance. This redundance exceeds the ordinary redundance one always encounters in an efficiently competitive market—that is, without some redundance, there can be no competition. (If the market needs 100 million barrels of oil per day, and

[35] Elinor Ostrom, *Understanding Institutional Diversity* (Princeton University Press 2005).

[36] Carlota Perez, *Technological Revolutions and Financial Capital, The Dynamics of Bubbles and Golden Ages* (Edward Elgar 2002) 90–99.

[37] *See* sections 2.5 and 3.4.

all producers but one fall out of the marketplace, the market is 'efficient' in the sense that it has rationalized lifting costs to the maximum extent possible—but it is also likely about to find itself on the receiving end of a significant price increase given the lack of competition). Redundance created by the bond of belonging is more than that. It actively looks to diversify risk and opportunity. (Say there are 100 million barrels of oil per day in the market with a potential to produce eight million more at short notice—we want these barrels to come from different places to make sure we are not deprived of our supply because the main transportation link has been interrupted due to armed conflict). By diversifying risk, we create greater resilience and greater reliability in energy value chains. The redundance absorbs potential shocks by reconnecting value chain links as needed to reroute inputs to where they are most needed. (Indeed, this is how Japan and Europe were able to make up for significant gas shortfalls after Japan phased out nuclear power following the Fukushima Daiichi accident and after Europe faced constraints in importing Russian gas following Russia's invasion of Ukraine.[38])

Redundant value chains are more difficult to manipulate. The risk of dependence therefore is precisely limited by diversifying risk and opportunity as broadly as feasible. This means that the bond of belonging in principle can provide a blueprint for an energy future that builds more redundance into the global energy system.

The bond of belonging also increases the room for energy innovation. The bond of belonging looks to increase energy agency to the maximum extent feasible. It therefore looks to place as many actors in as many parts of the energy value chain at or near the technological frontier.[39] It does not create redundance by supporting chronically inefficient firms. It creates redundance by providing incentives to be innovative in more places in light of the specific, specialized conditions found in those places that might give rise to a specific relative advantage in the energy marketplace. Some of those efforts will naturally fail. The bond of belonging does not insist on a rescue mission. Rather, it looks to support the next innovator to increase energy agency rather than to prop up the last failed one. By allowing inefficient firms to fail, the bond of belonging therefore also addresses inflation. It does not inject government money into inefficient production methods that will be reflected in a structurally permanent, and likely escalating, price increase. It instead creates regulatory marketplaces in which ideas can prove fruitful and increase energy productivity.

The bond of belonging creates a process that can navigate the perilous straights of energy dependence and energy stagflation. Problematically, it remains very

[38] Yep & Foo, 'How the Fukushima Crisis led to a Revolution in LNG Trading', (11 March 2021) S&P Global, https://www.spglobal.com/commodity-insights/en/news-research/blog/lng/031121-fukushima-crisis-japan-lng-trading-revolution-jkm, last accessed 7 January 2025; Pye et al, 'The Global Implications of a Russian Gas Pivot to Asia', (2025) 16 Nature Communications 386.

[39] Aghion (n 13), at 58–59.

abstract and, in its abstraction, demands potentially contradictory policymaking in practice. The question therefore is whether the concept of a broad, redundant, and innovative energy value chain is a theoretical fairytale. Can we fashion a realpolitik path to this kind of value chain configuration in the same way that we were able to fashion a realpolitik path to energy transition finance?

8.4 Growing to Balance

Turning a bond-of-belonging conception of energy value chains into reality in a competitive energy world is feasible. It begins with some of the same kind of 'defensive' measures that were already at the heart of trust building in the 'missing money' context. Yet, these kinds of 'defensive' measures are not enough to create the kind of broad value chains the bond of belonging contemplates. Rather, setting up these values chains requires short-term regulatory intervention (just as in the 'missing money' context, as well). The right type of short-term regulatory intervention is already typical in the global upstream oil and gas segment. As I will discuss in this section, it can usefully be applied to energy governance as a whole.

8.4(a) Defensive Tariffs, Quotas, and Bans

The obvious starting point for growing balanced global value chains is through tariffs and import quotas.[40] Both tariffs and import quotas protect the domestic market of the state imposing it for domestic value chain participants. It either makes it more expensive or even impossible for foreign competitors to enter the marketplace. This means that, over time, a larger proportion of domestic demand will be met by domestic supply, be it at a higher price point (ie cheaper imports would have been available to meet the same demand).[41]

Such measures could either be outright protectionist or they could be measures to maintain the competitiveness of a global marketplace. Protectionist tariffs look to substitute imports for domestically produced goods as means to industrialize.[42] Tariffs protect a nascent industry. This nascent industry, in turn, will drive economic growth by keeping more money in the economy, thus leaving it to be reinvested domestically rather than abroad. Such protectionist policies have a mixed

[40] For a discussion of US import quotas during the Eisenhower administration, *see* Daniel Yergin, *The Prize, The Epic Quest for Oil, Money, and Power* (Free Press 2012) 496–97.

[41] For a discussion of the literature, *see* Amiti et al, 'The Impact of the 2018 Tariffs on Prices and Welfare', (2019) 33 Journal of Economic Perspectives 187. The article notes the increase in costs from tariffs themselves for imports. It was arguably too early to establish the benefits of import substitution with regard to the 2018 tariffs.

[42] *See* Martin Daunton, *The Economic Government of the World 1933-2023* (Farrar, Straus & Giroux 2023) 107–10.

track record—in many instances, there is not yet a market worth capturing. In those instances, protectionism looks to both protect the local market and jump start an export economy.[43] Exports would then return the capital needed for domestic economic growth. Needless to say, the second part of this strategy in particular will strike other states as mercantilist—it seeks to take advantage of a largess in market access without reciprocity to compete with and overtake the economy to which one has now gained access.[44] When there is a strong domestic market, on the other hand, such measures can be a helpful tool to address domestic economic dislocation from a shift in production to cheaper foreign markets benefiting from, for example, lower labour costs.

Still, not all tariffs, quotas, or import bans are protectionist in this way. Rather, the same tools can also be deployed to prevent another state from using fiscal and industrial policy to gain an unfair trading advantage and thus achieve a dominant market position in the medium term. For instance, both the European Union and the United States suspect that the People's Republic of China supported its solar industry precisely to gain market power in both materials and in components.[45] The People's Republic of China has in fact achieved such a market position in about twenty years. Both the EU and the US have used tariffs and import bans in order to respond to Chinese industrial policies.[46]

The point of such defensive measures is not only to prop up national champions. Rather, the point is to protect global energy value chains against an overconcentration that was induced not by market forces but rather by policy interventions. Such an overconcentration has precisely the kind of geostrategic implications we discussed in Chapter 3.[47] They permit a state to exercise market power. Counteracting such market power therefore is a necessary mechanism to protect market resilience. In turn, this means that such measures are essential to protect the kind of broad value chains I am outlining in this chapter.

These defensive measures obviously are not enough. The market in its own right is likely to overconsolidate value chains as judged by the blueprint of the bond of belonging. To constitute such broad value chains therefore requires proactive measures as well as defensive ones.

Before turning to these proactive measures, the constellation, as we are developing it here, already highlights a potential problem: the proactive measures we

[43] *See ibid.*

[44] *See ibid* at 59-60.

[45] *See* Evenett, 'China-EU Solar Panel Trade Dispute: Rhetoric versus Reality', (5 June 2013) VoxEU, https://cepr.org/voxeu/columns/china-eu-solar-panel-trade-dispute-rhetoric-versus-reality, last accessed 7 January 2025; Wu & Salzman, 'The Next Generation of Trade and Environment Conflicts: The Rise of Green Industrial Policy', (2014) 108 Northwestern Law Review 401, 404.

[46] Wu & Salzman (n 45), at 404; for a discussion of solar energy-related trade disputes between the US and China, *see* Fang, 'A Never-Ending U.S. China Solar Trade War? The Uyghur Forced Labor Prevention Act and International Trade Law', (2024) 33 Minnesota Journal of International Law 189.

[47] *See* section 3.4.

take can be put in the light of anticompetitive trade practices. This, in turn, will trigger defensive measures. This will undermine the effectiveness of proactive measures. We therefore will need to provide for a link between both sets of measures at the end of this section to avoid the self-contradiction of which the last section warned.

8.4(b) Proactive measures and Missing Money

Broadening value chains through proactive measures replicates the 'missing money' problem. The 'missing money' problem arose because energy innovation lagged behind the need to realize public energy goods.[48] Consequently, realizing these public energy goods becomes a critical *policy* problem at a time when they have not yet been formulated as a critical *engineering* problem. Broadening value chains realizes a public energy good because it increases the resilience of the global energy system as a whole. Broadening value chains therefore resembles capacity markets.[49] Both aim to achieve a related outcome. In the context of capacity markets, that outcome is increasing both reliability and resilience of national energy systems. (Capacity markets increase available generation to meet expected peak loads and in doing so increase capacity to meet demand during unexpected, or less frequent, losses of capacity due to, for instance, unscheduled maintenance events.)[50] In the context of the broadening of energy value chains, this outcome is increasing the reliability of national energy systems and the resilience of the global energy system. (Broader value chains increase the available inputs to meet expected domestic energy demand and unexpected global value chain shortfalls.)[51]

In both instances, the demand for an increased reliability and resilience of energy systems cannot be met without regulatory intervention. In the capacity context, there is no incentive to install additional capacity for reasonably rare peak demand events.[52] In the value chain context, there is no market incentive to deconcentrate value chains, as such deconcentration would remove economies of scale.[53] The desired outcome therefore would not be a natural result of the application of market

48 *See* section 7.2.

49 *See* Todd S Aagaard & Andrew N Kleit, *Electricity Capacity Markets* (Cambridge University Press 2022).

50 *Ibid.*

51 *See* Sovacool & Mukherjee, 'Conceptualizing and Measuring Energy Security: A Synthesized Approach', (2011) 36 Energy 5343 (this concern fits under the availability rubric).

52 Aagaard & Kleit (n 49).

53 Bahar et al, 'Special Report on Solar PV Global Supply Chains' at 107, (August 2022) International Energy Agency, https://iea.blob.core.windows.net/assets/d2ee601d-6b1a-4cd2-a0e8-db02dc64332c/SpecialReportonSolarPVGlobalSupplyChains.pdf, last accessed 7 January 2025 ('In the absence of domestic demand, Chinese manufacturers had to improve their competitiveness. They therefore focused on economies of scale and integration of supply chain segments to reduce costs, increase exports and expand their global market share.')

forces from our current starting points. The only way to address the public need therefore is to intervene to create conditions in which it is economical for industry stakeholders, innovators, and investors to support the realization of the public energy good in question.

Importantly, broadening value chains is like the 'missing money' problem in another way, too. The 'missing money' problem is resolved when we create regulatory marketplaces that can meet the demand for public energy goods.[54] These regulatory marketplaces in principle are temporary. They serve as a bridge for innovation to catch up to the reverse salient in the relevant energy system and find a way to formulate it not just as a policy problem, but also as an engineering problem that could be solved more efficiently by means of new technology.[55] This means that broader value chains should become self-sustaining in the medium term due to the value increased reliability and resilience create.

Like the missing 'money problem' in the finance context, we need a catalyst to broaden value chains.[56] The 'hill' to create these value chains is too steep for the market to climb on its own. The regulatory catalyst overcomes this hill by starting a financial reaction to activate the desired result. Once this hill has been overcome though, the new state is reasonably stable in its own right. Broad and resilient value chains do not require constant regulatory support. They only need support to get started.

The first such catalyst is to arrange for market support to diversify the respective national energy mix. The more concentrated the energy mix, the more susceptible the national energy system is to disruption due to a shortness of supply in a critical value chain link.[57] By diversifying the energy mix, we take pressure off these links and allow for energy needs to be met by other means of energy generation.[58] Any energy mix that disproportionately favours a single form of energy therefore should look to diversify to achieve this greater resilience. (Notably, the threat to a value chain link can be geopolitical, commercial, or 'natural'. A state may impose an embargo.[59] A critical player might declare bankruptcy.[60] A storm or navigation error can close off a critical transportation node.[61] A diversified energy mix assists in anticipating each of these pressures by distributing the energy demand load across different value chains with different vulnerabilities.)

[54] Joskow, 'Capacity Payments in Imperfect Electricity Markets', (2008) 16 Utility Policy 159.
[55] *See* Hughes (n 23).
[56] *See* section 7.3.
[57] *See* Sovacool & Mukherjee (n 51).
[58] Yep & Foo (n 38).
[59] Garavini (n 9).
[60] *See* Sanzillo & Kunkel, 'New Fortress Energy, Leader of LNG Growth Bubble, Facing Bankruptcy', (22 November 2024) Institute for Energy Economics and Financial Analysis, https://ieefa.org/resources/new-fortress-energy-leader-lng-growth-bubble-facing-bankruptcy, last accessed 7 January 2025.
[61] Braw, 'What the Ever Given Taught the World', (10 November 2021) Foreign Policy, https://foreignpolicy.com/2021/11/10/what-the-ever-given-taught-the-world/, last accessed 7 January 2025.

Policymakers can create a marketplace for energy diversification in a myriad of ways. In the electricity context, they can provide dispatch priority to support diversification by advancing a certain source of electricity in the dispatch order.[62] This guarantees that the electricity in question will earn a return. Fiscal or tariff support similarly can diversify the energy mix.[63] Or, more crudely, a regulator can simply mandate a minimum portfolio standard.[64]

A diversified energy mix alone is still not sufficient. Each value chain for different energy sources can itself be concentrated.[65] We therefore need to create conditions in which value chains themselves broaden. One effective means to achieve such an outcome is for policymakers to include local content requirements in their respective national energy systems.[66]

Many oil and gas projects already contain such local content requirements. At the bidding stage for new oil and gas projects, international energy companies must specify how much value of the project will be assigned to approved local partners. This guarantees that these local partners will be part of the project even if economies of scale may otherwise suggest that an international services company would have received the project contract instead.[67] By insisting on local content, states in effect help to keep a strategic part of the upstream oil and gas value chain under domestic ownership and provide domestic employment.[68] Further, such a local content requirement frequently goes hand in hand with technology transfer regimes.[69] International partners must train local stakeholders in the use of technology and make the technology available for use. This, in turn, allows a broader business community to develop locally at the technological frontier, which then allows greater independence by the state in question by creating a broader energy and industrial domestic infrastructure.

This approach can be replicated outside of the oil and gas context. Policymakers can adopt a similar local content requirement to support critical parts of domestic

[62] Alessandro Rubino, Alessandro Sapia, & Massimo La Scala, *Handbook of Energy Economics and Policy* (Academic Press 2021) 365.

[63] *Ibid.*

[64] Klass, 'Energy and Eminent Domain', (2019) 104 Minnesota Law Review 659, 714.

[65] The value chain for solar energy is heavily concentrated in China. Bahar et al (n 53). Prior to Russia's invasion of Ukraine, Europe drew significant supply of natural gas from Russia. *See* 'Reliance on Russian Fossil Fuels in OECD and EU Countries', (July 2023) International Energy Agency, https://www.iea.org/data-and-statistics/data-product/reliance-on-russian-fossil-fuels-in-oecd-and-eu-countries, last accessed 7 January 2025.

[66] US Inflation Reduction Act of 2022, House Resolution 5376, 117th Congress §13101(g) (including local content requirements for incentives under the Act).

[67] *See* Pereira et al, 'Brazil's Local Content Requirement: Evolution, Lessons Learned & International Trade Limitations', (2024) 9 Oil and Gas, Natural Resources and Energy Journal 385.

[68] *See* Pereira et al, 'Local Content Policies in the Petroleum Industry: Lessons Learned', (2919) 4 Oil and Gas, Natural Resources and Energy Journal 631, 636–39.

[69] Ndulo, 'The African Continental Free Trade Area: Local Content Requirements As A Means to Addressing Africa's Productive Capacity Constraints', (2022) 43 Michigan Journal of International Law 61, 80.

energy value chains.[70] This approach is in fact either an express or an implicit component of many renewable energy policies.[71] The benefit of such an approach for domestic industry is obvious: domestic energy companies play on an uneven playing field due to the requirement that some domestic energy companies participate in the project in question.

This approach can also have global benefits. It increases the number of stakeholders capable of participating in energy value chains by exporting in case of foreign demand.[72] This increases the number of potential interlinkages between different buyers and sellers in that value chain. This, in turn, improves the resilience of the value chain in question.[73]

The global benefit becomes more pronounced when energy companies have the option to allocate the local content component of their respective projects. When the local content component completely blocks out foreign competition, local content providers do not have any incentive to innovate.[74] Yet, to the extent that local content can come from any part of the value chain, domestic providers are both in competition with each other and with foreign competitors. The logical conclusion is that only the most efficient domestic content provider for a particular project will benefit from local content requirements. Competition should push innovation. This innovation, in turn, should lead to breakthroughs that become self-sustaining even in the absence of a local content requirement.[75]

These policies have come under pressure from an international trade law perspective, with repeat findings by the dispute settlement body of the World Trade Organization (WTO) that such local content requirements violate the General Agreement on Tariff and Trade.[76] These conclusions, as well as many of the actions

[70] Indeed, the US Inflation Reduction Act has done just that. Pelton, 'Protection Protectionism in the WTO: A Reinterpretation of the General Exceptions to Protect the IRA's Local Content Requirements', (2024) 49 Columbia Environmental Law Journal 100, 111–18.

[71] Sourgens, Baldwin, & Banet (n 19), at 112.

[72] *See* Peirera et al (n 67).

[73] In many instances, exports from local content beneficiaries are limited. *See ibid.* This suggests that resilience can in fact increase cost due to a lack of competitiveness. Some of that lack of global competitiveness may well be an issue of economies of scale—providers are not able to access foreign markets even if they are able to support the domestic market. Yet, even here, there is a reasonable failure rate on the domestic side if support is withdrawn. *Ibid.* For a discussion of how to time such a withdrawal, *see infra*.

[74] *See* Peirera et al (n 67); Pereira et al (n 68).

[75] The breadth of this success remains open to question but can be improved through better local content requirement design. *See* Peirera et al (n 67); Pereira et al (n 68).

[76] *See eg* Appellate Body Report, Canada—Measures Relating to the Feed-in Tariff Program, WTO Doc WT/DS426/AB/R (6 May 2013); Appellate Body Report, Canada—Certain Measures Affecting the Renewable Energy Generation Sector, WTO Doc WT/DS412/AB/R (6 May 2013); Appellate Body Report, United States—Countervailing Duty Measures on Certain Products from China, WTO Cod WT/DS437/AB/R (18 December 2014); Appellate Body Report, India—Certain Measures Relating to Solar Cells and Solar Modules, WTO Doc WT/DS456/AB/R (16 September 2016); Panel Report, United States—Certain Measures Relating to the Renewable Energy Sector, WTO Doc WT/DS510/R (27 June 2019). For a summary of all WTO disputes, *see* Asmelash, 'The First Ten Years of WTO Jurisprudence on Renewable Energy Support: Has the Dust Settled Yet?', (2022) 21 World Trade Review 455. For a fuller analysis of trade law in the energy context, *see* Anna-Alexandra Marhold, *Energy*

that brought them about, are problematic.[77] In the first instance, there is no structural difference between renewable energy measures and local content requirements in the oil and gas context that have gone unchallenged before the WTO, suggesting that the challenge of renewable energy measures is opportunistic at best.[78] Further, this jurisprudence loses from view that every major modern advancement in (renewable) energy technology initially benefited from direct or indirect government support. For example, the renewable industry in the US was the direct beneficiary of US laws such as the Public Utility Regulatory Policies Act (PURPA), mandating that utilities purchase energy from small electricity producers.[79] The renewable energy industry in Germany was the direct beneficiary of feed-in tariffs for renewable energy.[80] In both cases, policies aimed at creating the domestic advantage in question by providing first mover money.[81] Blocking other states from emulating such a policy is functionally questionable. The industry segment in question could not have come into existence without government support. Global fairness therefore would suggest that each state have an equal opportunity to participate in such efforts.

This is not to say that such policies should be allowed to continue without any limitation. Rather, such policies should instead by embedded in a broader understanding of how energy innovation functions. Policy support is needed at the national installation phase of a new technology.[82] At this particular point in time, there is a limited commercial track record to establish how successful a new technology will be in the marketplace in question.[83] This increases the risk of adoption of the new technology. Risk, in turn, increases cost. States can mitigate this risk through credible support commitments for the new technology. Insisting that such credible commitments also include local content counter-intuitively helps international partners: it provides them with a local partner that is similarly invested in the success of a policy initiative. This local partner suggests that there is indeed a political and economic appetite for the new technology in the jurisdiction in question. While it increases the price of the project, such local content requirements

in International Trade Law: Concepts, Regulation and Changing Markets (Cambridge University Press 2021).

[77] Meyer, 'Free Trade, Fair Trade, and Selective Enforcement', (2018) 118 Columbia Law Review 491, 506–17.
[78] *Ibid.*
[79] Hornstein & Stoermer, 'The Energy Policy Act of 2005: PURPA Reform, the Amendments, and their Implications', (2006) 27 Energy Law Journal 25, 25–26.
[80] *See* Dotterud Leiren & Reimer, 'Germany: From Feed in Tariffs to Greater Competition', in Elin Lerum Boasson et al, *Comparative Renewable Policy: Political, Organizational and European Fields* (Routledge 2021) 81, 82.
[81] *See Renewable Power Pathways: Review of the U.S. Department of Energy's Renewable Energy Programs* (National Academy Press 2000) 99–101; Stephen G Gross, *Energy and Power, Germany in the Age of Oil, Atoms, and Climate Change* (Oxford University Press 2023) 218.
[82] *See* section 3.4.
[83] *See* section 7.3.

can diversify political risk by involving local stakeholders who are better able to gauge whether the policy initiative is likely to last than international stakeholders.[84] Having such local stakeholders therefore is helpful at this stage to prove that the market is in fact one that is receptive to the new technological approach.

New technology will at some point become fully self-supporting.[85] At this point, there is no need for further governmental support as there is a track record of profitability. This logic applies with similar force to the value chains supporting such projects. Local partners should learn as projects progress. Its respective value chain segment should itself become self-sustaining at this maturity point. It should be able to stand up to global competition at least for domestic deployment at this point.[86] It has a benefit of proximity and of understanding local market conditions. These benefits should suggest that once the energy market has become self-sustaining, the market segments supporting it should do so as well.

Returning to our discussion of renewable energy value chains from Chapter 3, we can now appreciate how one might reduce feed in tariffs without eroding domestic value chains. In Chapter 3, I outlined how the reduction of governmental feed-in tariff support allowed an opening for Chinese exporters to capture renewable energy markets like the German market.[87] The continued need for tariff support suggests that the technology could not yet fully stand on its own. The appropriate funding support therefore would be one that needed to reflect not just the cost of generation. It needed to bear in mind the need to bring the value chains supporting it across the threshold of providing an independently cost competitive product. A local content requirement would have provided an appropriate price signal in this context. A competitive approach to the support for renewable energy would likely look to a reverse auction approach—market actors would bid against each other to put a specific amount of renewable generation online. Rather than bidding up, they would bid 'down', that is, they would offer to accept a reduction in governmental support for the project. A local content requirement naturally changes this calculus.[88] A local content requirement forces up support prices as it still needs to support a local value chain.[89] A flexible approach that allows project

[84] In fact, the use of local joint venture partners is a classical political risk mitigation tool. *See* Frederick Stapenhurst, *Political Risk Around the North Atlantic* (St Martin's Press 1992) 115.

[85] An industry can become 'bankable' in the sense that it can attract lending for projects on its own merit. When an industry is bankable, actors within that industry still have to prove their own individual bankability. On this problem in the renewable energy value chain, *see* Connell, 'Becoming Bankable: How Renewable Energy Startups Can Deploy Equipment at Scale', (25 October 2018) Forbes, https://www.forbes.com/sites/energyinnovation/2018/10/25/becoming-bankable-how-renewable-energy-startups-can-deploy-equipment-at-scale/, last accessed 7 January 2025. For a fuller introduction, *see* Sourgens, Baldwin, & Banet (n 19), at 234–55.

[86] For a discussion of the practical limitations of such local content approaches, and best practices, *see* Peirera et al (n 67); Pereira et al (n 68).

[87] *See* section 3.4.

[88] Sourgens, Baldwin, & Banet (n 19), at 69.

[89] *See ibid.*

companies to satisfy the local content requirement in different ways creates competition even within the value chain to bring down costs. This means that reverse auctions with local content requirements should bring the support needed to zero over time. At this point, there would no longer be any need for the support for the segment in question—it should have innovated to the point of having achieved a relative advantage in the marketplace. At this stage, local content requirements therefore could be removed for the segment in question as it is no longer an efficient means to support energy innovation in energy value chains.

This approach again showcases the importance of combining local content requirements with a policy of grant-based innovation support. The point is to deliver alternative, efficient means to meet local value chain demands. Local content requirements provide an important means to shelter nascent domestic industries from the installation phase to maturity.[90] Yet, this alone is likely insufficient to encourage the commercialization of novel approaches to value chain needs. Grant-based funding to support practical research is critical to achieve this end, as discussed already in Chapter 7 in the financing context.[91] One famous grant-based research programme that has provided an innovation edge in the US in the defence context is the Defense Advanced Research Projects Agency (DARPA).[92] DARPA makes available feasibility, proof-of-concept, and venture capital funding for defence technologies.[93] The US has developed a similar financing approach in the energy context administered by the Advanced Research Projects Agency-Energy (ARPA-E).[94] Coordination between local content requirements and ARPA-E style research funding is likely to yield a better innovation-led approach to the development of materials and engineering solutions by domestic firms than a sole reliance on domestic content requirements by providing support for precommercial concepts as new value chains mature.[95]

This approach to value chain management is likely to support a move towards a regional consolidation of energy value chains.[96] Following the experiences of

[90] Silvia Tordo et al, *Local Content Policies in the Oil and Gas Sector, A World Bank Study* (International Bank for Reconstruction and Development 2013) 131.

[91] *See* section 7.3(b).

[92] Fukuyama, 'Challenges of Uncertainty: An Introduction', *in Blindside, How to Anticipate Forcing Events and Wild Cards in Global Politics* (Francis Fukuyama ed, Brookings Institution Press 2007) 1, 4.

[93] 'Proposal Submission Instructions', (27 February 2024) Defense Advanced Research Projects Agency, https://media.defense.gov/2024/Feb/27/2003400545/-1/-1/1/DARPA_STTR_24D_R2.PDF, last accessed 6 January 2025.

[94] 'Vision OPEN 2024', (22 May 2024) Advanced Research Projects Agency—Energy, https://arpa-e-foa.energy.gov/#FoaId6cc31453-6805-417c-967c-4df560ba2c88, last accessed 6 January 2025.

[95] *See* Bonvillian, 'The Once and Future DARPA', *in Blindside, How to Anticipate Forcing Events and Wild Cards in Global Politics* (Francis Fukuyama ed, Brookings Institution Press 2007) 57, 65–70.

[96] Press, 'Geopolitics of the Energy Transition: Energy Security' at 49, (2024) International Renewable Energy Agency, https://www.irena.org/-/media/Files/IRENA/Agency/Publication/2024/Apr/IRENA_Geopolitics_transition_energy_security_2024.pdf, last accessed 7 January 2025 ('Policy makers must fully understand the links between energy security and the supply chains for materials and related technologies. These are dynamic and can be managed with proactive policy action. Support for R&D to improve efficiency, find alternatives, shape product design and encourage innovation (Box

Covid-19 and energy insecurity in Europe, in particular following Russia's invasion of Ukraine, energy security advocates have counselled to shorten energy value chains.[97] A combination of local content requirements and innovation grant support can support such a shortening of value chains. It can provide regional solutions to regionally attractive components of national energy mixes.[98] Different neighbouring jurisdictions are likely to look for a comparative advantage in different parts of the affected value chains. This would lead to a stronger regional integration of national energy systems while providing a broader set of global alternatives in case of a failure in regionally integrated value chains.[99] Realpolitik and economic self-interest, in other words, would support a different and more just distribution of benefits and burdens within energy chains.

Just as importantly, this approach would also support a deconcentration of suppliers in global value chains.[100] Local content and innovation-led growth are likely to support smaller domestic suppliers with a relevant technological edge over their competitors to solve a particular, setting-relevant problem. Over time, it is of course likely that such innovators will be acquired by larger energy companies closer to the time of maturity of a particular technology.[101] Yet, the high capital costs of energy infrastructure and local know-how on the whole make it more likely that even in this context, much of the value chain will remain in place.[102] Further, innovation funding at this point will already look for new and novel solutions to more complex, related energy challenges.[103] Innovation-led support for local content providers therefore provides a helpful tool to manage a broadening

2.3) can reduce long term vulnerabilities and risks. Diversifying and shortening of supply chains is a priority, as well as making them more transparent, sustainable and responsible.')

[97] *See* Bahar, 'Renewables 2023: Analysis and Forecast to 2028' at 127, (January 2024) International Energy Agency, https://iea.blob.core.windows.net/assets/96d66a8b-d502-476b-ba94-54ffda84cf72/Renewables_2023.pdf, last accessed 7 January 2025 (noting the importance of industrial policy).

[98] Brinker, 'Redrawing the Solar Power Global Map with Regional Supply Chains', (10 March 2023) World Economic Forum, https://www.weforum.org/stories/2023/03/solar-power-regional-supply-chains/, last accessed 7 January 2025; Ribeiro & Holman, 'Regionalization of Battery Supply Chains Advances, But Challenges Persist', (30 September 2021) S&P Global, https://www.spglobal.com/commodity-insights/en/news-research/latest-news/energy-transition/093021-insight-regionalization-of-battery-supply-chains-advances-but-challenges-persist, last accessed 7 January 2025.

[99] Bricker (n 98); Ribeiro & Holman (n 98).

[100] For a discussion of the factors that typically deconcentrate value chains without local content requirements, *see* De Blasio & Zheng, 'Transition to a Low-Carbon Economy: An Evaluation Framework of Integration and Segmentation Scenarios' at 16–19, (August 2023) Harvard Kennedy School Belfer Center, https://www.belfercenter.org/sites/default/files/pantheon_files/files/publication/De%20Blasio%20Zheng_Energy%20Value%20Chains_FINAL.pdf, last accessed 7 January 2025. The integration of value chains is likely when a particular value chain component is closely related to the existing activity of a large energy stakeholder and is of significant strategic value. The only exception to this drive to integration is significant risk. Local content requirements can alleviate risk and shelter companies from integration at critical points in time when they might otherwise be acquired at a reasonably early point in time.

[101] *See ibid.*

[102] *See* Van de Graaf & Sovacool (n 5), at 74 (discussing the high cost of energy investments).

[103] Bonvillian (n 95), at 65–70.

of energy value chains without the need for an overly idealistic outlook on global energy governance. Prudent realpolitik gets us to a point within a reasonably adjacent neighbourhood.

This focus on small energy companies as innovation leaders may sound naively utopian. Yet, one of the largest energy revolutions of the early twenty-first century came precisely from such smaller energy companies. The hydraulic fracturing (known colloquially as fracking) revolution was the work of daring and innovative independent oil and gas companies. It did not come from oil majors or supermajors.[104] These smaller companies found a way profitably to exploit ever more marginal mineral interests through technological innovation.[105] They did so by building on known principles and technology by taking a risk. Their innovation and diligence utterly transformed the global energy landscape.[106] In their case, the needed support did not come from local content requirements. Instead, sky high energy prices, together with a private ownership regime of mineral reserves, permitted independent oil and gas companies to finance such risk taking.[107] Even here, however, the basic research into hydraulic fracturing as a means to address energy insecurity was a policy response to the energy insecurity in the US in the late 1970s.[108] This does not mean that the US government is responsible for the fracking revolution. The US government did not 'invent' hydraulic fracturing any more than Vice President Gore created the internet.[109] Still, government support in both instances had an important role to play in making available the tools with which independent entrepreneurs could take risks and experiment.

With these rudimentary tools in hand, independent oil and gas companies in Texas, Pennsylvania, North Dakota, and other shale plays resembled small farmers in Attica at the height of Athenian democracy. A strong property regime protecting investment in long-term work together with the hard and unrelenting work of comparatively small-scale cultivators in both cases changed productivity in a critical sector for their respective economies. Both provided the means by which their

[104] Hinton, 'The Seventeen-Year Overnight Wonder: George Mitchell and Unlocking the Barnett Shale', (2012) 99 Journal of American History 229.

[105] Golden & Wiseman, 'The Fracking Revolution: Shale Gas as a Case Study in Innovation Policy', (2015) 64 Emory Law Journal 955, 983–85.

[106] 'United States 2019 Review', (13 September 2019) International Energy Agency, https://iea.blob.core.windows.net/assets/7c65c270-ba15-466a-b50d-1c5cd19e359c/United_States_2019_Review.pdf, last accessed 7 January 2025.

[107] Middleton et al, 'The Shale Gas Revolution: Barriers, Sustainability, and Emerging Opportunities', (2017) 199 Applied Energy 88, 90.

[108] Steffy, 'How Much Did the Feds Really Help with Fracking', (31 October 2013) Forbes, https://www.forbes.com/sites/lorensteffy/2013/10/31/how-much-did-the-feds-really-help-with-fracking/, last accessed 6 January 2025.

[109] Kronenfeld & Kronenfeld, 'Al Gore, The Internet, and the National Library of Medicine', (2 July 2020) Circulating Now, https://circulatingnow.nlm.nih.gov/2020/07/02/al-gore-the-internet-and-the-national-library-of-medicine/, last accessed 7 January 2025.

countrymen prospered.[110] Both had a tenuous relationship with urbane culture and would likely be thought uncouth by the socialites in Athens or Manhattan. Yet, both provided an important counterweight to the increasing gravitational pull of wealth concentration in their respective societies. Both were financially successful—even if both could be undone with a single bad investment decision. World changing innovation can in fact come from such apparently small players. Good policy gives such innovators the tools to hand to take risks and alter the make-up of energy value chains in the process.

8.4(c) Avoiding a Feedback Loop

In principle, this approach to energy value chains secures the common energy good. It broadens energy value chains as far as is feasible and distributes benefits and burdens globally in a manner that is consistent with the goal of increasing global energy access. Yet, 'in principle' hides a problem. What is to prevent a state from acting anticompetitively in supporting its local energy industry? If subsidies for local content in critical energy chains is permissible, how are we to make sure that support is withdrawn in a timely manner? How do we prevent dumping?

A policy to broaden energy value chains can create a feedback loop. A feedback loop is a system in which an output itself becomes an input, distorting the next output. One example of such feedback is the loud sound when a microphone is placed too close to a speaker transmitting the sound captured by the microphone itself. Local content requirements can simply perpetuate non-competitive champions and allow these champions to undercut foreign competitors on price simply on the strength of local subsidies. This would lead us right back into the stagflation problem.[111] The typical answer is to beware of the beginnings. Yet, when we must accept these beginnings, how do we set an end?

The answer turns again on trust. In an environment of mutual trust, it is on the whole more likely that support mechanisms will function as intended. States will reduce the support for domestic producers at the right time to reduce the cost of energy for their respective populations, thus increasing overall productivity. This, in turn, will create globally accessible and mutually supporting energy markets. Yet, when we do not trust that each state will reduce support in a rational manner to lower domestic energy prices, this regime of local content and innovation support looks problematic.

[110] On the importance of such agriculture to the emergence of Athenian democracy and culture, *see* Victor Davis Hanson, *The Other Greeks, The Family Farm and the Agrarian Roots of Western Civilization* (The Free Press 1995).

[111] *See* section 8.2.

The classic realpolitik strategy again is able to reduce this risk significantly. Realpolitik does not trust blindly. It verifies. It responds to defection with a gradual policy intended to counter the effects of defection.[112] Such an approach in principle can increase barriers to entry for energy value chain inputs that benefited from undue foreign support. By reducing such market access, realpolitik can again rebalance the global energy system by imposing real costs for defection. The gradual and reciprocal nature of such a strategy is an adequate antidote to cheating. The absence of such cheating, on the other hand, increases trust on the margins.

Returning to our example of international trade cases complaining of undue support for domestic renewable energy champions by their respective governments, we can see how such a regime would in fact be mutually beneficial. Much of the litigation in question arose in 2015 and before.[113] At this point, utility-scale solar energy technology had not yet fully come into its own. It still required some—though less—governmental support.[114] At this point, it would be fair to increase the barriers to entry for key components of the renewable value chain to safeguard the health of domestic value chain segments. Doing so would not undercut the stated policy goal of foreign policymakers to help create a domestic alternative to foreign energy technology. Rather, it would allow the technology in question to incubate in its own national context. To the extent that incubation is wildly successful there is of course a risk that it will displace national champions in now importing economies. Yet, in this scenario, newly importing economies would see a material advantage in reduced energy costs. Complaining of such an innovation advantage would appear almost ironically self-defeating—it would seek to protect the domestic champions of the importing economy against superior foreign competition in a mature value chain. One can thus leave it to realpolitik responses to address the problem without needing to resort to international dispute resolution.

This still leaves the question of what to do with those earning a living by working for a displaced supplier. Reminding such employees of the logic of creative destruction is unlikely to be persuasive.[115] Life at the energy technological (and

[112] *See* section 3.5.

[113] Asmelash (n 76).

[114] Lazard's levelized cost of energy analysis in 2014 gave combined cycle gas generation an $11/MWh advantage over utility scale solar at the bottom end of the respective cost ranges ($61/MWh for combined cycle gas versus $72/MWh for utility scale solar). 'Lazard's Levelized Cost of Energy Analysis Version 8.0', (September 2014) Lazard, https://refman.energytransitionmodel.com/publications/1962, last accessed 7 January 2025. In 2015, this price advantage shifted to a $2/MWh advantage for solar thin film utility scale projects over combined cycle gas at the bottom end of the respective cost ranges ($52/MWh for combined cycle gas versus $50/MWh for utility scale solar). Given the unknown of interconnection and technology risk, government support was still important in 2015. As a side note, the cost reductions in solar at this crucial time were in part due to an increasing concentration of solar value chains in China. *See* section 3.4.

[115] *See* Weisman, 'How Democrats Lost the Working Class', (4 January 2025) New York Times, https://www.nytimes.com/2025/01/04/us/politics/democrats-working-class.html, last accessed 7 January 2025.

innovation) frontier is certainly turbulent. This turbulence itself has undesirable distributive consequences. The best way to address this concern is to support the next energy innovation that could provide employment to displaced stakeholders. Even here there remains a risk. Yet, the risk is not bottomless. Rather, it can be channelled into new energy innovation in broad, dynamic, cooperative global energy value chains.

8.5 Conclusion

Energy value chains are critical to the functioning of the global energy system. In this chapter, I have argued that these value chains can in fact be broadened in keeping with the overall theoretical outlook of this book. I have argued that such a broadening will require policy support. Yet, this policy support can be targeted in a manner consistent with realpolitik imperatives and in fact can check abuses by third states. Such a broad configuration of value chains is critical for an innovation-led, resilient global energy system.

This constellation of broad, regionally integrated, and diverse value chains serves two additional, critical goals. Firstly, it supports energy agency. There are more active stakeholders with an ability to make salient decisions that together constituted their energy systems. This increased agency supports the goal of greater human development through energy policy.

Further, such broader and regionally diverse energy value chains diversify the benefits and burdens from energy projects. It increases the number of participants who benefit from energy revenues. This distribution benefits society more than a fully concentrated value chain model by fostering innovation. Secondly, this constellation also diversifies burdens by placing more projects in more places to meet the same need. In both cases, this constellation of value chains supports the central goals of global, broad, and meaningful human development.

9
Rule of Law

9.1 Introduction

Implicit in the discussion of the last two chapters is the need for predictability in implementing energy finance and operating energy value chains. Financing is highly attuned to risk. A lack of predictability increases risk. It thus makes financing more expensive or altogether unavailable.[1] The same dynamic is at work in the day-to-day operation of energy value chains. Energy projects are among the most capital-intensive projects. Commercial actors will accept risk assignments only to the extent that both risk assignments and reward expectations can predictably be enforced. This is also true for the myriad of transactions needed along energy value chains to deliver needed materials and services to realize such projects.[2] We therefore do not just need money (finance) and stuff (value chains). We need an institution that can backstop the decisions and risk assignments by all of our relevant stakeholders at the conceptual or contracting stage when we implement those decisions and risk assignments.

This need is particularly pronounced in the energy context. Not only are energy projects hugely capital intensive,[3] this capital-intensive nature means that projects require a significant amount of time to become profitable for project sponsors and their investors as well as to yield the desired policy outcomes for regulators.[4] Given the dynamic nature of the energy world, this means that risk assignments must hold over the timeframe in which risks are bound to materialize and circumstances are bound to change. If there is no institution that can credibly enforce contractual decisions even against such a long-term horizon, it is unlikely that many energy projects will make it off the ground, given the risk sensitivities involved.

The premise of my discussion so far in this book has been a realpolitik view of mutual verification and gradual reaction by stakeholders to each other.[5] If I see that my neighbour does not keep to the rules, I will adjust to react to their defection. This, in turn, should incentivize rational actors to play fair, as an alternative course of action ultimately entails long-term losses for the defector.[6] Still, this

[1] *See* section 7.3.
[2] *See* section 8.2.
[3] Thijs van de Graaf & Benjamin K Sovacool, *Global Energy Politics* (Polity Press 2020) 74.
[4] Peter D Cameron & Michael C Stanley, *Oil, Gas, and Mining, A Sourcebook for Understanding the Extractive Industries* (World Bank 2017).
[5] *See* section 3.4.
[6] Robert Axelrod, *The Evolution of Cooperation* (Basic Books 1984) 58–62.

A Theory of Global Energy Governance. Frédéric Gilles Sourgens, Oxford University Press.
DOI: 10.1093/9780198950325.003.0009

realpolitik device imposed constraints of rational choice that may not always be realistic. Decisionmakers may be willing to trade small short-term gains for significant long-term losses because they will no longer be charged with resolving that later long-term problem.[7] Decisionmakers also may perceive situations differently, thus unknowingly increasing risk.[8] Decisionmakers finally may have sufficient leverage to believe themselves immune from long-term losses.

Realpolitik constraints of reciprocal defection do not suffice to provide such a level of predictability. They function best in a world of relative power parity.[9] They are inherently unstable.[10] Given the stakes, realpolitik alone therefore does not suffice to solve the systemic energy problems the world faces, whether it is alleviating energy poverty, combating climate change, etc.

During moments of significant upheaval, it is further likely that policy and market pressures will exacerbate beggar thy neighbour incentives. The global response to the Great Depression is one such example.[11] Though certainly significantly milder, the economic crises of 1970s as well as the continued aftermath of 2008 exhibit similar reactions.[12] This makes energy cooperation particularly challenging at the current moment of transition—realpolitik alone is likely to undermine rather than build trust at the geopolitical crossroads of the mid-2020s.

Global energy governance therefore needs a counterweight that can hold state, governmental, and commercial stakeholders alike to their word. This counterweight needs to shorten the time span, in which a 'defector' from a rational choice agreement will feel the relevant loss.[13] It also needs to provide a comparatively prompt remedy for a potentially injured party to reduce its assessment of its own risk exposure.[14] In short, it needs to provide an institution to foster cooperation when possible and to provide an adequate remedy when it is not.

This counterweight benefits everyone. It reduces political and commercial risk. It lowers the cost of capital. It makes more projects and transactions feasible for all

[7] *See* Dow, Han, and Sangiori, 'The Short-Termism Trap: Catering to Informed Investors with Limited Horizons', (13 August 2024) Harvard Law School Forum on Corporate Governance, https://corpgov.law.harvard.edu/2024/08/13/the-short-termism-trap-catering-to-informed-investors-with-limited-horizons/, last accessed 8 January 2025.

[8] Roger Fisher, William Ury & Bruce Patton, *Getting to Yes, Negotiating Agreement Without Giving in* (2nd edn, Houghton Mifflin Company 1991) 22–23.

[9] *See* Axelrod (n 6), at 58–62.

[10] *See* Kroenig, 'International Relations Theory Suggests Great-Power War Is Coming', (27 August 2022) Foreign Policy, https://foreignpolicy.com/2022/08/27/international-relations-theory-suggests-great-power-war-is-coming/#:~:text=Realists%20argue%20that%20multipolar%20systems,not%20out%20of%20the%20question., last accessed 7 January 2025.

[11] Martin Daunton, *The Economic Government of the World 1933-2023* (Farrar, Straus and Giroux 2023) 59–88.

[12] For a discussion, *see* Harold James, *Seven Crashes: The Economic Crises that Shaped Globalization* (Yale University Press 2023). James analyses both the immediate nationalist response and the opportunities for global realignment inherent in the crises. James thus suggests that the challenges can be overcome even as an initial reaction can in its own right be destabilizing.

[13] *See* Fisher, Ury & Patton (n 8), at 79.

[14] *Ibid.*

stakeholders. It therefore provides a public good at a minimum: it provides a non-rivalrous and non-excludable benefit to all energy stakeholders. As I will argue, it also provides a common energy good.[15] It exists in, and constitutes, a community with communal ends and communal means. It provides a critical common energy good by providing the tools necessary for diligence and vigilance to maintain and protect the global energy community.[16]

The counterweight we are looking for is the rule of law. Though what is included in the rule of law is itself contested, the literature distinguishes two kinds of rule of law. The first is the idea of a 'thin' rule of law.[17] A thin rule of law exists when decision-making follows an accepted process of decision and decisions are transparent, clear, generally applicable, prospective, consistent, relatively stable, fairly and consistently applied to like-situated actors, and reasonably acceptable to a majority of stakeholders it governs.[18] A thick rule of law adds a political morality to the thin version of the rule of law, which the rule of law also must serve on top of being acceptable to a majority of stakeholders.[19] Law defends a common good.[20] Even a thick rule of law, however, is premised in a process rather than an outcome—ends do not excuse the means even in this thicker conception.[21] Rather, means themselves are further constrained and defined.

In this chapter, I will begin by sketching what the rule of law means in the context of a global energy system that has internalized the bond of belonging in its decision-making processes. The bond of belonging looks to a thick rule of law to provide a common energy good. This thick rule of law is premised in the idea of shared ends of a global energy community. It therefore looks to global decisionmakers to make decisions to enforce risk assignments with these ends in mind. The decisionmakers in question are themselves international actors versed in the functioning of the energy system to understand these risk assignments. Their decisions are reasonably promptly enforced globally to secure a quick resolution of any energy disputes. The decisions themselves become reasonably well known so as to guide future projects and transactions and provide

[15] *See* section 6.3.

[16] *Ibid.*

[17] *See* Joseph Raz, *The Authority of Law* (2nd edn, Oxford University Press 2009) 3–52.

[18] Peerenboom, 'Let One Hundred Flowers Bloom, One Hundred School Contend: Debating Rule of Law in China', (2002) 23 Michigan Journal of International Law 471, 478–79. This list overlaps to a significant extent with the idea of rule of law in Lon Fuller's narrow reading of the natural law tradition. A thin rule of law therefore is not necessarily positivist. *See* Lon L Fuller, *The Morality of Law* (revised edn, Yale University Press 1969) 33–39.

[19] Peerenboom (n 18), at 472.

[20] *See* John Finnis, *Natural Law and Natural Rights* (Oxford University Press 1980) 316–17.

[21] *Ibid*; Niccolo Machiavelli, *Discourses on the First Decade of Titus Livius* (Ninian Hill Thomson trans, Kegan Paul, Trench & Co 1883) 42 ('For although the act condemn the doer, the end may justify him, and when, as in the case of Romulus, the end is good, it will always excuse the means'); Niccolò Machiavelli, *Tutte le Opere* (Mario Martelli ed, Sansoni Editore 1993) 90 ('Conviene bene, che, accusandolo il fatto, lo effetto lo scusi; e quando sia buono, come quello di Romolo, sempre lo scuserà; perchè collui che è violento per guastare, non quello che è per racconciare, si debbe riprendere.').

a means to backstop the global energy community with a ready enforcement mechanism.

I will then argue that progress towards such a conception of the rule of law is in fact achievable in a realpolitik energy world. A realpolitik perspective begins with a thin conception of the rule of law. This thin conception provides a means to make credible precommitment and no more. These credible precommitments, in turn, can then be enforced at a time of need through neutral and flexible decision-making processes such as international arbitration. These arbitral decisions, in turn, are readily enforceable around the world. As more decisions are made, the rules of engagement between stakeholders become clearer. Due to this firming up of rules of engagement, they become a community sharing in a common understanding of how energy governance ought to function in light of how it has functioned. As it does so, it progressively moves from a thin towards a thick understanding of the rule of law: the rule of law creates and then maintains community standards against which all stakeholders understand and negotiate their respective commitments.

The fact that realpolitik can bring about such a state of affairs does not mean that it must. It can just as well fail to take the necessary institutional actions. International commercial arbitration exists today and is reasonably effective following the conclusion of treaties like the 1958 New York Convention on the Recognition and Enforcement of Arbitral Awards.[22] Yet, there is significant retrenchment from this order, driven itself by realpolitik motivations.[23] While it is rational for realpolitik actors to maintain such institutions in a necessarily transnational energy system, realpolitik actors are precisely not always rational.

The failure of a realpolitik institution building is catastrophic for the global energy system, particularly at the current moment in time. Withdrawing from, or disbanding, institutions that can reduce risk for global energy value chain participants and global financial institutions will significantly increase the risk of energy investments. This, in turn, will limit energy options at precisely the time that more energy investment is needed to meet basic energy access, energy security, and environmental sustainability needs.

The best course to avoid such a result is to build on the existing institutions associated with the Washington consensus. These institutions have created a flexible, neutral, and transnational web of decisionmakers that are capable of enforcing precommitments. They can do so reasonably promptly. For now, their decisions are broadly enforceable around the world. The calls for reform of these institutions

[22] *See* New York Convention on the Recognition and Enforcement of Arbitral Awards, art V.

[23] *See* Michael Waibel et al, *The Backlash Against Investment Arbitration, Perceptions and Reality* (Kluwer Law 2010). This discussion focuses in the first place on investment arbitration. Yet, other critics have long employed a similar kind of critique against many forms of international arbitration involving sovereign interests (of which energy disputes would be an example). *See* M Sornarajah, *The International Law of Foreign Investment* (3rd edn, Cambridge University Press 2010).

therefore should be approached with caution.[24] The calls assert that the institutions in question unduly restrict the margin of policy-making of national regulators in particular. This complaint is of course very much the point of these institutions—precommitments must be enforced for the global energy system to function. This includes precommitments by policymakers. While some decisions of international decisionmakers are obviously of dubious merit—the international trade decisions undercutting domestic support mechanisms to broaden solar value chains being one obvious example—the institutions themselves are critical to efficient functioning of the global energy system and to its ability to deliver human development outcomes around the world.

Reform, while well-meaning, can be counterproductive when it attacks support pillars for the global institutional framework and with it, the thin rule of law itself. It should therefore focus on strengthening the authority of decisions by embedding them more strongly in our expectations of ends law must serve in global governance.[25] It should not insist on altering the decision-making processes themselves as any such attempt will simply undercut the ability of stakeholders credibly to assign central risks *ex ante* between themselves. Otherwise, it risks depriving the other institutions needed for the global energy system to function of their needed backstop. At this point of all points, a realpolitik only approach to global energy governance would be counterproductive to the point of being self-defeating.

9.2 Thick Rule of Law and the Bond of Belonging

Our conception of global energy governance pursuant to the bond of belonging requires the idea of a rule of law. The bond of belonging ties a community together. This community must cooperate to exploit communal resources. This exploitation of communal resources, in turn, must make reasonable use of resources and avoid waste. The idea of what constitutes reasonable use is also measured against the yardstick of a common energy good. As I have argued already, this common good seeks progressively to realize human development through cooperation within a shared energy community, in conditions of energy peace, abundance, and stewardship.[26]

The bond of belonging requires a strong normative guidepost to achieve this end. Cooperation frequently will take the form of voluntary, reciprocal commitments between stakeholders. The bond of belonging needs institutions that can

[24] For an excellent summary of the status of these reforms, *see* Arato, Claussen, & Langford, 'The Investor-State Dispute Settlement Reform Process: Design, Dilemmas and Discontents', (2023) 14 Journal of International Dispute Settlement 127.

[25] *See* Faccio, 'Investment Contracts and the Reform of Investment Arbitration: Towards Sustainability', (2023) 28 ICSID Review 625.

[26] *See* Part II.

enforce such commitments to strengthen trust between stakeholders and foster a shared ethos among community members.[27] In addition, the bond of belonging demands cooperation even when we do not enter into privity with each other. We owe other regard to each other just by virtue of our respective membership in a shared resource community.[28] The rules against waste and requiring reasonable use apply not because community members enter into a contract with each other.[29] They apply simply on the strength of the status of the community members—we are fellows in a resource community whether we agree to be or not (and frequently, we would rather not be fellows at all, as that would increase our own respective share of limited shared resources).[30]

In the national context, the rule of law straightforwardly backstops the bond of belonging. As I discussed in Chapter 2, balanced energy governance is a regulatory approach that sets incentives so as to bring private and public stakeholders together in realizing energy outcomes for the benefit of society as a whole.[31] The regulation in question applies law. For the most part, law follows the basic parameters of the thin rule of law—regulation follows an accepted, transparent, clear, generally applicable, prospective, consistent, relatively stable, fair, consistently applied, and generally accepted process of decision.[32] Some projects are caught in the regulatory cycle—the switch from one regulatory paradigm to another as energy cycles progress—leading to the potential of functionally retroactive regulation.[33] Yet, in these instances, national approaches do provide for fair compensation for affected stakeholders, in principle at least.[34] What is more, the very cyclical nature of energy regulation itself suggested a deeper regulatory logic to energy governance consistent with a thick rule of law. What explains the cyclical nature of regulatory approaches to energy governance is that regulation hopes to protect the common energy good by realigning incentives between relevant stakeholders to grow fair, secure, and sustainable energy access.[35] This common good is possible only in the context of a shared ethos, thus looking to a thick rule of law conception.[36] These

[27] *See* section 5.2(a).

[28] Carol M Rose, *Property and Persuasion: Essays on the History, Theory, and Rhetoric of Ownership* (Routledge 1994) 165–89; Pierce, 'Carol Rose Comes to the Oil Patch: Modern Property Analysis Applied to Modern Reservoir Problems', (2011) 19 Penn State Environmental Law Review 241, 245–46.

[29] *See* Frédéric G Sourgens & Leonardo Sempertegui, *Principles of International Energy Transition Law* (Oxford University Press 2023) 91–102.

[30] *See* Schremmer, 'Pore Space Property', (2021) Utah Law Review 1.

[31] *See* section 2.5.

[32] Peerenboom (n 18), at 478–79; Fuller (n 18), at 33–39.

[33] *See* Desierto & Sourgens, 'Investment Law and Decarbonisation', *in Decarbonization and the Energy Industry, Law, Policy and Regulation in Law-Carbon Energy Markets* (Tade Oyewunmi et al eds, Hart Publishing 2020) 157.

[34] One such example is litigation with regard to Germany's nuclear phase out. *See* Páez-Salgado, 'A Battle on Two Fronts: Vattenfall v. Federal Republic of Germany', (18 February 2021) Kluwer Arbitration Blog, https://arbitrationblog.kluwerarbitration.com/2021/02/18/a-battle-on-two-fronts-vattenfall-v-federal-republic-of-germany/, last accessed 9 January 2025.

[35] *See* section 2.5.

[36] Peerenboom (n 18), at 472.

regulatory approaches reach all the way down through the legal system and affect not just electricity regulation but also determine the property and contractual rights and obligations and delictual remedies for energy value chain participants and affected stakeholders.

There is an obvious problem in applying this understanding of the rule of law internationally. National sovereigns are charged with the attainment of the common good of their peoples.[37] 'Sovereignty' means to hold and use the highest governing authority.[38] There can be no global 'super' sovereign to regulate 'ordinary' sovereigns as well as cross-boundary relationships between stakeholders subject to different sovereigns. A rule of law therefore must find a different anchor.

One can straightforwardly provide such an anchor for a thin conception of the rule of law. In a thin conception of the rule of law, the source of my obligation in such a setting is my agreement to be bound.[39] States enter into treaties.[40] Energy value chain participants enter into contracts.[41] Such treaties and contracts, too, follow an accepted, transparent, clear, generally applicable, prospective, consistent, relatively stable, fair, consistently applied, and generally accepted process of decision-making.[42] I therefore do not submit to a higher authority—I simply precommit myself on the strength of my own word. The core question in the context of a thin rule of law is how to resolve legal disputes and enforce dispute resolution outcomes. Promises in contracts and treaties do not automatically police their own compliance. Consequently, parties wishing to bind each other legally will insist on a legal means of dispute resolution to secure compliance. One could look to standing dispute resolution fora in energy project host states. The standing dispute resolution bodies of host states are potentially problematic fora—they could have an appearance of bias in favour of a particular party or position.[43] Consequently, the logical thing to do is to rely on international fora. The most flexible such forum is arbitration—it does not require a standing court, can be tailored to the needs of a specific dispute, and can still provide a legal resolution.[44] Their limited competence further does not threaten the sovereignty of states—they simply resolve a simple dispute in accordance with rules agreed to by those states ahead of time.

[37] *See* ICESCR, art 2(1).

[38] For a discussion of sovereignty and its history, *see* Sourgens, 'Positivism, Humanism, and Hegemony: Sovereignty and Security for Our Time', (2006) 25 Penn State International Law Review 433.

[39] For a nuanced introduction to the role of consent in international law, *see* Samantha Besson ed, *Consenting to International Law* (Cambridge University Press 2024).

[40] Hollis, 'Do International Agreements Have a Consent Problem?', in Samantha Besson ed, *Consenting to International Law* (Cambridge University Press 2024) 137, 137–38.

[41] *See eg* Rudolf Dolzer, *Petroleum Contracts and International Law* (Oxford University Press 2018).

[42] Peerenboom (n 18), at 478–79; Fuller (n 18), at 33–39.

[43] Jan Paulsson, *The Idea of Arbitration* (Oxford University Press 2014) 106–08.

[44] On the nature of international arbitration, *see* Emmanuel Gaillard, *Aspects Philosophiques du Droit de l'Arbitrage International* (Brill Nijhoff 2008).

There are in fact international treaties about arbitration.[45] Arbitral awards, in turn, can either be enforced pursuant to those treaties or at the least, the treaties impose an obligation on states to recognize and abide by the awards.[46] There is thus a means to resolve disputes about, and enforce, obligations in a manner consistent with a thin rule of law in keeping with the basic premise of sovereign equality.

The thicker demands of the bond of belonging are more difficult to accommodate. The prohibition of waste and obligation of reasonable use do not arise from agreement or contract. They instead arise from the nature of a communal relationship or status.[47] The first question is how such thicker demands can create an obligation in the first place in the absence of a sovereign charged with the realization of the common good.

The bond of belonging provides a foothold. The bond of belonging means that the relationship in which I find myself is communal and has a common good.[48] Law in this context is a specified means to realize the common good.[49] (Law differs from other forms of decision-making in that it is an accepted, transparent, clear, generally applicable, prospective, consistent, relatively stable, fair, consistently applied, and generally accepted process of decision yielding specific answers in the context of specific situational prompts.)[50] Abiding by the law is necessary to realizing the common good.[51] The common good can only be realized through cooperation.[52] Cooperation, in turn, requires the kind of process of decision the law provides to coordinate specific actions to solve concrete problems.[53]

[45] 1907 Convention for the Pacific Settlement of International Disputes, art 37; New York Convention on the Recognition and Enforcement of Arbitral Awards, art V.

[46] *See* W Michael Reisman, *Systems of Control in International Adjudication and Arbitration, Breakdown and Repair* (Duke University Press 1992) 11–15

[47] *See* Rose (n 28), 165–89. I allude here to a movement in reverse to Maine's traditional view that law moves from 'primitive' status to agreement and contract. Henry Sumner Maine, *Ancient Law: Its Connection with the Early History of Society, and its Relation to Modern Ideas* (John Murray 1861) 169 ('Nor is it difficult to see what is the tie between man and man which replaces by degrees those forms of reciprocity in rights and duties which have their origin in the Family. It is Contract.'). The very point of the thick conception of the rule of law as I develop it brings it back to the notion of care as (synthetic) kinship in a shared resource community or, quite literally, 'common-wealth'. Working towards a common good is premised in a derivation of community from family rather than the idea of contract. Status as a fellow in community rather than privity determines the source of rights and obligations in community. Cicero, *De Oficiis* I.xvii.47-xvii *in Cicero Volume XXI: On Duties* (Walter Miller trans, Harvard University Press 1913) 51–61. The thin rule of law thus goes from status to contract. In a Tolkienian twist, the thick rule of law adds 'and back again'.

[48] *See* sections 2.4, 5.2, and 6.3.

[49] Finnis (n 20), at 315–16.

[50] Peerenboom (n 18), at 478–79; Fuller (n 18), at 33–39. Law differs from other decision-making processes because it is both authoritative, in the sense that it is accepted and expected, and controlling, in the sense that its demands are generally followed and can be enforced, through collective action or formal institutions, in case of need. Harold D Lasswell & Myres S McDougal, *Jurisprudence for a Free Society: Studies in Law, Science and Policy* (New Haven Press 1992).

[51] Finnis (n 20), at 315–16.

[52] *See* section 5.2(a).

[53] I can only participate in a practice and realize its goals to the extent that that there are reasonably clear principles and rules. In section 5.2(a), I borrowed McIntyre's example of chess as a practice.

I therefore must act consistently with the law to act consistently with the bond of belonging.[54]

This still leaves the question of how to make this thicker understanding of the rule of law controlling. How do we enforce it? It might be tempting to suggest that such a truly controlling order requires a global court of general jurisdiction of some kind. Yet, this suggestion is inconsistent with the parameters in which we operate. Our starting point is that there is no sovereign above the state. A global court of general jurisdiction with the power to make the kind of decisions inherent in a thick rule of law would itself act as a sovereign, given the very broad, purposive remit of law in a thick rule of law context. Such law by definition radiates beyond text and assists in making policy judgements.[55] A supranational decisionmaker who could prescribe how to make such policy judgements as a matter of course would act essentially as a regulator of last resort.[56] This is inconsistent with the diffuse organization of world society.[57] (It is also not availing to say that states should simply consent to such broad compulsory jurisdiction. First, the point of the nature of the underlying obligations in question is that they exist beyond privity. Bringing them within the realm of privity *substantively* provides a snapshot instead of integrating the dynamic nature of obligations in question. Second, consenting to such a broad compulsory jurisdiction is only a *jurisdictionally* temporary solution as such consent can also be withdrawn. One could rejoin that consent must be given irrevocably. This rejoinder takes us out of

Alasdair MacIntyre, *After Virtue* (2nd edn., University of Notre Dame Press 1984) 187. The practice of chess is possible only if fellow participants play the game by the same rules. Otherwise, chess is not chess. One should not, however, over-read the chess analogy. Rules in practices are not akin to rules in boardgames (in the sense that they are known *a priori* before playing the game and are close to immutable). Rather, rules are the kind of inductive rules we establish on the basis of family resemblances between situations we recognize as meaningfully functionally alike. *See* Ludwig Wittgenstein, 'Philosophische Untersuchungen', *in Werkausgabe* (Suhrkamp Verlag 1984).

[54] One might object that this is a circular argument. A thick rule of law is premised in a common good so if there is a common good there is a way to justify a thick rule of law. This appears to assume the existence of a common good rather than proving it. In the context of resource communities, or commons, one can prove the existence of a common good in a non-circular way. I can only benefit from my rights if everyone in the commons acts to preserve and maintain the commons. The commons is the common good for each member because the resource community tragically collapses if we act otherwise. There is thus an external validation for the existence of a common good. We do not assume that it exists. We can prove its existence against the background of the tragedy of the commons and catastrophe of the anticommons. *See* section 2.2–2.5.

[55] W Michael Reisman, *The Quest for World Order and Human Dignity in the Twenty-First Century: Constitutive Process and Individual Commitment* (Brill Nijhoff 2012).

[56] Alexis de Tocqueville, 'De la Démocratie en Amérique I (1835)', *in* André Jardin ed, *Bibliothèque de la Pléiade: Tocqueville Œuvres II* (Gallimard 1992) 3, 167–70 ('Dans les mains des sept juges fédéraux reposent incessamment la paix, la prospérité, l'existence même de l'Union. Sans eux, la Constitution est une œuvre morte; c'est à eux qu'en appelle le pouvoir exécutif pour résister aux empiètements du corps législatif; la législature, pour se defender des entreprises du pouvoir exécutif; l'Union, pour se faire obéir des États; les États, pour repousser les prétentions exagérées de l'Union; l'intérêt public contre l'intérêt prive; l'esprit de conservation contre l'instabilité démocratique.')

[57] *See* Reisman (n 46), at 26.

a truly consensus-based understanding of why the court would have jurisdiction in the first place.)

The first answer is that the thicker understanding of law informs decision-making without in fact being justiciable in the same way as consensual obligations incurred in treaties and contracts. Law informs how we approach policy questions. It does not dictate a single answer. Rather, it eliminates what we may not do and provides a toolkit to understand how we might solve a particular problem.[58] Here, law is a tool to engage within a community and not a means to compel specific conduct. The rule of law still operates through institutions—ministries of foreign affairs and energy or environment, in-house counsel in large energy companies, and advisors in non-governmental organizations. It just does not operate through judicial or quasi-judicial bodies.

This first answer is incomplete. If it were the complete answer, law would be a prudential rather than controlling process of decision-making. It would advise but could not in fact compel. I therefore can pragmatically ignore its counsel when it suits me. In doing so, I would undermine the ability to realize the common good, as we established that abiding by the law is a necessary condition for its realization.[59] How then do we give law bite without creating judge-sages to stand alongside Plato's philosopher kings?[60]

The answer lies in the fact that the rule of law is not a blunt instrument. This is particularly the case for the thick rule of law. It does not set up clear single-answer, single-path problem solutions.[61] It requires instead discerning judgement that takes multiple facets of the common good into account at the same time. It must *integrate* these frequently inconsistent demands into a single whole.[62] This single decision typically reverberates through a myriad of legal relationships. Many of these relationships, in turn, are privity-based. In the energy context, for instance, a regulator may have entered into a power purchase agreement with an independent power producer operating a coal-fired power plant. When a regulator makes a decision premised in its understanding of law and this decision facially impairs the

[58] Reisman (n 55), at 183–89.
[59] Finnis (n 20), at 315–16.
[60] *See* Ronald Dworkin, *Laws' Empire* (Harvard University Press 1986) 238–44 (introducing 'Judge Hercules').
[61] Reisman (n 55), at 183–89. This, of course, is precisely the opposite of the Dworkinian approach to adjudication. *See* Dworkin (n 60), at 126–28. For an introduction to Dworkin's 'one-right-answer' thesis and its theoretical context and evolution, *see* Brian Bix, *Law, Language and Legal Determinacy* (Oxford University Press 1995) 77–132.
[62] *See* Desierto, '"Stringent Due Diligence", Duties of Cooperation and Assistance to Climate Vulnerable States, and the Selective Integration of External Rules in the ITLOS Advisory Opinion on Climate Change and International Law', (3 June 2024) EJILTalk, https://www.ejiltalk.org/stringent-due-diligence-duties-of-cooperation-and-assistance-to-climate-vulnerable-states-and-the-selective-integration-of-external-rules-in-the-itlos-advisory-opinion-on-climate-change-and-inte/, last accessed 9 January 2025.

expected return of the independent power producer, the dispute may end up in arbitration pursuant to the project documents.[63] The decision-making process leading up to the impairment of the return of the independent power producer will now be subject to legal scrutiny. Specifically, did the independent power producer assume the risk of the regulatory action in question in light of the overall legal framework as it found it? If the answer is 'yes', the impairment of expected returns did not breach the underlying agreement between the independent power producer and its regulator. Conversely, decisions that rely on invocations of the common good and broader legal mandates of environmental protection pretextually can in fact create liability for the state and the regulator under international treaties containing an arbitration clause or under contract.[64] The question therefore is not if the thick rule of law reaches international legal decision-making but *how* it does so. The answer to this how is that it reaches obliquely and asks if the policy judgement by states is consistent with the legal obligations of the state seen as a whole (including, of course, the project documents.) The question then becomes whether the manner in which the rule of law guided decision-making was tenable—whether it followed the process of decision prescribed by the thick rule of law.[65] It is not what the correct policy answer for the regulator would have been under the circumstances.

The international institutions upon which the thick rule of law relies in the energy context therefore are the same institutions that are also at the heart of the thin rule of law. Typically, they will be arbitral tribunals operating on the basis of consent. This consent is typically anchored in a broader set of obligations to which it relates.[66] These institutions confirm that law is indeed controlling even if they cannot compel single answers to all problems. In many instances, that means that the thicker aspects of the rule of law operate only at the policy-making and project structuring stage. They do not become cudgels to compel judicial solutions even to pressing problems.[67] They operate instead in the background to reinforce the idea of a community and to integrate the common good in day-to-day decision-making without subjecting that decision-making to the caprice of white knight lawyering.

[63] For a discussion of one such example (albeit involving domestic and investment treaty arbitrations as opposed to contractual arbitration), *see* Putter, 'The Netherlands Coals Phase-Out and the Resulting (RWE and Uniper) ICSID Arbitrations', (24 August 2021) Kluwer Arbitration Blog, https://arbitrationblog.kluwerarbitration.com/2021/08/24/the-netherlands-coal-phase-out-and-the-resulting-rwe-and-uniper-icsid-arbitrations/, last accessed 9 January 2025.

[64] *Rockhopper Italia SpA v Italy*, ICSID Case No ARB/17/14, award (23 August 2022).

[65] *See Fraport AG Frankfurt Airport Services Worldwide v Philippines*, ICSID Case No ARB/03/25, annulment (23 December 2010), ¶¶ 44–45, 112.

[66] For a discussion, *see* Berger, 'Contractual Arbitration Clauses and Non-Contractual Claims', (2023) 40 Journal of International Arbitration 105.

[67] *See* Sourgens & Sempertegui (n 29), at 299–326.

9.3 Rule of Law Stabilization of Energy Realpolitik

The bond of belonging describes the energy world as it could be once we have solved the tragedies of the commons and anticommons in the global energy system.[68] Yet, both tragedies of the commons and anticommons are precisely tragic because realpolitik incentive structures of relative advantage in low trust environments encourage sub-ideal outcomes. These sub-ideal outcomes over time completely erode the common resource base, meaning that it is cold comfort to stakeholders standing in front of a now desolate commons that alternative paths were theoretically available.[69]

The critical question is how do we make these paths more than theoretically available and embed them instead in realpolitik energy governance. Here, the rule of law is again critical. As I will argue in this section, we must begin with a thin conception of the rule of law. The thin rule of law is a credible backstop for precommitments. It can confirm that such commitments will be enforced. In doing so, it generates outcomes that increase the reason to trust in cooperation. As the thin rule of law begins to weave a tapestry of predictable and mutually beneficial cooperative outcomes with each new precedent of a successful project or international cooperative endeavour, it shows us that we are in fact connected by a bond of belonging in resource community that benefits all of its members. This realization, in turn, can further strengthen and hold together the global energy system by means of the rule of law. A properly constituted thin rule of law is therefore critical to avoiding the catastrophic consequences of unreasonable and wasteful use of the energy resource community. It makes possible the proper functioning of energy finance and value energy chains. It is the map that can keep us on course when expediency draws even critical energy stakeholders off course.

I will conclude this section in noting that an energy world governed even by a thin rule of law is not a foregone conclusion. It requires effort to conceive, construct, and maintain. It takes significantly less effort to unravel it. Once it is in the process of unravelling, a failing rule of law raises the spectre of a vicious lawless cycle. This lawless cycle over time infects all stakeholders with despair in any cooperative future. It increasingly accelerates action that destroys common resource bases and sets incentives that further precipitate their unreasonable and wasteful use. The global energy system in the 2020s finds itself at a decision point that could lead down either path—as the energy system has done in the context of past crises. If we do not want to look back at the desolate remains of a ruined global energy commons some thirty years hence, now is the time to choose.

[68] *See* sections 2.2–2.3.

[69] *See* Hardin, 'The Tragedy of the Commons', (1968) 162 Science 1243; Heller, 'The Tragedy of the Anticommons: A Concise Introduction and Lexicon', (2013) 76 Modern Law Review 6.

9.3(a) Verification and Credible Precommitment

The central refrain for constituting the institutions that can successfully govern the global energy system is 'trust but verify'.[70] If we can trust but verify, we can finance investments in needed energy systems even—and particularly—when innovation has not yet caught up to critical energy policy problems.[71] In these instances, there is a missing money problem to deliver public energy goods.[72] This missing money problem can only be solved through collective action—and yet collective action takes trust and resources. Both are only possible if there are credible verification mechanisms.[73] The same is true at the next logical step of building out the projects and initiatives we have financed. We now need energy value chains—the stuff and services—to translate money into outcomes. Here, too, we need to be able to trust but verify that the value chains we are building are going to last and stand up to the stress of both expected and unexpected disruptions and even catastrophes.[74]

This idea of trust but verify in the first place needs a means to make meaningful commitments.[75] Such commitments are precisely of the kind that define the thin rule of law. That is, they are transparent, clear, generally applicable, prospective, consistent, relatively stable, fairly and consistently applied to like-situated actors, and reasonably acceptable to a majority of the stakeholders it governs.[76] Such commitments relinquish an option (ie to act inconsistently with the commitment).[77] They further change behaviour in others who have now come to rely on the commitment, for instance by making commitments of their own.

To take a mundane everyday example: say my children must complete their homework to receive their allowance and that I check that they can complete their homework if they want to go and see a movie with friends on a school night. If one of my children has a homework assignment due in a month, 'I will do my homework' is likely not a meaningful commitment for me to feel good about letting the

[70] *See* sections 5.3, 7.4(a), and 8.4(c).

[71] *See* section 7.4(a).

[72] *See* section 7.4.

[73] *See* section 7.4(a).

[74] *See* section 8.4(c).

[75] *See* Ratner, 'Precommitment Theory and International Law: Starting a Conversation', (2003) 81 Texas Law Review 2055; Ginsburg, Chernykh, & Elkins, 'Commitment and Diffusion: How and Why National Constitutions Incorporate International Law', (2008) University of Illinois Law Review 201, 210–27; Peters, 'Precommitment Theory Applied to International Law: Between Sovereignty and Triviality', (2008 University of Illinois Law Review 239, 241–46; Schelling, 'Strategies of Commitment', in Thomas Schelling, *Strategies of Commitment and Other Essays* (Harvard University Press 2006) 1, 6, 8–9.

[76] Peerenboom, 'Let One Hundred Flowers Bloom, One Hundred Schools Contend: Debating Rule of Law in China', (2002) 23 Michigan Journal of International Law 471, 478–79. This list overlaps to a significant extent with the idea of rule of law in Lon Fuller's narrow reading of the natural law tradition. A thin rule of law therefore is not necessarily positivist. *See* Lon L Fuller, *The Morality of Law* (revised edn, Yale University Press 1969) 33–39.

[77] Schelling (n 75), at 6, 8–9; Peters (n 75), at 241 (quoting Thomas Schelling's canonical definition of precommitment).

child go to see a movie the same night the assignment was given. It is not concrete enough. For example, it does not tell me when and how the work will be done (in assembly at school on the day it is due technically counts as 'doing my homework' and yet is not what a parent would have in mind). The commitment therefore must be both more *transparent* and *clearer*. ('I will start my homework after breakfast this Saturday and if I am not done in two hours will continue after breakfast on Sunday and every following weekend in the same way until it is done.') If I have more than one child, it is on the whole helpful if I exact similar commitments from each child when they have homework—that is, the commitment is meaningful if it is part of a generally applicable set of expectations. The commitment is obviously prospective—committing to doing last term's homework is comparatively meaningless. I also cannot randomly overlook that one child did not in fact submit homework as required but enforce the rule for the other etc.

Commitments in the energy governance context follow the same pattern. Commitments are meaningful because they are verifiable and predictable. In the context of an energy project, I know what risk is being assigned to whom and what circumstances alter the risk assignment. I know that similar risk assignments have been successful in the past (ie the party taking the risk could in fact shoulder it.) The only way in which I can make such commitments is to make them with specificity and in the manner of a contractual covenant. The rule of law is helpful precisely because it specifies what I need to know to have confidence that each party understands what risks and obligations it is assuming, what reward it receives, and that each can count on the reciprocal commitment of the other. Once we have these elements in place, it is possible to begin trusting and relying because we know what each party must do so that I can trust them.[78] There are clear rules and benchmarks that allow me to measure our respective performance.

Making commitments is not enough. The idea of trust and reliance requires the second element of verification.[79] To be meaningful, commitments must be both verifiable and verified. Concrete commitments such as the ones drafted by competent lawyers in contracts or treaties are verifiable in principle. Yet, we also need a verification mechanism.

This verification mechanism is not the same thing as a dispute resolution facility. Say that I enter into a contract with a Texas-based space entrepreneur to build me a mansion on Mars to my own specifications. It is drafted by a competent lawyer and subject to Texas law and I can sue the Texas-based space entrepreneur in the state courts of Texas. Unless I know whether a mansion on Mars has been built to my specifications, I do not know whether or when I need to sue. It is also on the whole unwise simply to trust the space entrepreneur's word. I need to be able to verify construction *independently*. I therefore need to account for a

[78] *Ibid.*
[79] Ginsburg, Chernykh, & Elkins (n 75), at 210.

verification mechanism for the rule of law to be of meaningful help to me. In many instances, the answer will be obvious—just go and look whether the performance has been rendered. In other instances, like the Mars example, it is not nearly as obvious. Many energy projects in principle would have similar problems of access to needed performance data to understand whether one has a dispute. These verification problems are contractually resolved ahead of time, for instance by defining the performance testing to be done prior to acceptance of a powerplant, the creation of 'punch lists' detailing additional work to bring a plant up to contractual standards following the performance test, and the requirements for the issuance of a certificate of completion once additional work has been performed.[80]

Such verification mechanisms are essential for the transparent functioning of commitment devices. They address information asymmetries inherent in global energy projects and global energy diplomacy. Without such verification mechanisms, attempts at precommitment would fail. A statement is only a meaningful commitment to the extent it can induce reliance.[81] Reliance here does not have to mean a detrimental change in position in light of the commitment. It can also mean making a return commitment as part of contractual negotiations. These return commitments only make sense if a counterparty can evaluate the strength of the commitment—and the risk of non-performance. The stronger the belief that performance is secure, the more valuable the commitment. Verification mechanisms are critical to assess one's ability to determine performance and overcome information asymmetries.

Once there is a meaningful way to make commitments and a means to verify that they have been met, it is possible to address the key problem for commons governance. There is a means to address the trust deficit that undercuts the potential for cooperation.[82] The thin rule of law therefore is a critical toolkit to transact out of tragedy in both the finance and in the energy value chain space. It provides the language within which we can formulate meaningful commitments and the structures that make them verifiable. Given the incentive structure of greater long-term rewards from cooperation, if the trust and information deficits in the commons governance situation can be overcome, this toolkit is critical to escaping tragedy.

9.3(b) Arbitration as Flexible and Neutral Enforcement Mechanism

Verification alone is frequently not enough. The thin rule of law requires, among other things, that laws are consistently applied and are relatively stable.[83]

[80] Panos Konstanin & Margarete Konstanin, *The Power Supply Industry, Best Practice Manual for Power Generation and Transport, Economics and Trade* (Springer 2018) 243–45.

[81] Peters (n 75), at 241.

[82] *See* Elinor Ostrom, *Understanding Institutional Diversity* (Princeton University Press 2009) 97–98.

[83] Peerenboom (n 18), at 478–79; Fuller (n 18), at 33–39.

Commitments are such laws for the parties whom they concern. Treaty commitments and internationally binding unilateral declarations of states are international legal obligations.[84] They are 'law' in the sense intended by the thin rule of law. The same is true for contractual commitments in transnational trade—those commitments are the law of the parties.[85] To be consistently applied and relatively stable, the verification that such commitments have not been fulfilled must lead to a remedy for the injured party.[86] Short of such a remedy, commitments are not consistently applied. The more inconsistently they are applied, the more unstable they become because one cannot trust on the face of a statement that looks like a commitment, that it will in fact be treated as binding by the party making it. The more this is the case, the less purchase a thin international rule of law would have. It would precisely not elicit the trust that is needed to overcome the tragedies of the commons and anticommons.

Structurally, this means that the thin rule of law additionally requires a web of binding dispute resolution mechanisms to address this problem. As I have outlined already in the context of the bond of belonging, such mechanisms indeed exist and are habitually used by energy stakeholders.[87] This dispute resolution mechanism is international arbitration. In the commercial context, international arbitration is the preferred means of dispute resolution for transnational transactions.[88] In the public international law context, arbitration exists alongside adjudication. Yet adjudication essentially functions as arbitration in that it is only accessible on the basis of a specific consent.[89] The key difference is that in international adjudication, one does not select the arbitrators for the specific dispute. Yet, given that states typically do have a direct input into the selection of international judges, this difference, while still important, is not as categorical as it might seem.

Arbitration in principle can provide the right kind of backstop for verification. It can provide a neutral and trusted third party means to resolve any outstanding legal or factual disputes.[90] It can then compel that an injured party be made whole. By agreeing to arbitration, parties indicate that they have fully agreed to internalize the cost of non-compliance at the outset. This, in turn, does in fact tie the committing party to its word because it no longer has the ability freely to change its mind. It is thus stuck.

[84] Sourgens, 'Climate Commons Law: The Transformative Force of the Paris Agreement', (2017) 50 NYU Journal of International Law & Politics 885.

[85] ICC Case No 5485, award (18 August 1987), ¶ 42, available at https://www.trans-lex.org/205485, last accessed 10 January 2025.

[86] O'Flaherty, 'Ubi Jus Ibi Remedium', (1999) 45 Loyola Law Review 527, 531.

[87] *See* section 9.2.

[88] Gallagher et al, '2021 International Arbitration Survey: Adapting Arbitration to a Changing World', (2021) Queen Mary University of London/White & Case, https://www.whitecase.com/publications/insight/2021-international-arbitration-survey, last accessed 10 January 2025.

[89] Reisman (n 46).

[90] Paulsson (n 43).

International arbitration has a further systemic benefit. With each decision, it provides greater clarity as to how parties can assign risks and what the scope of their commitments is. It thus provides data points to assess the strength and meaning of future commitments.[91] This means that with each decision, the stability of the international commitment edifice should strengthen because we know more and thus can insist on a different structure or formulation to protect our own rights and interests. 'Trust but verify' now has a different quality because we know what we get when verification comes up short. We also know what coming up short means. We therefore are better prepared to make future commitments.

Still, critical areas of state-to-state energy relationships do not benefit from such dispute resolution as a backstop for verification. For instance, while the UN Charter codifies a prohibition against the unilateral use of force except in cases of self-defence, in most instances states do not consent to the resolution of disputes.[92] The rule looks like a mandatory treaty commitment.[93] Yet, there is no ready recourse in case of breach. Further, even if there were, the means to enforce an international judgment or arbitral award against a party deemed to have used force unlawfully are comparatively limited. Such promises are less valuable as commitments even though they are part of international law. They are enforced only through diplomatic means—diplomatic means that are frequently deployed to meet realpolitik needs. There are thus critical gaps in the thin international rule of law.

These gaps are not fatal. They rather are 'offshore zones' of weaker legal organization.[94] So long as international stakeholders can understand how states actually conduct themselves when they make certain kinds of promises without dispute resolution, they can understand that some conduct in fact is a breach of an important legal norm. This understanding does not defeat the thin rule of law. So long as areas of likely breaches can be isolated and the kind of breaches and their triggers predictably identified, commitments can readily be understood, albeit in a discounted fashion. Here, reliance will look different. It will include the risk of breach in its planning and build redundancies around it. Cooperation will be shallower than it might otherwise be. Yet, it does not go away—in part because the absence of dispute resolution commitments already indicates that such putative commitments, while not worthless, are certainly worth less than commitments with binding dispute resolution mechanisms in place.

The key to avoiding destabilizing outcomes, therefore, must be both evasive and proactive. Energy policy-making must be evasive in the sense of avoiding predictable triggers for critical breaches of international legal obligations such as the use

[91] *See* Klaus-Peter Berger, *The Creeping Codification of the New Lex Mercatoria* (2nd edn, Kluwer 2010).

[92] *See* UN Charter, arts 2(4), 51.

[93] *Ibid.*

[94] *See* Reisman (n 55).

of force. Energy policy and project choices that heighten essential security concerns of affected states are not worth the geostrategic dislocation they may cause.

For example, the Nord Stream and Nord Stream 2 pipelines increased geopolitical risk in Central and Eastern Europe by upsetting the strategic balance between Russia, Ukraine, and Germany. I discussed the economic and energy incentives that informed Germany's energy policy in favour of Russian gas imports in Chapter 3.[95] Germany required an inexpensive feedstock to complement its investment in renewable energy.[96] Russian pipeline gas was a natural choice. Germany also pursued a (hesitant) policy of moving Ukraine closer into the European orbit (and away from Russia) at the same time.[97]

These two policies were in tension with one another. German energy policy created realpolitik vulnerabilities by assigning Russian gas a central role in the functioning of the German energy system.[98] At the same time, German foreign policy of bringing Ukraine closer to the EU was read as a realpolitik threat to Russia's essential security interests in the region.[99] This threat became acute after the 'Euromaidan' in 2014.[100] The 'Euromaidan' was a movement to protest against Ukrainian president Yanukovych's decision not to enter into a trade agreement with the EU and pivoting towards Russia instead.[101] The Euromaidan culminated in a power-sharing agreement between the protesters and President Yanukovych brokered with EU and Russian involvement (though, auspiciously, not signed by the Russian representative).[102] Within twenty-four hours, President Yanukovych fled the country.[103] Russia now apparently saw a national security threat to its

[95] *See* sections 3.3–3.4.

[96] *See* Mormann, Reicher, & Hanna, 'A Tale of Three Markets: Comparing Renewable Energy Experiences of California, Texas, and Germany', (2016) Stanford Environmental Law Journal 55 (discussing the need for fast-ramping, easy to dispatch power to balance German electricity demand); Sabadus, 'Putin's Energy Weapon: Europe Must Be Ready for Russian Gas Blackmail', (8 July 2022) Atlantic Council, https://www.atlanticcouncil.org/blogs/ukrainealert/putins-energy-weapon-europe-must-be-ready-for-russian-gas-blackmail/, last accessed 22 January 2025.

[97] Contemporaneous reports noted the tension between Ukrainian integration into the EU and the German Russia policy, thus highlighting the fact that the ongoing EU–Ukraine negotiations were seen within Germany as a geostrategic choice. Germany arguably ended up sitting between both seats. Yet, from a Russian perspective, the choice by Germany to proceed knowing of the tension would not have been de-escalatory. *See* Pöhle, 'Germany's Ukraine Problem', (19 December 2013) Deutsche Welle, https://www.dw.com/en/german-foreign-minister-tackles-ukraine-quandary/a-17309710, last accessed 22 July 2025.

[98] Sabadus (n 96).

[99] *See* Walker, 'Ukraine's EU Trade Deal Will Be Catastrophic, Says Russia', (22 September 2013) Guardian, https://www.theguardian.com/world/2013/sep/22/ukraine-european-union-trade-russia, last accessed 22 January 2025.

[100] Shelest, 'Ukraine's Euromaidan: Questions from the (R)evolution', (21 February 2014) NATO Defense College Research Report.

[101] Diuk, 'EUROMAIDAN: Ukraine's Self-Organizing Revolution', (March/April 2014) 176 World Affairs 9.

[102] Higgins & Kramer, 'Ukraine Has Deal, but Both Russia and Protesters Appear Wary', (21 February 2014) New York Times, https://www.nytimes.com/2014/02/22/world/europe/ukraine.html, last accessed 22 January 2025.

[103] Higgins & Kramer, 'Archrival Is Freed as Ukraine Leader Flees', (22 February 2014) New York Times, https://www.nytimes.com/2014/02/23/world/europe/ukraine.html, last accessed 22 January 2025.

Black Sea Fleet base in Crimea and moved to secure Crimea by military force.[104] This, in turn, led to Western rebukes.[105]

The geostrategic incentives facilitated escalation by appearing to present an acute national security threat to Russia in Ukraine from Germany and Europe at the same time as creating a significant energy dependence by Germany and Europe on Russia. Energy policy did not structure around this tension but rather structured into it. It did so due to a continued belief that energy engagement could continue in the tradition of German *Ostpolitik* engagement with the USSR during the Cold War to de-escalate tensions in the late 2000s and 2010s with Russia.[106] As German hesitation in 2013 should already have signalled, *Ostpolitik* energy policy approaches only functioned when they are combined with transparently de-escalatory foreign policy.[107] Here, it did not. Instead, *Ostpolitk*-style energy policy unintentionally increased tensions by providing realpolitik tools to cow a perceived adversary.

Energy policy-making must also be proactive. It must look to support a global energy constellation that moves away from legal 'offshore zones' and towards more firmly established legal 'islands' with a far more well-developed organization with significantly more robust authority structures and dispute resolution mechanisms.[108] Such energy policy-making looks to finance and build value chains that assist in de-escalating essential security concerns. Building a robust market for liquified natural gas is one such example. Liquified natural gas could step in in times of energy crises—whether it was the Fukushima Daiichi accident or Russia's invasion of Ukraine—because there was in fact a robust legal landscape for the global LNG trade.[109] This legal landscape included price reopening agreements in long-term supply agreements that allowed the development of a gas market autonomous of oil.[110] These price reopeners, importantly, were enforceable and enforced

[104] 'Putin Says He Decided to Take Crimea Just Hours after Yanukovych's Ouster', (9 March 2015) Eurasianet, https://eurasianet.org/putin-says-he-decided-to-take-crimea-just-hours-after-yanukovychs-ouster, last accessed 22 January 2025; Kononczuk, 'Russia's Real Aims in Crimea', (13 March 2014) Carnegie Endowment for Peace, https://carnegieendowment.org/research/2014/03/russias-real-aims-in-crimea?lang=en, last accessed 22 January 2025. While Kononczuk generally ascribes motives to influence the outcome of Ukrainian constitutional arrangements after the Maidan, he notes the special place of Sevastopol in Russia's self-understanding.

[105] *See* Oona Hathaway & Scott Shapiro, *The Internationalists: How a Radical Plan to Outlaw War Remade the World* (Simon & Schuster 2017) 309–11, 390–94.

[106] *See* Stephen G Gross, *Energy and Power, Germany in the Age of Oil, Atoms and Climate Change* (Oxford University Press 2023).

[107] *See* Pöhle (n 97).

[108] *See* Reisman (n 55).

[109] Yep & Foo, 'How the Fukushima Crisis led to a Revolution in LNG Trading', (11 March 2021) S&P Global, https://www.spglobal.com/commodity-insights/en/news-research/blog/lng/031121-fukushima-crisis-japan-lng-trading-revolution-jkm, last accessed 7 January 2025; Pye et al, 'The Global Implications of a Russian Gas Pivot to Asia', (2025) 16 Nature Communications 386.

[110] Anway et al, 'The Evolution of Natural Gas Price Review Arbitrations', in *The Guide to Energy Arbitrations* (6th edn, 24 May 2024), https://globalarbitrationreview.com/guide/the-guide-energy-arbitrations/sixth-edition/article/the-evolution-of-natural-gas-price-review-arbitrations, last accessed 10 January 2025.

through international arbitration.[111] This web of transactions helped to diversify global gas supplies.[112] It further moved them to a place of greater certainty purely by means of legal statecraft, and created predictability where none existed before.

In sum, dispute resolution is an important component of the thin rule of law. International arbitration provides a key guarantee for its implementability. Yet, simply including an arbitration clause in core project documents is insufficient. Dispute resolution is not universal. There are many important areas in which dispute resolution is sparse. The task of global energy policy and dealmaking is to de-risk global energy value chains by moving more and more volume towards balanced, comparatively 'safe' trading structures that avoid geopolitical flashpoints and secure core transaction channels through international arbitration mechanisms.

This strategy is plainly feasible. The arbitral infrastructure exists. Integrating supply chains into a comparatively lower risk world energy order is possible. One can structure transactions so as to render potential points of disagreement more plainly justiciable by integrating potentially problematic projects in a broader, geopolitically innocuous market. Here, dispute resolution can help create certainty. It can create trust without also sparking unintended geopolitical conflict. Policy-making and business can work together to achieve this goal. To do so, they must work with a keen eye to the legal tools available to verify and enforce precommitments in the energy space. Yet, existing realpolitik answers to energy insecurities amply suffice to achieve this aim. Trust but verify requires skill. It does not require impossible feats of clairvoyance.

9.3(c) The Spectre of a Vicious Lawless Cycle

Even as the thin rule of law promises to be an effective backstop for the other institutions and processes I have discussed in this third part of the book, its success in helping to order global energy governance is not a foregone conclusion. A prudent employment of the thin rule of law ties energy governance to the firm 'islands' of international lawfulness—the areas of international and transnational law that dependably deliver predictable decisions and thus increase the value of commitments about energy.[113] An imprudent employment of the thin rule of law becomes lost at sea in the 'offshore' zones of international lawfulness. Rather than being evasive and proactive, such a course is foolhardy and indecisive, thus increasing the risks of decay in the thin rule of law. This decay holds within it a spectre of lawlessness.

[111] *Ibid.*
[112] Yep & Foo (n 109); Pye (n 109).
[113] *See* Reisman (n 55).

Before I outline how such lawlessness can engage a reverse vicious cycle fuelling tragedies of the commons and anticommons in energy governance, I need to define what I mean by lawlessness. There is a school of thought that denies that such a thing as lawlessness actually exists in its own right.[114] Certainly, the thinking goes, there is such a thing as an absence of the predictable application of the rule of law in a particular problem field.[115] But this is simply a relative absence that can be overcome by means of creative and insightful lawyering.[116] In a way, this school of thought views the absence of a robust rule of law in a particular field like the absence of light in the dead of a rainy night. The night certainly is dark and may even thwart some forms of lighting like lighting a candle. Still, the darkness is not force in its own right. Darkness does not extinguish whatever light we bring to it. It simply currently lacks light. This can certainly be inconvenient and dangerous when trying to find one's way. Still, there is no such thing as 'darkness' or 'lawlessness'. There simply is a relative absence of light or law that can and must be overcome by human ingenuity.

This assessment is sadly too optimistic. Lawlessness does have a logic of its own. It is not the absence of law. It is a process in its own right that actively opposes the commitment processes supporting a thin rule of law. When we think of lawlessness as the absence of law, we make a critical error. We already espouse a legal perspective. Our starting point is that there is a process, which we think of as the rule of law, and that this process is lacking in a particular space. This perspective assumes too much. The thin rule of law as we have discussed it so far is a social process as well as a legal process. It is a process in which we can make precommitments because those precommitments lead to authoritative and controlling decisions in the future.[117] Lawlessness is problematic because it undercuts the very process by which precommitments make sense. Precommitments are simply hollow words rather than signals leading to authoritative, controlling, and predictable decisions in the future. What happens is the very opposite of what was promised. Promises are simply a ruse to take by force or guile whatever one can to secure a short-term advantage, no matter the long-term consequences. In this social process, we teach each other to do the very opposite of the thin rule of law. We offer something that looks like a commitment but actually functions as its very opposite. It is a 'simulacrum' or Trojan horse to overcome realpolitik defences to a direct attack.[118]

This kind of lawlessness exerts a kind of gravitational pull.[119] Just as the rule of law is self-reinforcing because we observe that predictable outcomes follow from

[114] *See ibid* at 20–21, 117–23, 170–91.
[115] *Ibid* at 190–91.
[116] *Ibid.*
[117] *See* Rattner (n 75); Ginsburg, Chernykh, & Elkins (n 75); Peters (n 75).
[118] *See* Jean Baudrillard, *Simulacres et Simulation* (Gallimard 1981); Virgil, 'Aeneid', *in Virgil, Eclogues, Georgics, Aeneid, Books 1–6* (trans GH Fairclough, rev GP Good, Harvard University Press, 1999), 318–32.
[119] Sourgens, 'The End of Law: The ISIL Case Study for Comprehensive Study of Lawlessness', (2015) 39 Fordham International Law Journal 355.

input, lawlessness is also self-reinforcing. We see that commitments are useful tools to blur the battlelines to one's advantage. What is more, what was once an inconceivable violation of legal commitments now becomes a foregone realpolitik conclusion. The successive discussions in US international legal circles whether and to what extent there is a qualitative difference between Russia's invasion of Ukraine in 2022 and the US's invasion of Iraq in 2003 and whether and to what extent a potential Russian acquisition of Crimea by force undermines the post-Second World War legal order are a testament to such a spiral.[120] The same process is already underway in the context of another key node for global energy value chains—the South China Sea. The social processes at work do not rework the law.[121] They are beginning to eviscerate it.

The thin rule of law can withstand this gravitation pull of lawlessness to a point. When 'offshore zones' of international law are clearly marked on international legal maps, one can circumnavigate and even reintegrate them.[122] When the logic of 'offshore zones' becomes a social force to rival the thin rule of law in the organization of key nodes in the global energy system, it is no longer possible to circumnavigate or integrate. Now, the rule of law and lawlessness enter into a direct competition with each other as rival social forces.[123] The thin rule of law is not well equipped to win this contest. The very tool it needs to be effective—the possibility of credible commitment—is being weaponized against it when too many Trojan horses advance on too many critical fronts.

In this situation, the underlying logic of selfish, short-term choice in the commons becomes again the most rational choice for each actor. If I cannot trust, I must take. Not only must I take to have. I must take to deprive my rival. I cannot trust supposed commitments so that we each take less. I therefore have to take more particularly whenever such a supposed commitment is made as it is only the opening move of a ruse to take in its own right. This process is a powerful accelerant to destroy in a short period of time what took decades to build. Its spectre is upon us today as a realistic governance principle for the global energy system. If it were to succeed, it would even overwhelm realpolitik responses as realpolitik could no longer distinguish between defection and cooperation. It would read cooperation as covert attack. In this energy war of all against all, no one could win.

[120] Hakimi & Brunk, 'Russia, Ukraine, and the Future World Order', (2022) 116 American Journal of International Law 687; Hakimi & Brunk, 'The Prohibition of Annexations and the Foundations of Modern International Law', (2024) 118 American Journal of International Law 417.

[121] Desierto, 'China's Maritime Law Enforcement Activities in the South China Sea', (2020) 96 International Law Studies 257.

[122] Reisman (n 55), at 20–21, 117–23, 170–91.

[123] Carl Schmitt, *Der Begriff des Politischen* (Duncker & Humblot 1932).

9.4 Keeping to Consensus

There currently is a public sentiment that the legal institutions holding up the so-called Washington consensus are deeply flawed. Current criticism dangerously overshoots its mark. Much of the criticism aims to discredit the precommitment mechanism needed for the thin rule of law to work. The criticism advances that international arbitration is a mode of dispute resolution that is a 'businessman's court' and as such biased against bona fide regulatory interventions in the energy market.[124] Implicitly, international energy arbitrations do not enforce the precommitments made by regulators to energy industry partners. They instead allegedly create liability for states or state entities in international arbitration out of nothing. In addition, this criticism argues that international investment protection treaties also are dangerous because these treaties make available an additional, non-contractual recourse to arbitration.[125] These investment tribunals then allegedly misuse treaty language that host states shall accord fair and equitable treatment to investments of protected foreign investors, who are nationals of their respective treaty counterparty.[126]

This criticism targets the very precommitment mechanism needed for the thin rule of law to function. It does not allege that some arbitral tribunals at times err. Rather, the criticism is more categorical. Arbitration is problematic because it systemically creates liability in the absence of a prior precommitment by a state or state-owned counterparty. According to the criticism, one cannot trust international arbitral awards because they are the result of an international arbitral process. This process allegedly invents precommitments.

This criticism of international arbitration plays into the themes of the cycle of lawlessness I discussed in the last section.[127] Something that looks like the rule of law is not. One therefore cannot trust the very legal institutions needed to protect the thin rule of law. If such an attack on the institutional framework holding up international energy governance is successful, it does not help regulators. It does not provide regulatory freedom. It instead deprives state regulators of the means to approach industry stakeholders in a manner that will in fact be treated as a credible precommitment. There will be no credible means to enforce a commitment that could induce an industry stakeholder to make an investment decision. Investors therefore will have to invest without such a credible precommitment. If they do so at all, investors and sponsors will naturally wish to receive significantly greater

[124] Gus van Harten, *Investment Treaty Protection and Public Law* (Oxford University Press 2008).

[125] Sen Warren, 'The Transpacific Partnership Clause Everyone Should Oppose', (25 February 2015) Washington Post, https://www.washingtonpost.com/opinions/kill-the-dispute-settlement-language-in-the-trans-pacific-partnership/2015/02/25/ec7705a2-bd1e-11e4-b274-e5209a3bc9a9_story.html, last accessed 11 January 2025.

[126] van Harten (n 124).

[127] *See* section 9.3(c).

risk premiums for such projects. This, in turn, means that fewer projects will be possible.

The institutions holding up the Washington consensus—international arbitration, international investment treaties, etc—are essential to the functioning of the thin rule of law. They are also inherently innocuous. International arbitration for the most part allows the parties to choose their arbitrators.[128] Most parties are represented by highly competent lawyers in international arbitration. The idea that all arbitrators are biased because they are arbitrators cannot hold water. The parties can choose whom they wish to serve as their arbitrator, so long as the person passes an independence and impartiality screen (eg one cannot appoint a state official as arbitrator in a dispute involving the same state).[129] The parties can therefore choose the expertise they deem most important. Arbitration outcomes are highly sensitive to inputs. The critique of international arbitration, including investment arbitration, as presented therefore cannot be correct. Arbitral decisions can be wrong. That said, this is not an inherent flaw of arbitration. It is simply a fact of life that in any process there will be better and worse outcomes. Arbitration is no exception.

The substantive attack of the Washington consensus also goes too far in other respects. The Washington consensus is a reaction to a particular moment in time. It arose as a reaction to a significant role of the state in the economy. In this context, it suggested that privatization and liberalization of the economy together with strong property protections and a fiscal regime friendly to investment would help generate needed economic growth to overcome structural problems in the world economy. The Washington consensus did not misdiagnose that there were such structural problems. The United States prior to the Washington consensus' emergence was stuck in stagnation and inflation (stagflation). At the same time, much of the Global South also pointed to structural inequities in the world economy harming Global South economies. European economies were similarly in a state of limbo. There thus were structural problems to which the Washington consensus legitimately responded.[130]

This is not to say that liberalization and privatization are always the answer. As the discussion of the missing 'money problem' made clear, the state has an important role to play in energy governance alongside the private sector.[131] The Washington consensus therefore is part of a broader process of balanced global

[128] *See* Arif Ali et al, *The International Arbitration Rulebook: A Guide to Arbitral Regimes* (Kluwer 2019).

[129] 'International Guidelines on Conflicts of Interest in International Arbitration', (25 May 2024) International Bar Association, https://www.ibanet.org/document?id=Guidelines-on-Conflicts-of-Interest-in-International-Arbitration-2024, last accessed 22 January 2025.

[130] Daunton (n 11). Daunton is a critic of the implementation of the Washington consensus. He does however outline that the consensus itself has significant internal variations and outlines the history to which it responds.

[131] *See* section 7.2.

economic and global energy balance. It does not have to prescribe a single best method of energy governance—nor indeed did it ever pretend to do so. Instead, the Washington consensus built the institutions necessary to support highly integrated global supply chains. These highly integrated global supply chains, in turn, increased productivity and the potential for human development. As I have argued in Chapter 8, we need to add to these value chains and broaden them, not abolish them, in order to meet the goals of international energy governance. If we hope to achieve this end, we need the institutions created by the Washington consensus.

At the same time, it is true that there exists a 'growth-only' strain within the Washington consensus.[132] As I have argued, this growth-only strain aims at the wrong end—growth rather than human development.[133] Yet, this observation, too, is one that comes from within the consensus. The World Bank is a core constitutive institution of the Washington consensus. The Bank looked to human development as much as to economic growth as part of its lending decisions historically. It also does so currently. In fact, the International Finance Corporation Performance standards embed development in core decision-making functions.[134] Again, this is not to say that the Bank is a perfect champion of human development at all times. It is just to say that the Washington consensus is indeed consistent with, rather than inimical to, a human development lens.

If we wish to make the thin rule of law work as a governance tool of the global energy system, we will need to build on the institutions that are central to the Washington consensus. Attacking them will undermine our ability to gain purchase for the thin rule of law. Ignoring them deprives us of expertise that was instrumental in building the very finance and value chain processes we now wish to improve.

This is not to say that the Washington consensus does not need reform. Any governance tool does as circumstances change. In the context of the Washington consensus, this reform must be to integrate additional perspectives in its decision-making matrices. It must begin to take onboard the different strains of legal commitments at the heart of the thick rule of law. It must take seriously the demands of the right to development.[135] In our context, this means it must take into account the fair distribution of benefits and burdens of energy growth. The reform of the consensus therefore should be internal and not external. It should look to remind the relevant actors of the ends of global energy governance. It is to embed them in a progressive realization of the global bond of belonging. This task, too, is inherently feasible, as the discussion throughout the book has hopefully shown.

[132] Daunton (n 11).
[133] *See* section 5.3.
[134] For a discussion, *see* Sourgens & Sempertegui (n 29), at 200–18.
[135] *See* Desierto (n 62).

9.5 Conclusion

Global energy governance without the rule of law is impossible. The rule of law protects our ability to make credible commitments. These credible commitments can slowly build the trust needed to avoid the wasteful and unreasonable use of global energy resources. As I have argued, the key to building such a rule of law is to begin in a thin rule of law. This thin rule of law looks to build flexible institutions that can verify that commitments have been kept and provide a flexible and neutral remedy in international arbitration in case they do not. Over time, this thin rule of law can in fact create the trust needed to support the development of global energy finance and global energy value chains. It helps to mitigate risks. This risk mitigation makes much of the growth needed in the global energy system to respond to the dual threats of energy poverty and climate change adaptation possible. As we build such a framework, the thin rule of law in fact can integrate a growing set of legal demands in its decision-making process. As it does so, it supports a slow switch to energy governance premised in a thick rule of law aiming at building a global energy order premised in a bond of belonging. This framework replicates almost all of the institutions of the current global energy law system. It refocuses these institutions in substance to better understand their respective roles in the governance of the global energy system.

PART IV

PERSPECTIVES

10
Systems and Choices

10.1 Introduction

This conclusion hopes to bring together the themes of this book one more time. The book has ranged the gamut from domestic to global energy governance. It has introduced ends and means. The question that remains to be answered one more time is—why should we care? How should we proceed? And what is our ultimate goal?

This chapter briefly draws together the answer to these three questions. It begins by introducing the three choices global energy governance permits: tragedy, realpolitik, or cooperative innovation. These three choices are particularly acute at the current point in time. Climate change presents unique challenges for energy governance. Not only that, but energy transition itself is becoming geopolitically contentious. The idea of an energy tragedy of the commons at this point in time is therefore not a hyperbole or hypothetical. It is a very real prospect. Seeing that other choices are available at this point in particular is practically relevant.

Noting these three choices is not enough. We need to find our paths away from the one that leads to the tragedy of the commons. As I have argued throughout the book, the beginning of this path is not one that asks for utopian levels of global trust. To the contrary, the beginning of any path to global energy governance is to look to vigilant realpolitik. This vigilant realpolitik must do more than simply formulate foreign policy. It must formulate a holistic domestic and global energy policy. Yet, as it does so, it can benefit from global cross-stabilization. This cross-stabilization requires effective means of precommitment. As we venture down the path of precommitment, we now have the option of leaning more firmly into its successes. This is the point where we need to structure to support global faith that cooperation will hold. Yet, even here, this structure is not utopian. It is practical. And it is largely built.

Finally, I will sketch why the effort and faith are worth it. Energy is critical to development. Energy cooperation that supports development empowers us. This empowerment is mutually beneficial. It is non-rivalrous and self-supporting. It propels human capabilities. It allows us to live flourishing lives. This is as good a 'why' as any a governance approach could hope to support. It is the 'why' of this book.

The overall theme of this book has been one to look to moderation. Extreme proposals are hardly ever solutions. Building coalitions, providing checks and

A Theory of Global Energy Governance. Frédéric Gilles Sourgens, Oxford University Press. © Frédéric Sourgens 2025.
DOI: 10.1093/9780198950325.003.0010

balances, stacking weights against counterweights, that is what makes most good solutions work. It means that we take a little from everyone. Yet, in taking a little from everyone, we need to know what it is that we are meant to build and support. In organizing our thinking around a bond of belonging to the global energy system, we can find such a measure of moderation—does our action strengthen the global energy system? Does it make it more responsive to our needs and more resilient in and sustainable to our environment? Moderation thus is moderation with a purpose. As such, it stands a chance of guiding us to solutions even when the voices of extremism are loud and temptations to heed them strong.

10.2 Three Choices

There are three choices we can make. The first of these choices does not really feel like a choice. It is action out of constraint. That action is to give in to misaligned incentives and play out the tragedy of the commons and anticommons. The second choice is to refuse to accept constraint. Instead, this second choice looks shrewdly for a way out of an impasse by acting solely for one's own interest and survival. This choice brings the predictability of realpolitik. There is security. Yet, there is also much sacrificed in the name of security. Finally, we have a third choice. That third choice is to cooperate in a global energy commons governed by a bond of belonging. This path is risky because it creates vulnerabilities to those who seek to take advantage, free ride, and coopt. Yet, it is also the path that ultimately gets us the greatest return on our energy resources. It is innovative. It is growth-oriented. It is empowering.

I do not need to say much about the first choice. It is not a choice. It is an accident. It is an abdication of agency as much as it is a despair of invention. The first choice brings us back to Hardin's commons and Heller's anticommons. The global energy system is a shared space. It is shared at the points where national energy systems interconnect through the value chains that power energy systems everywhere. These value chains are the conveyer belts that bring us the inputs to make all of currently commercial energy approaches work. These value chains have to rely on inputs from many places around the world and thus connect us together, whether we want to be connected or not.

The Hardin-Heller world is dystopian. In this world, we are perfectly aware that current use patterns are unreasonable—they erode the resource base we need to make the global energy system work. They destroy the real economy as well as the energy system. Still, the problem is that we have no power to stop the use patterns on our own. If we stop, we just harm ourselves. We do not make the world better for anyone. We just make it worse. Therefore, we should not even try. We should take all we can and give in to the fact that there was nothing to be done.

Climate change is an excellent illustration of this Hardin-Heller world. Addressing climate change is a collective action problem. It is difficult to overcome because it seems to hit at the heart of the global energy system: using affordable energy is exacerbating climate change. If I address climate change, I lose productivity. I am no longer competitive. My adversaries gladly relocate my businesses with the lure of cheaper energy. This cheaper energy is more greenhouse gas intensive than it was before I started working on addressing climate change. My action to address climate change sped it up and impoverished me. So I lean into existing energy systems to the hilt to get us much as I can while I can get it. In the end, I do not even try to act. I simply surrender to circumstance.

Hardin and Heller painted this world to dissuade us from living in it. It is therefore reasonably straightforward that we should under no circumstances fall into patterns that lead to it. Still, incentive structures mean that it is the easiest world to live in. It is the default world. Everything else takes skill and effort. Hardin's and Heller's world is where we end up if we do not even try. It is also where we end up if we fail and become discouraged. Still, because it is the world we inhabit if we fail to act, it is the most certain of the three. It is the world in which our sole financial plan in life is to win the lottery and yet we do not buy a ticket.

Luckily, we have other choices. We can in fact choose to act. We can brave adversity.

The second choice is to act to help myself and only myself. This is Machiavelli's world (the Machiavelli of the Prince, not the Discourses). In this world, I do everything to protect myself. The spring of self-preservation gets me to try again and again to escape the consequences of Hardin and Heller world. I know that falling into the default position means that my own survival is threatened. As that is the worst of all outcomes, I will work together to avoid this fate. Still, I trust no one. Also, when no one is looking, I will cheat every time to gain every advantage I can get. In this world, I believe that only the strongest survive. I therefore will do everything I can to weaken others and strengthen myself.

John D Rockefeller, the businessman, is an excellent illustration of this approach. Rockefeller built an oil empire by learning how to cooperate with others. Every time Rockefeller cooperated, though, he used the opportunity to weaken his competitors. He worked with the railways to move his oil. Part of the agreement was that every barrel of oil transported by his competitors on the railways was subject to an additional fee that went to him. He therefore made it more expensive for his competitors to move oil and also profited from the surcharge. There was cooperation. This cooperation was a relentless drive to concentrate market power.

In this world, all stakeholders have better learnt how to answer a Rockefeller like a Rockefeller. Everyone will act with distrust. Yet, everyone will also look for opportunities to work together to help themselves. This cooperation plays out in a framework of constant vigilance and verification to avoid the ruse I expect. Still, over time we can in fact come to work according to rules of the game. These rules of the game allow us to take some advantage. Yet, if all sides know the rules and everyone works diligently, the rules work to a dynamic equilibrium. Everyone gets to escape from Hardin-Heller world. Escape still has a price. There is a lot we simply cannot do because we cannot trust enough that it will work to our own advantage. Every time this happens, our rule is to forego an opportunity so as to prevent my partner from gaining a relative advantage. It does not matter whether I can be certain that I will be better off; I need to make sure that everything I do maintains my relative standing in the community. Better off is only ever better off in comparison to my peers with one exception. That one exception is survival.

Machiavelli's world is not a world we would dream to inhabit. It is harsh. It is unforgiving. Still, as perilous as it is, it is a world that will help us survive so long as we are adept at playing by the rules. The rules, luckily, are learnable. Just as helpfully, the rules are set up for the strong to swallow the weak. The strong know the rules. So there is a mechanism that keeps the collective on a path to stay out of Hardin-Heller world. The system can keep functioning even in the face of many who blunder. Blunder is simply a step by the powerful towards greater concentration of power. The system works.

The third choice is to act for myself and for my community. This world is Athens before the Plague or Rome before Octavian. In this world, we recognize that we are connected by a bond of belonging. I know that flourishing is only possible in my community. For my community to do well, I must do well. The inverse is also true: I can only flourish if my community thrives. So I have to band together with people like me to protect my commonwealth. When I do so, I am assured of their work for common good, as well. In this world, we can set the foundations for an order premised in innovation and growth that solves problems by thinking about them harder and engineering a solution to overcome them. In this world, we can in fact build what we plan because we can work together to deliver each of the pieces we need for our invention. Our ingenuity can turn seemingly barren landscapes into the backbone of a national economy and culture (think the Athenian farm or contemporary breakthrough energy projects) and build complex infrastructure to overcome resource scarcities (think aqueducts or transmission networks).

The deployment of fracking and horizontal drilling by independent oil companies in the Barnett Shale in Texas and its adoption in the Marcellus Shale in Pennsylvania and Ohio, the Bakken in North Dakota, the Permian Basin in Texas and New Mexico, and beyond is one example of this model. Small companies used their superior knowledge of geology and took a risk on marginal resources. They could take this risk because they could rely on partners who could provide much of the equipment and many of the services needed to attempt to develop oil and gas resources in this way. These companies were fiercely competitive with each other. Yet, they also worked with an ethos so strong that the law happily defers to it—good oilfield practices. In doing so, they have inverted the energy world to turn the US from an oil and gas importer to a leading oil and gas exporter. In essence, they have brought on a new global energy order. Their work has laid the groundwork for next generation geothermal energy projects and generated electricity from geological heat with a closed loop steam-turbine system.

Their example stacks energy technologies rather than choosing between them. The Texas power infrastructure supporting oil and gas development is relying heavily on wind and solar power generation. One of the largest oil producers in the Permian Basin is a leading innovator in direct CO_2 capture. US natural gas is a critical fuel to balance global renewable energy markets with fast-ramping, easy to dispatch electricity. It is an example of an integrated, competitive, growth-oriented, 'all of the above' energy transition energy community.

This is the world I want to inhabit. It is about human capability. It is about innovation. It is about delivering needed energy resources to improve living conditions. Just as importantly, it is about working in community—my community. It is the sense of belonging that empowers me and helps me empower my peers. We work our way out of Hardin-Heller world by inverting Hardin-Heller world. The fear of others that paralysed us becomes the joy of the teamwork that empowers us.

10.3 Two Paths

Global energy governance can thus take two paths. The first path is to choose realpolitik. At its heart, the realpolitik path is about preserving energy agency. Preserving energy agency in the first place is to avoid becoming dependent for critical inputs to one's own national energy system on a single set of suppliers over whom one does not have ultimate control. The perhaps best way of avoiding such dependence is to subsume strategic parts of energy value chains under one's own national control. Success at such a policy means that one is not subject to foreign domination. Rather, one is able to exercise global power oneself.

In a complex energy world, this exercise of power should only ever be partial. For a state to have complete energy control would require that state to gain strategic control over a critical part of energy value chains for each part of the energy mix. Allowing a state to gain such a position would in its own right amount to a critical failure in realpolitik by its peers. This is not to say that states will not each attempt to gain such a strategic position in as large a number of energy value chains as possible. As multiple states do so, they will each naturally end up balancing out the efforts of the other. What results is a dynamic balance of power that is constantly tested by states as they seek to gain a position in energy value chains critical to their own energy agency.

A good exercise of energy realpolitik must integrate domestic and international energy policymaking into a single energy policy. States can capture control over critical links in energy value chains because domestic energy policies at the synergy stage of the energy cycle create openings for consolidation. This consolidation presents an opportunity to seize parts of the value chain by providing structural price incentives just as consolidation is beginning to take shape. Preventing such consolidation into lasting dominance over critical supplies by a geopolitical actor requires domestic energy policymaking that anticipates the global realpolitik incentives set by domestic energy policy. Global policymaking historically has been adept in doing so outside of moments of systemic crisis like the oil shocks of the 1970s. Energy policymaking in the 2020s again begins to internalize the lesson. Whether it will do so successfully—and permanently—remains to be seen.

Good energy realpolitik is ultimately cooperative. If the goal of realpolitik is to limit dominance by any one state or stakeholder over critical links in the energy value chain, we must deconcentrate those value chains. Deconcentration of value chains means that states and private stakeholders will need to cooperate to realize national energy policy goals, achieve a competitive return on investment, and continue to innovate in turn to improve energy policy outcomes and grow returns on investment. Such cooperation needs credible mechanisms to make and enforce precommitments. It therefore needs an international rule of law. This international thin rule of law functions best when energy value chains are integrated in a way that there is always a way practically to enforce precommitments without having to go to the home jurisdiction of the stakeholder against whom enforcement is sought. In that home jurisdiction, that stakeholder is more likely to receive a home court advantage. Globally integrated financial flows and supply chains reduce this risk by increasing the number of fora in which enforcement action is possible. Reducing the risk of enforcement increases the value of precommitments. Increasing the value of precommitments makes it more rational to cooperate more broadly. What is more, it means that one can use cooperation as a means to counterbalance potential breaches of precommitment in some relationships ahead of time by contracting around it.

The goal of a good realpolitik ultimately is to stabilize the dynamics of energy equilibria. Stabilizing energy equilibria provides greater energy security in its own right by providing greater predictability. This predictability can then feed in to reducing costs. This, in turn, makes energy more available domestically, thus leading to a potentially virtuous cycle. Global energy cooperation makes realpolitik sense if it helps to stabilize deconcentrated global energy relationships that make it difficult (if not impossible) for states to gain dominance over critical parts of any one value chain.

Once we have arrived at this point, energy governance paths fork. On the one hand, we continue with realpolitik and secure individual goals. On the other hand, we can use successful precommitment experiences to transform the aggregate of a myriad of individual international relationships in global value chains into a global energy community. We can make a governance switch from using global energy value chains to meet the demands of national energy systems (plural) to a true form of global energy governance (singular) that works to support national energy systems and brings a deeper benefit of integration and cooperation to solving common issues all energy stakeholders share with significantly greater efficiency than would be possible at the purely national stage. This path follows the logic of the bond of belonging.

The path of the bond of belonging does not require us to act radically differently from good realpolitik. The same precommitment devices that hold together realpolitik energy cooperation also hold together global governance according to the bond of belonging. We do not need to give up the security of realpolitik governance. Instead, this second path simply uses a mechanism that has been helpful in bringing about a modicum of stability to otherwise volatile realpolitik exchange more frequently and more intensely. It understands that as we create a global energy system cooperatively, we get more out of it if we act to improve the global system in its own right. Improving the global system in its own right means to benefit from the opportunities it provides by bringing more innovators to conceiving of critical energy problems and solving them and bringing more resources to bear to implement those solutions without falling into the trap of value chain concentration.

Obviously, this mode of energy governance must provide a greater return to each participant than not participating. The growth in innovation we can expect, as well as the additional material resources we can bring to bear. The dynamics of innovation and energy diffusion therefore should work in favour of such a result.

In addition, this mode of energy governance cannot itself lead to a loss of energy autonomy by any participant. It cannot grant ultimate decision-making authority to a global proto-energy regulator or 'globalist cabal'. It also cannot provide an opportunity for one state to capture critical parts of energy value chains while everyone else lets their guard down. The mechanism of the bond of belonging should prevent both results. The key to greater cooperation through stronger precommitment is that it aims at the progressive deconcentration and diversification of energy value chains. This, in turn, means that energy decision-making in principle is actively devolved to a greater group of stakeholders. The bond of belonging uses cooperation as an anti-elitist device by lowering barriers to entry into key parts of the energy value chain by making available a specialized group of partners to whom one can out-source critical functions that otherwise could only be fulfilled in a fully vertically integrated enterprise (setting up a competitive vertically integrated enterprise, needless to say, is significantly more capital intensive, thus increasing barriers to entry). It also looks to distribute those value chains in more places around the world. This means that it is on the whole more difficult to capture.

The bond of belonging looks to a networked and flat mode of global energy governance. In this flat mode of energy governance, each participant has a sense of belonging to the whole and acts for the good of the whole. Still, each participant is its own master. It has full agency and acts independently within the network. It builds a thick rule of law—a community held together by law—because each can see an equal opportunity to realize their own ends and their own flourishing.

10.4 One Goal

No matter the path, energy governance ultimately has one overarching goal. That goal is to provide the means to as many people as possible to realize human flourishing. Energy is critical to every human capability we need to thrive. Energy is the core ingredient to be more productive with less physical effort. It is the critical substitution tool that frees us up to be more productive while also having greater creative agency. The more we deliver energy, the more we empower people. The more we empower people, the more they have the ability to live a dignified, fulfilled, and flourishing life.

One can express this goal in different terms. One way to say the same thing is that the goal of energy governance is human development. Human development is about securing the resources, institutions, and relationships to improve not just the physical wellbeing of members of society. Human development similarly is about improving agency. It is about giving greater ability to more people to guide their own lives according to their own designs. It is about giving them a sense that their own decisions matter to who they are and how they are in the world. Energy is critical to this because of what it can do to limit chores that would otherwise require long and hard labour, for instance through in-home food refrigeration, to increase the ability to connect to the outside world through mobile phones and internet access, and to learn and exchange ideas with a global community receptive to their inputs.

Beyond this, energy is responsible for inputs to almost every other 'security'—food security, water security, shelter, etc. A realpolitik view is about increasing national security. National security sounds like a geostrategic question. It obviously is that. Yet, it is also about these securities. These securities are critical to limiting the potential for national dependence. The more people have basic securities, the less likely they are to grant outsized concessions to foreign powers in exchange for basic goods and services. Realpolitik is therefore about providing a nationally independent means to secure this goods and services through equal access to the global market—including a global energy market permitting such entry. Human development and energy realpolitik are thus not two opposite extremes on a governance scale. They are flipsides of the same coin.

One could also say that such governance is about the progressive realization of human rights. Human development is itself a human right. This human right, in turn, is not separate and distinct from other rights. Rather, it looks to their collective fulfilment and realization. Development is what happens when all rights are appropriately progressively realized. Development can only happen if there is international cooperation. This international cooperation means that we must work together to provide the means (financial, technical, and physical) for development to societies currently still at the margins. We must act as catalysts to overcome the obstacles they face to development. This role of catalyst means that once the reaction is fully underway, we do not need to continue to support it externally. Rather, we now get the return benefit of a partner who in turn supports the global system on which we all draw.

Energy is a critical catalyst. The human rights discourse therefore should see energy and energy access as perhaps the key component to realizing development more broadly. Yet, if we look at development in this way, we have difficulty remaining in a realpolitik frame. We would cooperate to be a catalyst not simply because it makes us better off. (It does make us better off in the long run by deconcentrating value chains in the future.) Instead, we would cooperate because we act for the good of a shared community as well. We recognize that we ought to be a catalyst not just because it makes us better off. We ought to be a catalyst because we belong together and our own development is critically tied together. Nowhere is this truer than in the global energy system.

10.5 Conclusion

In this book, I have made a case for global energy governance that is sensitive to the nature of the global energy system. I have argued that this global energy system must be understood in light of its constituent national energy systems and the value chains that hold them together. I have therefore argued that there is no such thing as 'national' energy policy and 'global' energy policy. Both are the same thing because both are constituted by the other. This has significant repercussions for how we approach energy governance.

This approach to energy governance must follow the logic of how energy works. It must follow the internal logic of energy systems. This internal logic, on the one hand, showed us that there is a basic energy cycle. This energy cycle binds together the forces of capital, innovation, and regulation. Capital looks for returns. Innovation can yield such returns when it addresses a critical problem limiting how we can produce and consume energy. When we solve this problem, we become exponentially more productive—this, in turn, means that capital can achieve exponentially greater returns. Yet, it can do so only in the context of a marketplace for the new energy approach. This new marketplace can only exist with the state—with regulation setting up how the marketplace functions. The energy cycle then follows the path of innovation as its first successful diffusion sets off a frenzy that overexpands in core energy markets, building on the early success of first adopters. Frenzy leads to hangovers. In these hangovers, we need to right-size incentives in the marketplace to deliver needed energy at an appropriate price. Once the market is right-sized, we get to the full diffusion of the energy paradigm but do so at the cost of ever decreasing returns as we have found every efficiency to exploit in its delivery. Consequently, we must look for the next exponential gain to fund and the cycle begins again.

The overarching point I hope my reader takes away from this book is that energy governance (global or domestic) tries to stabilize energy cycles. Stabilizing energy cycles is meant to achieve something. It provides progressively cheaper, more resilient, and sustainable energy to a growing number of people. Stabilizing energy cycles stands in a line of other similar endeavours. For example, global monetary policy is about the stabilization of monetary and economic cycles. It does so to support stable and fair global economic growth. A more distant example is the idea of stabilizing constitutional cycles by means of good constitutional government.

My argument throughout the book was that both the global energy system and national energy systems function like commons. I have sketched that this commons can best be governed by means of concerted action held together by a bond of belonging. This bond of belonging provided the through line between national energy systems and the global energy system. It also explained the relationship between regulators, innovators, and finance in the progression of domestic energy cycles. In the end, I hope that this conception of the bond of belonging is both descriptively and normatively helpful in addressing the challenges of the current climate transition. Descriptively, my hope is that the bond of belonging makes visible relationships that have as of yet only been addressed piecemeal rather than as a whole. By describing the relevant governance processes as inherently interconnected, my hope is that we can gain a stronger understanding of where and why governance responses succeed or fail. Normatively, I hope that the bond of belonging provides a yardstick to address the deep distributive challenges energy policy will have to address, particularly at the current moment in time. This normative yardstick is not intended as absolute. Rather, it is intended as a means to improve upon existing metrics of global realpolitik. It thus is not utopian or abstract. Instead, the goal is to provide a means to approximate policies that can bring greater stability to the global energy system. Greater stability means moderation. Greater stability means increasing the beneficiaries from global energy flows. Greater stability means sharing the burdens of the energy system among more shoulders to give everyone a reason to buy in. This model of energy governance can help us not only to overcome the energy challenges of the middle of the twenty-first century. It is a model that helps us harness innovation, growth, and development to conceive of a world in which energy supports a world of prosperity through energy peace, energy abundance, and energy stewardship. This world is as realistic a prospect as the dystopian vision of climate collapse and war of all against all. All it takes to make it a reality is choice, action—agency. I hope this book has shown that such agency is always open to us. I also hope that it has shown that choosing it means choosing it together.

Select Bibliography

Aagard Todd S & Kleit Andrew, *Electricity Capacity Markets* (Cambridge University Press 2022).

Aagaard & Kleit, 'Too Much Is Never Enough: Constructing Energy Capacity Market Demand', (2022) 43 Energy Law Journal 79.

Abbott, '"Trust but Verify": The Production of Information in Arms Control Treaties and Other International Agreements', (1993) 26 Cornell International Law Journal 1.

Acemoglu Daron & Robinson James A, *The Narrow Corridor, States, Societies, and the Fate of Liberty* (Penguin 2019).

Adams, 'Economic Growth, Inequality, and Poverty, Findings from a New Dataset', (February 2003) World Bank Group, https://openknowledge.worldbank.org/server/api/core/bitstreams/fe3b85f2-bcc5-56bd-ba40-fdb450626f38/content, last accessed 6 October 2024.

Adams et al, 'Macroeconomic Policy and Poverty Reduction', (August 2001) International Monetary Fund, https://www.imf.org/external/pubs/ft/exrp/macropol/eng/, last accessed 6 October 2024.

Aghion Philippe, Antonin Céline, & Bunel Simon, *The Power of Creative Destruction, Economic Upheaval and the Wealth of Nations* (Harvard University Press 2021).

Ahdieh, 'The Visible Hand: Coordination Functions of the Regulatory State', (2010) 95 Minnesota Law Review 578.

Alderman, 'Investors Punish France Over Budget Turmoil', (2 December 2024) New York Times, https://www.nytimes.com/2024/12/02/business/frances-credit-rating.html#:~:text=France%20is%20in%20worse%20fiscal,the%20country's%20gross%20domestic%20product, last accessed 11 December 2024.

Alessandri & Gazzini, 'The Impact of Gas Supply Shocks in Europe', (25 July 2023) Center for Economic Policy Research, https://cepr.org/voxeu/columns/impact-gas-supply-shocks-europe, last accessed 4 May 2024.

Ali Arif et al, *The International Arbitration Rulebook: A Guide to Arbitral Regimes* (Kluwer 2019).

Alunni Andrea, *Innovation Finance and Technology Transfer: Funding Proof of Concept* (Routledge 2019).

Amiti et al, 'The Impact of the 2018 Tariffs on Prices and Welfare', (2019) 33 Journal of Economic Perspectives 187.

Al-Qahtani Ayed S, *World Oil Outlook 2045* (Organization of Petroleum Exporting Countries 2023).

Alston Philip & Goodman Ryan, *International Human Rights* (Oxford University Press 2013).

Alvarez YR et al, *Status and Trends in Spent Fuel and Radioactive Waste Management* (International Atomic Energy Agency 2022).

Anderson, 'Europe's Dependence on Russian Natural Gas: Perspectives and Recommendations for a Long-term Strategy', (September 2008) George C Marshall European Center for Security Studies, https://www.marshallcenter.org/en/publications/occasional-papers/europes-dependence-russian-natural-gas-perspectives-and-recommendations-long-term-strategy-0, last accessed 18 August 2024.

Anderson Owen L et al, *Oil and Gas Law and Taxation* (West Academic 2017).

Anderson Owen L et al, *International Petroleum Law and Transactions* (Rocky Mountain Mineral Law Foundation 2020).

André et al, 'Rising Energy Prices and Productivity: Short-Run Pain, Long-Term Gain?', (23 May 2023) Organisation for Economic Co-operation and Development Economics Working Paper No 1755, https://one.oecd.org/document/ECO/WKP(2023)8/en/pdf#:~:text=The%20estimates%20suggest%20that%20a,gains%20in%20the%20medium%20term, last accessed 7 October 2024.

Andruleit et al, 'Reserves, Resources and Availability of Energy Resources' at 37–38, (December 2013) German Federal Institute for Geosciences and Natural Resources (BGR), https://www.bgr.bund.de/EN/Themen/Energie/Downloads/energiestudie_2013_en.pdf;jsessionid=17D704B1546E57D7441A22581077EE5B.internet012?__blob=publicationFile&v=2, last accessed 16 September 2024.

Anghie Antony, *Imperialism, Sovereignty and the Making of International Law* (Cambridge University Press 2004).

Annas Julia, *Intelligent Virtue* (Oxford University Press 2011).

Anway et al, 'The Evolution of Natural Gas Price Review Arbitrations', *in The Guide to Energy Arbitrations* (6th edn, 24 May 2024), https://globalarbitrationreview.com/guide/the-guide-energy-arbitrations/sixth-edition/article/the-evolution-of-natural-gas-price-review-arbitrations, last accessed 10 January 2025.

Appelbaum Binyamin, *The Economists' Hour, False Prophets, Free Markets, and the Fracture of Society* (Little, Brown & Co 2019).

Arango & Kamin, '"Will Pay Any Amount": Private Firefighters Are in Demand in L.A.', (12 January 2025) New York Times, https://www.nytimes.com/2025/01/12/us/private-firefighters-la-wildfires.html, last accessed 21 January 2025.

Arato, Claussen & Langford, 'The Investor-State Dispute Settlement Reform Process: Design, Dilemmas and Discontents', (2023) 14 Journal of International Dispute Settlement 127.

Aristotle, 'Nicomachean Ethics', *in The Complete Works of Aristotle, The Revised Oxford Translation* (Jonathan Barnes ed, WD Ross & JO Urmson trans, Princeton University Press 1984) 1729.

Aristotle, *Politics: Book 1, in The Complete Works of Aristotle: The Revised Oxford Translation* (Jonathan Barnes ed, Princeton University Press, 1984) 1986.

Asmelash, 'The First Ten Years of WTO Jurisprudence on Renewable Energy Support: Has the Dust Settled Yet?', (2022) 21 World Trade Review 455.

Astor, 'As Gas Prices Went Up, So Did the Hunt for Electric Vehicles', (8 April 2022) New York Times, https://www.nytimes.com/2022/04/08/climate/gas-prices-electric-vehicles.html#:~:text=As%20Gas%20Prices%20Went%20Up,Vehicles%20%2D%20The%20New%20York%20Times, last accessed 20 January 2025.

Atkins et al, 'Rekindling US Productivity for a New Era', (16 February 2023) McKinsey Global Institute, https://www.mckinsey.com/mgi/our-research/rekindling-us-productivity-for-a-new-era, last accessed 6 October 2024.

Axelrod Robert, *The Evolution of Cooperation* (Basic Books 1984).

Badger et al, 'They Used to Be Ahead in the American Economy. Now They've Fallen Behind', (26 October 2024) New York Times, https://www.nytimes.com/interactive/2024/10/26/upshot/census-relative-income.html, last accessed 29 October 2024.

Bahar et al, 'Special Report on Solar PV Global Supply Chains', (August 2022) International Energy Agency, https://iea.blob.core.windows.net/assets/d2ee601d-6b1a-4cd2-a0e8-db02dc64332c/SpecialReportonSolarPVGlobalSupplyChains.pdf, last accessed 7 January 2025.

Bahar, 'Renewables 2023: Analysis and Forecast to 2028', (January 2024) International Energy Agency, https://iea.blob.core.windows.net/assets/96d66a8b-d502-476b-ba94-54ffda84cf72/Renewables_2023.pdf, last accessed 7 January 2025.

Balkin, 'Deconstructive Practice and Legal Theory', (1987) 96 Yale Law Journal 743.

Balmaceda Margarita, *Russian Energy Chains: The Remaking of Technopolitics from Siberia to Ukraine to the European Union* (Columbia University Press 2021).

Baker, 'U.S. Renewables M&A: A Cautious Road to Recovery?', (4 November 2024) White & Case, https://mergers.whitecase.com/highlights/us-renewables-ma-a-cautious-road-to-recovery#!, last accessed 22 January 2025.

Bane, 'Making Methane from CO2: Carbon Capture Grows More Affordable', (2 September 2021) U.S. Department of Energy Pacific Northwest National Laboratory, https://www.pnnl.gov/news-media/making-methane-co2-carbon-capture-grows-more-affordable, last accessed 6 December 2024.

Banerjee Abhijit & Duflo Ester, *Good Economics for Hard Times* (Public Affairs 2019).

Barry & Winfield, 'As Summer Breezes Fade, Sweltering Europeans Give Air Conditioning a Skeptical Embrace', (2 August 2023) Associated Press, https://apnews.com/article/air-conditioning-ac-extreme-heat-europe-3f1b8ad9275297da02ae137a72b77a8d, last accessed 11 December 2024.

Bartlett Robert, *The Making of Europe: Conquest, Colonization, and Cultural Change 950-1350* (Princeton University Press 1993).

Baudrillard Jean, *Simulacres et Simulation* (Gallimard 1981).

Berger Klaus-Peter, *The Creeping Codification of the New Lex Mercatoria* (2nd edn, Kluwer 2010).

Berger, 'Contractual Arbitration Clauses and Non-Contractual Claims', (2023) 40 Journal of International Arbitration 105.

Besson Samantha ed, *Consenting to International Law* (2024).

Betolli, 'Renewable-Energy Development in a Net-Zero World: Disrupted Supply Chains', (17 February 2023) McKinsey & Co, https://www.mckinsey.com/industries/electric-power-and-natural-gas/our-insights/renewable-energy-development-in-a-net-zero-world-disrupted-supply-chains, last accessed 20 January 2025.

Biebricher Thomas ed, *The Oxford Handbook of Ordoliberalism* (Oxford University Press 2022).

Bix Brian, *Law, Language and Legal Determinacy* (Oxford University Press 1995).

Blankenship et al, 'Pathways to Commercial Liftoff: Next-Generation Geothermal Power', (March 2024) US Department of Energy, https://liftoff.energy.gov/wp-content/uploads/2024/03/LIFTOFF_DOE_NextGen_Geothermal_v14.pdf, last accessed 18 November 2024.

Bodansky Daniel, Brunée Jutta, & Rajamani Lavanya, *International Climate Change Law* (Oxford University Press 2017).

Bonvillian, 'The Once and Future DARPA', *in Blindside, How to Anticipate Forcing Events and Wild Cards in Global Politics* (Francis Fukuyama ed, Brookings Institution Press 2007) 57.

Borgonovi et al, 'The Effect of the EU Fit for 55 Packages on Labour Markets and the Demand for Skill', (28 July 2023) OECD Social, Employment and Migration Working Papers No. 297, https://www.oecd.org/en/publications/the-effects-of-the-eu-fit-for-55-package-on-labour-markets-and-the-demand-for-skills_6c16baac-en.html, last accessed 9 December 2024.

Boyd, 'Decommodifying Electricity', (2024) 97 Southern California Law Review 937.

Boyle Nicholas, *Goethe, The Poet and the Age, Volume 1: The Poetry of Desire* (Oxford University Press 1991).

Brandenburger & Nalebuff, 'The Rules of Co-opetition', (January/ February 2021) Harvard Business Review, available at https://hbr.org/2021/01/the-rules-of-co-opetition, last accessed 26 March 2024.

Bratspies, '"Underburdened" Communities', (2022) 110 California Law Review 1933.

Brauers, 'Liquified National Gas Expansion Plans in Germany: The Risk of Gas Lock-in under Energy Transition', (2021) 76 Energy Research & Social Science 102059.

Braw, 'What the Ever Given Taught the World', (10 November 2021) Foreign Policy, https://foreignpolicy.com/2021/11/10/what-the-ever-given-taught-the-world/, last accessed 7 January 2025.

Brinker, 'Redrawing the Solar Power Global Map with Regional Supply Chains', (10 March 2023) World Economic Forum, https://www.weforum.org/stories/2023/03/solar-power-regional-supply-chains/, last accessed 7 January 2025.

Brumfiel, 'The World Is Running Out of Helium. Here's Why It Matters', (8 November 2019) National Public Radio, https://www.npr.org/2019/11/01/775554343/the-world-is-constantly-running-out-of-helium-heres-why-it-matters, last accessed 5 December 2024.

Brundtland Gro Harlem, *World Commission on Environment and Development, Our Common Future* (UNDP 1987).

Bryce Robert, *A Question of Power, Electricity and the Wealth of Nations* (Public Affairs 2020).

Callen, 'Gross Domestic Product: An Economy's All', (2020) International Monetary Fund, https://www.imf.org/en/Publications/fandd/issues/Series/Back-to-Basics/gross-domestic-product-GDP#:~:text=GDP%20is%20composed%20of%20goods,the%20residents%20of%20a%20country, last accessed 6 October 2024.

Calliess Gralf-Peter & Zumbansen Peer, *Rough Consensus and Running Code: A Theory of Transnational Private Law* (Hart Publishing 2010).

Cambou & Smis, 'Permanent Sovereignty over Natural Resources from A Human Rights Perspective: Natural Resources Exploitation and Indigenous Peoples' Rights in the Arctic', (2013) 22 Michigan State International Law Review 347.

Cameron Peter, *Competition in Energy Markets: Law and Regulation in the European Union* (Oxford University Press 2002).

Cameron Peter D & Stanley Michael C, *Oil, Gas, and Mining, A Sourcebook for Understanding the Extractive Industries* (World Bank 2017).

Carlier, 'Vehicles in Operation in U.S. Q1 2018-Q2 2024', (5 December 2024) Statistica, https://www.statista.com/statistics/859950/vehicles-in-operation-by-quarter-united-states/, last accessed 20 January 2025.

Casselman, 'U.S. Economy Grew at 3.3% Rate in Latest Quarter', (25 January 2024) New York Times, https://www.nytimes.com/2024/01/25/business/economy/economy-q4-gdp.html, last accessed 29 October 2024.

Chalamoud-Trapiers Annie, *Le Droit des Biens* (2nd edn, Breal, 2007).

Chandler, 'The Evolution of Modern Global Competition', *in Competition in Global Industries* (Michael Porter ed, Harvard University Press 1986) 405.

Cherneski, 'An Unacknowledged Adversary: Carl Schmitt, Joseph Schumpeter, and the Classical Doctrine of Democracy', (2017) 29 Critical Review 447.

Childs William R, *The Texas Railroad Commissions: Understanding Regulation in America to the Mid-Twentieth Century* (Texas A&M University Press 2005).

Choudhury, 'Commodities 2024: Price Slump in 2023 Clouds Outlook for Voluntary Carbon Markets', (5 January 2024) S&P Global, https://www.spglobal.com/commodity-insights/en/news-research/latest-news/energy-transition/010524-price-slump-in-2023-clouds-outlook-for-voluntary-carbon-market, last accessed 9 December 2024.

Cicero, 'De Legibus' *in Cicero, The Republic & The Laws* (Niall Rudd trans, Oxford University Press 1998).

Cicero, 'De Oficiis' I.xvii.47-xvii *in Cicero Volume XXI: On Duties* (Walter Miller trans, Harvard University Press 1913).

Claeys, 'Jefferson Meets Coase: Land-Use Torts, Law and Economics, and Natural Property Rights', (2010) 85 Notre Dame Law Review 1379.

Clark Christopher, *Iron Kingdom, The Rise and Downfall of Prussia, 1600-1947* (Penguin 2007).

Clark Christopher, *The Sleepwalkers: How Europe Went to War in 1914* (HarperCollins 2013).

Clift, 'French Responses to the Global Economic Crisis: The Political Economy of "Post-Dirigisme" and New State Activism', *in The Consequences of the Global Financial Crisis: The Rhetoric of Reform and Regulation* (Wyn Grant & Graham Wilson eds, Oxford University Press 2012) 206.

Cockrell, 'I'm a Therapist to the Super-Rich: They Are as Miserable as Succession Makes Out', (22 November 2021) The Guardian, https://www.theguardian.com/commentisfree/2021/nov/22/therapist-super-rich-succession-billionaires, last accessed 17 October 2024.

Coleman, 'State Energy Cartels', (2021) 42 Cardozo Law Review 2247.

Connell, 'Becoming Bankable: How Renewable Energy Startups Can Deploy Equipment at Scale', (25 October 2018) Forbes, https://www.forbes.com/sites/energyinnovation/2018/10/25/becoming-bankable-how-renewable-energy-startups-can-deploy-equipment-at-scale/, last accessed 7 January 2025.

Cooper, 'A Note on Deregulation on Natural Gas Prices', (1982) 2 Brookings Paper on Economic Activity 371.

Corbeau & Mitrova, 'Russia' Gas Export Strategy: Adapting to the New Reality', (21 February 2024) Columbia Center on Global Energy Policy, https://www.energypolicy.columbia.edu/publications/russias-gas-export-strategy-adapting-to-the-new-reality/#:~:text=Russia%20has%20also%20been%20in,and%20India)%20gas%20pipeline%20project, last accessed 1 September 2024.

Corey, 'The Averch and Johnson Proposition: A Critical Analysis', (1971) 2 Bell Journal of Economics and Management Science 358.

Cozzi Laura, *Net Zero by 2050, A Roadmap for the Global Energy Sector* (International Energy Agency 2021).

Cozzi Laura et al, *World Energy Outlook 2022* (International Energy Agency 2022).

Cribbet, 'Concepts in Transition: The Search for A New Definition of Property', 1986 University of Illinois Law Review 1.

Cristi, 'Carl Schmitt: Decisionism', *in The Oxford Handbook of Ordoliberalism* (Thomas Biebricher ed, Oxford University Press 2022) 243.

Daintith Terence & Hancher Leigh, *Energy Strategy in Europe: The Legal Framework* (De Gruyter 1986).

Dante, 'Paradiso, Canto XXI', *in Dante Alighieri, La Divina Commedia Vol 6* (Gaetano Ferraro 1830) 163.

Daunton Martin, *Wealth and Welfare, An Economic and Social History of Britain 1851-1951* (Oxford University Press 2007).

Daunton Martin, *The Economic Government of the World: 1933-2023* (Farrar, Straus Giroux 2023).

Dawes, 'What's Plaguing Voluntary Carbon Markets?', (2 February 2024) Center for Strategic & International Studies, https://www.csis.org/analysis/whats-plaguing-voluntary-carbon-markets, last accessed 9 December 2024.

de Blasio & Zheng, 'Transition to a Low-Carbon Economy: An Evaluation Framework of Integration and Segmentation Scenarios' at 16–19, (August 2023) Harvard Kennedy School Belfer Center, https://www.belfercenter.org/sites/default/files/pantheon_files/files/publication/De%20Blasio%20Zheng_Energy%20Value%20Chains_FINAL.pdf, last accessed 7 January 2025.

de Tocqueville Alexis, 'De la Démocratie en Amérique I (1835)', *in Bibliothèque de la Pléiade: Tocqueville Œuvres II* (André Jardin ed, Gallimard 1992).

Derrida Jacques, *De la Grammatologie* (Les éditions de minuit 1967).

Desierto Diane A, *Public Policy in International Economic Law, The ICESCR in Trade, Finance, and Investment* (Oxford University Press 2015).

Desierto & Sourgens, 'Investment Law and Decarbonisation', *in Decarbonization and the Energy Industry, Law, Policy and Regulation in Law-Carbon Energy Markets* (Tade Oyewunmi et al eds, Hart Publishing 2020) 157.

Desierto, 'China's Maritime Law Enforcement Activities in the South China Sea', (2020) 96 International Law Studies 257.

Desierto, '"Stringent Due Diligence", Duties of Cooperation and Assistance to Climate Vulnerable States, and the Selective Integration of External Rules in the ITLOS Advisory Opinion on Climate Change and International Law', (3 June 2024) EJILTalk, https://www.ejiltalk.org/stringent-due-diligence-duties-of-cooperation-and-assistance-to-climate-vulnerable-states-and-the-selective-integration-of-external-rules-in-the-itlos-advisory-opinion-on-climate-change-and-inte/, last accessed 9 January 2025.

Diffenbaugh & Burke, 'Global Warming Has Increased Global Economic Inequality', (2019) 116 Proceedings of the National Academy of Sciences of the United States of America 9808-9813.

Diuk, 'EUROMAIDAN: Ukraine's Self-Organizing Revolution', (March/ April 2014) 176 World Affairs 9.

Dochuk, 'Blessed by Oil, Cursed with Crude: God and Black Gold in the American Southwest', (2012) 99 Journal of American History 51.

Dolzer Rudolf & Schreuer Christoph, *Principles of International Investment Law* (2nd edn, Oxford University Press 2012).

Dolzer Rudolf, *Petroleum Contracts and International Law* (Oxford University Press 2018).

Domke, 'American Protection Against Foreign Expropriation in the Light of the Suez Canal Crisis, (1957) 105 University of Pennsylvania Law Review 1033.

Doshi Rush, *The Long Game: China's Grand Strategy to Displace American Order* (Oxford University Press 2021).

Doshi, 'As Europe Deindustrializes, Can Economic Suicide Be Avoided?' (10 May 2024) Forbes, https://www.forbes.com/sites/tilakdoshi/2024/05/09/as-europe-deindustrializes-can-economic-suicide-be-avoided/, last accessed 9 December 2024.
Dotterud Leiren & Reimer, 'Germany: From Feed in Tariffs to Greater Competition', *in Comparative Renewable Policy: Political, Organizational and European Fields* (Elin Lerum Boasson, Merethe Dotterud Leiren, & Jørgen Wettestad eds, Routledge 2021) 81.
Dow, Han, and Sangiori, 'The Short-Termism Trap: Catering to Informed Investors with Limited Horizons', (13 August 2024) Harvard Law School Forum on Corporate Governance, https://corpgov.law.harvard.edu/2024/08/13/the-short-termism-trap-catering-to-informed-investors-with-limited-horizons/, last accessed 8 January 2025.
Drahos Peter, *Survival Governance: Energy and Climate in the Chinese Century* (Oxford University Press 2021).
Dreisbach & Staib, 'Hat Kiew die Nord-Stream-Pipelines gesprengt?', (15 June 2023) Frankfurt Allgemeine Zeitung, https://www.faz.net/aktuell/politik/ausland/ukraine-hat-kiew-die-nord-stream-pipelines-gesprengt-18964913.html, last accessed 28 August 2024.
Dreves, 'Working Out the Details of a Circular Solar Economy', (22 April 2024) US Department of Energy National Renewable Energy Laboratory, https://www.nrel.gov/news/program/2022/working-out-the-details-of-a-circular-solar-economy.html, last accessed 6 December 2024.
Duane, 'Regulation's Rationale: Learning from the California Energy Crisis', (2002) 19 Yale Journal on Regulation 471.
Duda et al, 'Carbon Dioxide Enhanced Oil Recovery, Untapped Domestic Energy Supply and Long Term Carbon Storage', (March 2010) U.S. Department of Energy National Energy Technology Laboratory, https://www.netl.doe.gov/sites/default/files/netl-file/co2_eor_primer.pdf, last accessed 6 December 2024.
DuVivier, 'Preventing Wind Waste', (2021) 71 American University Law Review 1.
Dworkin Ronald, *Laws' Empire* (Harvard University Press 1986).
Dyal-Chand, 'Sharing the Climate', (2022) 122 Columbia Law Review 581.
Edwards Sebastian, *The Chile Project: The Story of the Chicago Boys and the Downfall of Neoliberalism* (Princeton University Press 2023).
Encyclical Letter 'Laudatio Si' of the Holy Father Francis on Care for our Common Home (24 May 2015).
Encyclical Letter 'Fratelli Tutti' of the Holy Father Francis on Fraternity and Social Friendship (3 October 2020).
Ergen & Kohl, 'Rival Views of Economic Competition', (2022) 20 Socio-Economic Review 937.
Eriksson and Hack, 'Production of Metallurgical- Grade Silicon in an Electric Arc Furnace' *in SGTE Casebook* (Klaus Hack ed, 2nd edn, Woodhead Publishing 2008) 415.
Espinoza et al, 'The Political Economy of Rent-Seeking: Evidence from Spain's Support Policies for Renewable Energy', (2021) 14 Energies 4197.
Evans & Pearce, 'Mapped: The World's Coal Power Plants', (26 March 2020) Carbon Brief, https://www.carbonbrief.org/mapped-worlds-coal-power-plants/, last accessed 12 August 2024.
Evenett, 'China-EU Solar Panel Trade Dispute: Rhetoric versus Reality', (5 June 2013) VoxEU, https://cepr.org/voxeu/columns/china-eu-solar-panel-trade-dispute-rhetoric-versus-reality, last accessed 7 January 2025.
Faccio, 'Investment Contracts and the Reform of Investment Arbitration: Towards Sustainability', (2023) 28 ICSID Review 625.
Fang, 'A Never-Ending U.S. China Solar Trade War? The Uyghur Forced Labor Prevention Act and International Trade Law', (2024) 33 Minnesota Journal of International Law 189.
Farber, Tsuji, & Jing, 'Thinking Globally, Acting Locally: Lessons from the U.S., Japan, and China', (2021) 82 Ohio State Law Journal 953.
Farnsworth, 'Legal Remedies for Breach of Contract', (1970) 70 Columbia Law Review 1145.
Favennec Jean-Pierre, *The Geopolitics of Energy* (Editions Technip 2011).
Fellmeth Aaron X & Horwitz Maurice, *Guide to Latin in International Law* (Oxford University Press 2009).

Ferris, 'Why Hybrid Sales Surge as EV Sales Flatten', (4 April 2024) CNBC, https://www.cnbc.com/2024/04/04/why-hybrid-sales-surge-as-ev-sales-flatten.html, last accessed 4 May 2024.

Finley, *Is Saudi Arabia Quietly Trying To Help Europe's Oil Consumers?*, (5 May 2022) Forbes, https://www.forbes.com/sites/thebakersinstitute/2022/05/04/is-saudi-arabia-quietly-trying-to-help-europes-oil-consumers/, last accessed 28 June 2024.

Finley & Mikulska, 'Wielding the Energy Weapon: Differences Between Oil and Natural Gas', (26 June 2023) Baker Institute Center for Energy Studies Report, https://www.bakerinstitute.org/research/wielding-energy-weapon-differences-between-oil-and-natural-gas#:~:text=Russia%20has%20tried%20to%20use,Russia's%20military%20actions%20in%20Ukraine, last accessed 14 April 2024.

Finnis John, *Natural Law and Natural Rights* (Oxford University Press 1980).

Fisher Roger, Ury William, & Patton Bruce, *Getting to Yes, Negotiating Agreement Without Giving in* (2nd edn, Houghton Mifflin Company 1991).

Fletcher, 'Strict Subordination: The Origins of Civil Control of Military Power in State Constitutions', (2023) 14 Harvard National Security Journal 254.

Fraley, 'Liability for Unintentional Nuisances: How the Restatement of Torts Almost Negligently Killed the Right to Exclude in Property Law', (2018) 121 West Virginia Law Review 419.

Fujii-Takamoto, 'Strategic Competition in the Pacific: A Case for Kiribati', (7 December 2022) Journal of Indo-Pacific Affairs, https://www.airuniversity.af.edu/JIPA/Display/Article/3237885/strategic-competition-in-the-pacific-a-case-for-kiribati/, last accessed 11 December 2024.

Fukuyama Francis, *Identity: The Demand for Dignity and the Politics of Resentment* (Profile Books 2018).

Fukuyama, 'Challenges of Uncertainty: An Introduction', *in Blindside, How to Anticipate Forcing Events and Wild Cards in Global Politics* (Francis Fukuyama ed, Brookings Institution Press 2007).

Fuller Lon L, *The Morality of Law* (revised ed., Yale University Press 1969).

Gaillard Emmanuel, *Aspects Philosophiques du Droit de l'Arbitrage International* (Brill Nijhoff 2008).

Gallagher et al, '2021 International Arbitration Survey: Adapting Arbitration to a Changing World', (2021) Queen Mary University of London/White & Case, https://www.whitecase.com/publications/insight/2021-international-arbitration-survey, last accessed 10 January 2025.

Garavini Giuliano, *The Rise and Fall of OPEC in the Twentieth Century* (Oxford University Press 2019).

Gathii, 'Food Sovereignty for Poor Countries in the Global Trading System', (2011) 57 Loyola Law Review 509.

Gathii, 'Beyond China's Human Rights Exceptionalism in Africa: Leveraging Science, Technology and Engineering for Long-Term Growth', (2013) 51 Columbia Journal of Transnational Law 664.

Gearino, 'One State Generates Much, Much More Renewable Energy Than Any Other—and It's Not California', (9 March 2023) Inside Climate News, https://insideclimatenews.org/news/09032023/inside-clean-energy-texas-renewables/#:~:text=Texas%20has%20produced%20more%20gigawatt,thanks%20largely%20to%20wind%20energy, last accessed 4 May 2024.

Gelles, 'The Unmistakable Backdrop of COP29', (12 November 2024) New York Times, https://messaging-custom-newsletters.nytimes.com/dynamic/render?uri=nyt%3A%2F%2Fnewsletter%2F551102f3-9524-56ff-9ee2-12933766f221, last accessed 18 November 2024.

Getachew Adom, *Worldmaking After Empire: The Rise and Fall of Self-Determination* (Princeton University Press 2019).

Giovanni & Bercovich, 'Legal Empowerment in Informal Settlements: Lessons on Using the Law to Overcome Urban Exclusion and Poverty in the Global South', (2021) 54 NYU Journal of International Law & Politics 93.

Gold, 'The Year the Texas Legislature Changed the Energy Game Forever', (November 2023) Texas Monthly, https://www.texasmonthly.com/news-politics/the-year-the-texas-legislature-changed-the-energy-game-forever/, last accessed 6 November 2024.

Golden & Wiseman, 'The Fracking Revolution: Shale Gas as a Case Study in Innovation Policy', (2015) 64 Emory Law Journal 955.

Goldman, 'An Introduction to the French Law of Government Procurement Contracts', (1987) 20 George Washington Journal of International Law and Economics 461.

Goodman, 'America's Oil Country Increasingly Runs on Renewables', (18 September 2024) New York Times, https://www.nytimes.com/2024/09/18/us/texas-grid-renewables-battery-storage-solar.html, last accessed 7 January 2025.

Gordley James et al, *An Introduction to the Comparative Study of Private Law* (2nd edn, Cambridge University Press 2021).

Graham, 'German Government Averts Crisis with a Budget Agreement for Europe's Largest Economy', (5 July 2024) Associated Press, https://apnews.com/article/germany-budget-agreement-stimulus-coalition-a95dbc1d92c70ee2c10e921b8a5e0762, last accessed 7 September 2024.

Grewal David Singh, *Network Power, The Social Dynamics of Globalization* (Yale University Press 2008).

Gross Stephen G, *Energy and Power, Germany in the Age of Oil, Atoms, and Climate Change* (Oxford University Press 2023).

Gül Timur, *Global EV Outlook 2023, Catching Up With Climate Ambitions* (International Energy Agency 2023).

Guillot, 'Environmental Justice in Pollution Hotspots and Sections 7 & 15 of the Charter: The Case of the Aamjiwnaang Community in Chemical Valley', (2023) 53 Environmental Law 273.

Hadiprayitno, 'Poverty', *Realizing the Right to Development* (Office of the High Commissioner on Human Rights 2013) 137.

Hajiyeva, 'Gaullism as a Legacy of Charles De Gaulle', (6 July 2017) Modern Diplomacy, https://moderndiplomacy.eu/2017/07/06/gaullism-as-a-legacy-of-charles-de-gaulle/, last accessed 13 September 2024.

Hakimi & Brunk, 'Russia, Ukraine, and the Future World Order', (2022) 116 American Journal of International Law 687.

Hakimi & Brunk, 'The Prohibition of Annexations and the Foundations of Modern International Law', (2024) 118 American Journal of International Law 417.

Hallam, 'A Polysilicon Learning Curve and the Materials Requirements for Broad Electrification with Photovoltaics by 2050', (2022) 6 Solar RLL 220458.

Hamilton, 'Causes and Consequences of the Oil Shock of 2007-08', (2009) Brookings Papers on Economic Activity 215.

Handl, 'Territorial Sovereignty and the Problem of Transnational Pollution', (1975) 69 American Journal of International Law 50.

Hanson Victor Davis, *The Other Greeks, The Family Farm and the Agrarian Roots of Western Civilization* (Free Press 1995).

Hardin, 'The Tragedy of the Commons', (1968) 162 Science 1243.

Harper, 'Vital Signs 2020: Industrial Base Could Struggle to Surge Production in Wartime', (24 January 2020) National Defense Magazine, https://www.nationaldefensemagazine.org/articles/2020/1/24/industrial-base-could-struggle-to-surge-production-in-wartime, last accessed 9 December 2024.

Hathaway Oona & Shapiro Scott J, *The Internationalists: How a Radical Plan to Outlaw War Remade the World* (Simon & Schuster 2017).

Hathaway, 'Path Dependence in the Law: The Course and Pattern of Legal Change in a Common Law System', (2001) 86 Iowa Law Review 601.

Heffron & McCauley, 'Achieving Sustainable Supply Chains through Energy Justice', (2014) 123 Applied Energy 435.

Heidegger Martin, *Sein und Zeit* (Max Niemeyer Verlag 1993).

Heller Michael, *The Gridlock Economy: How Too Much Ownership Wrecks Markets, Stops Innovation and Costs Lives* (2008).

Heller, The Tragedy of the Anticommons: Property in Transition from Marx to Markets, (1998) 111 Harvard Law Review 621.

Heller, 'Common Interest Developments at the Crossroads of Legal Theory', (2005) 37 Urban Lawyer 329, 330–32.

Heller, 'The Tragedy of the Anticommons: A Concise Introduction and Lexicon', (2013) 76 Modern Law Review 6.

Helliwell, 'Comparative Macroeconomics of Stagflation', (1988) 26 Journal of Economic Literature 1.

Heraclitus, *Fragments* (Brooks Haxton trans, Viking 2001).

Herman, 'Classical Social Theories and the Doctrine of "Abuse of Rights"', (1977) 37 Louisiana Law Review 747.

Hestermeyer, 'Reality or Aspiration? Solidarity in Environmental and World Trade Law', *in Coexistence, Cooperation and Solidarity: Liber Amicorum Rüdiger Wolfrum* (Holger Hestermeyer et al eds, Martinus Nijhoff 2012) 45.

Higgins & Kramer, 'Ukraine Has Deal, but Both Russia and Protesters Appear Wary', (21 February 2014) New York Times, https://www.nytimes.com/2014/02/22/world/europe/ukraine.html, last accessed 22 January 2025.

Higgins & Kramer, 'Archrival Is Freed as Ukraine Leader Flees', (22 February 2014) New York Times, https://www.nytimes.com/2014/02/23/world/europe/ukraine.html, last accessed 22 January 2025.

Hinton, 'The Seventeen-Year Overnight Wonder: George Mitchell and Unlocking the Barnett Shale', (2012) 99 Journal of American History 229.

Hochschild, 'I Spent 5 Years With Some of Trump's Biggest Fans. Here's What They Won't Tell You', (October 2016) Mother Jones, https://www.motherjones.com/politics/2016/08/trump-white-blue-collar-supporters/, last accessed 29 October 2024.

Hogan, 'Follow the Missing Money: Ensuring Reliability at Least Cost to Consumers in Transition to a Low-Carbon Power System', (2017) 30 Electricity Journal 55.

Hollis, 'Do International Agreements Have a Consent Problem?', *in Consenting to International Law* (Samantha Besson ed, 2024) 137.

Holtzman Hannah, *Through a Nuclear Lens, France, Japan, and Cienema from Hiroshima to Fukushima* (State University of New York Press 2024).

Home, 'West Challenges China's Critical Minerals Hold on Africa', (18 February 2024) Reuters, https://www.reuters.com/markets/commodities/west-challenges-chinas-critical-minerals-hold-africa-2024-02-16/, last accessed 2 September 2024.

Honoré, 'Ownership', *in Oxford Essays in Jurisprudence* 113 (Anthony G Guest ed, Oxford University Press 1961) 113.

Hornstein & Stoermer, 'The Energy Policy Act of 2005: PURPA Reform, the Amendments, and their Implications', (2006) 27 Energy Law Journal 25.

Hughes Thomas P, *Networks of Power, Electrification in Western Society 1880-1930* (Johns Hopkins University Press 1983).

Hummer et al, 'Just 15 Countries Account for 98% of New Coal-Power Developments', (3 September 2024) Carbon Brief, https://www.carbonbrief.org/guest-post-just-15-countries-account-for-98-of-new-coal-power-development/, last accessed 11 December 2024

Humpert, 'Germany Continues to Import Russian Natural Gas Through Belgium and the Netherlands', (27 February 2024) High North News, https://www.highnorthnews.com/en/germany-continues-import-russian-natural-gas-through-belgium-and-netherlands#:~:text=Germany%20stopped%20directly%20importing%20Russian,through%20supplies%20from%20its%20neighbors, last accessed 6 August 2024.

Ingersol, 'Small Modular Reactors (SMRs) for Producing Nuclear Energy: International Developments', *in Handbook on Small Modular Reactors* (2nd edn, Daniel T Ingersoll & Mario D Carelli eds, Elsevier 2021) 29.

Jacobs, 'Dramatic Photos Show How Radically Dubai Has Changed in 50 Years', (14 December 2018) Business Insider, https://www.businessinsider.com/dramatic-photos-show-how-radically-dubai-has-changed-in-50-years-2018-12, last accessed 29 October 2024.

Jakob, 'The Future of Coal in a Carbon-Constrained Climate', (2020) 10 Nature Climate Change 704.

James Harold, *Seven Crashes: The Economic Crises that Shaped Globalization* (Yale University Press 2023).

Jamet, 'Air Conditioning Is "Exacerbating the Climate Crisis" But How Many Europeans Use It?', (18 June 2024) Euronews, https://www.euronews.com/green/2024/06/18/air-conditioning-use-has-more-than-doubled-in-europe-since-1990, last accessed 11 December 2024.

Wilson Jones Mark, *Principles of Roman Architecture* (Yale University Press 2000).

Johnson & Persico, 'Broadband Internet Access, Economic Growth, and Wellbeing', (May 2024) National Bureau of Economic Research Working Paper 32517, https://www.nber.org/system/files/working_papers/w32517/w32517.pdf, last accessed 6 November 2024.

Jones, 'The U.S. Defense Industrial Base Is Not Prepared for a Possible Conflict with China', (2024) Center for Strategic & International Studies, https://features.csis.org/preparing-the-US-industrial-base-to-deter-conflict-with-China/, last accessed 9 December 2024.

Joskow, 'Lessons Learned From Electricity Market Liberalization', (2008) 29 Energy Journal 9.

Joskow, 'Capacity Payments in Imperfect Electricity Markets', (2008) 16 Utility Policy 159.

Kagan Donald, *The Outbreak of the Peloponnesian War* (Cornell University Press 1969).

Kahn Matthew E, *Adapting to Climate Change, Markets and the Management of an Uncertain Future* (Yale University Press 2021).

Kahn et al, 'Long-Term Macroeconomic Effects of Climate Change: A Country-Country Analysis', (October 2019) IMF Working Paper, https://www.imf.org/-/media/Files/Publications/WP/2019/wpiea2019215-print-pdf.ashx, last accessed 11 November 2024.

Kanet & Sussex, 'Introduction: Russia, Eurasia and the New Geopolitics of Energy', *in Russia, Eurasia and the New Geopolitics of Energy, Confrontation and Consolidation* (Matthew Sussex and Roger Kanet eds, Palgrave 2015) 1.

Karnitschnig, 'Why Merkel Chose Russia over US on Nord Stream 2', (16 July 2021) Politico, https://www.politico.eu/article/vladimir-putin-german-chancellors-nord-stream-russia-energy-angela-merkel/, last accessed 17 August 2024.

Kędzierski, 'At All Costs. Germany Shifts to LNG', (28 April 2023) Center for Eastern Studies, https://www.osw.waw.pl/en/publikacje/osw-commentary/2023-04-28/all-costs-germany-shifts-to-lng, last accessed 7 September 2024.

Kelliher & Farinella, 'The Changing Landscape of Federal Energy Law', (2009) 61 Administrative Law Review 611.

Kelly & Wiseman, 'No Easy Transmission Fixes', (December 2016) North American Windpower, https://www.akingump.com/a/web/53869/NAW1612_Akingump.pdf, last accessed 4 May 2024.

Kennedy, 'Biophysical Economic Interpretation of the Great Depression', (2023) 27 Journal of Industrial Ecology 1197.

Kennedy, 'Energy Constraints on Macroeconomic Paradigms', (2024) 226 Ecological Economics 108361.

Kent James, *Commentaries on American Law Volume 2* (O Halsted 1827).

Kintisch, 'Technologies', *in Climate Engineering and the Law, Regulation and Liability for Solar Radiation Management and Carbon Dioxide Removal* (Michael B Gerrard & Tracy Hester eds, Cambridge University Press 2018) 28.

Klass Alexanda B & Wiseman Hannah J, *Energy Law* (Foundation Press 2017).

Klass, 'Takings and Transmission', (2013) 91 North Carolina Law Review 1079.

Klass, 'Energy and Eminent Domain', (2019) 104 Minnesota Law Review 659.

Klass & Chan, 'Cooperative Clean Energy', (2021) 100 North Carolina Law Review 1.

Klass & Wilton, 'Local Power', (2022) 75 Vanderbilt Law Review 93.

Klass et al, 'The Key to Electric Grid Reliability: Modernizing Governance', (Mar 2024) University of Pennsylvania Kleinman Center for Energy Policy, https://kleinmanenergy.upenn.edu/wp-content/uploads/2024/03/KCEP-Paper-15-Key-to-Electric-Grid-Reliability.pdf, last accessed 7 December 2024.

Kleit, 'The Texas Electricity Two-Step' (Fall 2023) Regulation, https://www.cato.org/regulation/fall-2023/texas-electricity-two-step, last accessed 17 July 2024.

Hongju Koh Harold, *The Trump Administration and International Law* (Oxford University Press 2018).

Koh 'Triptych's End: A Better Framework to Evaluate 21st Century International Lawmaking', (2017) 126 Yale Law Journal Forum 338.
Kononczuk, 'Russia's Real Aims in Crimea', (13 March 2014) Carnegie Endowment for Peace, https://carnegieendowment.org/research/2014/03/russias-real-aims-in-crimea?lang=en, last accessed 22 January 2025.
Konstanin Panos & Konstanin Margarete, *The Power Supply Industry, Best Practice Manual for Power Generation and Transport, Economics and Trade* (Springer 2018).
Koskenniemi Martti, *The Gentle Civilizer of Nations, The Rise and Fall of International Law 1870-1960* (Cambridge University Press 2004).
Kramer & Anderson, 'The Rule of Capture—An Oil and Gas Perspective', (2005) 35 Environmental Law 899.
Kroenig, 'International Relations Theory Suggests Great-Power War Is Coming', (27 August 2022) Foreign Policy, https://foreignpolicy.com/2022/08/27/international-relations-theory-suggests-great-power-war-is-coming/#:~:text=Realists%20argue%20that%20multipolar%20systems,not%20out%20of%20the%20question, last accessed 7 January 2025.
Kronenfeld & Kronenfeld, 'Al Gore, The Internet, and the National Library of Medicine', (2 July 2020) Circulating Now, https://circulatingnow.nlm.nih.gov/2020/07/02/al-gore-the-internet-and-the-national-library-of-medicine/, last accessed 7 January 2025.
Kwon, 'Rent and Rent-Seeking in Renewable Energy Support Policies: Feed-in Tariff vs. Renewable Portfolio Standards', (2015) 44 Renewable & Sustainable Energy Review 676.
Largey, 'La place du contrat dans le domaine de l'approvionnement en électricité, en droit suisse', *in La Contractualisation en Droit Public* (Véronique Boillet et al eds, Schulthess 2021) 175.
Lasswell Harold & McDougal Myers S, *Jurisprudence for a Free Society* (Martinus Nijhoff 1992).
Leal-Arcas, 'Sustainability, Common Concern, and Public Goods', (2017) 49 George Washington International Law Review 801.
Lee Hoesung et al, *Climate Change 2023: Synthesis Report. Contribution of Working Groups I, II and III to the Sixth Assessment Report of the Intergovernmental Panel on Climate Change* (Intergovernmental Panel on Climate Change 2023).
Lee et al, 'How the Tiny Island City-State of Singapore Fights Rising Sea Levels', (10 October 2023) Time Magazine, https://time.com/6322111/singapore-fights-rising-sea-levels-climate-change/, last accessed 11 December 2024.
Leffer, 'The AI Boom Could Use a Shocking Amount of Energy', (13 October 2023) Scientific American, https://www.scientificamerican.com/article/the-ai-boom-could-use-a-shocking-amount-of-electricity/, last accessed 13 January 2025.
Leich, 'Arms Control and Disarmament', (1988) 82 American Journal of International Law 341.
Lempriere, 'China Responsible for 95% of New Coal Power Construction in 2023, Report Says', (11 April 2024) CarbonBriefs, https://www.carbonbrief.org/china-responsible-for-95-of-new-coal-power-construction-in-2023-report-says/#:~:text=China%20accounted%20for%2095%25%20of,the%20global%20coal%20power%20industry, last accessed 3 May 2024.
Leslie, 'Food Deserts, Racism, and Antitrust Law', (2022) 110 California Law Review 1717.
Levinson, 'The Brooding Omnipresence of Carl Schmitt in Contemporary Jurisprudence: Reflections on William Scheuerman's *The End of Law:* Carl Schmitt in the 21st Century', (2020) 47 Philosophy & Social Criticism 178.
Levit, 'A Bottom-Up Approach to International Lawmaking: The Tale of Three Trade Finance Instruments', (2005) 30 Yale Journal of International Law 125.
Lewin, 'Comparative Nusiance', (1989) 50 University of Pittsburg Law Review 1009.
Li et al, 'Life Cycle Sustainability Assessment and Circularity of Geothermal Power Plants', (2023) 35 Sustainable Production and Consumption 141.
Li, 'Scaling Up Climate Finance for Emerging Markets and Developing Economies', (27 February 2023) International Monetary Fund, https://www.imf.org/en/News/Articles/2023/02/28/sp022823-scaling-up-climate-finance-for-emerging-markets-and-developing-economies, last accessed 11 December 2024.
Lianos, 'Population and State-State Economy in Plato and Aristotle', (2022) 7 Population and Sustainability 123.

Linsey, 'Climate Change: Atmospheric CO2', (12 May 2023) US National Oceanic Atmospheric Administration, https://www.climate.gov/news-features/understanding-climate/climate-change-atmospheric-carbon-dioxide#:~:text=The%20increase%20between%202021%20and,dioxide%20in%202022%20was%20418.56, last accessed 26 March 2024.

Lipke et al, 'Trust and Trade-offs: How to Manage Europe's Green Technology Dependence on China', (29 May 2024) European Council on Foreign Relations, https://ecfr.eu/publication/trust-and-trade-offs-how-to-manage-europes-green-technology-dependence-on-china/, last accessed 9 December 2024.

Lipton, '"The Coal Industry Is Back", Trump Proclaimed. It Wasn't', (18 October 2020) New York Times, https://www.nytimes.com/2020/10/05/us/politics/trump-coal-industry.html, last accessed 4 May 2024.

Lipton, Searcey, & Forsythe, 'Race to the Future: What to Know About the Frantic Quest for Cobalt', (7 December 2021) New York Times, https://www.nytimes.com/2021/11/20/world/china-congo-cobalt-explained.html, last accessed 28 August 2024.

Lovins, 'Energy Strategy: The Road Not Taken?', (October 1976) 55 Foreign Affairs 65.

Lowenfeld Andreas, *International Economic Law* (2nd edn, Oxford University Press 2008).

Luhmann Niklas, *Theory of Society, Volume 1* (Rhodes Barrett trans, Stanford University Press 2012).

MacIntyre Alastair, *After Virtue* (2nd edn, University of Notre Dame Press 1984).

McGlade Christophe et al, *The Oil and Gas Industry in Net Zero Transitions* (International Energy Agency 2024).

McNamee, 'Department of Energy and Related Commissions', *in Mandate for Leadership, The Conservative Promise, Project 2025 Presidential Transition Project* (Paul Dans & Steven Groves eds, Heritage Foundation 2023).

McLain & Rattner, 'How Electric Vehicles Are Losing Momentum with U.S. Buyers, in Charts', (27 December 2023) Wall Street Journal, https://www.wsj.com/business/autos/electric-vehicle-demand-charts-7d3089c7, last accessed 4 May 2024.

Machiavelli Niccolo, *Discourses on the First Decade of Titus Livius* (Ninian Hill Thomson trans, Kegan Paul, Trench & Co 1883).

Machiavelli Niccolò, *Tutte le Opere* (Mario Martelli ed, Sansoni Editore 1993).

Mackey et al, 'Estimates of Lithium Mass Yields from Produced Water Sources from the Devonian-aged Marcellus Shale', (2024) 14 Scientific Reports 8813.

Maine Henry Sumner, *Ancient Law: Its Connection with the Early History of Society, and its Relation to Modern Ideas* (John Murray 1861).

Maj, 'Energy Without Russia —The Consequences of the Ukraine War and EU Sanctions on the Energy Sector in Europe' at 4, (2023) Friedrich-Ebert-Stiftung Country Report Poland, https://library.fes.de/pdf-files/bueros/budapest/20475.pdf, last accessed 16 September 2024.

Mandhana, 'In Beijing's Quest for Control of the South China Sea, a New Flashpoint Emerges', (25 August 2024) Wall Street Journal, https://www.wsj.com/world/asia/in-beijings-quest-for-control-of-the-south-china-sea-a-new-flashpoint-emerges-5ac29fc5, last accessed 28 August 2024.

Martin Jamie, *The Meddlers, Sovereignty, Empire, and the Birth of Global Economic Governance* (Harvard University Press 2022).

Marhold Anna-Alexandra, *Energy in International Trade Law, Concepts, Regulations and Changing Markets* (Cambridge University Press 2021).

Masters, *July 2023:* 'Earth's Hottest Month on Record', (14 August 2023) Yale Climate Connections, https://yaleclimateconnections.org/2023/08/july-2023-earths-hottest-month-on-record/, last accessed 25 March 2024.

Mattingly Daniel C, *The Art of Political Control in China* (Cambridge University Press 2020).

Meyer, 'Free Trade, Fair Trade, and Selective Enforcement', (2018) 118 Columbia Law Review 491.

Middleton et al, 'The Shale Gas Revolution: Barriers, Sustainability, and Emerging Opportunities', (2017) 199 Applied Energy 88.

Miller, 'Mississippi Economic Outlook', (Spring 2023) Mississippi State Economist, http://www.mississippi.edu/URC/downloads/outlook/0423mseo.pdf, last accessed 7 October 2024.

Mills et al, 'Qatar LNG Sales to Key Asian Markets Confronted by US, UAE Rivalry', (21 October 2024) Reuters, https://www.reuters.com/business/energy/qatar-lng-sales-key-asian-markets-confronted-by-us-uae-rivalry-2024-10-21/, last accessed 20 January 2025.
Milov, 'Oil, Gas, and War: The Effect of Sanctions on the Russian Energy Industry' at 3, (May 2024) Atlantic Council, https://www.atlanticcouncil.org/wp-content/uploads/2024/05/Oil-gas-and-war-Vladimir-Milov.pdf, last accessed 28 August 2024.
Mikaelsson et al, 'Executive Summary', *in European Climate Risk Assessment*, (2024) European Environmental Agency EEA Report 01/2024.
Mitchell Timothy, *Carbon Democracy: Political Power in the Age of Oil* (Verso Book 2011).
Möller & Walwei, 'Die Agenda 2010 war ein unerwarteter Erfolg', (14 March 2013) Die Zeit, https://www.zeit.de/wirtschaft/2013-03/agenda2010-reformen-erfolg, last accessed 17 August 2024.
Mommer, 'The New Governance of Venezuelan Oil' at 35–36, (April 1998) Oxford Institute for Energy Studies WPM 23.
Mommsen Theodor, *Römisches Staatsrecht, Dritter Band* (Verlag von S Hirzel 1887).
Montoya & Ewing, 'How Many Electric Cars Are There in the U.S.?' (17 July 2024) Edmunds, https://www.edmunds.com/electric-car/articles/how-many-electric-cars-in-us.html, last accessed 20 January 2025.
Mormann, Reicher, & Hanna, 'A Tale of Three Markets: Comparing Renewable Energy Experiences of California, Texas, and Germany', (2016) Stanford Environmental Law Journal 55.
Mtambierweki, 'Biotechnology and International Law Within the North-South Context', (2001) 14 Transnational Lawyer 103.
Mulder Nicholas, *The Economic Weapon, The Rise of Sanctions as a Tool of Modern War* (Princeton University Press 2022).
Munro, 'The Proposed German Petroleum Monopoly', (1945) 4 American Economic Review 315.
Murtazashvili Ilia & Piano Ennio, *The Political Economy of Fracking, Private Property, Polycentricity, and the Shale Revolution* (Routledge 2018).
Muthuraj & Mekonnen, 'Recent Progress in Carbon Dioxide (CO_2) as Feedstock for Sustainable Materials Development: Co-polymers and Polymer Blends', (2018) 145 Polymer 348.
Nan & Moseley, 'The Expansion of China's Generation Capacity' at 1, (July 2011) World Bank PPP Insights, https://ppp.worldbank.org/public-private-partnership/sites/ppp.worldbank.org/files/documents/China_Energy_v1n1_0.pdf, last accessed 12 August 2024.
Ndulo, 'The African Continental Free Trade Area: Local Content Requirements As A Means to Addressing Africa's Productive Capacity Constraints', (2022) 43 Michigan Journal of International Law 61.
Neuman William, *Things Are Never So Bad That They Can't Get Worse: Inside the Collapse of Venezuela* (St Martin's Publishing 2022).
Newbury & Kanya-Forstner, 'French Policy and the Origins of the Scramble for Africa', (1969) 10 Journal for African History 253.
Nolan et al, 'Political Risk Insurance and Guarantees from Public Providers', *in Transnational Law of Public Contracts* (Mathias Audit & Stephan Schill eds, Bruylant 2016) 737.
Nordhaus William D, *The Spirit of Green, The Economics of Collision and Contagions in a Crowded World* (Princeton University Press 2021).
Nozick Robert, *Anarchy, State, and Utopia* (Basic Books 1974).
Nussbaum, 'Non-Relative Virtues: An Aristotelian Account', *in The Quality of Life* (Martha Nussbaum & Amartya Sen eds, Oxford University Press 1993) 242.
Nussbaum Martha C, *The Fragility of Goodness: Luck and Ethics in Greek Tragedy and Philosophy* (Cambridge University Press 2001).
Nussbaum Martha C, *Creating Capabilities: The Human Development Approach* (Harvard University Press 2011).
O'Connell & Day, 'Natural Law as Source of Extrapositive Norms', *in Oxford Handbook of the Sources of International Law* (Jean d'Aspremont & Samantha Besson eds, Oxford University Press 2018) 562.

O'Connell, 'The Arc Towards Justice and Peace', *in Arcs of Global Justice: Essays in Honor of William A. Schabas* (Margaret M de Guzman & Diane Amann eds, Oxford University Press 2018) 467.

O'Donoghue, 'What's Going on with the West's Largest Transmission Line in Decades?', (30 June 2023) Deseret News, https://www.deseret.com/utah/2023/6/30/23773218/transwest-express-transmission-line-renewable-energy-wyoming-wind-western-power-grid/#:~:text=The%20TransWest%20Express%20Project%20will%20connect%20three%20planning%20regions%20in,to%20Nevada%2C%20California%20and%20Arizona, last accessed 26 June 2024.

O'Flaherty, 'Ubi Jus Ibi Remedium', (1999) 45 Loyola Law Review 527.

Olawuyi Damilola S et al eds, *Net Zero and Natural Resources Law, Sorvereignty, Security, and Solidarity in the Clean Energy Transition* (Oxford University Press 2024).

Osofsky & Levit, 'The Scale of Networks?: Local Climate Change Coalitions', (2008) 8 Chicago Journal of International Law 409.

Ostrom Elinor, *Understanding Institutional Diversity* (Princeton University Press 2009).

Ostrom Elinor, *Governing the Commons: The Evolution of Institutions for Collective Action* (Cambridge University Press 2015).

Ovidius Naso Publius, *Tritia. Ex Ponto* (AL Wheeler trans, Harvard University Press 1924).

Oyewunmi Tade et al eds, *Decarbonization and the Energy Industry, Law, Policy and Regulation in Law-Carbon Energy Markets* (Hart Publishing 2020).

Páez-Salgado, 'A Battle on Two Fronts: Vattenfall v. Federal Republic of Germany', (18 February 2021) Kluwer Arbitration Blog, https://arbitrationblog.kluwerarbitration.com/2021/02/18/a-battle-on-two-fronts-vattenfall-v-federal-republic-of-germany/, last accessed 9 January 2025.

Paris, 'Oil Tanker Attacked by Houthis Is at Risk of Leaking in Red Sea', (28 August 2024) Wall Street Journal, https://www.wsj.com/world/oil-tanker-attacked-by-houthis-is-at-risk-of-leaking-in-red-sea-15672593, last accessed 28 August 2024.

Parks Tim, *Medici Money: Banking, Metaphysics, and Art in Fifteenth-Century Florence* (Atlas Books 2005).

Paulsson Jan, *The Idea of Arbitration* (Oxford University Press 2014).

Peerenboom, 'Let One Hundred Flowers Bloom, One Hundred Schools Contend: Debating Rule of Law in China', (2002) 23 Michigan Journal of International Law 471.

Pelton, 'Protection Protectionism in the WTO: A Reinterpretation of the General Exceptions to Protect the IRA's Local Content Requirements', (2024) 49 Columbia Environmental Law Journal 100.

Penn, 'Oil Companies Expand Offshore Drilling, Pointing to Energy Needs', (3 May 2024) New York Times, https://www.nytimes.com/2024/05/03/business/energy-environment/shell-offshore-oil-gulf-of-mexico.html, last accessed 4 May 2024.

Peplow, 'Lithium-ion Battery Recycling Goes Large', (19 November 2023) Chemical & Engineering News, https://cen.acs.org/environment/recycling/Lithium-ion-battery-recycling-goes/101/i38, last accessed 6 December 2024.

Perez Carlota, *Technical Revolutions and Financial Capital, The Dynamics of Bubbles and Golden Ages* (Edward Elgar 2003).

Pereira et al, 'Local Content Policies in the Petroleum Industry: Lessons Learned', (2919) 4 Oil and Gas, Natural Resources and Energy Journal 631.

Pereira et al, 'Brazil's Local Content Requirement: Evolution, Lessons Learned & International Trade Limitations', (2024) 9 Oil and Gas, Natural Resources and Energy Journal 385.

Peters, 'Precommitment Theory Applied to International Law: Between Sovereignty and Triviality', (2008) University of Illinois Law Review 239.

Petit Eugene, *Traité Élémentaire du Droit Romain* (Rousseau 1906).

Pettit Philip, *A Theory of Freedom and Government* (Oxford University Press 1997).

Pickerel, 'China's Share of World's Polysilicon Production Grows from 30% to 80% in Just One Decade', (27 April 2022) Solar Power World, https://www.solarpowerworldonline.com/2022/04/chinas-share-of-worlds-polysilicon-production-grows-from-30-to-80-in-just-one-decade/, last accessed 8 August 2024.

Pierce, 'Carol Rose Comes to the Oil Patch: Modern Property Analysis Applied to Modern Reservoir Problems', (2011) 19 Penn State Environmental Law Review 241.

Pillay Navanethem, *Human Rights, Health, and Poverty Reduction Strategies* (World Health Organization 2008).

Pilling David, *The Growth Delusion: Wealth, Poverty, and the Well-Being of Nations* (Penguin 2018).

Pocock JGA, *The Ancient Constitution and the Feudal Law, Study of English Historical Thought in the Seventeenth Century* (Cambridge University Press 1987).

Pocock JGA, *The Machiavellian Moment, Florentine Political Thought and the Atlantic Republican Tradition* (2nd edn, Princeton University Press 2003).

Podshivalov, 'Models of Actio Negatoria in the Law of Russia and European Countries', (2019) 7 Russian Law Journal 128.

Pöhle, 'Germany's Ukraine Problem', (19 December 2013) Deutsche Welle, https://www.dw.com/en/german-foreign-minister-tackles-ukraine-quandary/a-17309710, last accessed 22 July 2025.

Porter Michael E, *Competitive Advantage: Creating and Sustaining Superior Performance* (Free Press 2008).

Posner, 'The Ethical and Political Basis of the Efficiency Norm in Common Law Adjudication', (1980) 8 Hofstra Law Review 487.

Posner & Sykes, 'Efficient Breach of International Law: Optimal Remedies, 'Legalized Noncompliance', and Related Issues, (2011) 110 Michigan Law Review 243.

Pound Roscoe, *Readings in Roman Law* (Jacob North & Co 1906).

Press Elizabeth, *Geopolitics of Energy Transition: Critical Minerals* (IRENA 2023).

Press, 'Geopolitics of the Energy Transition: Energy Security' at 49, (2024) International Renewable Energy Agency, https://www.irena.org/-/media/Files/IRENA/Agency/Publication/2024/Apr/IRENA_Geopolitics_transition_energy_security_2024.pdf, last accessed 7 January 2025.

Purdy, 'The American Transformation of Waste Doctrine: A Pluralist Interpretation', (2006) 91 Cornell Law Review 653.

Putter, 'The Netherlands Coals Phase-Out and the Resulting (RWE and Uniper) ICSID Arbitrations', (24 August 2021) Kluwer Arbitration Blog, https://arbitrationblog.kluwerarbitration.com/2021/08/24/the-netherlands-coal-phase-out-and-the-resulting-rwe-and-uniper-icsid-arbitrations/, last accessed 9 January 2025.

Pye et al, 'The Global Implications of a Russian Gas Pivot to Asia', (2025) 16 Nature Communications 386.

Rabinovich, 'Israel: The Impact of the Peace Treaty', (1980) 78 Current History 5.

Rappeport, 'U.S. National Debt Tops $35 Trillion for First Time', (29 July 2024) New York Times, https://www.nytimes.com/2024/07/29/us/politics/national-debt-35-trillion.html, last accessed 11 December 2024.

Rajamani & Bodansky, 'The Paris Rulebook: Balancing International Prescriptiveness with National Discretion', (2019) 68 International & Comparative Law Quarterly 1023.

Rapawy, 'Federal Mandate Procedures', (1999) 36 Harvard Journal on Legislation 571.

Rapier, 'How the Shale Boom Turned the World Upside Down', (21 April 2017) Forbes, https://www.forbes.com/sites/rrapier/2017/04/21/how-the-shale-boom-turned-the-world-upside-down/, last accessed 16 July 2024.

Rapier, 'How the U.S. Became the World's Top LNG Exporter', (5 January 2024) Forbes, https://www.forbes.com/sites/rrapier/2024/01/05/how-the-us-became-the-worlds-top-lng-exporter/, last accessed 17 August 2024.

Rasool et al, 'Crafting a Robust U.S. Carbon Border Adjustment Mechanism', (8 August 2024) Center for Strategic & International Studies, https://www.csis.org/analysis/crafting-robust-us-carbon-border-adjustment-mechanism, last accessed 20 January 2025.

Rattner, 'Precommitment Theory and International Law: Starting a Conversation', (2003) 81 Texas Law Review 2055.

Rawls John, *A Theory of Justice* (Harvard University Press 1971).

Rawls John, *Political Liberalism* (Columbia University Press 1993).
Raz Joseph, *The Authority of Law* (2nd edn, Oxford University Press 2009).
Reinsch & Arrieta-Kenna, 'A Dark Spot for the Solar Energy Industry: Forced Labor in Xinjiang', (19 April 2021) Center for Strategic & International Studies, https://www.csis.org/analysis/dark-spot-solar-energy-industry-forced-labor-xinjiang#:~:text=The%20polysilicon%20components%20are%20produced,polysilicon%20factories%20in%20the%20world, last accessed 9 August 2024.
Reagan President, 'Farewell Address to the American People', (12 January 1989) New York Times, https://www.nytimes.com/1989/01/12/news/transcript-of-reagan-s-farewell-address-to-american-people.html, last accessed 9 December 2024.
Reisman W Michael, *Systems of Control in International Adjudication and Arbitration, Breakdown and Repair* (Duke University Press 1992).
Reisman W Michael, *The Quest for World Order and Human Dignity in the Twenty-First Century: Constitutive Process and Individual Commitment* (Brill Nijhoff 2012).
Ribeiro & Holman, 'Regionalization of Battery Supply Chains Advances, But Challenges Persist', (30 September 2021) S&P Global, https://www.spglobal.com/commodity-insights/en/news-research/latest-news/energy-transition/093021-insight-regionalization-of-battery-supply-chains-advances-but-challenges-persist, last accessed 7 January 2025.
Richardson, 'Reframing Ameliorative Waste', (2017) 65 American Journal of Comparative Law 335.
Righetti & Schremmer, Waste and the Governance of Private and Public Property, (2022) 93 University of Colorado Law Review 609.
Roberts Sean R, *The War no the Uyghurs* (Princeton University Press 2020).
Roeben, 'What Drives OPEC Production Policy', (2024) 17 Journal of World Energy Law & Business 19.
Röpke Wilhelm, *A Humane Economy, The Social Framework of the Free Market* (Elizabeth Henderson trans, 3rd edn, Intercollegiate Studies Institute 1998).
Rose, 'The Hope Case and Public Utility Valuation in the States', (1954) 54 Columbia Law Review 188.
Rose Carol M, *Property and Persuasion: Essays on the History, Theory, and Rhetoric of Ownership* (Routledge 1994).
Rose, 'Privatization—The Road to Democracy', (2006) 50 Saint Louis Law Journal 691.
Rosenblatt Helena, *The Lost History of Liberalism, From Ancient Rome to the Twenty-First Century* (Princeton University Press 2018).
Rubino Alessandro, Sapia Alessandro, & La Scala Massimo, *Handbook of Energy Economics and Policy* (Academic Press 2021).
Runde 'The U.S. Exim Bank in an Age of Great Power Competition', (18 June 2024) Center for Strategic & International Studies, https://www.csis.org/analysis/us-exim-bank-age-great-power-competition, last accessed 11 December 2024.
Sabadus, 'Putin's Energy Weapon: Europe Must Be Ready for Russian Gas Blackmail', (8 July 2022) Atlantic Council, https://www.atlanticcouncil.org/blogs/ukrainealert/putins-energy-weapon-europe-must-be-ready-for-russian-gas-blackmail/, last accessed 22 January 2025.
Sabel Charles F & Victor David G, *Fixing the Climate, Strategies for an Uncertain World* (Princeton University Press 2022).
Sadik-Zada, 'Back to the Future: Revisiting Perspectives on Nuclear Fusion and Juxtaposition to Existing Energy Sources', (2024) 290 Energy 129150.
Salacuse Jeswald, *The Three Laws of International Investment: National, Contractual, and International Frameworks for Foreign Capital* (Oxford University Press 2013).
Sandalow David et al, *Guide to Chinese Climate Policy 2022* (Oxford Institute for Energy Studies 2022).
Sanzillo & Kunkel, 'New Fortress Energy, Leader of LNG Growth Bubble, Facing Bankruptcy', (22 November 2024) Institute for Energy Economics and Financial Analysis, https://ieefa.org/resources/new-fortress-energy-leader-lng-growth-bubble-facing-bankruptcy, last accessed 7 January 2025.

Saul Ben et al, *The International Covenant on Economic, Social and Cultural Rights: Commentary, Cases, and Materials* (Oxford University Press 2014).
Schelling, 'Strategies of Commitment', *in Strategies of Commitment and Other Essays* (Thomas Schelling ed, Harvard University Press 2006) 1.
Schmitt Carl, *Politische Theologie, Vier Kapitel zur Lehre von der Souveränität* (Duncker & Humblot 1922).
Schmitt Carl, *Der Begriff des Politischen* (Duncker & Humblot 1932).
Schremmer, 'Pore Space Property', (2021) Utah Law Review 1.
Schremmer, A Unifying Doctrine of Subsurface Property Rights, (2022) 46 Harvard Environmental Law Review 525.
Schumpeter Joseph A, *Capitalism, Socialism and Democracy* (Harper 1976).
Schumpeter Joseph A, *The Theory of Economic Development, An Inquiry into Profits, Capital, Credit, Interest, and the Business Cycle* (Redvers Opie trans, Transaction Publishers 1984).
Seddon, Stognei, Foy, & Leahy, 'Russia-China Gas Pipeline Deal Stalls over Beijing Price Demands', (2 June 2024) Financial Times, https://www.ft.com/content/f7a34e3e-bce9-4db9-ac49-a092f382c526, last accessed 1 September 2024.
Seely, 'Texas Power Grid Update', (2024) 63 South Texas Law Review 429.
Segrave Kerry, *The Electric Car in America, 1890-1922* (McFarland 2019).
Sen Amartya, *Development as Freedom* (Knopf 1999).
Sen Amartya, *The Idea of Justice* (Belknap Press 2009).
Shackelford, 'The Law of Cyber Peace', (2017) 18 Chicago Journal of International Law 1.
Shackelford, 'On Climate Change and Cyber Attacks: Leveraging Polycentric Governance to Mitigate Global Collective Action Problems', (2020) 18 Vanderbilt Journal of Entertainment & Technology Law 653.
Shaffer, 'Governing the Interface of U.S.-China Trade Relations', (2021) 115 American Journal of International Law 622.
Shelest, 'Ukraine's Euromaidan: Questions from the (R)evolution', (21 February 2014) NATO Defense College Research Report.
Siegel, 'Senate Republicans Introduce Climate Bill – Aimed at China', (2 November 2024) Politico, https://www.politico.com/news/2023/11/02/senate-gop-climate-bill-china-00124909, last accessed 9 December 2024.
Simpson, 'Lithium Prices in Free Fall: Implications for Clean Energy Transition in the Private Sector', (1 February 2024) Bradley Intelligence Report, https://www.bradley.com/insights/publications/2024/02/lithium-prices-in-free-fall-implications-for-clean-energy-transition-in-the-private-sector, last accessed 4 May 2024.
Sing, 'China's Risky Answer to Wall of Debt Is More Debt', (18 June 204) Reuters, https://www.reuters.com/breakingviews/chinas-risky-answer-wall-debt-is-more-debt-2024-06-17/, last accessed 11 December 2024.
Skinner Quentin, *The Foundations of Modern Political Thought, Volume One: The Renaissance* (Cambridge University Press 1978).
Skinner Quentin, *Liberty Before Liberalism* (Cambridge University Press 1998).
Skinner Quentin, *Visions of Politics* (Cambridge University Press 2012).
Skinner, 'Two Concepts of Citizenship', (1993) 55 Tijdschrift voor Filosofie 403.
Skocpol Theda, *States & Social Revolutions, A Comparative Analysis of France, Russia & China* (Cambridge University Press 1979).
Slaughter Anne-Marie, *A New World Order* (Princeton University Press 2004).
Smil Vaclav, *Energy and Civilization—A History* (MIT Press 2017).
Smithson-Paul et al, 'Decommissioning Case Study, Circular Economy in the Wind Sector – Summary', (29 April 2024) Catapult, https://tethys.pnnl.gov/sites/default/files/publications/Smithson-Paul_et_al_2024.pdf, last accessed 6 December 2024.
Snyder Timothy, *Bloodlands: Europe Between Hitler and Stalin* (Basic Books 2010).
Sohn, 'The New International Law: Protection of the Rights of Individuals Rather than States', (1982) 32 American University Law Review 1.

Sorkin et al, *Biden, Oil and the Middle East*, (14 July 2022) New York Times, https://www.nytimes.com/2022/07/14/business/dealbook/biden-saudi-arabia-oil-middle-east-netflix.html, last accessed 28 June 2024.

Sornarajah M, *The International Law of Foreign Investment* (3rd edn, Cambridge University Press 2010).

Sourgens Frédéric G, *Good Faith in Transnational Law: A Pluralist Account* (Brill Nijhoff 2022).

Sourgens Frédéric G & Sempertegui Leonardo, *Principles of International Energy Transition Law* (Oxford University Press 2023).

Sourgens Frederic G, Banet Catherine, & Baldwin Teddy, *The Transnational Law of Renewable Energy* (Oxford University Press 2024).

Sourgens, 'Positivism, Humanism, and Hegemony: Sovereignty and Security for Our Time', (2006) 25 Penn State International Law Review 433.

Sourgens, 'The End of Law: The ISIL Case Study for Comprehensive Study of Lawlessness', (2015) 39 Fordham International Law Journal 355.

Sourgens, 'Climate Commons Law: The Transformative Force of the Paris Agreement', (2017) 50 NYU Journal of International Law & Politics 885.

Sourgens, 'States of Resistance', (2019) 14 Duke Journal of Constitutional Law & Public Policy 91.

Sourgens, 'Cyber-Nuisance', (2021) 42 University of Pennsylvania Journal of International Law 1005.

Sourgens, 'A Parisian Consensus', (2022) 60 Columbia Journal of Transnational Law 657.

Sourgens, 'Diligent Zero', (2022) 75 SMU Law Review 417.

Sourgens, 'Energy Lessons from the Ukraine Crisis', (24 February 2022) EJILTalk!, https://www.ejiltalk.org/energy-lessons-from-the-ukraine-crisis/, last accessed 4 December 2024.

Sourgens, 'The Dark Sun Network', (2023) 94 University of Colorado Law Review 681.

Sourgens, 'Bundles of Freedom', (2024) Rutgers Law Review 393.

Sourgens, 'Climate Prevention', (2025) 36 Georgetown Environmental Law Review (forthcoming).

Sourgens, 'Polyrelativity', (2025) 52 Pepperdine Law Review (forthcoming).

Soustelle, 'France and Europe, A Gaullist View', (1952) 30 Foreign Affairs 545.

Sovacool & Mukherjee, 'Conceptualizing and Measuring Energy Security: A Synthesized Approach', (2011) 36 Energy 5343.

Spector, 'Two Conceptions of Justice and the Dystopia of Global Justice', (2015) 52 San Diego Law Review 1077.

Stapenhurst Frederick, *Political Risk Around the North Atlantic* (St Martin's Press 1992).

Steffy, 'How Much Did the Feds Really Help with Fracking', (31 October 2013) Forbes, https://www.forbes.com/sites/lorensteffy/2013/10/31/how-much-did-the-feds-really-help-with-fracking/, last accessed 6 January 2025.

Steiner George, *After Babel: Aspects of Language and Translation* (2nd edn, Oxford University Press 1992).

Steiner George, *Antigones: How the Antigone Legend Has Endured in Western Literature, Art, and Thought* (Yale University Press 1996).

Storrow, 'How Coal Failed Texas in the Deep Freeze', (18 March 2021) E&E News, https://www.eenews.net/articles/how-coal-failed-in-the-texas-deep-freeze/, last accessed 6 November 2024.

Strange Susan, *The Retreat of the State, The Diffusion of Power in the World Economy* (Cambridge University Press 1996).

Subedi, 'Declaration on the Right to Development', (2021) United Nations Audiovisual Library of International Law, https://legal.un.org/avl/pdf/ha/drd/drd_e.pdf, last accessed 6 October 2024.

Sunstein Cass, *Laws of Fear, Beyond the Precautionary Principle* (Cambridge University Press 2005).

Tagliapietra Simone, *Global Energy Fundamentals, Economics, Politics and Technology* (Cambridge University Press 2020).

Talus Kim, *EU Energy Law and Policy, A Critical Account* (Oxford University Press 2013).

Tanserksley & Rappeport, 'New Plan to Target Russia's Oil Revenue Brings Debate in White House', (7 July 2024) New York Times, https://www.nytimes.com/2024/07/07/us/politics/russia-oil-ukraine-shadow-fleet.html, last accessed 28 August 2024.

Taylor, 'Global Military Spending Hits Record $2.2 Trillion Amid Multiple Wars', (13 February 2024) Washington Post, https://www.washingtonpost.com/world/2024/02/13/nato-spending-russia-ukraine-trump/, last accessed 26 March 2024.

Terzi Alessio, *Growth for Good, Reshaping Capitalism to Save Humanity from Climate Catastrophe* (Harvard University Press 2022).

Theramus, 'Was Volatility in the Price of Oil a Cause of the 2008 Financial Crisis', (8 December 2009) The Oil Drum, available at https://www.resilience.org/stories/2009-12-08/was-volatility-price-oil-cause-2008-financial-crisis/, last accessed 25 January 2025.

Thomas, 'Slow EV Sales Are Proving Problematic for Australia's Lithium Miners', (30 January 2024) Mining Technology, https://www.mining-technology.com/news/slow-ev-sales-are-proving-problematic-for-australias-lithium-miners/, last accessed 4 May 2024.

Tolkien John RR, *The Lord of the Rings* (HarperCollins 2021).

Tomain, 'The Persistence of Natural Monopoly', (2002) 16 Natural Resources & Environment 242.

Tomuschat Christian, *Human Rights: Between Idealism and Realism* (3rd edn, Oxford University Press 2014).

Tonrey, 'Distributed Energy Resources: How Utilities Have Stared Death in the Face and Emerged Victorious', (7 July 2023) Kleinman Center for Energy Policy, https://kleinmanenergy.upenn.edu/commentary/blog/distributed-energy-resources-how-utilities-have-stared-death-in-the-face-and-emerged-victorious/, last accessed 3 November 2024.

Tordo Silvia et al, *Local Content Policies in the Oil and Gas Sector, A World Bank Study* (International Bank for Reconstruction and Development 2013).

Trovall, 'Why Have Texas' Electric Bills Gotten More Expensive and Volatile?, (24 May 2024) Houston Public Media, https://www.houstonpublicmedia.org/articles/news/2024/05/24/488578/why-have-texas-electric-bills-gotten-more-expensive-and-volatile/, last accessed 17 July 2024.

Tubiana et al, 'Between Crises and Decarbonisation: Realigning EU Climate and Energy Policy for the New 'State of the World'', (July 2022) EUI Florence School of Regulation Policy Brief 2022/42, https://cadmus.eui.eu/bitstream/handle/1814/74737/QM-AX-22-042-EN-N.pdf?sequence=1&isAllowed=y, last accessed 4 May 2024.

Uhlenhuth, 'Power from the Prairie Aims to Link West Coast Sun with Prairie Wind', (24 November 2020) Energy News Network, https://energynews.us/2020/11/24/power-from-the-prairie-aims-to-link-west-coast-sun-with-midwest-wind/, last accessed 9 June 2024.

van de Graaf Thijs & Sovacool Benjamin K, *Global Energy Politics* (Polity 2020).

van Harten Gus, *Investment Treaty Protection and Public Law* (Oxford University Press 2008).

van Nuffel et al, 'Sector Coupling: How Can It Be Enhanced in the EU to Foster Grid Stability and Decarbonise?' at 7, (November 2018) Policy Department for Economic, Scientific and Quality of Life Policies European Parliament, https://www.europarl.europa.eu/RegData/etudes/STUD/2018/626091/IPOL_STU(2018)626091_EN.pdf, last accessed 6 December 2024.

Vargas, 'CEO Board Update', (23 April 2024) Electric Reliability Council of Texas, https://www.ercot.com/files/docs/2024/04/22/5%20CEO%20Update.pdf, last accessed 17 July 2024.

Vermeule Adrian, *Common Good Constitutionalism* (John Wiley 2022).

Viernes, 'Oversupply, Low Prices for Cobalt to Persist in 2024 as Demand Slips', (27 December 2023) S&P Global, https://www.spglobal.com/commodityinsights/en/market-insights/latest-news/metals/122723-oversupply-low-prices-for-cobalt-to-persist-in-2024-as-demand-slips, last accessed 1 September 2024.

Vince et al, 'What Is Happening and Where in the World of RTOs and ISOs?', (2006) 27 Energy Law Journal 65.

Viñuales Jorge, *The International Law of Energy* (Cambridge University Press 2022).

Virgil, 'Aeneid', *in Virgil, Eclogues, Georgics, Aeneid, Books 1–6* (GH Fairclough trans, GP Good rev, Harvard University Press 1999).

Waibel Michael et al, *The Backlash Against Investment Arbitration, Perceptions and Reality* (Kluwer Law 2010).

Wälde, 'Renegotiating Acquired Rights in the Oil and Gas Industries: Industry and Political Cycles Meet the Rule of Law', (2008) 1 Journal of World Energy Law & Business 55.

Walker, 'Ukraine's EU Trade Deal Will Be Catastrophic, Says Russia', (22 September 2013) Guardian, https://www.theguardian.com/world/2013/sep/22/ukraine-european-union-trade-russia, last accessed 22 January 2025.

Waltz Kenneth N, *Theory of International Politics* (Random House 1979).

Wang, 'China's Impressive Rate of Nuclear Construction, What Do Fast Chinese-Led Builds Mean for Nuclear's Future?', (5 March 2024) Breakthrough Institute, https://thebreakthrough.org/issues/energy/chinas-impressive-rate-of-nuclear-construction#:~:text=The%20Chinese%20nuclear%20project%20construction,to%20just%20over%207%20years, last accessed 3 May 2024.

Ward-Glenton, 'German Energy Prices Are so High They're Driving Companies to Relocate, Industry Body Says', (21 June 2023) CNBC, https://www.cnbc.com/2023/06/21/high-german-energy-prices-are-seeing-some-companies-relocate-bdi.html last accessed 26 August 2024.

Warner, 'Gaullist Foreign Policy', (1965) 21 The World Today 112.

Sen Warren, 'The Transpacific Partnership Clause Everyone Should Oppose', (25 February 2015) Washington Post, https://www.washingtonpost.com/opinions/kill-the-dispute-settlement-language-in-the-trans-pacific-partnership/2015/02/25/ec7705a2-bd1e-11e4-b274-e5209a3bc9a9_story.html, last accessed 11 January 2025.

Welton & Eisen, 'Clean Energy Justice: Charting an Emerging Agenda', (2019) 43 Harvard Environmental Law Review 307.

Weisbach & Sunstein, 'Climate Change and Discounting the Future: A Guide for the Perplexed', (2009) 27 Yale Law and Policy Review 433.

Weisman, 'How Democrats Lost the Working Class', (4 January 2025) New York Times, https://www.nytimes.com/2025/01/04/us/politics/democrats-working-class.html, last accessed 7 January 2025.

Williams, "Can International Legal Principles Play a Positive Role in Resolving Central and East European Transboundary Environmental Disputes', (1995) 7 Georgetown International Environmental Law Review 421.

Williams and others, 'A Guide to the Circular Carbon Economy (CCE)' King Abdullah Petroleum Studies and Research Center (August 2020).

Winton, 'Europe To Buy Nearly 9 Million Fewer EVs By 2030 Than Expected: Report', (8 April 2024) Forbes, https://www.forbes.com/sites/neilwinton/2024/04/08/europe-to-buy-nearly-9-million-fewer-evs-by-2030-than-expected-report/?sh=3113e0fa239e, last accessed 4 May 2024.

Wiseman, 'Expanding Regional Renewable Governance', (2011) 35 Harvard Environmental Law Review 477.

Wiseman & Osofsky, 'Dynamic Energy Federalism', (2013) 72 Maryland Law Review 773.

Wittgenstein Ludwig, 'Philosophische Untersuchungen', *in Werkausgabe* (Suhrkamp Verlag 1984) 255.

Wolfrum Rüdiger, *Solidarity and Community Interest: Driving Forces for Interpretation and Development of International Law* (Brill Nijhoff 2021).

Woo, 'A Wholesale Electricity Market Design sans Missing Money and Price Manipulation', (2019) 134 Energy Policy 110988.

Wu & Salzman, 'The Next Generation of Trade and Environment Conflicts: The Rise of Green Industrial Policy', (2014) 108 Northwestern Law Review 401.

Wyns Arthur et al, *The Health Argument for Climate Action, A COP26 Special Report on Climate Change and Health* (World Health Organization 2021).

Yep & Foo, 'How the Fukushima Crisis led to a Revolution in LNG Trading', (11 March 2021) S&P Global, https://www.spglobal.com/commodity-insights/en/news-research/blog/lng/031121-fukushima-crisis-japan-lng-trading-revolution-jkm, last accessed 7 January 2025.

Yergin Daniel, *The Prize, The Epic Quest for Oil, Money & Power* (Free Press 2092).

Yergin Daniel, *The Quest, Energy, Security, and the Remaking of the Modern World* (revised edn, Penguin 2012).

Yergin Daniel, *The New Map: Energy, Climate, and the Clash of Nations* (Random House 2020).
Yergin, 'Ensuring Energy Security', (2006) 85 Foreign Affairs 69.
Zhao, 'Cost–Benefit Analysis of Distributed Energy Systems Considering the Monetization of Indirect Benefits', (2024) 16 Sustainability 820.
Zile, 'Judicial Control of Land Use in France', (1960) 45 Cornell Law Review 288.
'British Rationing Ends Next Summer', (6 November 1952) New York Times, https://timesmachine.nytimes.com/timesmachine/1953/11/06/84070351.html?pageNumber=11, last accessed 29 October 2024.
Renewable Power Pathways: Review of the U.S. Department of Energy's Renewable Energy Programs (National Academy Press 2000).
'Schröder will Kohle und Klima schützen', (17 September 2003) Frankfurter Allgemeine Zeitung, https://www.faz.net/aktuell/wirtschaft/energiepolitik-schroeder-will-kohle-und-klima-schuetzen-1112446.html, last accessed 17 August 2024.
'E.On Hatches Plan for Germany's First LNG Import Terminal', (26 October 2005) Energy Intelligence, https://www.energyintel.com/0000017b-a7a9-de4c-a17b-e7eb89700000, last accessed 20 January 2025.
Levelized Cost of Energy 3.0 (February 2009) Lazard, https://www.solarthermalworld.org/sites/default/files/lazard2009_levelizedcostofenergy.pdf, last accessed 30 September 2024.
'New Electric Generating Plants in Texas Since 1995', (October 2013) Texas Public Utility Commission, https://ftp.puc.texas.gov/public/puct-info/industry/maps/elecmaps/gentable.pdf, last accessed 17 July 2024.
'Levelized Cost and Levelized Avoided Cost of New Generation Resources in the Annual Energy Outlook 2014', US Energy Information Administration (April 2014), https://www.eia.gov/outlooks/archive/aeo14/pdf/electricity_generation_2014.pdf, last accessed 29 April 2024.
'Lazard's Levelized Cost of Energy Analysis Version 8.0', (September 2014) Lazard, https://refman.energytransitionmodel.com/publications/1962, last accessed 7 January 2025.
'What We Have Learned, Principles of Truth and Reconciliation', (2015) Truth and Reconciliation Commission of Canada, https://ehprnh2mwo3.exactdn.com/wp-content/uploads/2021/01/Principles_English_Web.pdf, last accessed 1 November 2024.
'Putin Says He Decided to Take Crimea Just Hours after Yanukovych's Ouster', (9 March 2015) Eurasianet, https://eurasianet.org/putin-says-he-decided-to-take-crimea-just-hours-after-yanukovychs-ouster, last accessed 22 January 2025.
'Republic of Indonesia, The Indonesian Carbon Capture Storage (CCS) Capacity Building Program, CCS for Coal-Fired Power Plants in Indonesia', (June 2015) World Bank, https://documents1.worldbank.org/curated/en/563781468284373788/pdf/FINAL-OK2-Jun-2415Cov-reduced-with-WB-cover.pdf, last accessed 12 August 2024.
'Closing the Loop, New Circular Economy Package', (January 2016) European Parliament, https://www.europarl.europa.eu/RegData/etudes/BRIE/2016/573899/EPRS_BRI%282016%29573899_EN.pdf, last accessed 5 December 2024.
'United States 2019 Review', (13 September 2019) International Energy Agency, https://iea.blob.core.windows.net/assets/7c65c270-ba15-466a-b50d-1c5cd19e359c/United_States_2019_Review.pdf, last accessed 7 January 2025.
'More U.S. Coal-Fired Power Plants are Decommissioning as Retirements Continue', (26 July 2019) U.S. Energy Information Administration, https://www.eia.gov/todayinenergy/detail.php?id=40212, last accessed 16 July 2024.
'Industry Power Prices in Germany: Extraordinarily High—and Low', (4 December 2019) Clean Energy Wire, https://www.cleanenergywire.org/industrial-power-prices-and-energiewende, last accessed 20 January 2025.
'Mapped: The World's Coal Power Plants', (26 March 2020) Carbon Brief, https://www.carbonbrief.org/mapped-worlds-coal-power-plants/#:~:text=Global%20coal%20capacity%20grew%20in,1%2C066GW%20to%202%2C045GW, last accessed 20 January 2025.
'IEA US Shale Upstream Cost Index, 2005-2020', (27 May 2020) International Energy Agency, https://www.iea.org/data-and-statistics/charts/iea-us-shale-upstream-cost-index-2005-2020, last accessed 20 January 2025.

'Installed Capacity in India, 2000-2020, and Projections up to 2040 in the Stated Policies Scenario', (27 October 2020) International Energy Agency, https://www.iea.org/data-and-statistics/charts/installed-capacity-in-india-2000-2020-and-projections-up-to-2040-in-the-stated-policies-scenario, last accessed 12 August 2024.

'South Korea Looked Just Like North Korea 50 Years Ago', (26 July 2021) Business Insider Asia, https://www.businessinsider.in/stock-market/south-korea-looked-just-like-north-korea-50-years-ago-photos/slidelist/21199867.cms, last accessed 29 October 2024.

'Key World Energy Statistics 2021', (September 2021) International Energy Agency, https://iea.blob.core.windows.net/assets/52f66a88-0b63-4ad2-94a5-29d36e864b82/KeyWorldEnergyStatistics2021.pdf, last accessed 25 March 2024.

'The February 2021 Cold Weather Outages in Texas and the South Central United States', (16 November 2021) US Federal Electricity Regulatory Commission, https://www.ferc.gov/media/february-2021-cold-weather-outages-texas-and-south-central-united-states-ferc-nerc-and, last accessed 4 November 2024.

U.S. Inflation Reduction Act of 2022, House Resolution 5376, 117th Congress.

'The Net Zero Transition, What It Would Cost, What It Would Bring' at 5, (January 2022) McKinsey & Co, https://www.mckinsey.com/~/media/mckinsey/business%20functions/sustainability/our%20insights/the%20net%20zero%20transition%20what%20it%20would%20cost%20what%20it%20could%20bring/the-net-zero-transition-what-it-would-cost-and-what-it-could-bring-final.pdf, last accessed 26 March 2024.

'How Heavily Does Germany Rely on Russian Energy?', (4 May 2022) The Economist, https://www.economist.com/the-economist-explains/2022/05/04/how-heavily-does-germany-rely-on-russian-energy, last accessed 6 August 2024.

'Japan Natural Gas Security Policy', (18 August 2022) International Energy Agency, https://www.iea.org/articles/japan-natural-gas-security-policy, last accessed 20 January 2025.

'Qatar Signs Gas Export Deal with Germany', (29 November 2022) Deutsche Welle, https://www.dw.com/en/qatar-signs-gas-export-deal-with-germany/a-63923323, last accessed 30 November 2024.

'Key Findings From the Global Religious Futures Project', (21 December 2022) Pew Research, https://www.pewresearch.org/religion/2022/12/21/key-findings-from-the-global-religious-futures-project/, last accessed 29 October 2024.

'China: Coal', (2023) International Energy Agency, https://www.iea.org/countries/china/coal, last accessed 21 January 2025.

'Oil Dependence and U.S. Foreign Policy 1850-2023', (2023) Council on Foreign Relations, https://www.cfr.org/timeline/oil-dependence-and-us-foreign-policy, last accessed 30 November 2024.

'Levelized Cost of Energy+', (April 2023) Lazard, https://www.lazard.com/research-insights/2023-levelized-cost-of-energyplus/, last accessed 29 April 2024.

'Mexico Power Plant Purchases Touted as 'New Nationalization', (4 April 2023) Associated Press, https://apnews.com/article/mexico-spain-electricity-plants-purchase-ae10392607ee263c2bc87b0fbe2ae9d7, last accessed 3 May 2024.

'German Politicians Split as Last Nuclear Plants Close', (16 April 2023) Deutsche Welle, https://www.dw.com/en/german-politicians-split-as-last-nuclear-plants-close/a-65332978, last accessed 20 January 2025.

'Venture Global LNG Signs 20-Year Contract with German Energy Firm', (22 June 2023) Reuters, https://www.reuters.com/business/energy/venture-global-lng-signs-20-year-contract-with-german-energy-firm-2023-06-22/, last accessed 7 September 2024.

'Reliance on Russian Fossil Fuels in OECD and EU Countries', (July 2023) International Energy Agency, https://www.iea.org/data-and-statistics/data-product/reliance-on-russian-fossil-fuels-in-oecd-and-eu-countries, last accessed 7 January 2025.

'Climate Change Impacts Are Increasing for Americans', (14 November 2023) National Oceanic and Atmospheric Administration, https://www.noaa.gov/news-release/climate-change-impacts-are-increasing-for-americans, last accessed 10 December 2024.

'Carbon Capture and Storage in the United States', (December 2023) Congressional Budget Office, https://www.cbo.gov/system/files/2023-12/59345-carbon-capture-storage.pdf, last accessed 9 December 2024.

Fact Sheet, 'Supporting Renewable Energy and Environmental Export', (2024) US Export-Import Bank, https://www.exim.gov/about/special-initiatives/ctep/fact-sheets/supporting-renewable-energy-environmental-exports#:~:text=Since%201992%2C%20EXIM%20has%20had,for%2018%2Dyear%20repayment%20terms, last accessed 11 February 2024.

'Sustainable Development Goal 11', (2024) United Nations Statistics Division, https://unstats.un.org/sdgs/report/2023/goal-11/#:~:text=The%20world's%20population%20reached%208,70%20per%20cent%20by%202050, last accessed 26 August 2024.

'Biodiversity', (2024) United Nations System of Environmental Economic Accounting, https://seea.un.org/content/biodiversity, last accessed 29 October 2024.

'Human Development Index', (2024) United Nations Development Programme, https://hdr.undp.org/data-center/human-development-index#/indicies/HDI, last accessed 29 October 2024.

'Medium and Long-Term Loan Guarantee', (2024) Export-Import Bank of the United States, https://www.exim.gov/solutions/loan-guarantee, last accessed 11 December 2024.

'Critical Grid Infrastructure to Connect the West', (2024) TransWest Express, https://www.transwestexpress.net, last accessed 26 June 2024.

'Don't Mess With Texas – Origin Story', (2024) Don't Mess With Texas, https://www.dontmesswithtexas.org/about-us/, last accessed 5 December 2024.

'France: Energy Mix', (2024) International Energy Agency, https://www.iea.org/countries/france/energy-mix, last accessed 3 May 2024.

'Fusion in Brief', (2024) UK Atomic Energy Authority Culham Centre for Fusion Energy, https://ccfe.ukaea.uk/fusion-energy/fusion-in-brief/, last accessed 5 December 2024.

'Germany: Coal', (2024) International Energy Agency, https://www.iea.org/countries/germany/coal, last accessed 21 January 2025.

'Market for Electricity', (2024) PJM Learning Center, https://learn.pjm.com/electricity-basics/market-for-electricity.aspx#:~:text=The%20clearing%20price%20for%20electricity,on%20the%20Markets%20%26%20Operations%20homepage, last accessed 26 June 2024.

'Vatican Media Live', (2024) The Holy See, https://www.comunicazione.va/en/servizi/live.html, last accessed 29 October 2024.

'Utah's Coal Resources', (2024) Utah Office of Energy Development, https://geology.utah.gov/apps/energy-resources/?page=Coal, last accessed 26 June 2024.

'Solar Explained', (19 January 2024) U.S. Energy Information Administration, https://www.eia.gov/energyexplained/solar/solar-energy-and-the-environment.php, last accessed 20 January 2025.

'Beneath the Rubble: Documenting Devastation and Loss in Mariupol', (8 February 2024) Human Rights Watch, https://www.hrw.org/feature/russia-ukraine-war-mariupol#:~:text=On%20May%2017%2C%20Ukrainian%20forces,a%20place%20of%20shallow%20graves, last accessed 1 September 2024.

'Retirements of U.S. electric generating capacity to slow in 2024', (20 February 2024) U.S. Energy Information Administration, https://www.eia.gov/todayinenergy/detail.php?id=61425#:~:text=Coal%20retirements%20are%20scheduled%20to,age%20of%20operating%20coal%20units, last accessed 16 July 2024.

'Proposal Submission Instructions', (27 February 2024) Defense Advanced Research Projects Agency, https://media.defense.gov/2024/Feb/27/2003400545/-1/-1/1/DARPA_STTR_24D_R2.PDF, last accessed 6 January 2025.

'Rechte Rheinstrecke wird erneuert', (29 February 2024), Frankfurter Allgemeine Zeitung, https://www.faz.net/aktuell/rhein-main/rechte-rheinstrecke-wird-erneuert-19555370.html, last accessed 16 July 2024.

'Distribution of Voting Power', (31 March 2024) African Development Bank, https://www.afdb.org/en/documents/afdb-statement-voting-powers-31-march-2024, last accessed 11 December 2024.

'The United States Was the World's Largest Liquefied Natural Gas Exporter in 2023', (1 April 2024) U.S. Energy Information Administration, https://www.eia.gov/todayinenergy/detail.php?id=61683, last accessed 17 August 2024.

'Experts React. The U.S. Just Reimposed Sanctions on Venezuela. What Does that Mean for Energy Markets and Venezuela's Election?', (18 April 2024) Atlantic Council, https://www.atlanticcouncil.org/blogs/new-atlanticist/experts-react/experts-react-venezuela-sanctions-election/, last accessed 28 July 2024.

'China Wants Ability to Invade Taiwan by 2027, U.S. Admiral Says', (24 April 2024) Nikkei Asia, https://asia.nikkei.com/Editor-s-Picks/Interview/China-wants-ability-to-invade-Taiwan-by-2027-U.S.-admiral-says, last accessed 9 December 2024.

'Nuclear Power in France', (25 April 2024) World Nuclear Association, https://world-nuclear.org/information-library/country-profiles/countries-a-f/france, last accessed 3 May 2024.

'U.S. Energy-Related Carbon Dioxide Emissions, 2023', (25 April 2024) U.S. Energy Information Administration, https://www.eia.gov/environment/emissions/carbon/, last accessed 10 December 2024.

'2023 State of the Market Report for the ERCOT Electricity Markets', (May 2024) Potomac Economics, https://www.potomaceconomics.com/wp-content/uploads/2024/05/2023-State-of-the-Market-Report_Final.pdf, last accessed 4 November 2024.

'Economic Forecast for Germany', (15 May 2024) European Commission, https://economy-finance.ec.europa.eu/economic-surveillance-eu-economies/germany/economic-forecast-germany_en, last accessed 2 September 2024.

'Vision OPEN 2024', (22 May 2024) Advanced Research Projects Agency – Energy, https://arpa-e-foa.energy.gov/#FoaId6cc31453-6805-417c-967c-4df560ba2c88, last accessed 6 January 2025.

'Levelized Cost of Energy+', (June 2024) Lazard, https://www.lazard.com/media/xemfey0k/lazards-lcoeplus-june-2024-_vf.pdf, last accessed 20 January 2025.

'Russia Government's Oil Revenue Was Up Almost Up 50% in June', (3 July 2024) Bloomberg, https://www.bloomberg.com/news/articles/2024-07-03/russian-government-s-oil-revenue-was-up-almost-50-in-june?embedded-checkout=true, last accessed 28 August 2024.

'Offshore Wind: Strategies for Uncertain Times', (12 July 2024) McKinsey & Co, https://www.mckinsey.com/industries/electric-power-and-natural-gas/our-insights/offshore-wind-strategies-for-uncertain-times, last accessed 30 November 2024.

'The Global Fusion Industry in 2024', (16 July 2024) Fusion Industry Association, https://www.fusionindustryassociation.org/wp-content/uploads/2024/07/2024-annual-global-fusion-industry-report.pdf, last accessed 18 November 2024.

'NATO's Response to Russia's Invasion of Ukraine', (19 July 2024) NATO Report, https://www.nato.int/cps/en/natohq/topics_192648.htm, last accessed 28 August 2024.

'Ukraine weist Bericht zu Nord Stream zurück', (15 August 2024) Frankfurt Allgemeine Zeitung, https://www.faz.net/aktuell/politik/ukraine-weist-anschuldigungen-zu-nord-stream-zurueck-19921953.html, last accessed 28 August 2024.

'Safety of Nuclear Reactors', (23 August 2024) World Nuclear Association, https://world-nuclear.org/information-library/safety-and-security/safety-of-plants/safety-of-nuclear-power-reactors, last accessed 5 December 2024.

'German Inflation Sinks to 1.9% in August', (29 August 2024) Deutsche Welle, https://www.dw.com/en/german-inflation-sinks-to-19-in-august/a-70081684, last accessed 2 September 2024.

'Revisions Show US Economy Grew Faster, 2021–23, Boosting Real Incomes', (26 September 2024) The White House, https://www.whitehouse.gov/cea/written-materials/2024/09/26/revisions-show-us-economy-grew-faster-2021-23-boosting-real-incomes/, last accessed 7 October 2024.

Executive Order 'Putting America First in International Environmental Agreements', (20 January 2025) The White House, https://www.whitehouse.gov/presidential-actions/2025/01/putting-america-first-in-international-environmental-agreements/, last accessed 21 January 2025.

Table of Treaties & Treaty Instruments

1907 Convention for the Pacific Settlement of International Disputes.
UN Charter (1945).
Universal Declaration of Human Rights (1948).
European Convention on Human Rights (1950).
New York Convention on the Recognition and Enforcement of Arbitral Awards (1958).
International Convention on Civil and Political Rights (1966).
American Convention on Human Rights (1969).
Declaration on Principles of International Law concerning Friendly Relations and Co-operation among States in Accordance with the Charter of the United Nations, (24 October 1970) UN General Assembly Resolution 2625 (XXV).
African Charter on Human and Peoples' Rights (1981).
Committee for Economic, Social, and Cultural Rights, General Comment No. 3 (The Nature of States Parties Obligations) (14 December 1990).
Asian Human Rights Charter (1998).
Committee on Economic, Social, and Cultural Rights, General Comment No 12 (Right to Adequate Food) (14 May 1999).
General Comment No 21 (Right of Everyone to Take Part in Cultural Life) (20 November 2009).
Committee on Economic, Social, and Cultural Rights, General Comment No 13 (Right to Education) (8 December 1999).
Committee on Economic, Social, and Cultural Rights, General Comment No 14 (Right to Health) (12 May 2000).
Smith, 'Indigenous Peoples and Boarding Schools, A Comparative Study', (26 January 2009) United Nations Permanent Forum on Indigenous Issues, UN Document Number E/C.19/CRP.1, https://www.un.org/esa/socdev/unpfii/documents/IPS_Boarding_Schools.pdf last accessed 1 November 2024.
UN Guiding Principles on Business and Human Rights (2011).
Committee on Economic, Social and Cultural Rights, General Comment No. 4 (Right to Adequate Housing) (13 December 2014).
Paris Agreement (2015).
'Transforming Our World: The 2030 Agenda for Sustainable Development', (25 September 2015) United Nations General Assembly Resolution 70/1.
Human Rights Committee, General Comment No 36 (Right to Life) (3 September 2019).
Secretary Pompeo, 'On the U.S. Withdrawal from the Paris Agreement', (4 November 2019) U.S. State Department, https://2017-2021.state.gov/on-the-u-s-withdrawal-from-the-paris-agreement/, last accessed 4 May 2024.
'EU Member States Sign an Agreement for the Termination of Intra-EU Bilateral Investment Treaties', (5 May 2020) European Commission, https://finance.ec.europa.eu/publications/eu-member-states-sign-agreement-termination-intra-eu-bilateral-investment-treaties_en, last accessed 9 June 2024.
Second Nationally Determine Contribution of the United States of America (15 April 2021), https://unfccc.int/sites/default/files/NDC/2022-06/United%20States%20NDC%20April%2021%202021%20Final.pdf, last accessed 4 May 2024.
Glasgow Climate Pact (2021)
Boyd (Special Rapporteur on Human Rights and the Environment), 'The Right to a Clean, Healthy, and Sustainable Environment', (12 January 2022) UN Doc. A/HRC/49/53.
The Human Right to a Clean, Healthy and Sustainable Environment, GA Res 76/ 3000 (28 July 2022) UN Doc A/ 76/ L.75 (2022).
UN Draft Convention on the Right to Development with commentaries (6 April 2022).
First Global Stocktake (2023)

Table of Cases

ICC Case No 5485, award (18 August 1987), ¶ 42, https://www.trans-lex.org/205485, last accessed 10 January 2025.
Advisory Opinion on Climate Change, ITLOS Decision No 31 (21 May 2024).
Badoit v André, Lyon, 18 avril 1856, DP [1856] 2 199
Appellate Body Report, Canada—Measures Relating to the Feed-in Tariff Program, WTO Doc WT/DS426/AB/R (6 May 2013).
Appellate Body Report, Canada—Certain Measures Affecting the Renewable Energy Generation Sector, WTO Doc WT/DS412/AB/R (6 May 2013).
Coastal Oil & Gas Corp v Garza Energy Tr, 268 SW3d 1, 13–17 (Tex 2008).
Forissier v Chaverot, Req, 10 juin 1902, DP [1902] 1 454.
Fraport AG Frankfurt Airport Services Worldwide v Philippines, ICSID Case No ARB/03/25, annulment (23 December 2010).
Appellate Body Report, India—Certain Measures Relating to Solar Cells and Solar Modules, WTO Doc WT/DS456/AB/R (16 September 2016).
Mfrs' Gas & Oil Co v Indiana Nat Gas & Oil Co, 57 NE 912, 915 (Ind 1900).
Neubauer v Germany, 1 BvR 2656/18 (Mar 24, 2021).
Pierson v Post, 3 Cai R 175 (New York 1805).
Rockhopper Italia SpA v Italy, ICSID Case No ARB/17/14, award (23 August 2022).
Spur Industries, Inc v Del E Webb Development Co, 494 P2d 700 (Arizona 1972).
United States—Countervailing Duty Measures on Certain Products from China, Appellate Body Report, WTO Cod WT/DS437/AB/R (18 December 2014).
United States—Certain Measures Relating to the Renewable Energy Sector, Panel Report, WTO Doc WT/DS510/R (27 June 2019).
HR 20 December 2019, NJ 2020, 41 mnt. J Spier (De Staat der Nederlanden/Stichting Urgenda).
Verein KlimaSeniorinnen Schweiz v Switzerland, European Court of Human Rights, Application No 53600/20, judgment (9 April 2024).

Index

For the benefit of digital users, indexed terms that span two pages (e.g., 52–53) may, on occasion, appear on only one of those pages.

Acemoglu, Daron 25, 99–100, 155–56, 162, 185, 255–56
AEG 81
Aghion, Philippe 99–100, 155–56, 165–66, 255–56, 259, 262
Ali, Arif 300
Alston, Philip 148, 149
Anderson, Owen 18, 20–21, 40–41, 58, 73–74, 110, 166, 207–8
Anghie, Antony 105–6, 157–58
Annas, Julia 70
anticommons 12–13, 36–37, 43–44, 79–80, 97, 98, 99, 120, 121, 227, 306
  anticommons governance 37–38, 45–46, 223–24, 288, 291–92, 297
  disaster of the anticommons 36, 43, 44–45, 47, 49, 169
  Holy Roman Empire, and 46, 47
  relationship to commons 36–37, 45
  Zollverein, and 47, 48
Aquinas, Thomas (Saint) 63
Arato, Julian 19, 280–81
arbitration 280, 281, 283–84, 286–87, 291–96, 299–300, 302
  1907 Convention for the Pacific Settlement of International Disputes 283–84
  1958 New York Convention on the Recognition and Enforcement of Arbitral Awards 280
  Investor-State arbitration 280
Aristotle 47, 63, 75, 141, 142, 143–44, 145, 158, 185
Austria-Hungary 83
Axelrod, Robert 110, 129–30, 172, 192–93, 277–78

Balmaceda, Margarita 5, 93–94, 107
batteries 28, 30, 105, 191–92, 216, 236, 271–72
Baudrillard, Jean 297
Berger, Klaus-Peter 287, 293
Berlin 67–68, 72, 74–75, 79, 81, 131, 229
Berliner Electrizitäts-Werke (BEW) 68, 72, 74, 79, 81
Besson, Samantha 141, 283–84
Bilateral Investment Treaties *see* International Investment Agreements
Bodansky, Daniel 195–96, 241, 242
bond of belonging
  in general 35–76
  battle of the systems/ universal system, and 53–54, 60, 205–10
  care, and 202–4
  global nature of 116–20, 121, 125, 126, 240–41, 301
  human capabilities, and 142, 143–44
  polycentricity of belonging 261
  shock therapy, and 54–55, 61
  virtue, and 64, 177
Bovari & Company 81
Boyle, Nicholas 46, 47
Brazil 83–84, 267
Brundtland, Gro Harlem 212–13
Brunnée, Jutta 242

California 37–38, 43–44
Cameron, Peter D. 17–18, 26–27, 277
Chicago 81, 229
China, People's Republic 4–5, 24, 25, 85, 86, 88–92, 94, 96, 105, 106–7, 113, 114, 170, 237–39, 243, 245, 248–49, 264, 275
Cicero, Marcus Tullius 141, 177, 178, 284
Clark, Christopher 47–48, 74–75, 82–83
Claussen, Kathleen 280–81
climate change
  adaptation 8–9, 140, 164, 216–17, 219–20, 224, 243–48, 251, 302
  carbon capture utilization and storage (CCUS) 14, 113–14, 214–15, 236, 238–39, 240, 242
  decarbonization *see* mitigation
  direct air capture 14, 81–82, 214–15, 232, 238–39, 240, 242
  first Global Stocktake 13, 216
  glasgow Climate Pact 13, 14, 15–16, 240–41
  greenhouse gases
    CO_2 8, 39–40, 42, 89–90, 119–20, 170, 215–16, 232, 236
    methane (CH_4) 8

climate change (*cont.*)
mitigation 22, 98–99, 191, 195–96, 236–43
Paris Agreement 13, 14, 29, 99, 195–96, 224, 238–39, 240–43, 250–51
Paris Rulebook 240–41
solar radiation management 81–82, 216–17
coal 5, 8, 29, 30, 41–42, 43–44, 61–62, 65, 74–75, 79, 81, 82, 89–90, 93–94, 96–97, 107, 108, 109, 113, 119–20, 170, 242–43, 252, 286–87
cobalt 105–6
Coleman, James W. 20
collective action 40–42, 44–45, 49–50, 120, 289, 307
common good
circular economy, and 214–16
energy abundance, and 210–12
energy peace, and 205–10
energy stewardship, and 212–17
friendship as a model, and 202–3
public good, versus 205–6
reciprocity, and 218–19
thick version of 202–4
thin version of 199–202
commons
commons, definition of 36
commons governance 15–17, 45, 49, 55, 74–75, 79–80, 175–80, 194, 284–85, 291–92, 298
energy system as common pool resource 258, 314
global nature of 97–101, 104, 106, 107–8, 110, 111–12, 114–16
human development and 180–87
neighbourliness/ *troubles de voisinage*, and 15–16, 41, 55–56, 125, 143, 181–82, 216
polycentric governance 63, 64, 175, 261
tragedy of the commons 12–13, 16–17, 37–38, 39–42, 121, 169, 213–14, 223–24, 288, 297, 305, 306
Commonwealth Edison Co. 68, 81
communitarian ethics 55–56, 63
competition 69, 70–72, 95, 99–100, 113–14, 117–18, 155–56, 162, 174, 185, 188–92, 226, 243, 252, 255, 258–60, 261–62, 268, 270–71, 275, 298
co- opetition 16–17, 55–56, 99–100
cooperation
agency, and 129–30, 188–89, 305
anticommons, and 47–48
civic virtue, and 177, 178, 179–80, 185, 187
climate change, and 15–16, 39–40, 243–44, 246–47
Commons, and 97–98
Competition, and 16–17, 174
as an end 170–71, 173–74, 176–77, 184, 189, 196, 197, 199, 218
Energy transition finance, and 233–34, 238–41
Flourishing, and 164
Human rights duty to cooperate 180–83, 185, 187
Innovation, competition, and 78–79
as a means 172, 173, 175–76, 197, 198–99, 200–2, 218
Mutual benefit, and 189–90, 191
Public utility model, and 67–68, 74
Realpolitik, and 99, 111–16, 117–20, 170, 185–87, 192–97, 202, 218, 307–8, 310–11
Rule of law, and 278, 281–82, 284–85, 288, 291, 293, 298
Social practice as 176, 179
Solidarity, and 183–84
Technology transfer, and 165–66
'Thick' decision-making, and 190–91, 208–9
Trust, and 178–79, 305
Universal system as 191–92
Value chain participation, and 12
Covid-19 135, 271–72
critical problem
climate change, as 224, 240–41
in general 11–12, 66, 74, 82, 83, 84, 112, 227–28
missing money problem, and 230–31, 232
policy, and 115, 190–91, 208–9, 233
reverse salient, and 67, 80–81, 95, 229, 230

Daintith, Terence 18–19
Dante Alighieri 173
Daunton, Martin 51, 185–86, 187, 199–200, 205, 206, 243, 246, 248–49, 263–64, 278, 300, 301
De Gaulle, Charles General (President) 116
Democratic Republic of Congo 105
Desierto, Diane A. 141, 146, 154, 282–83, 286–87, 297–98, 301
Deutsche Bank 67–68
development
economic development 131–40
climate change, and 140
distributive problems, and 135
economic globalization, and 138
economic waste 136
gross domestic product (GDP) 131–32

growth 132–33
Kaldor-Hicks efficiency, and 137
Pareto optimal distribution and, and 137
poverty reduction, and 133–35
human development 140
African Charter on Human and Peoples' Rights (ACHPR) 146, 147, 148, 150, 152
agency, and 142, 145, 148, 154
American Convention on Human Rights (AmCHR) 146, 147, 148, 149, 151, 152
Asian Human Rights Charter (AHRC) 146, 147, 148, 149, 150, 151, 152
care, and 142
common good, and 142, 147
deliberation, and 166, 167
distributive problems, and 148–49, 154–55, 159–61, 164
empowerment as 152, 156–64
environmental sacrifice zones, and 165
European Convention on Human Rights (ECHR) 146–48, 152
friendship, and 141
human capabilities, and 143–44
human development index 127–28
human flourishing, and 141, 142, 144–45
International Covenant on Civil and Political Rights (ICCPR) 127, 146–49, 152, 180–81, 186–87, 189, 211
International Covenant on Economic, Social, and Cultural Rights (ICESCR) 148–54, 159, 164, 180–82, 186–87, 205–6, 260
Kaldor-Hicks efficiency, and 155
practice, and 143
progressive realization 127, 143–44, 149, 162–63, 164, 166, 170–71, 182, 207, 257, 260, 301
right to belonging 147, 152
right to bodily integrity 146, 150
right to care for others 147, 152
right to educated, discerning judgement 152
right to environmental stewardship 153
right to freedom of thought 147, 151
right to health 150, 151, 153
right to life 146, 149
right to play 153
right to political and material agency 148, 154
UN Draft Convention on the Right to Development 154–55, 182–83, 186–87, 259–60
development finance 98, 224–25, 242–43, 246, 247–50
dignified life *see* dignity
dignity 3–4, 135, 143, 147, 149–51, 152, 175–76, 312
Dolzer, Rudolf 210, 283–84
Doshi, Rush 237–38, 245
Drahos, Peter 24, 71–72
Dworkin, Ronald 286–87

economic crises
Great Depression 65, 278
Great Recession 65
stagflation 254, 255–57
Edison, Thomas 41
Pearl Street Power Station 41–42, 52–53
Egypt 102
electricity
distributed generation & transmission 160
generation 3–4, 8, 18, 20–21, 22–23, 30, 32, 60–61, 65, 79, 84–85, 87, 95–96, 113–14, 118–19, 191–92, 308–9
transmission 18, 20, 22–23, 29–30, 43–44, 52–53, 80–81, 118, 229, 232–33, 252, 267
energy cycle
bubbles *see* frenzy
downswing/ deployment phase 66, 68–69, 73
frenzy 66, 68–69, 70–72, 73
irruption 66, 70, 73, 74, 261
maturity 68–69, 70–71, 73, 270, 271
synergy 68–69, 71–72, 191–92
upswing/ installation phase 66, 67, 74, 87
energy cycle & geopolitics
during frenzy 82–87, 88, 91–92, 93–94, 95–96, 114, 138, 170, 313–14
during irruption 80–84, 85–86, 88, 91–92, 95
during maturity 81, 87, 95–97, 116–17, 119, 170, 272–73
during synergy 87–94, 114, 116–17, 121, 170, 309–10
value chain lengthening 84, 85, 87–88
energy governance paradigms
authoritarian command & nationalization 14–15, 22–32, 45–46, 48–49, 71–73, 117, 120, 169, 175, 225
balanced governance 64–75, 227–28, 254, 257–63
liberalization 14–15, 26–32, 33–34, 69–72, 78–79, 117, 162, 169, 300–1
Friedman, Milton 69
missing money problem and 225–28
utility model 14–15, 18–19, 21–22, 23, 169, 227–28, 229

energy governance paradigms (*cont.*)
feed in tariffs, and 84–85, 86, 87, 91–92, 114, 231, 268–69, 270–71, 310
natural monopoly and 20
energy transition
all of the above/ hybrid approach 12, 14, 309
coordination transition 232–33
cost of 13–14, 24, 224, 254
innovation transition 229–30
missing money transition 230–33
path dependence 254
energy trilemma 10–12, 166, 199, 204, 210–11, 217–18, 219, 223, 251
affordability/ access 4–5, 6, 7, 9, 10, 13, 19, 21, 22, 26, 32, 42, 49, 72, 82, 89–90, 112, 136, 138, 160, 163, 170, 199
security 10–11, 20–21, 23, 31–32, 51, 62, 64, 69, 87–88, 92, 104–5, 112, 118–19, 126, 136, 170, 186, 188–90, 199, 204, 205–10, 310
sustainability 10–11, 112, 186–87, 190, 199, 204, 210–11, 212–17, 280 *see also* climate change
energy value chains
bond of belonging as constituting force 261–62
competing value chains 51, 258
concentration of 113, 138, 165, 168, 193, 200, 256–57, 266, 267, 275, 311
de-concentration of 162, 168, 170, 175, 193, 194, 200, 209–10, 255, 259–60, 265–66, 272–73, 310
feedback loops 108–9, 261, 274–76
horizontal relationships 51, 258–60
innovation, and 252, 253–54, 256, 258–61, 262, 265, 266, 268, 269–74
integrated value chains 174, 252, 271–72, 276, 300–1, 309, 310, 311
local content requirements, and 165–66, 208, 267–74
market power, and 12, 50, 113–14, 168, 193, 201, 255, 264, 307
redundancy 16, 29–31, 115, 258–59, 262, 293
solar value chains 81–82, 88, 89–90, 275
stagflationary policies, and 255–56
support mechanisms: dispatch priority 267
support mechanisms: portfolio standards 267
tariffs, and 263–74
technological frontier, and 81, 86, 99–100, 119, 155–56, 159, 165–66, 172, 275–76
vertical relationships 257–59
wind value chains 107
European Union (EU) 5, 31–32, 118–19, 214–15, 237–38, 243–44, 245, 264, 267, 294–95

finance
bankability, and 246
development finance 246–51
guarantees 248
political risk insurance 248
proof-of-concept finance 271
Finnis, John 155, 201–3, 208–9, 279, 284–85, 286
Ford Model T 83
France 4–5, 23, 46, 116
Francis, Holy Father 140
Fukushima Daiichi 116, 261–62, 295–96
Fukuyama, Francis 135, 144–45, 157–58, 173, 175–76, 271
Fuller, Lon L. 279, 282–85, 289, 291–92

Gaillard, Emmanuel 283–84
Garavini, Giuliano 65–66, 77–79, 97–98, 101–2, 106, 116, 255, 266
gas *see* natural gas
Gathii, James T. 180–81, 189
General Electric 81
geopolitics
energy cooperation, and 97–98, 99–100, 117–20, 192–93, 233–34, 243–44
energy nationalism, and 111–16
energy rivalry/ energy realpolitik, and 53–54, 74–75, 79–80, 99, 100–11, 125, 130, 138, 167
equilibrium/ balance of power, and 5–6, 110, 193, 200–2, 234, 240, 309, 310
'missing power' problem, and 235–36, 237–38, 240–41, 243
nuclear disarmament analogue of climate negotiations, and 239–40
prisoner's dilemma, and 110, 129–30
prudent realpolitik, and 113, 114–15, 117–18, 272–73
reciprocity, and 201, 203, 218–19, 224–25, 238–39, 240, 245, 250–51, 275, 278, 281–82, 290
Germany
Nord Stream 1 Pipeline 92, 93–94, 103–4, 109, 294
Nord Stream 2 Pipeline 294
Ostpolitik 295
Stromeinspeisungsgesetz 86
Getachew, Adom 116, 205
Ginsburg, Tom 289, 290, 297
Goethe, Johann Wolfgang 47
Goodman, Ryan 148, 149

Gordley, James 178
Grewal, David Singh 256

Hancher, Leigh 18–19
Hanson, Victor Davis 145, 162, 166, 178–80, 273–74
Hardin, Garrett 17, 36, 39, 44, 97–98, 288, 306, 307–8, 309
Hathaway, Oona A. 103, 254, 294–95
Heffron, Raphael 212–13
Heidegger, Martin 63, 142
Heller, Michael A. 17, 36, 43–44, 45–46, 51–52, 97, 98, 288, 306–9
Hollis, Duncan 283–84
Honoré, Anthony M. 58
Hoplite warfare 178–79
Hughes, Thomas P 11, 16–17, 18, 41–42, 52–53, 60, 61, 66, 67–68, 74, 77–78, 79, 80–82, 95, 99–100, 115, 155–56, 160–61, 190–91, 195, 206, 208–9, 211, 229, 232, 258, 266
humanist tradition 63, 162

innovation
  innovation frontier 99–100, 119, 156, 159, 172
  main mechanism 8, 33–34, 53–55, 60–61, 65–66, 73, 80–81, 82, 85–86, 155, 162, 165–66, 174–75, 191–92, 200, 224, 227–30, 262, 289
  technology forcing/ subsidies 22, 25–26, 84–85, 190, 230–33, 271
intellectual property 3, 100–1, 189
intergovernmental Panel on Climate Change (IPCC) 8–9, 13, 14, 39–40, 213, 214–15, 216–17, 232, 236
International Energy Agency (IEA) 3, 8, 14, 23, 50, 51–52, 85, 92, 94, 96, 170, 191, 265–66, 267, 271–72, 273
International Finance Corporation (IFC) 301
International Investment Agreements 21–22, 35, 280, 281, 286–87, 300
Israel 101–2, 245
Italy 107, 286–87

James, Harold 6, 278
Johnson, Lyndon B. (Congressman/ Senator/ President) 160–61
Joskow, Paul L. 70, 225–26, 227, 235–36, 266
judgement 125, 142, 143, 149, 154, 162–63, 207, 251, 285–87

Kagan, Donald 144–45, 260–61
Kahn, Matthew E. 8–9, 11–12, 140, 159–60, 243–44
Klass, Alexandra B. 18–19, 22, 160–61, 163, 164, 226, 267
Koh, Harold Hongju 195
Koskenniemi, Martti 185–86
Kramer, Bruce 40–41, 58

Langford, Malcolm 281
Lasswell, Harold 40–41, 176, 284–85, 291–92
Leal-Arcas, Rafael 205
lending/lenders 20, 61–62, 98–99, 206, 246, 248–49, 270, 301
liberty 25, 46, 129–30, 146, 147, 148, 150, 151, 152, 154, 158, 173, 260
lithium 28, 191–92
Lovins, Amory 160–61
Lowenfeld, Andreas 22–23
Luhmann, Niklas 22–23

McDougal, Myers S. 40–41, 176, 284–85, 291–92
MacIntyre, Alasdair 141, 142, 143, 144–45, 158, 173, 176, 184, 284–85
Machiavelli, Niccolò 5–6, 63, 279, 307, 308
Maine, Henry Sumner 284
manganese 83–84
Merkel, Angela Dr. (Chancellor) 93
Meyer, Timothy 268–69
Mitchell, Timothy 5, 74–75
Mommsen, Theodor 177

NATO 103
natural gas 78–79, 93–94, 109, 214–15, 218, 309
  gas-fired power plants 30, 161, 209
  hydraulic fracturing, and 94
  liquified natural gas (LNG) 3, 60, 92, 94, 113, 201, 295–96
Netherlands, the 9, 78–79, 286–87
Nkrumah, Kwame (Prime Minister/ President) 116
Nordhaus, William D. 139
North-South Dialogue 65–66, 78–79, 96–97, 102
Nozick, Robert 148
nuclear energy 23, 24, 60–61, 116, 118–19, 160–61, 214–15
  fusion 215–16
  Messmer plan 23
  nuclear exit 93–94, 109, 209–10, 261–62, 282–83
  small modular reactors 185–86, 201–2
nuisance *see* reasonable use
Nussbaum, Martha 3–4, 16, 110–11, 128–29, 141, 142, 143–44, 147, 153, 177, 186

O'Connell, Mary Ellen 141, 203–4
Obama, Barack H. (President) 29
oil
  in general 31, 36, 39, 41, 52, 59, 65, 73–75, 78–79, 82–83, 92, 103, 104, 173–74, 191–92, 200, 207–8, 252, 253, 254, 258, 261–62, 267–69, 273, 308–9
  hydraulic fracturing *see* natural gas: hydraulic fracturing
  oil shock/ Arab oil embargo 69–70, 78–79, 97–98, 101–2, 309–10
  petrol/ gasoline 83
  Standard Oil 307
Osofsky, Hari 3, 195
Ostrom, Elinor 15–16, 17, 20, 37–38, 39, 40–42, 49–50, 57, 58, 63, 97–98, 99–100, 110, 162, 175–76, 178–80, 190, 195, 202, 218, 238, 261, 291
Ovid, Publius Naso 173

Pascal, Blaise
  Pascal's wager 128–29
Paulsson, Jan 283–84, 292
Peerenboom, Randall 279, 282–85, 289, 291–92
Perez, Carlota 7, 8, 54–55, 65–74, 80–97, 170, 191–92, 230, 261
Peters, Anne 289, 291, 297
Petit, Eugene 56
petroleum *see* oil
Pettit, Philip 129–30, 141, 260
Pierce, David 16–17, 36, 39, 41, 97–98, 104, 281–82
Pocock, John Greville Agard 5–6, 46
Poland 118, 131
political risk 21–22, 92, 115, 121, 219, 248, 269–70, 294
polysilicon 82, 85, 88, 89, 113–14, 257–58
Porter, Michael E. 50, 255
Posner, Eric A. 201–2
Posner, Richard A. (Judge) 137, 139, 155
Pound, Roscoe 184
pricing
  arbitrage 40
  capacity markets, and 227, 265
  levelized Cost of Energy 25–26, 30, 60–62, 84–85, 89–90, 275
  market price 225–26
  rate-based pricing 70, 234
Project 2025 112–15
Putin, Vladimir Vladimirovich (President) 93–94, 294–95

Qatar 3, 118, 201

Rajamani, Lavanya 195–96, 240–41, 242
Ratner, Steven R. 289, 297
Rawls, John 4, 128–29, 133, 173, 203
Raz, Joseph 279
Reagan, Ronald (President) 102, 239–40
realpolitik *see* geopolitics
reasonable use
  abuse of right, and 56, 57, 60, 63–64
  fair opportunity, and 59, 62, 63–64, 69, 70, 115, 116, 178, 179, 180–81, 183, 190, 194, 258
  nuisance, and 57, 62–63
Reisman, W. Michael 175–76, 283–84, 285–87, 292, 293, 295–96, 298
reverse salient *see* critical problem
revolutions
  1789 46
  1848 47–48
  Industrial Revolution 48, 60–61, 105–6
Righetti, Tara K. 57, 104, 180–81
Robinson, James A. 25, 99–100, 155–56, 162, 185, 255–56
Rockefeller, John D. 173–74, 307–8
Romania 82–83
Roman law 110
  Actio negatoria/ servitudes 56, 57
  Comitia tributa 177
  Obligatio in solidum 184
Röpke, Wilhelm 188, 190, 259
Rose, Carol M. 36, 39, 57, 180–81, 229–30, 281–82, 284
Royal Dutch Shell 83
rule of law
  bond of belonging, and 279–80, 281–87
  'islands' 295–96
  lawlessness 296–98, 299–300
  'offshore zones' 293, 295–96, 298
  precommitment 280–81, 288, 289–91, 296, 297, 299–300, 305, 310–11
  reliance 290, 291, 293
  remedies, and 291–92
  'thick' 279–80, 281–88, 301, 302
  'thin' 279, 280, 281, 282–84, 287, 288, 291–92, 293, 296, 297, 298, 299–302
  transparency, and 218, 279, 282–85, 289–90, 291, 295
Russia 31, 83, 92, 93–94, 102–3, 106–7, 108, 109, 113, 118, 245, 294–95

Sabel, Charles F. 17

Salacuse, Jeswald 73
Saudi Arabia 51–52, 212
Saul, Ben 164
Schelling, Thomas 289
Schmitt, Carl 49, 53–54, 63, 162, 298
Schremmer, Joseph A. 40–41, 57, 59, 104, 115, 180–81, 281–82
Schreuer, Christoph 210
Schröder, Gerhard (Chancellor) 93–94
Schumpeter, Joseph A 7, 54–55, 65–66
Sen, Amartya 134–35, 143–44
Shackelford, Scott J. 39–40
Siemens 67–68
Skinner, Quentin 162, 173, 177
Slaughter, Anne-Marie 17, 195, 206
Smil, Vaclav 3, 4–5, 8, 14, 17–18, 54–55, 126, 189–90, 212–13
Snyder, Timothy 131
social practice 143, 144–45, 155–56
Sohn, Louis B. 180–81
solar energy 8, 22, 25–26, 29, 30, 43–44, 60–62, 81, 84–85, 86, 92, 93–94, 161, 209, 216, 309
Solidarity 183–84, 185–86, 187
Sophocles 176–77
Sornarajah, Muthucumaraswamy 280
South Africa 87
South China Sea 103–4, 297–98
Sovacool, Benjamin 8, 20, 77, 118, 252, 254, 265, 266, 272–73, 277
sovereignty 104, 180–81, 283–84
Soviet Union 131, 239–40
Sprague, Frank Julian 80–81
Steiner, George 158, 176–77
Strange, Susan 27, 155
Sunstein, Cass 25–26, 140
Switzerland 9, 18

Talus, Kim 18, 23, 26–27, 29–30, 69–70
technology-forcing *see* innovation: technology forcing
Terzi, Alessio 132–33, 217–18
Tesla, Nikola 52–53
Texas 3, 16–17, 18–19, 29, 55–56, 71, 161, 213–14, 273–74, 308–9
  Pedernales Electric Cooperative 160–61
Thatcher, Margaret (Prime Minister) 102
Tocqueville, Alexis de 285–86
Tolkien, John Ronald Reuel 204, 284
Tomuchat, Christian 164
transportation 8, 51–52, 65, 82–83, 101, 105, 238–39, 252, 261–62, 266
  electric vehicles 28, 50–53, 105–6
  internal combustion engine 28, 51–52, 82–84
Trump, Donald J. (President) 112, 116

Ukraine 294, 295
  Crimea 92
  Euromaidan 294–95
  Russian invasion of 31, 51–52, 78–79, 102–3, 108, 109, 131, 261–62, 271–72, 295–96, 297–98
  Yanukovych, Victor F. (President) 294–95
United Arab Emirates 212
  Abu Dhabi 244–45
  Dubai 131
United Kingdom 14
United Nations Charter 205–6
United States of America 3, 20, 43–44, 61–62, 69–70, 78–79, 81, 82–83, 86, 92, 94, 101–2, 103, 105, 112, 118, 139, 174, 200, 237–39, 241–42, 243–44, 245, 246, 264, 300
  Advanced Research Projects Agency-Energy (ARPA-E) 271
  Defense Advanced Research Projects Agency (DARPA) 271
  Energy Policy Act (2005) 268–69
  Inflation Reduction Act (IRA) 267–68
  Public Utility Regulatory Policies Act (PURPA) 268–69
uranium 43–44, 252
Utah 43–44

value chains *see* energy value chain
Van de Graaf, Thijs 8, 20, 77, 118, 252, 254, 272–73, 277
van Harten, Gus 299
Venezuela 103
Vermeule, Adrian 55–56, 141, 143–45, 155, 158
Victor, David G 17
Viñuales, Jorge 77
Virgil, Publius Maro 297
virtue *see* cooperation: civic virtue and
von Rathenau, Emil 67–68

Waibel, Michael 280
Wälde, Thomas 21
Waltz, Kenneth 5–6, 12, 50, 98, 108–9, 193, 199–200, 235
Warren, Elizabeth (Senator) 299
Washington consensus 280–81, 299, 300–1
waste 19, 41, 49, 57–59, 63–64, 68, 69, 70, 100–1, 107, 121, 125–26, 129–30, 136–38, 169, 171, 193, 196–97, 198, 202, 214–15, 216, 281–82, 284

water governance analogy 37–38, 39, 40–41, 57
wind energy 5, 22, 29, 30, 43–44, 60–62, 84–85, 86, 107, 108, 161, 201–2, 216, 309
Wiseman, Hannah J. 3, 18–19, 22, 30, 43–44, 174, 273
Wittgenstein, Ludwig 153, 284–85
Wolfrum, Rüdiger 183, 184, 185, 186, 187
World Trade Organization (WTO) 85, 268–69

Yergin, Daniel 18–19, 20, 60, 70, 77–78, 83, 101–2, 199–200, 205, 263